Ludovic
Debeurme

renée

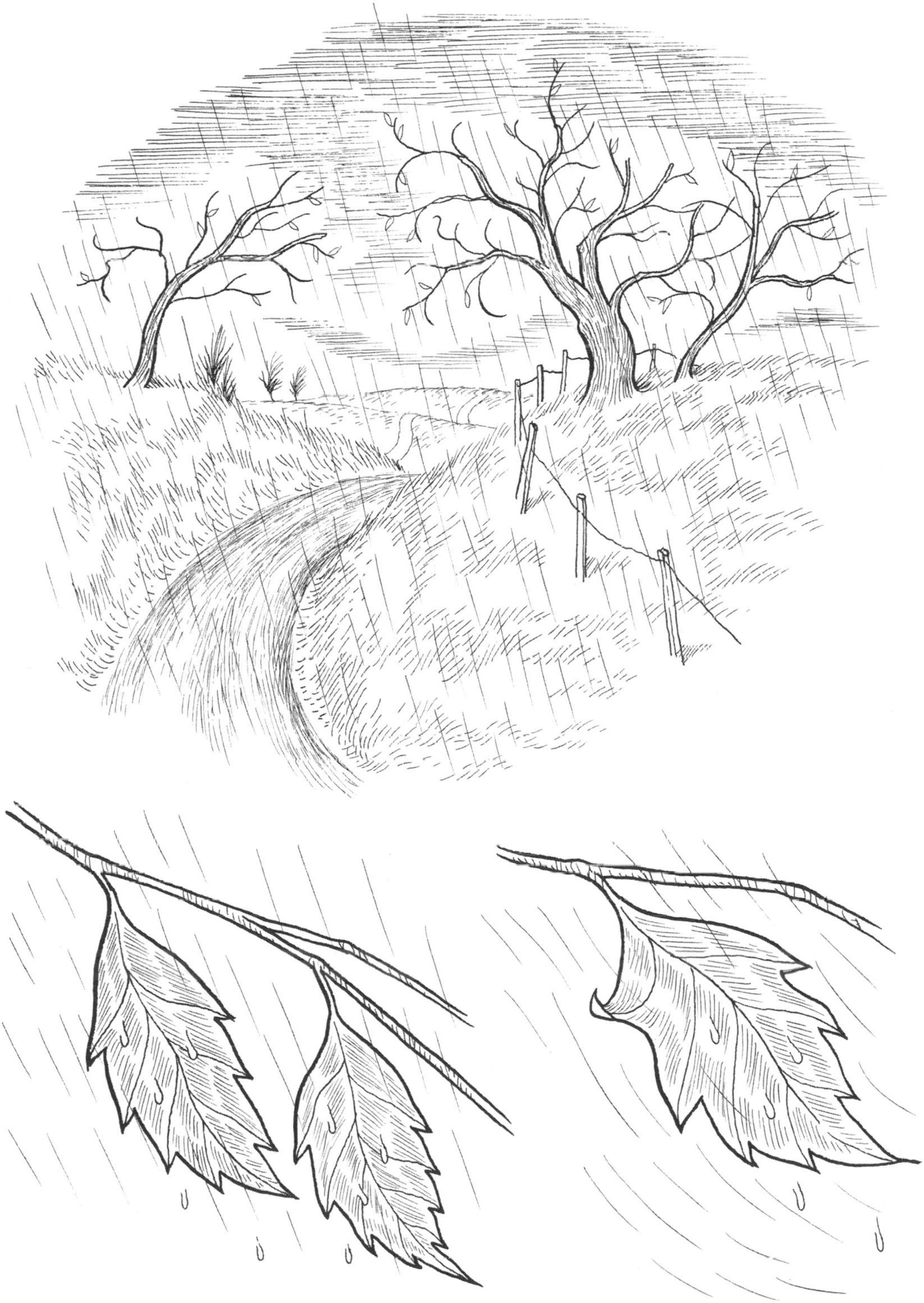

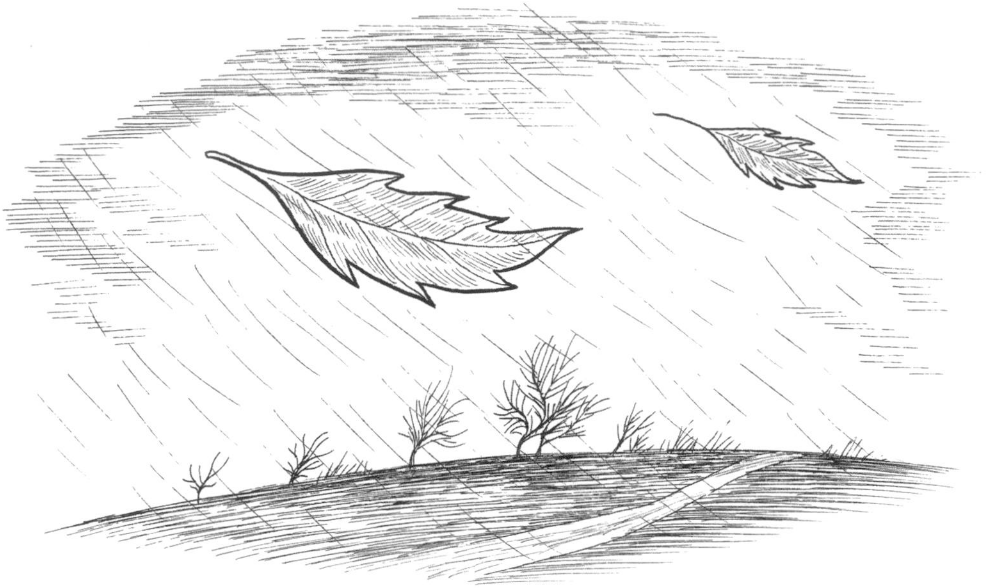

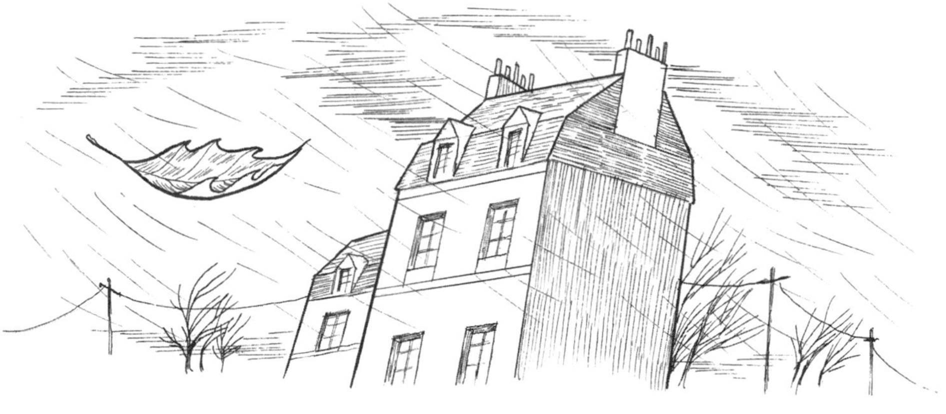

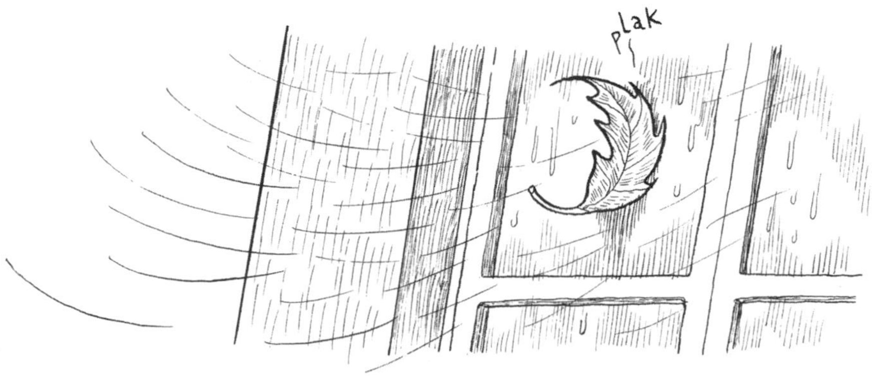
plak

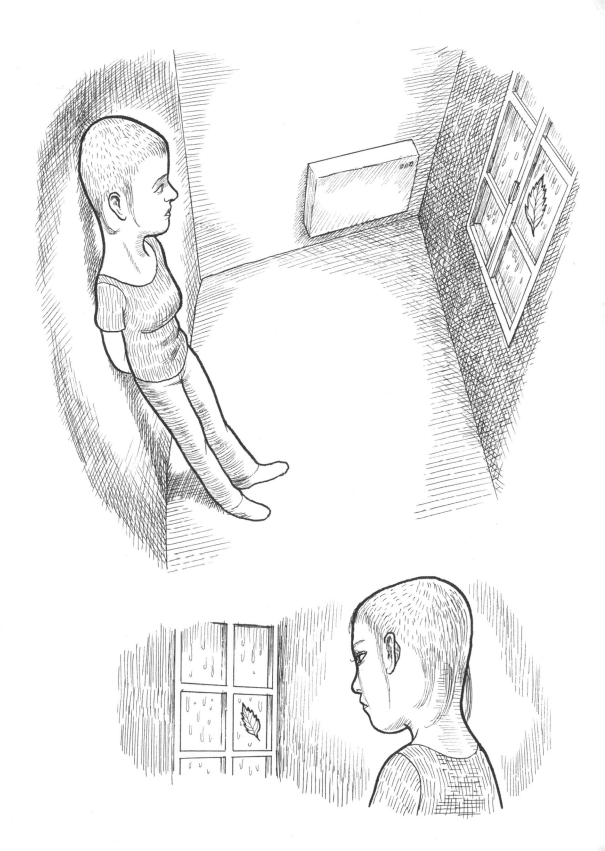

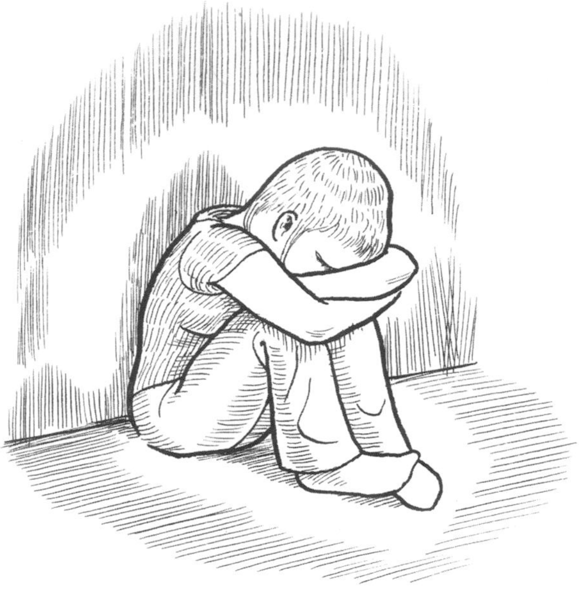

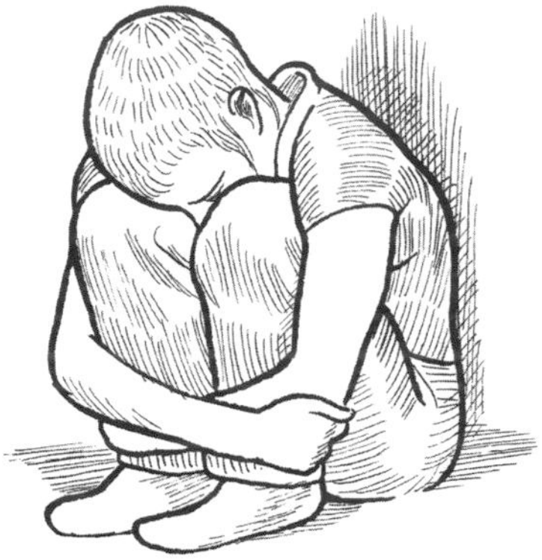

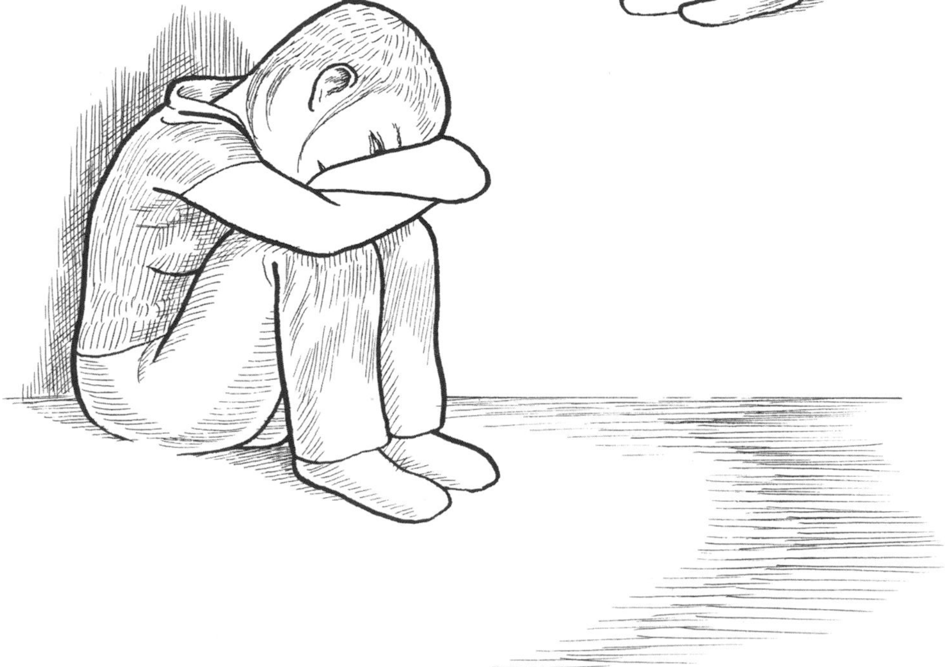

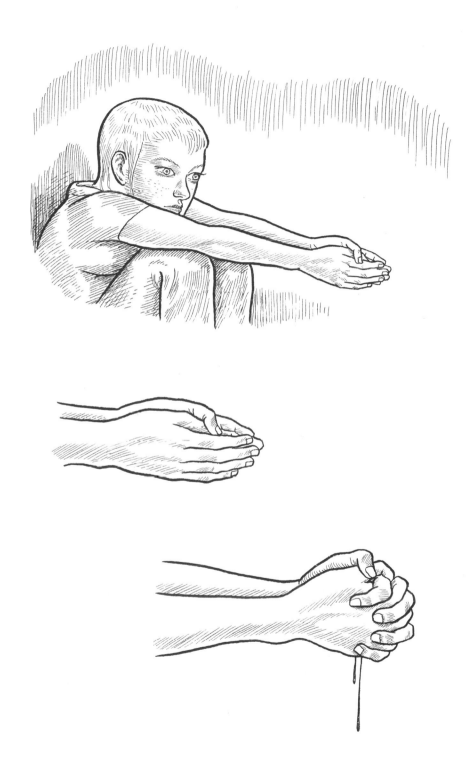

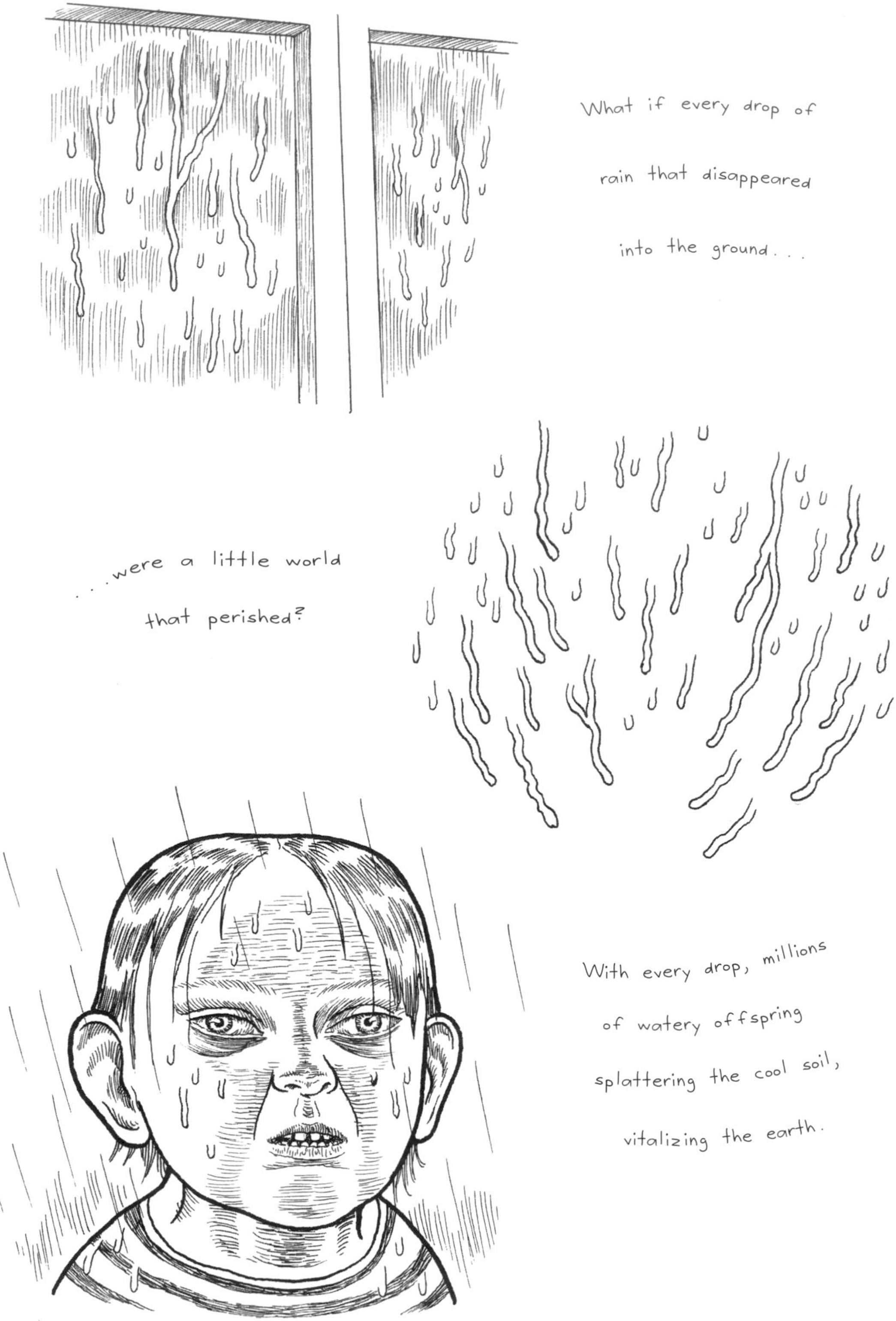
What if every drop of rain that disappeared into the ground...
...were a little world that perished?
With every drop, millions of watery offspring splattering the cool soil, vitalizing the earth.

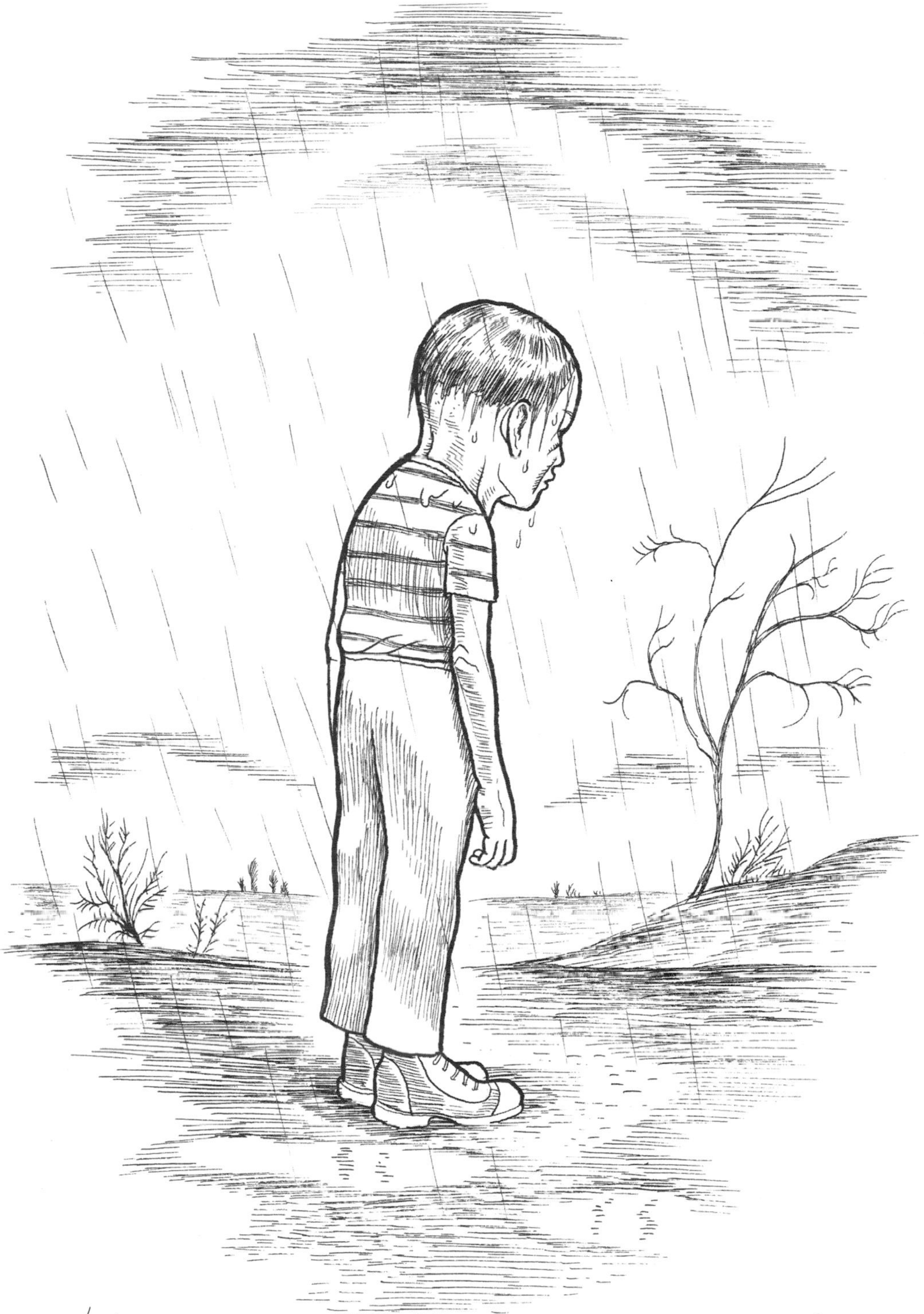

I think I am a river that must, now and then, be allowed to run. . .

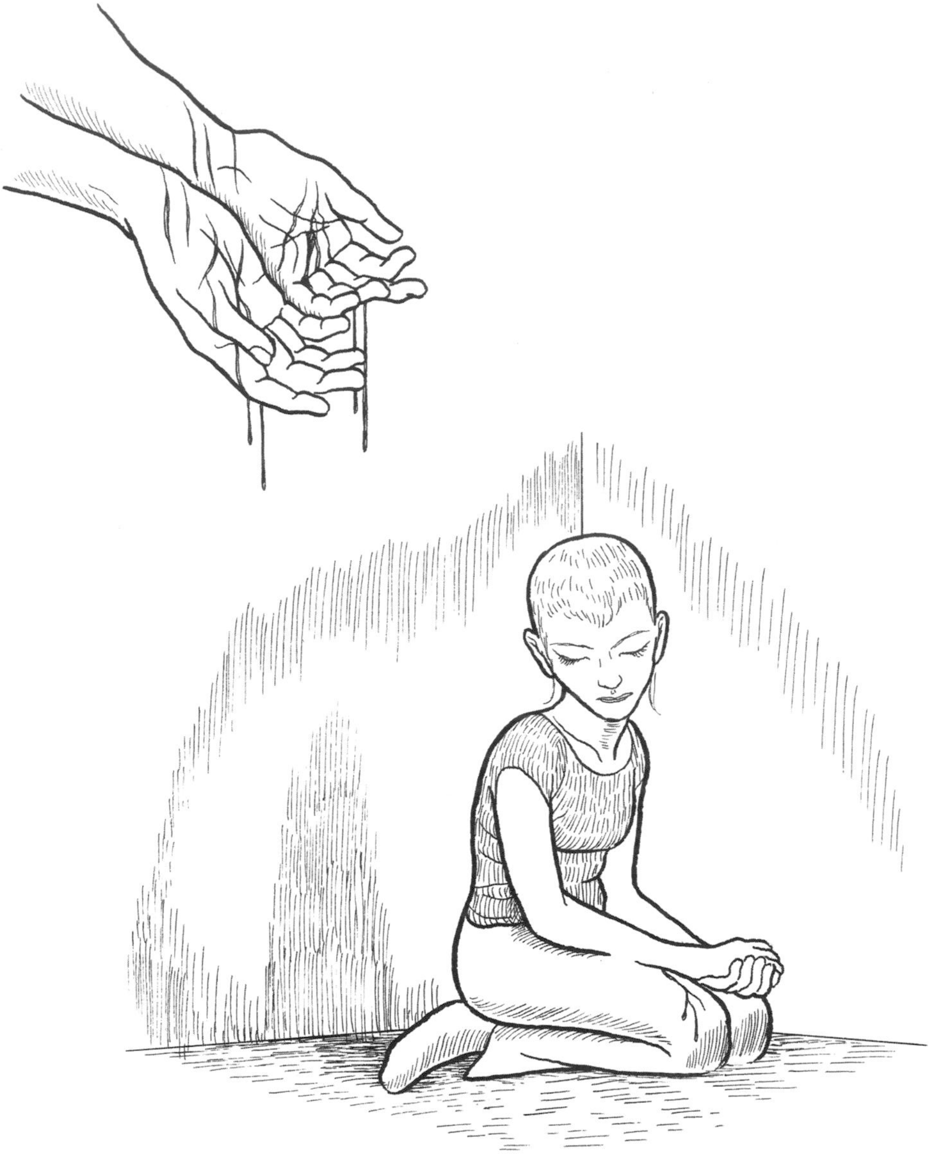

. . . so that all the rage and evil flee through it . . .

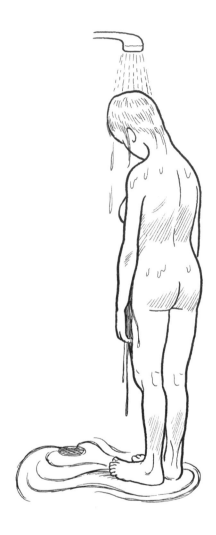

...the blood in the water disappearing for good.

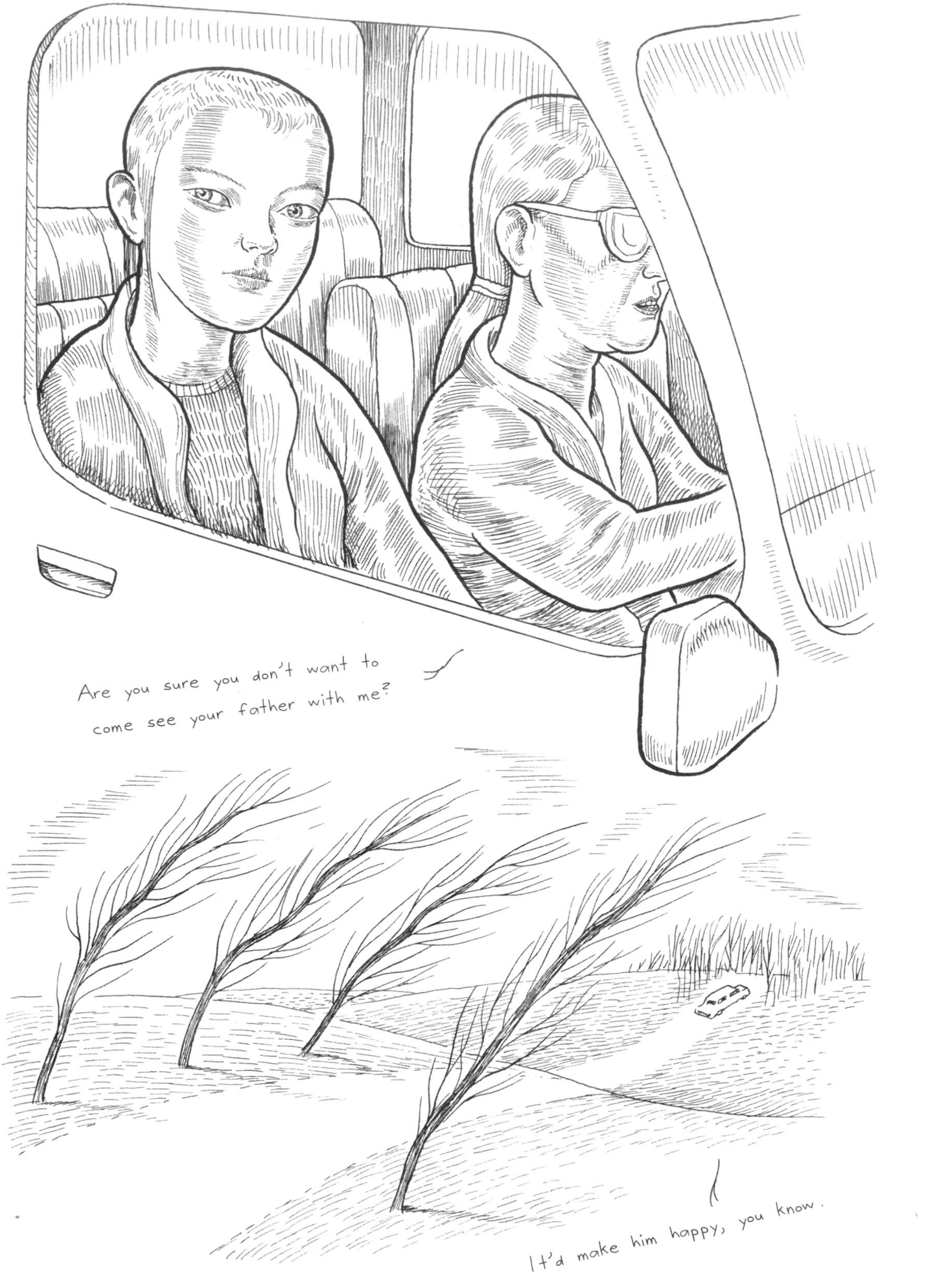
Are you sure you don't want to come see your father with me?
It'd make him happy, you know.

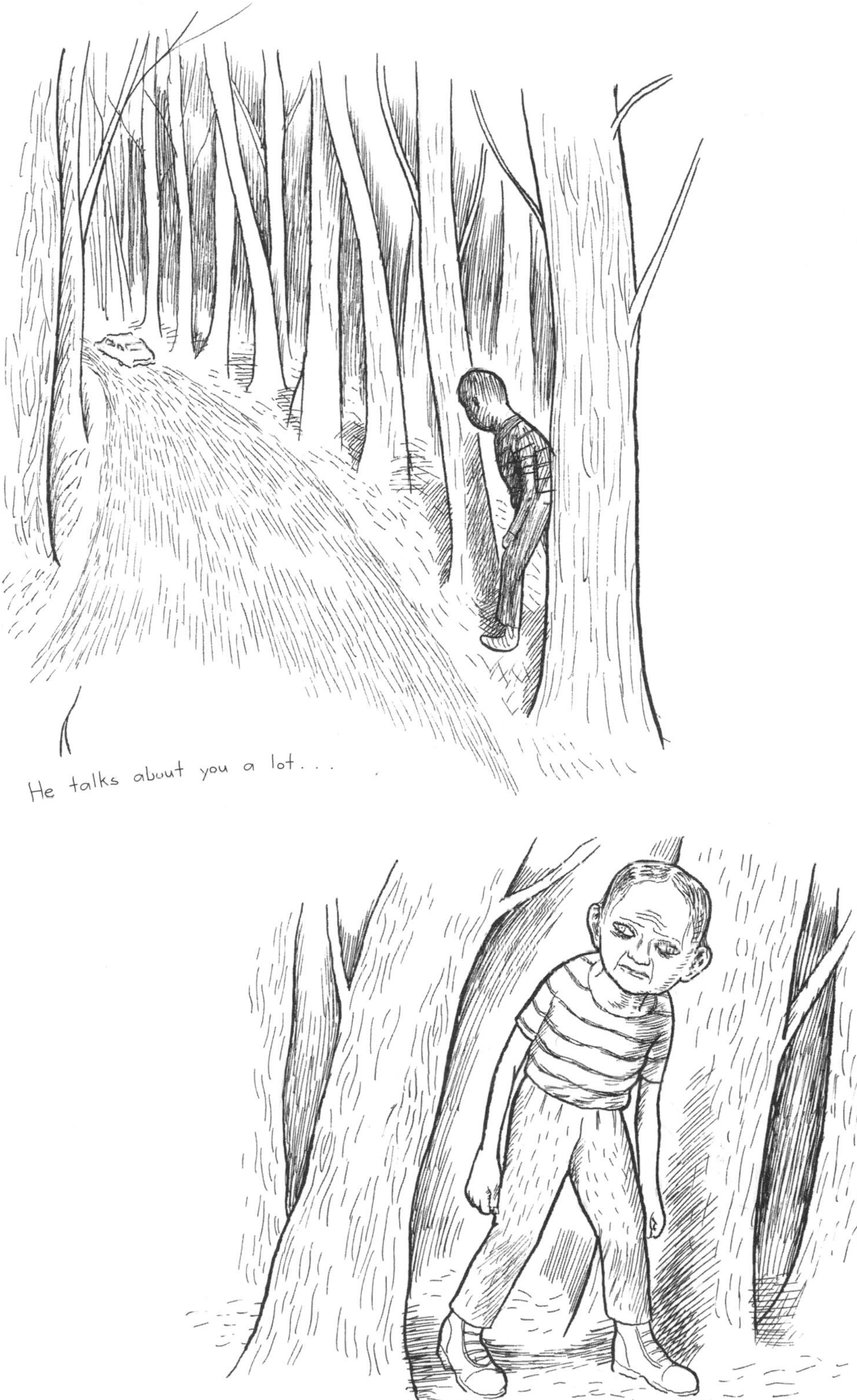
He talks about you a lot...

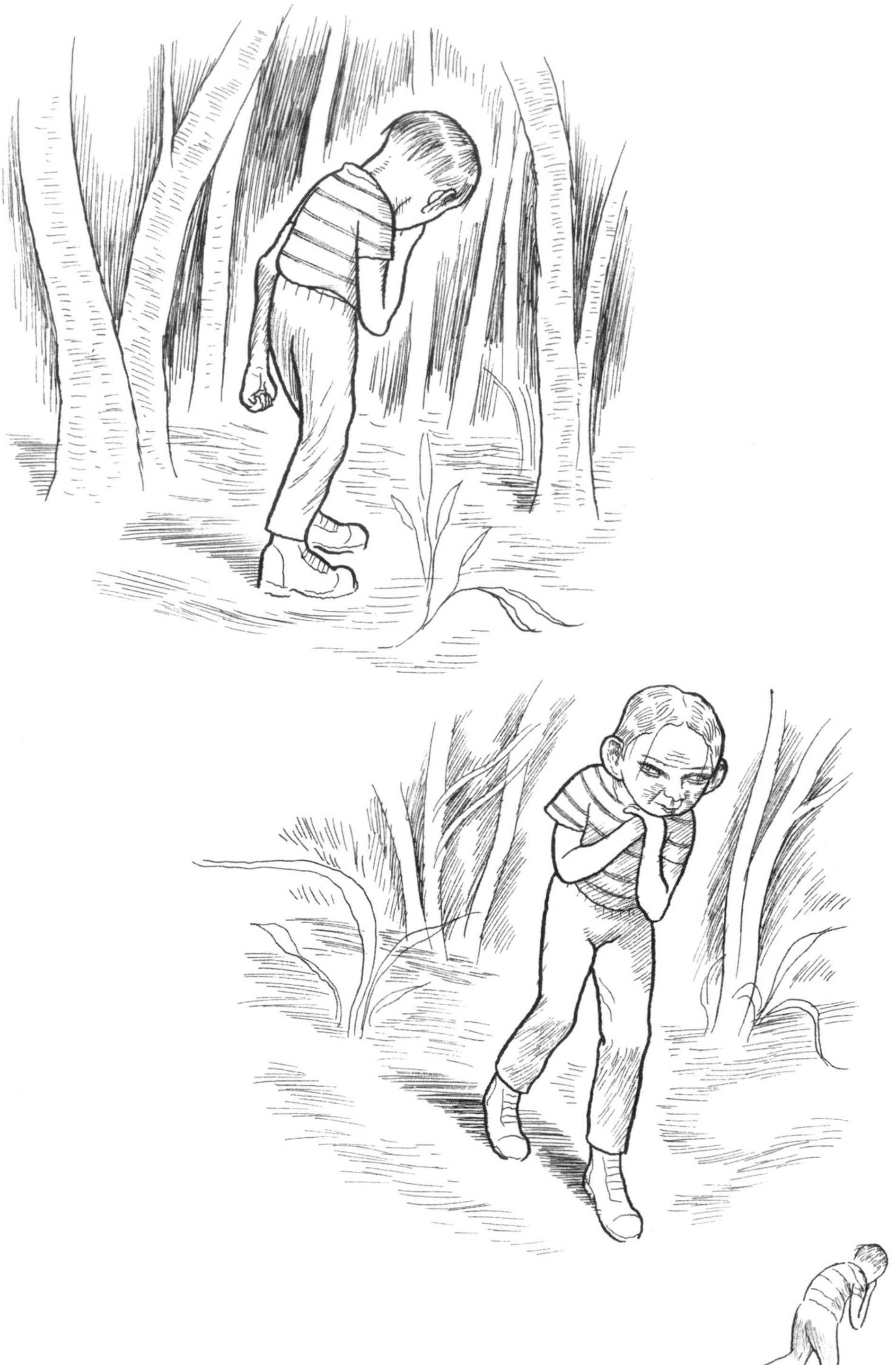

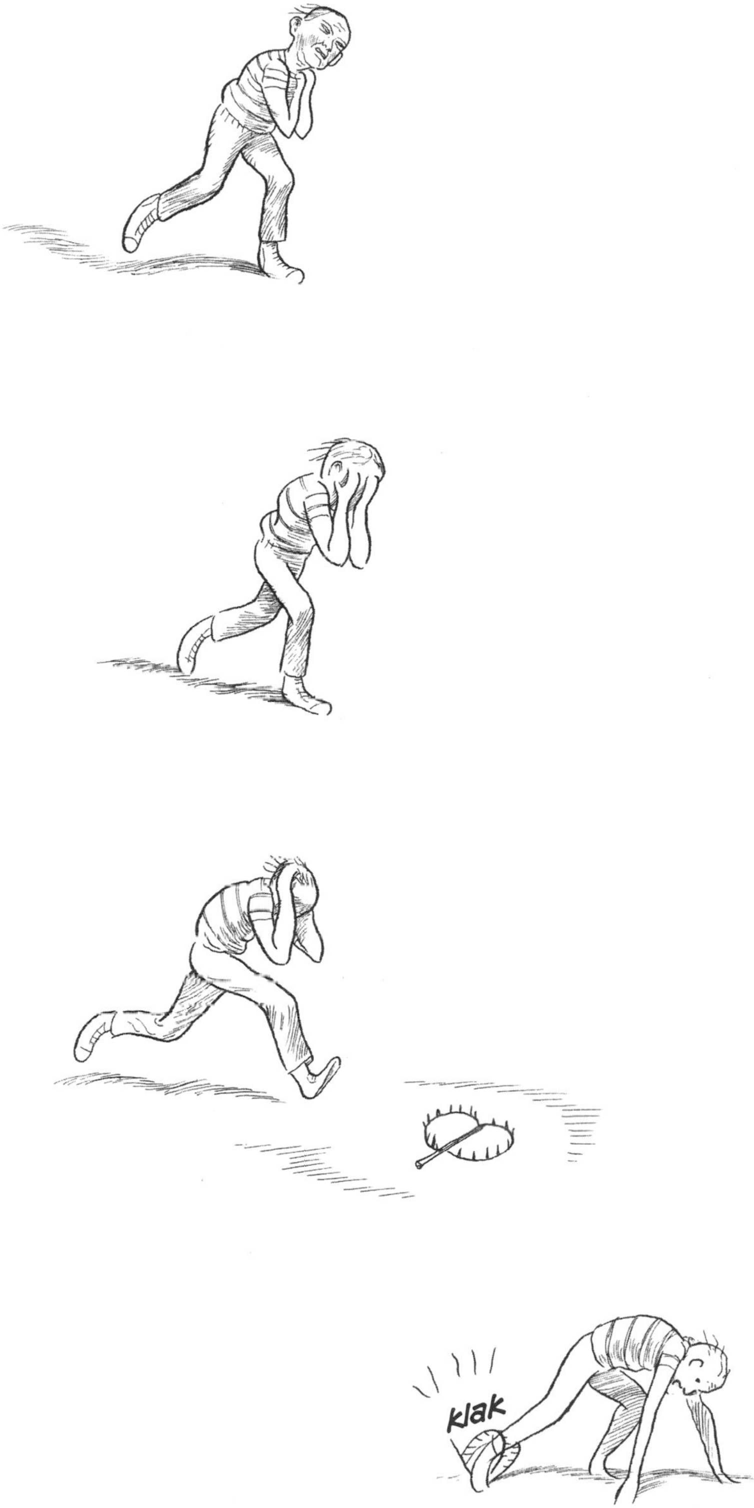
klak

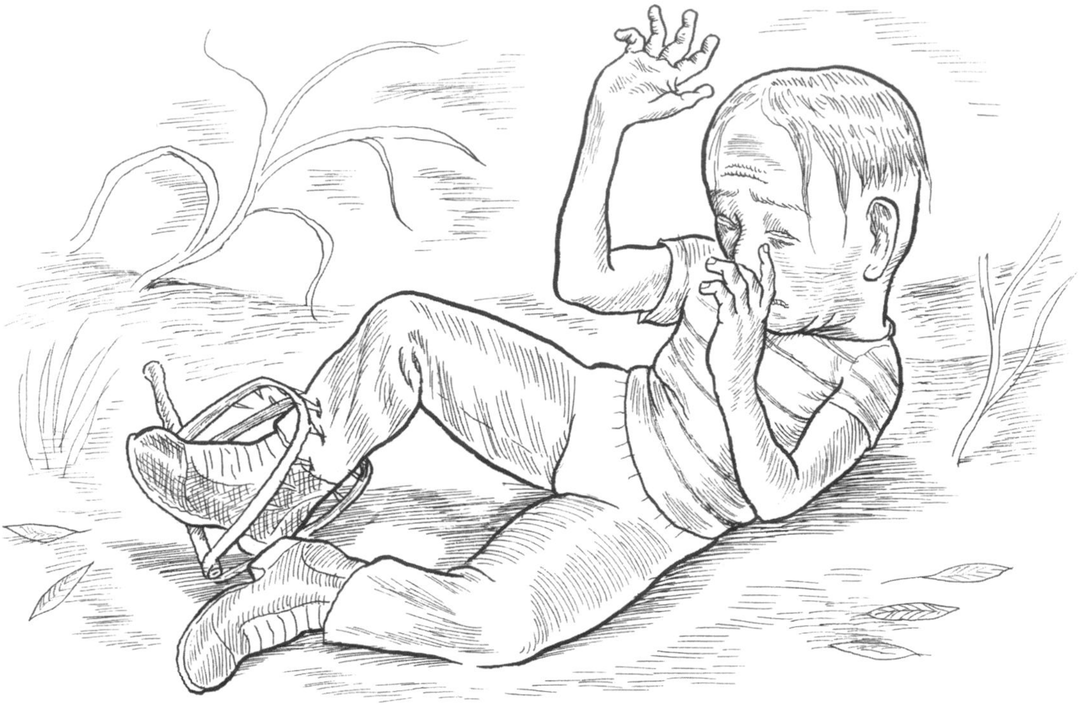

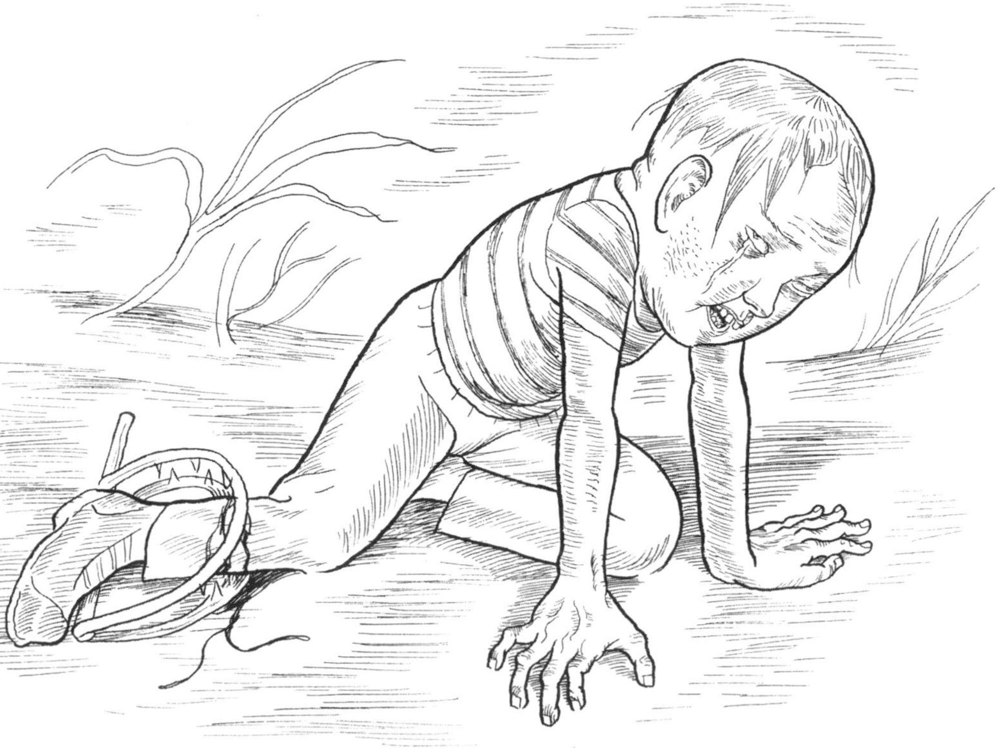

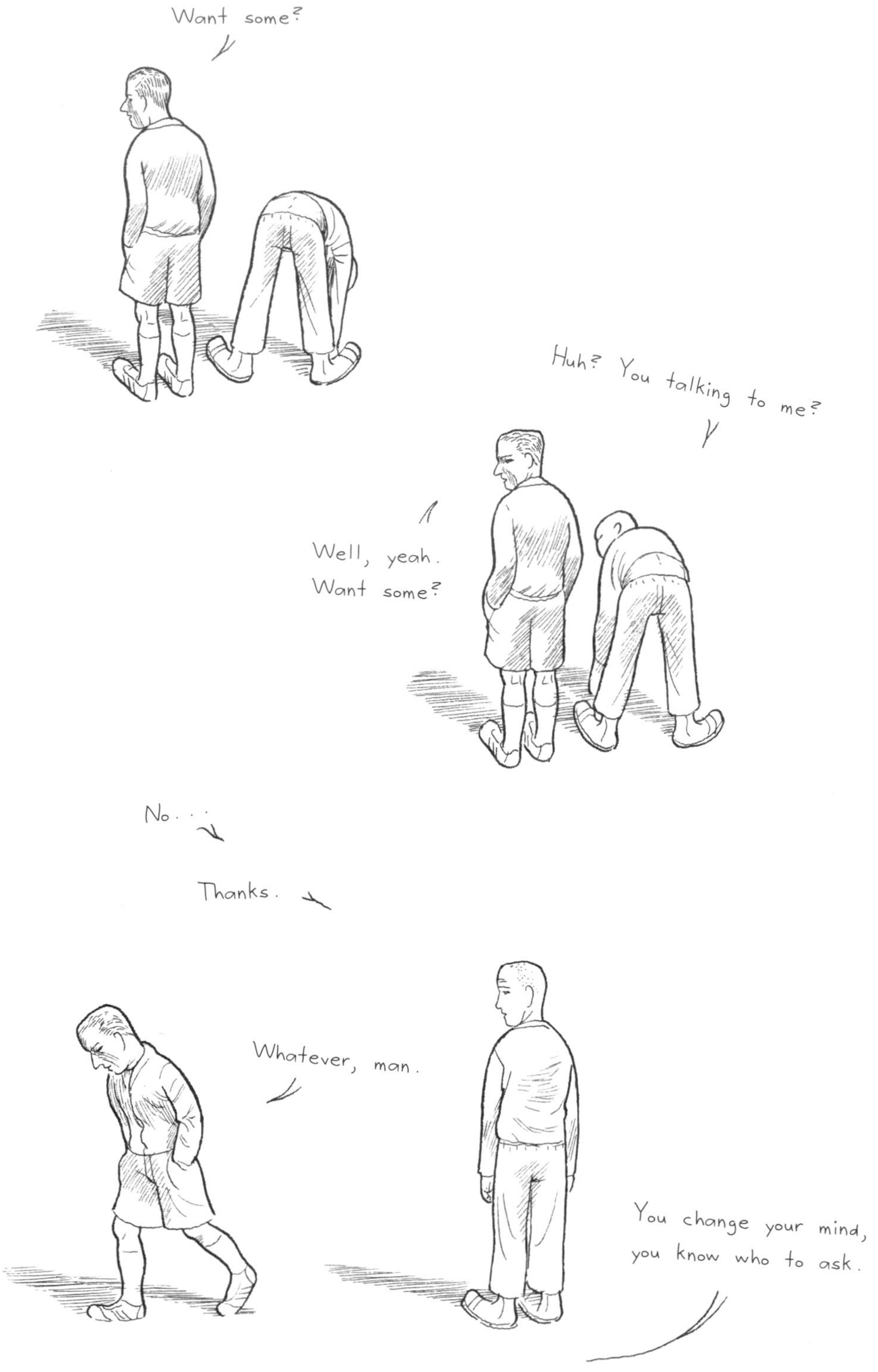
Want some?
Huh? You talking to me?
Well, yeah.
Want some?
No...
Thanks.
Whatever, man.
You change your mind,
you know who to ask.

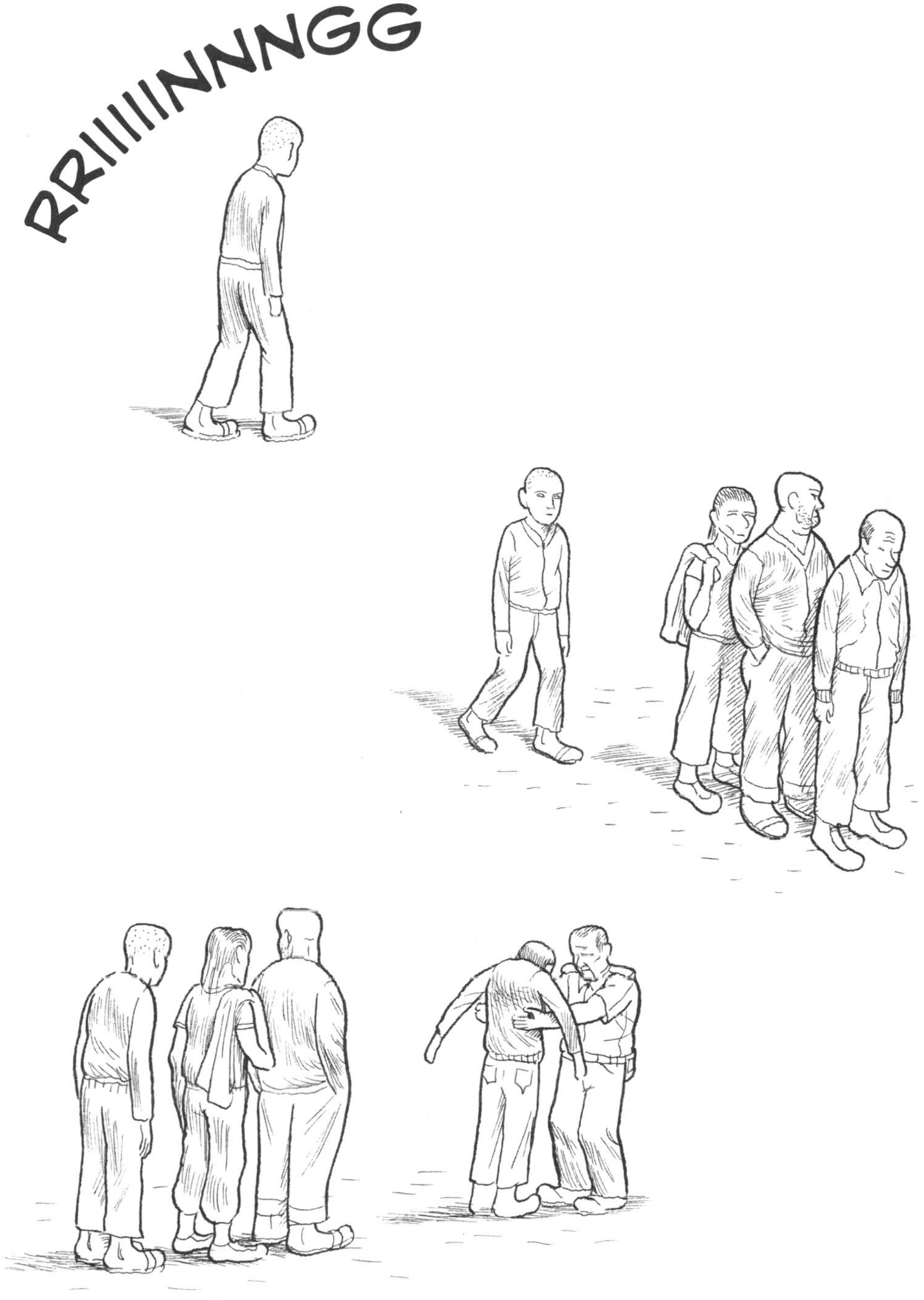
RRIIIIINNNGG

CLANK-CLANK

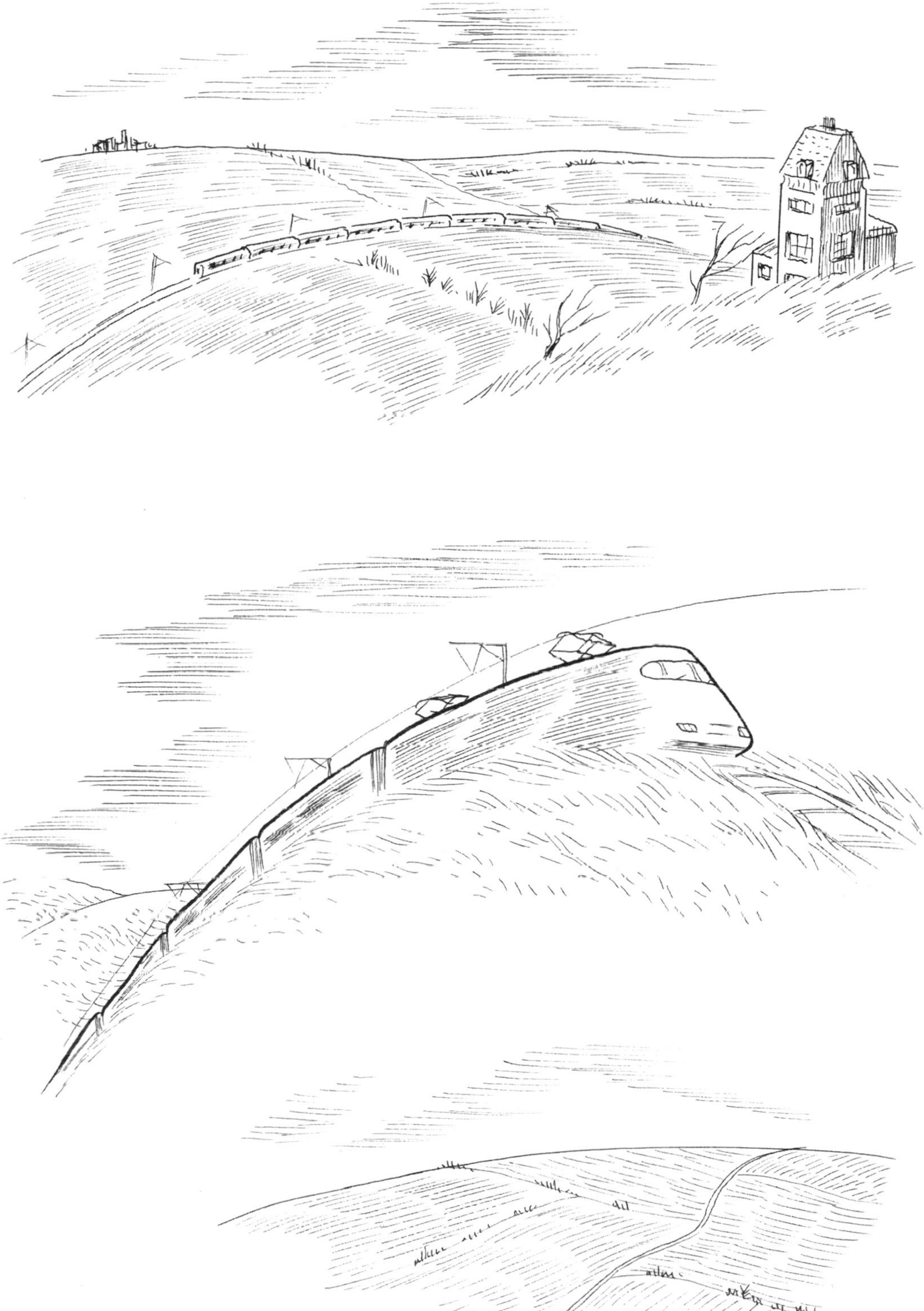

You're so ugly when

you're sleeping...

...poor schmuck.

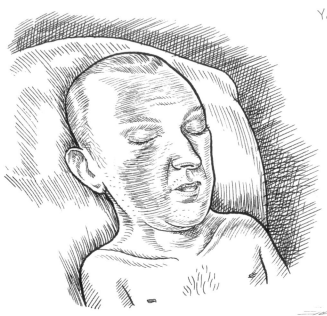

Your too-thin lips make little

sucking motions...

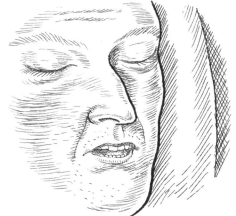

It's pathetic.

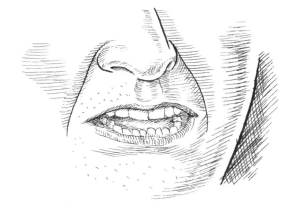

Your fat heavy eyelids...
hefting tons with
every flutter.

You're soft.

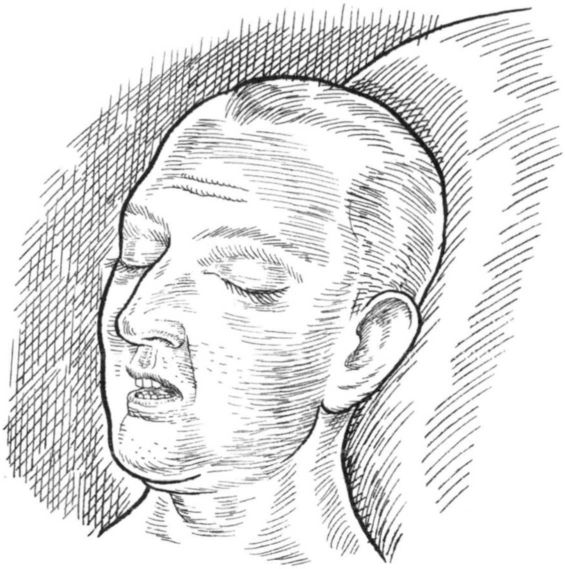

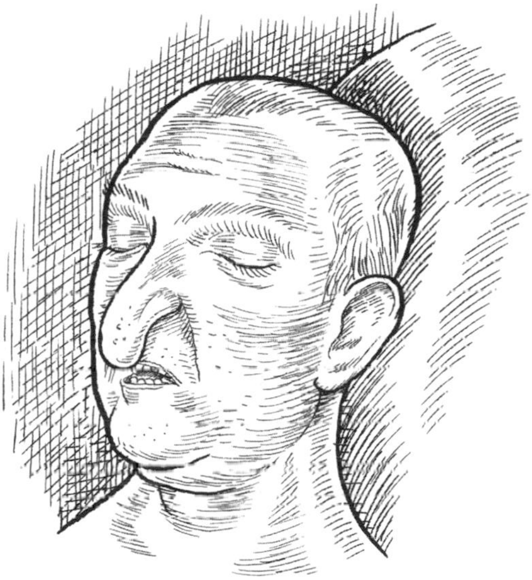

Everything about
you is soft.

You're from a race
of soft men.

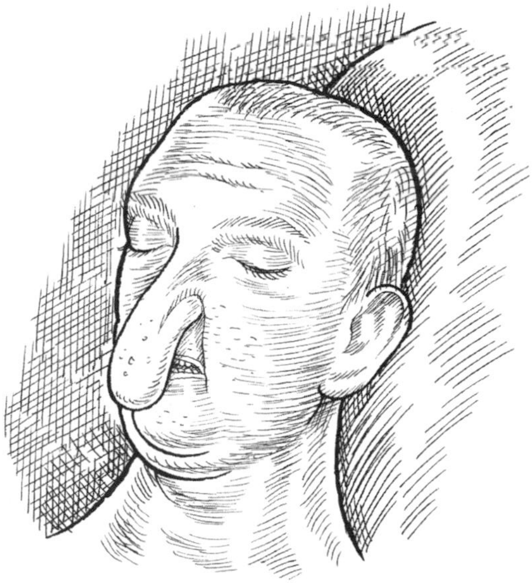

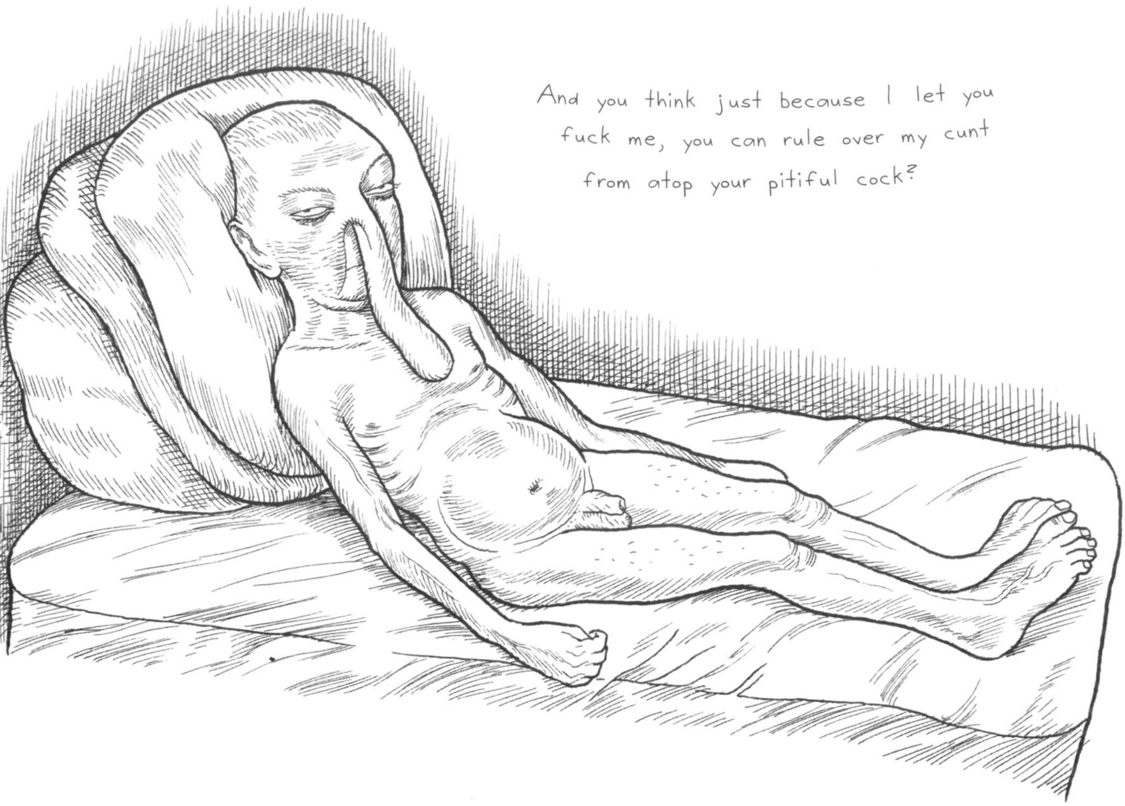
And you think just because I let you fuck me, you can rule over my cunt from atop your pitiful cock?

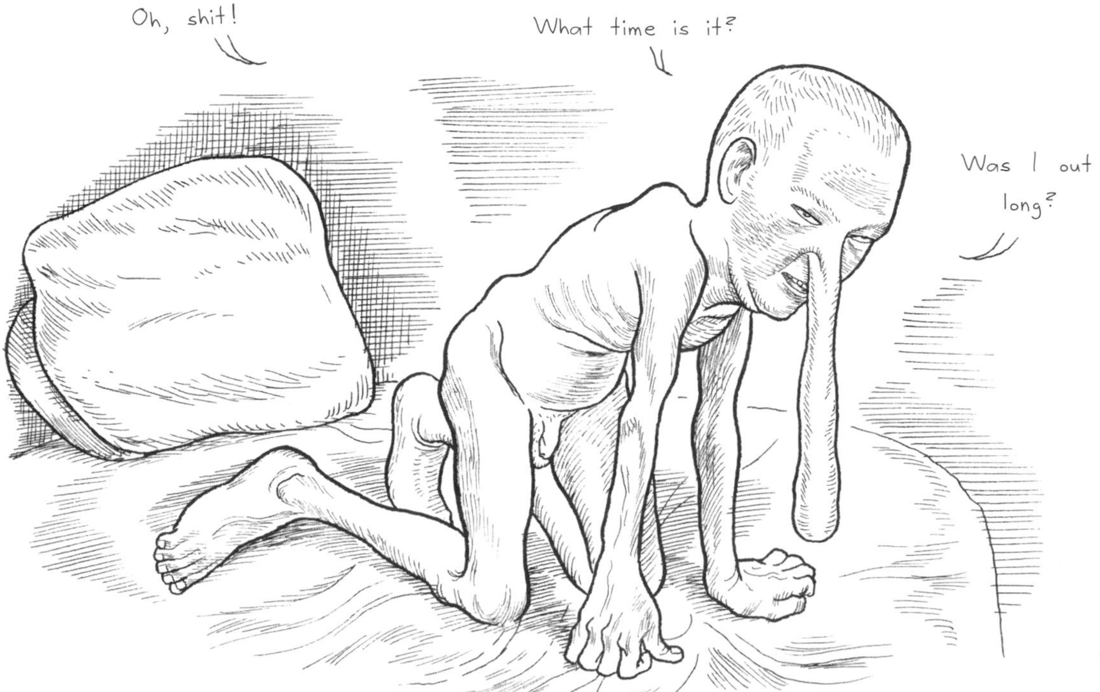
Oh, shit!
What time is it?
Was I out long?

That does it! I'm screwed!

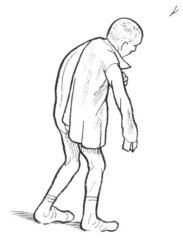

Goddammit, why didn't you wake me?

I knew it.

I'm screwed.

Do you want us to stop seeing each other!? Is that it?

Did you do it on purpose?

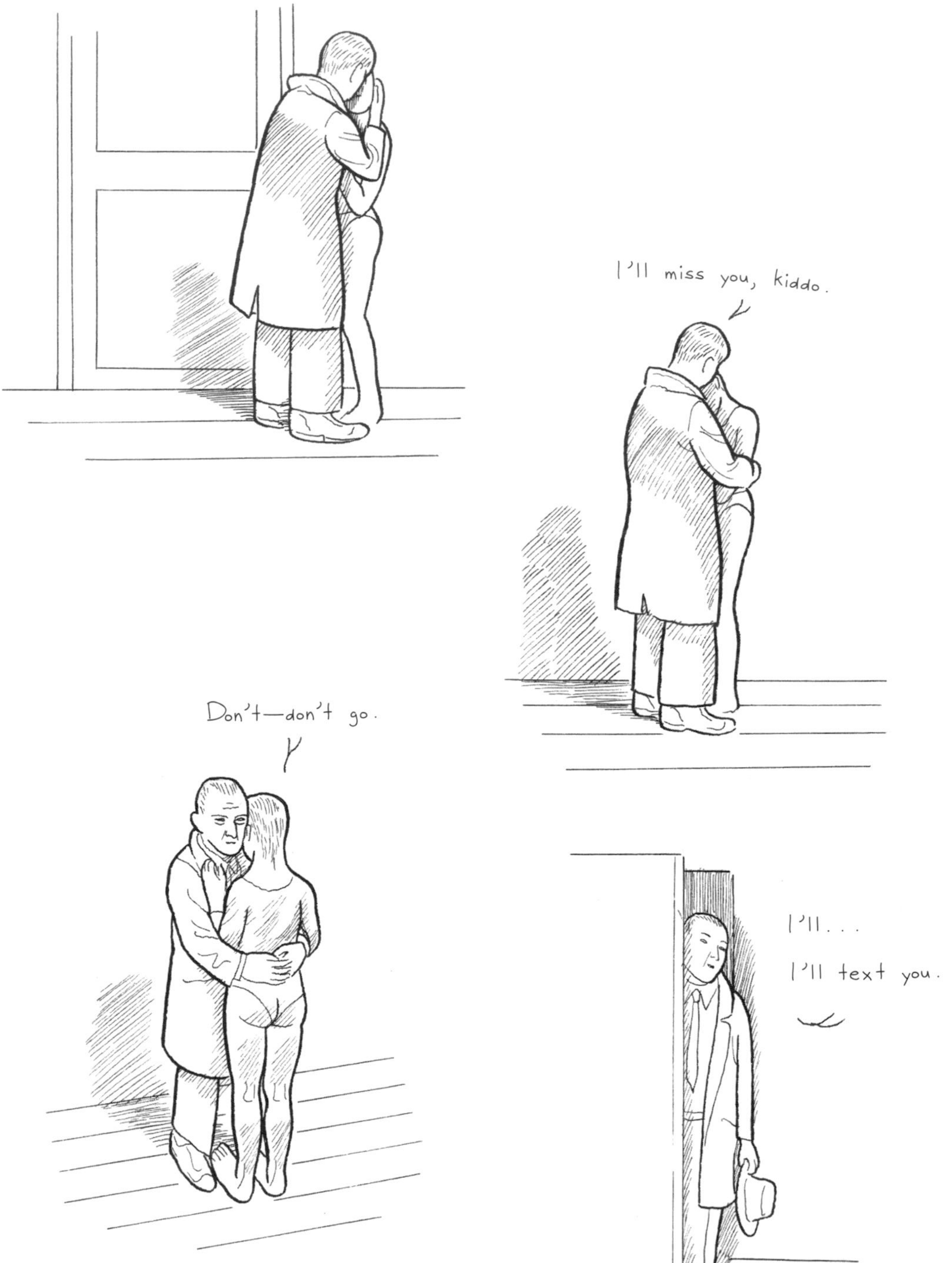
I'll miss you, kiddo.
Don't—don't go.
I'll...
I'll text you.

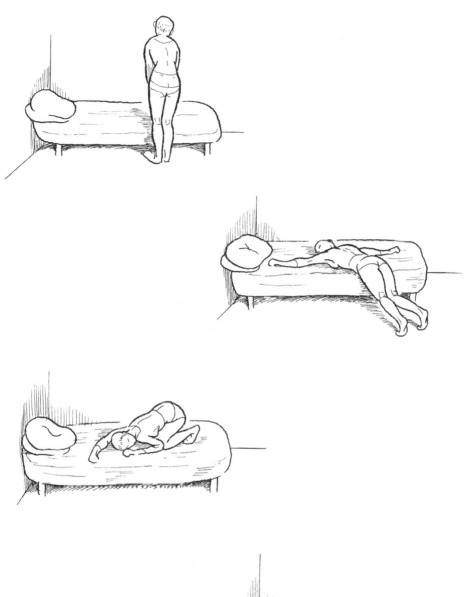

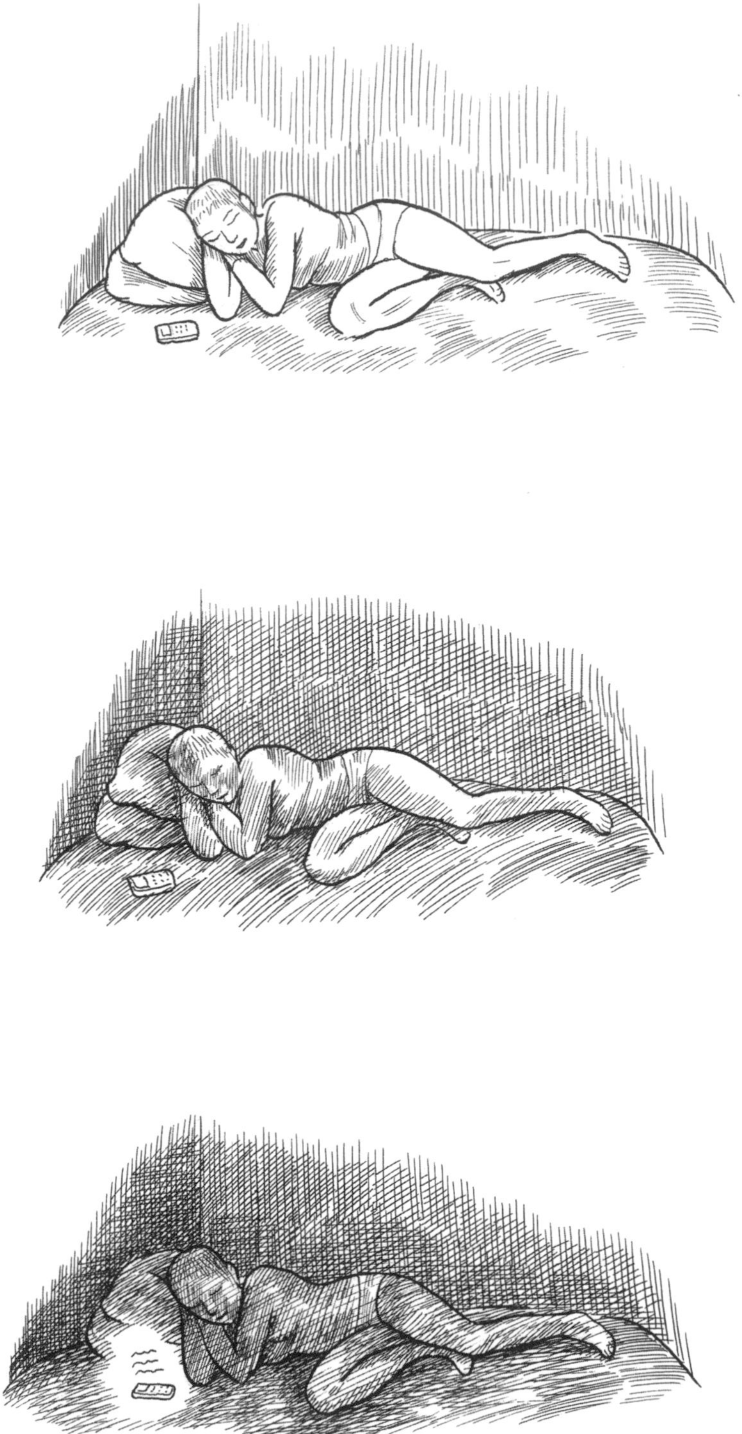
bzzz
bzzz
bzzz

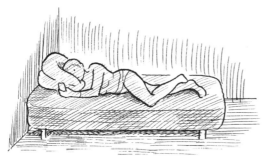

You're my
wonderful
Renée.

The dark sun that obsesses me and
haunts my days.

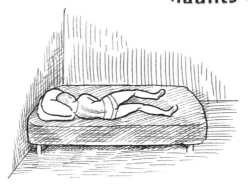

My magical, beautiful love.

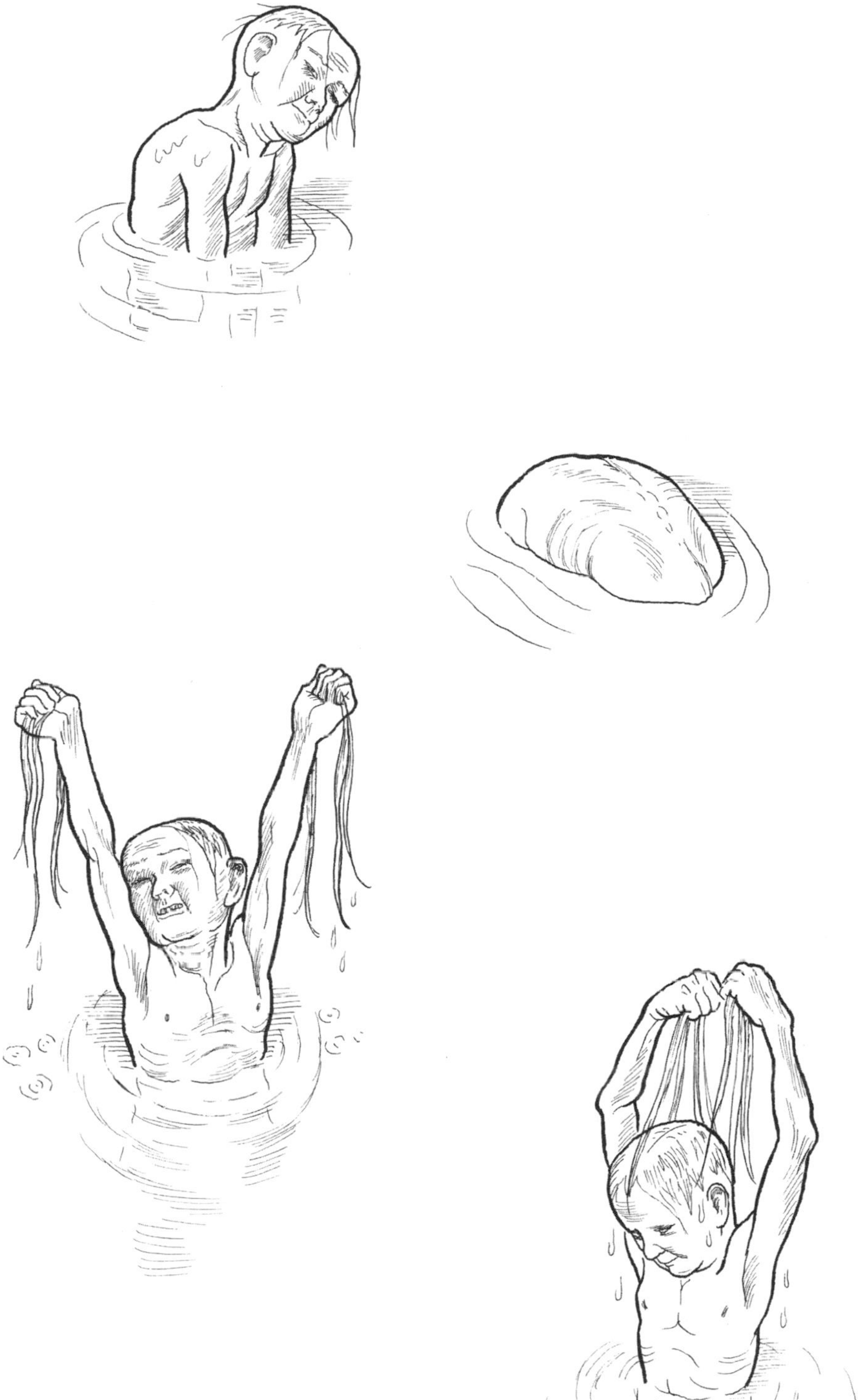

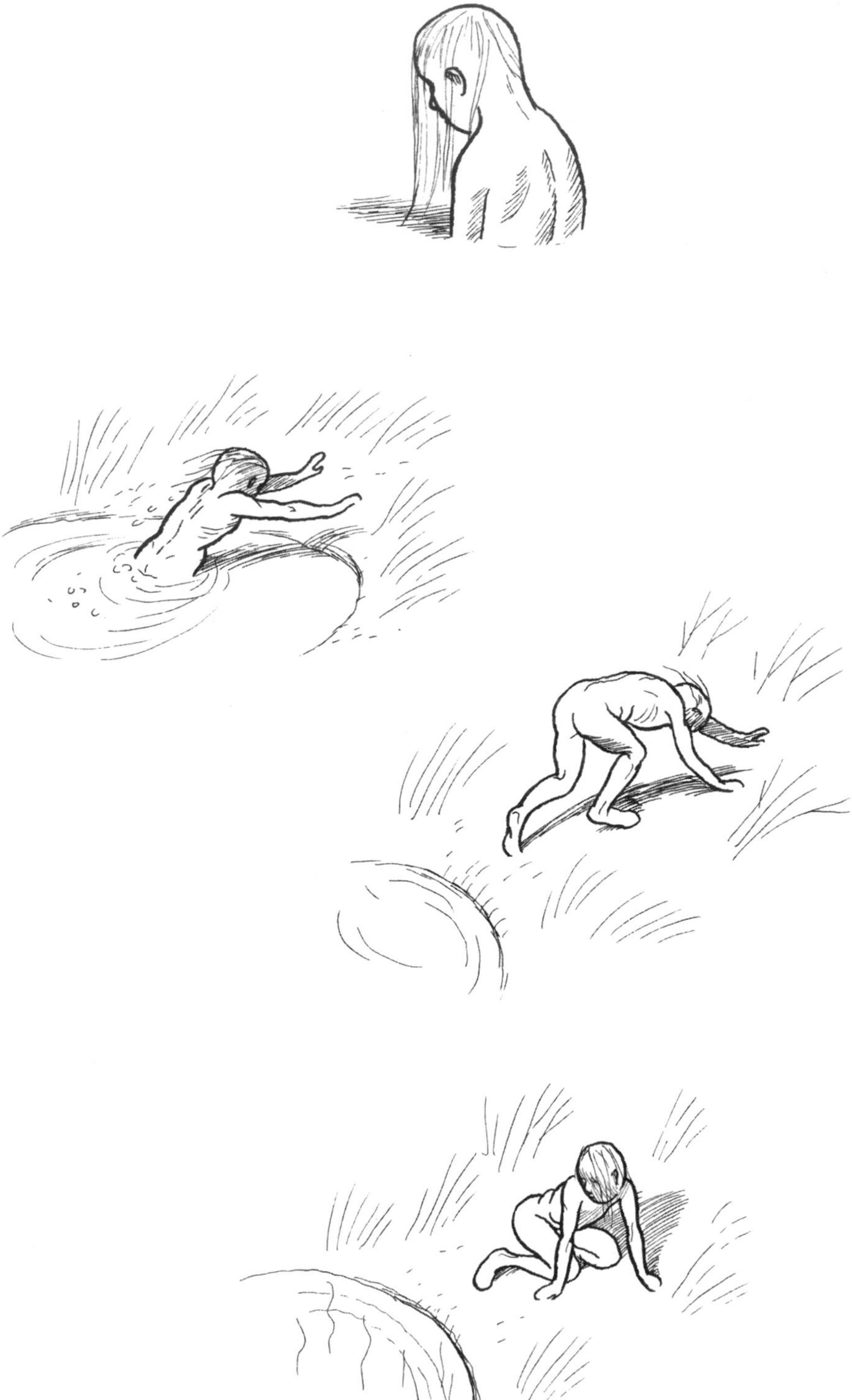

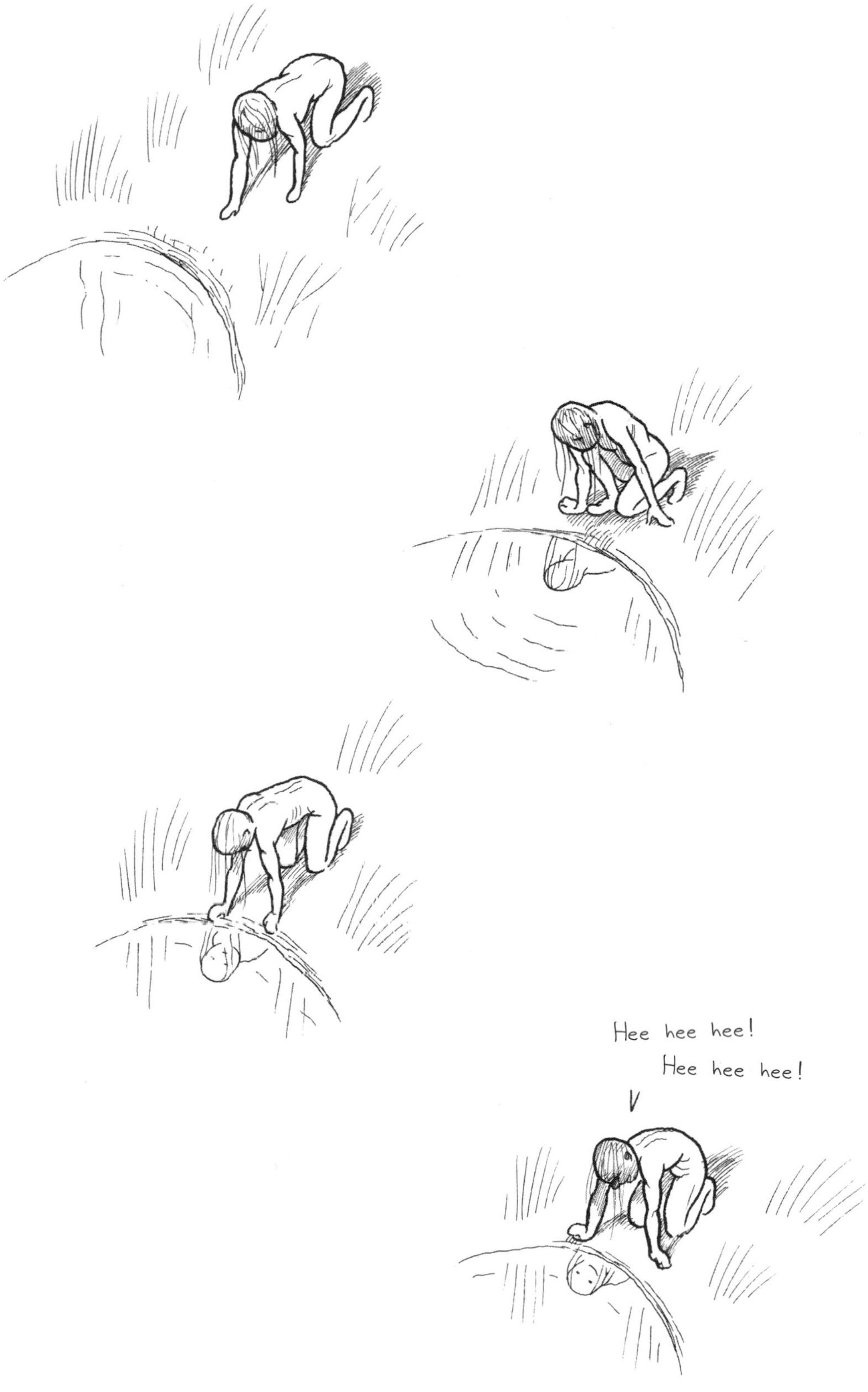
Hee hee hee! Hee hee hee!

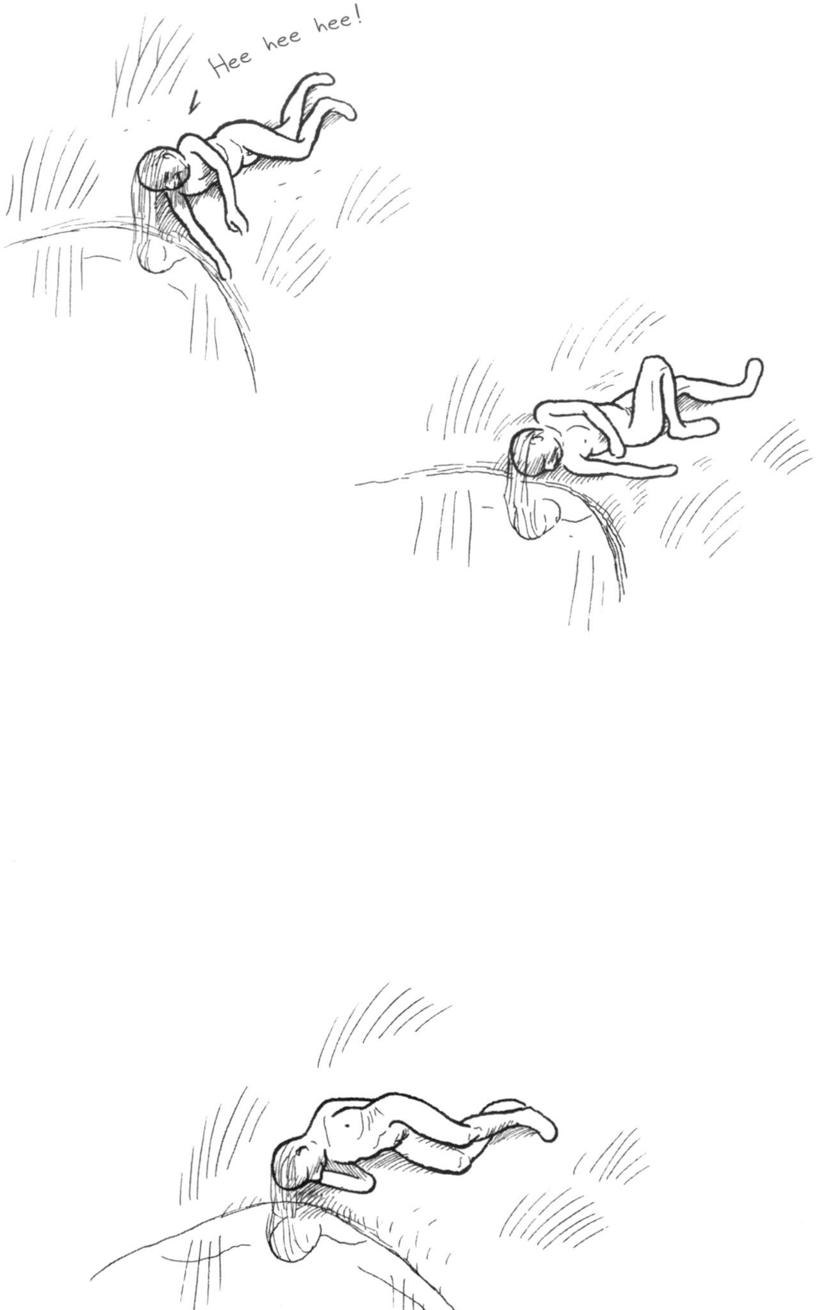
Hee hee hee!

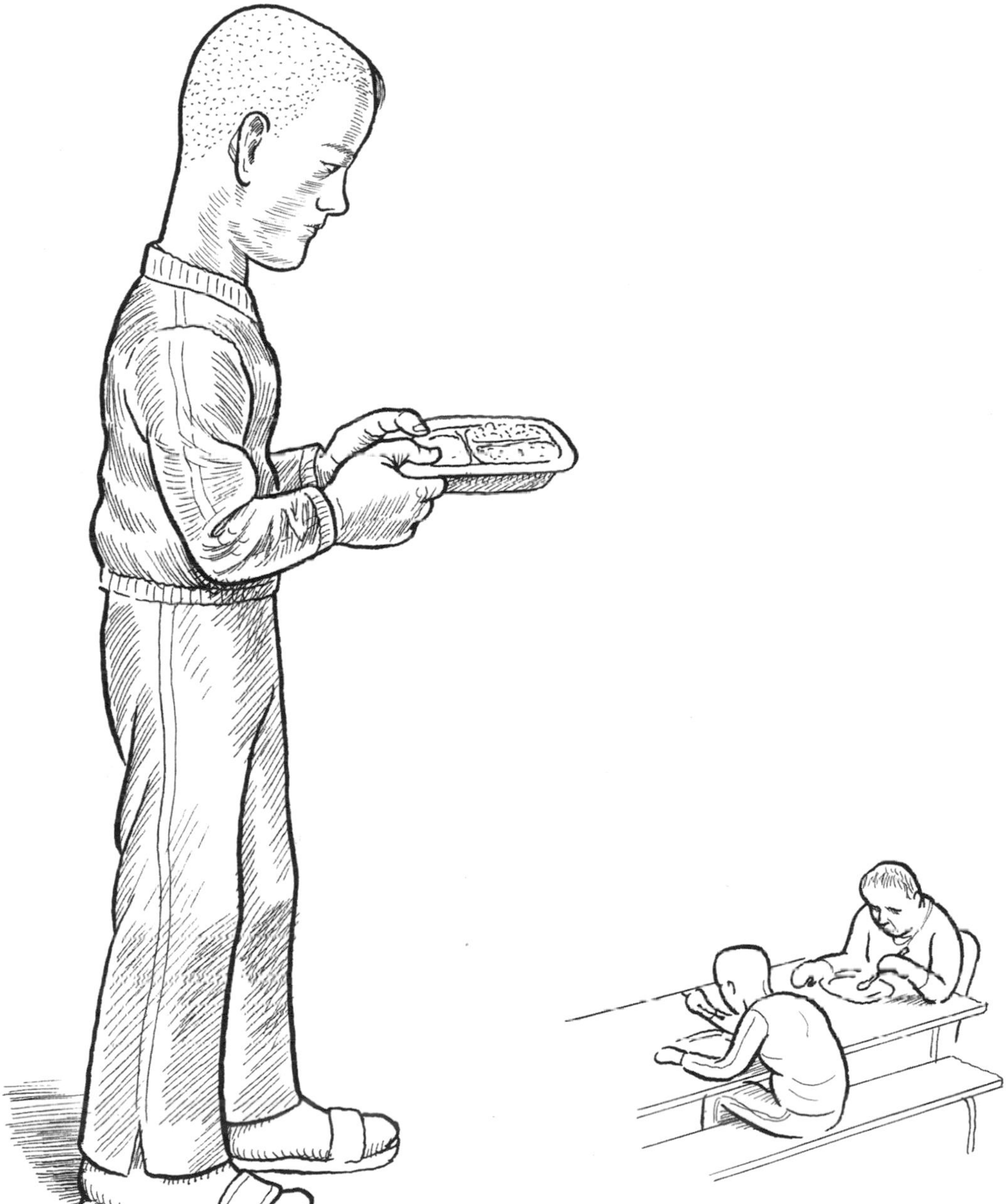

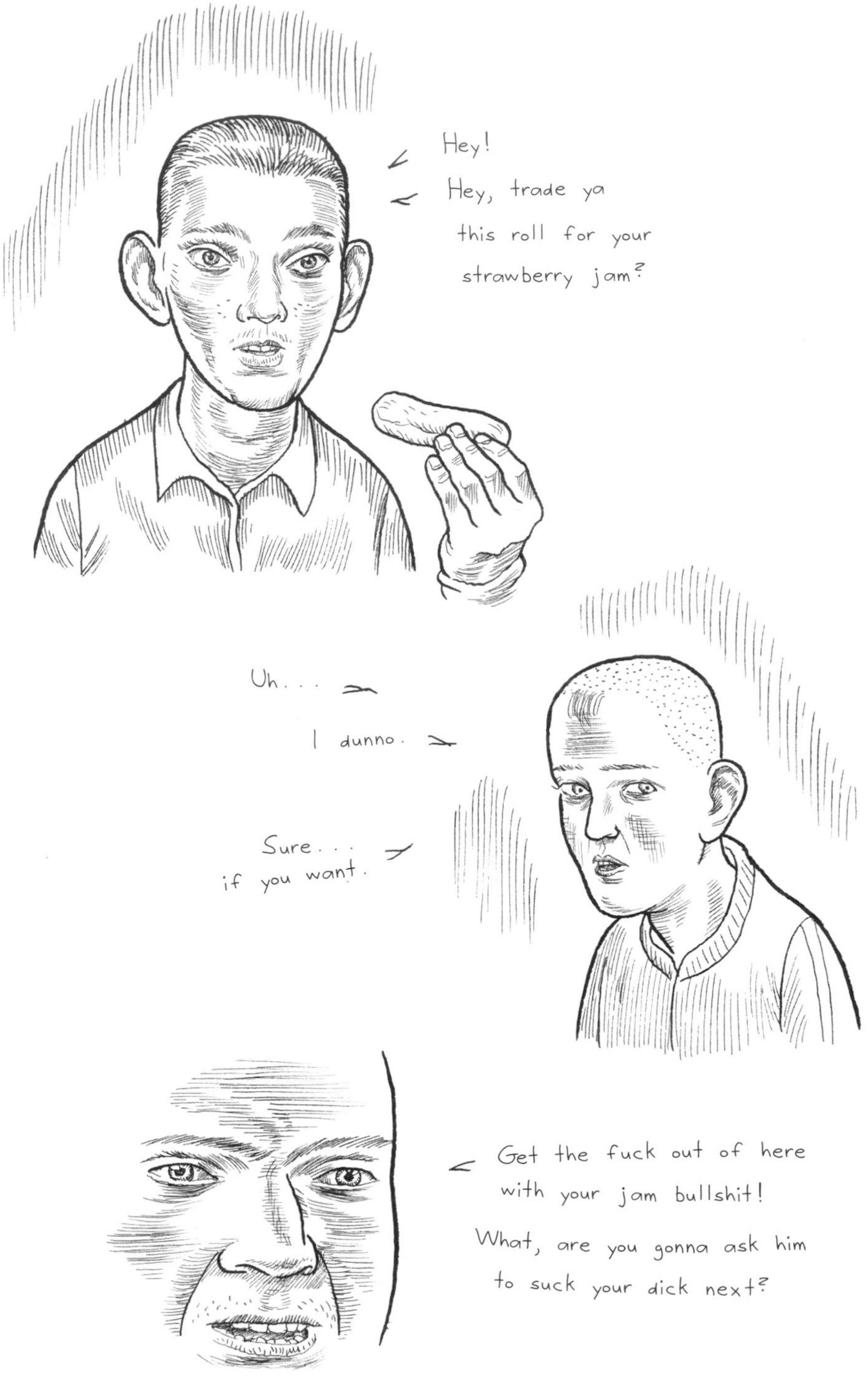
Hey!
Hey, trade ya this roll for your strawberry jam?
Uh...
I dunno.
Sure... if you want.
Get the fuck out of here with your jam bullshit!
What, are you gonna ask him to suck your dick next?

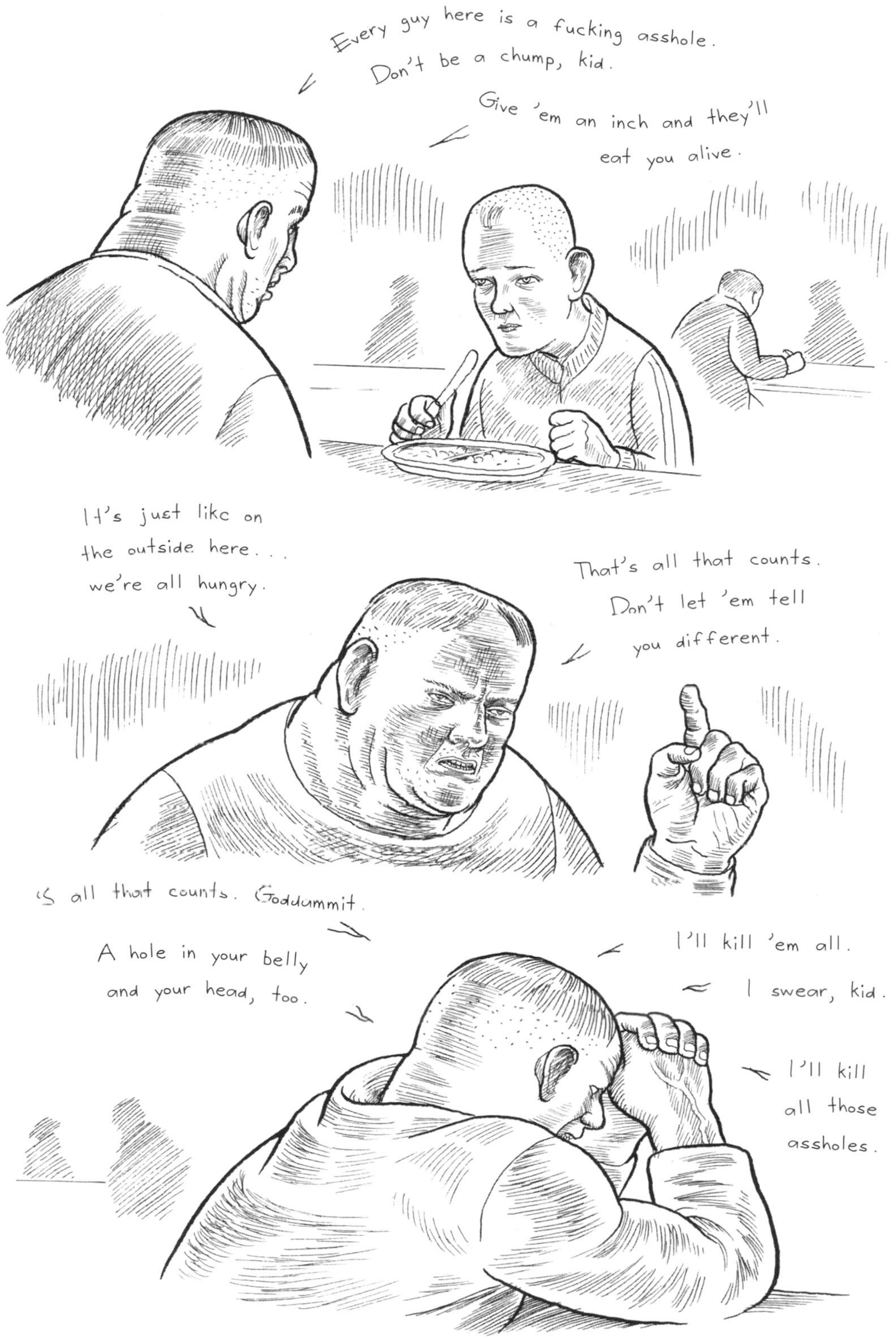
Every guy here is a fucking asshole.
Don't be a chump, kid.
Give 'em an inch and they'll eat you alive.
It's just like on the outside here... we're all hungry.
That's all that counts. Don't let 'em tell you different.
is all that counts. Goddammit.
A hole in your belly and your head, too.
I'll kill 'em all.
I swear, kid.
I'll kill all those assholes.

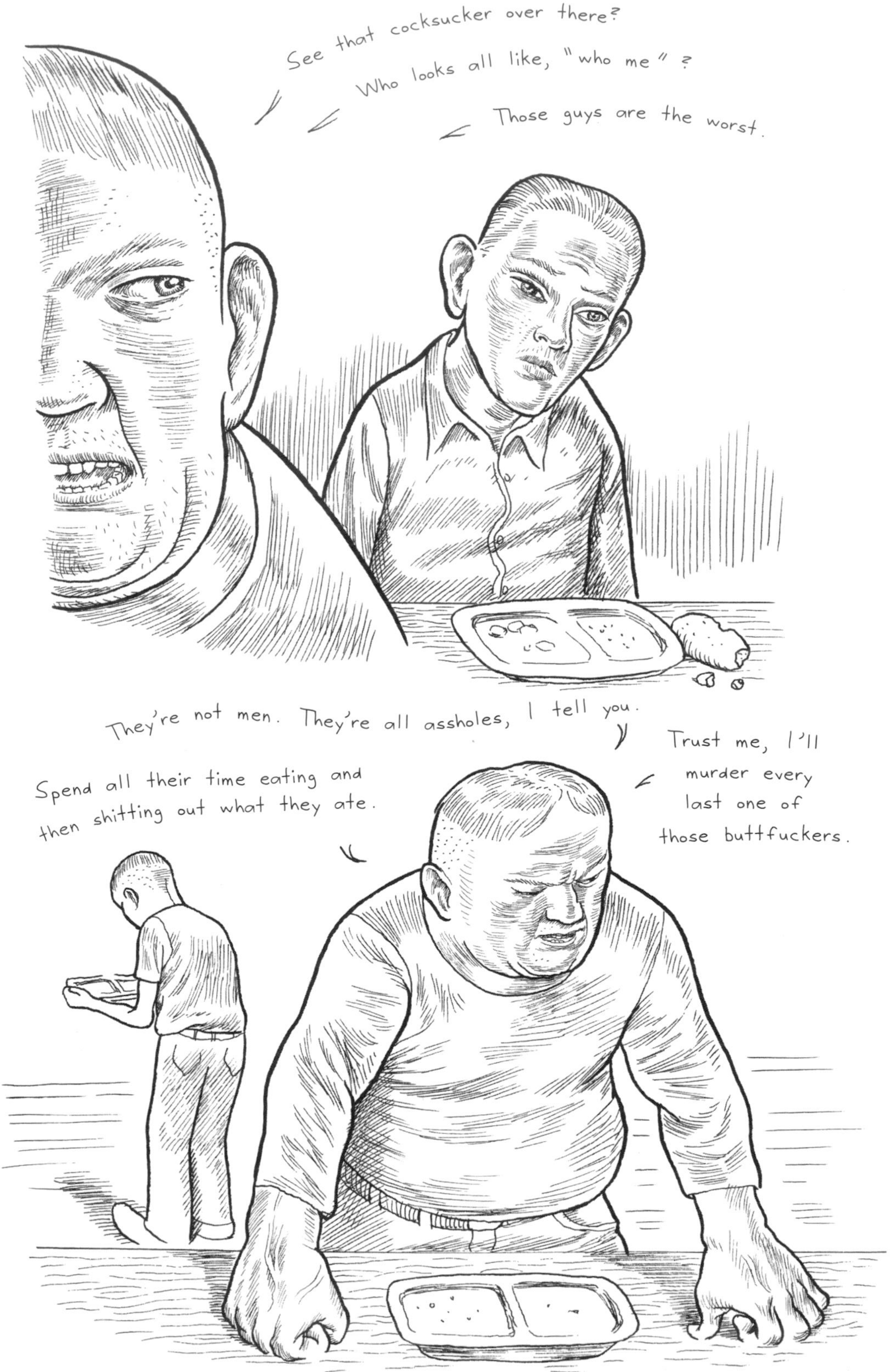

See that cocksucker over there?
Who looks all like, "who me"?
Those guys are the worst.
They're not men. They're all assholes, I tell you.
Spend all their time eating and then shitting out what they ate.
Trust me, I'll murder every last one of those buttfuckers.

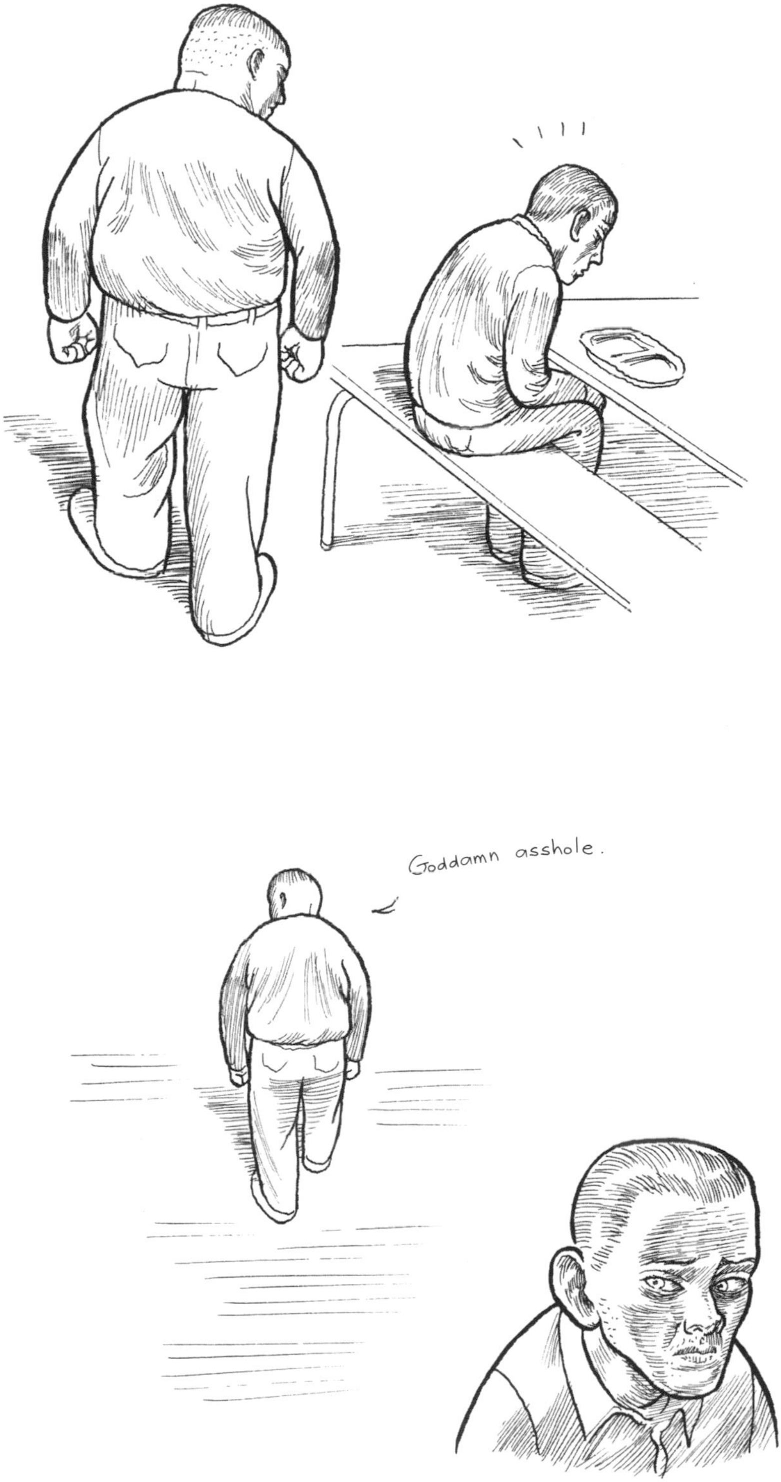
Goddamn asshole.

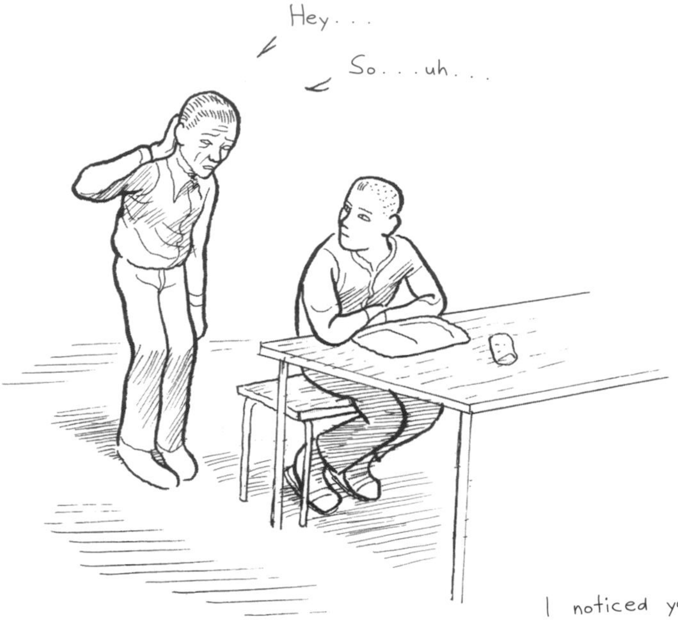
Hey...
So...uh...

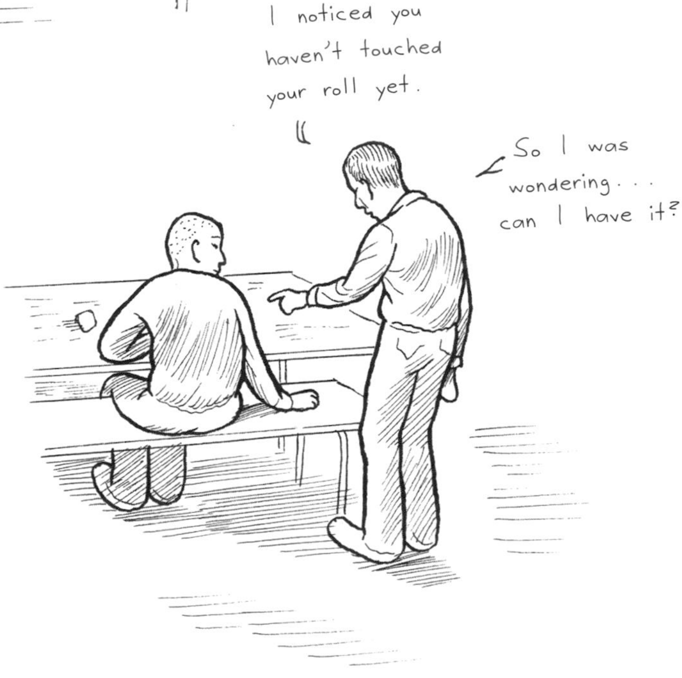
I noticed you haven't touched your roll yet.
So I was wondering... can I have it?

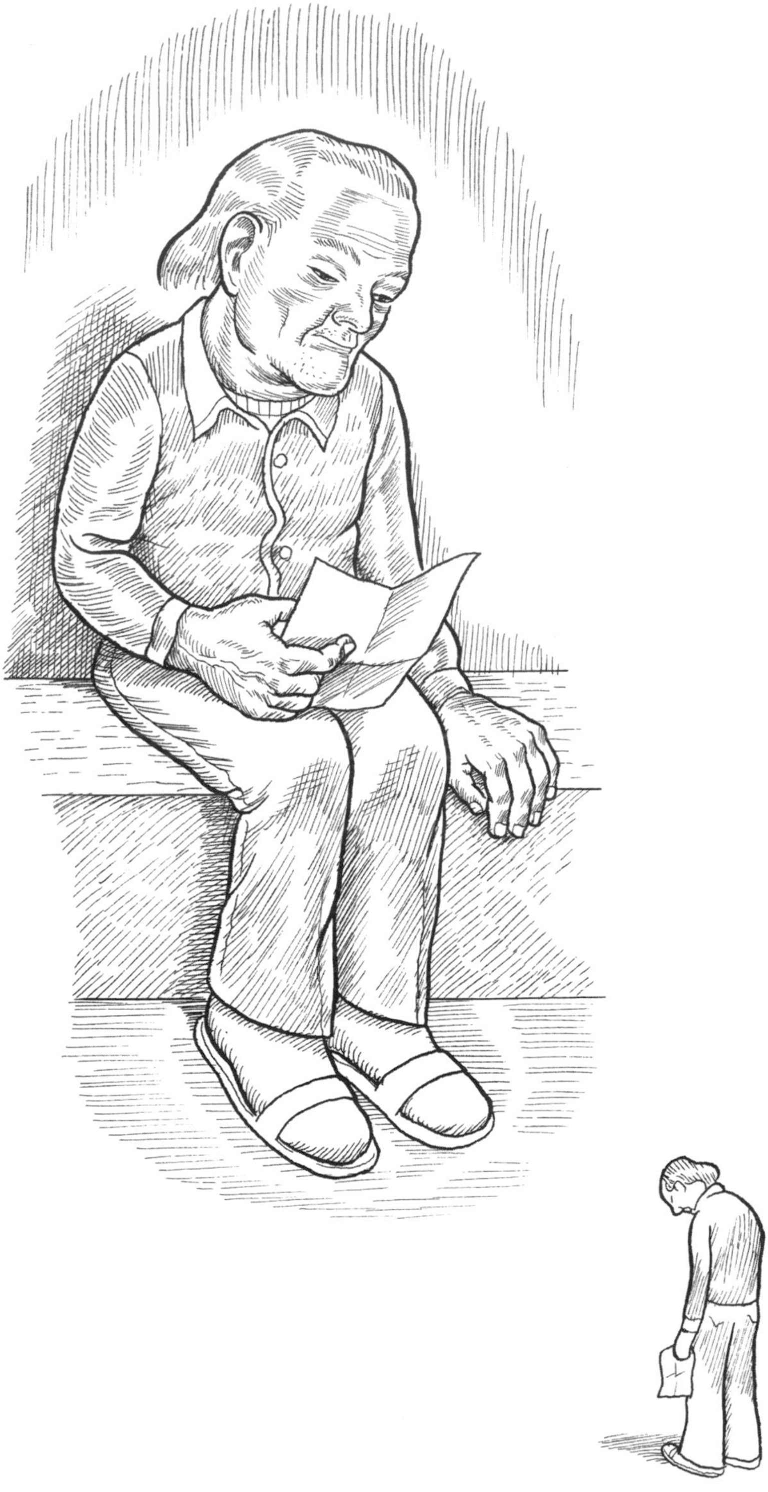

Mmph. . .

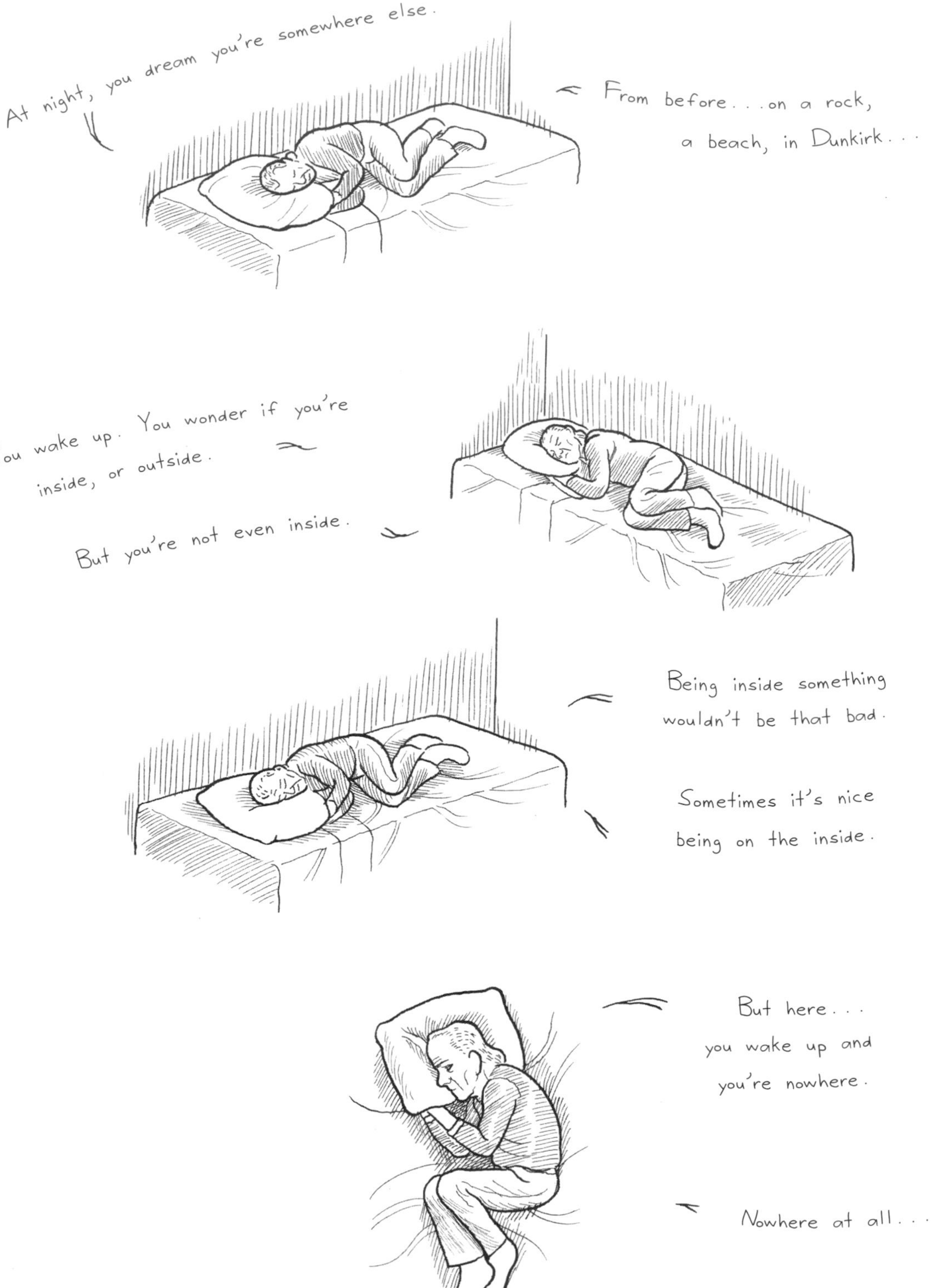
At night, you dream you're somewhere else.
From before... on a rock, a beach, in Dunkirk...
You wake up. You wonder if you're inside, or outside.
But you're not even inside.
Being inside something wouldn't be that bad.
Sometimes it's nice being on the inside.
But here... you wake up and you're nowhere.
Nowhere at all...

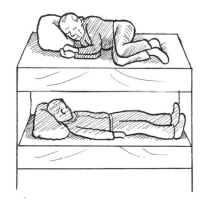

Hey, you got someone
on the outside?

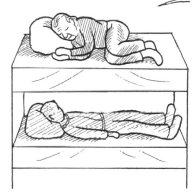

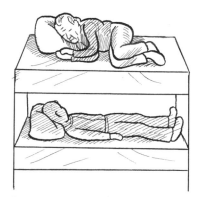

Yeah, I think.

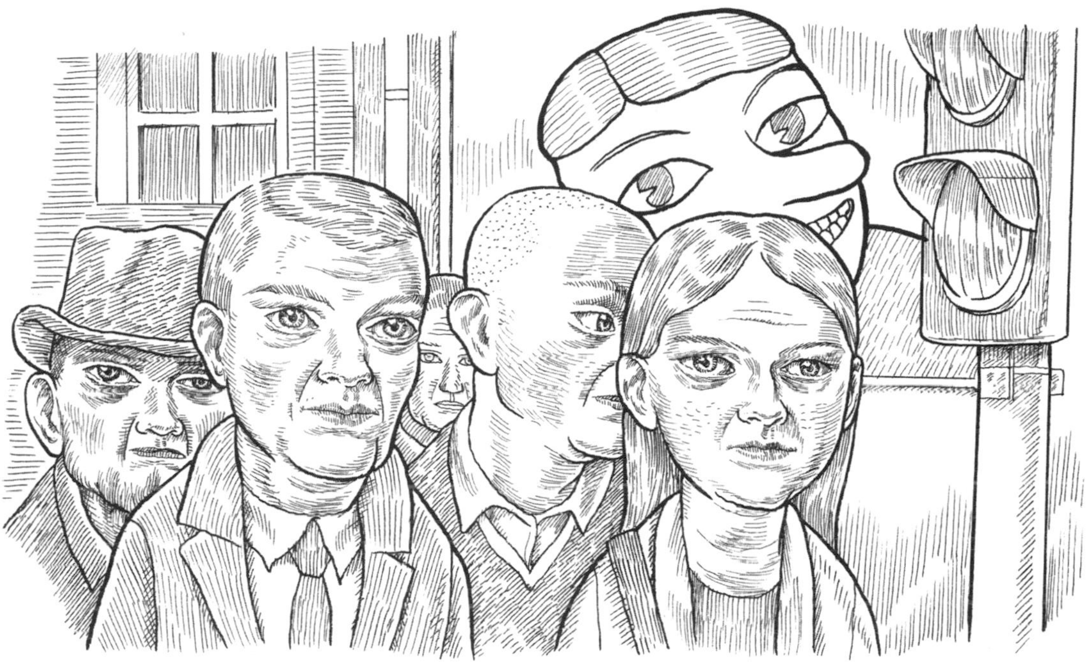

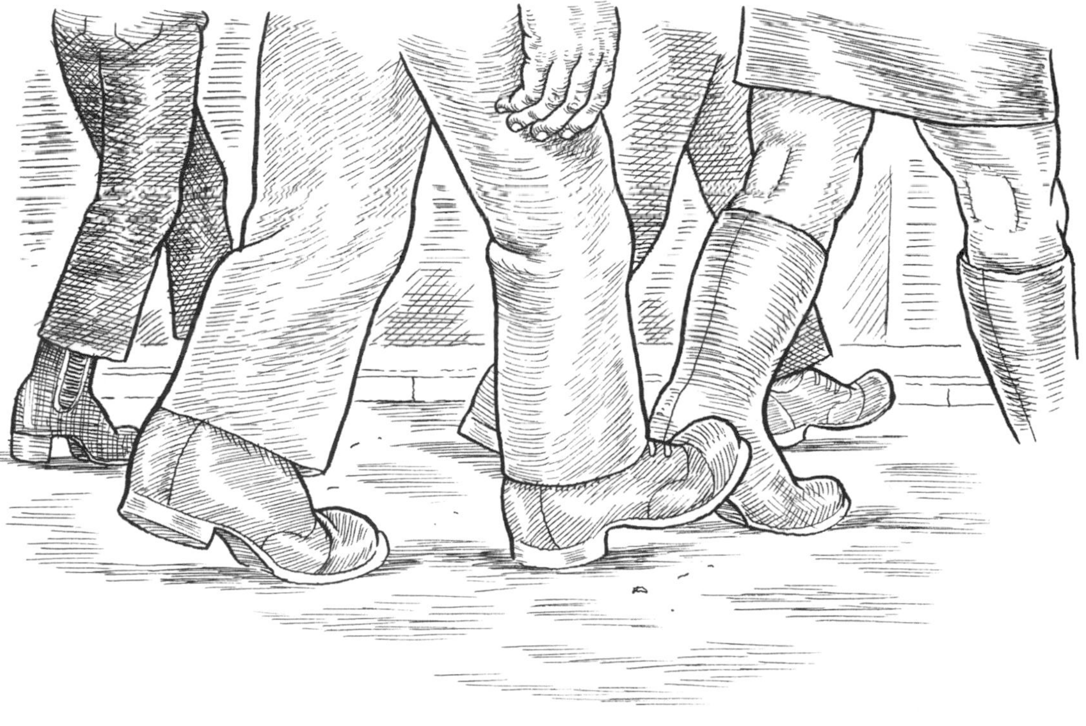

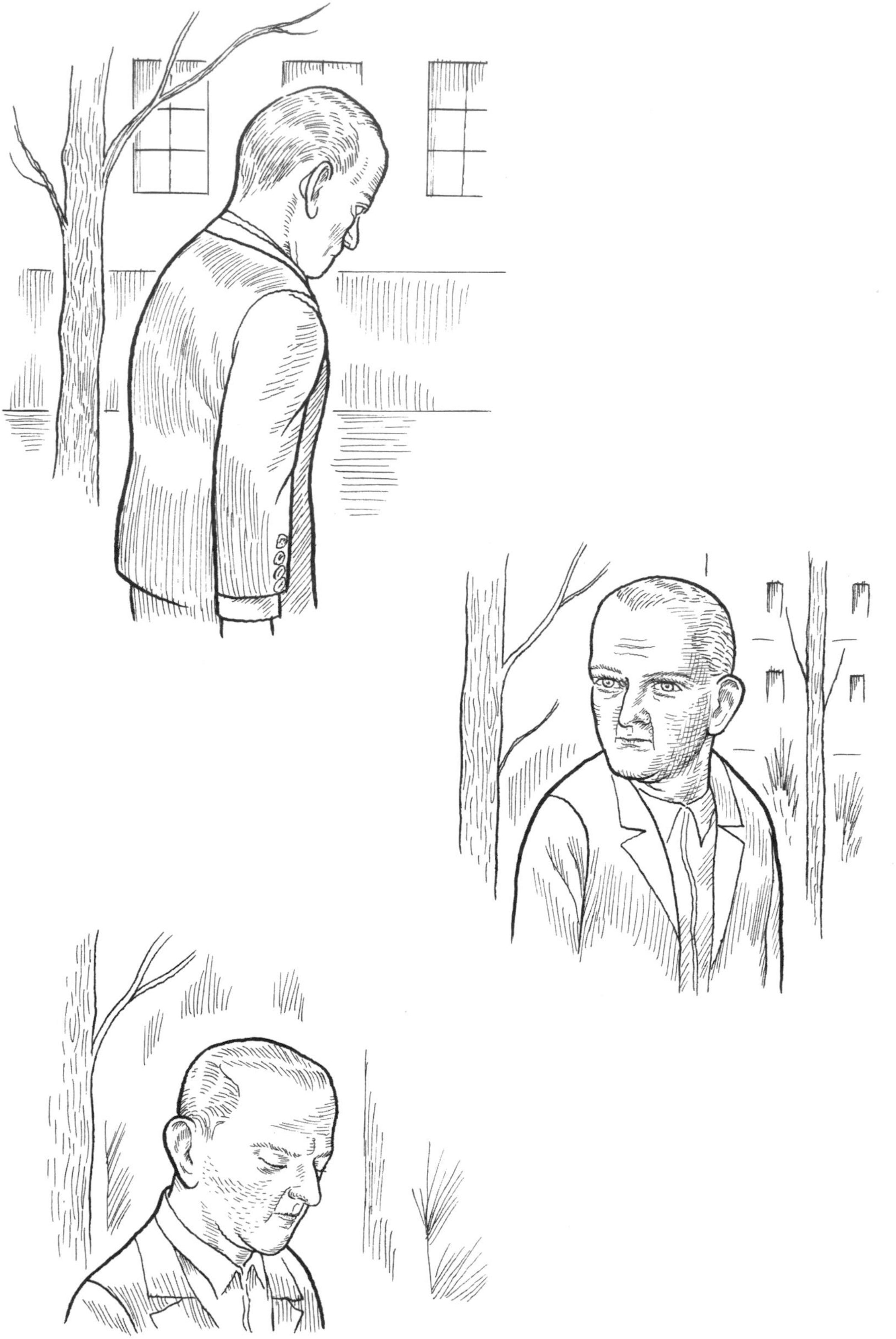

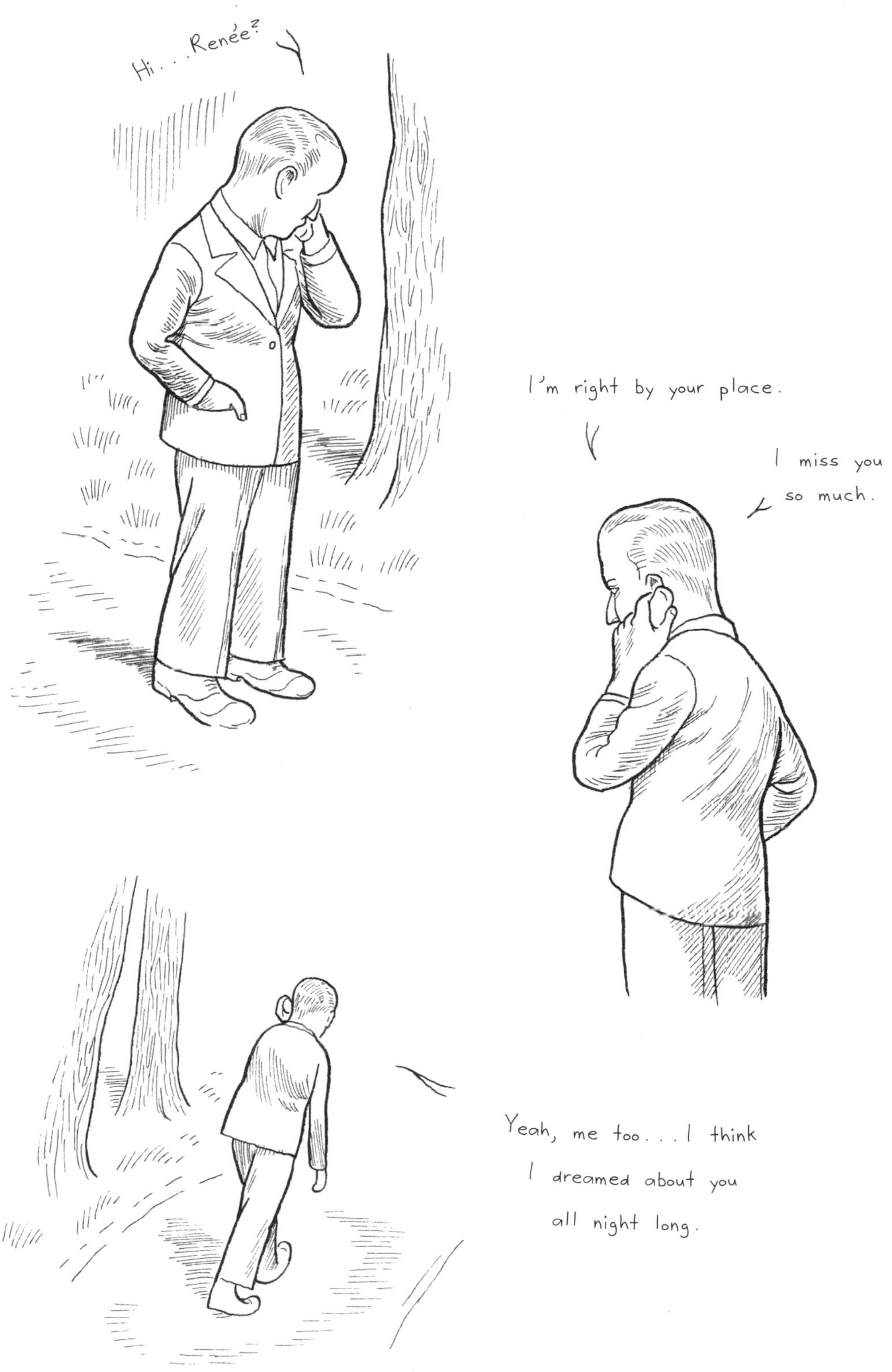
Hi. . .Renée?
I'm right by your place.
I miss you so much.
Yeah, me too. . . I think I dreamed about you all night long.

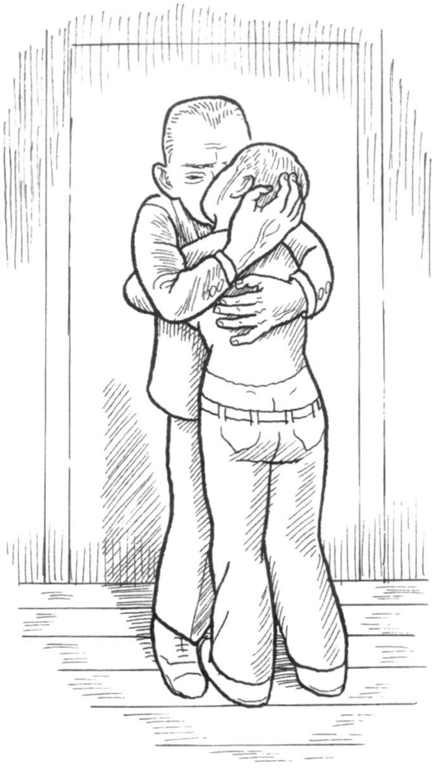
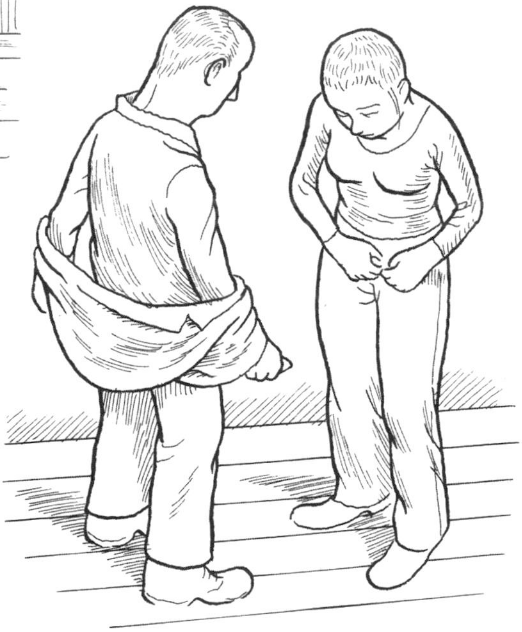
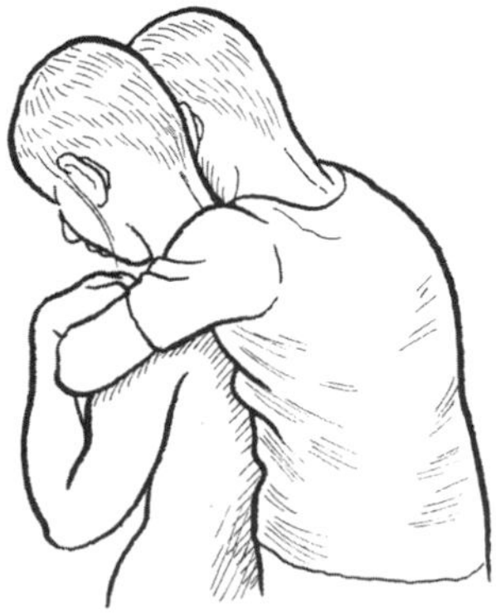

Goddamn...

Fuck me, fuck me hard.

I'm your whore.

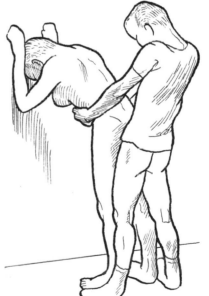

Fucking destroy me.

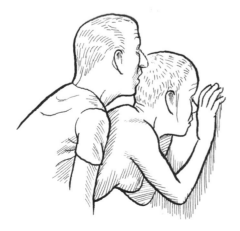

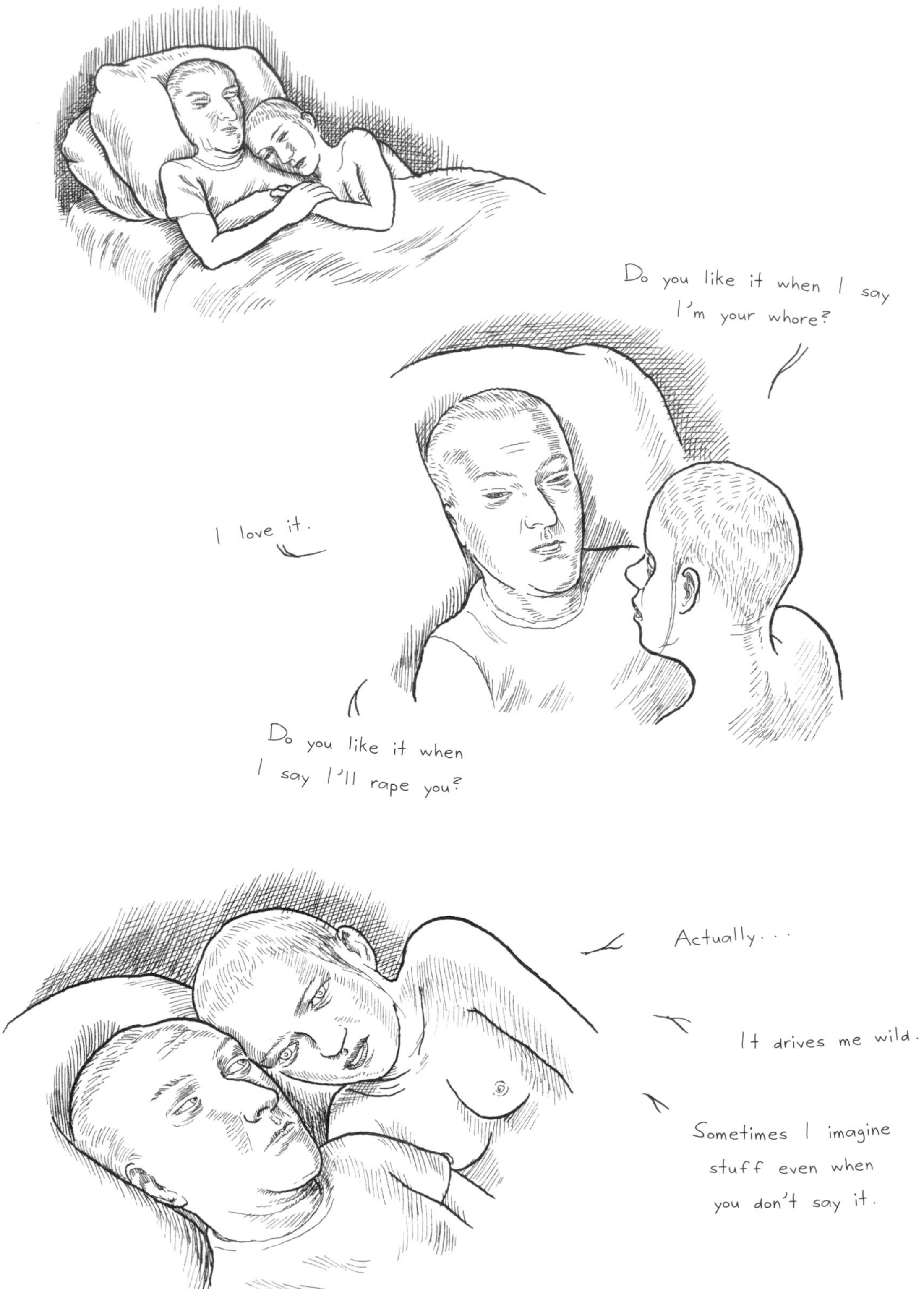
Do you like it when I say I'm your whore?
I love it.
Do you like it when I say I'll rape you?
Actually...
It drives me wild.
Sometimes I imagine stuff even when you don't say it.

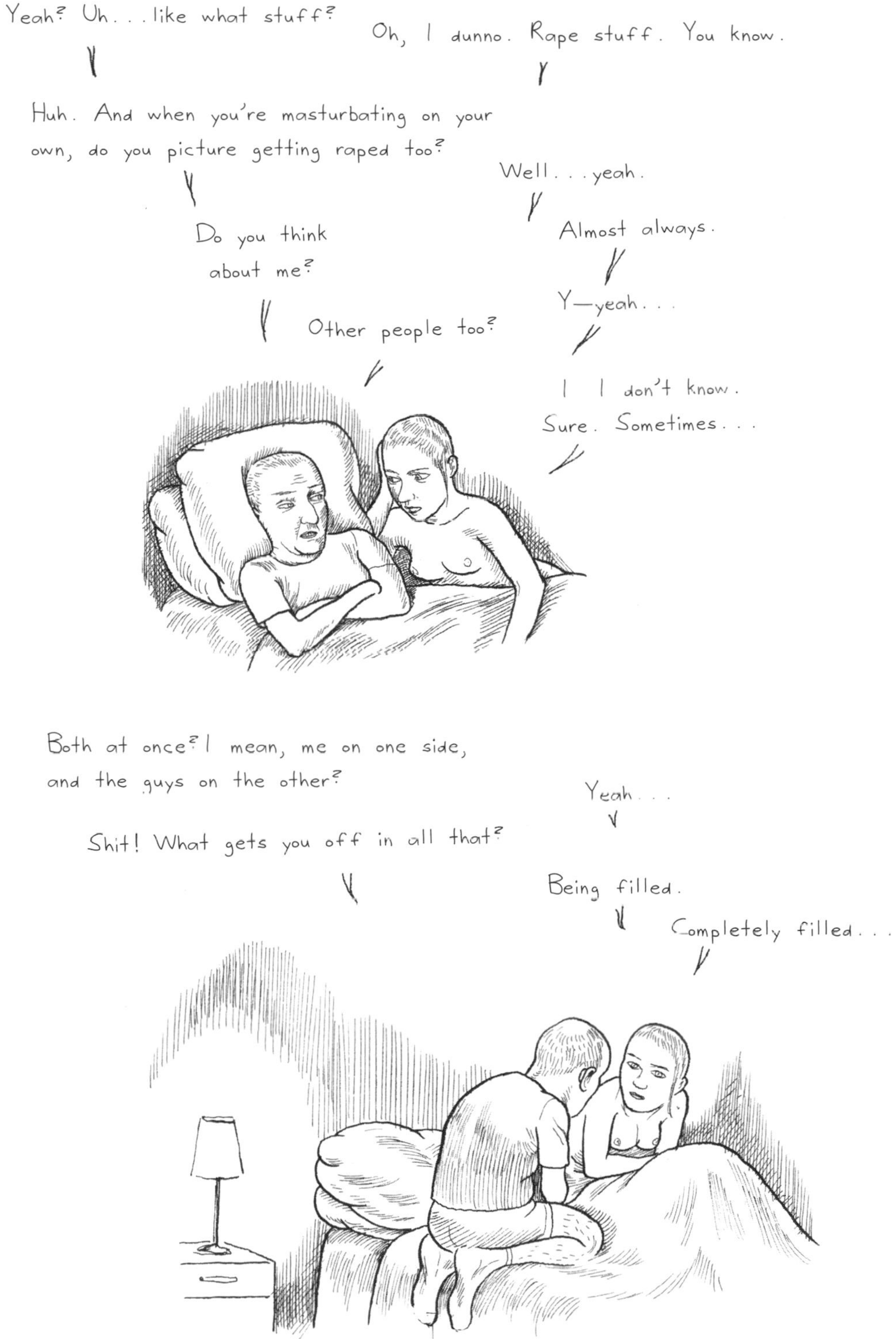
Yeah? Uh...like what stuff?
Oh, I dunno. Rape stuff. You know.
Huh. And when you're masturbating on your own, do you picture getting raped too?
Well...yeah.
Almost always.
Do you think about me?
Y—yeah...
Other people too?
I I don't know. Sure. Sometimes...
Both at once? I mean, me on one side, and the guys on the other?
Yeah...
Shit! What gets you off in all that?
Being filled.
Completely filled...

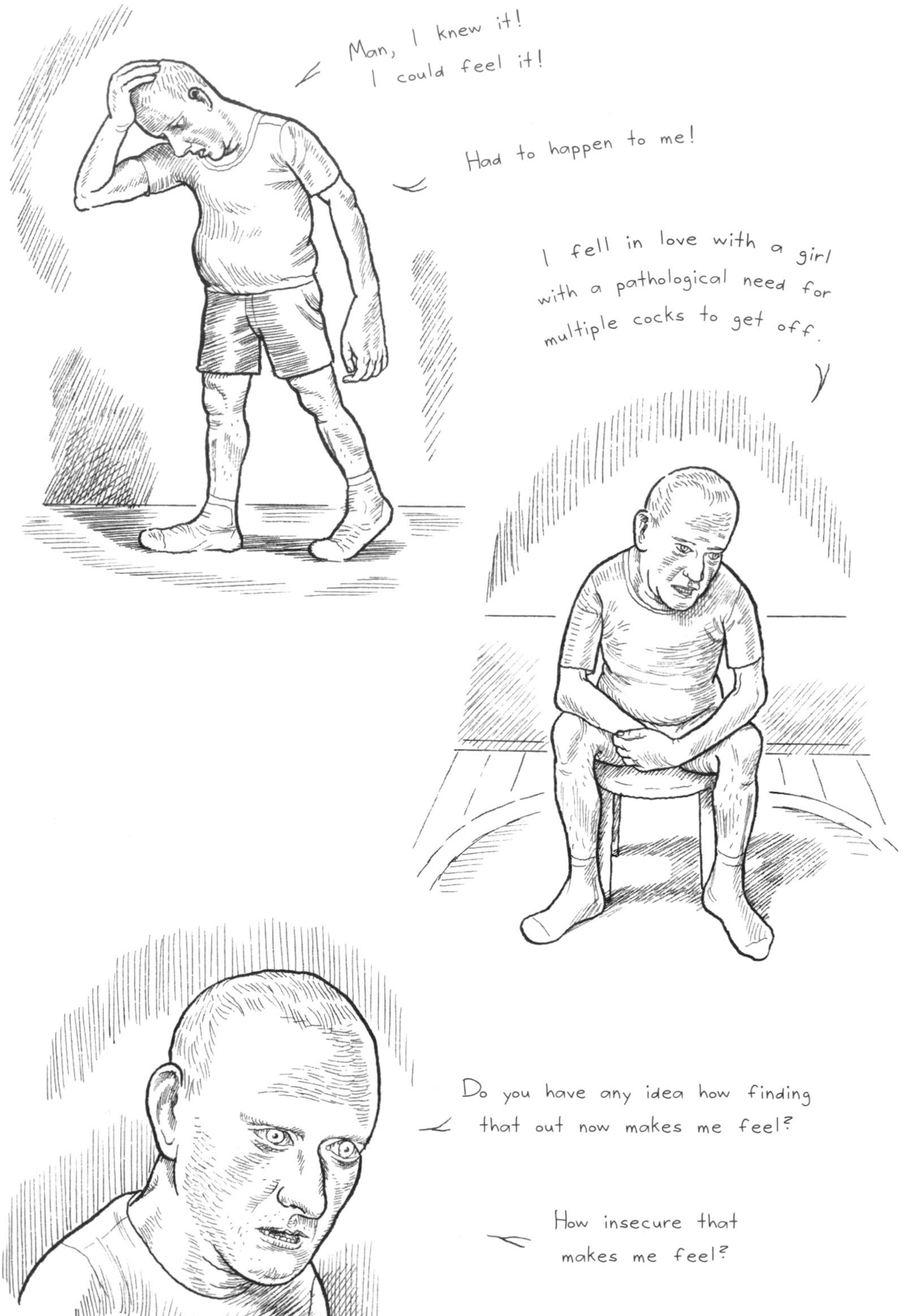
Man, I knew it!
I could feel it!
Had to happen to me!
I fell in love with a girl with a pathological need for multiple cocks to get off.
Do you have any idea how finding that out now makes me feel?
How insecure that makes me feel?

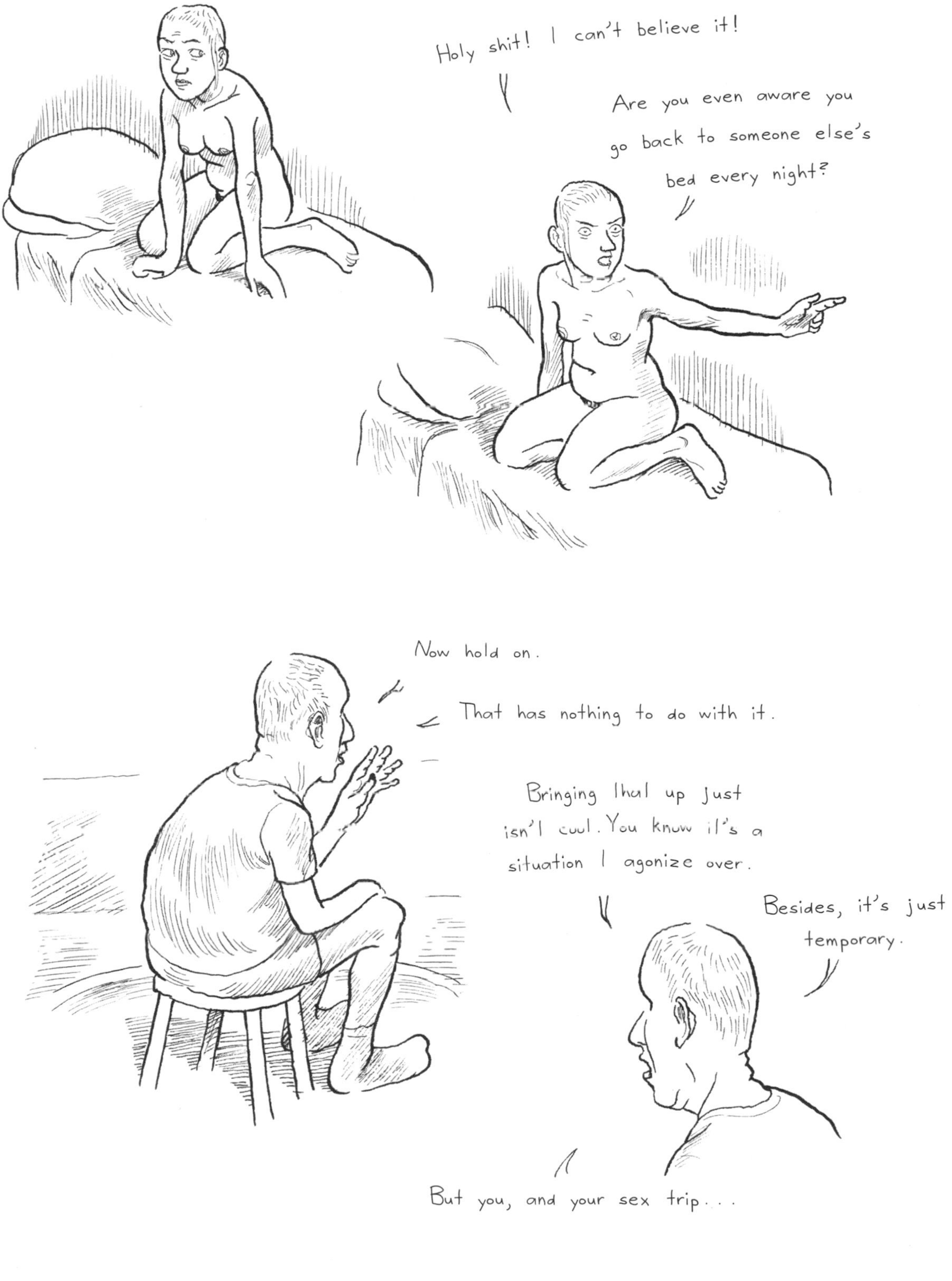
Holy shit! I can't believe it!
Are you even aware you go back to someone else's bed every night?
Now hold on.
That has nothing to do with it.
Bringing that up just isn't cool. You know it's a situation I agonize over.
Besides, it's just temporary.
But you, and your sex trip...

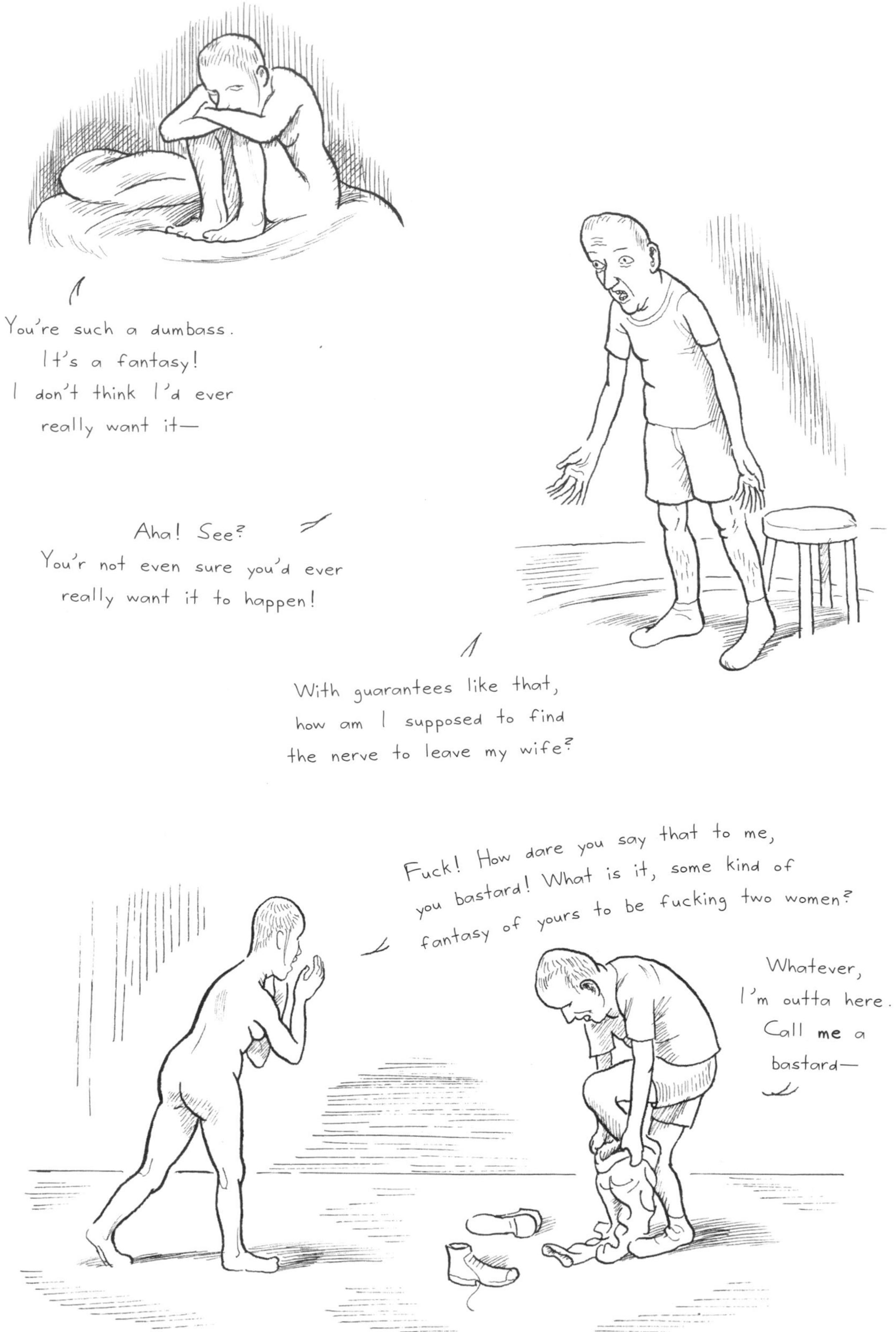
You're such a dumbass. It's a fantasy! I don't think I'd ever really want it—
Aha! See? You'r not even sure you'd ever really want it to happen!
With guarantees like that, how am I supposed to find the nerve to leave my wife?
Fuck! How dare you say that to me, you bastard! What is it, some kind of fantasy of yours to be fucking two women?
Whatever, I'm outta here. Call **me** a bastard—

WHAM

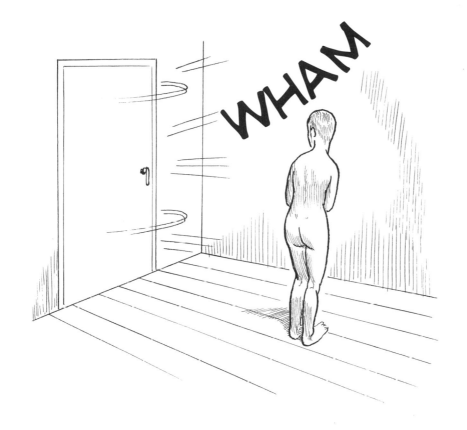

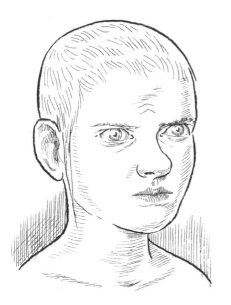

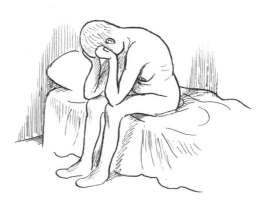

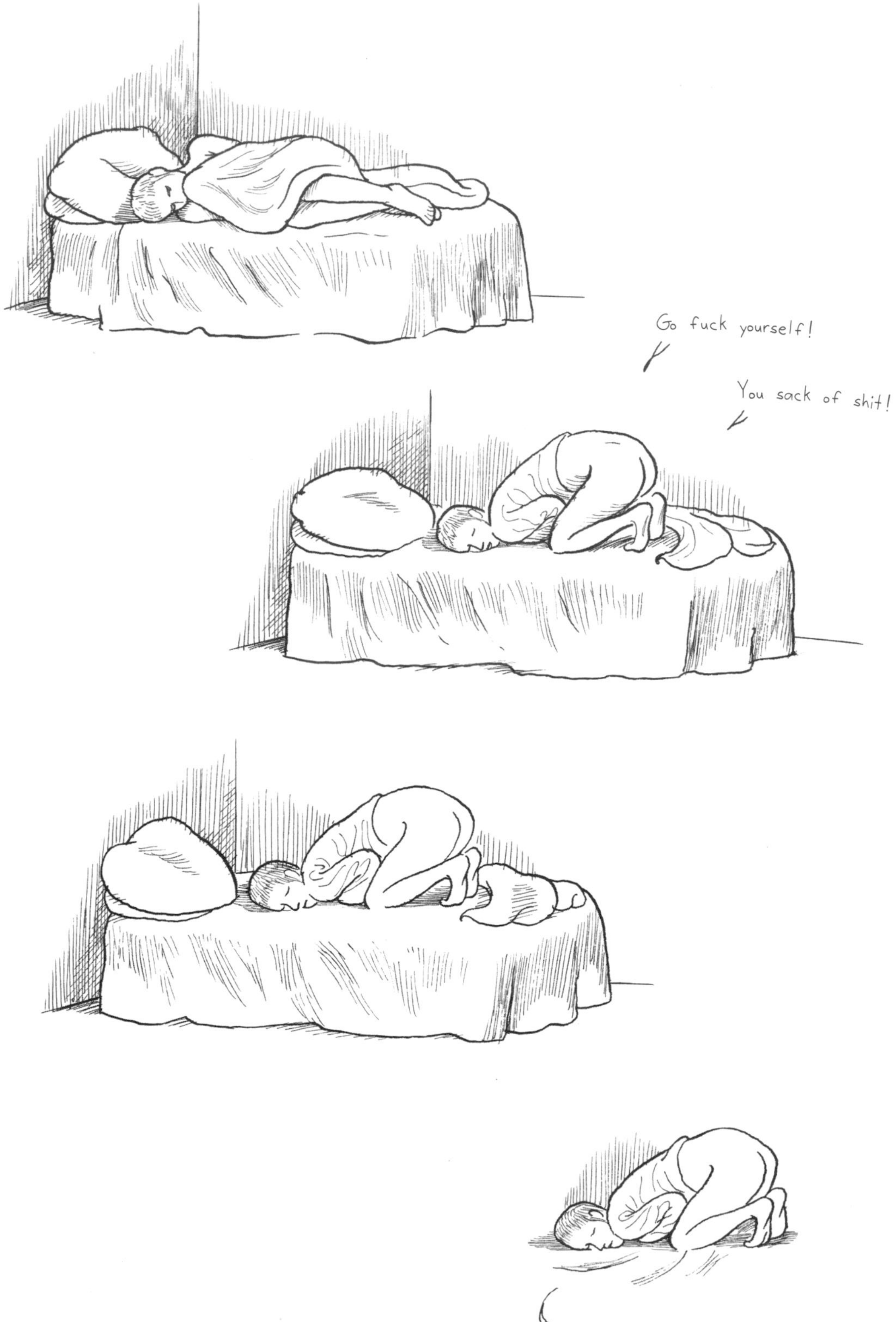
Go fuck yourself!
You sack of shit!
Sack of shit!

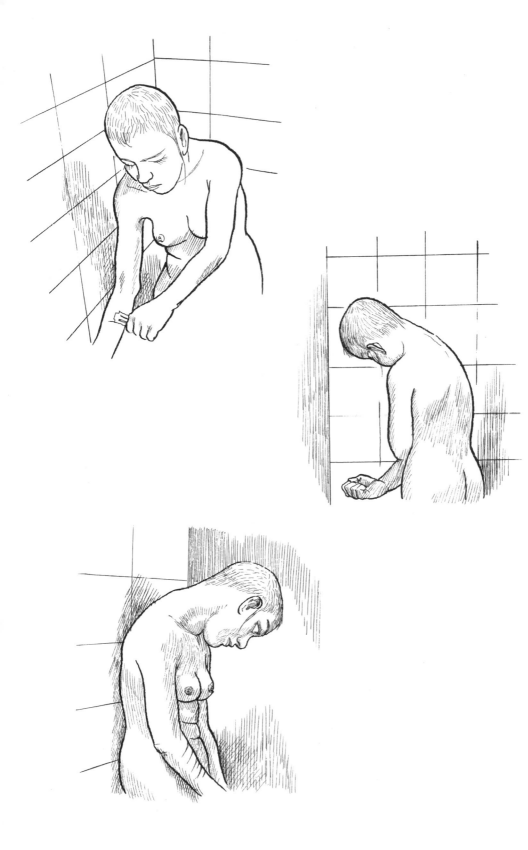

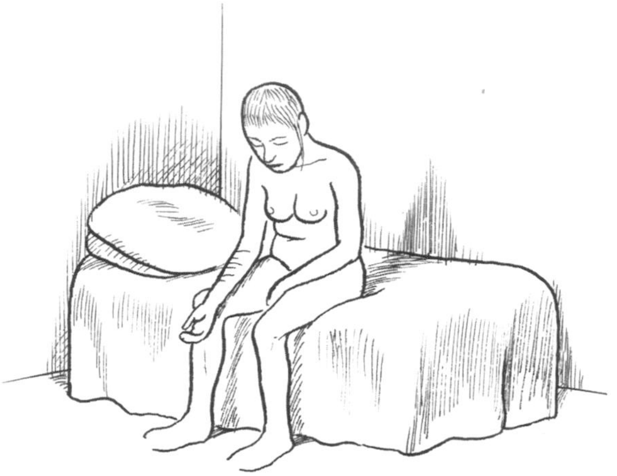

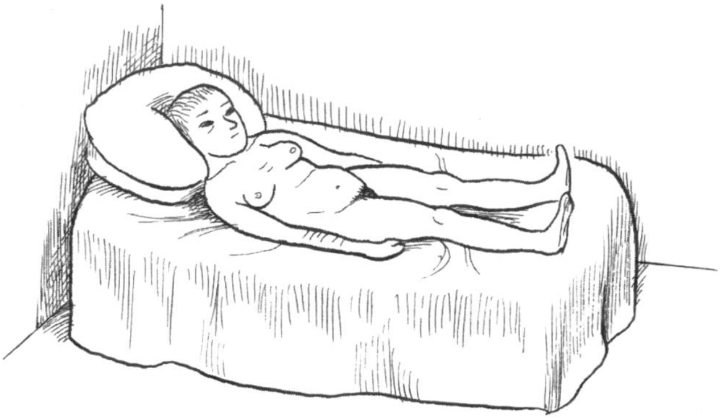

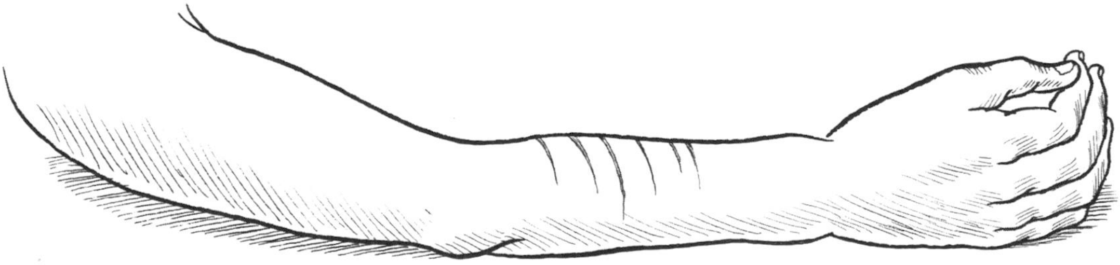

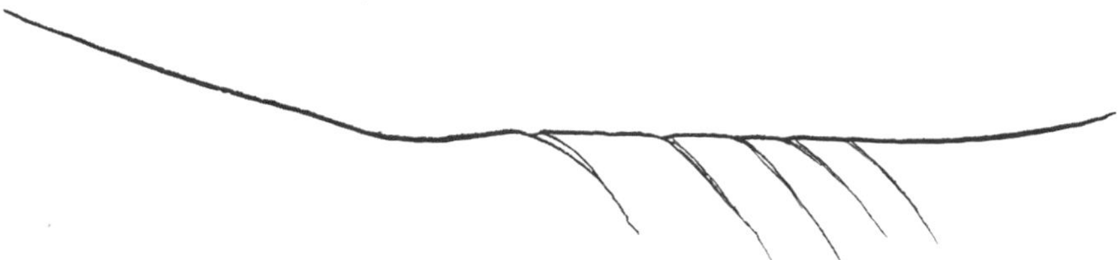

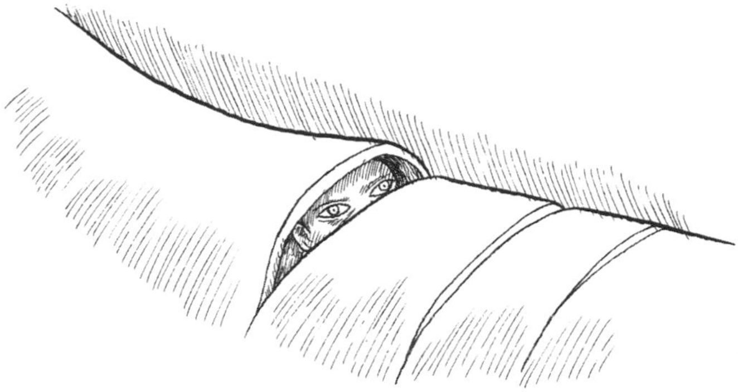

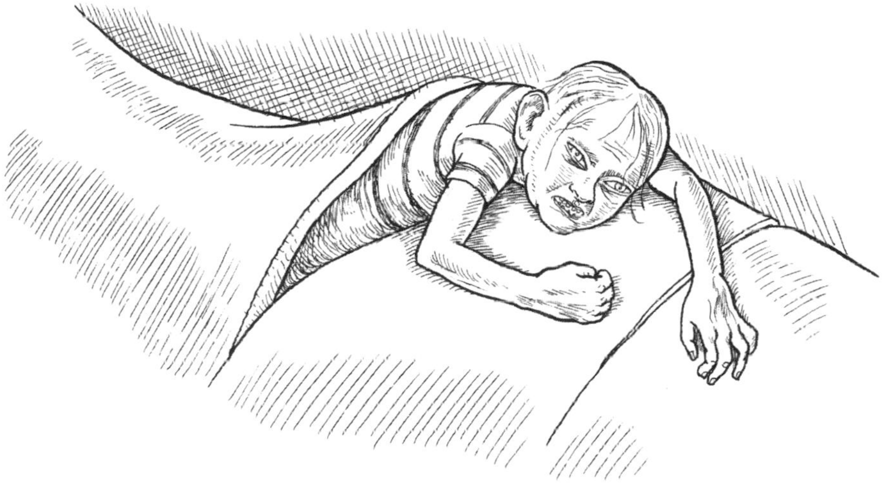

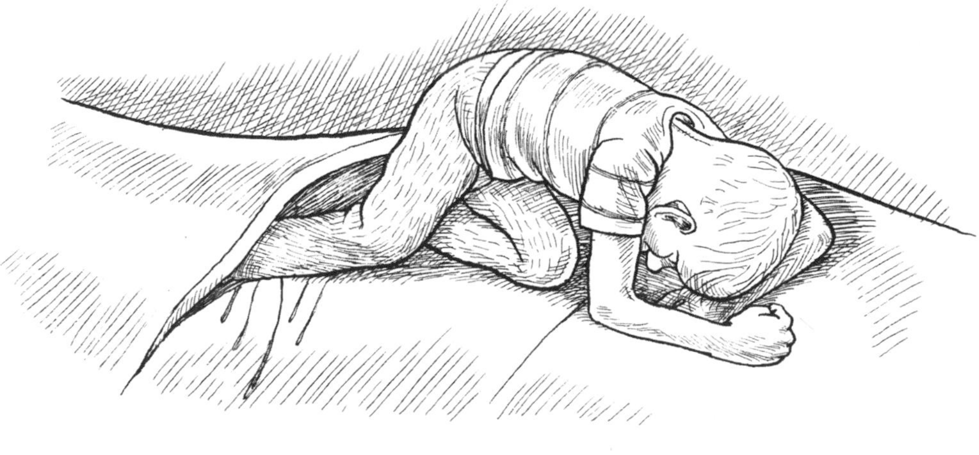

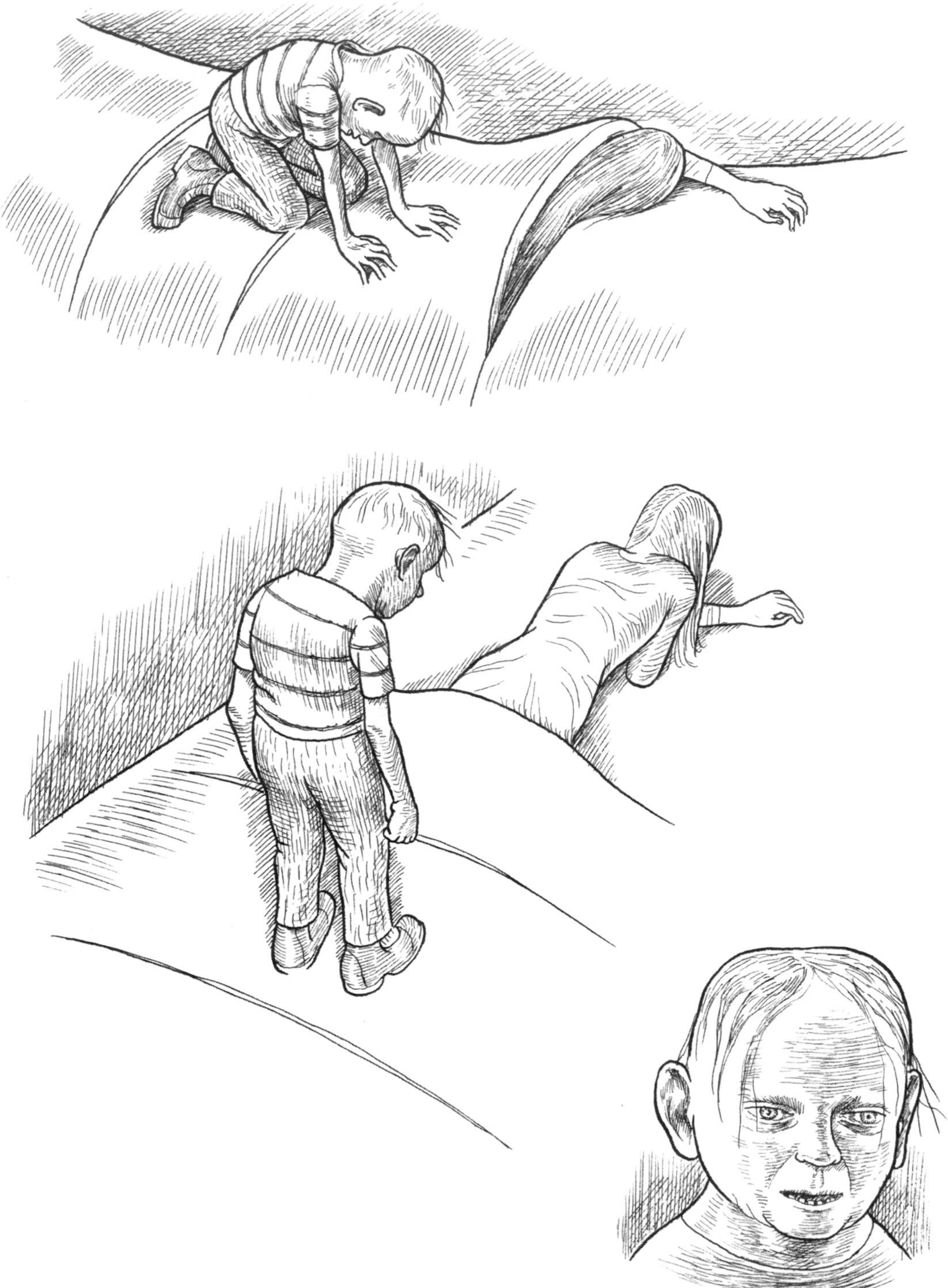

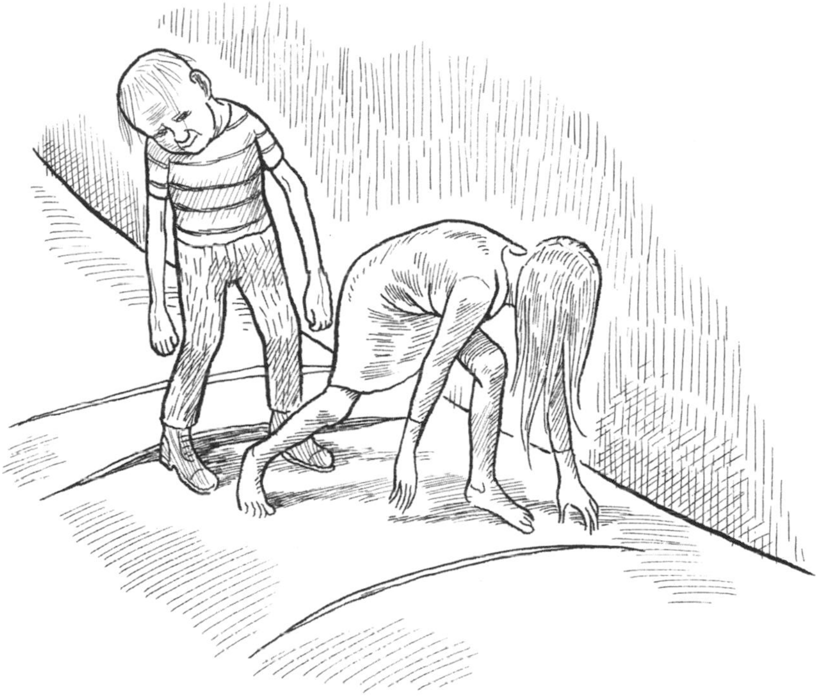
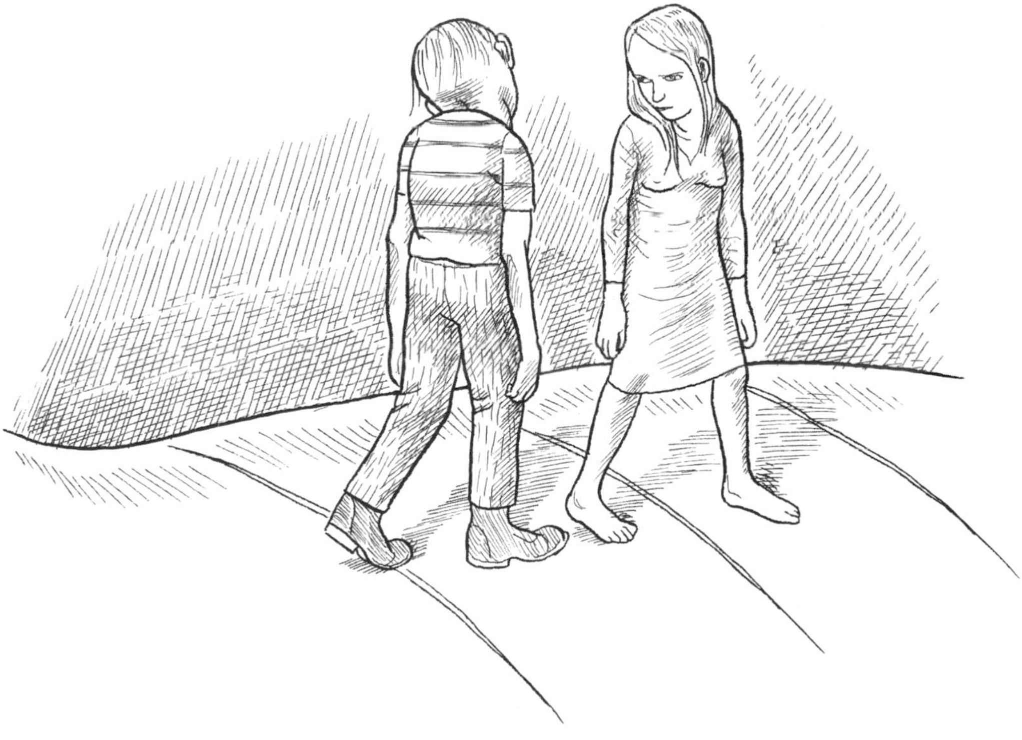

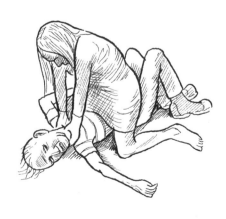

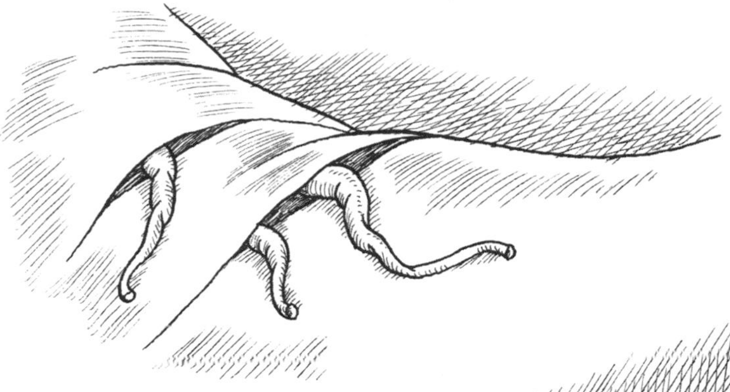

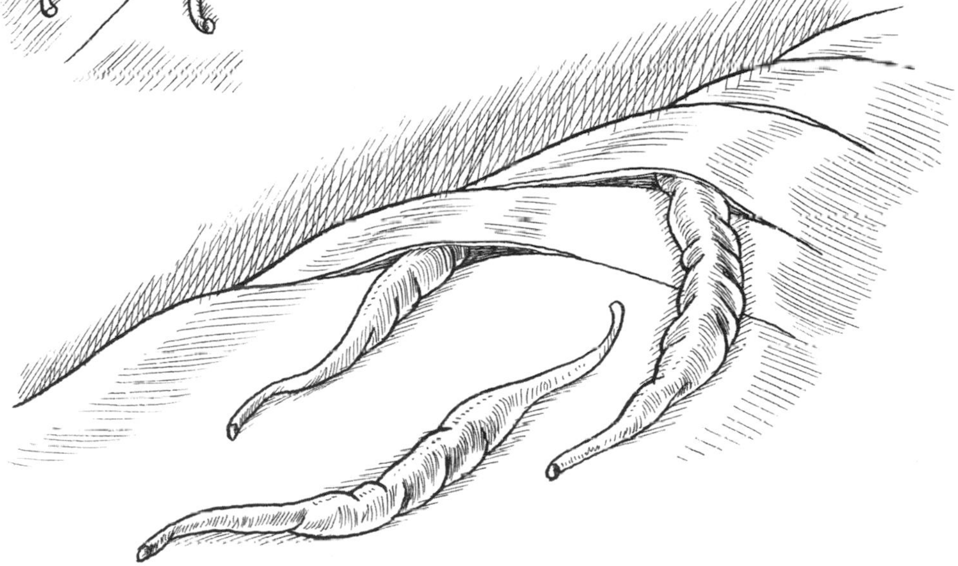

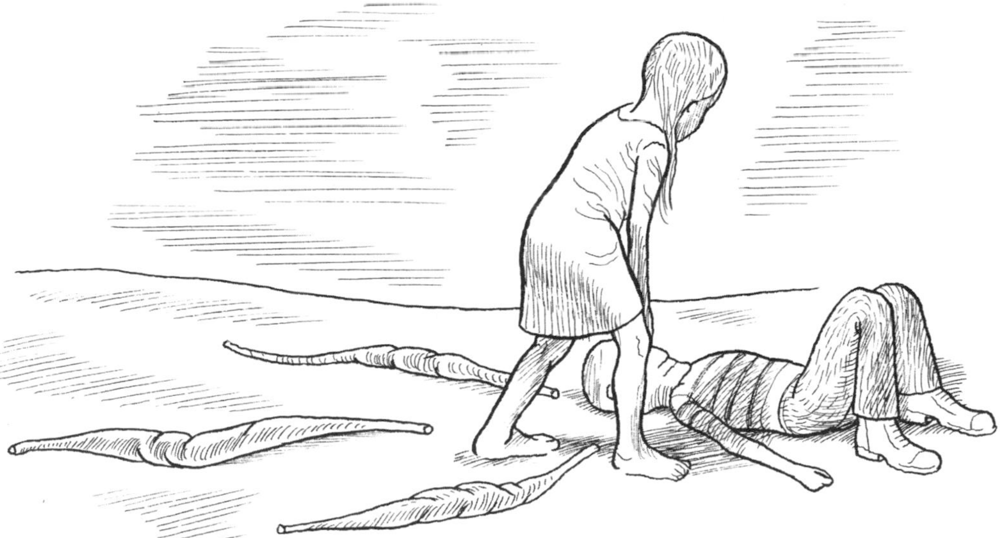

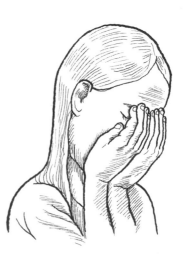

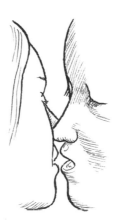

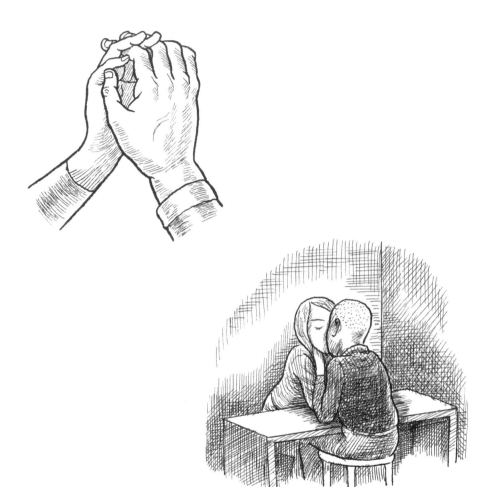

Visiting hours are over!

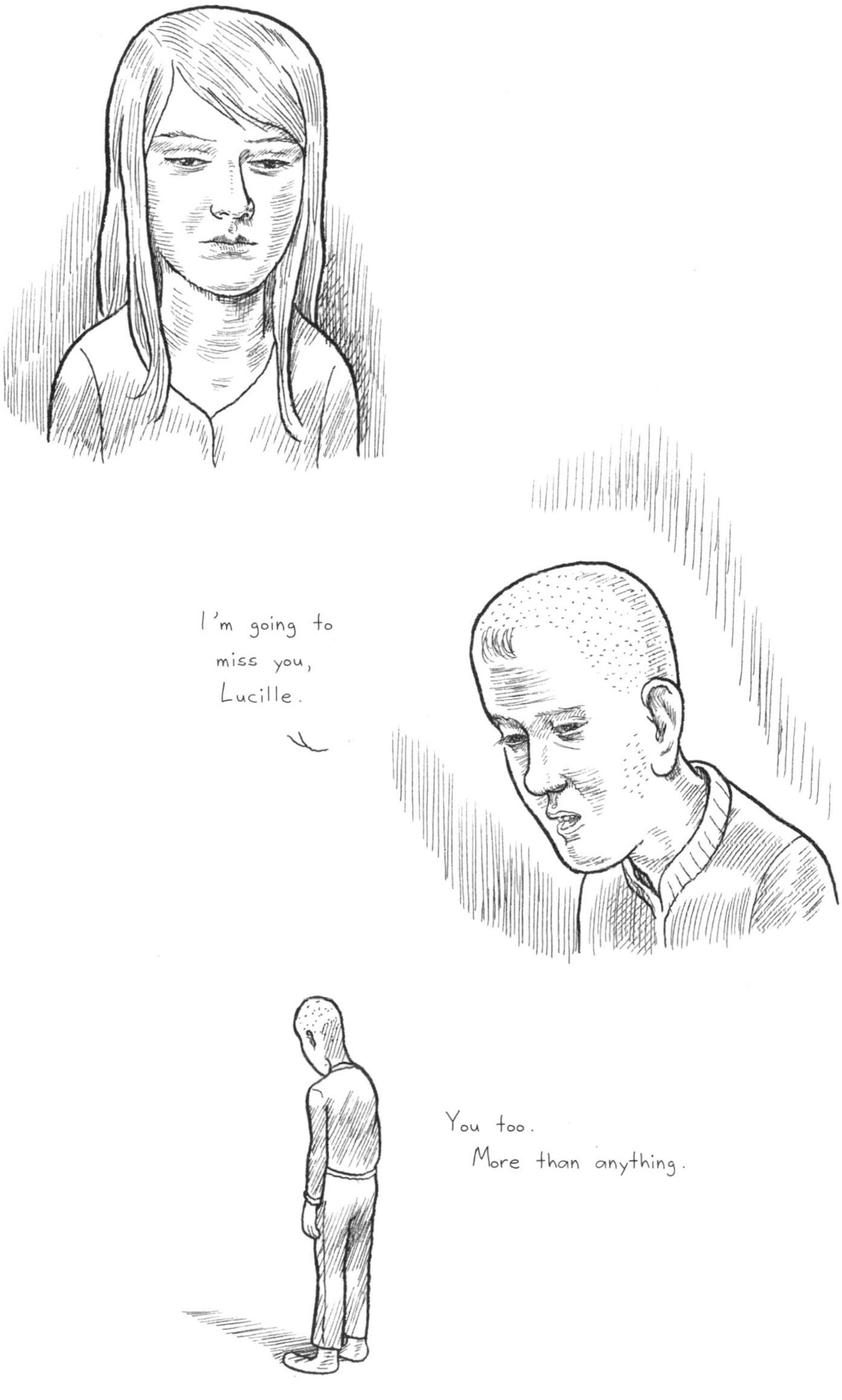
I'm going to miss you, Lucille.
You too. More than anything.

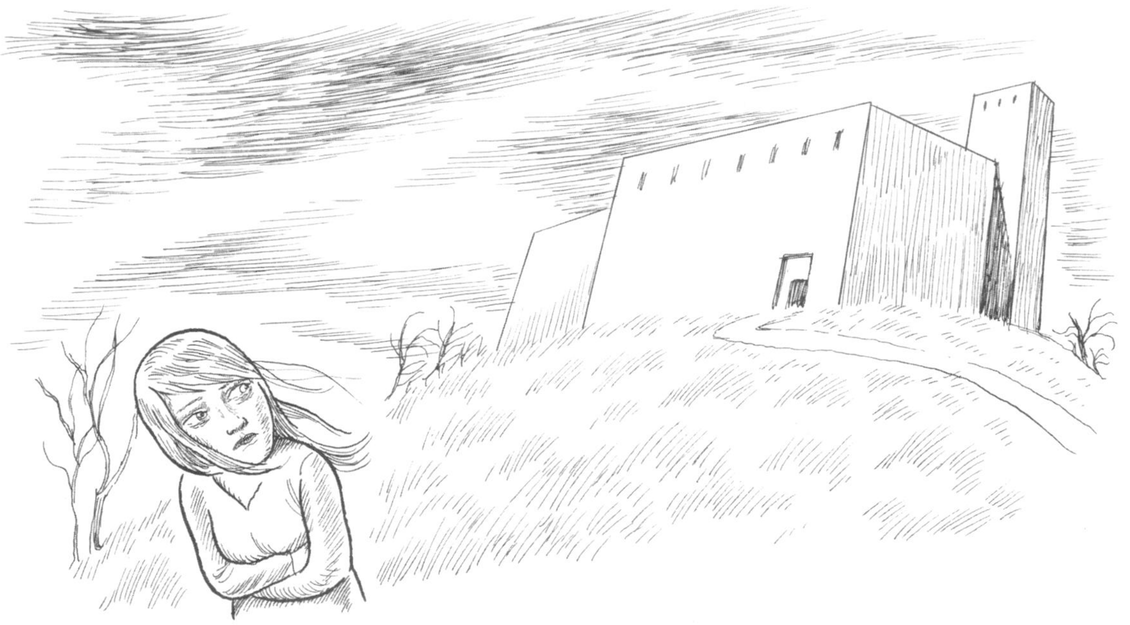

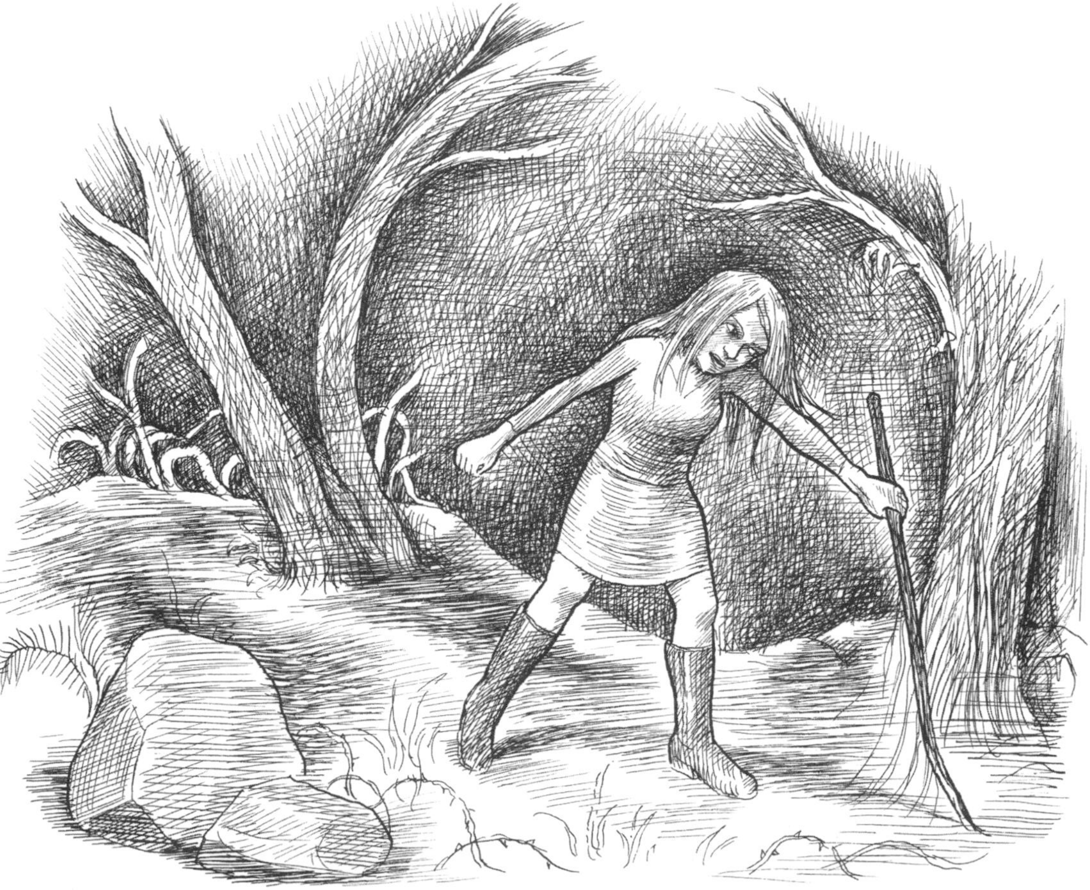

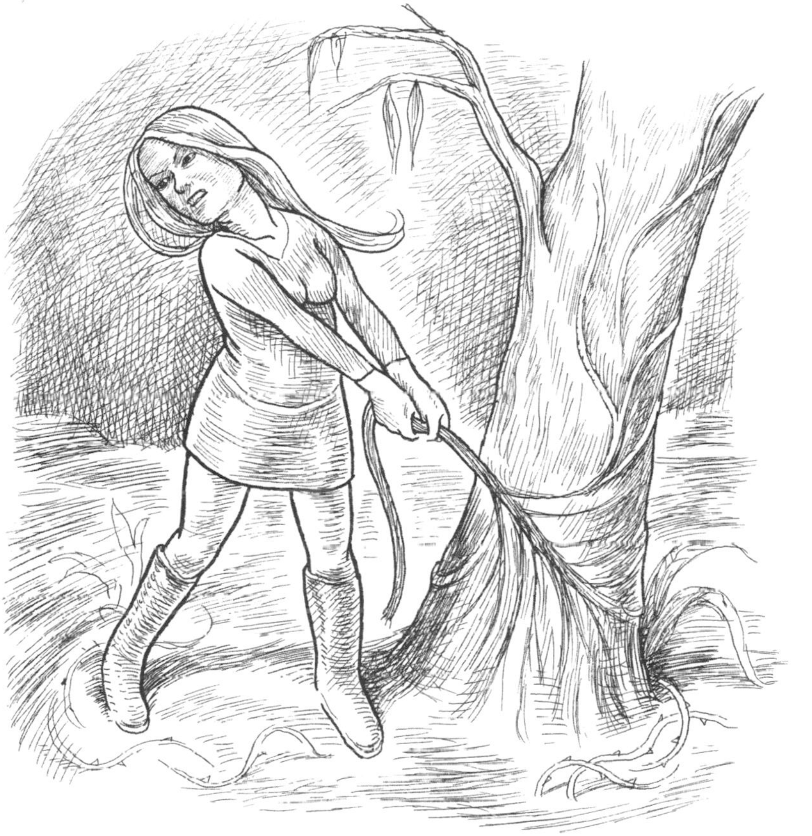

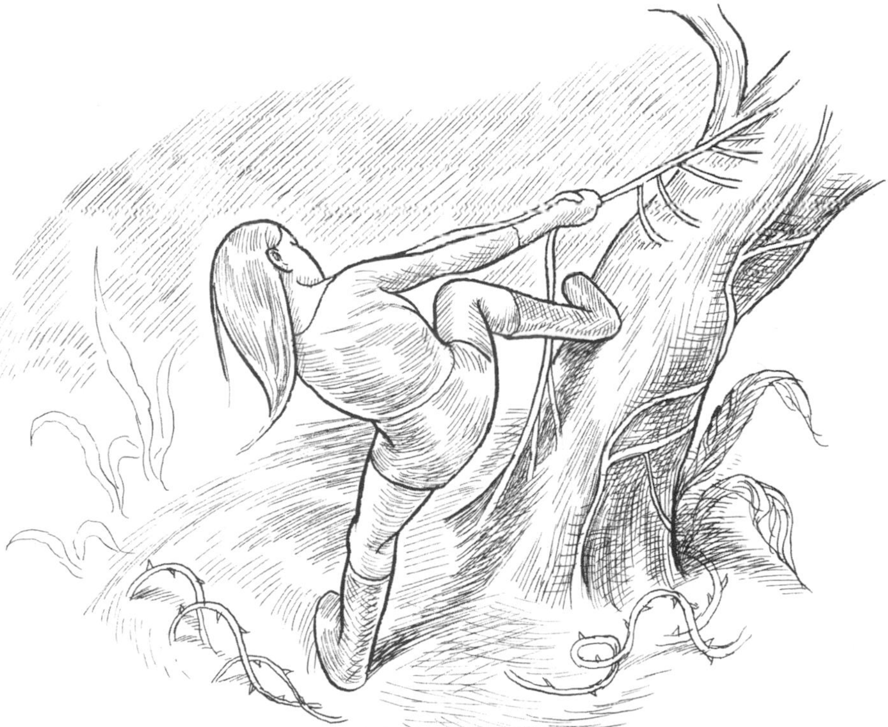

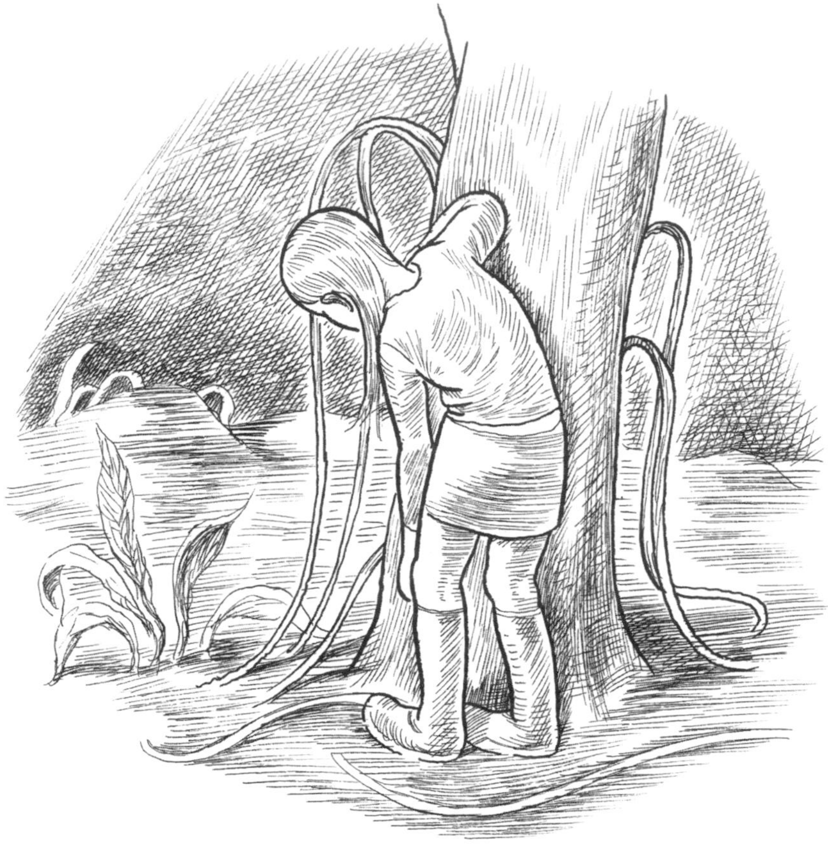

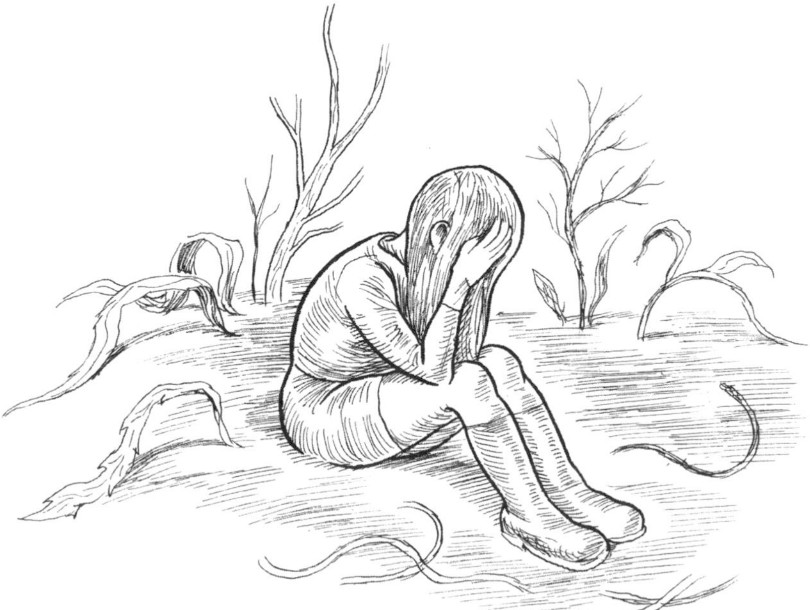

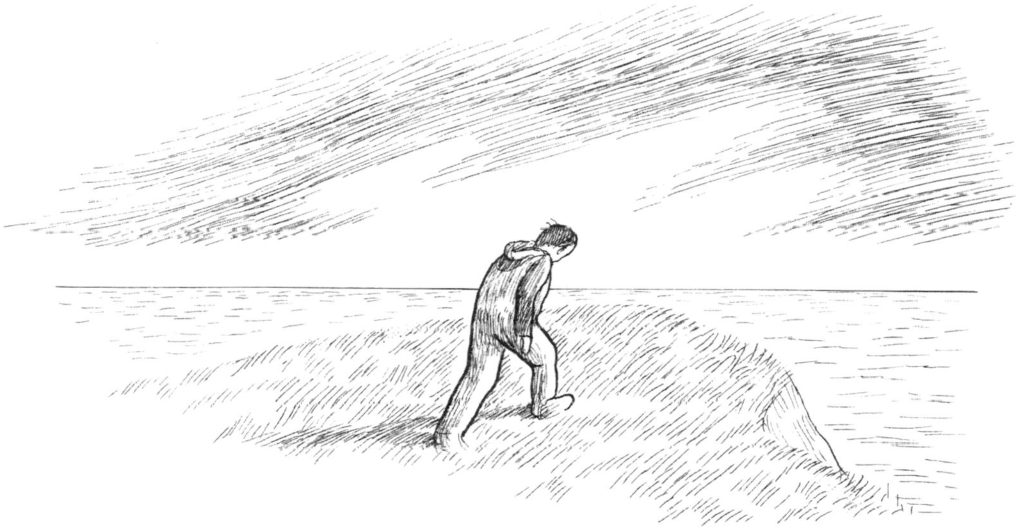

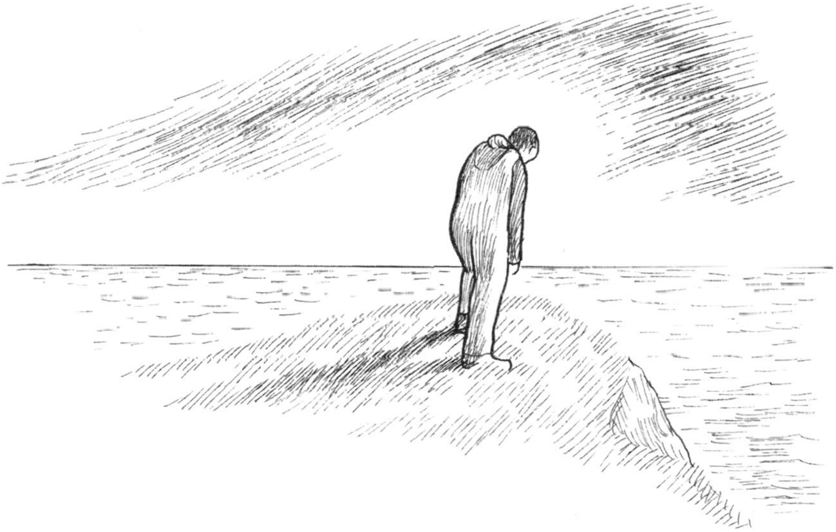

There it is. . .the sea. A giant sheet pocked with ridges, peaks, and moving tears.

It always knocks me right out. Flat on my back. With its force. Without its surface rising to meet me or spilling so much as a drop.

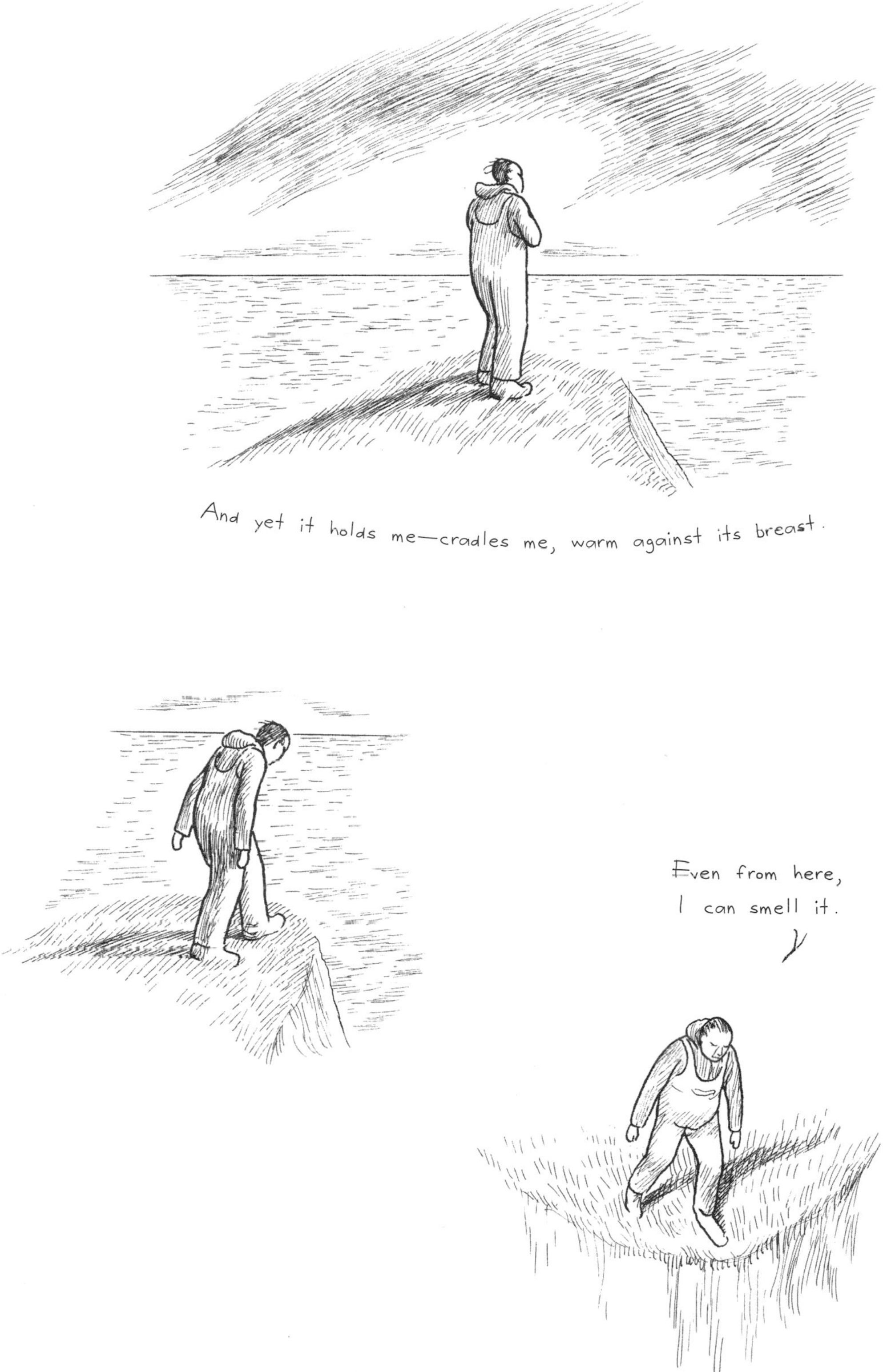
And yet it holds me—cradles me, warm against its breast.
Even from here, I can smell it.

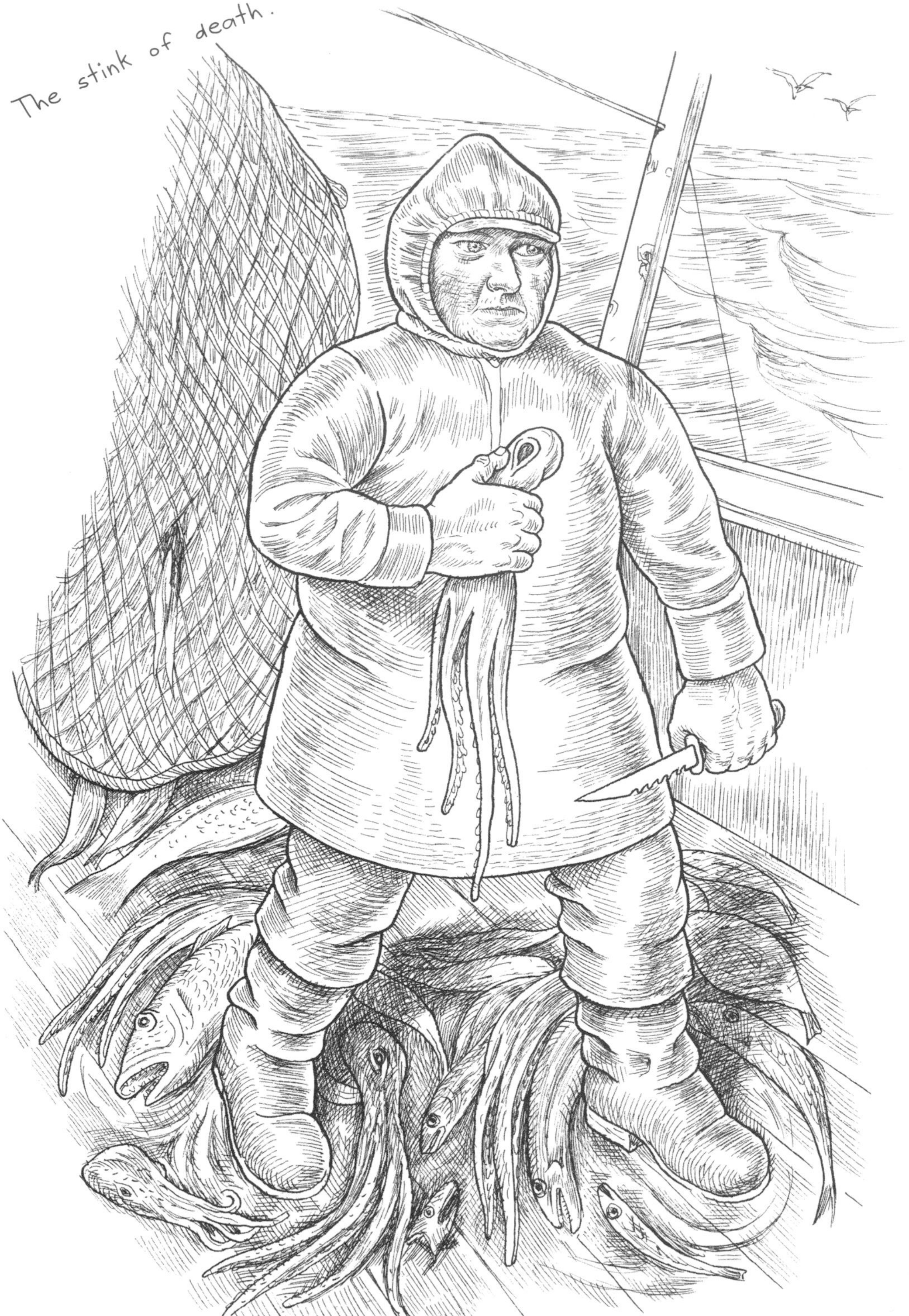
The stink of death.

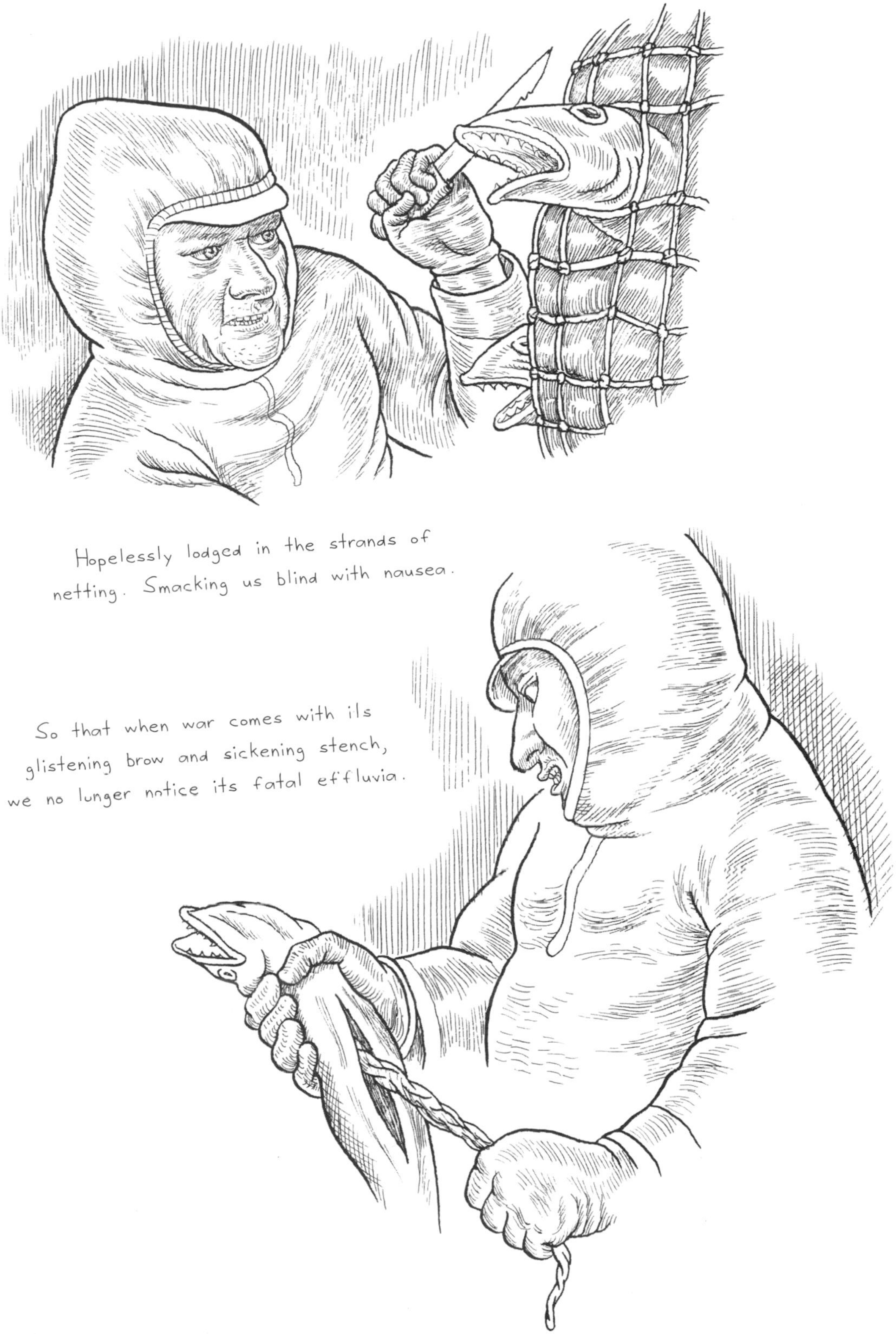
Hopelessly lodged in the strands of netting. Smacking us blind with nausea.
So that when war comes with ils glistening brow and sickening stench, we no lunger notice its fatal effluvia.

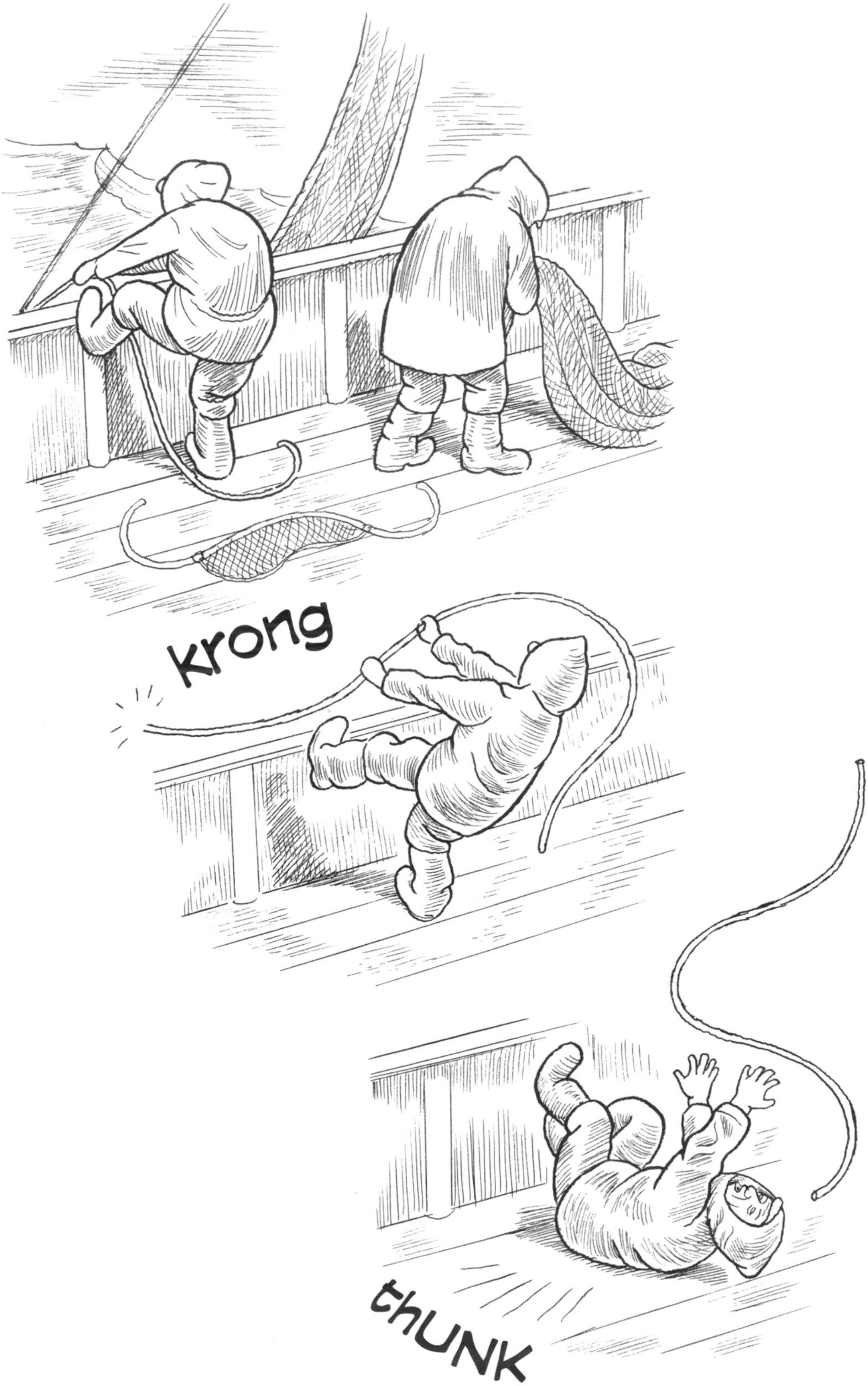
krong
thUNK

ha-ha!
ha-ha!

Ha-Ha!
Ha-Ha!

Ha-Ha!

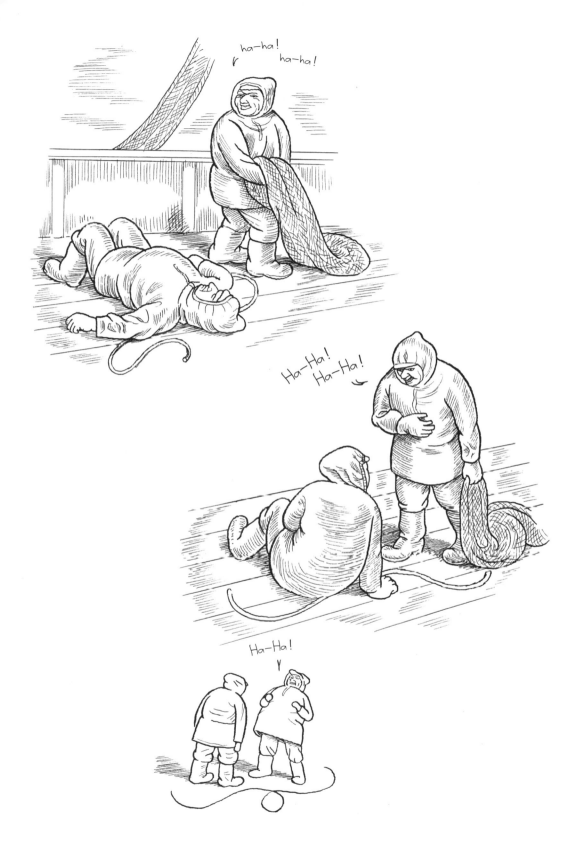

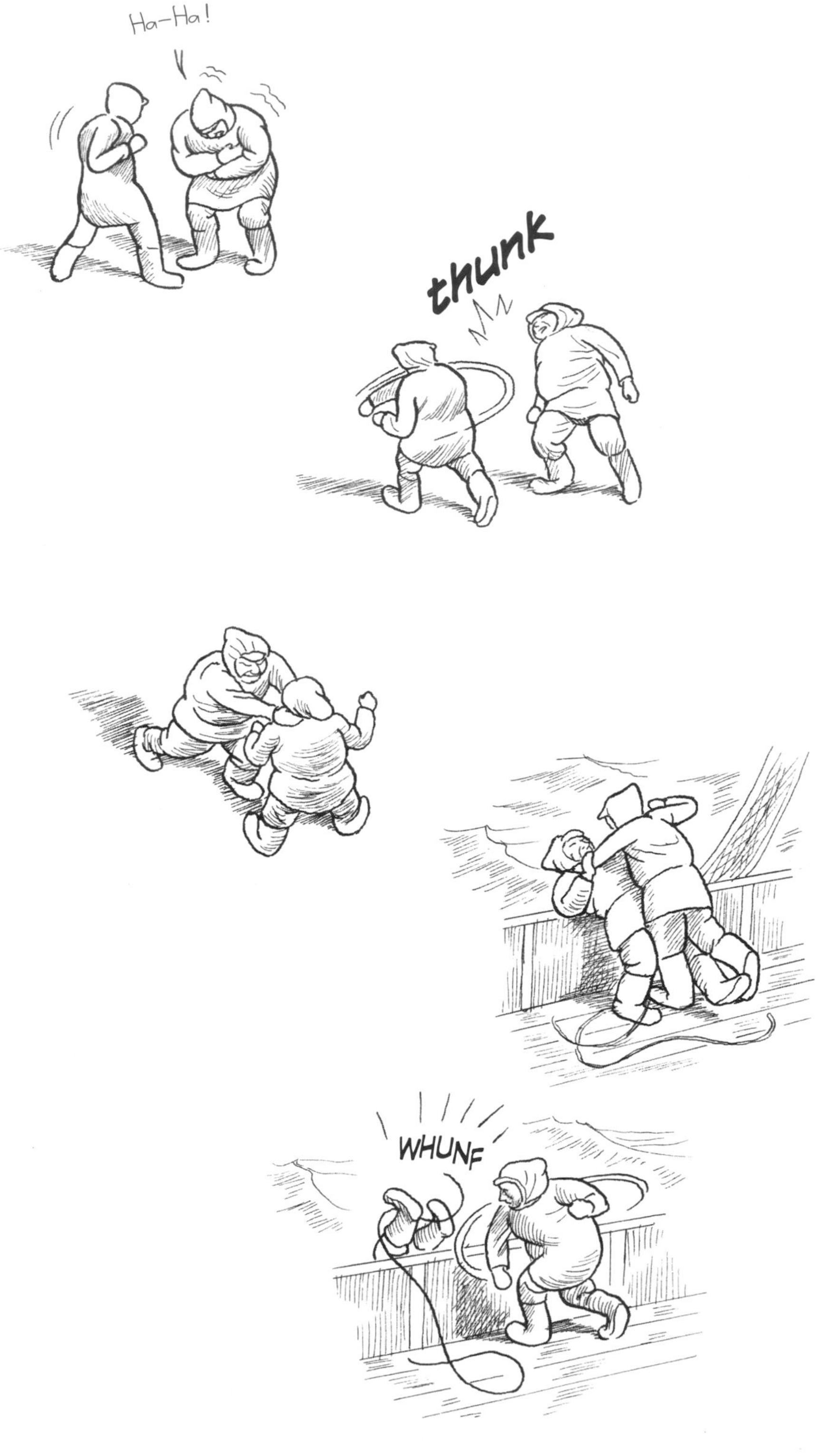
Ha-Ha!
thunk
WHUNF

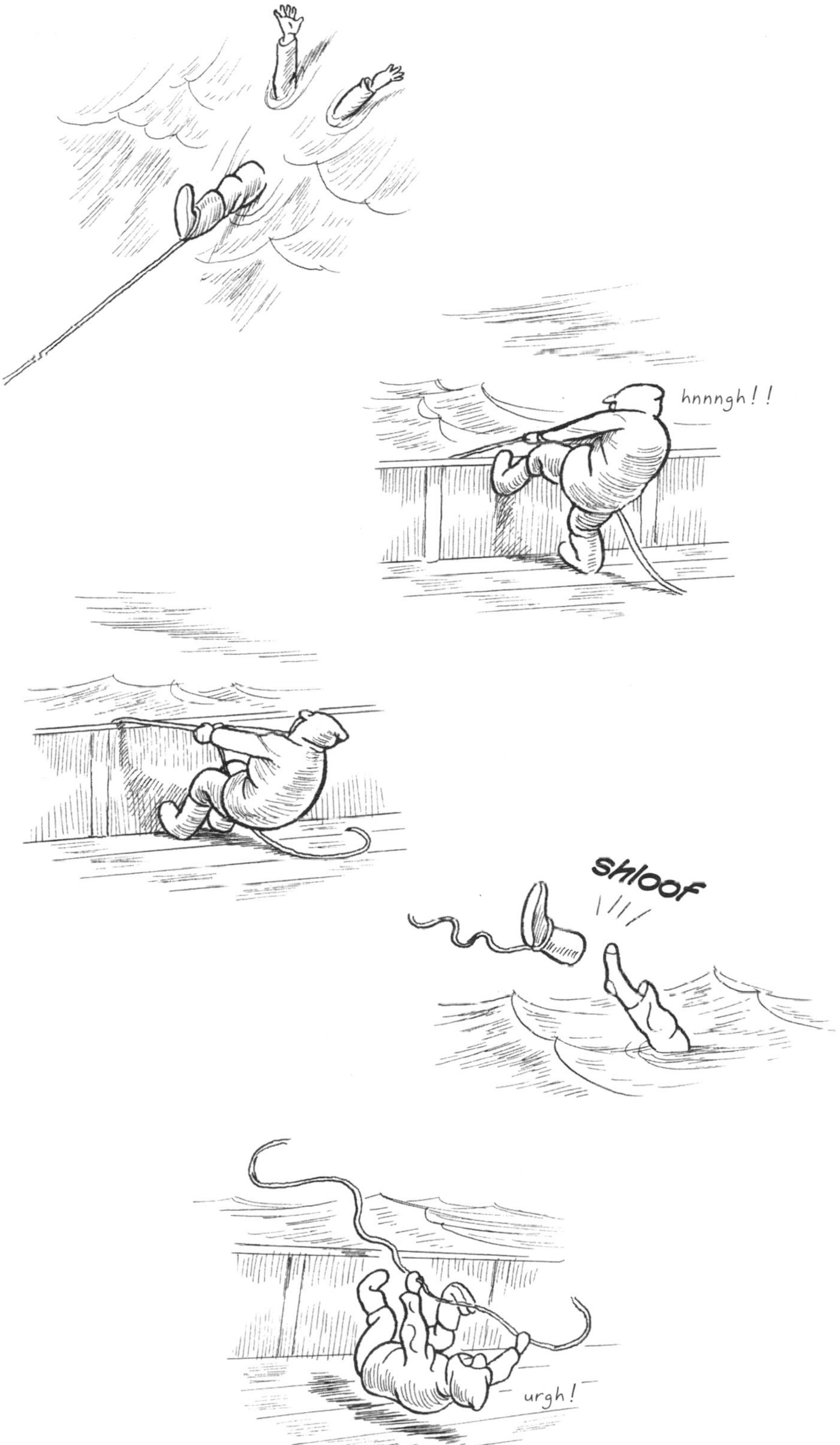
hnnngh!!
shloof
urgh!

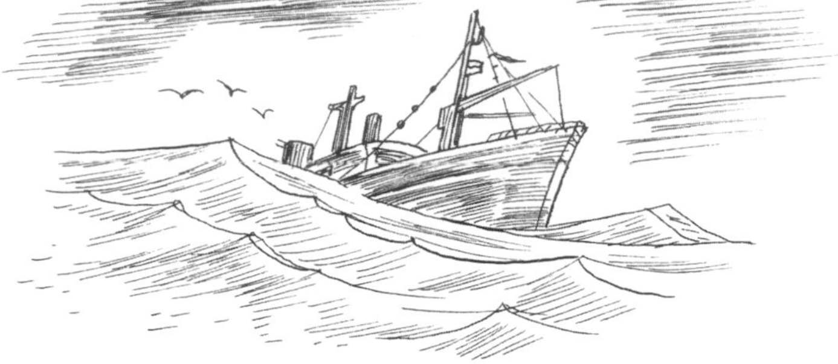

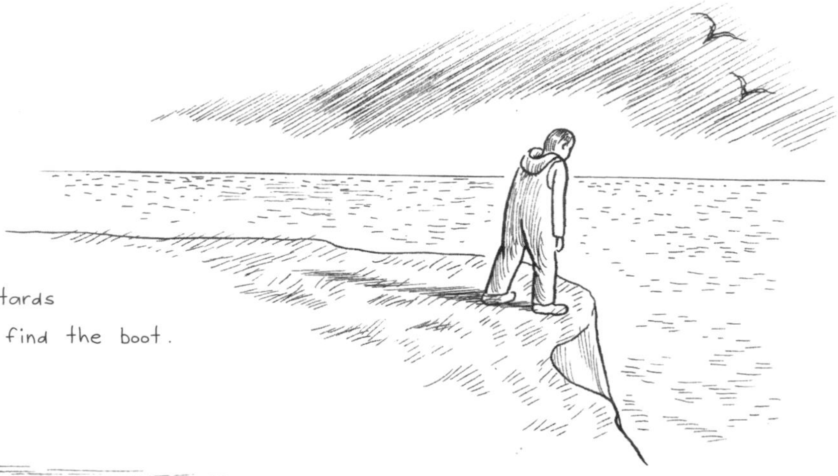

Those bastards
never did find the boot.

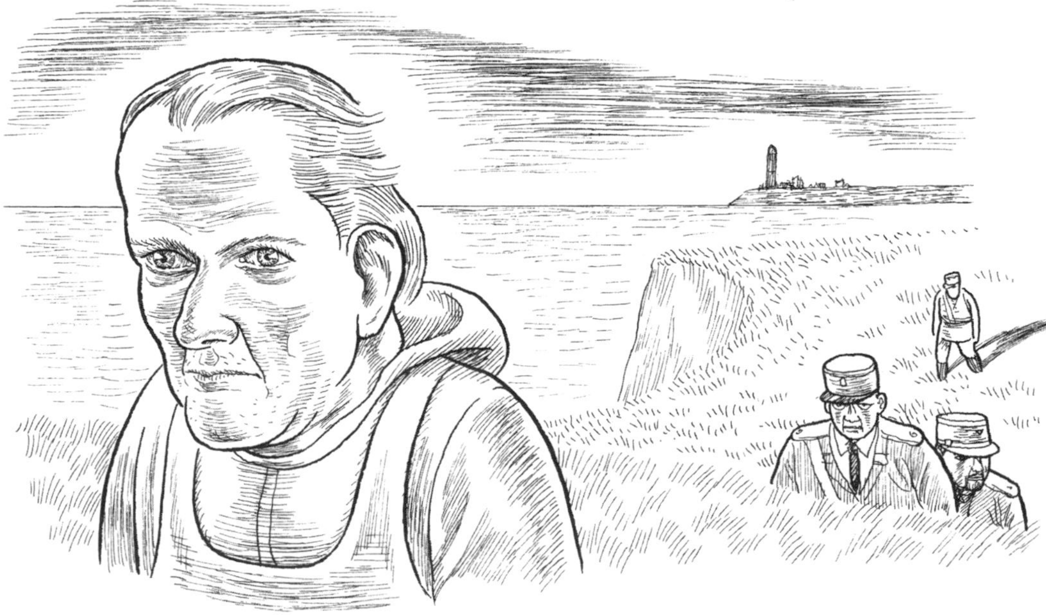

Just the traces my blows had left on his face...

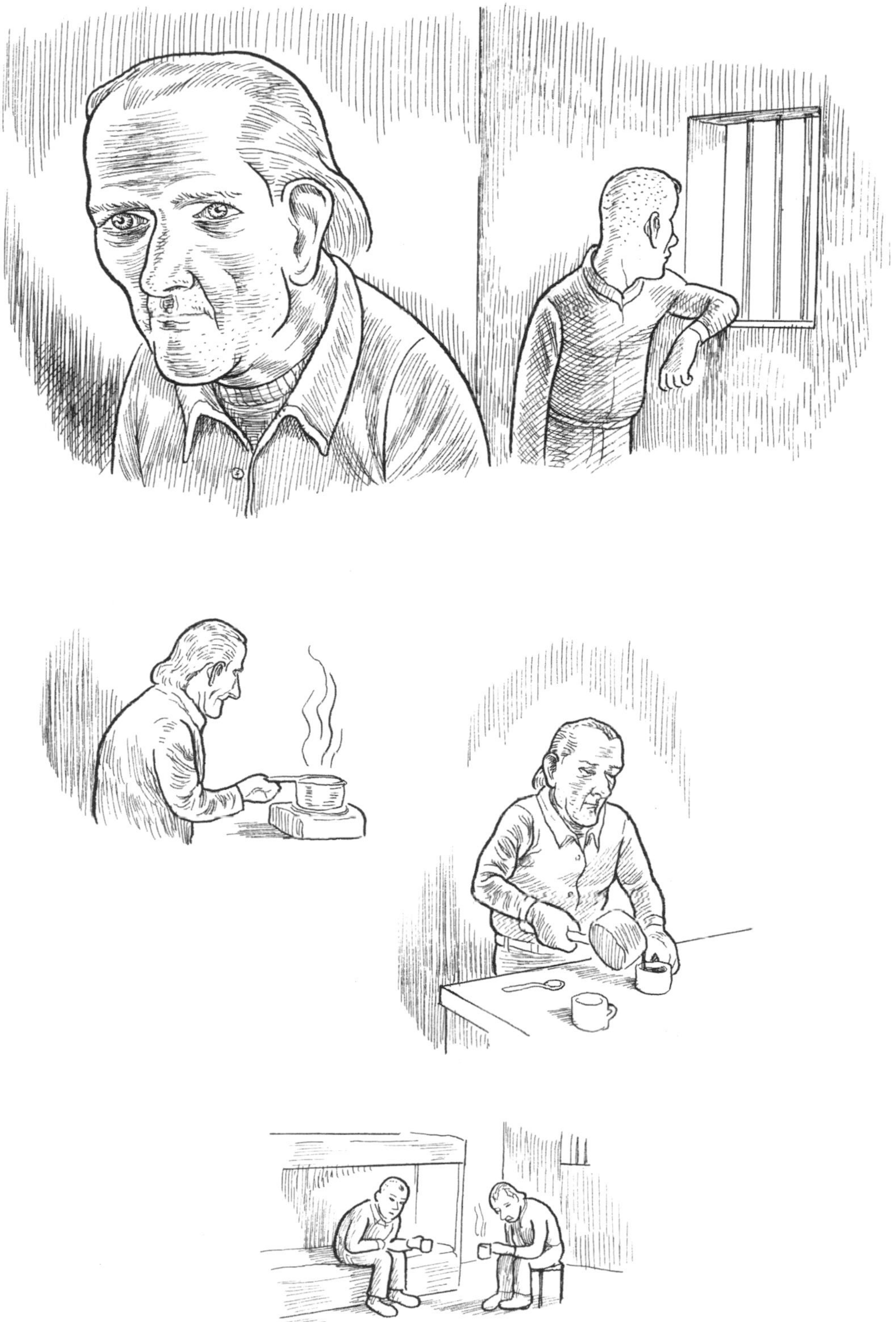

One morning . . .

I will walk on carpets of
greasy leaves.

My steps will crush
bulbs of wild garlic.

I'll wait for the smell from the crumpled stalks
to rise up along my thighs.

That's all I'll do.

Breathe in that nature smell.

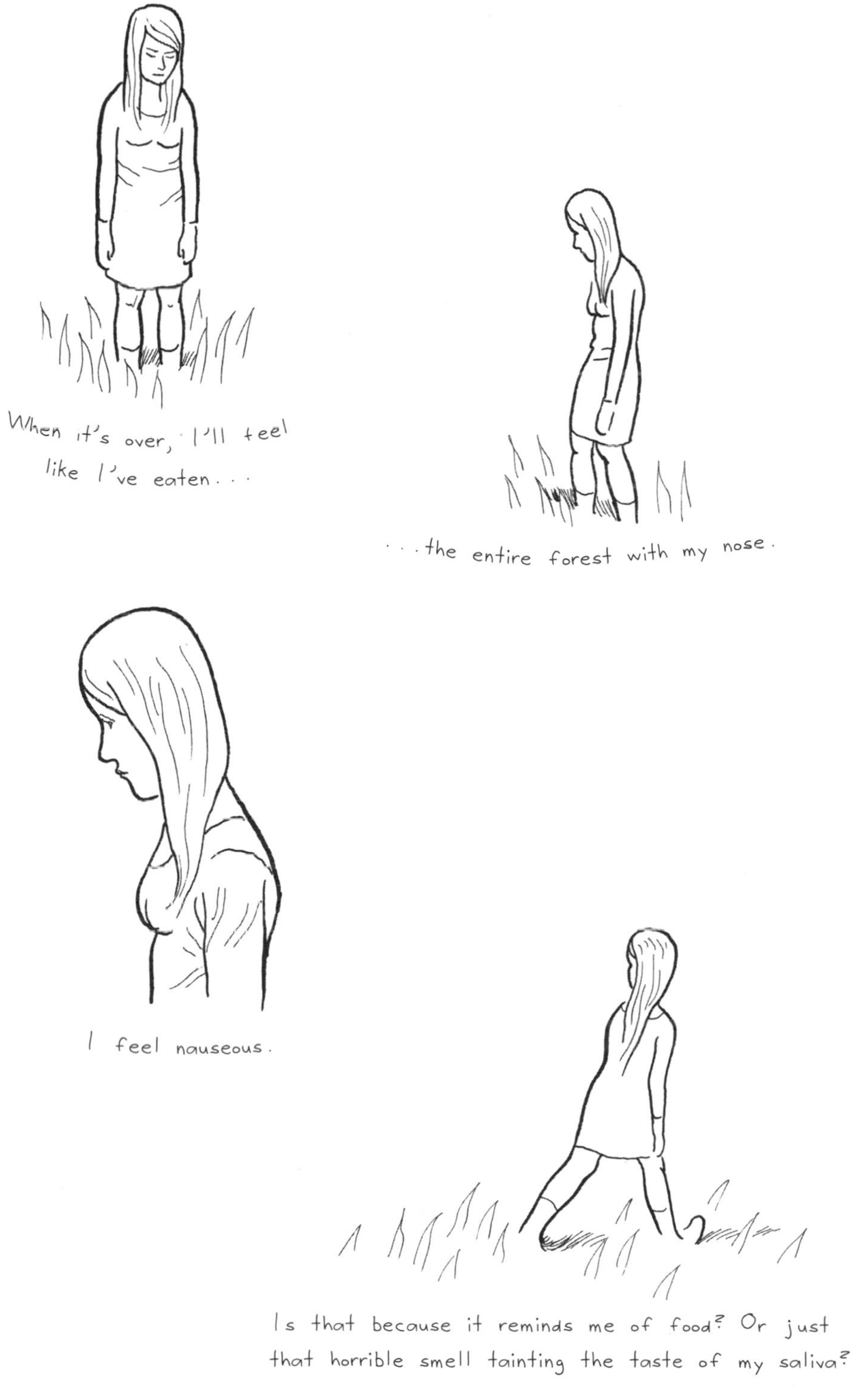
When it's over, I'll feel like I've eaten...
...the entire forest with my nose.
I feel nauseous.
Is that because it reminds me of food? Or just that horrible smell tainting the taste of my saliva?

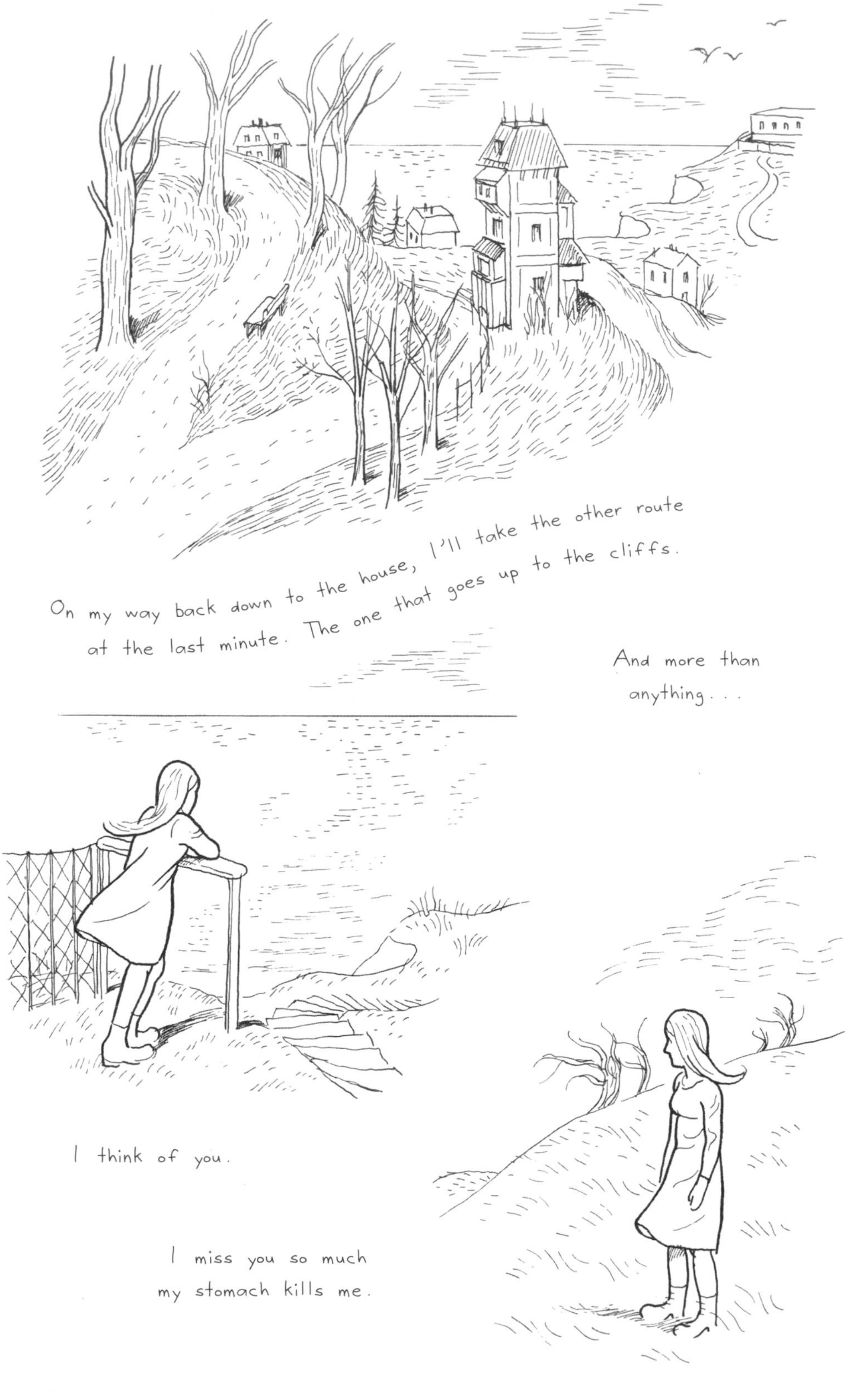
On my way back down to the house, I'll take the other route at the last minute. The one that goes up to the cliffs.
And more than anything . . .
I think of you.
I miss you so much my stomach kills me.

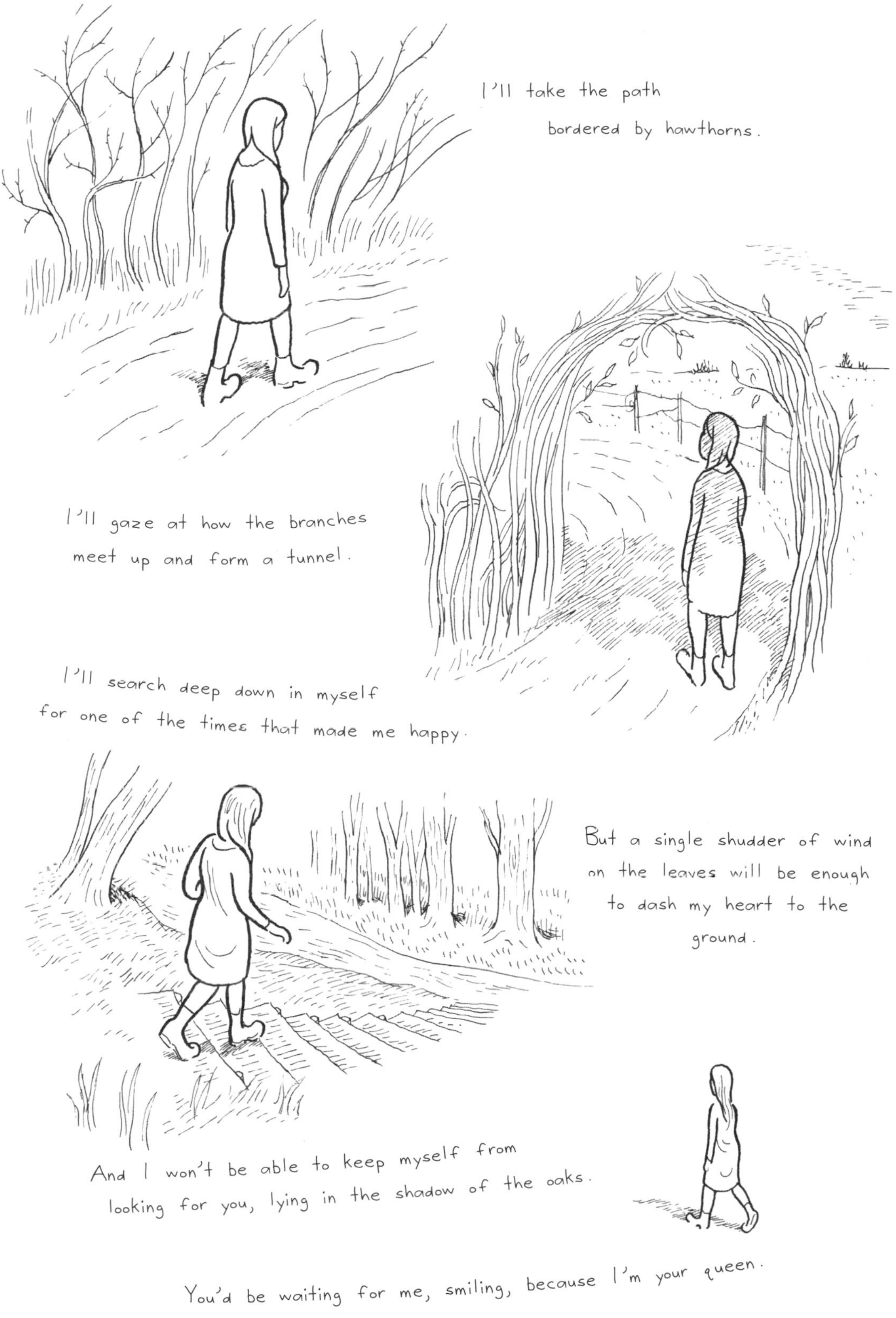
I'll take the path
bordered by hawthorns.
I'll gaze at how the branches
meet up and form a tunnel.
I'll search deep down in myself
for one of the times that made me happy.
But a single shudder of wind
on the leaves will be enough
to dash my heart to the
ground.
And I won't be able to keep myself from
looking for you, lying in the shadow of the oaks.
You'd be waiting for me, smiling, because I'm your queen.

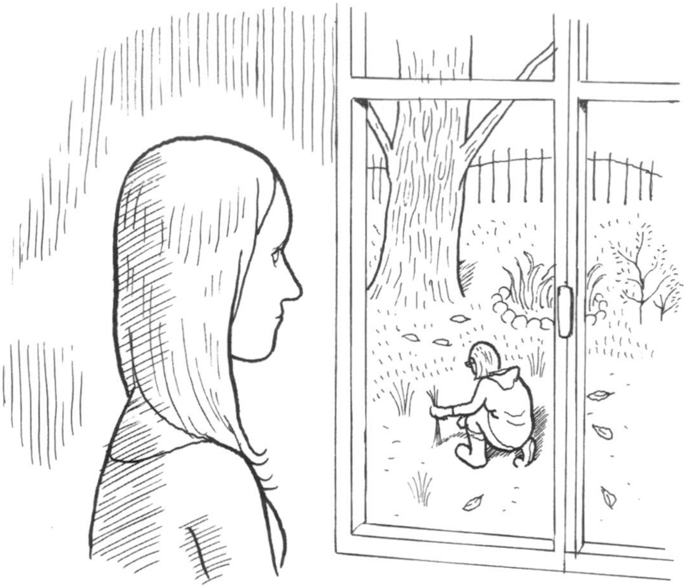

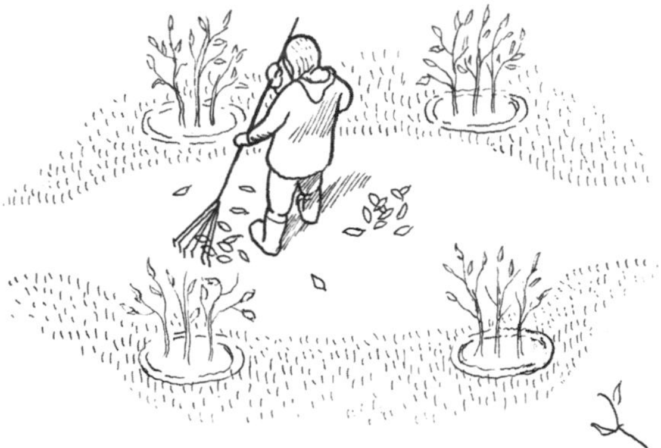

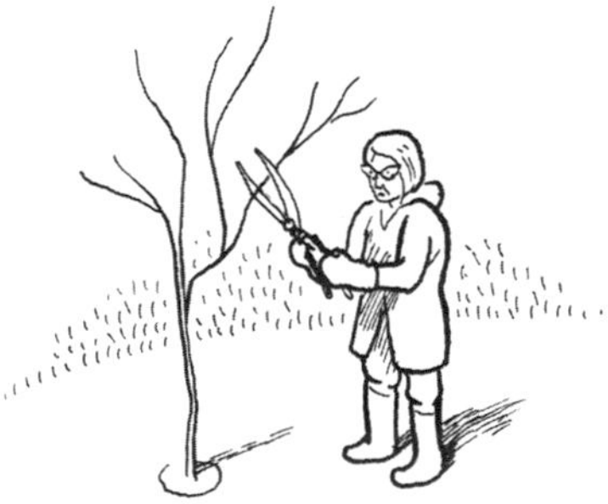

Trimming, neatening,

cutting back, laying out . . .

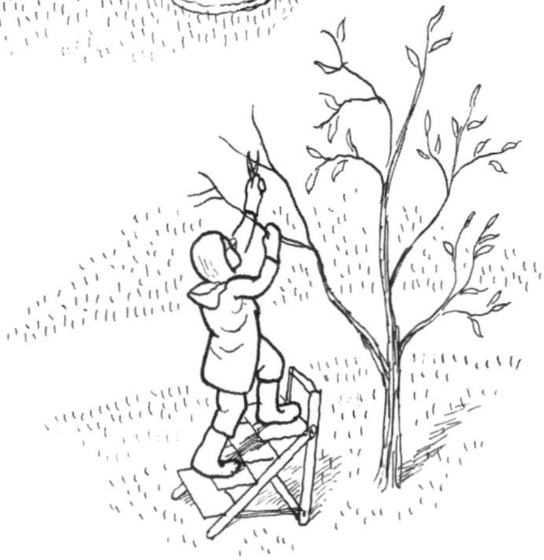

It's clear my mother thinks she makes the flowers grow.

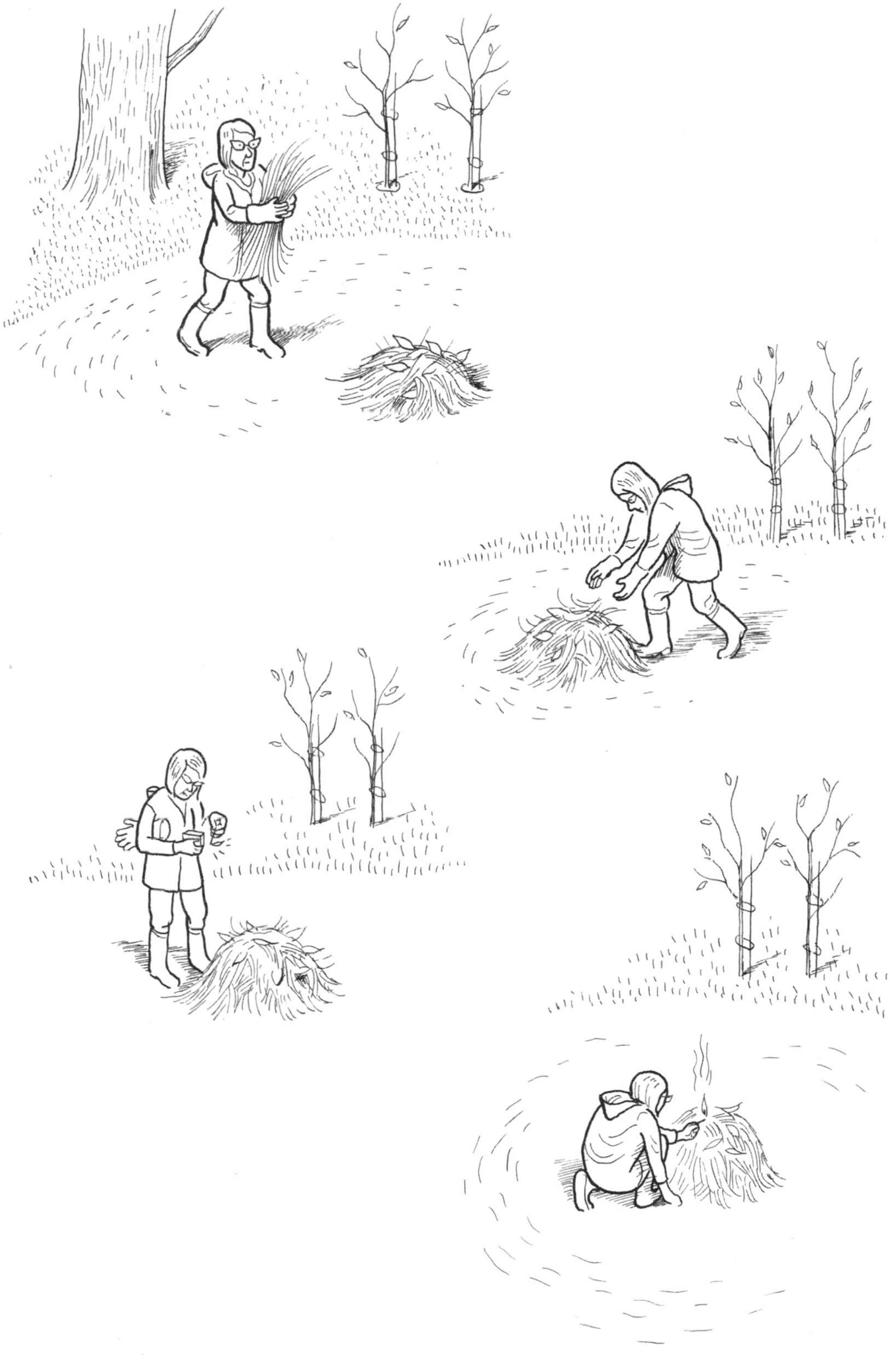

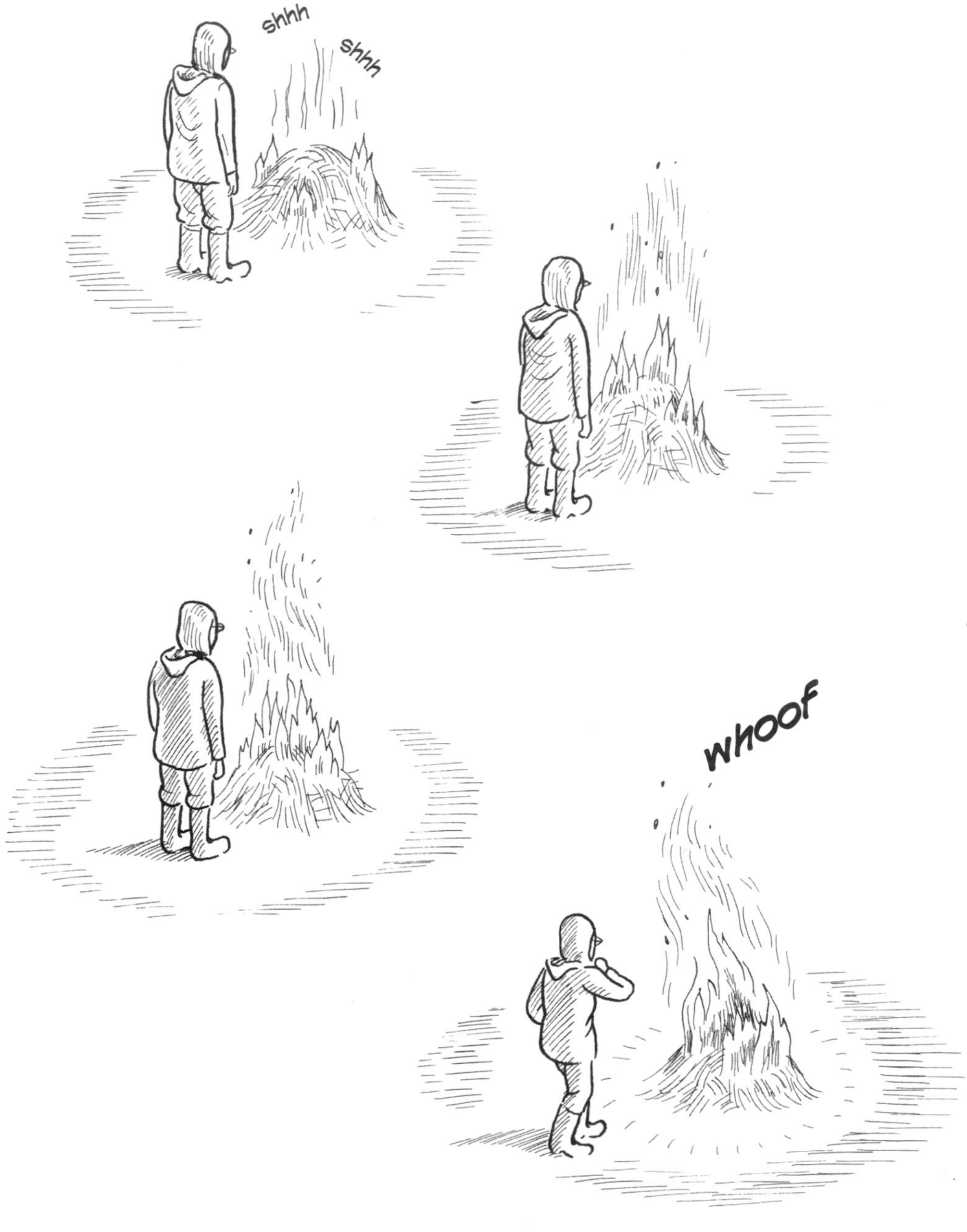
shhh
shhh
WHOOF

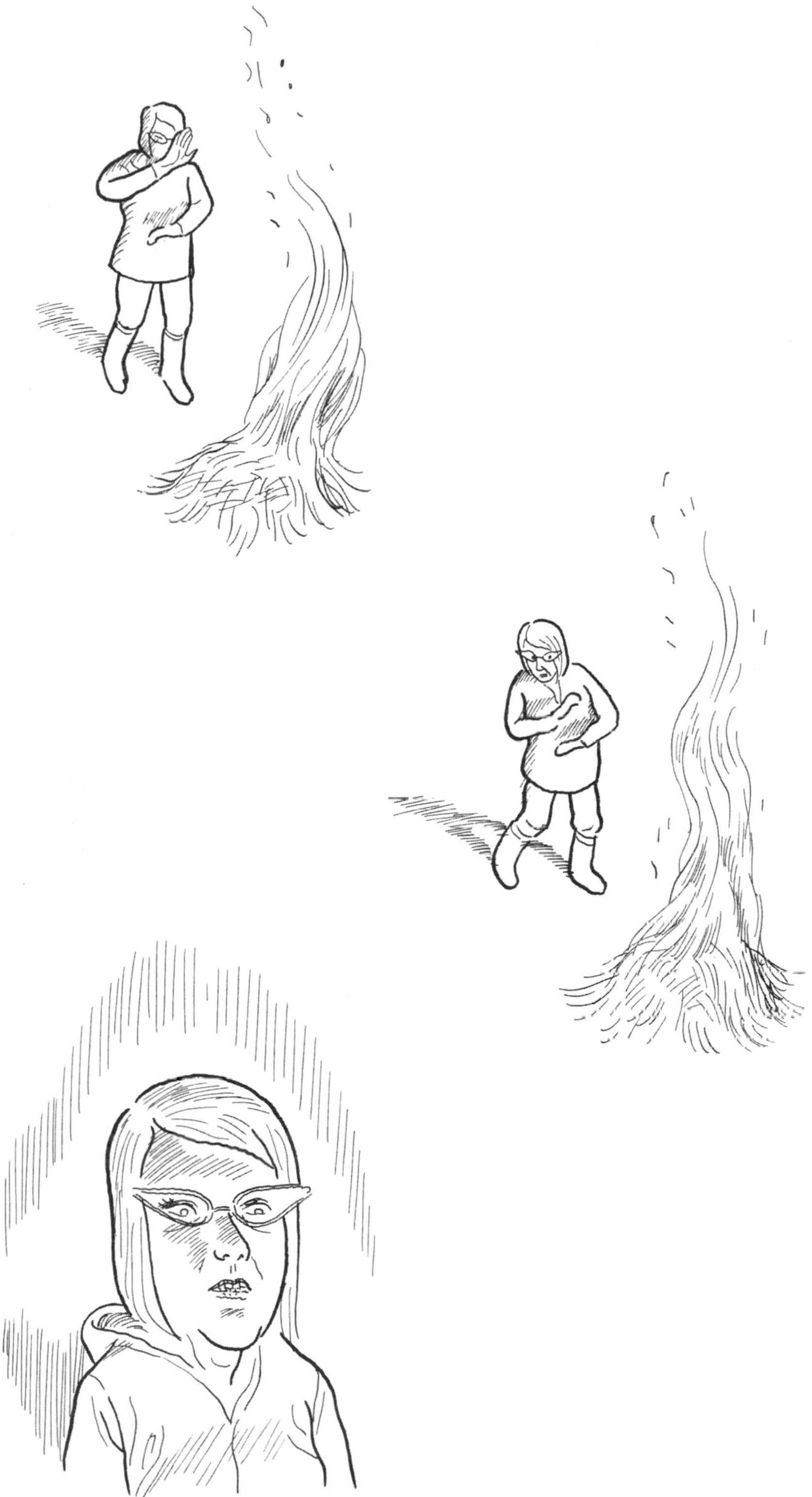

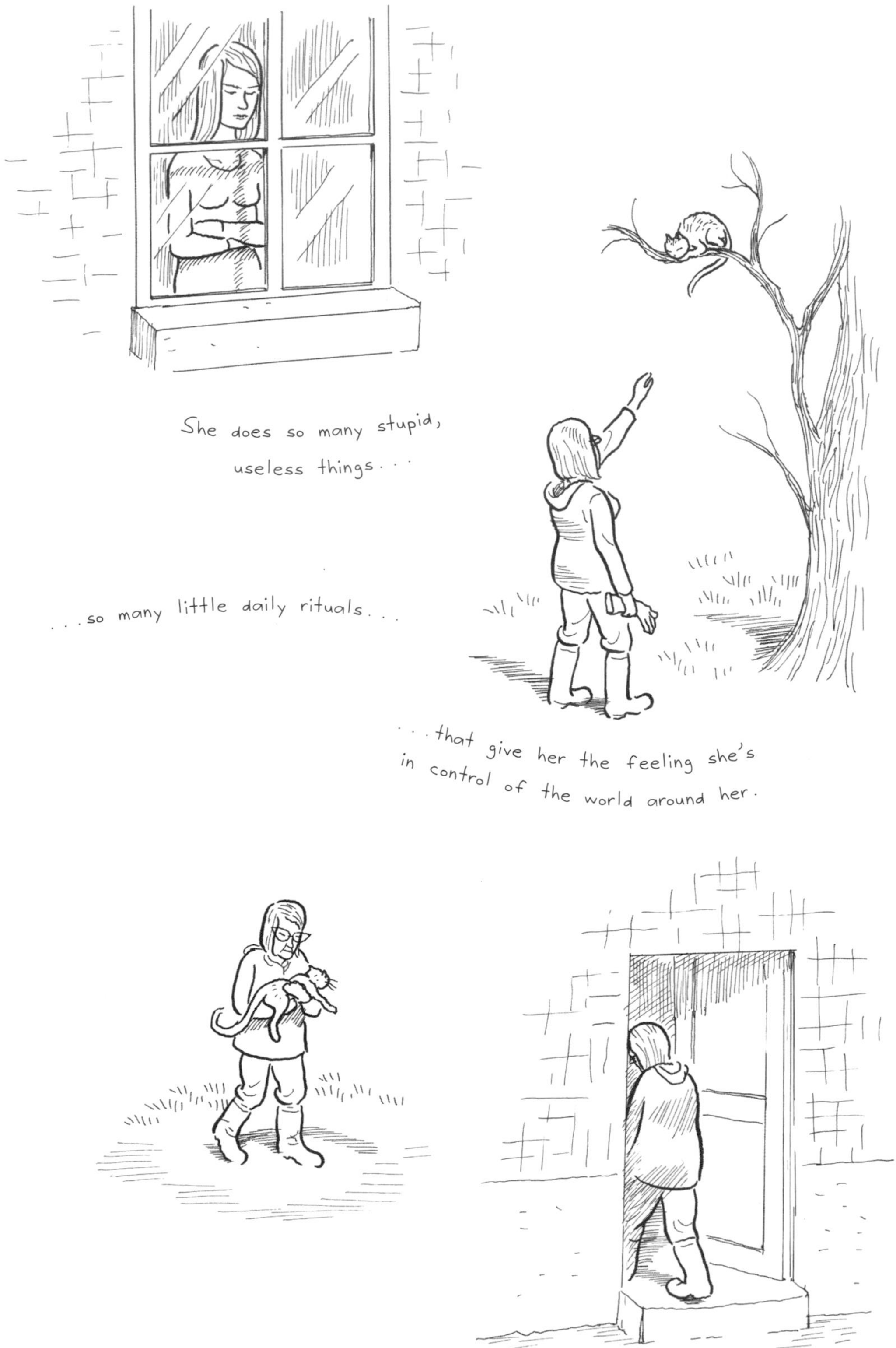
She does so many stupid, useless things...
...so many little daily rituals...
...that give her the feeling she's in control of the world around her.

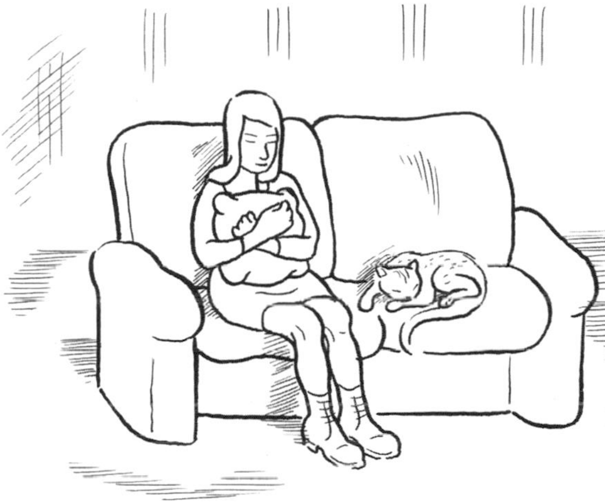

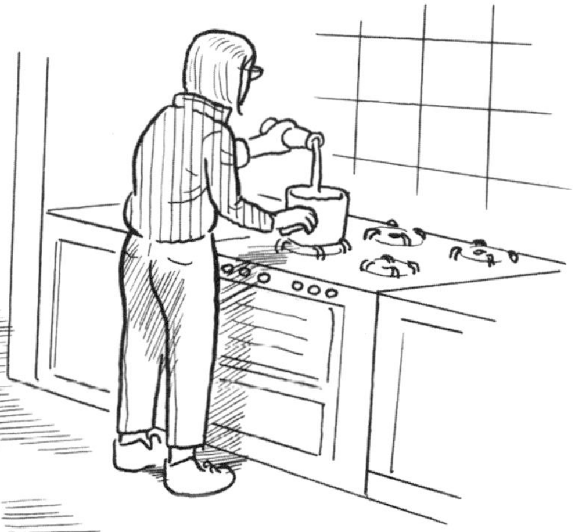

I never noticed...

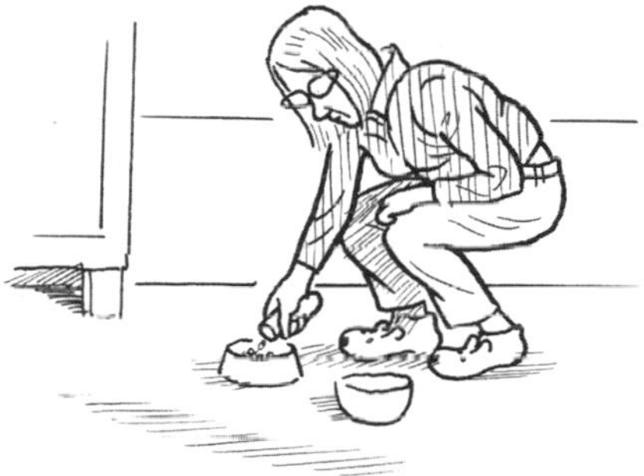

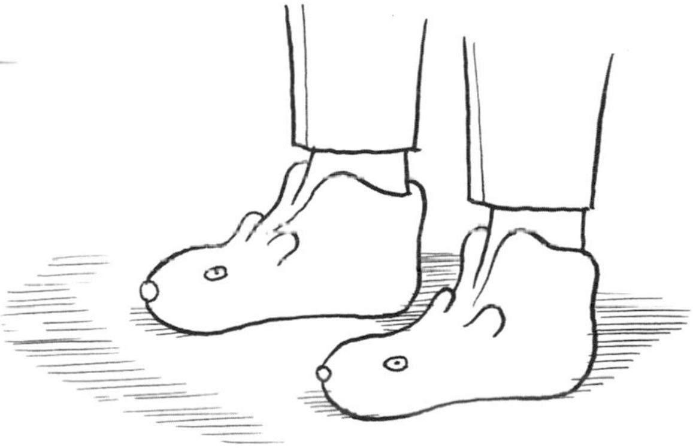

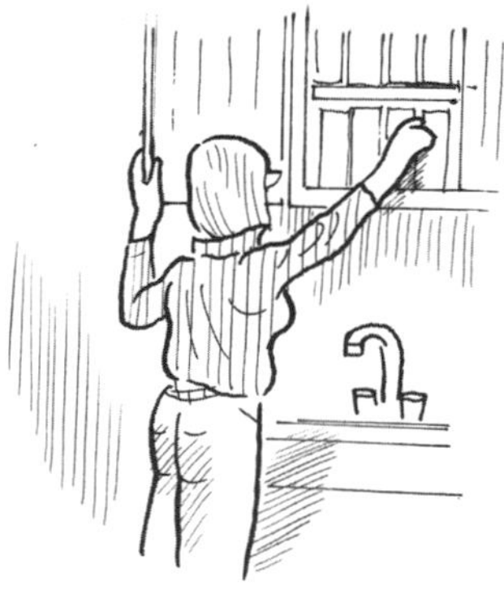

...all her little quirks before.

Now, I not only see them, but I think I can even feel what creeps just behind them.

And that builds up deep inside...

So strongly—

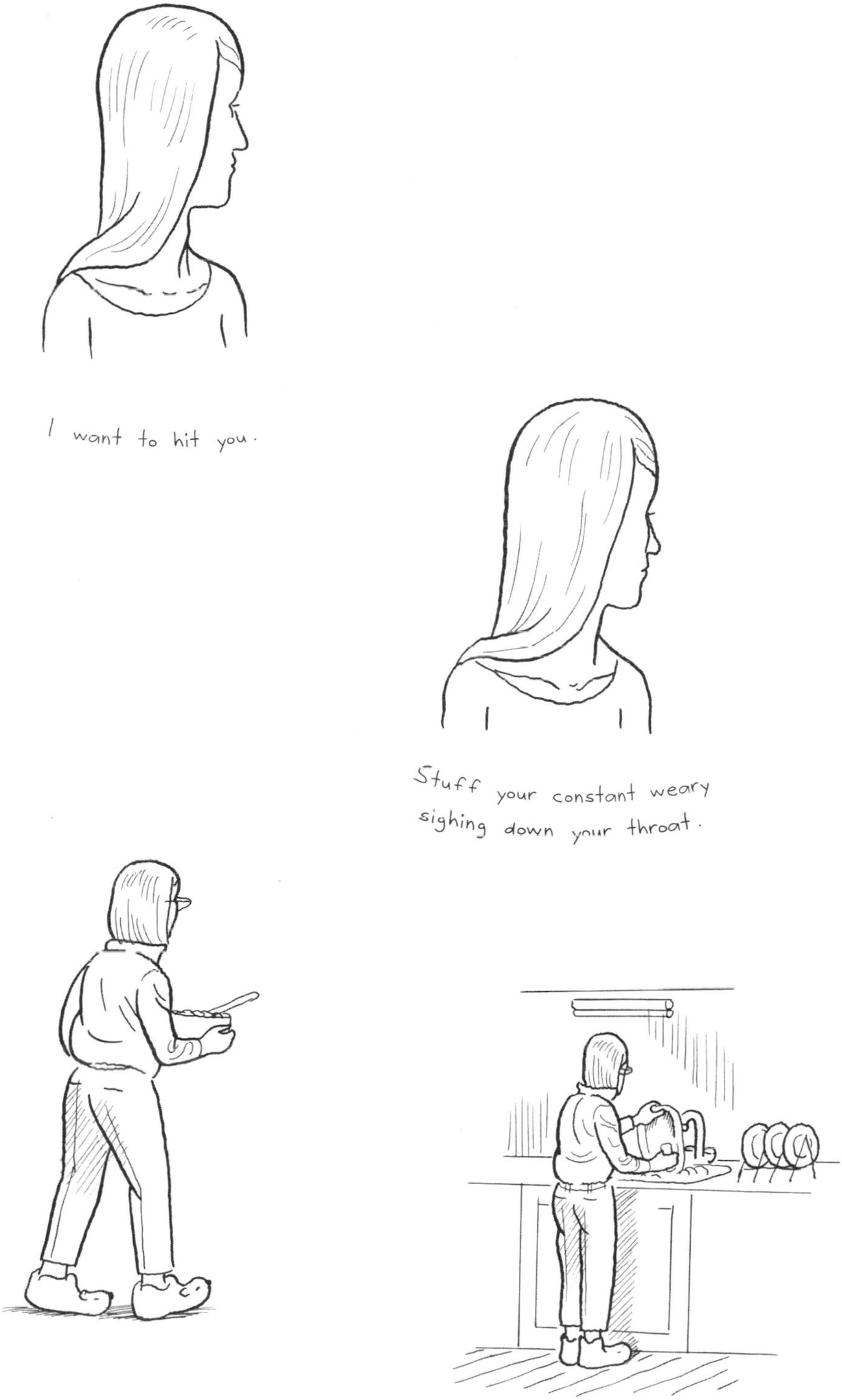
I want to hit you.
Stuff your constant weary sighing down your throat.

Use a fork to open your eyes so you'll finally
see how stupid you are.

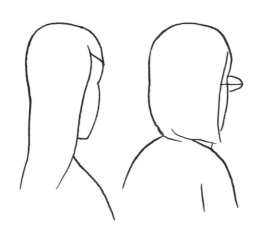

But I love you.

I love you so much.

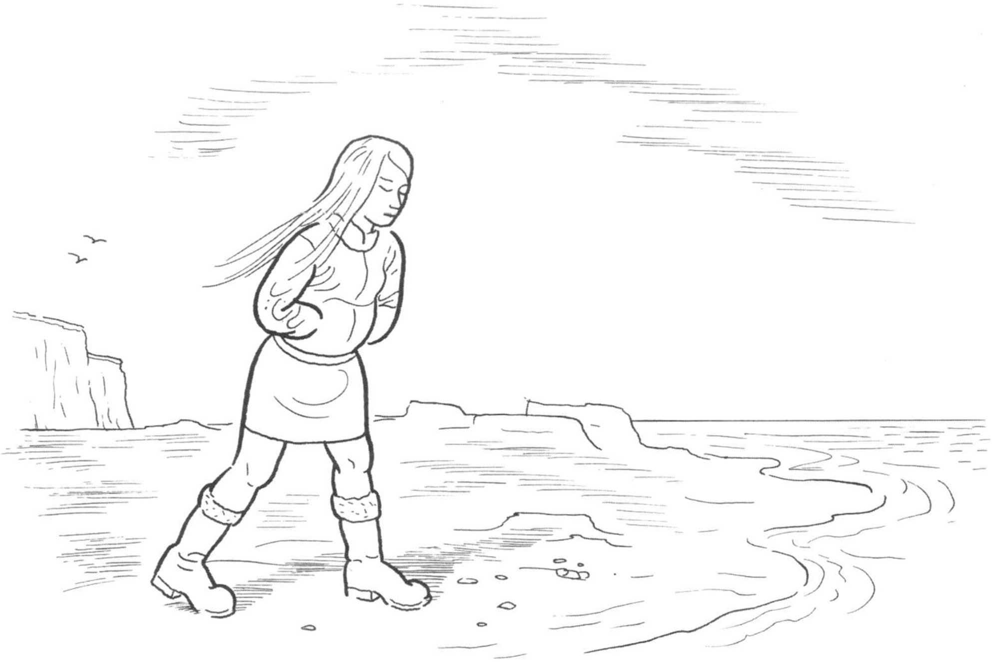

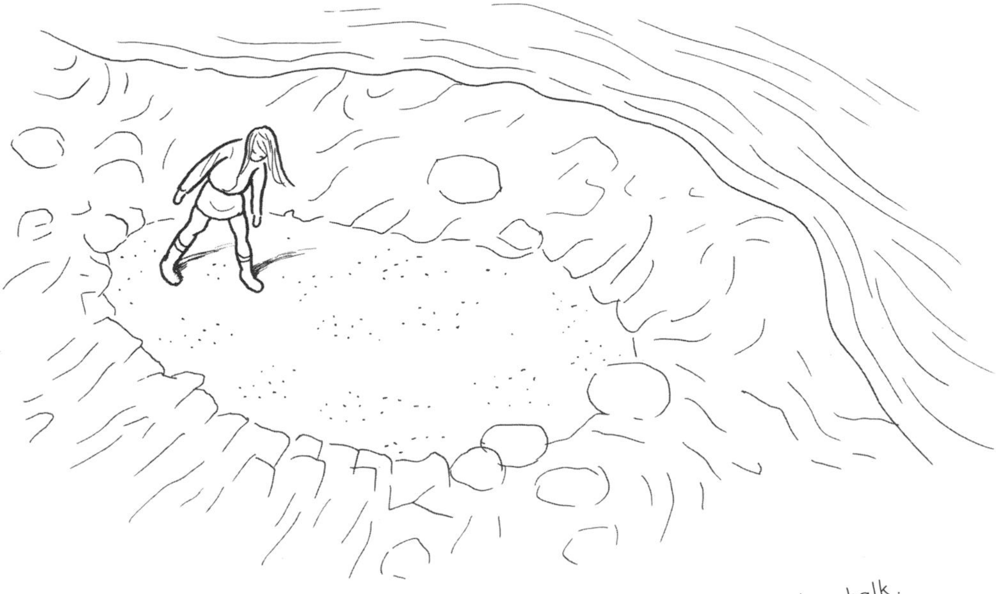

When the ocean draws back, there are bits of yellow, dirty chalk.

They form a fragile borderland. A path between air and water.
Half the time they're drowning, and the other half burning
in the sunlight.

They're rounded like old hills from the ocean tossing them around,
I think. But I can't recall the moon maps they made.

I don't know what they used to be like anymore. I just remember how
overjoyed I was to find once, at low tide, a sandbank caught
between the rocks.

It was like a little island.
No one had ever set foot there.

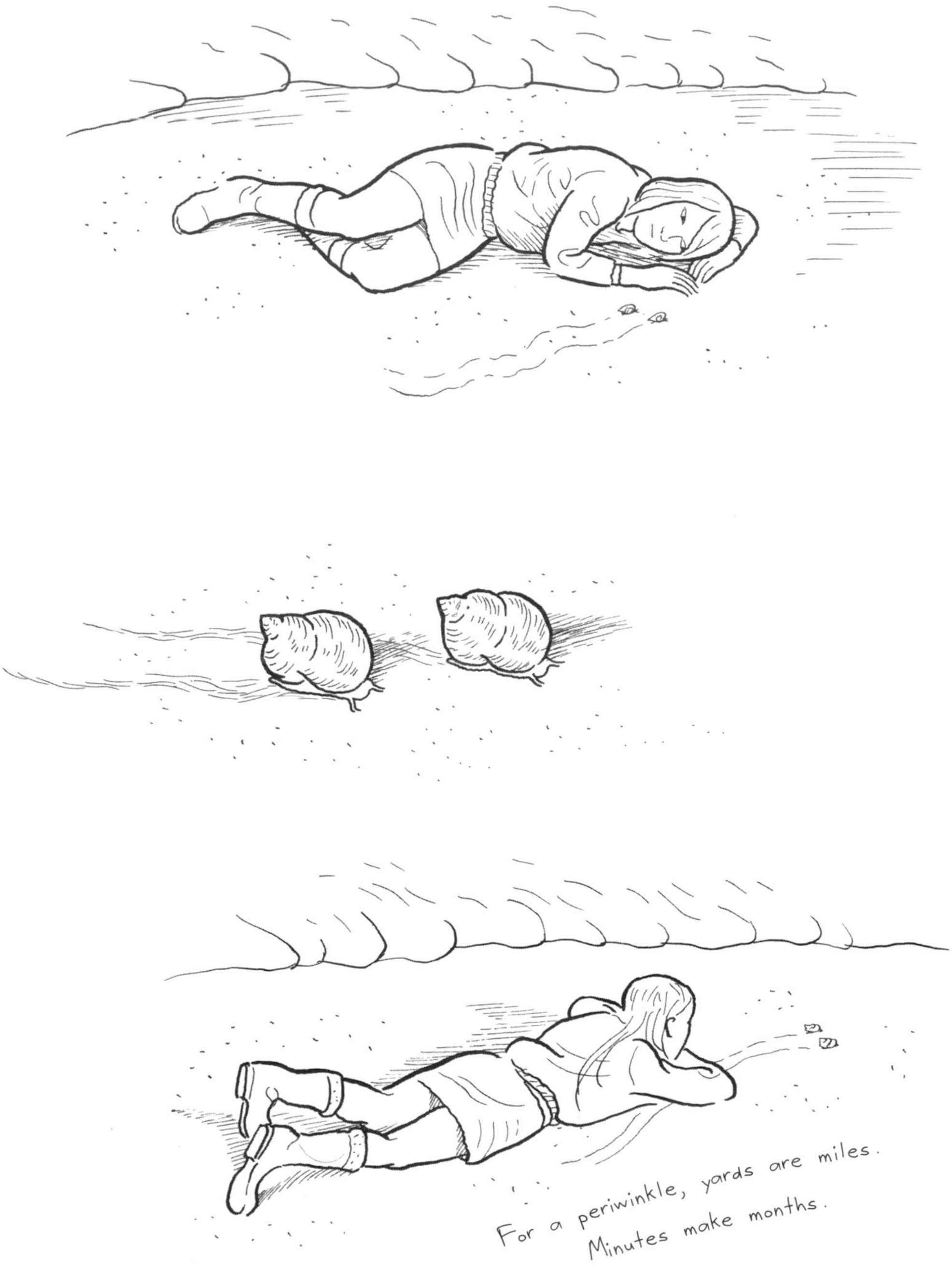
For a periwinkle, yards are miles.
Minutes make months.

And there's the sea, to sweep them away before they've reached the far chalk shore...

If I carried them there in my hands . . .

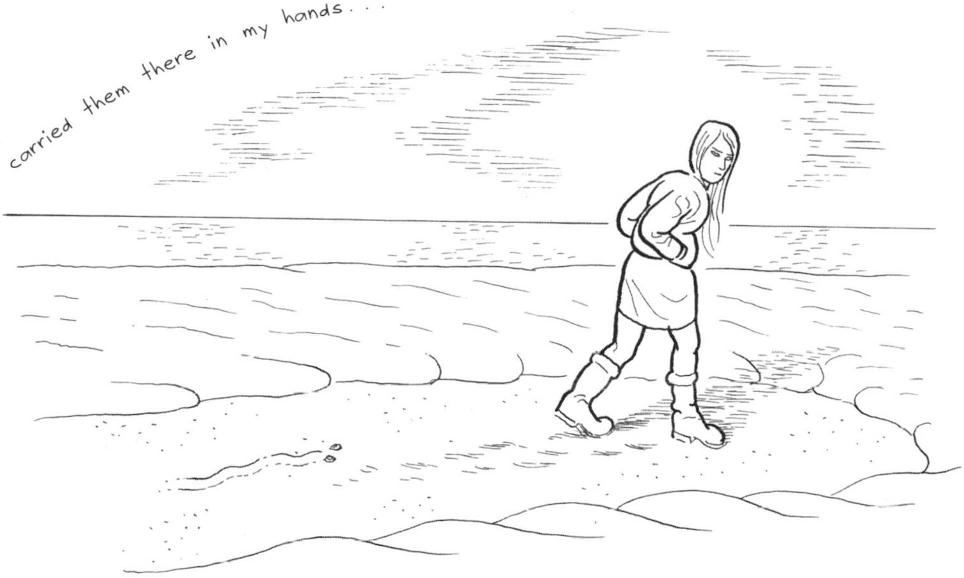

. . . I might be leading them astray. Who knows the true, winding path of a sea snail?

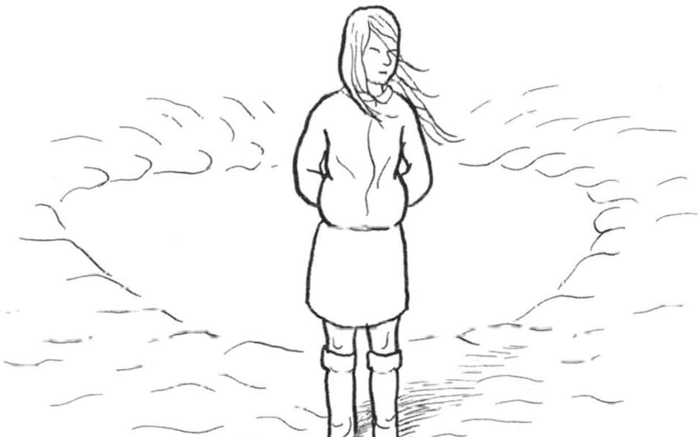

I want the hours, months, years until you are released to become the seconds of a periwinkle.

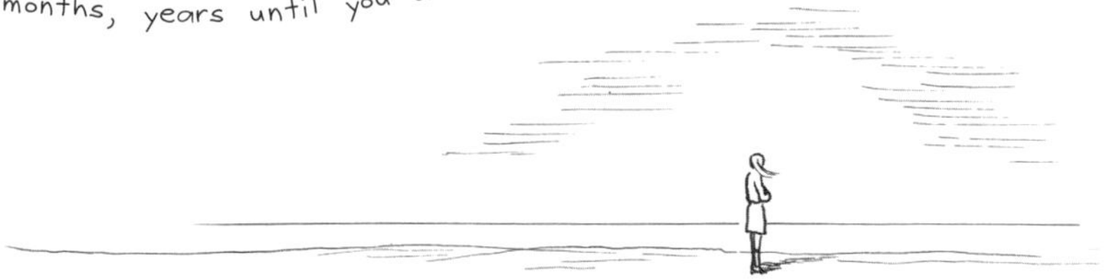

For some magnificent hand to sweep away the senseless time keeping us apart.

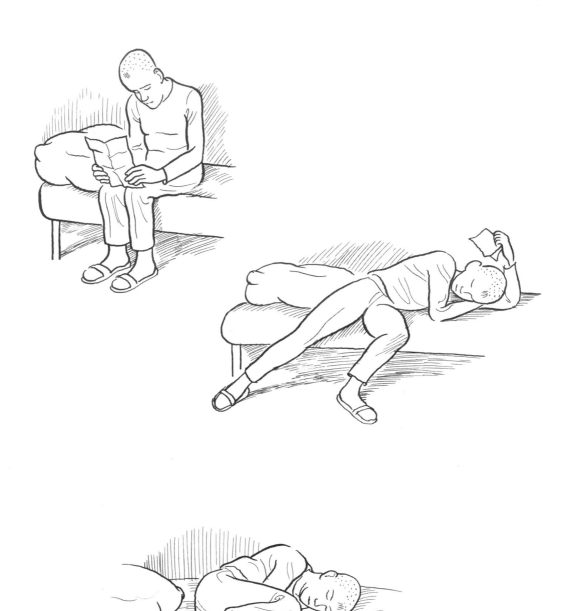

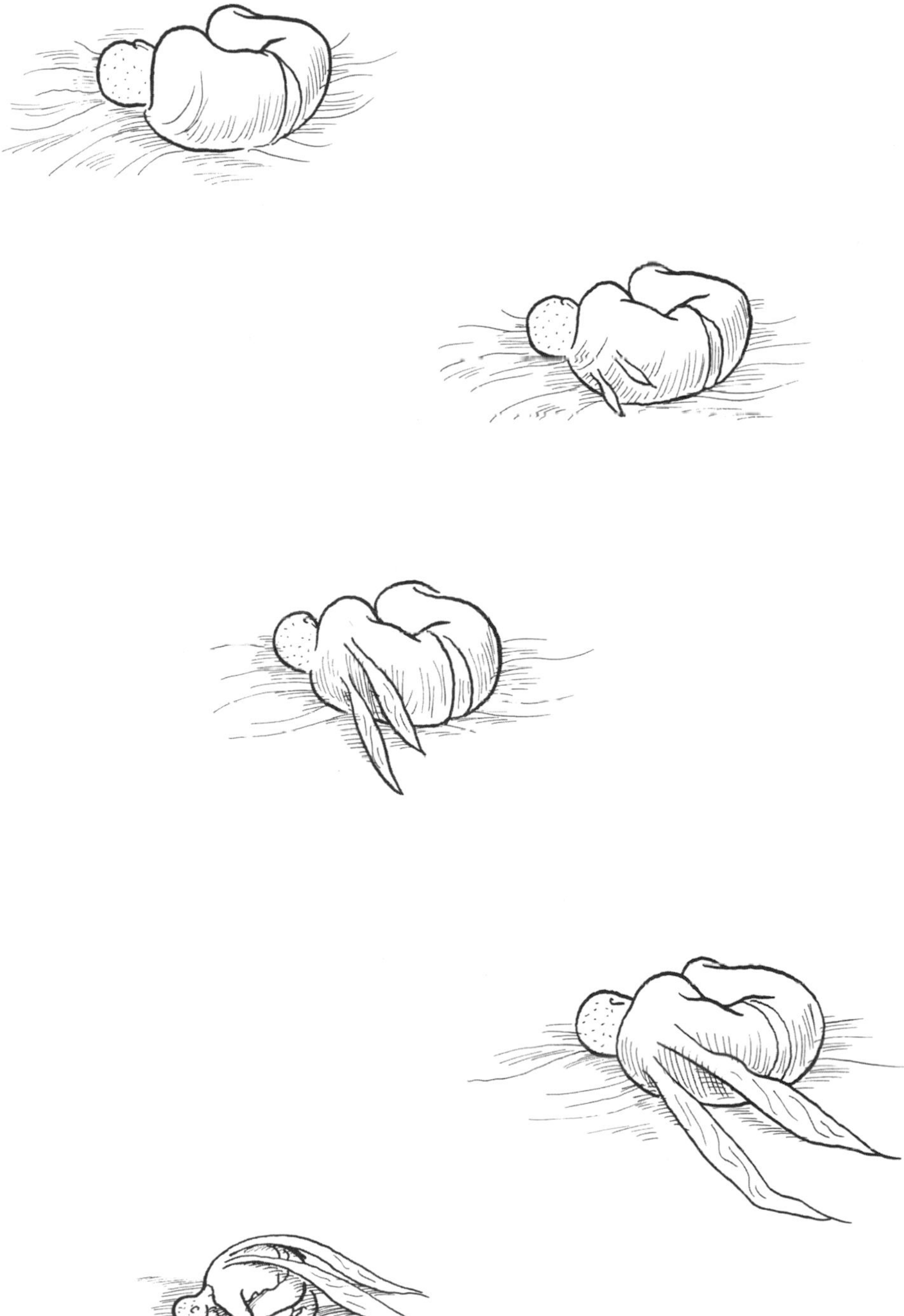

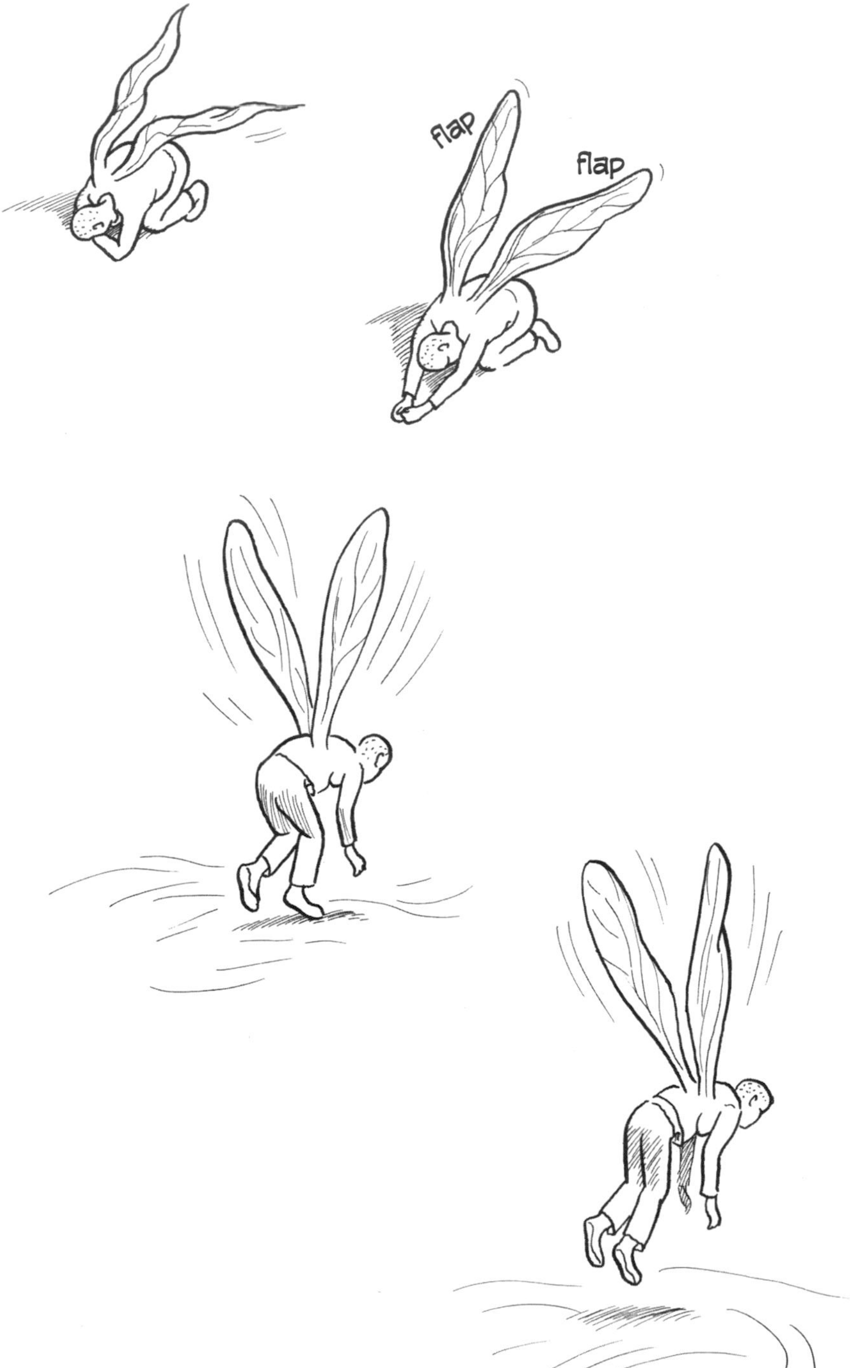
flap
flap

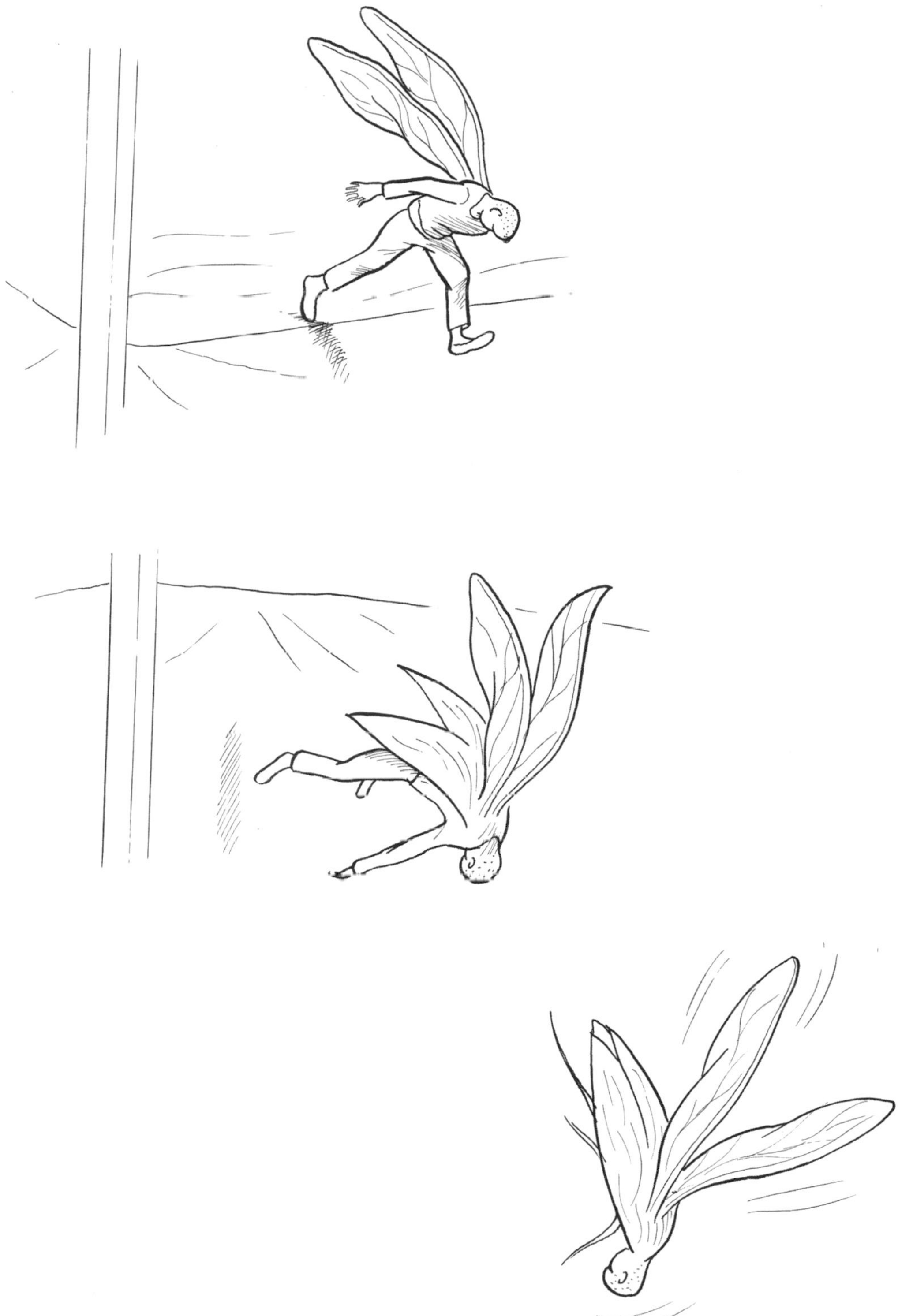

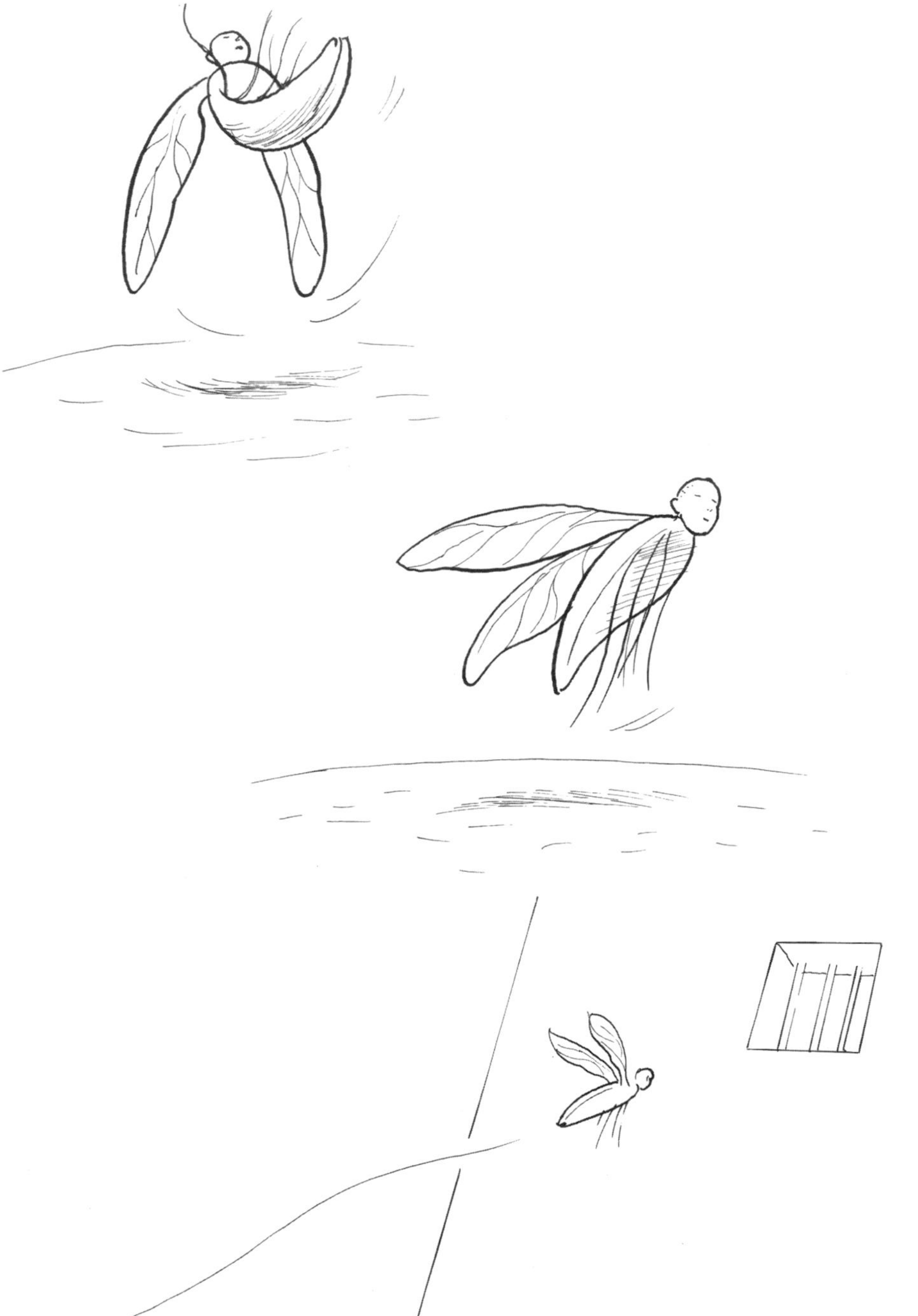

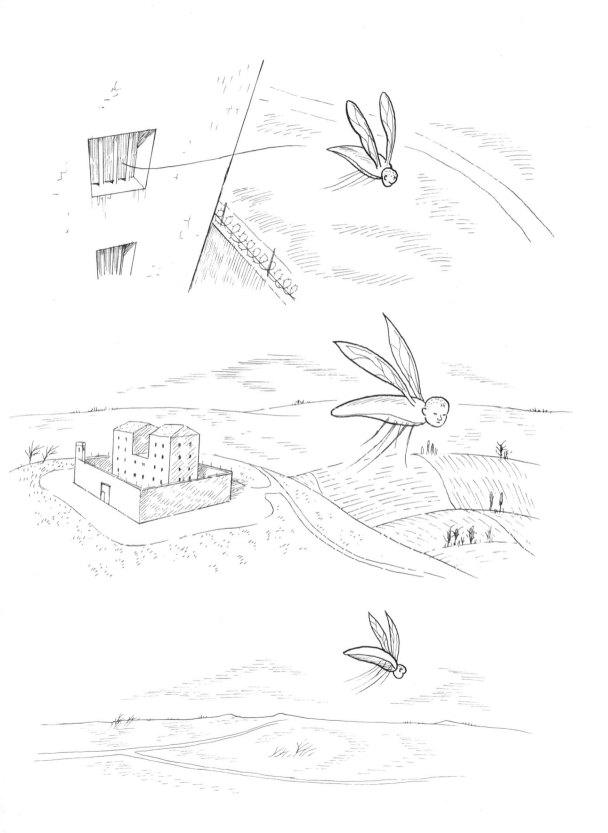

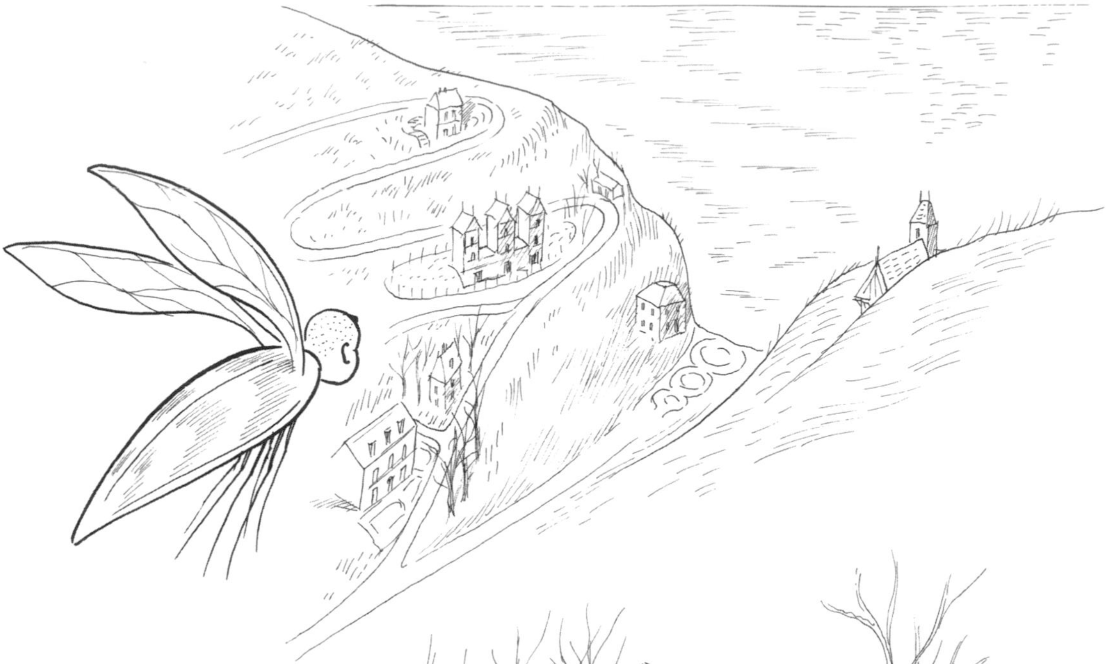

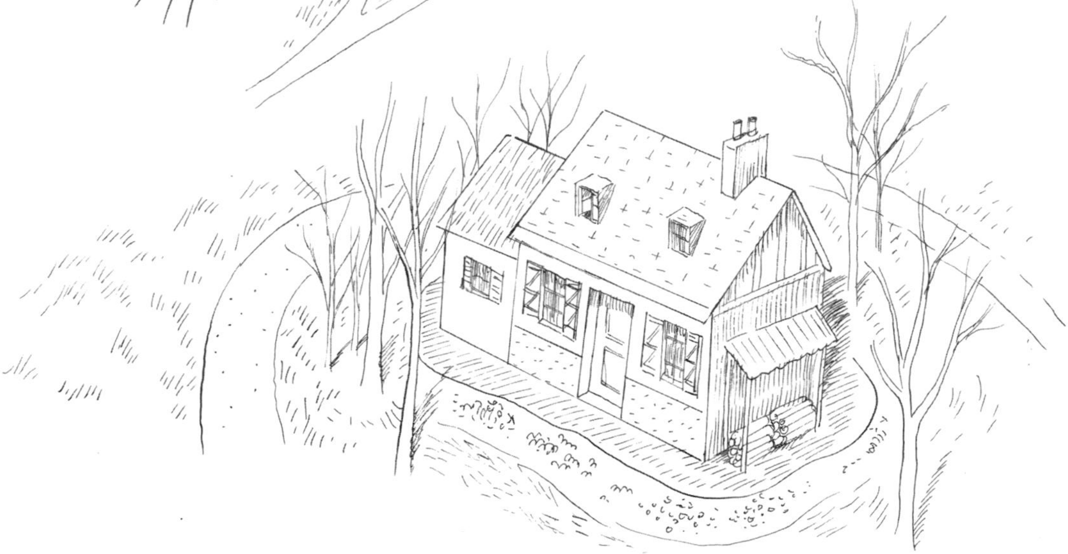

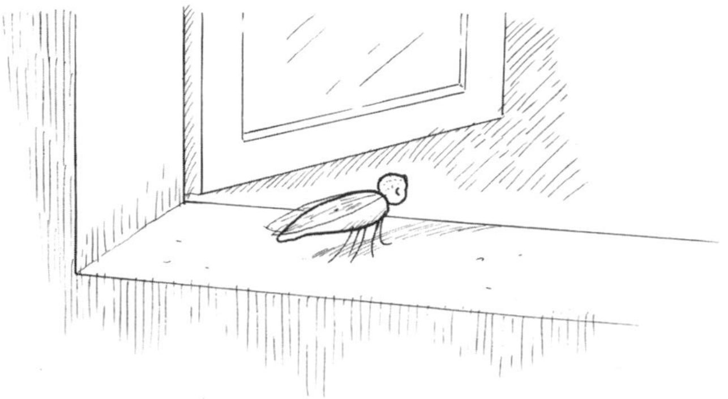

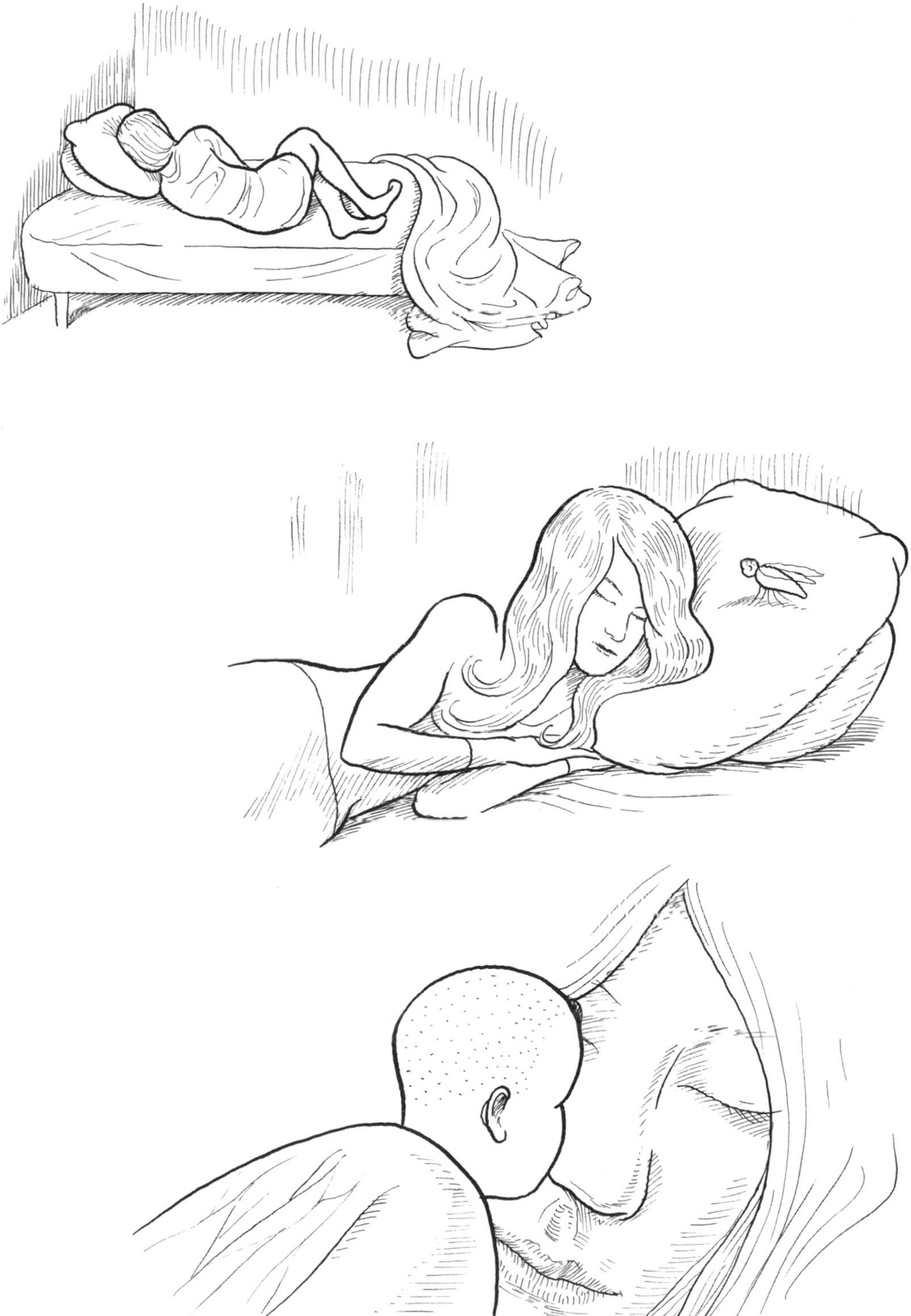

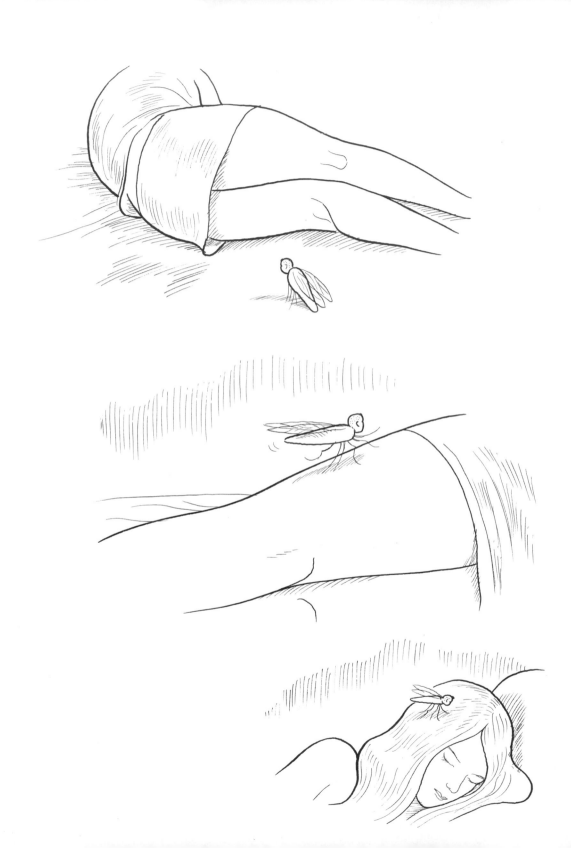

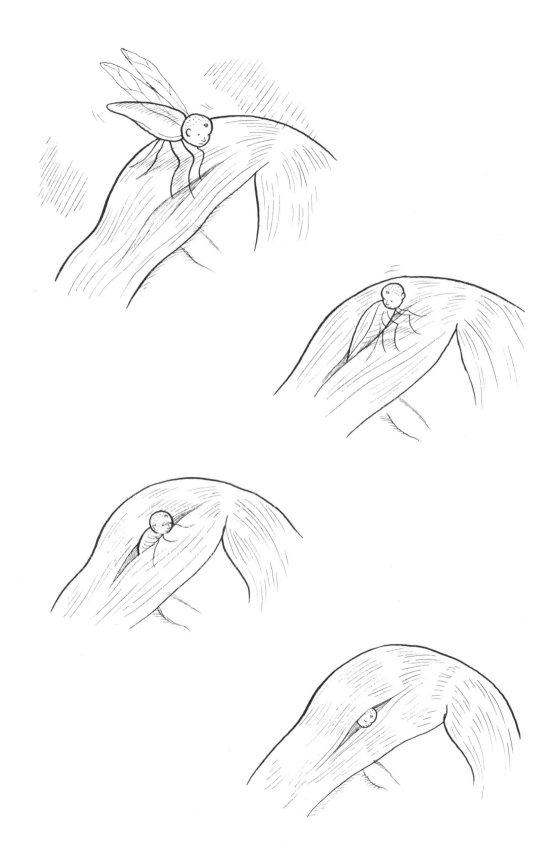

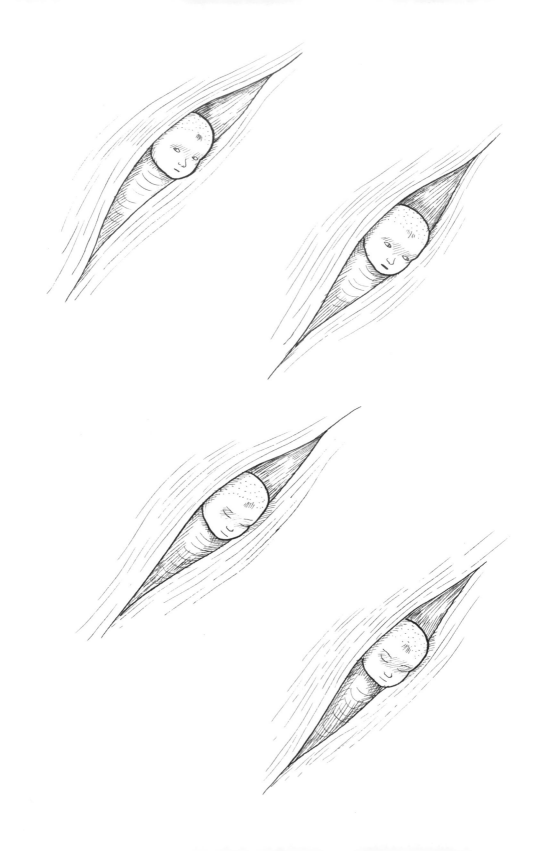

sob

sob

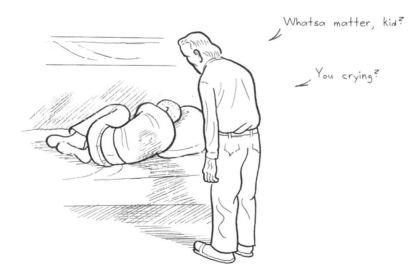

Whatsa matter, kid?

You crying?

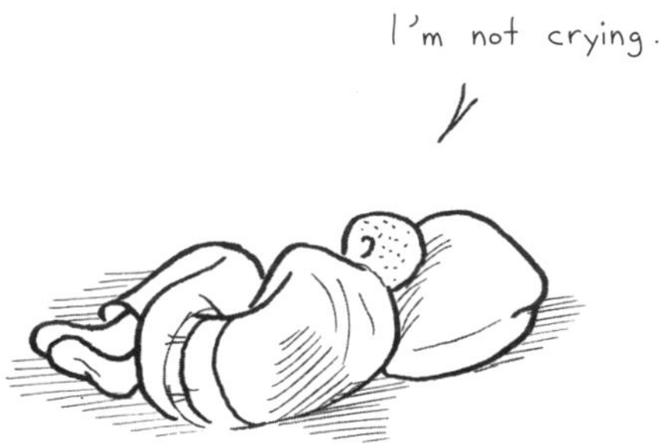
I'm not crying.

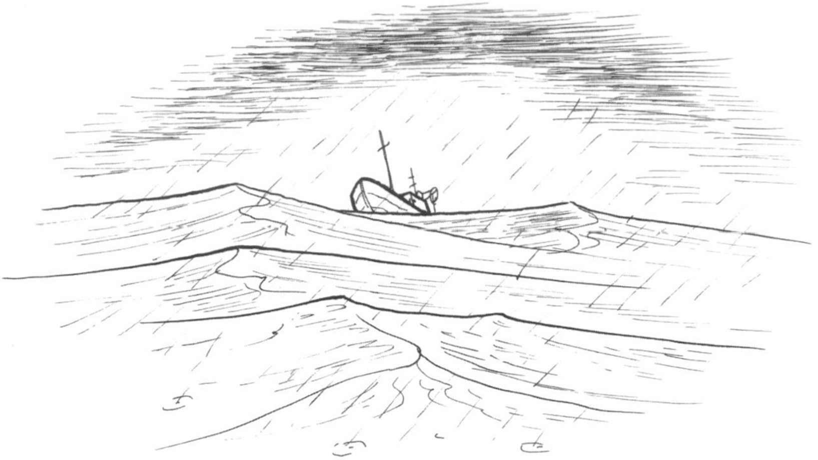

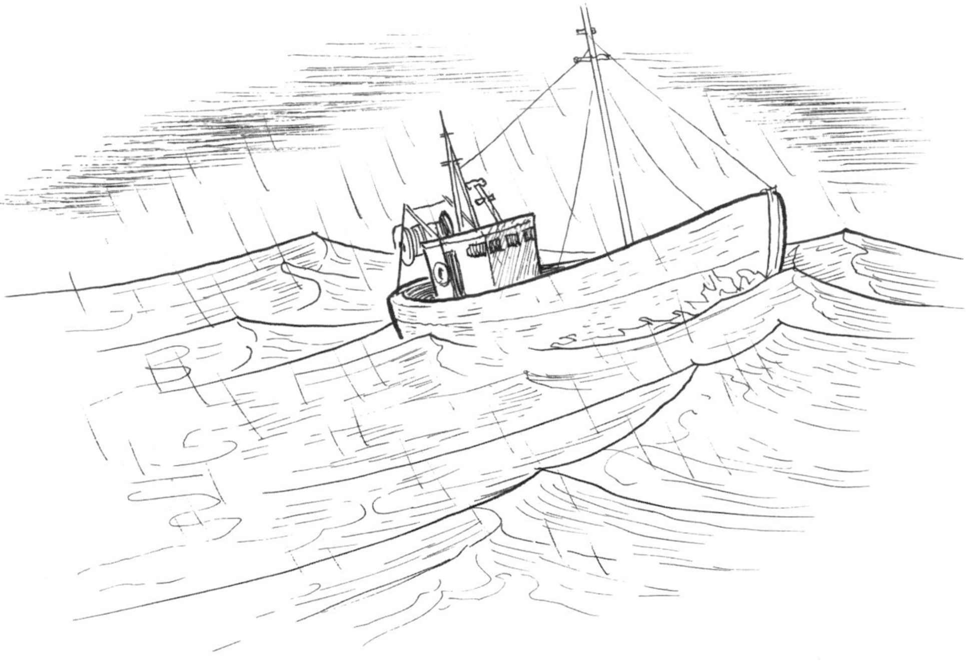

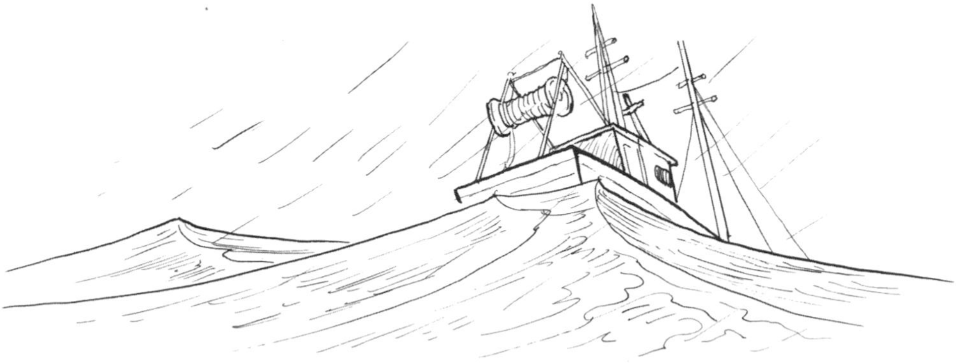

It was a family of sailors.

Goddamn madmen.

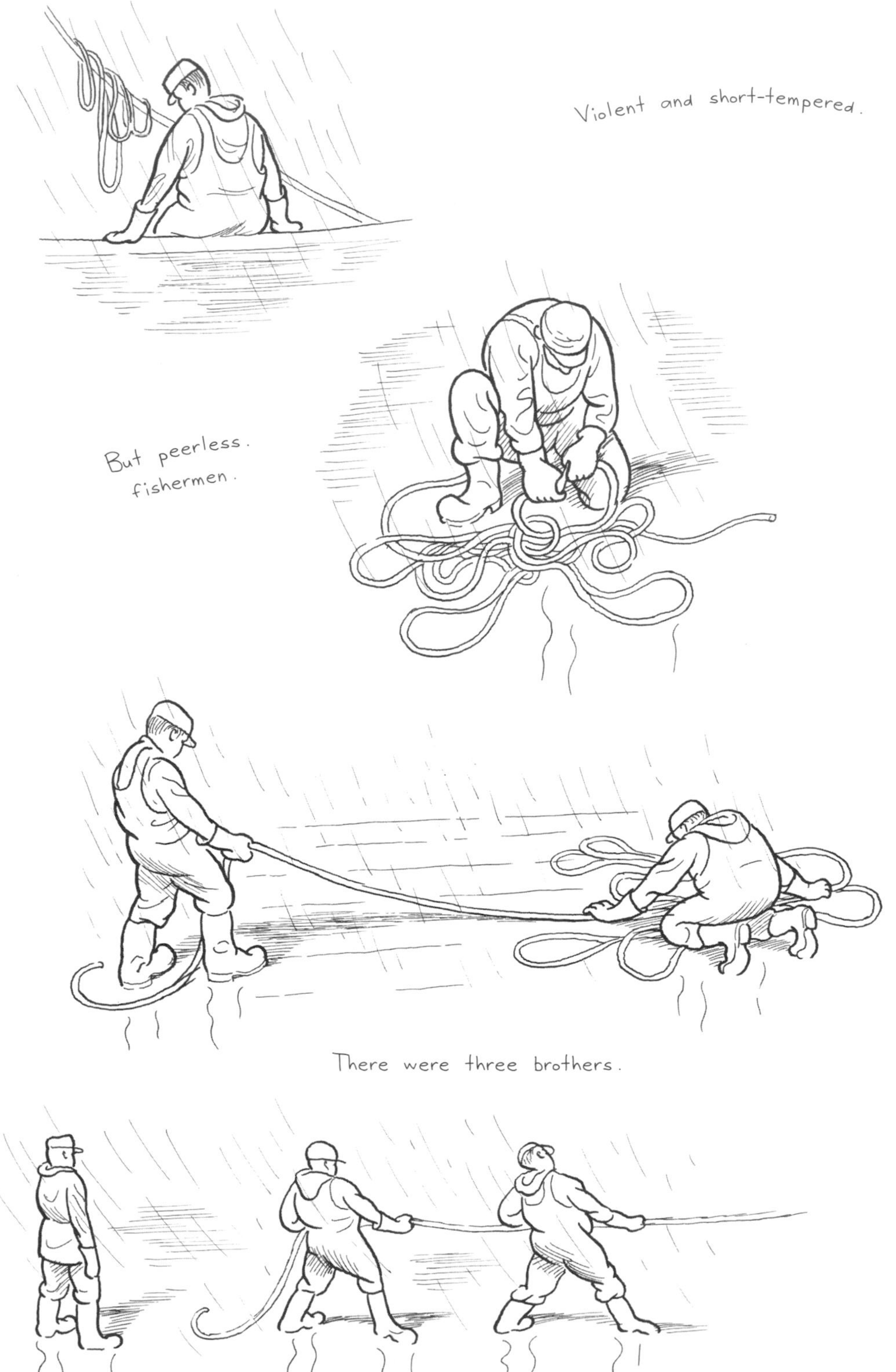
Violent and short-tempered.
But peerless.
fishermen.
There were three brothers.

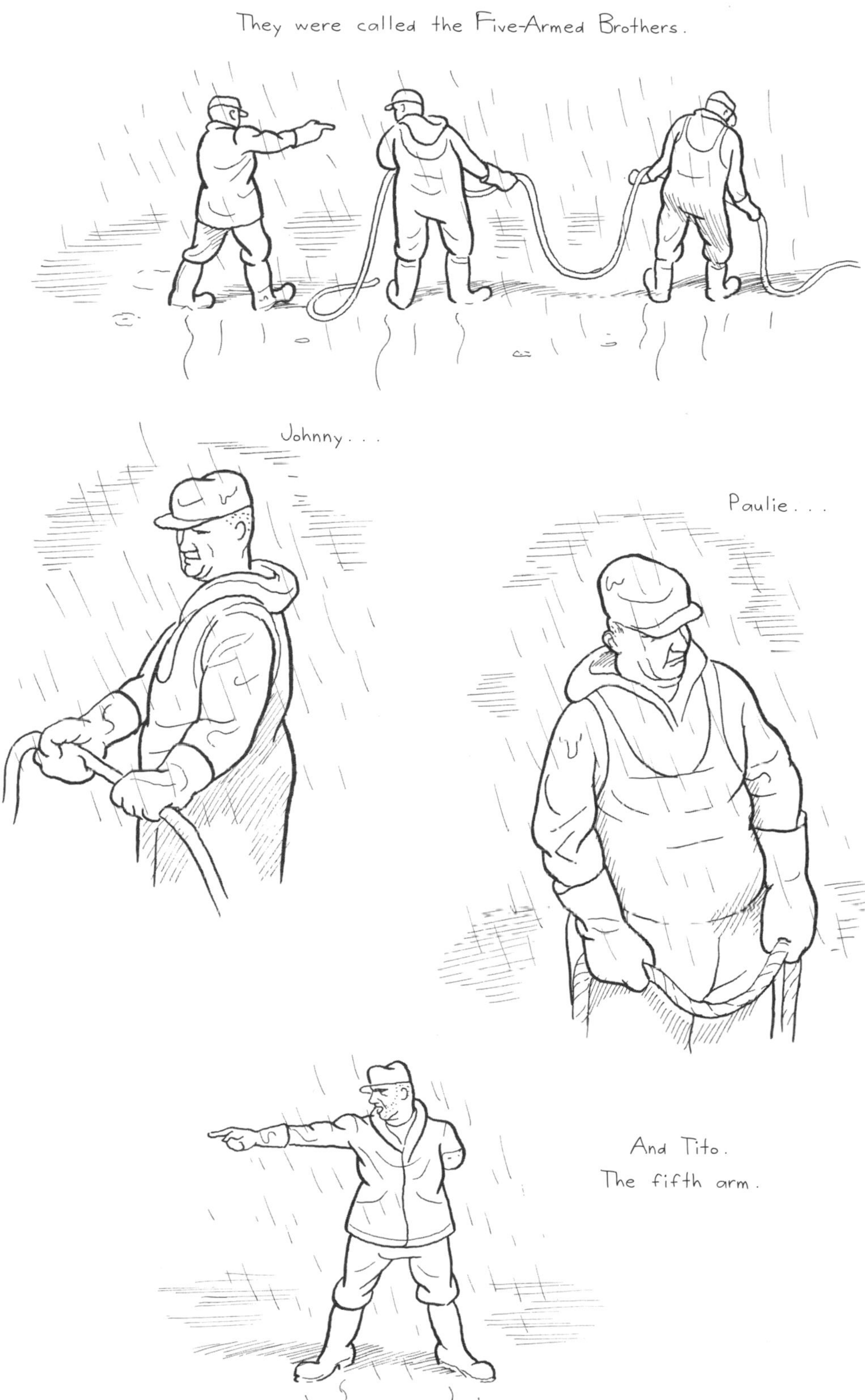
They were called the Five-Armed Brothers.
Johnny...
Paulie...
And Tito.
The fifth arm.

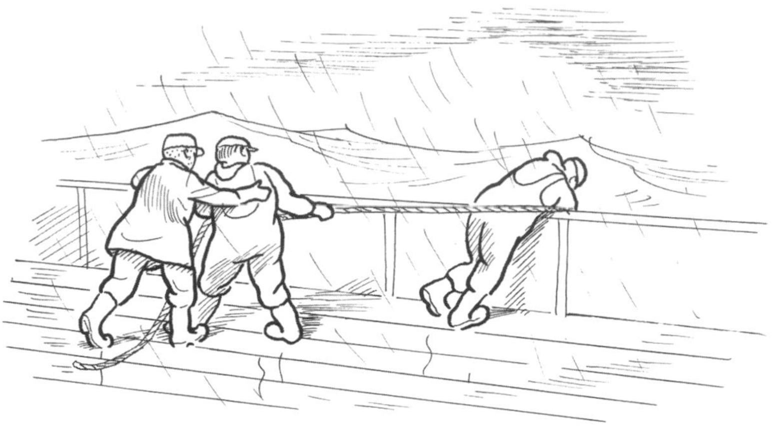

They weren't good men.

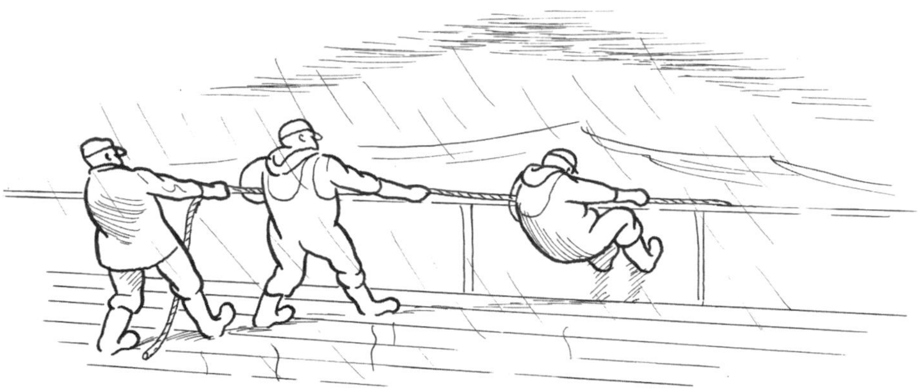

Most everything they did when not on a boat
brought them and those around them unhappiness.

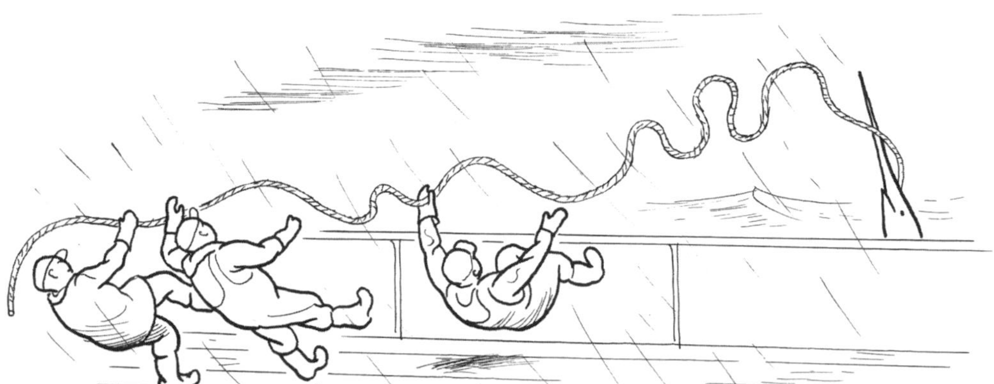

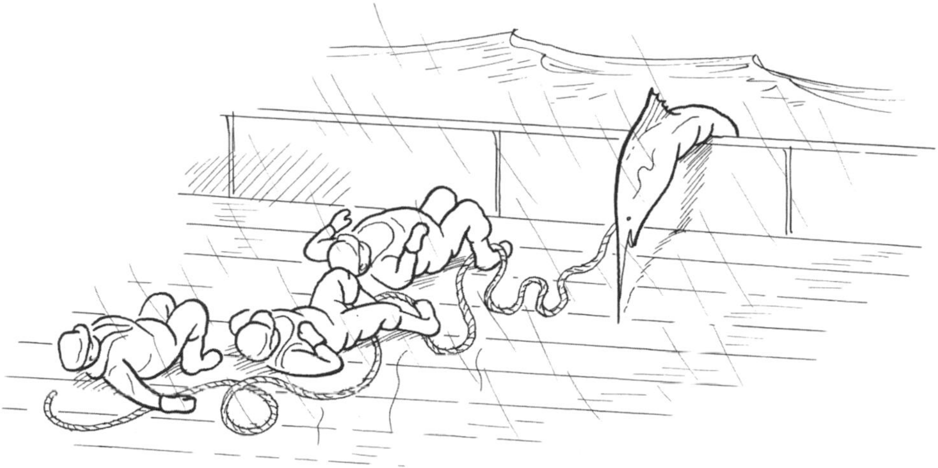

But in the middle of the ocean, far from ports and other men, it was like their anger no longer had a refuge . . .

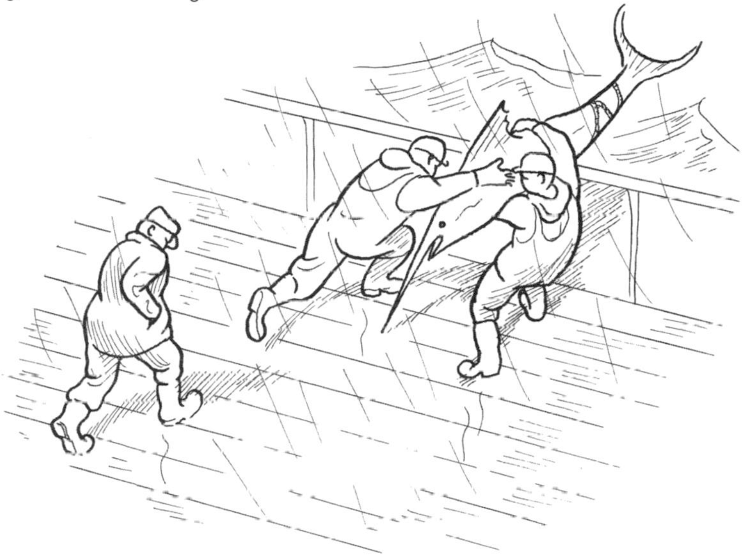

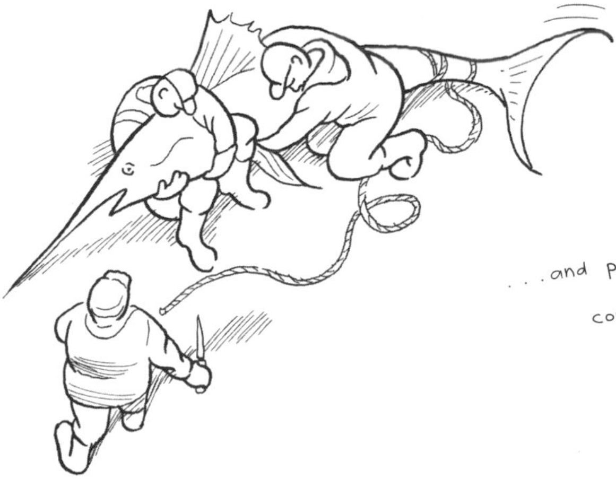

. . . and poured itself utterly and completely into the sea.

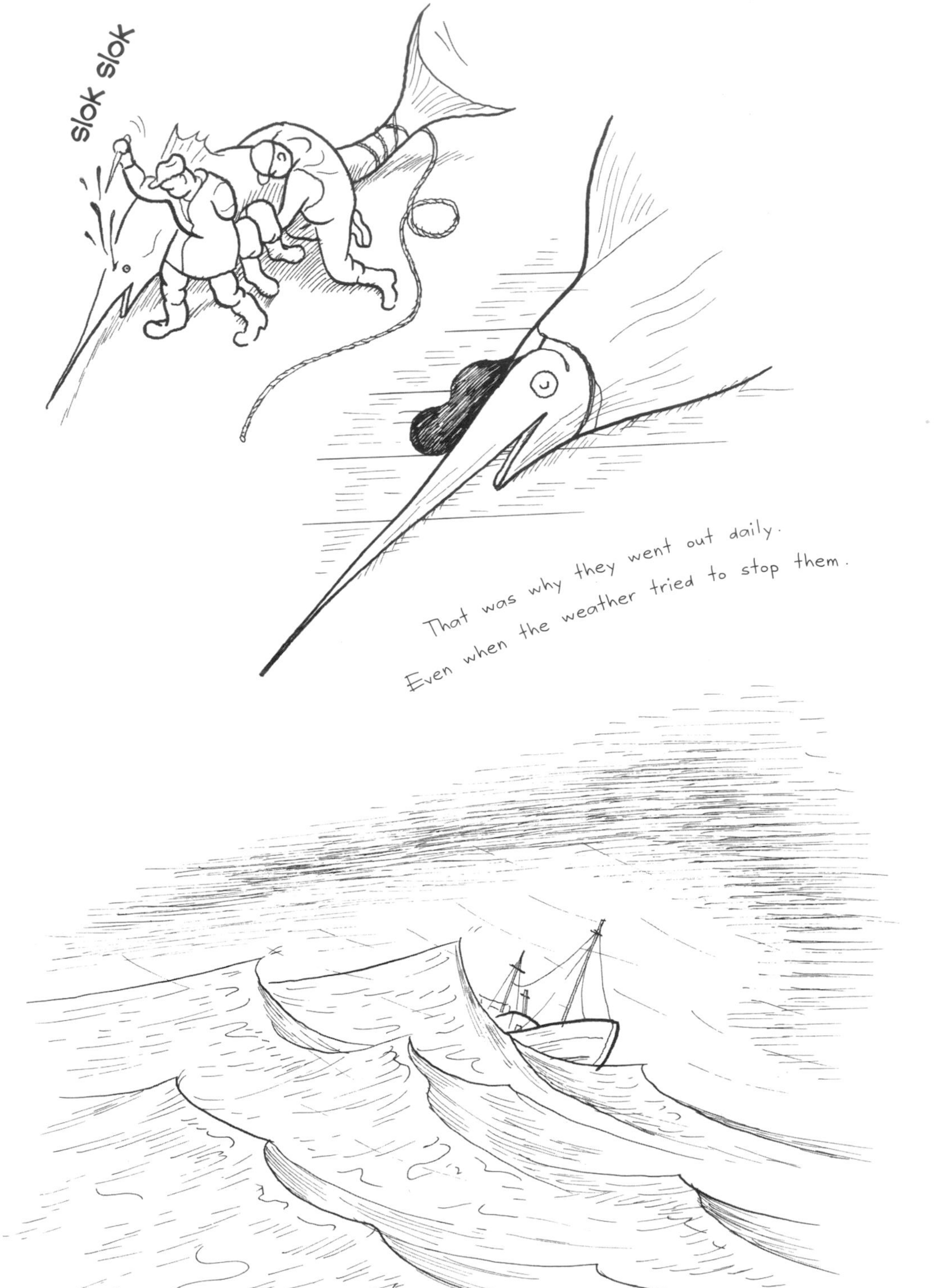
slok slok
That was why they went out daily.
Even when the weather tried to stop them.
Especially when the weather tried to stop them.

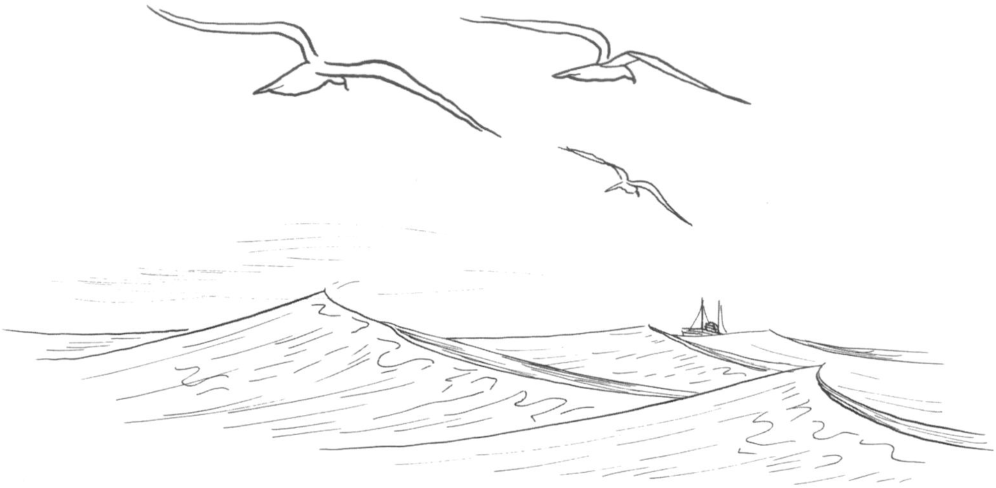

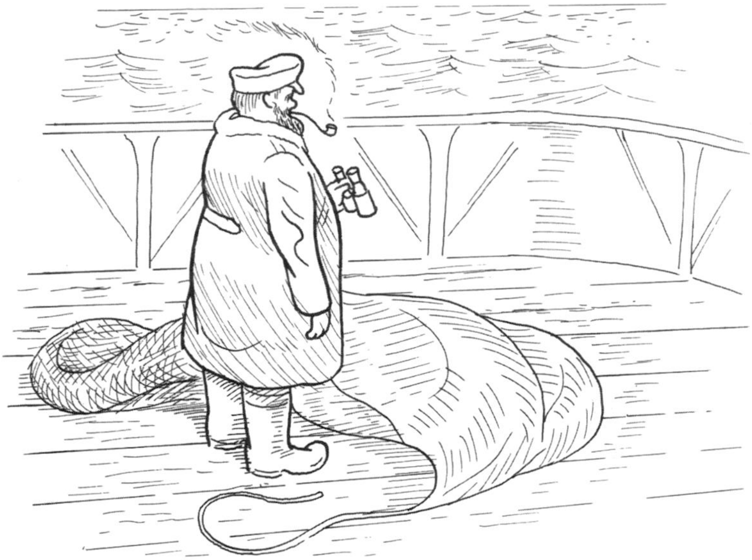

Their father. . .

Their uncle. . .

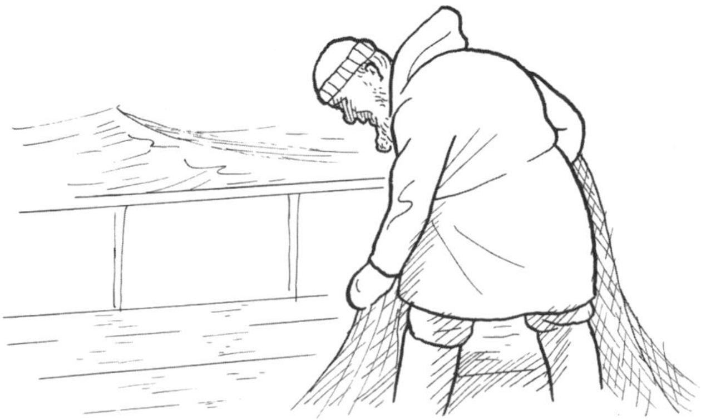

Before them, it had been the same.

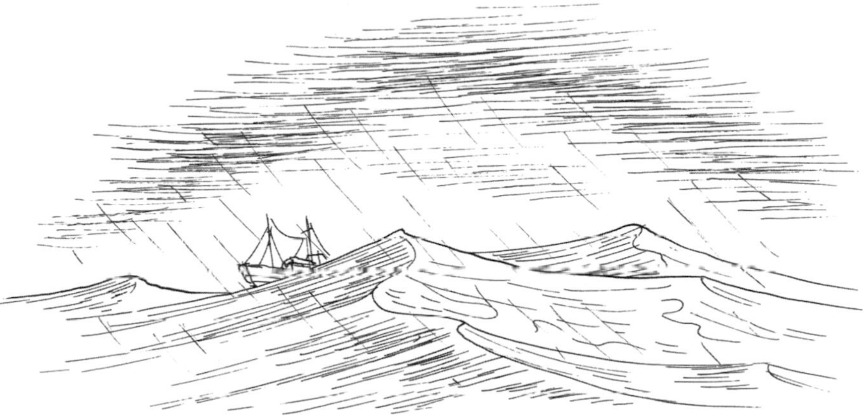

Out to sea when other sailors were hurrying home, as a black wind assailed the water's surface.

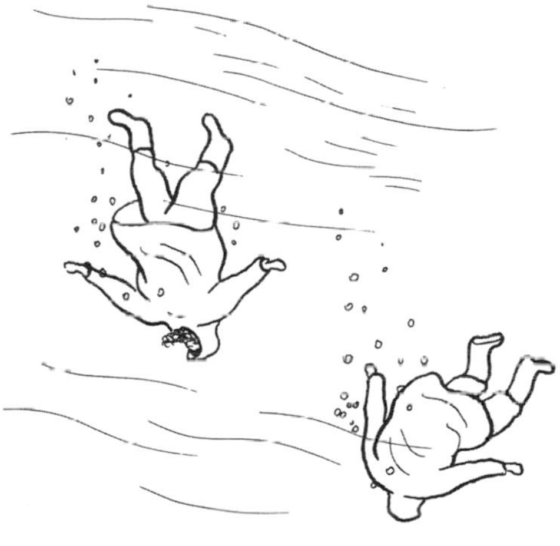

They wound up leaving their slickers in the depths.

Cauls...

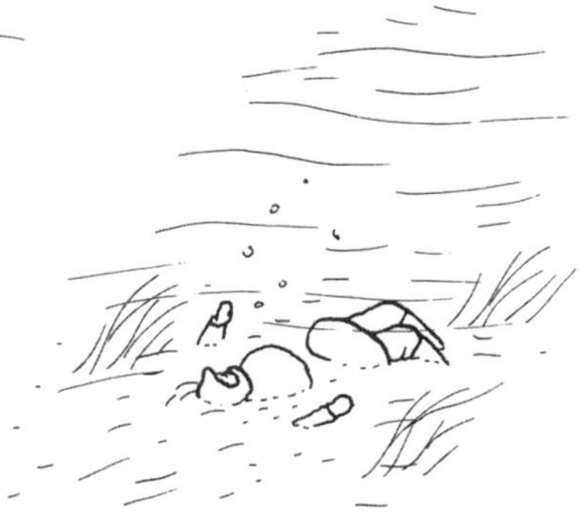

The three brothers—children at the time—knew the tale.

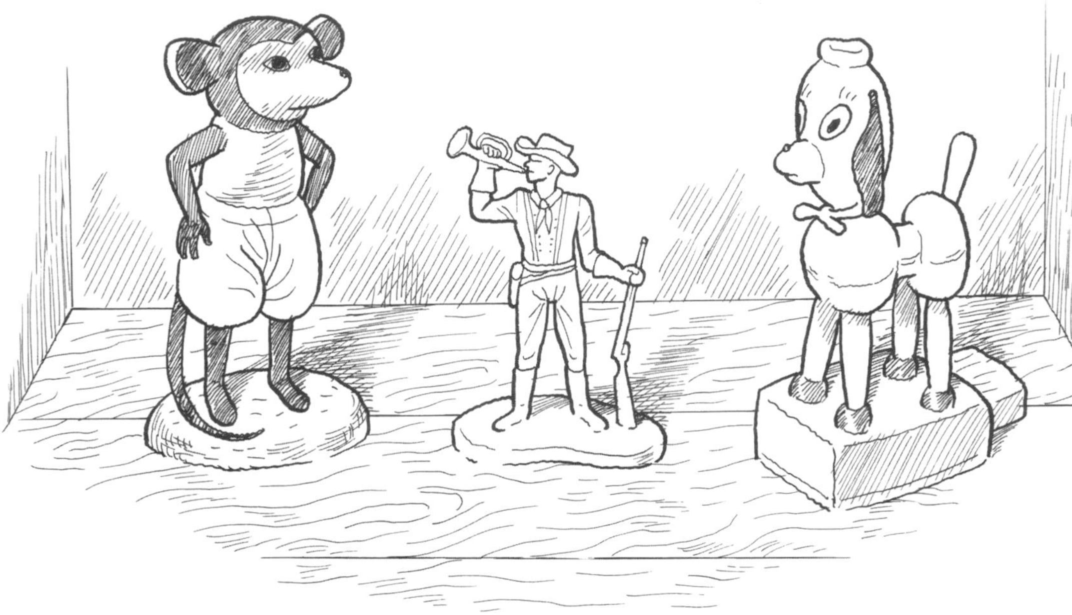

A kind of family curse.

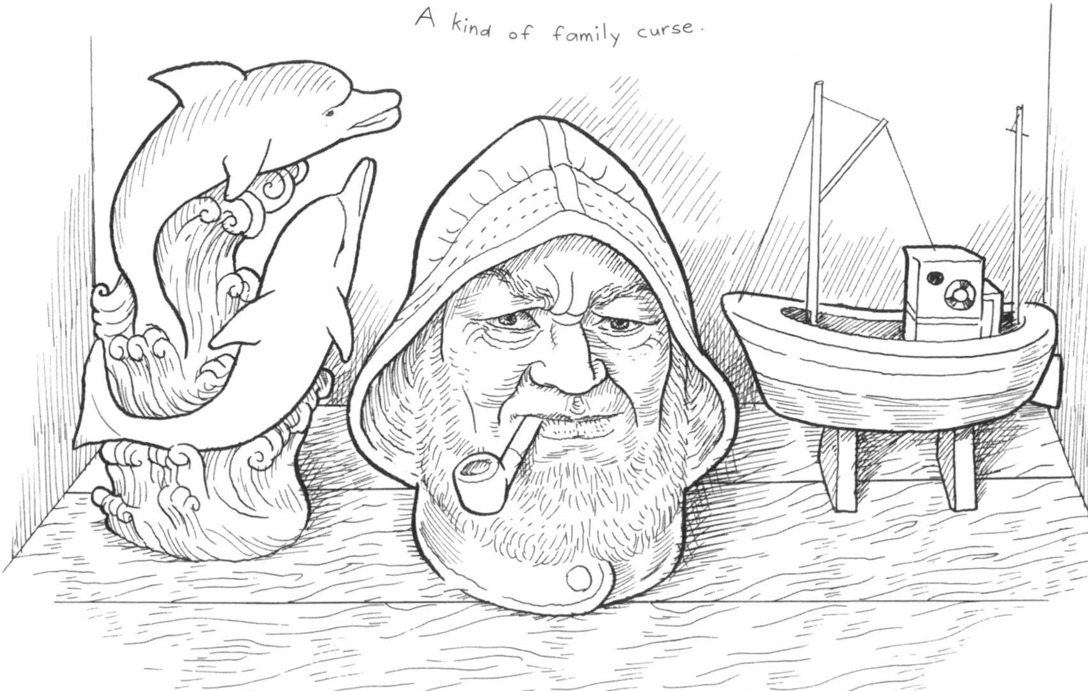

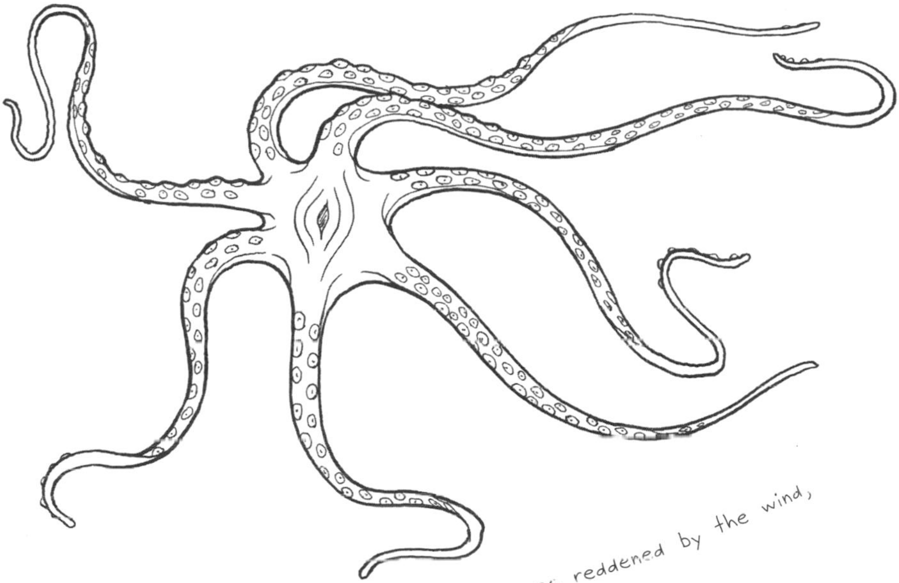

They chose the path of night storms, faces reddened by the wind,
and gasoline motors gunned and raring.

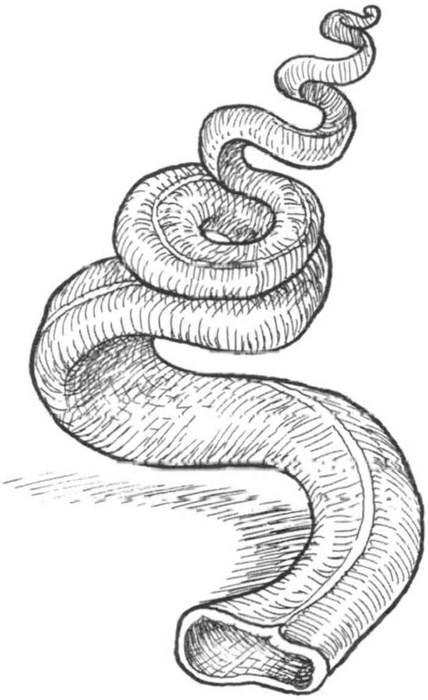

Johnny was the first to be lost.
Beneath a misshapen wave.
A water giant.

The sea is blind. And deaf...
But it howls. Yes, howls...War songs...
Bombarding the hull...Liquid meteors...

It sinks mad
trawlers.

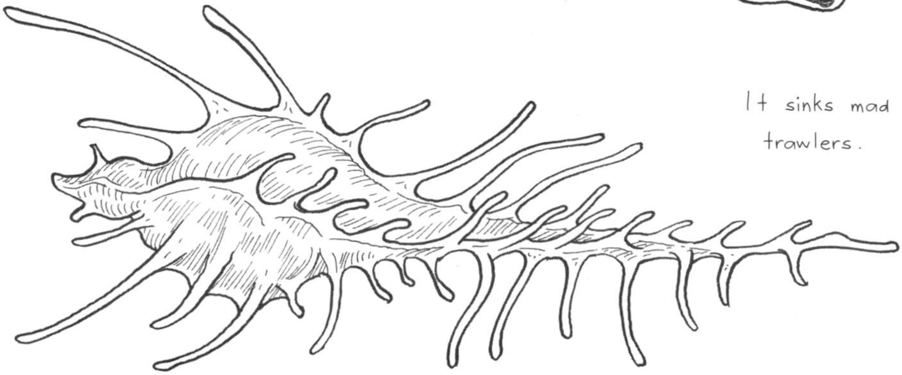

That was when they became a legend. A family of consumed and brutal sailors. Madmen...

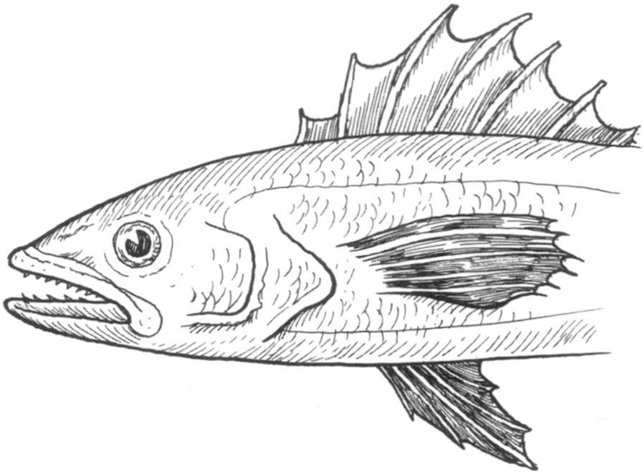

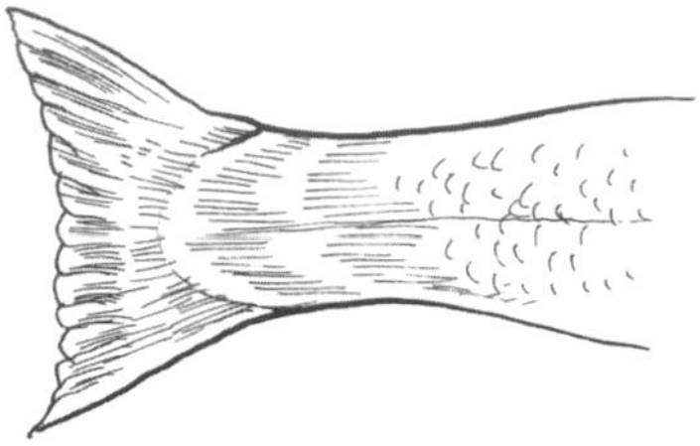

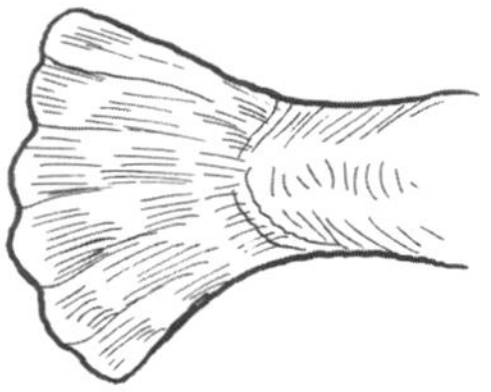

One night when the worst of all tides had raised pillars of water to shatter them in salvos against two seawalls. The Five-Armed Brothers, alone at sea, to and fro in the narrow channel leading to the harbor.

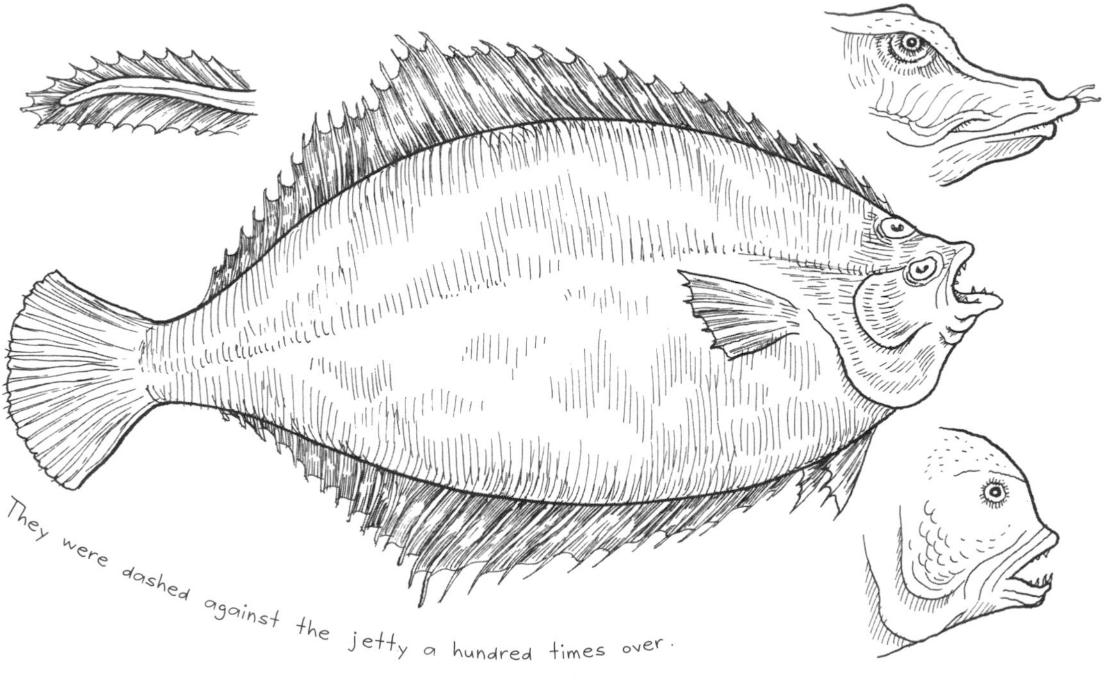

They were dashed against the jetty a hundred times over.

In the morning, after hours of sullen defiance, they slipped like a breath from atop a wave five stories high...

The two brothers returned to the safety of the harbor,
where the whole town was clapping and crying.

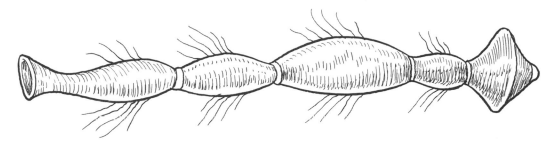

"We thought you'd died..." They had a habit of vanishing alone.
At sea. But this time their madness was plain for all to see.
They were the surviving members of a family swallowed whole. Heroes.

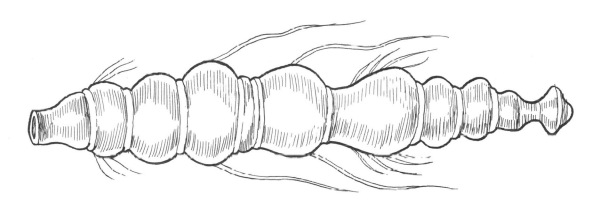

The brothers headed out again. Tito went a few months later, carried off by a
fickle net that caught his only arm.
Like a mullet or a conger eel, returning to the sea.

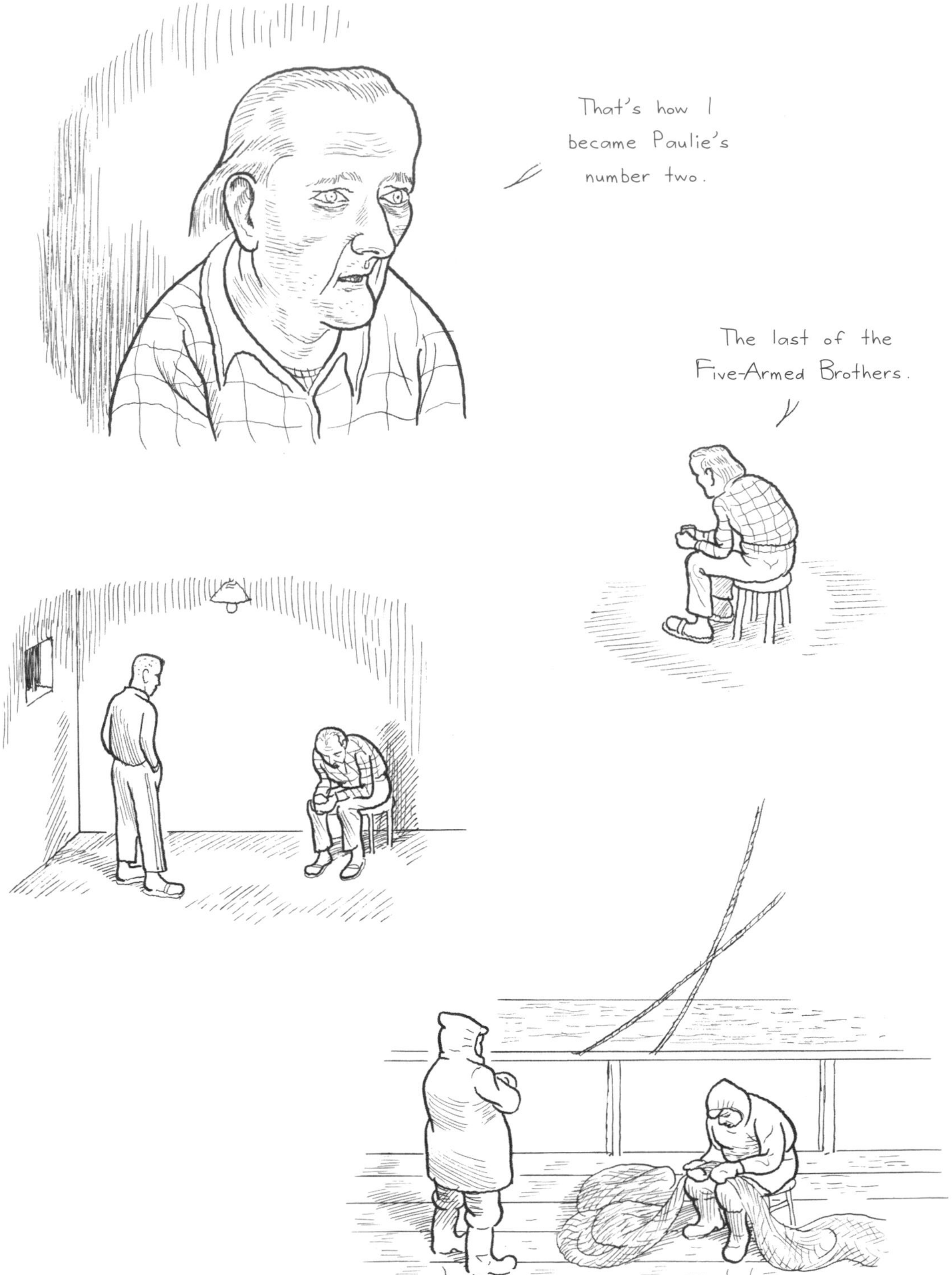
That's how I became Paulie's number two.
The last of the Five-Armed Brothers.

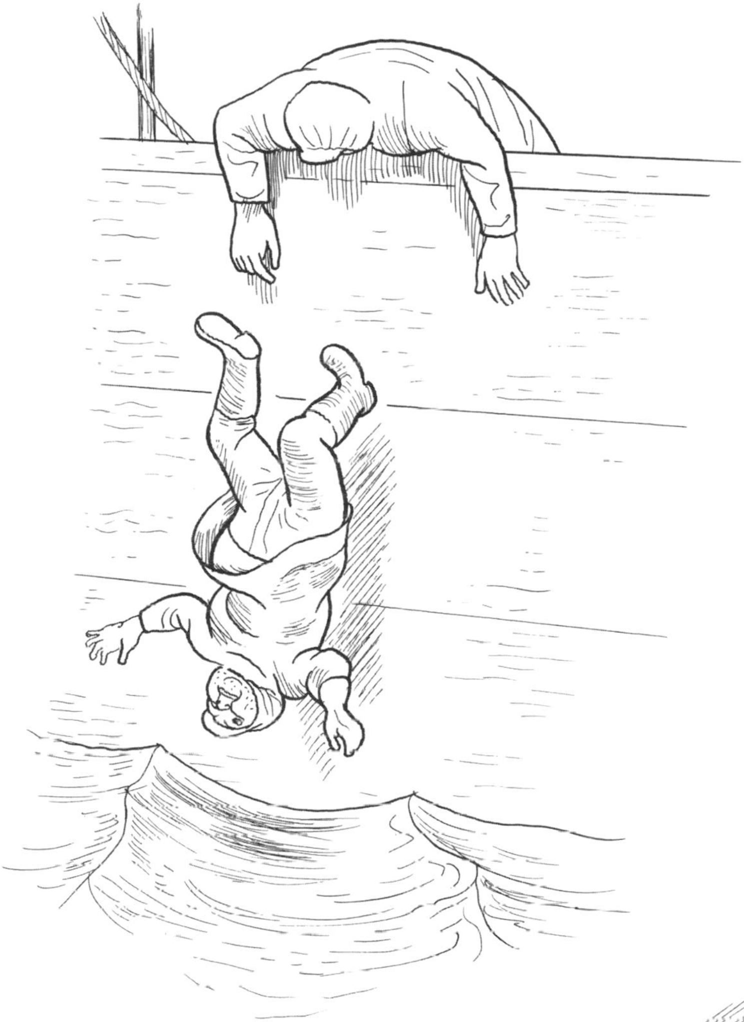
A bad, scornful man.
He didn't deserve what happened to him. But what could I do? Those boys were cursed.

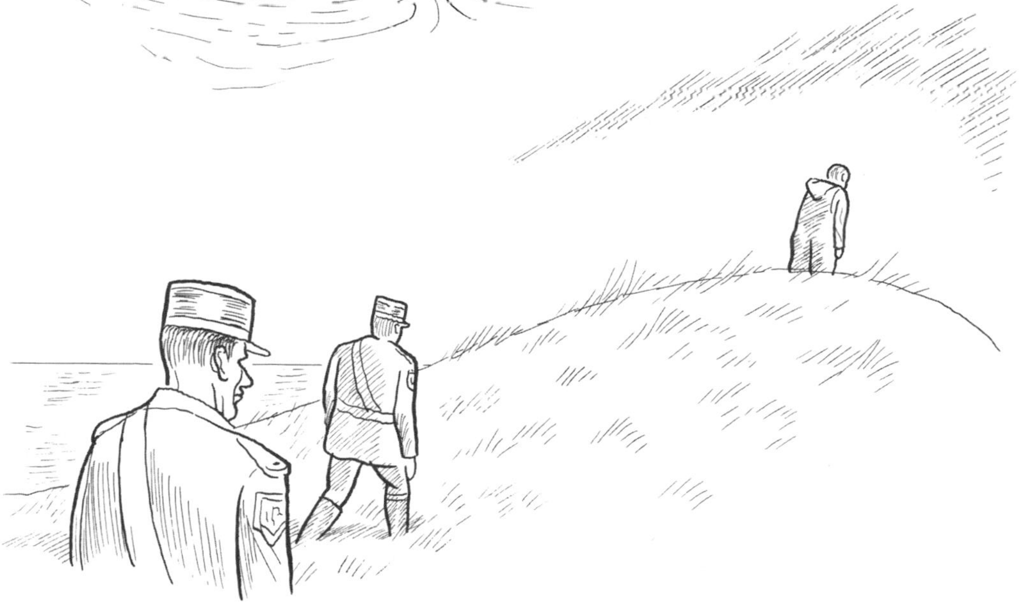

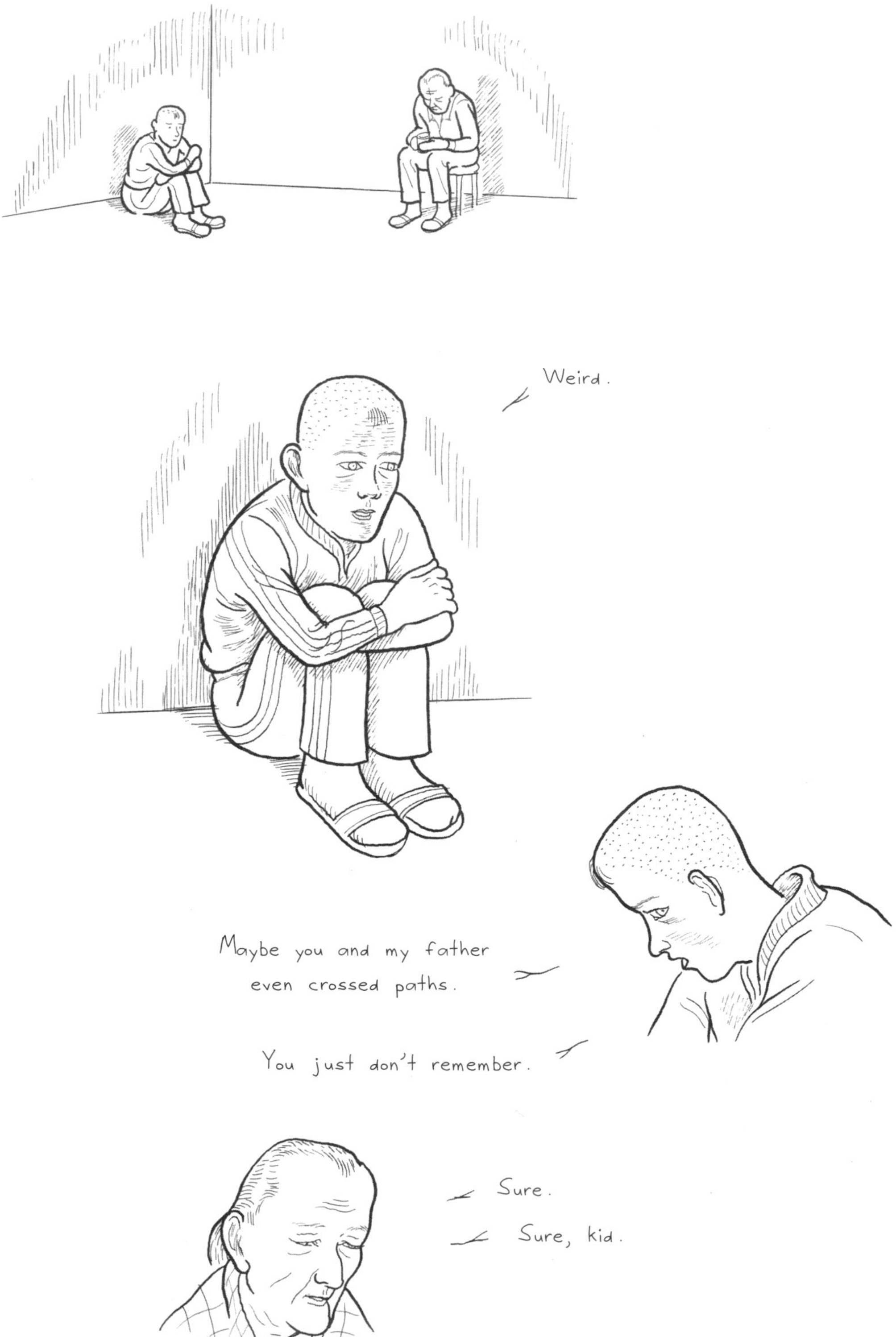
Weird.
Maybe you and my father even crossed paths.
You just don't remember.
Sure.
Sure, kid.

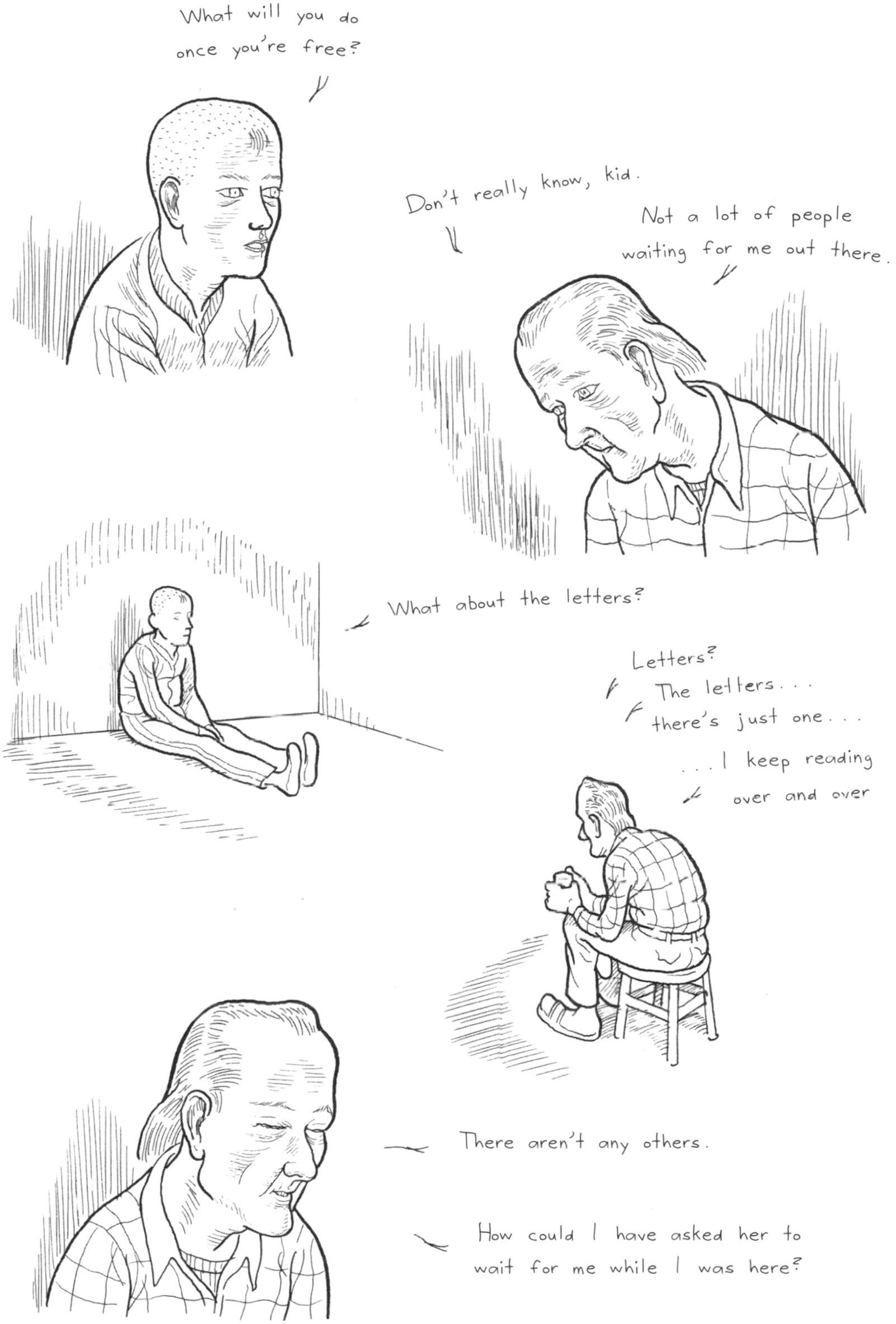
What will you do once you're free?
Don't really know, kid.
Not a lot of people waiting for me out there.
What about the letters?
Letters?
The letters...
there's just one...
...I keep reading over and over
There aren't any others.
How could I have asked her to wait for me while I was here?

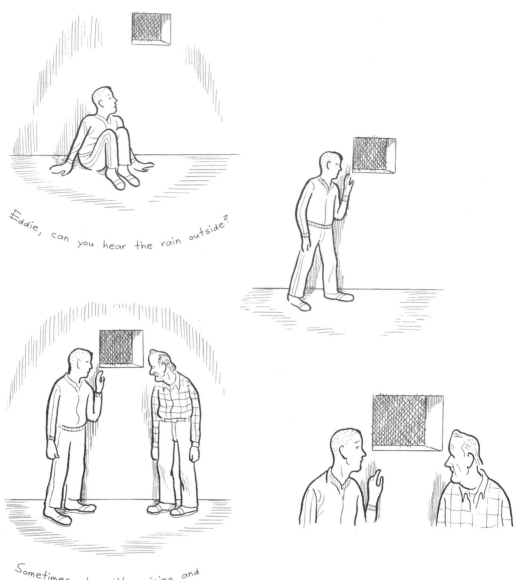

Eddie, can you hear the rain outside?

Sometimes when it's raining and windy, I can smell the damp woods all the way from here.

It's like smells travel better by night...

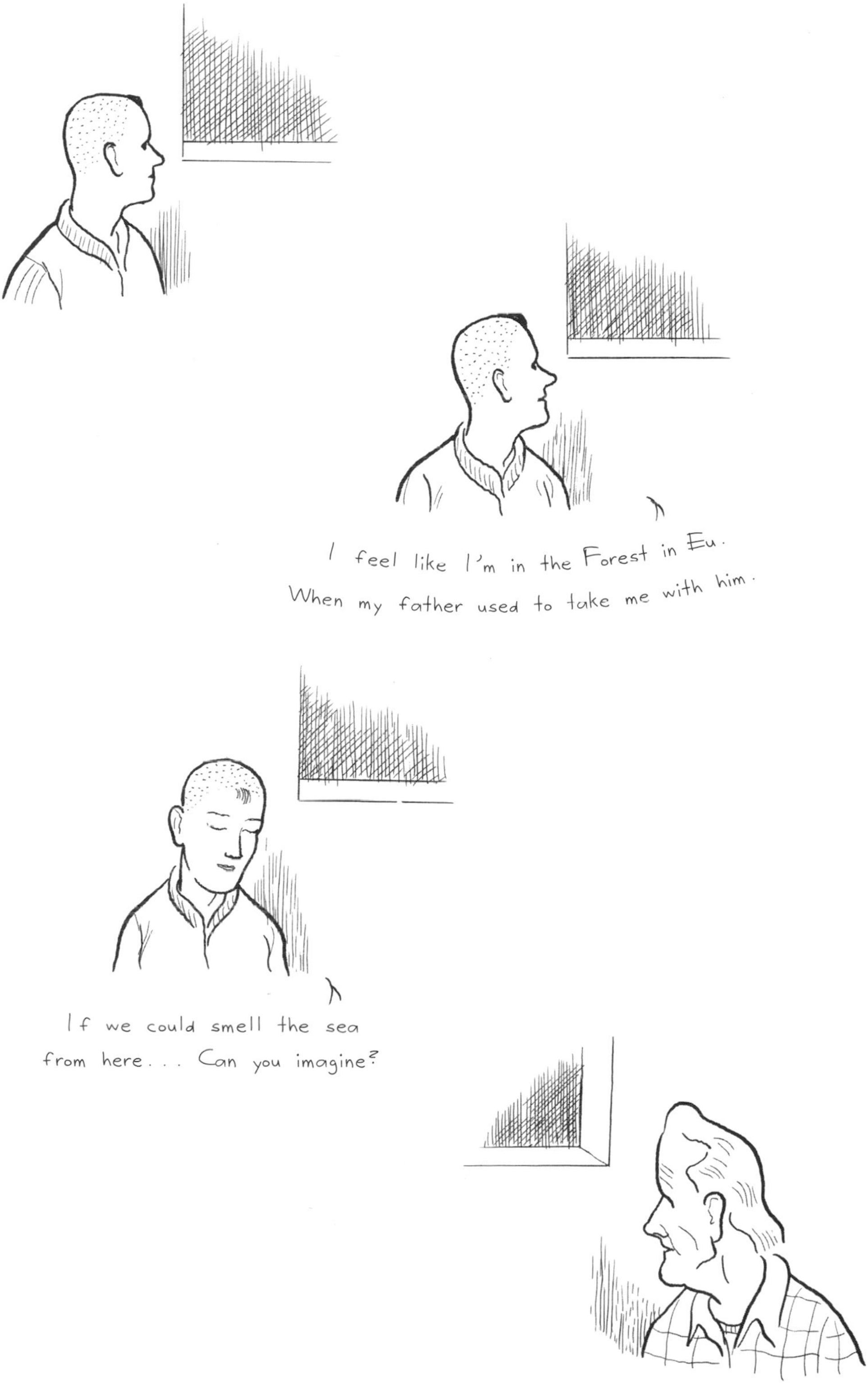
I feel like I'm in the Forest in Eu.
When my father used to take me with him.
If we could smell the sea
from here... Can you imagine?

Y'know, Eddie... I thought of something.

For when you get out of here.

I figured—

You could live at my mother's for a while.

You're totally nuts, kid!

Who'd want a codger like me?
An ex-con to boot!

Actually... I talked to her
about it already.
She's said yes.

Besides, you'll be kind of
like a grandpa to my
little brother and sister.

Oh!

Well... kid,
I mean...

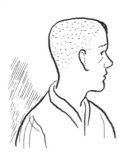

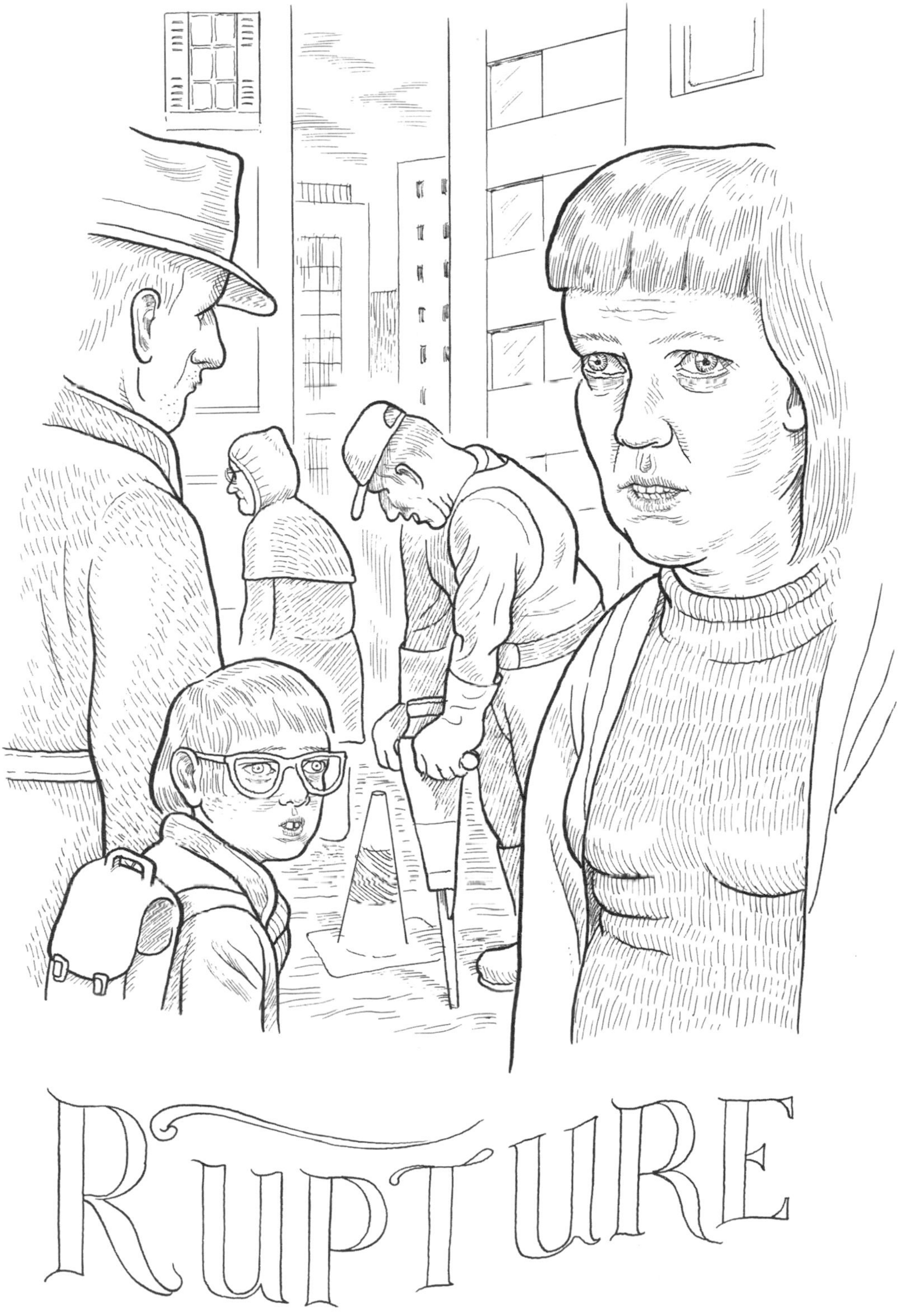

RUPTURE

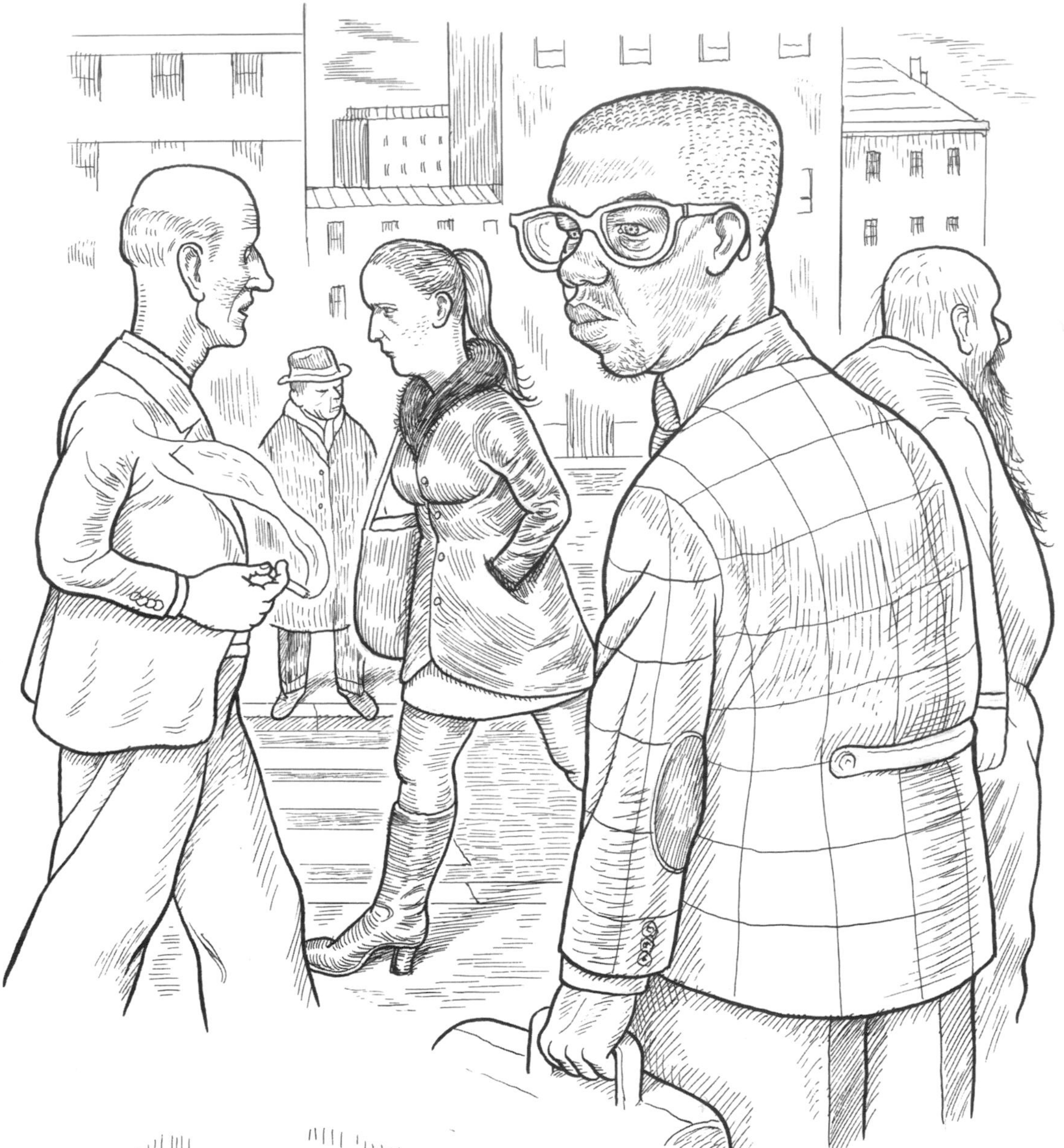

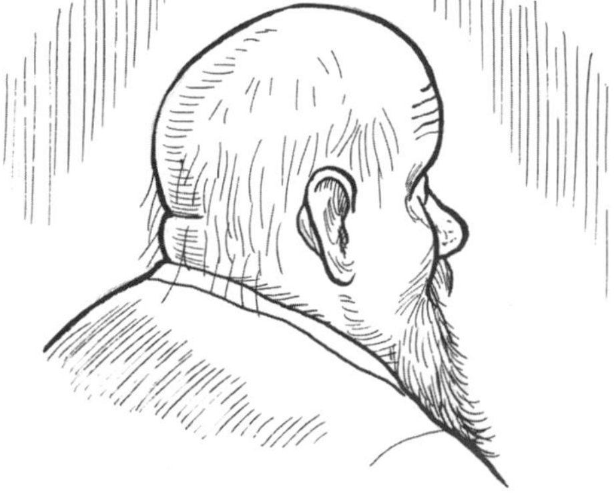

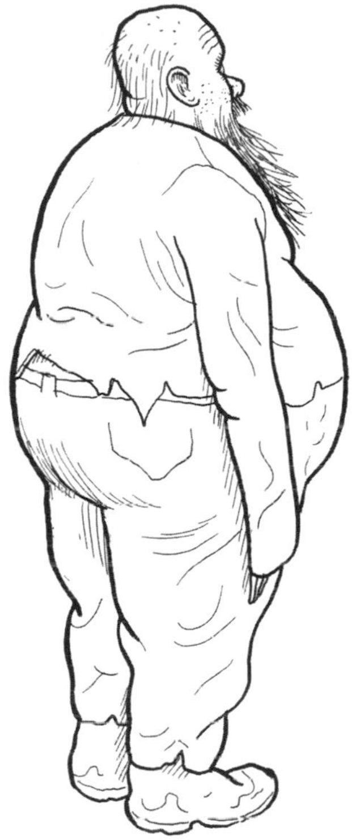

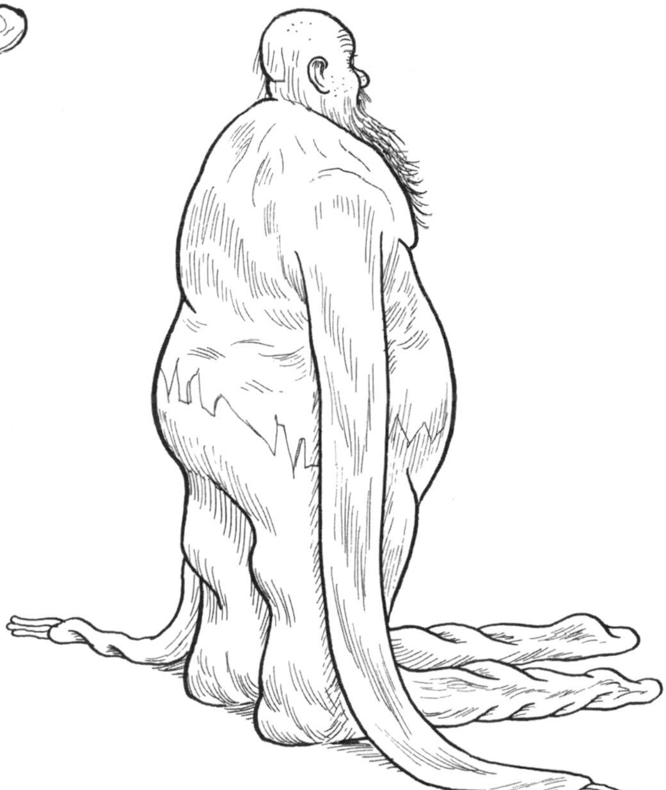

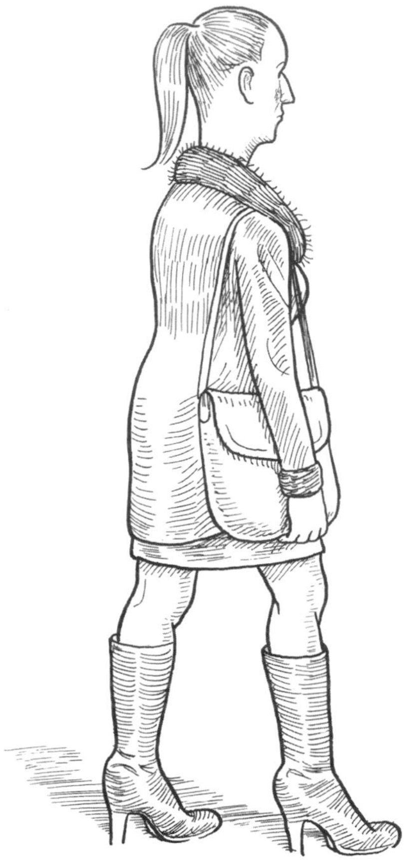
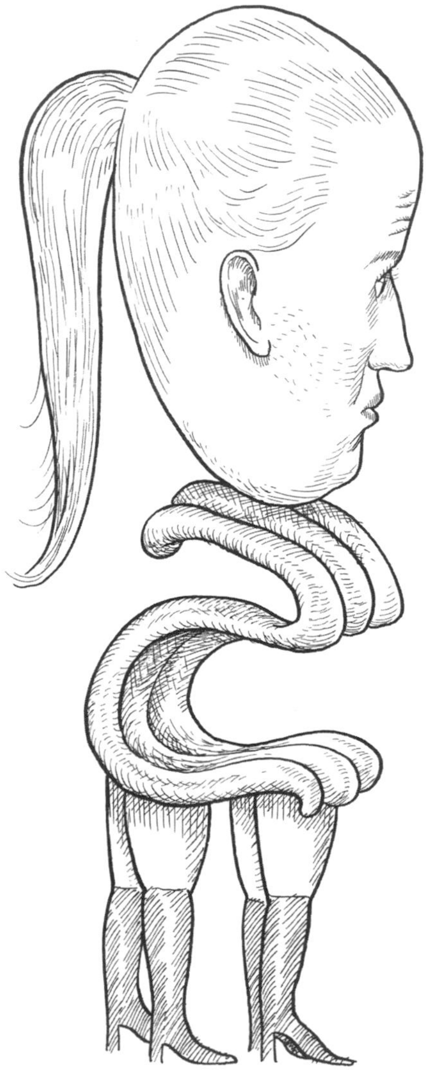

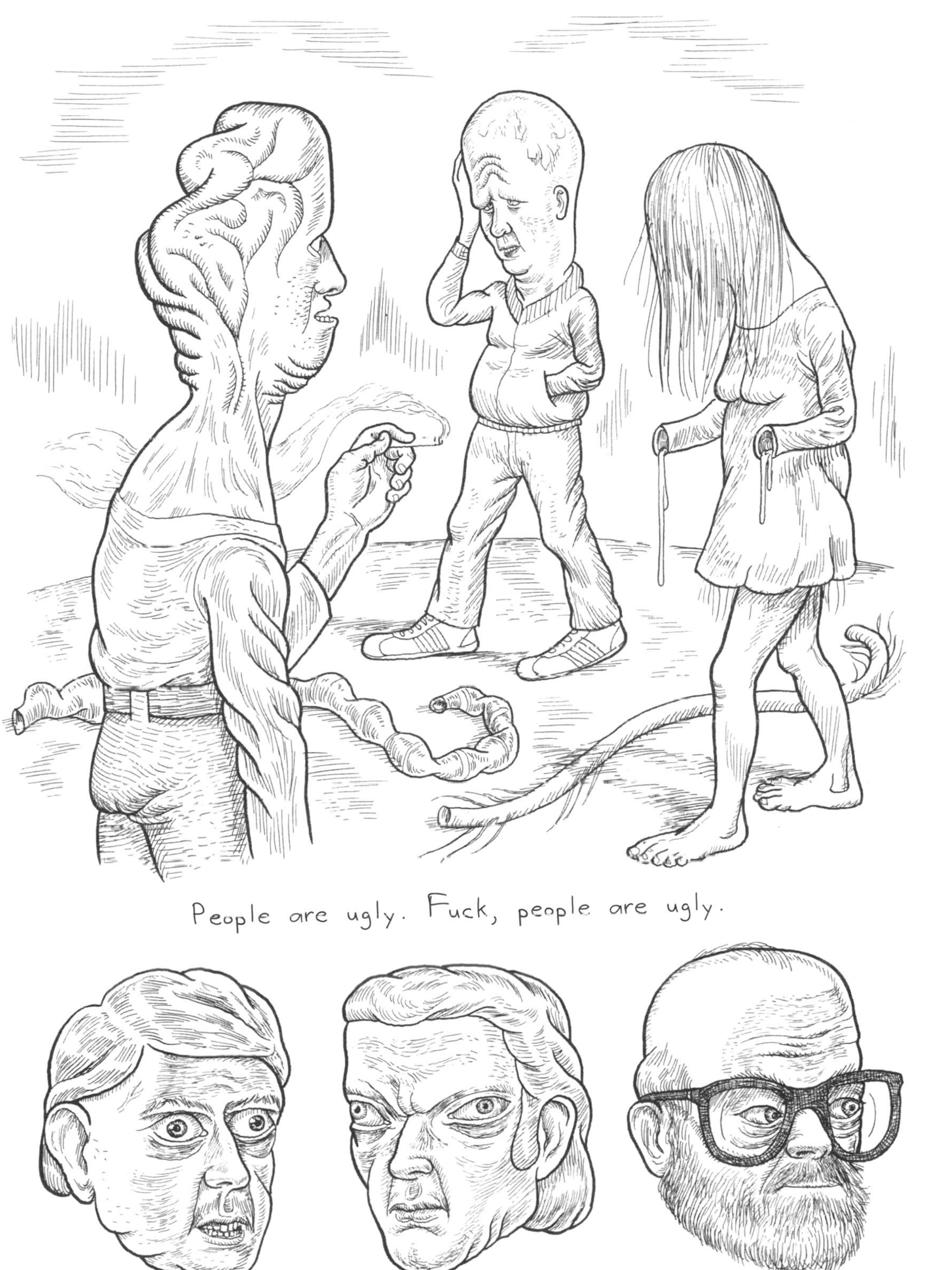
People are ugly. Fuck, people are ugly.

You'd definitely be the ugliest of them all...

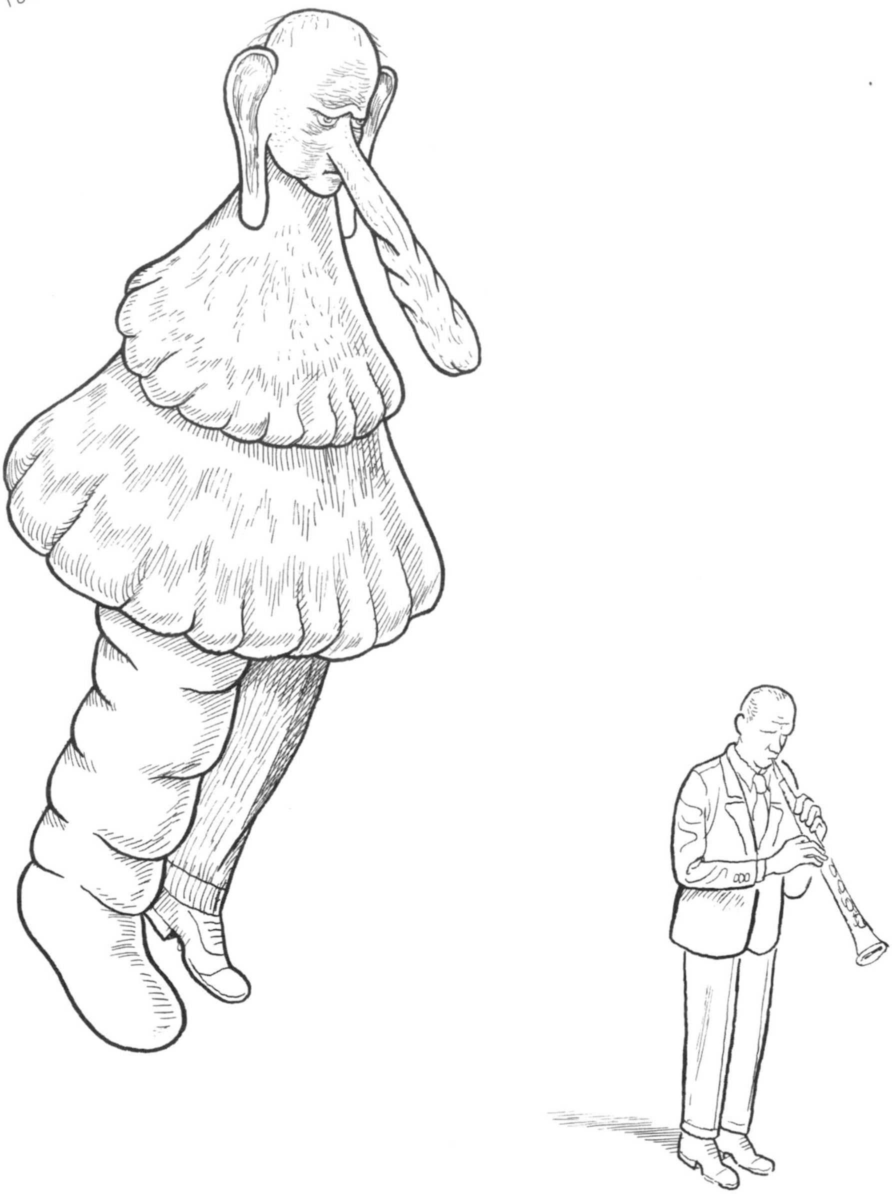

If music didn't make a divine, inestimable poet of you.

That night . . . a moving elegy leapt from
your lips and into the room.

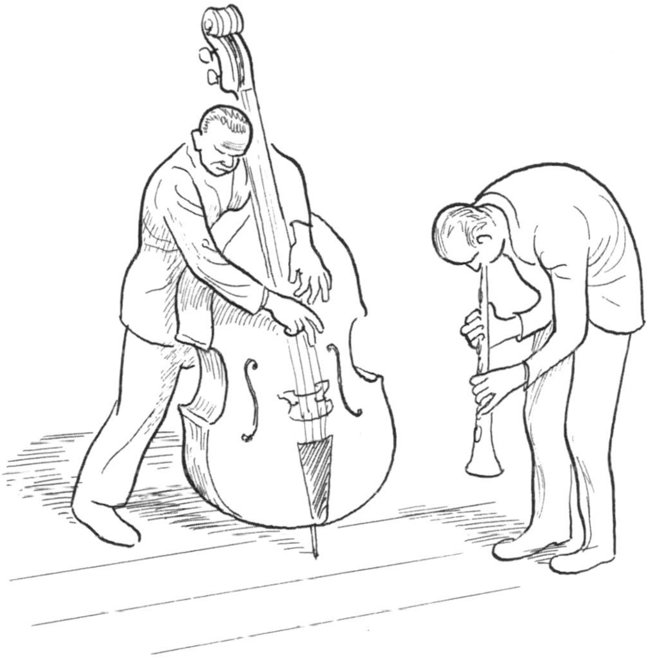

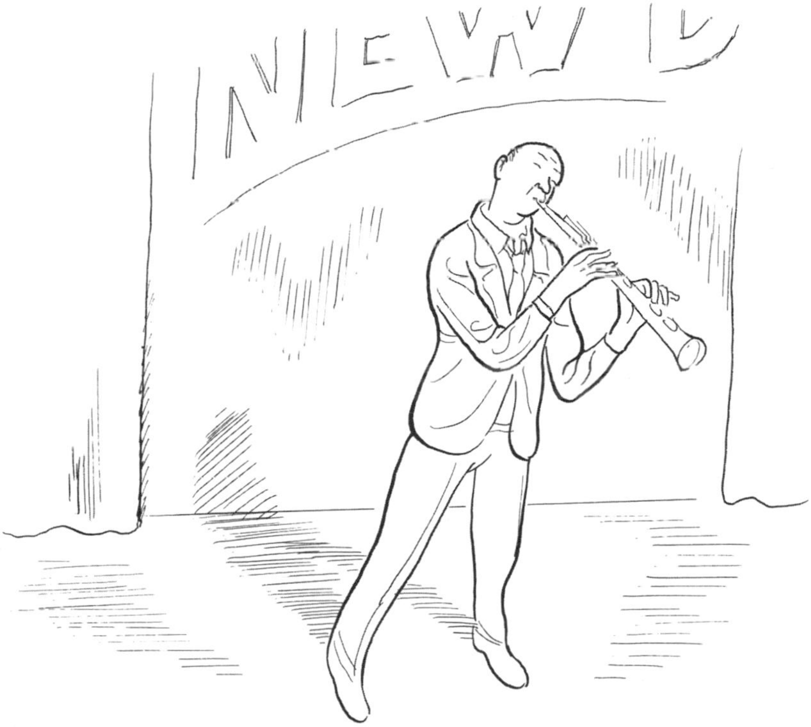
NEW

It didn't sound like anything...
but it touched me.

How could I put it in words?

They had a lot of drinks before they left. I followed them.

I waited a minute for the other two to get a bit of a lead, and then I went up to him.

He was humming convoluted little bars of jazz. He had a slight stoop.

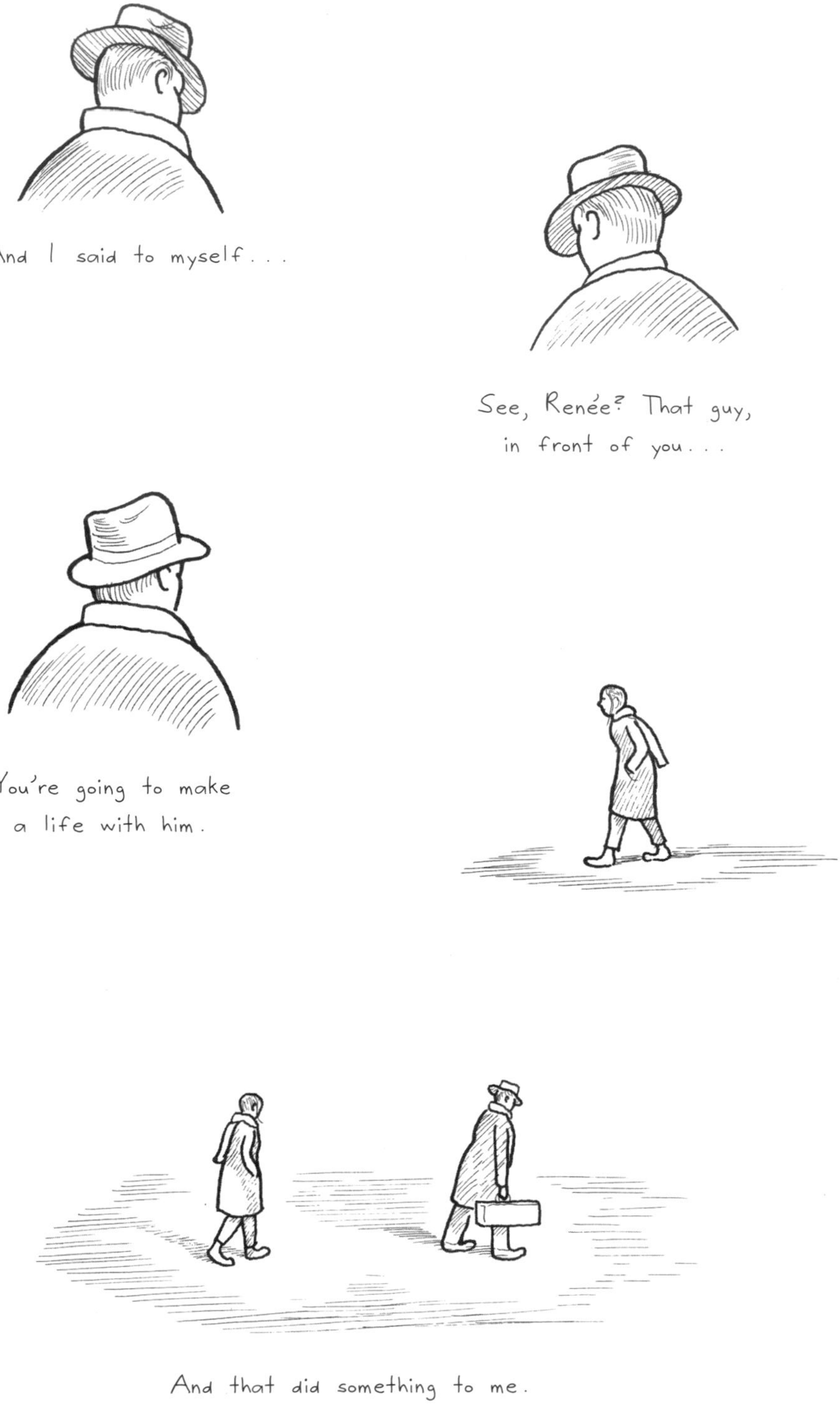
And I said to myself . . .
See, Renée? That guy, in front of you . . .
You're going to make a life with him.
And that did something to me.

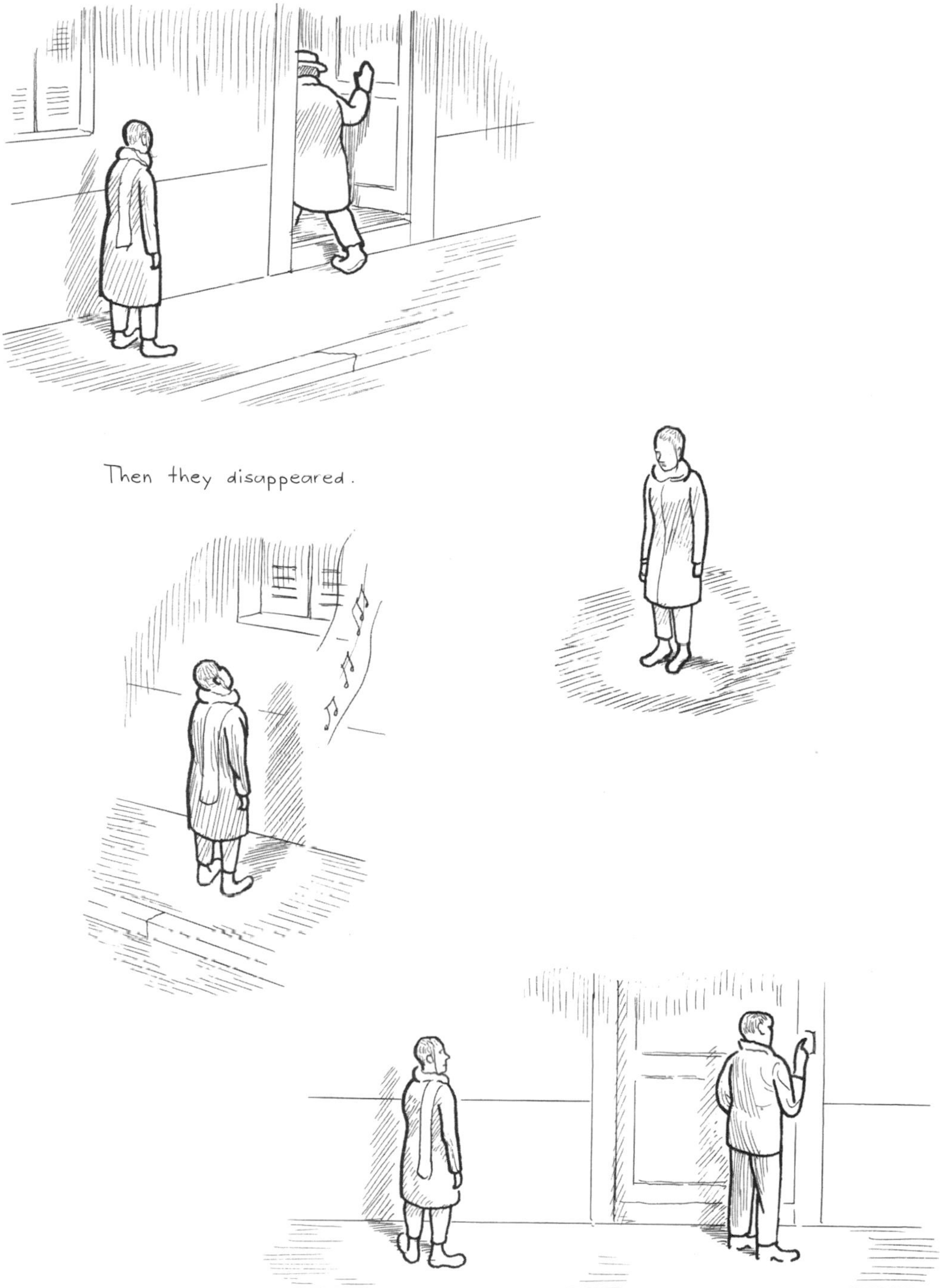
Then they disappeared.

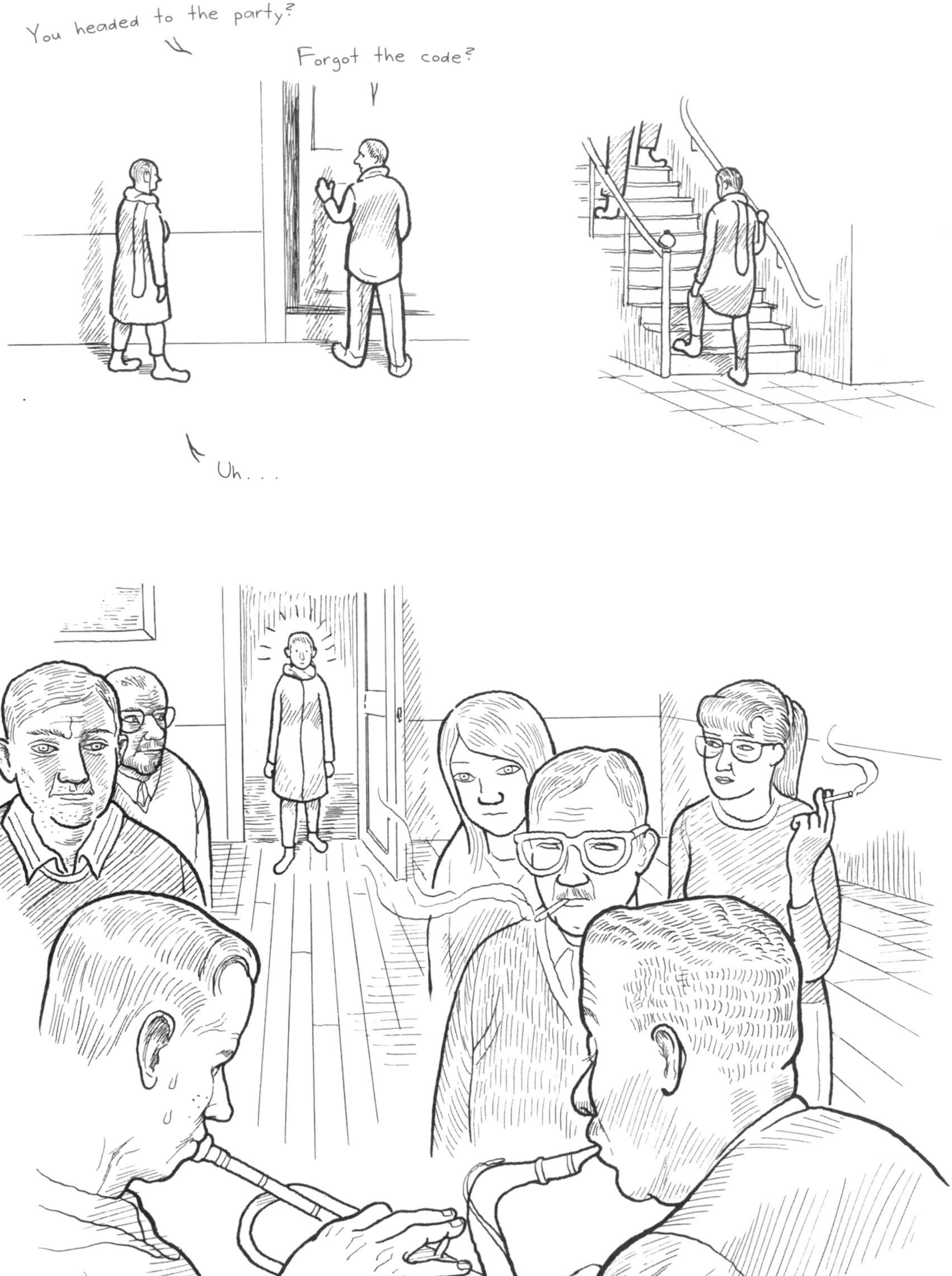
You headed to the party?
Forgot the code?
Uh...

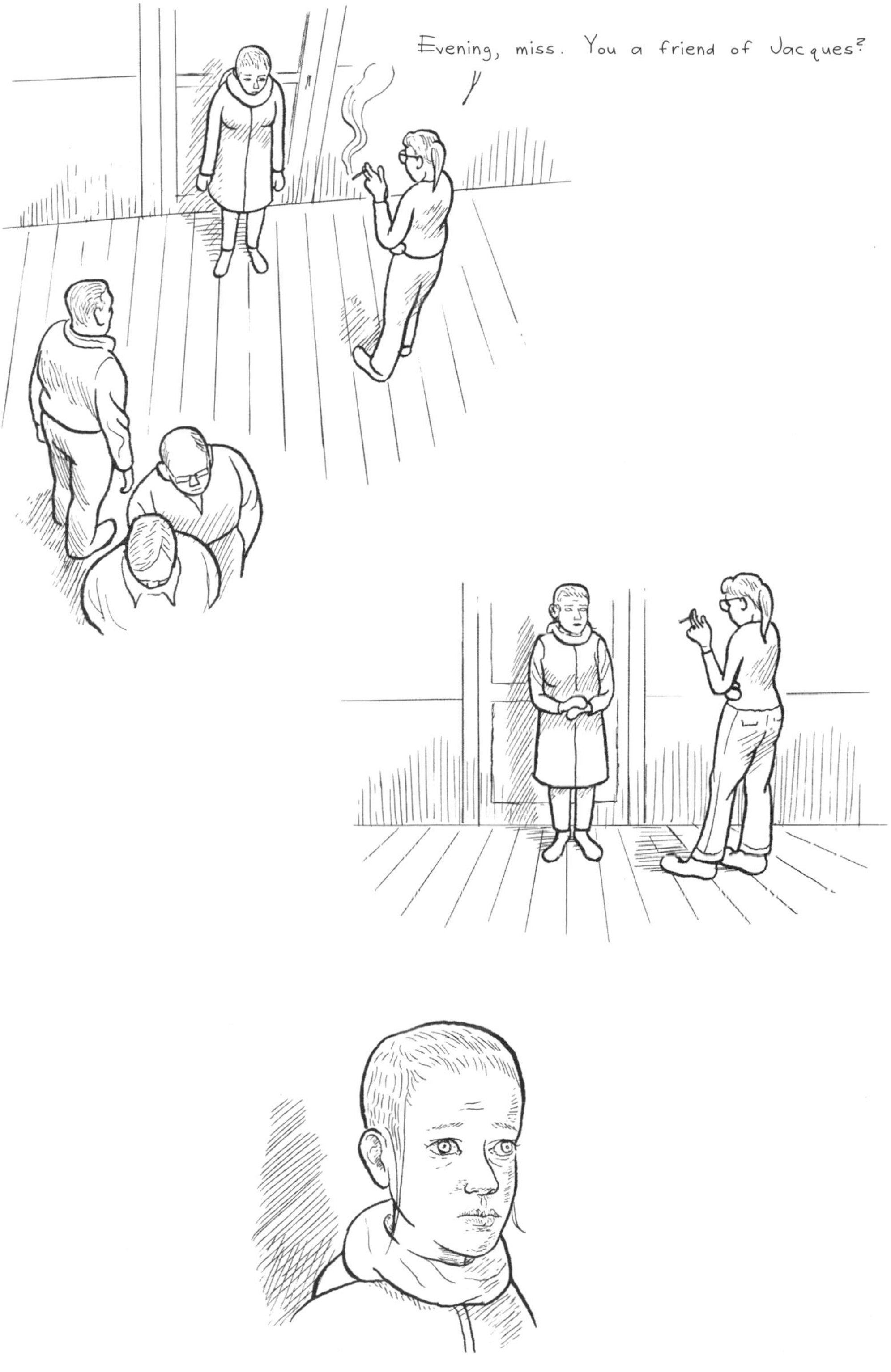
Evening, miss. You a friend of Jacques?

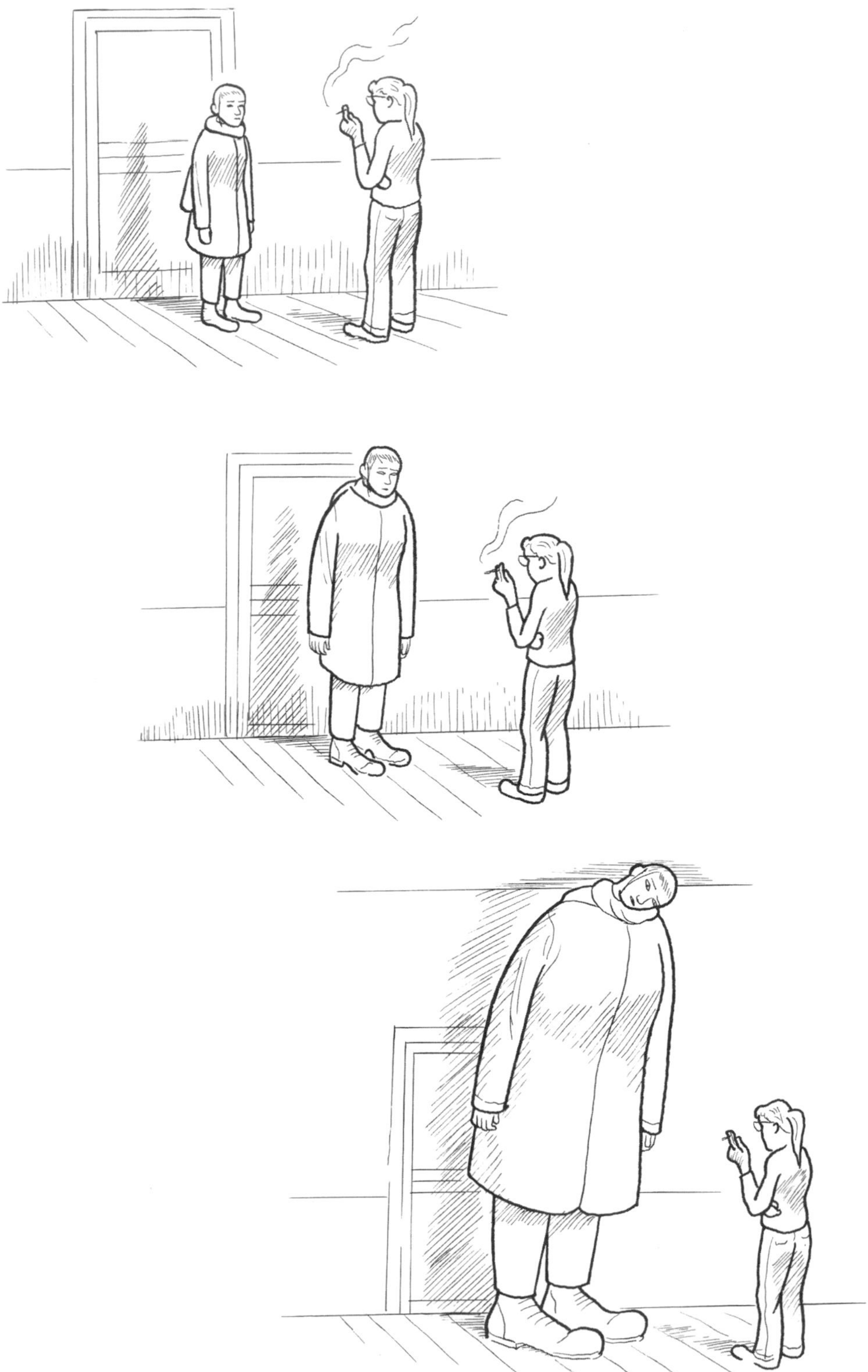

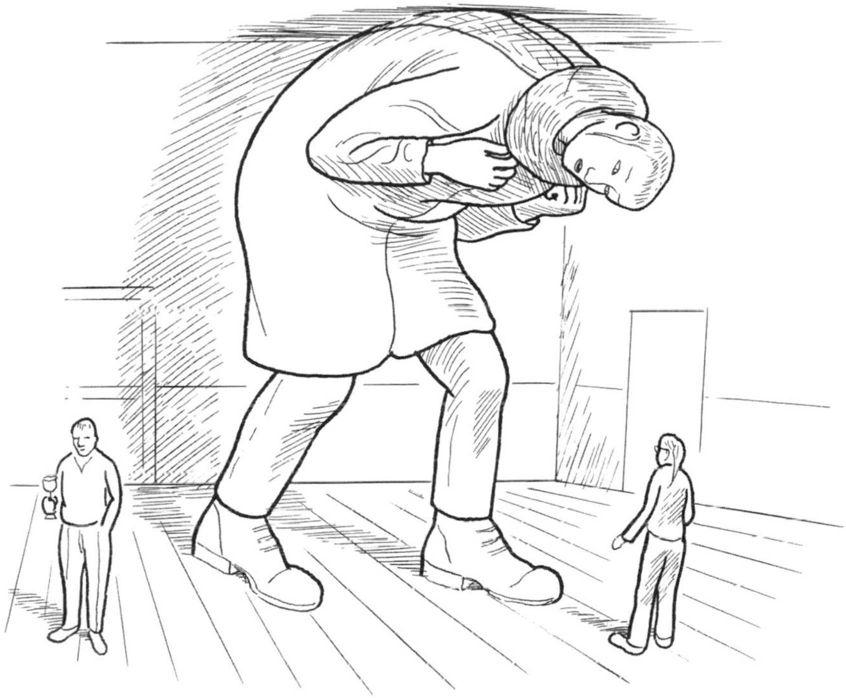

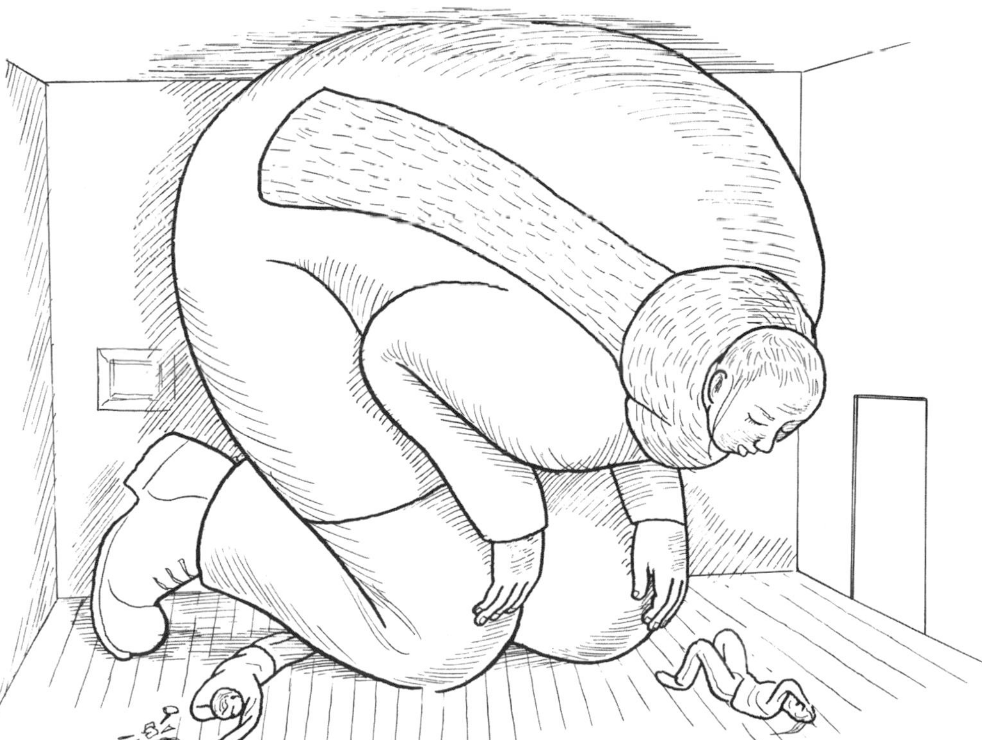

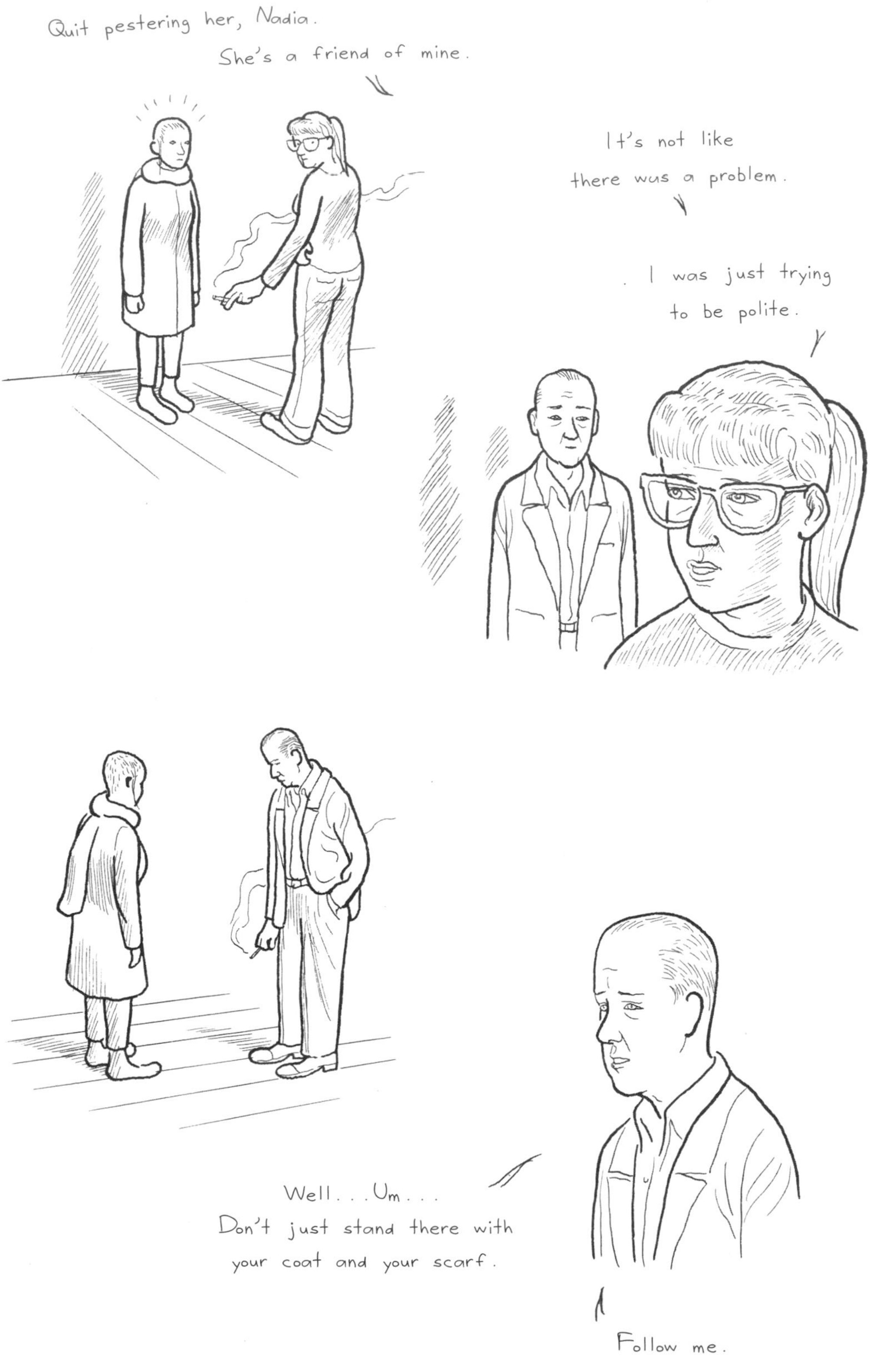
Quit pestering her, Nadia.
She's a friend of mine.
It's not like there was a problem.
. I was just trying to be polite.
Well. . . Um. . .
Don't just stand there with your coat and your scarf.
Follow me.

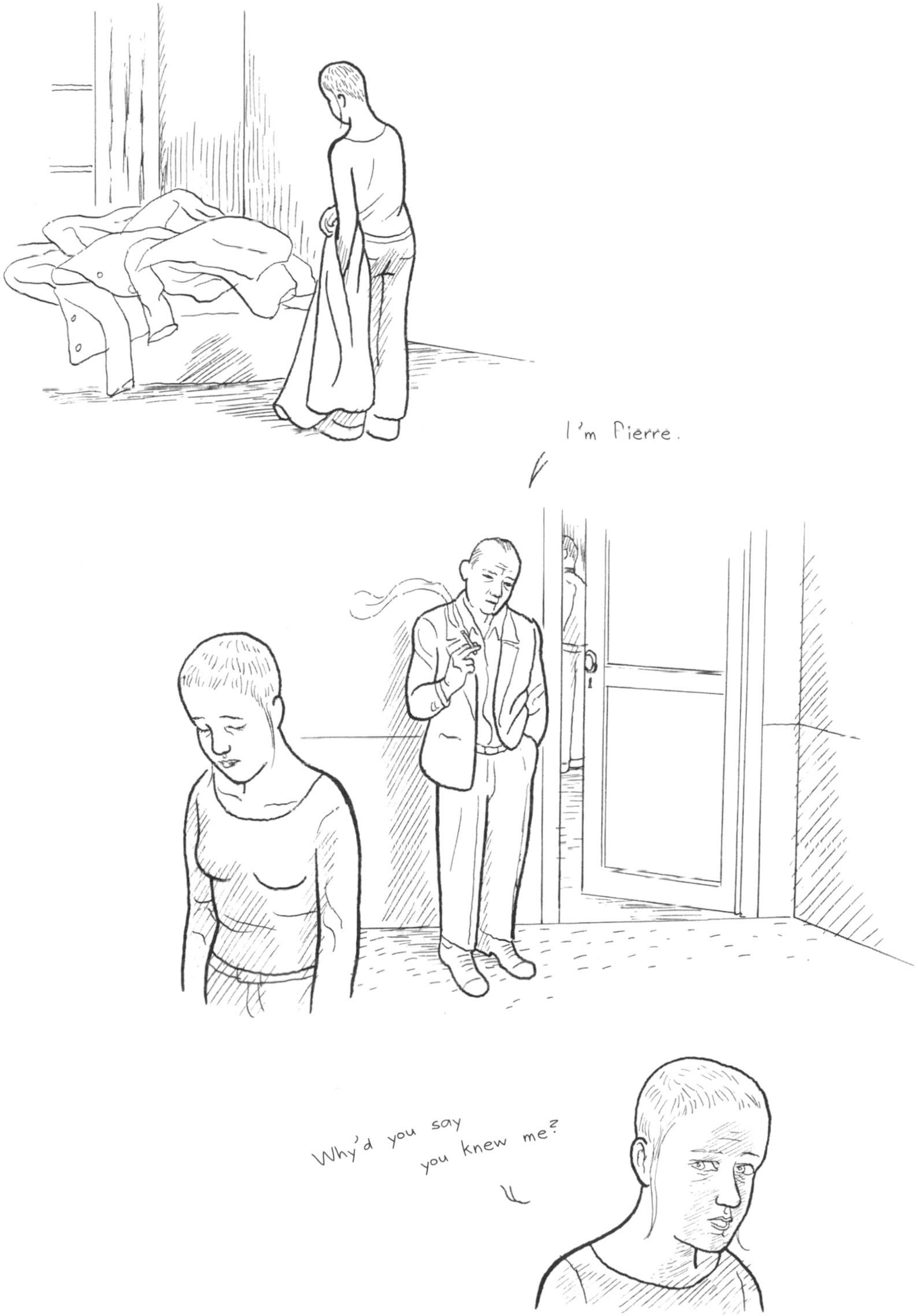
I'm Pierre.
Why'd you say you knew me?

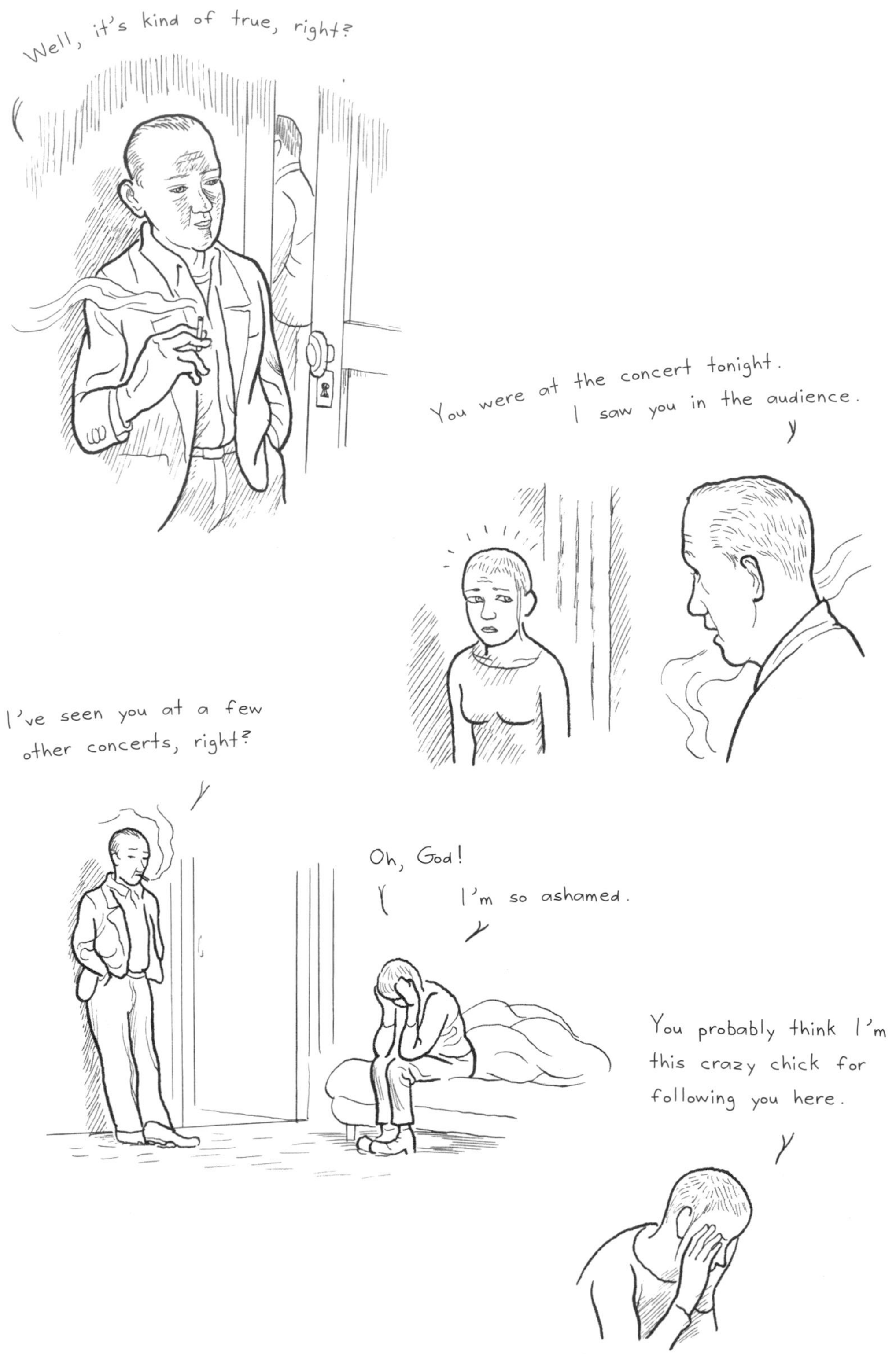

Well, it's kind of true, right?
You were at the concert tonight. I saw you in the audience.
I've seen you at a few other concerts, right?
Oh, God!
I'm so ashamed.
You probably think I'm this crazy chick for following you here.

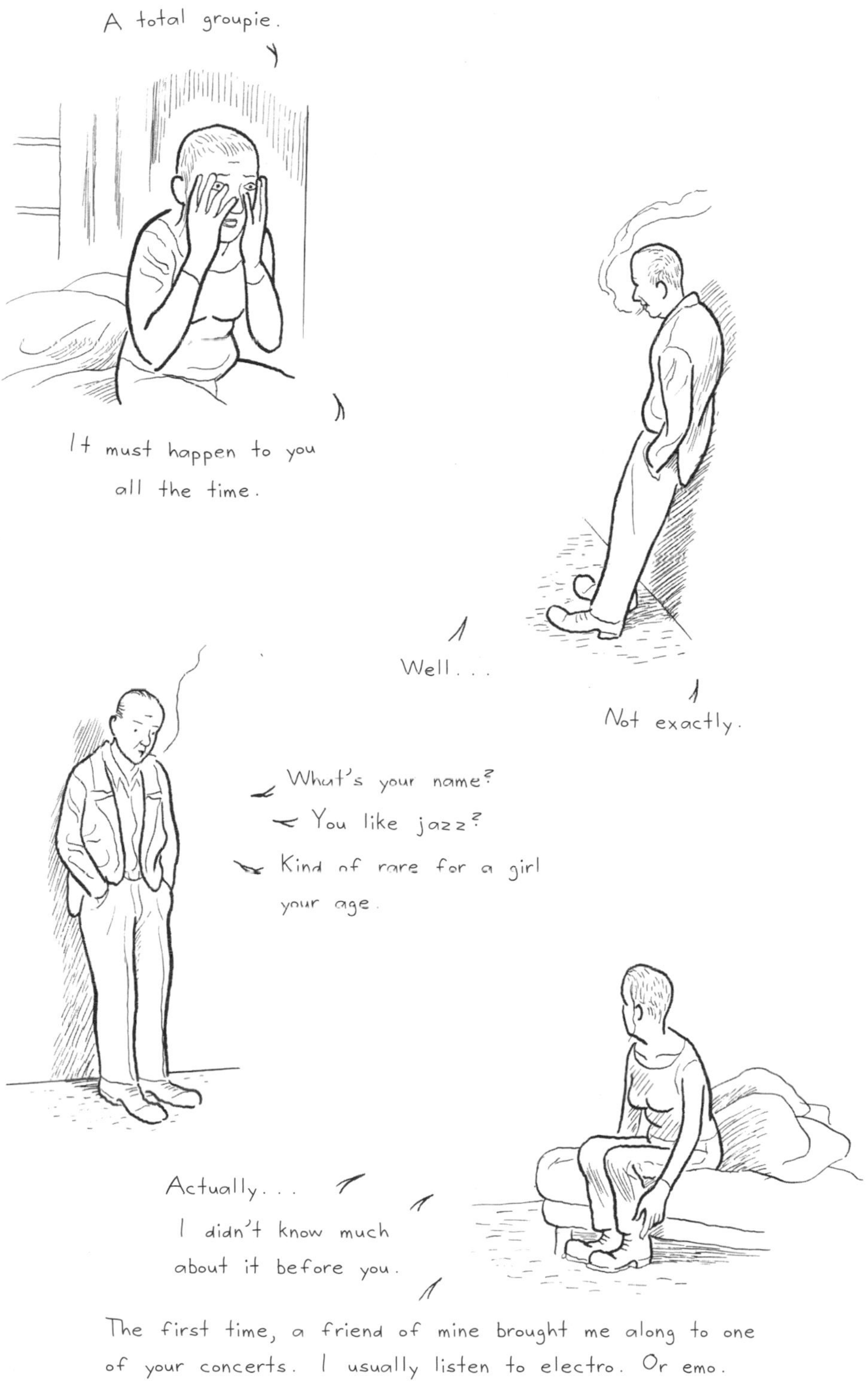
A total groupie.
It must happen to you all the time.
Well...
Not exactly.
What's your name?
You like jazz?
Kind of rare for a girl your age.
Actually...
I didn't know much about it before you.
The first time, a friend of mine brought me along to one of your concerts. I usually listen to electro. Or emo.

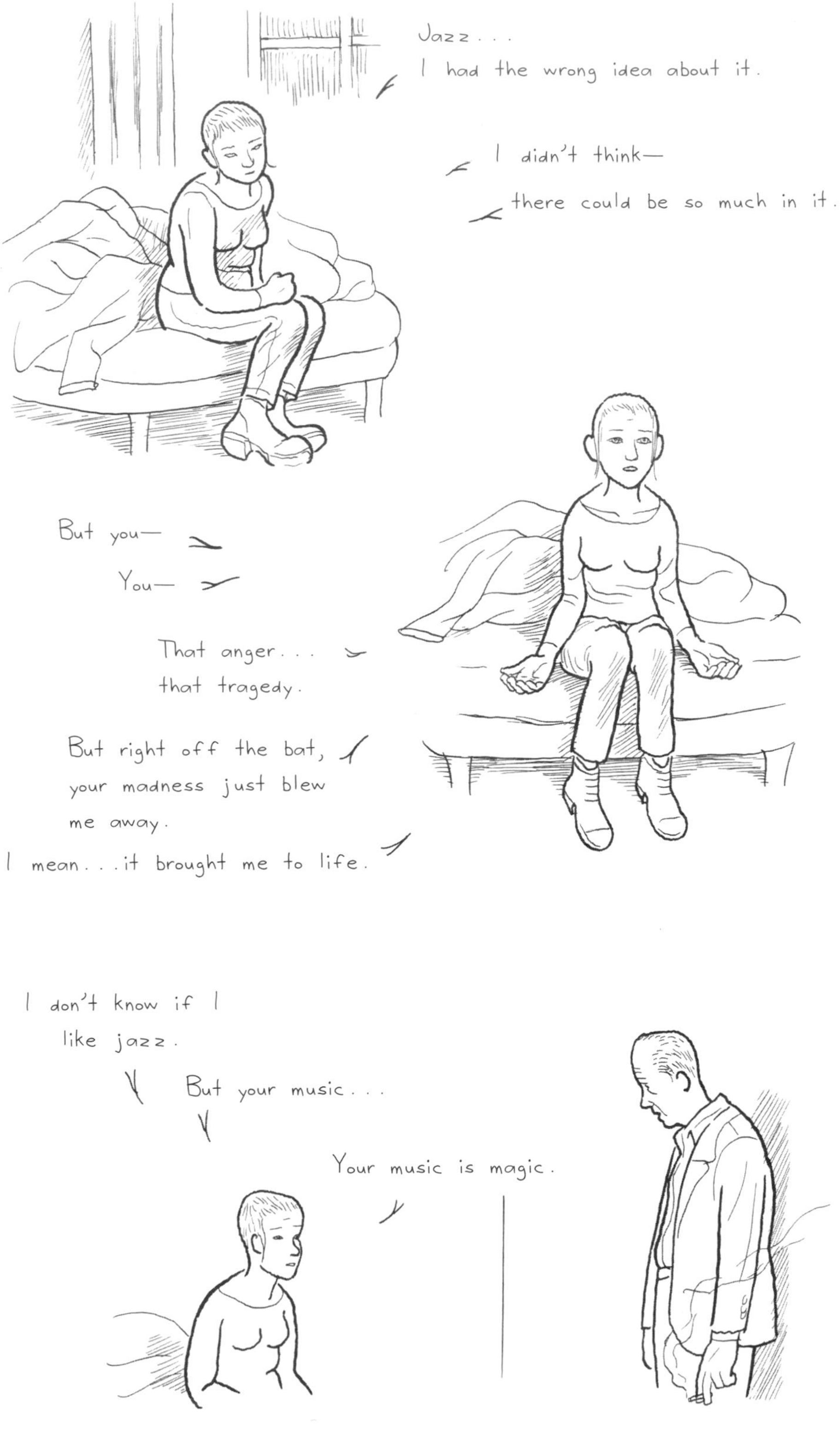
Jazz . . .
I had the wrong idea about it.
I didn't think—
there could be so much in it.
But you—
You—
That anger . . . that tragedy.
But right off the bat, your madness just blew me away.
I mean . . . it brought me to life.
I don't know if I like jazz.
But your music . . .
Your music is magic.

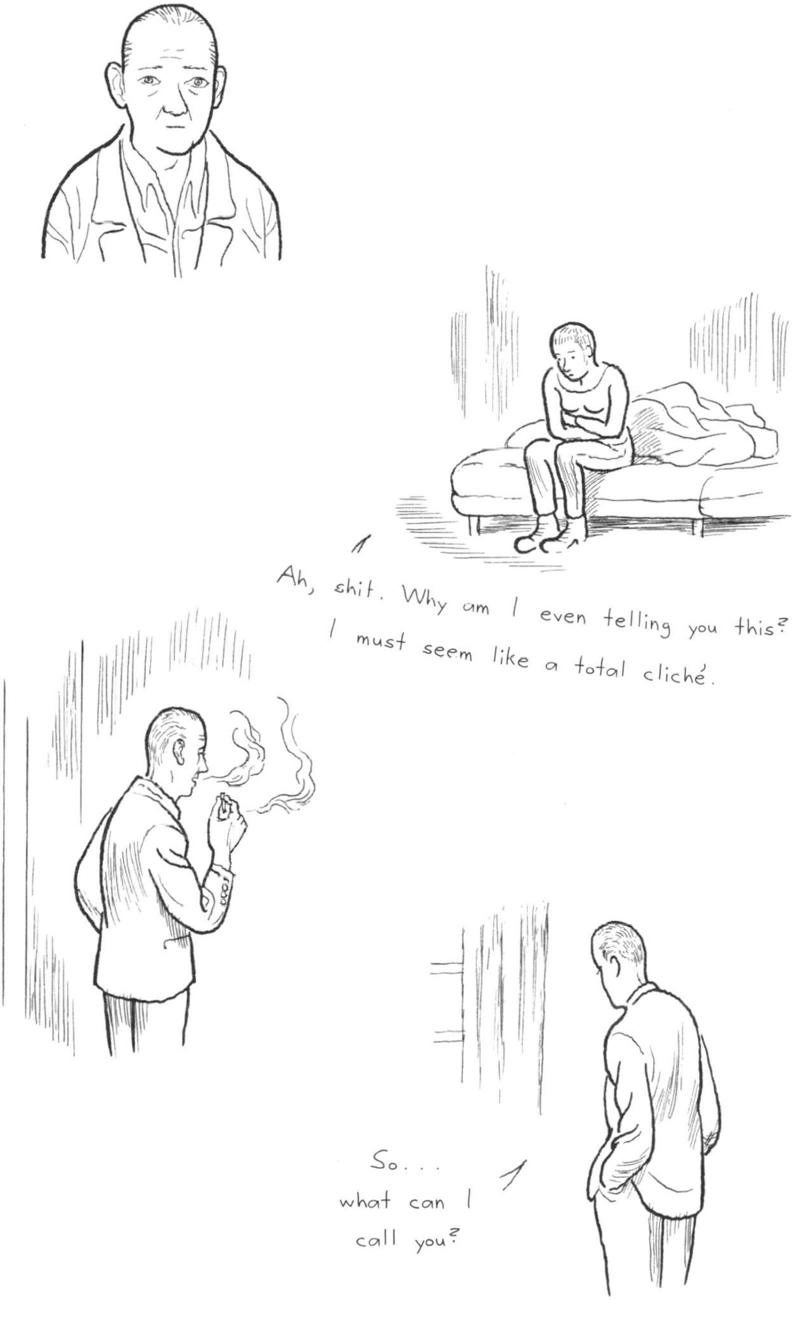
Ah, shit. Why am I even telling you this?
I must seem like a total cliché.
So...
what can I
call you?

Then he played with
the other musicians.
The rest of the night.

He was burning
with brilliance.

We were all watching
him, but when his eyes
opened. . . I think he
was looking at me.

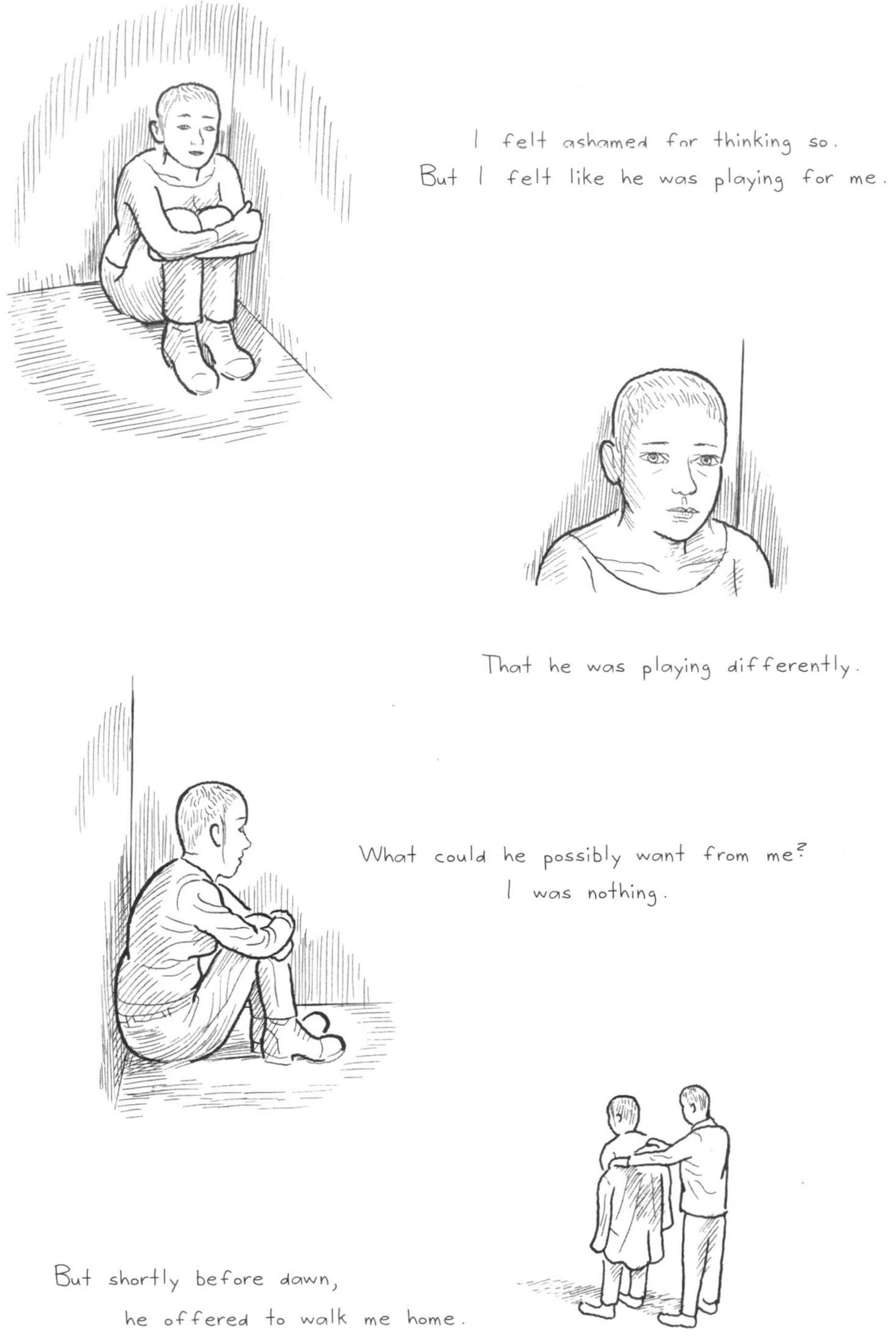
I felt ashamed for thinking so.
But I felt like he was playing for me.
That he was playing differently.
What could he possibly want from me?
I was nothing.
But shortly before dawn,
he offered to walk me home.

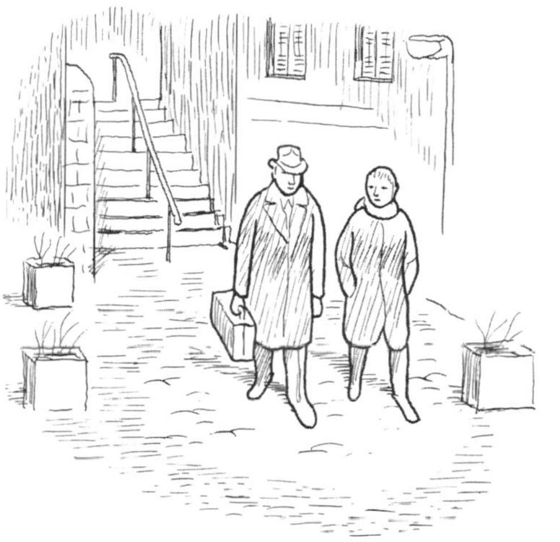
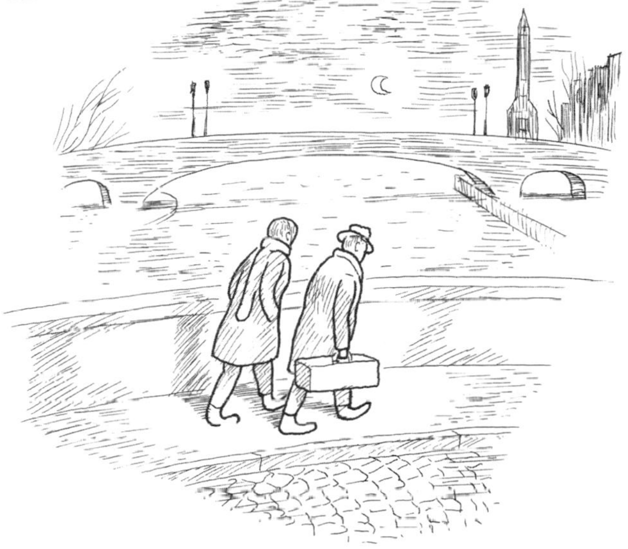
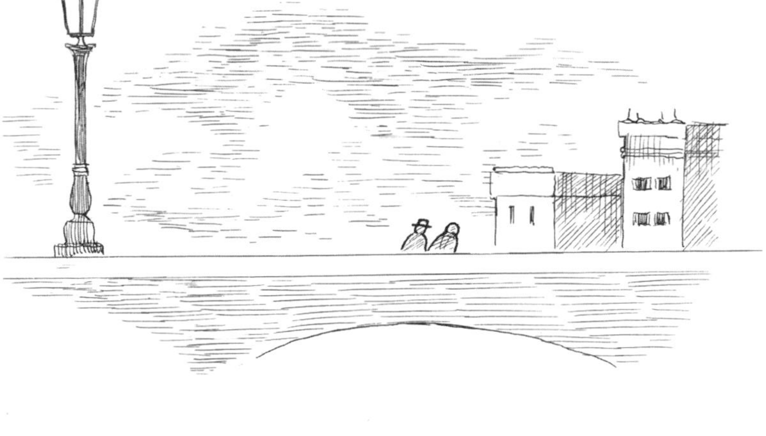

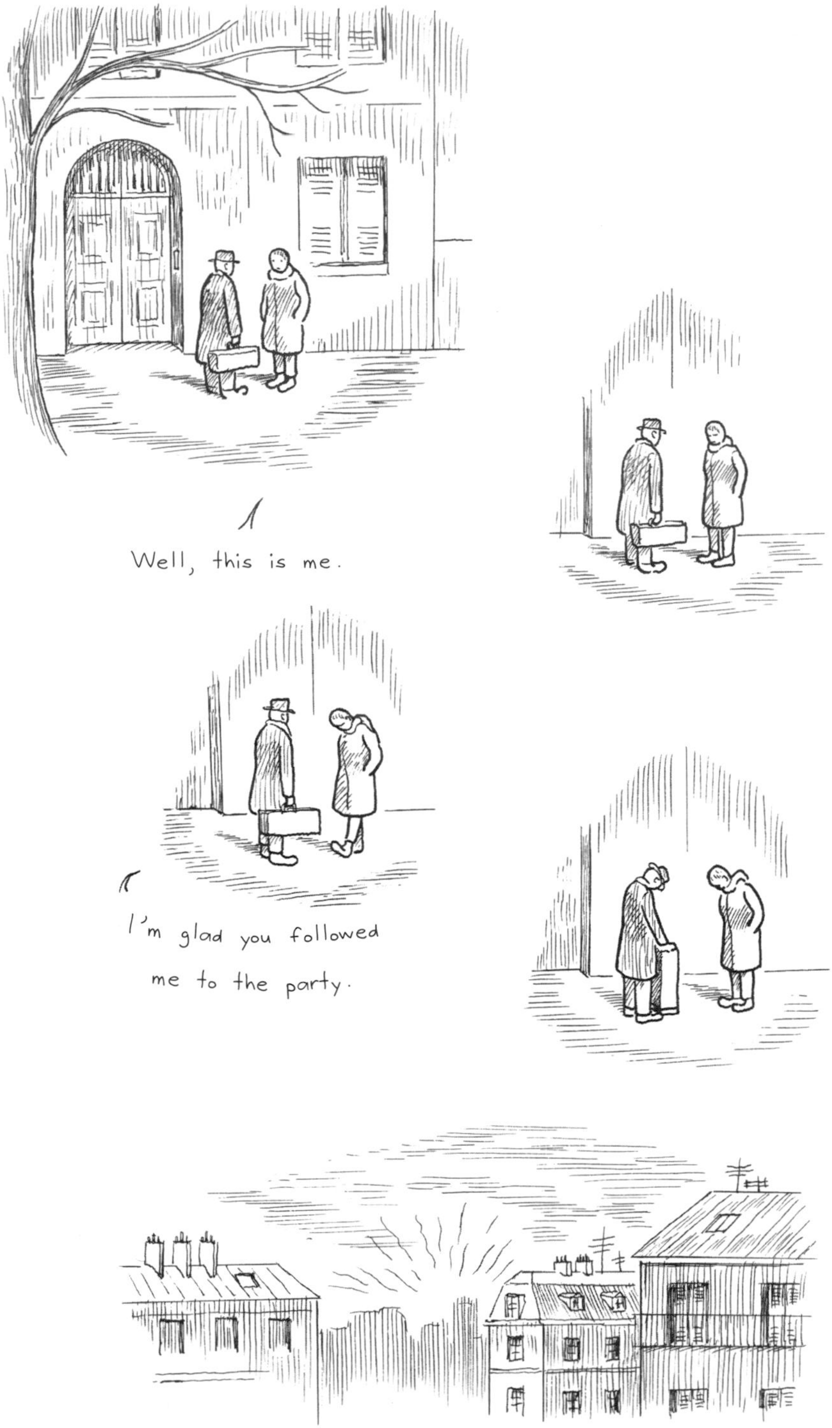
Well, this is me.
I'm glad you followed me to the party.

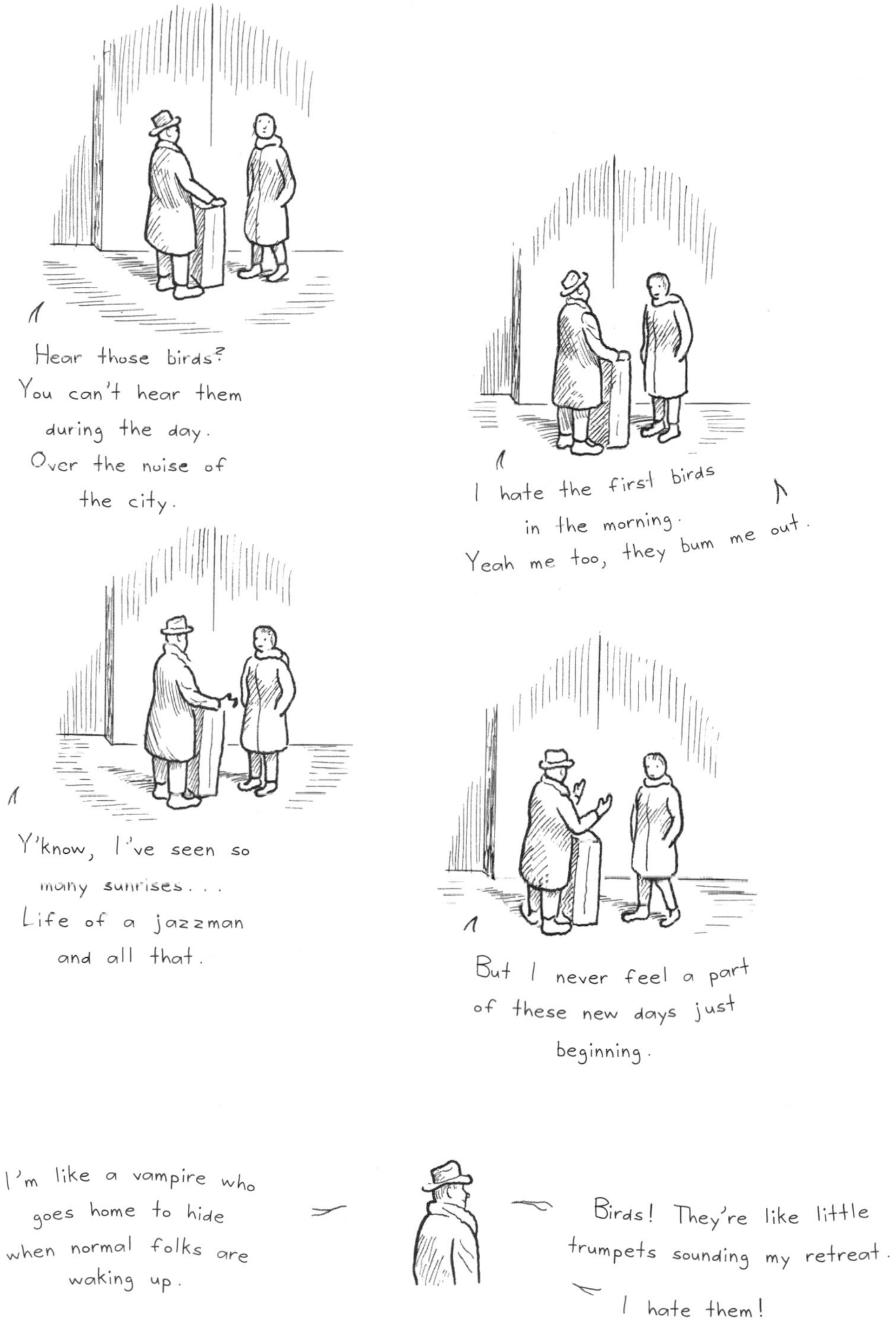
Hear those birds? You can't hear them during the day. Over the noise of the city.
I hate the first birds in the morning.
Yeah me too, they bum me out.
Y'know, I've seen so many sunrises... Life of a jazzman and all that.
But I never feel a part of these new days just beginning.
I'm like a vampire who goes home to hide when normal folks are waking up.
Birds! They're like little trumpets sounding my retreat.
I hate them!

Ha ha!

Uh . . . Mr. Vampire . . .
Pierre . . . do you want to
come up and see my room?

It can be a tomb
to shelter you.

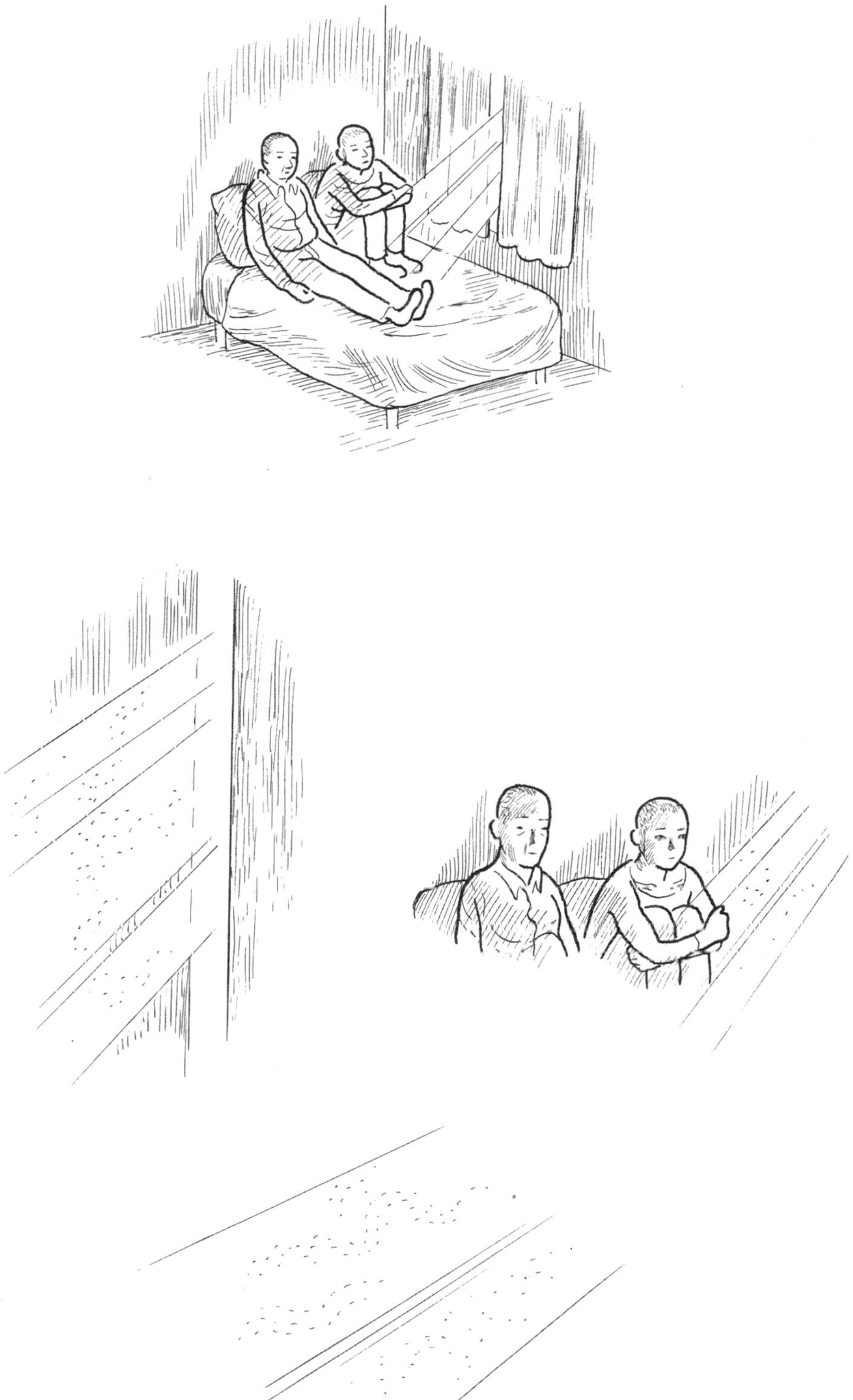

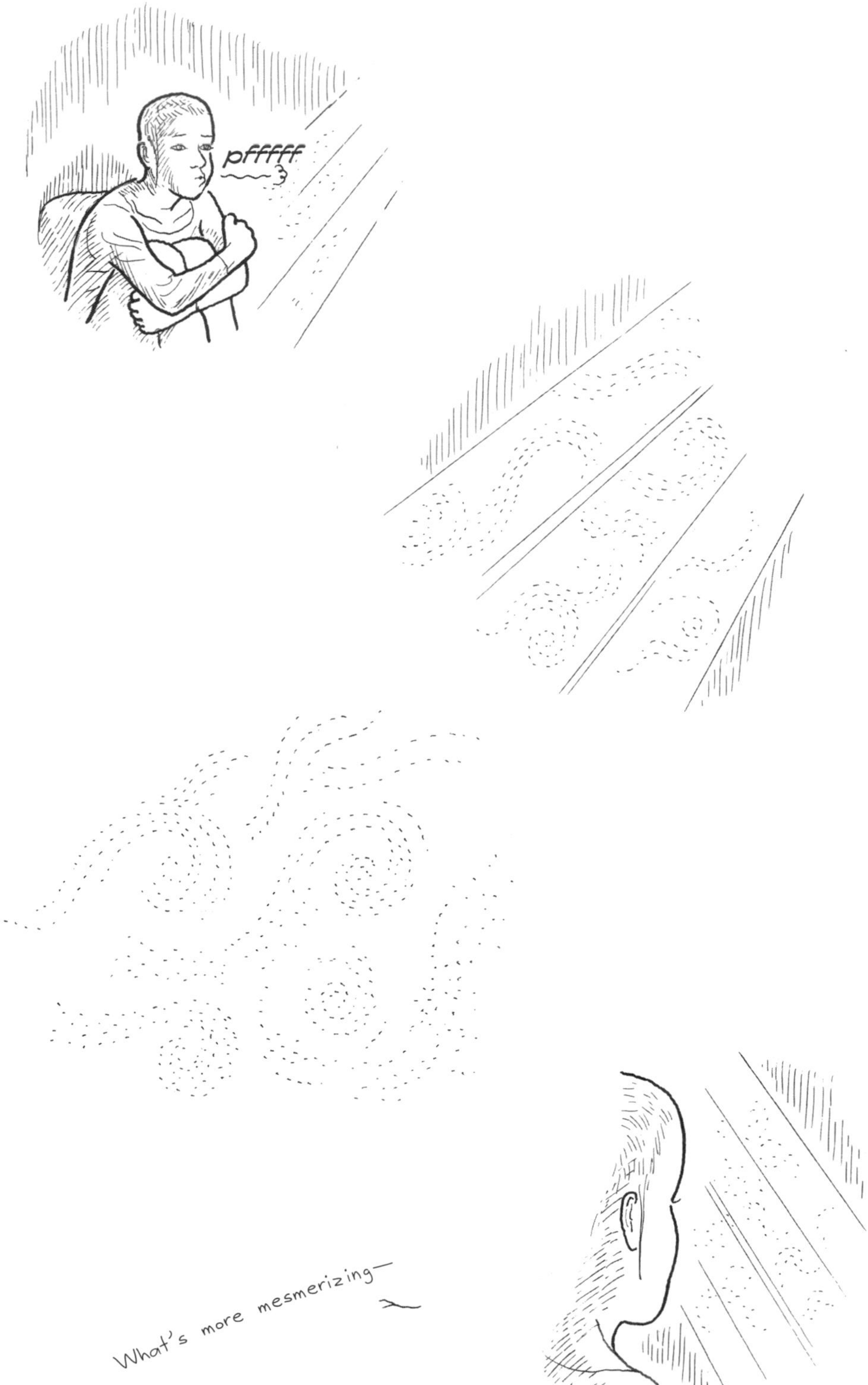
pfffff
What's more mesmerizing—

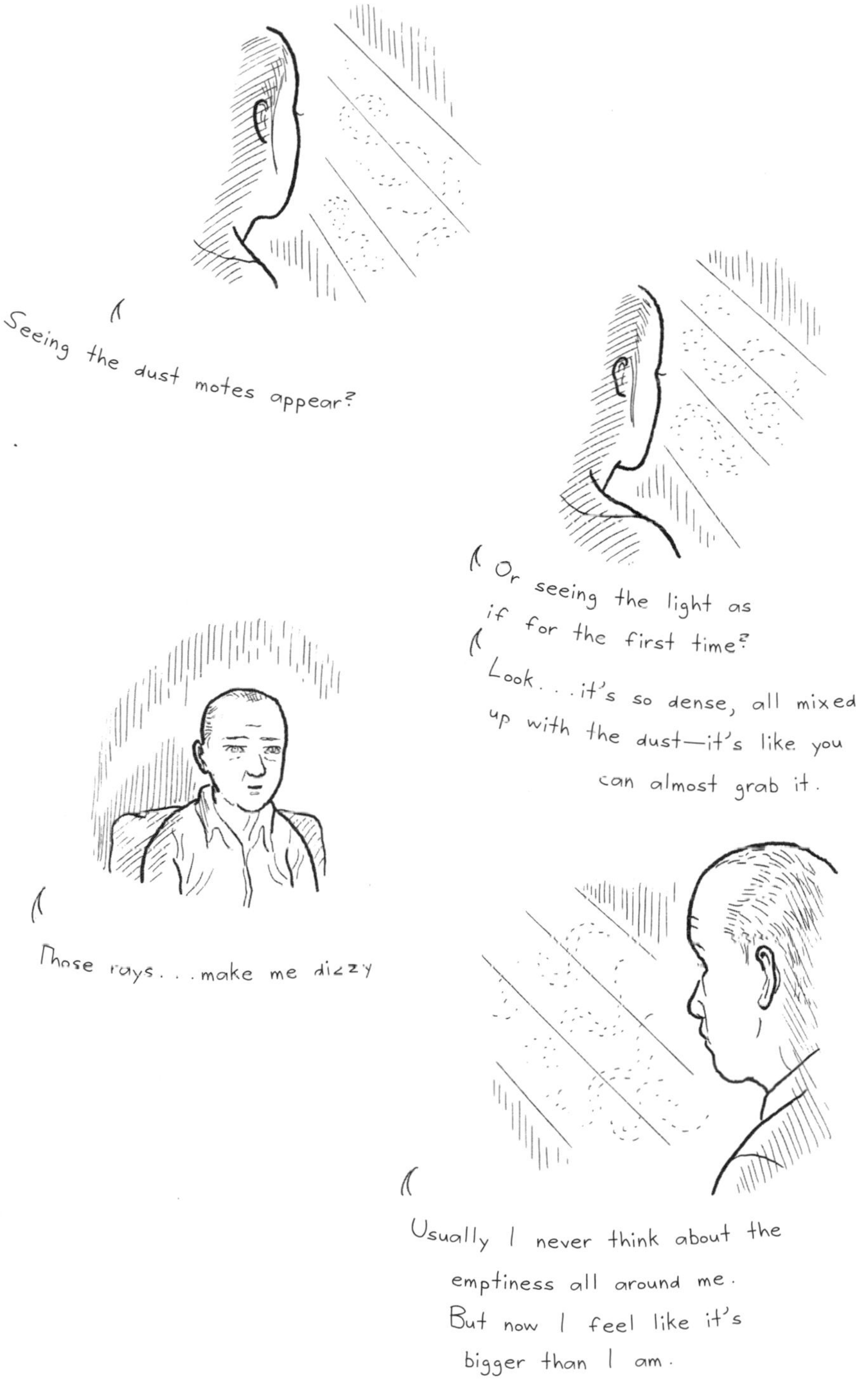
Seeing the dust motes appear?
Or seeing the light as if for the first time?
Look...it's so dense, all mixed up with the dust—it's like you can almost grab it.
Those rays...make me dizzy
Usually I never think about the emptiness all around me. But now I feel like it's bigger than I am.

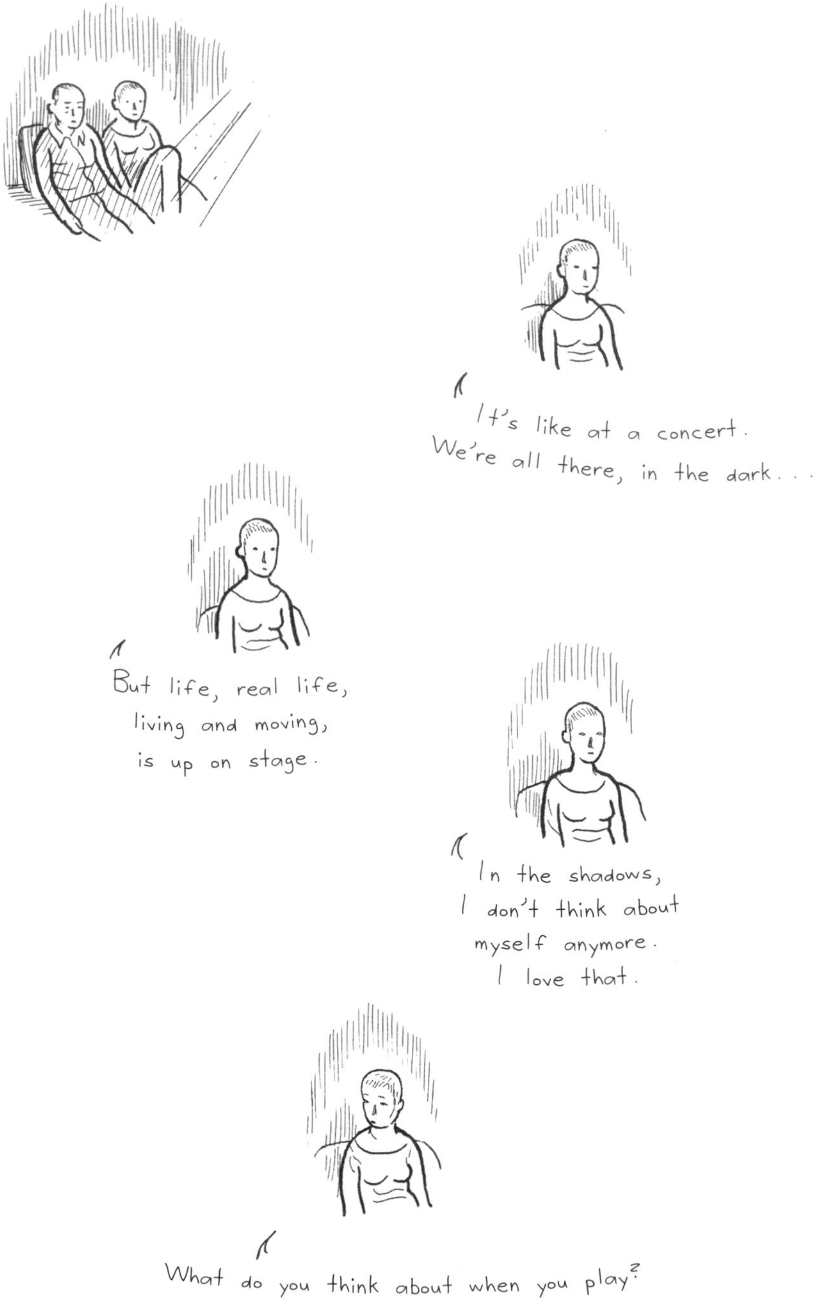
It's like at a concert. We're all there, in the dark...
But life, real life, living and moving, is up on stage.
In the shadows, I don't think about myself anymore. I love that.
What do you think about when you play?

Nothing.

I mean, I try.

But when I was playing
at the party earlier...
and I looked at you...

I was thinking about
you when I was playing.

You're so beautiful...

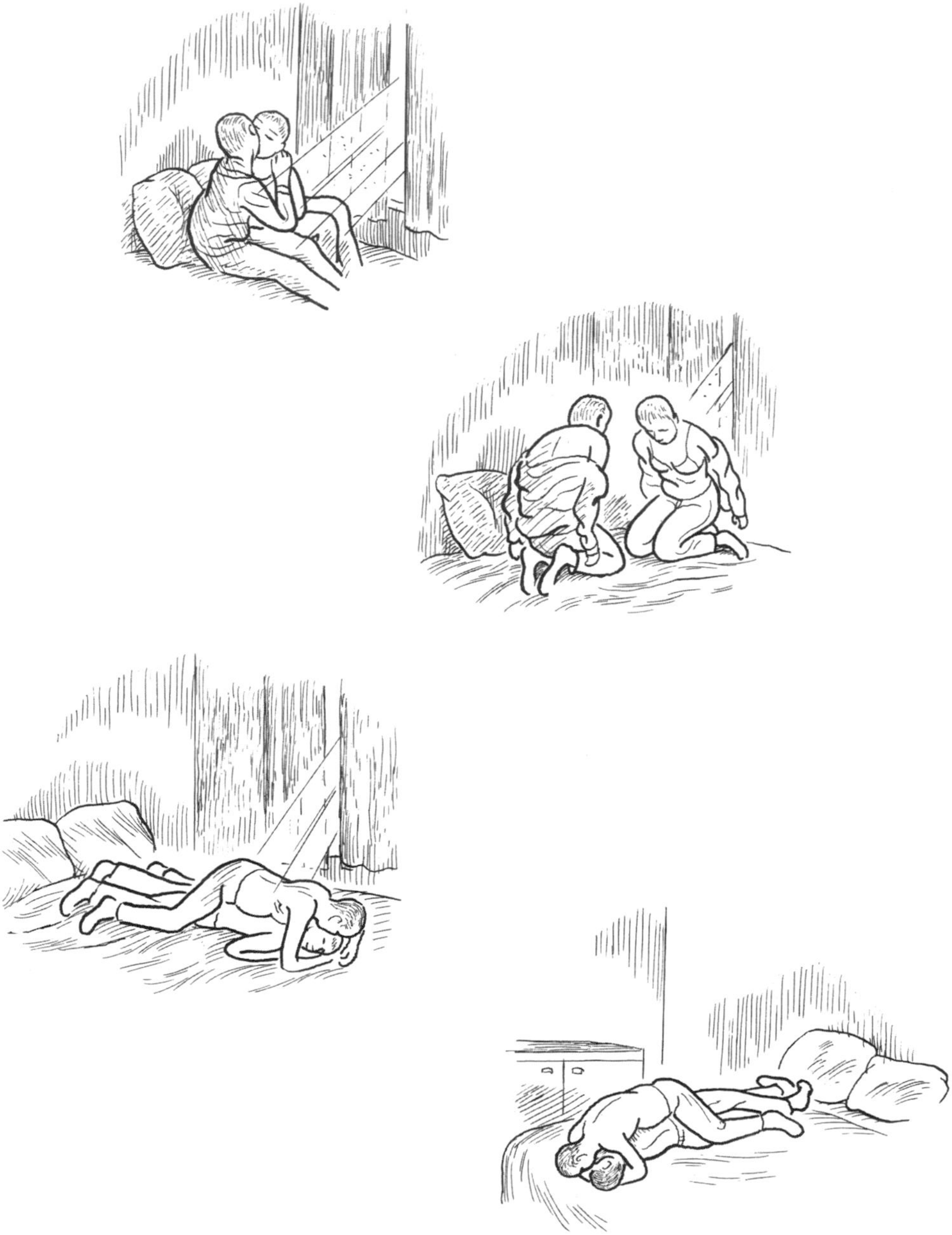

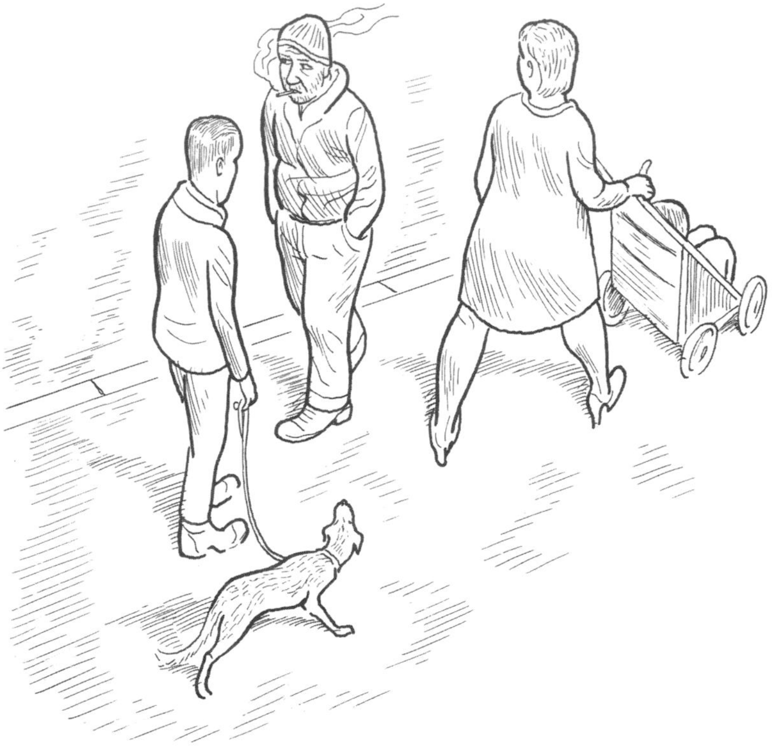

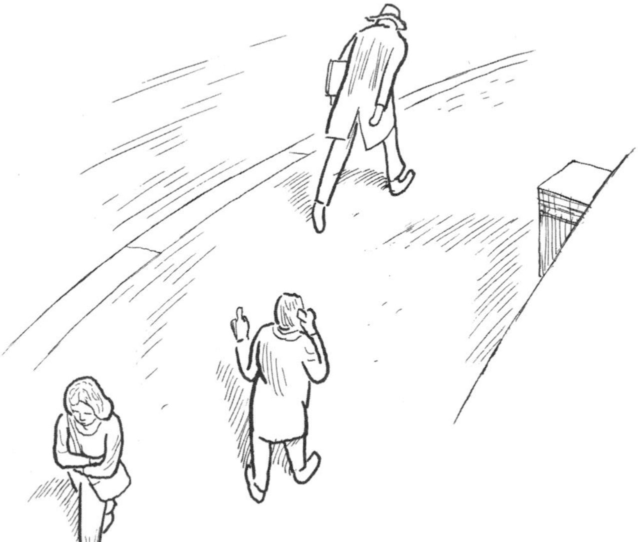

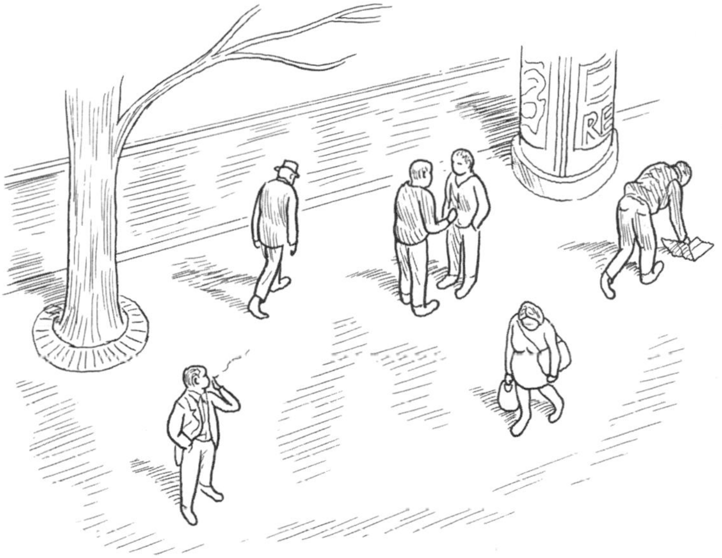

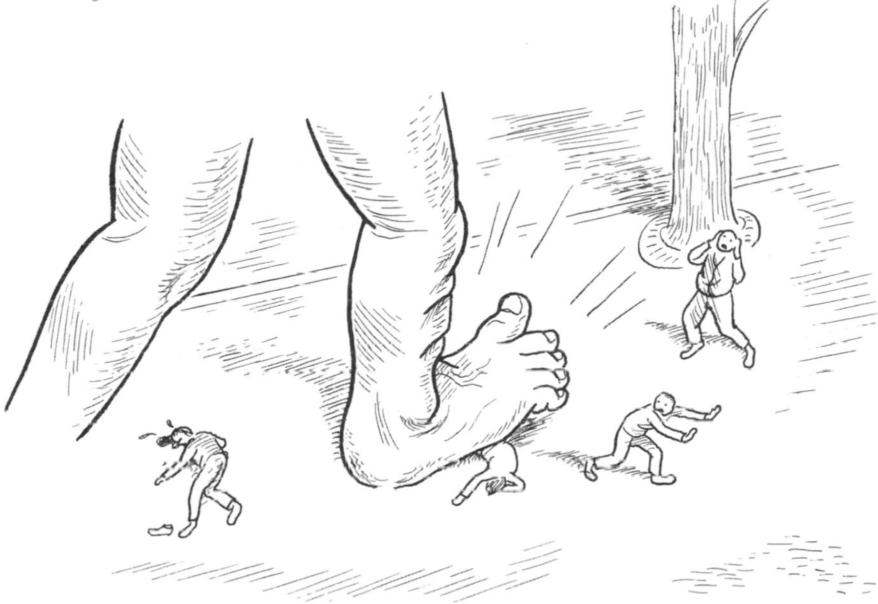

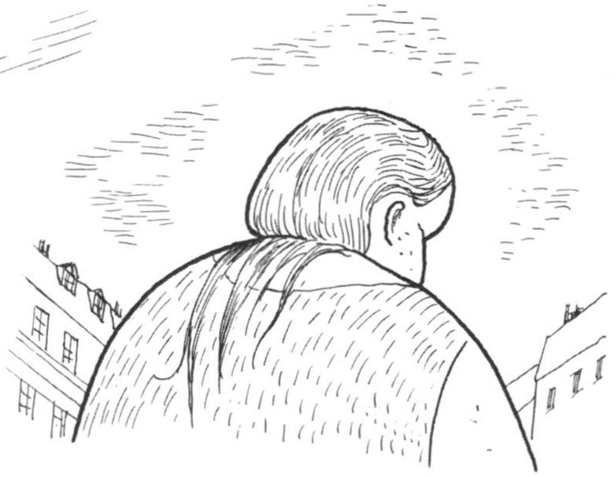

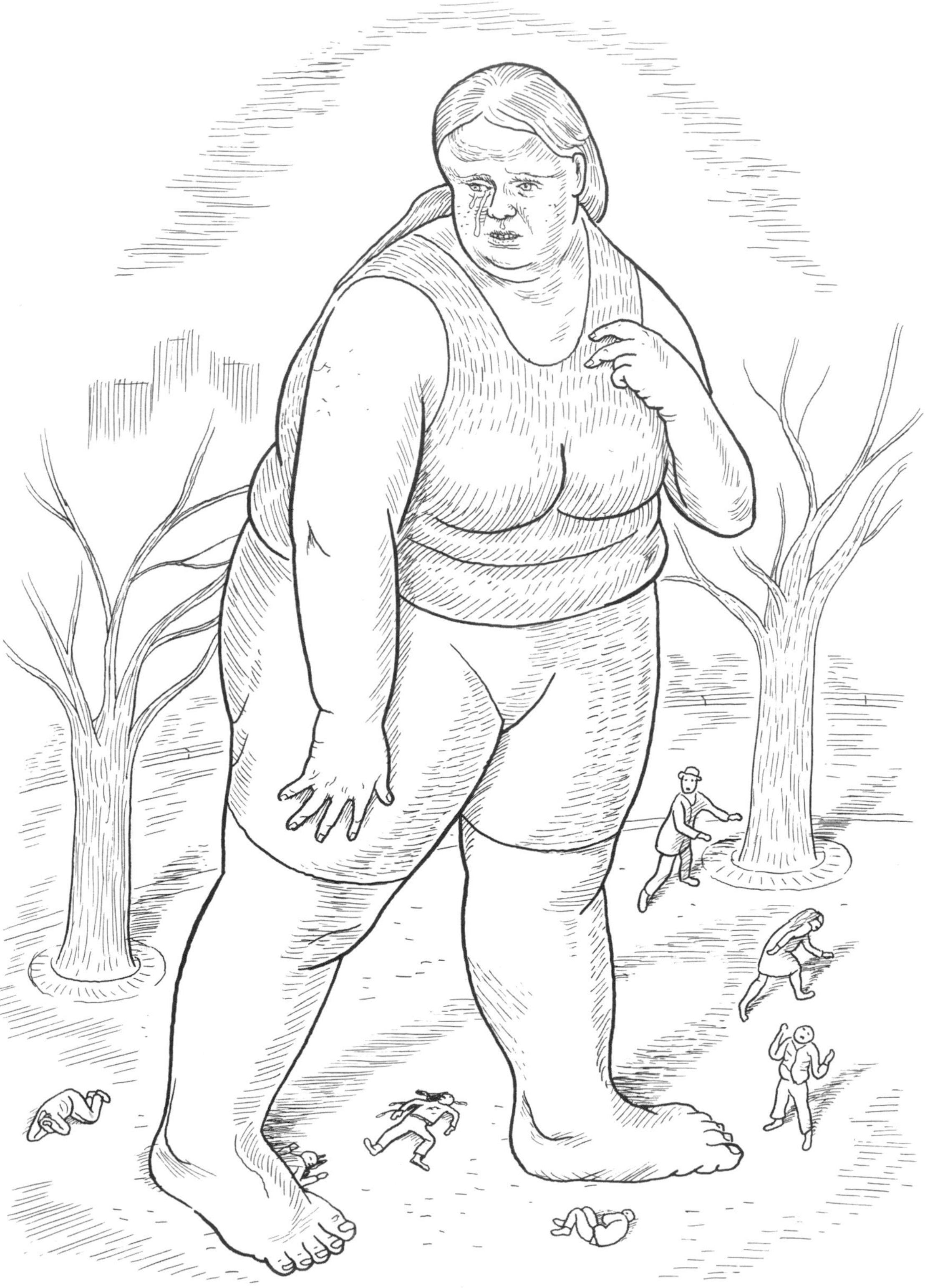

It was violent.

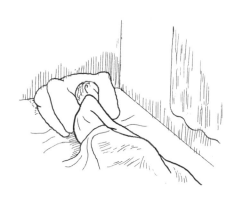

Pierre...his anger...
It captivates me.

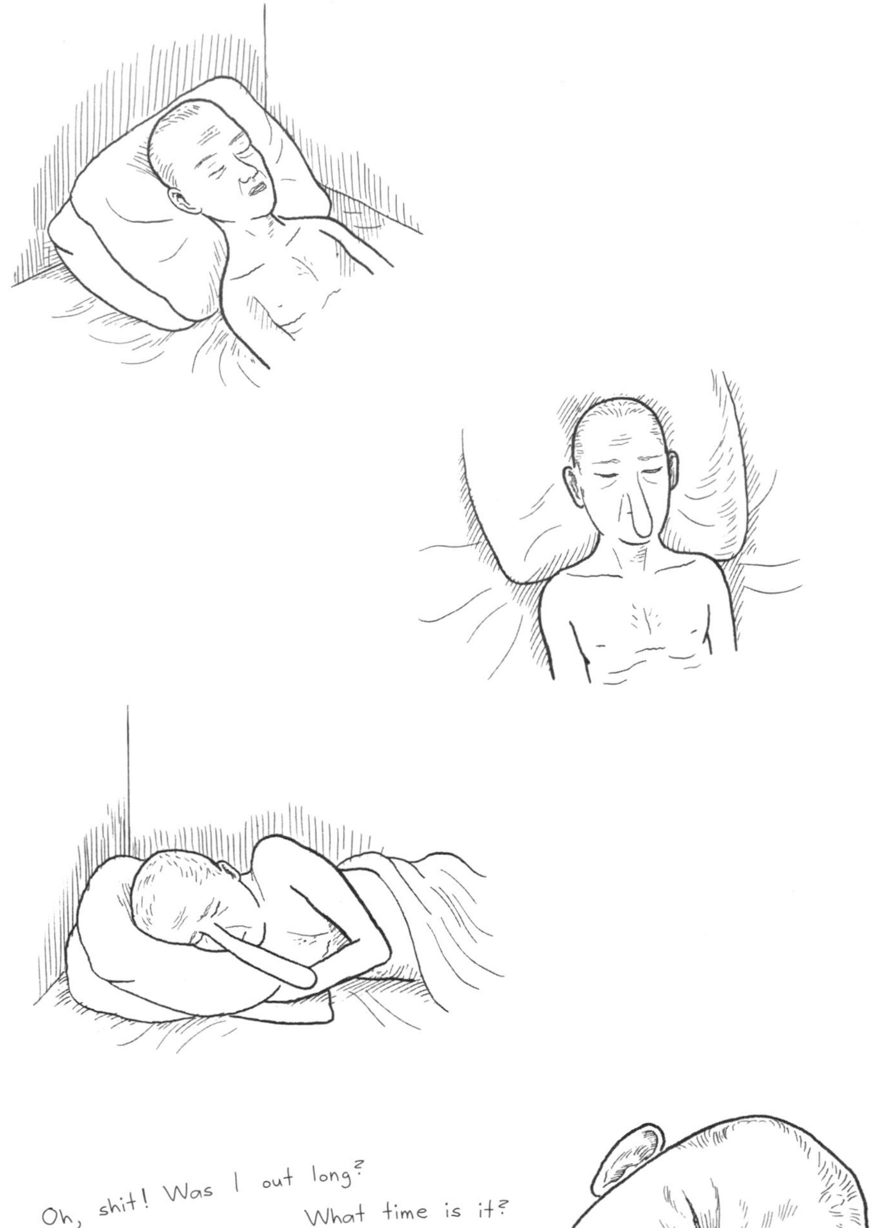
Oh, shit! Was I out long?
What time is it?

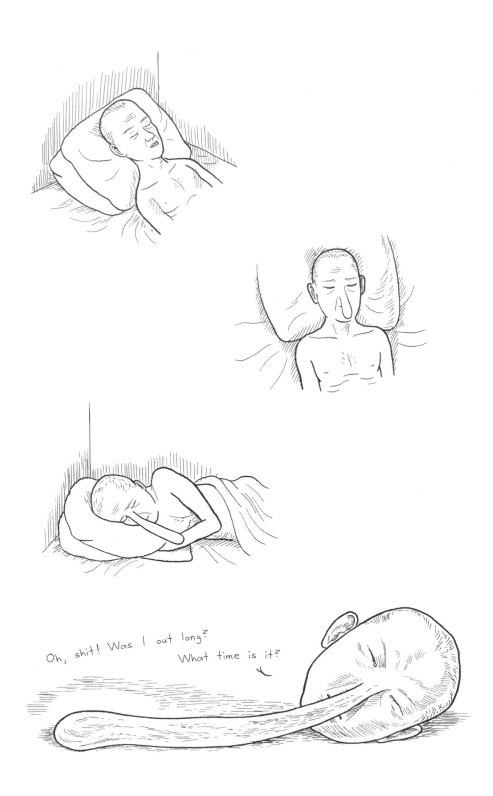

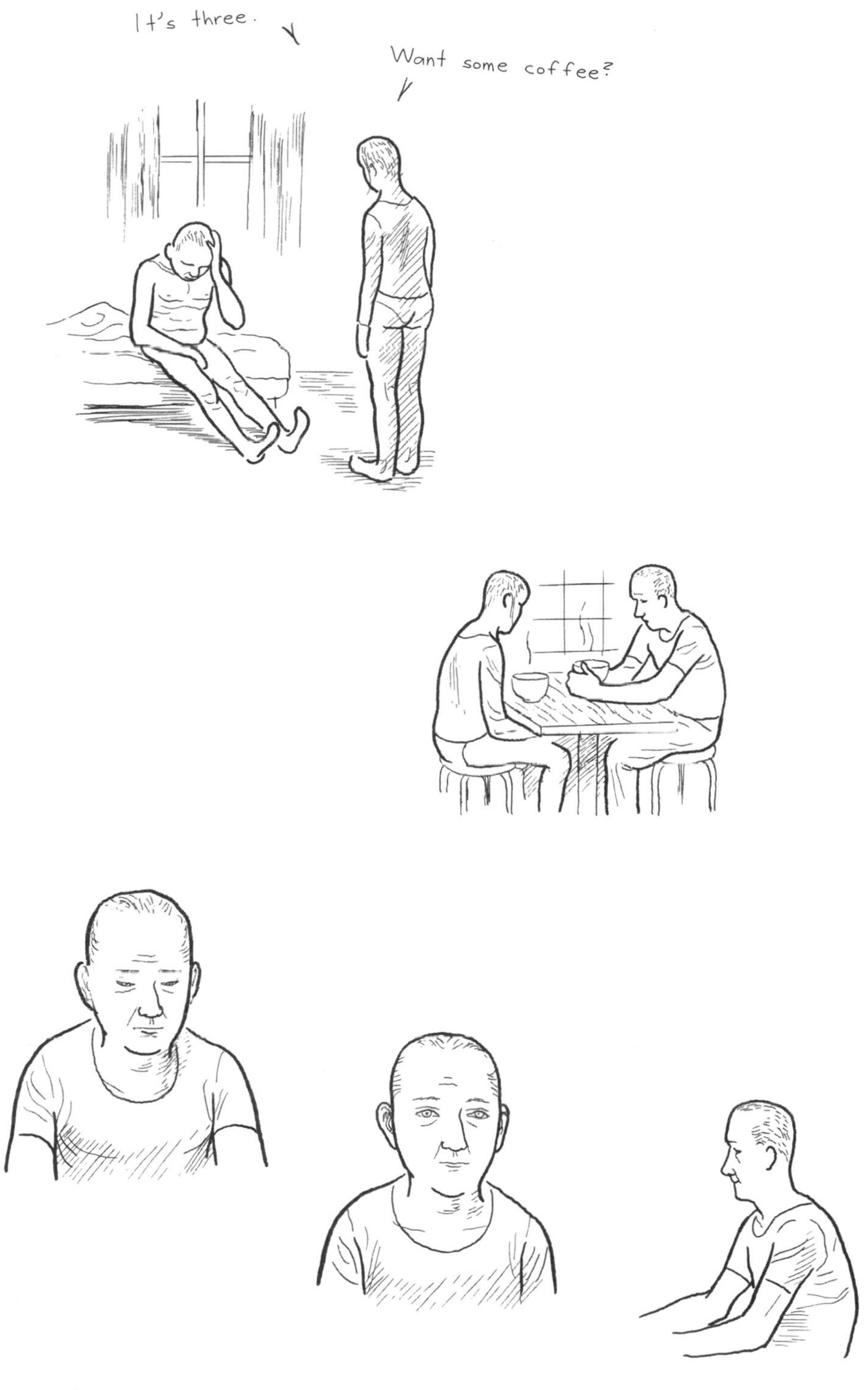
It's three.
Want some coffee?

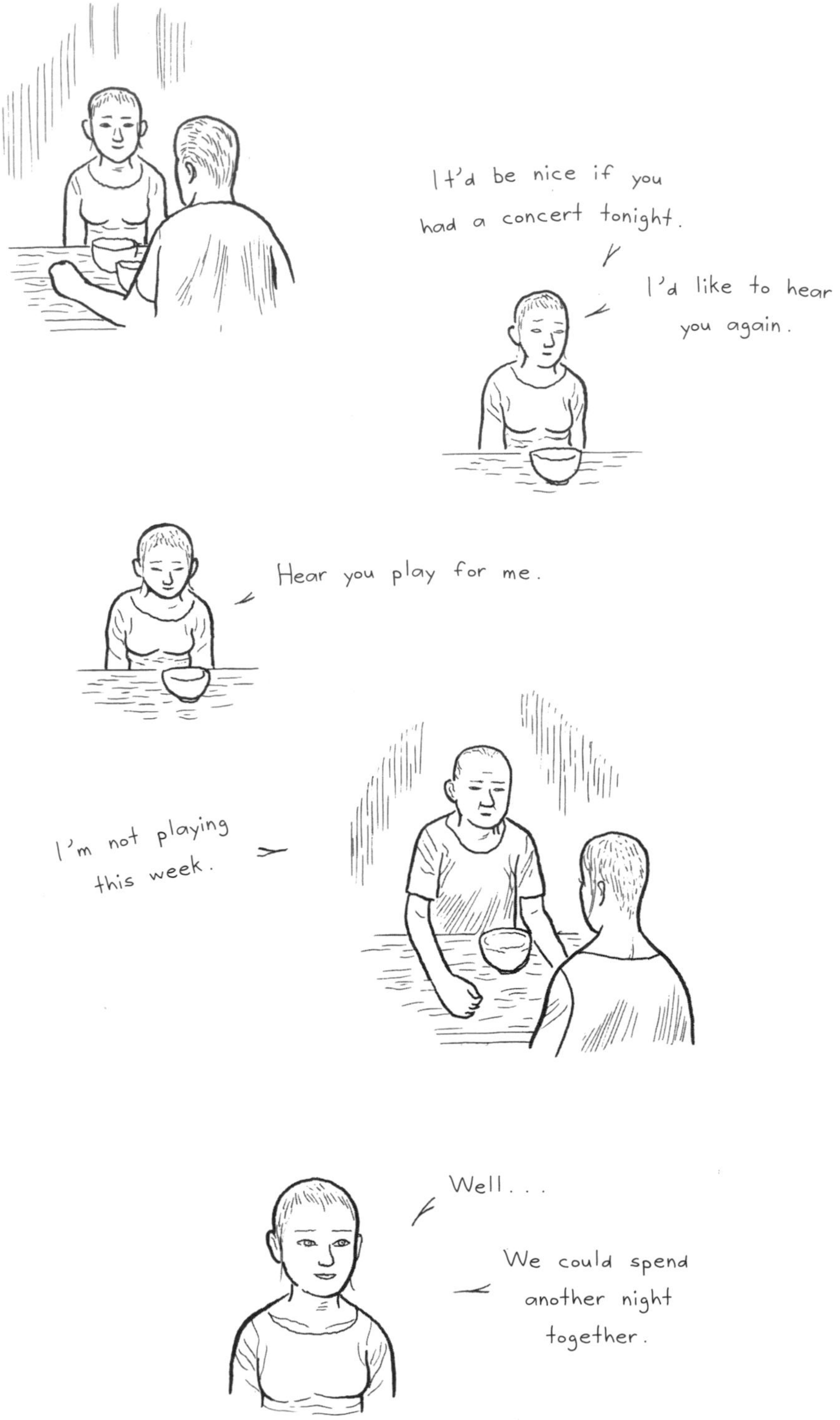
It'd be nice if you had a concert tonight.
I'd like to hear you again.
Hear you play for me.
I'm not playing this week.
Well...
We could spend another night together.

I can't, Renée...

I live with someone.

Why didn't you tell me before?

I was afraid to drive you away.

So? That might've been better, right?

Renée, you're important to me.
I know that already.

I never thought this'd be
just a one-night stand.

If you want to
see me again . . .

I'd be happy.

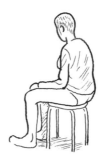

iramsso

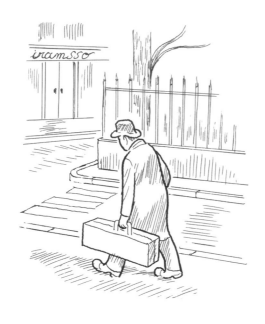

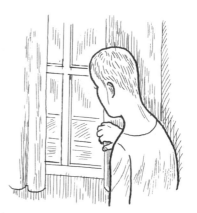

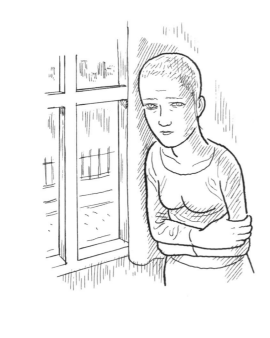

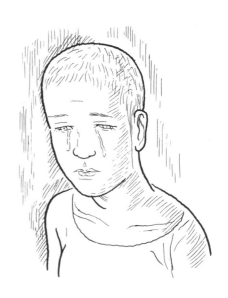

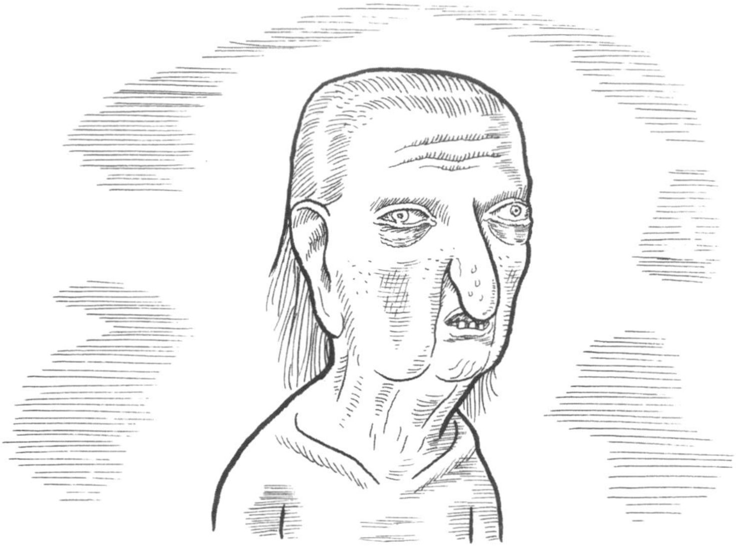

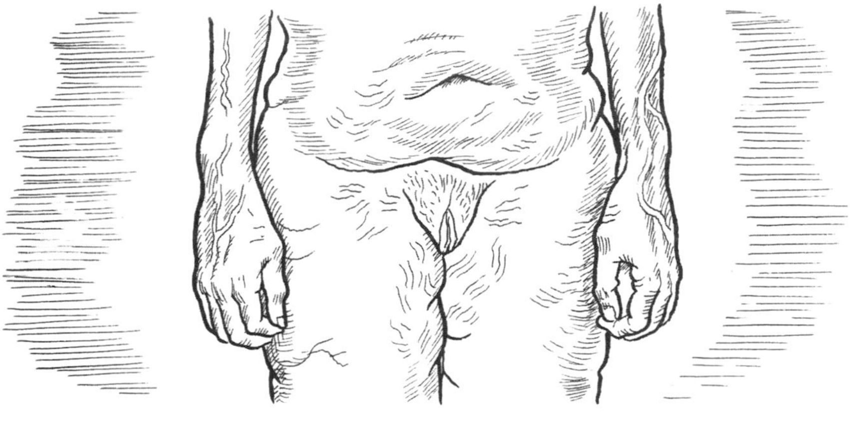

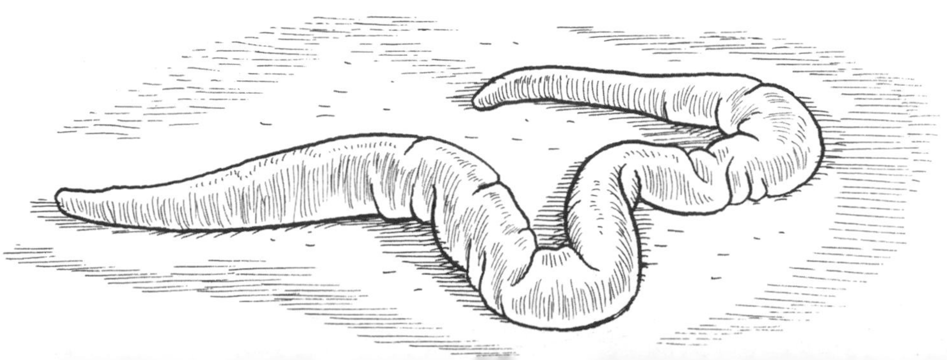

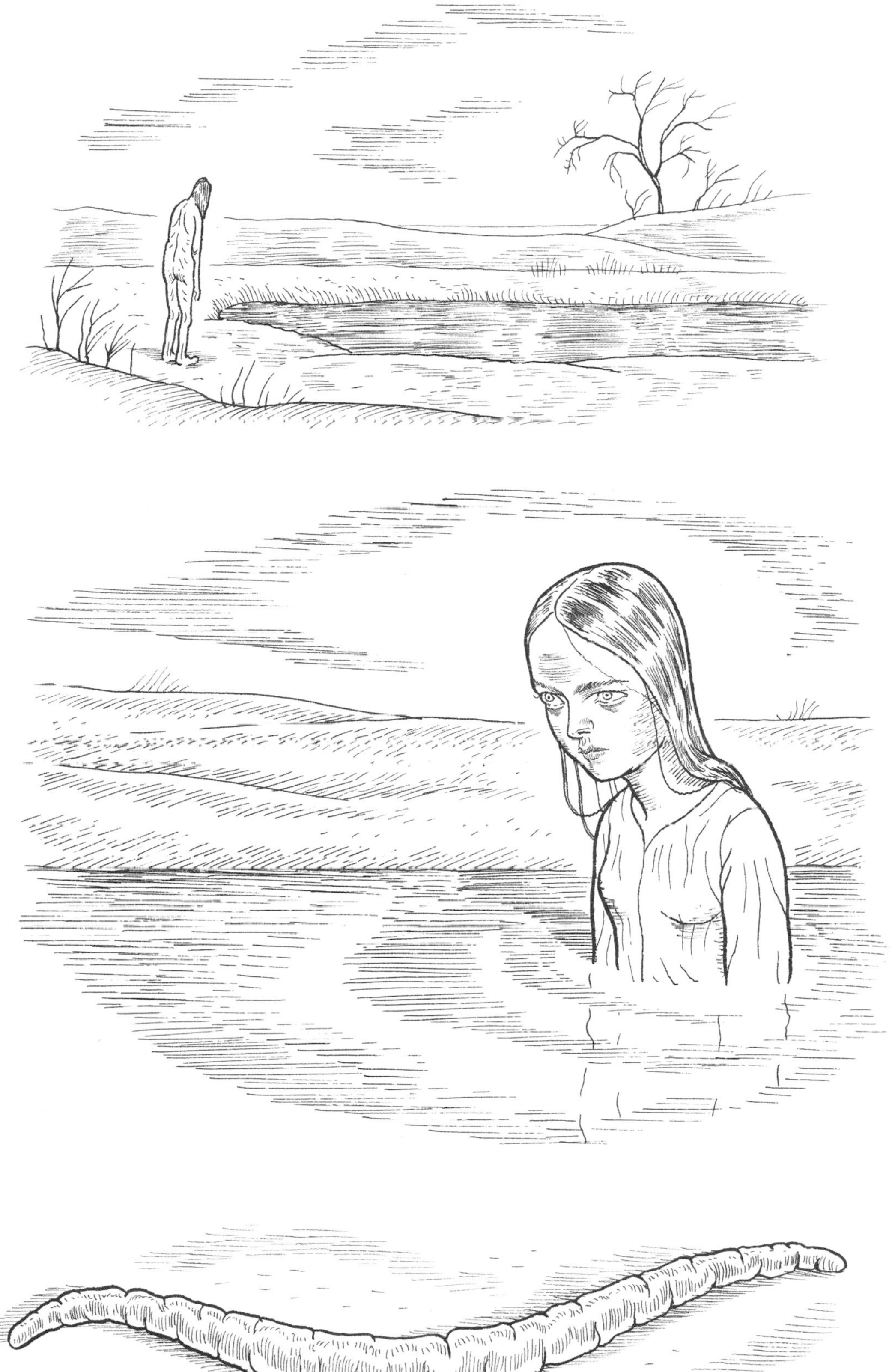

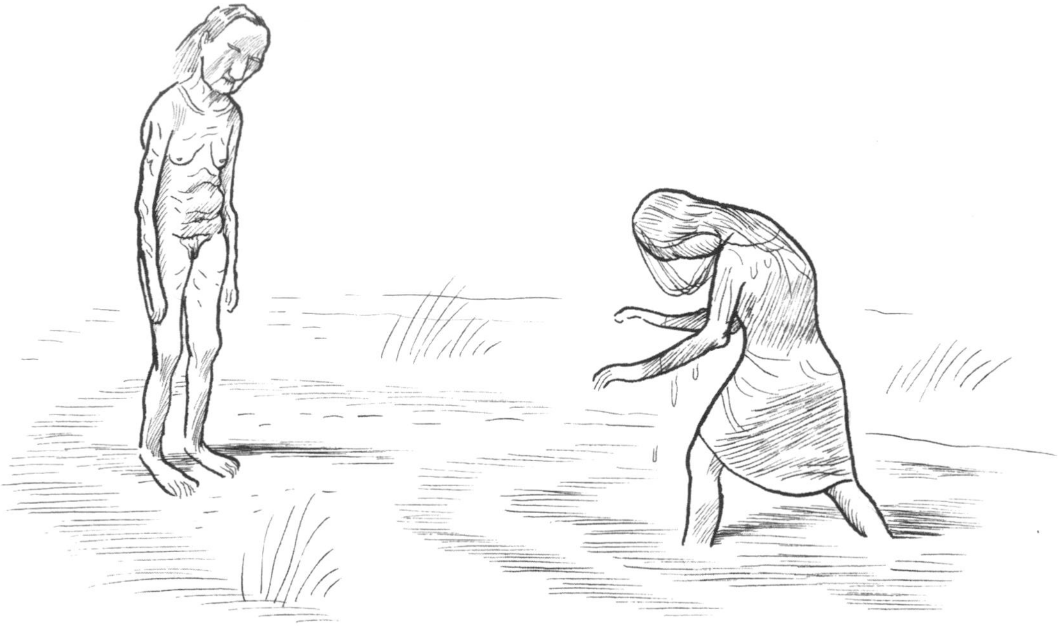

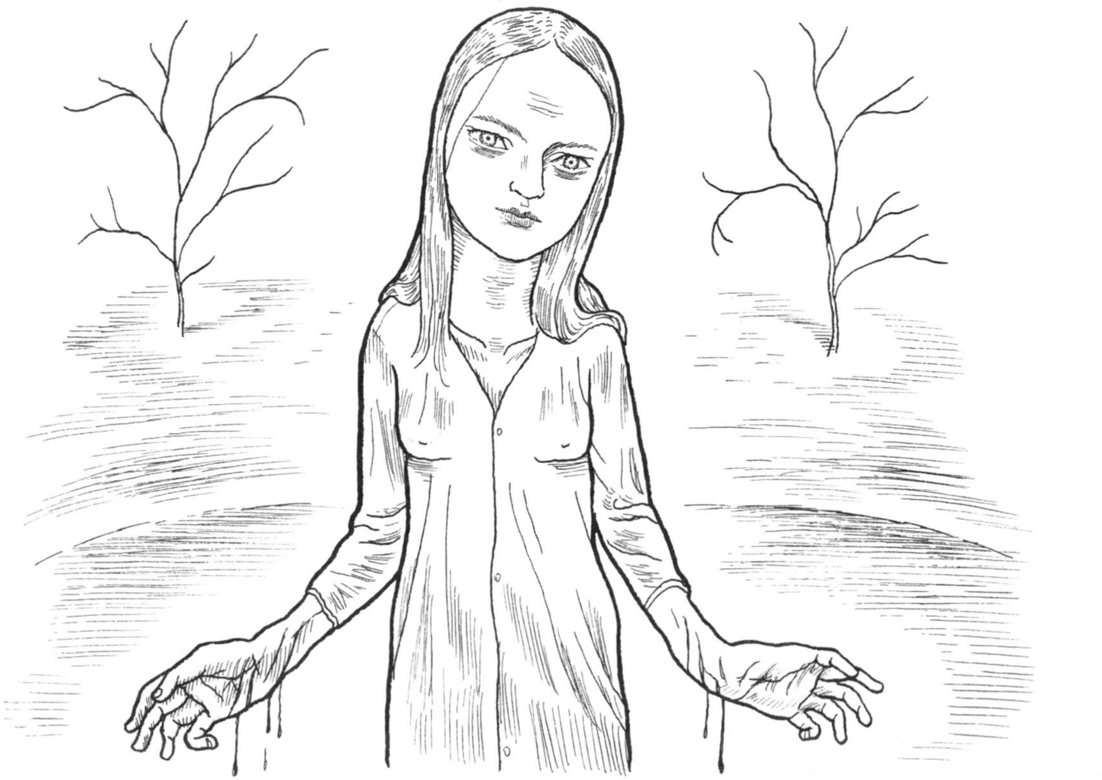

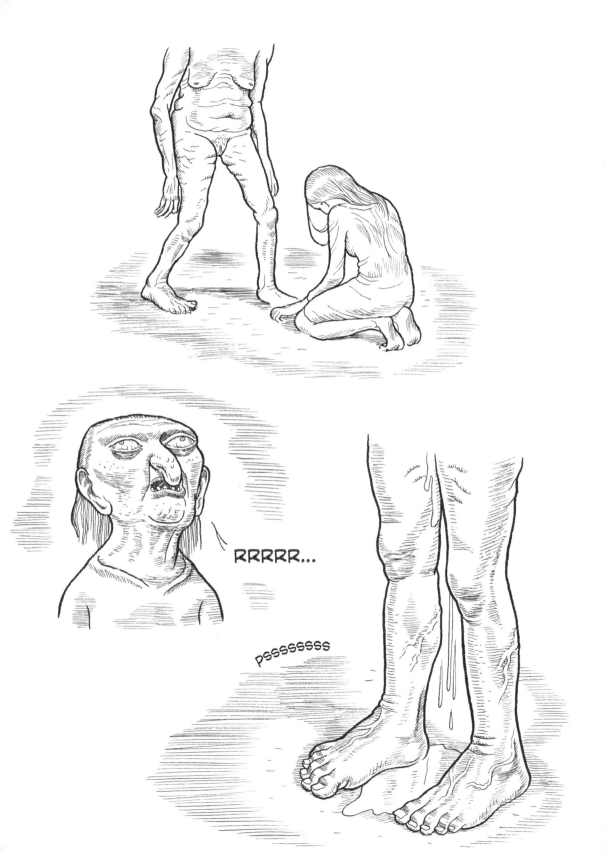

RRRRR...

PSSSSSSSS

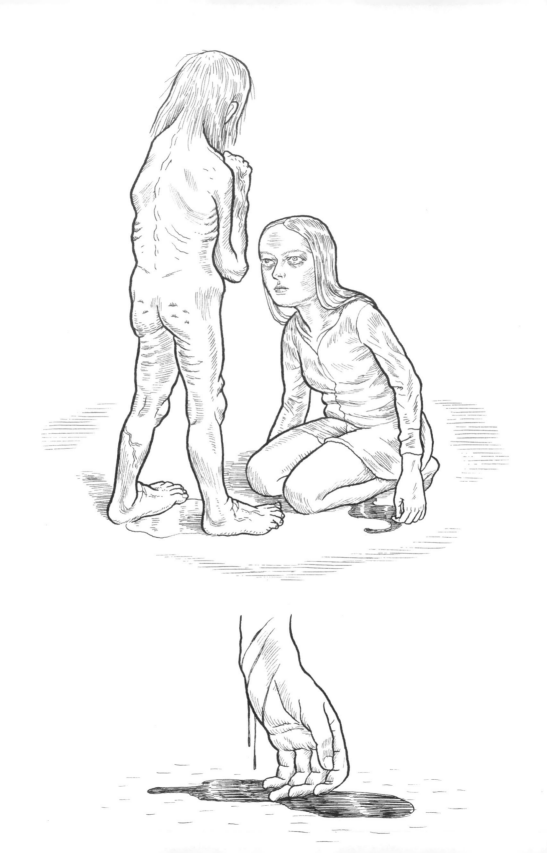

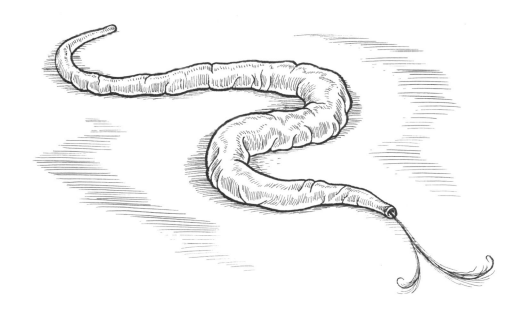

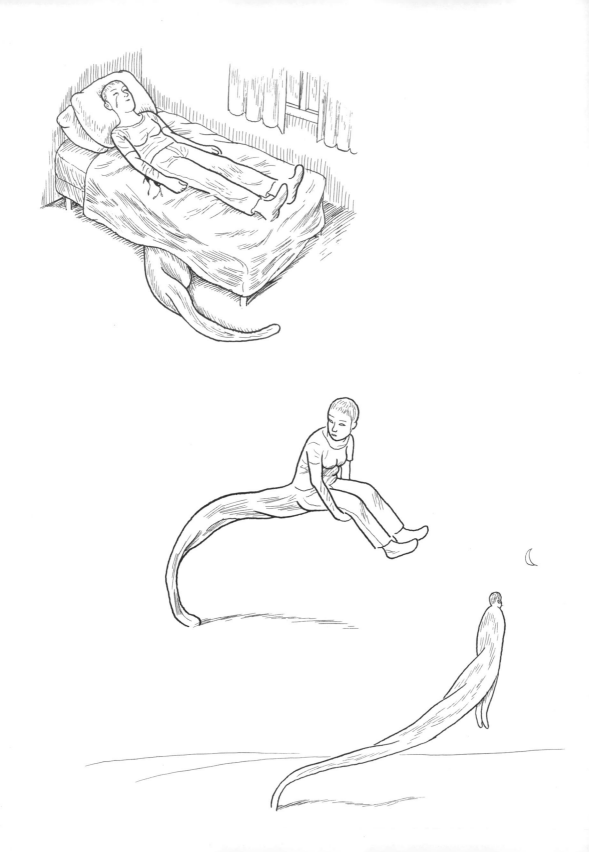

There are mystical knives that bury themselves in the flesh
of young girls beneath the weight of a boy.

I'd give those boys a thousand hairs from my head if they'd
weave them into purity ribbons to wear around their blind cocks.

It's so hard to have to fight against yourself.

You win so little...for everything you leave along the way.

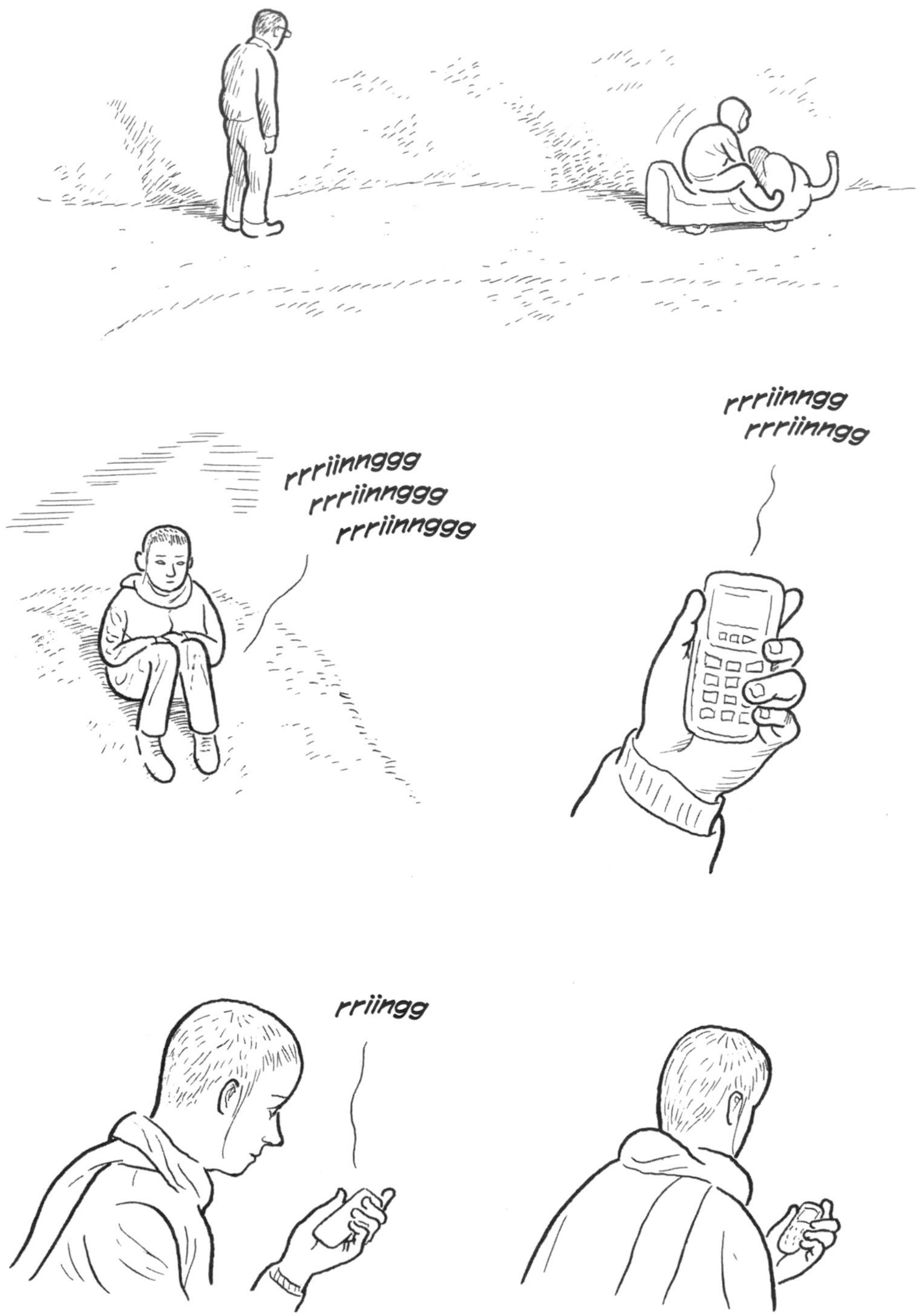
rrriinnggg
rrriinnggg
rrriinnggg
rrriinngg
rrriinngg
rriingg

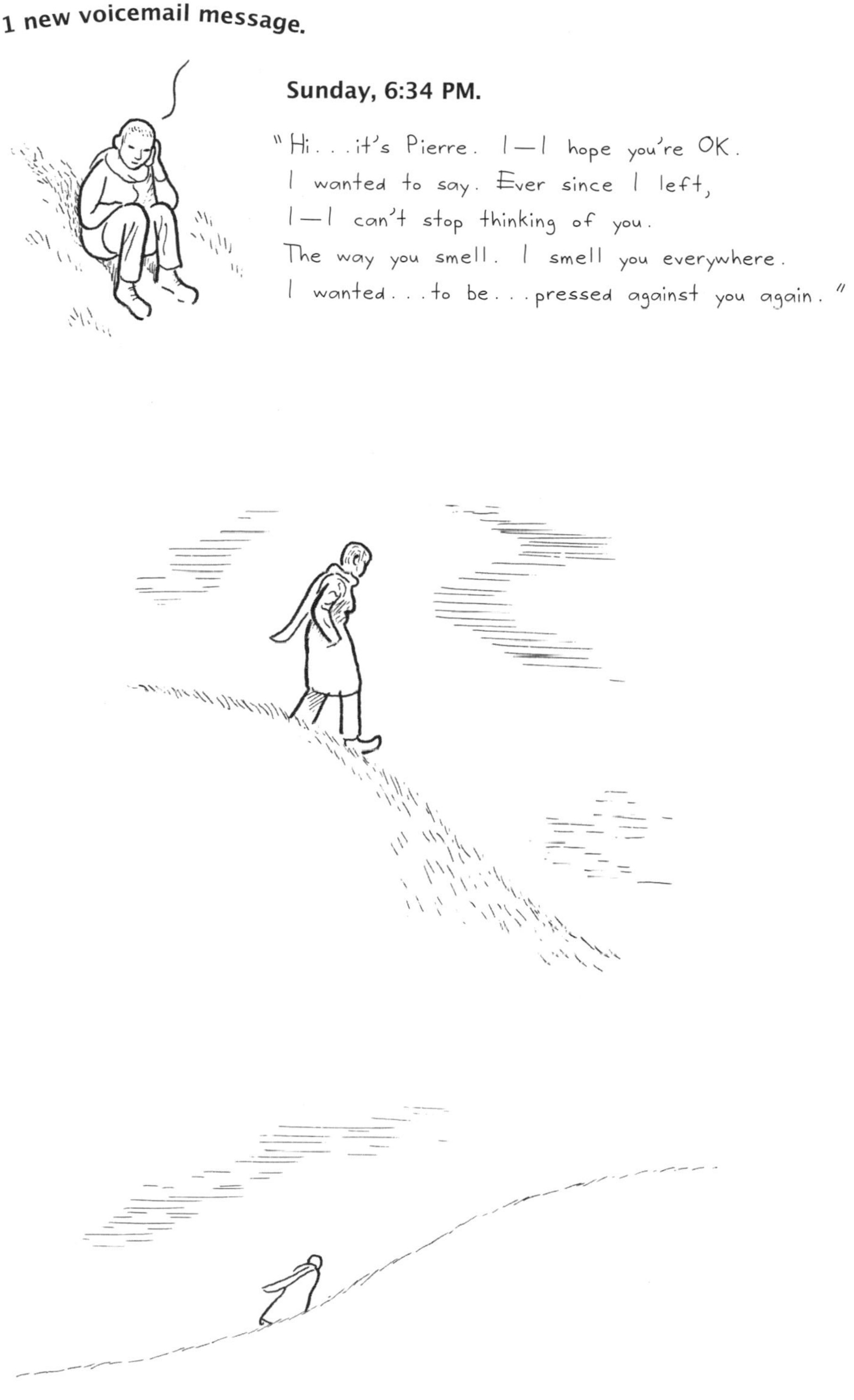
1 new voicemail message.
Sunday, 6:34 PM.
"Hi...it's Pierre. I—I hope you're OK.
I wanted to say. Ever since I left,
I—I can't stop thinking of you.
The way you smell. I smell you everywhere.
I wanted...to be...pressed against you again."

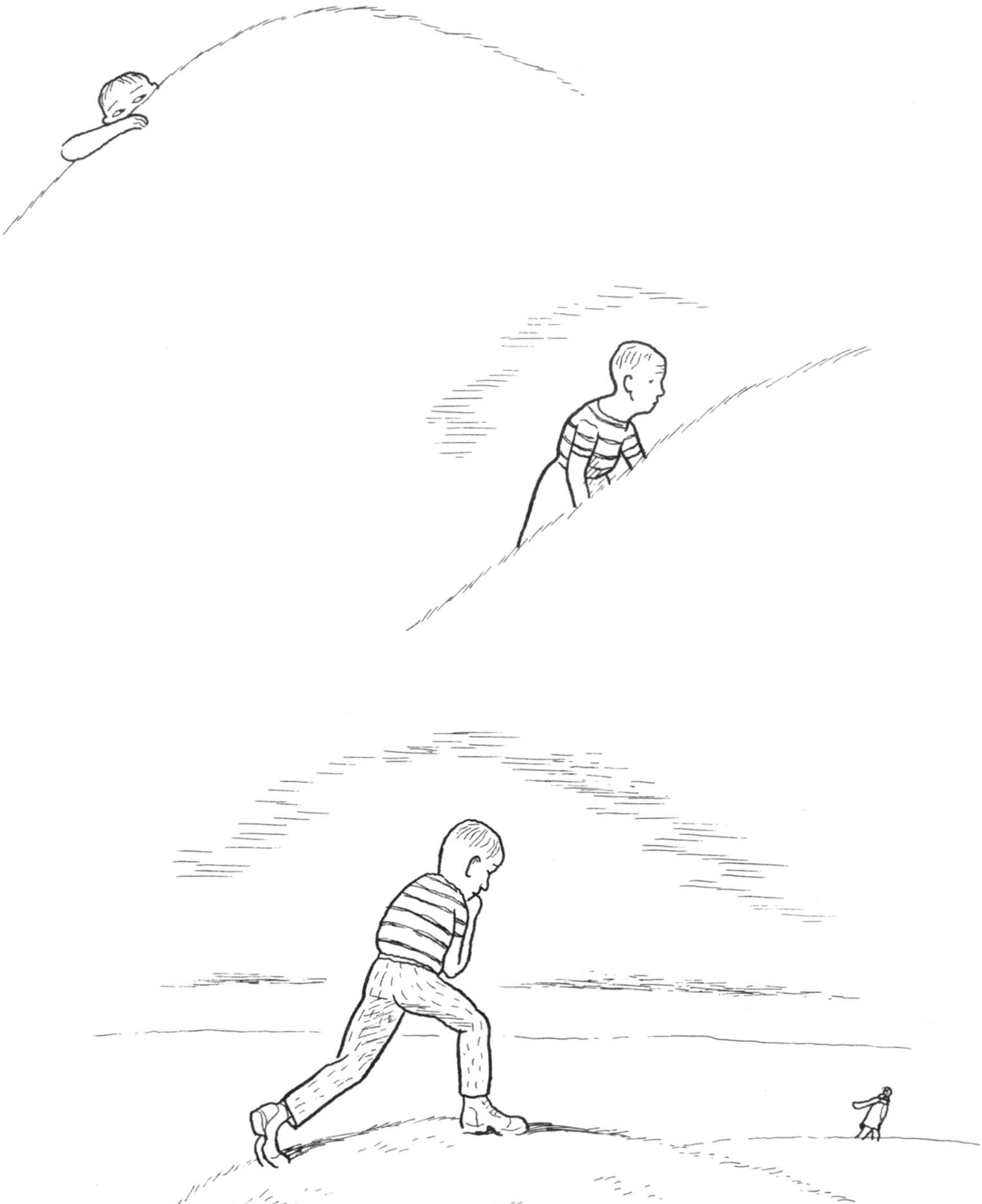

Hey, Arthur! Say hello to your new cellmate!

FENSTER

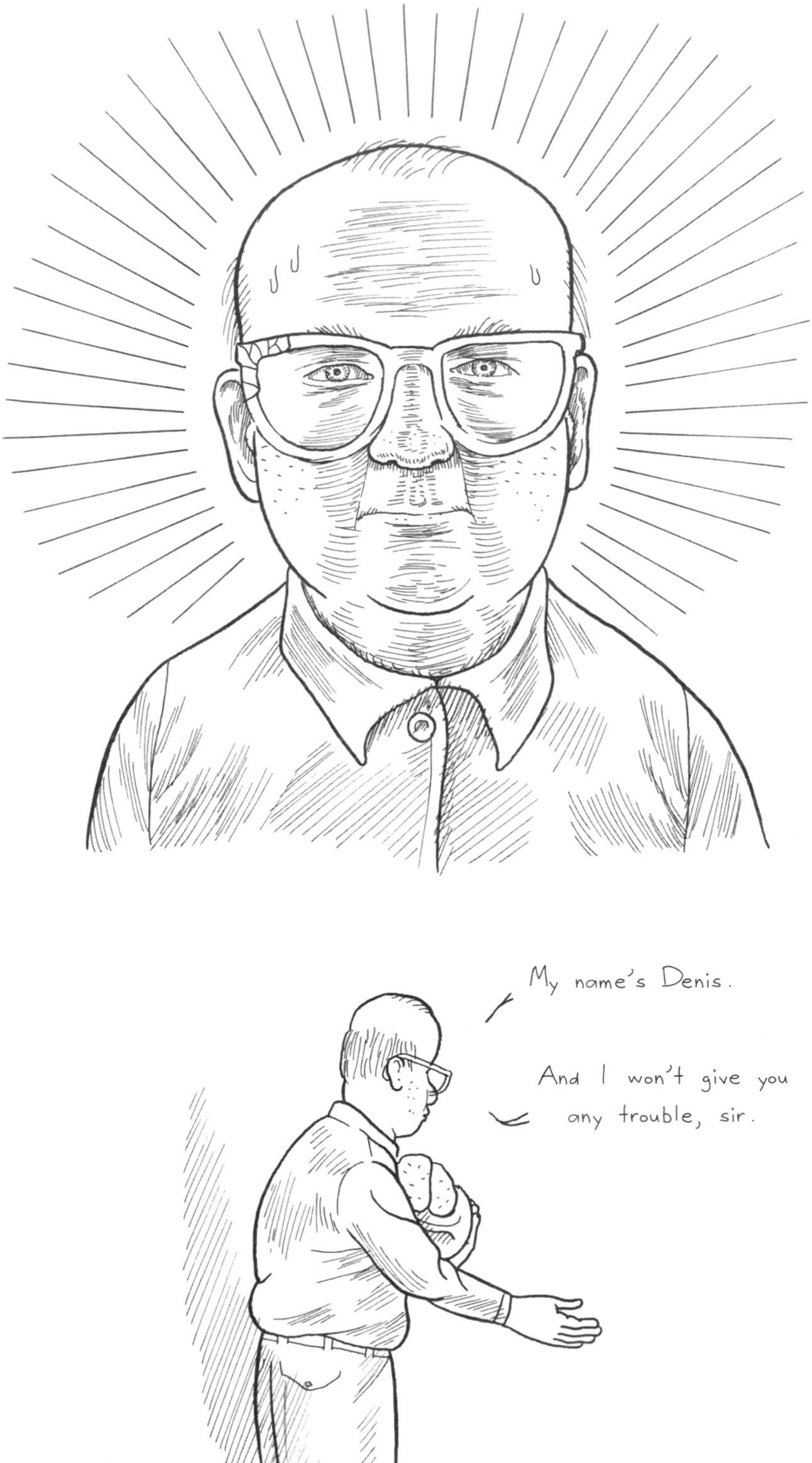
My name's Denis.
And I won't give you any trouble, sir.

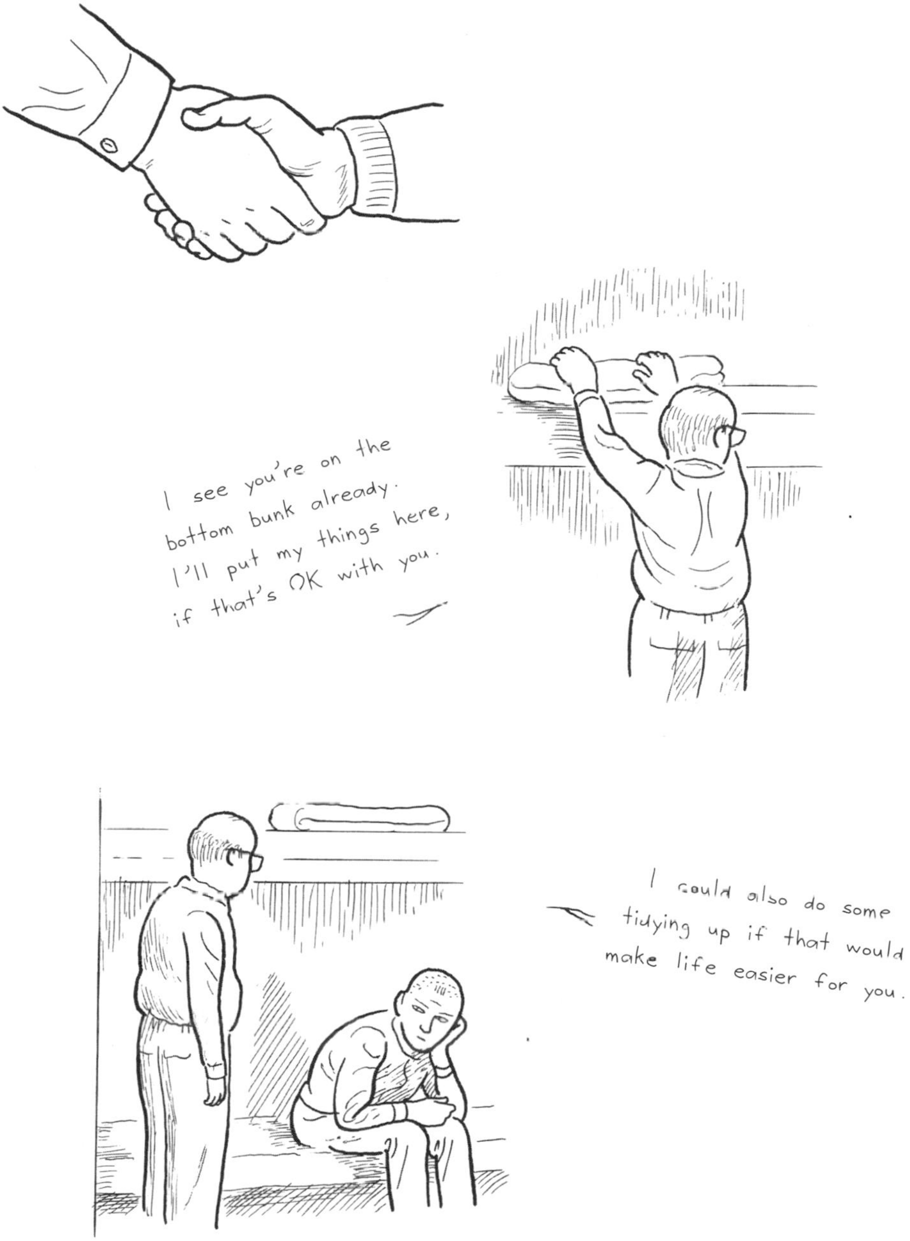
I see you're on the bottom bunk already. I'll put my things here, if that's OK with you.
I could also do some tidying up if that would make life easier for you.

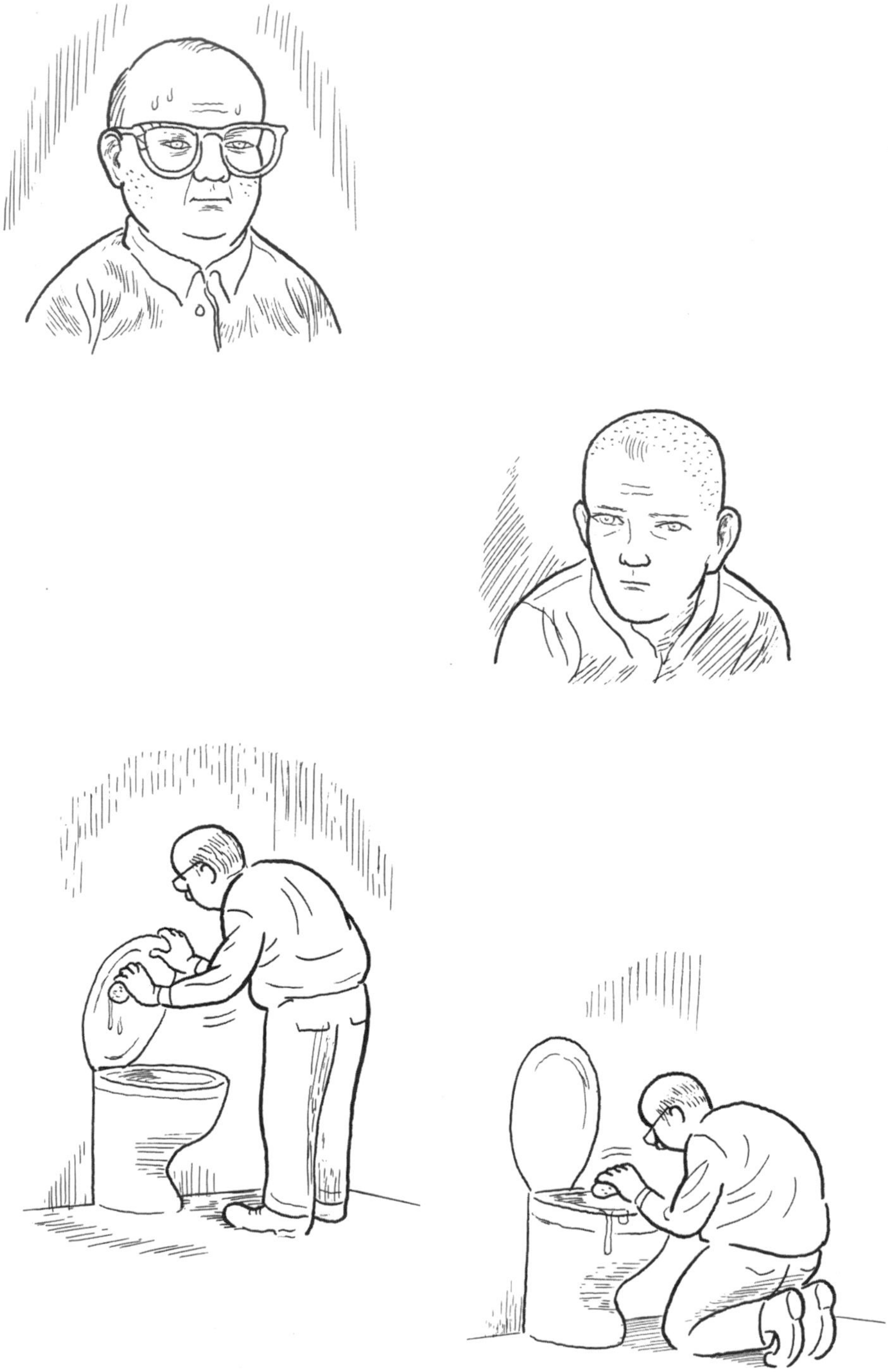

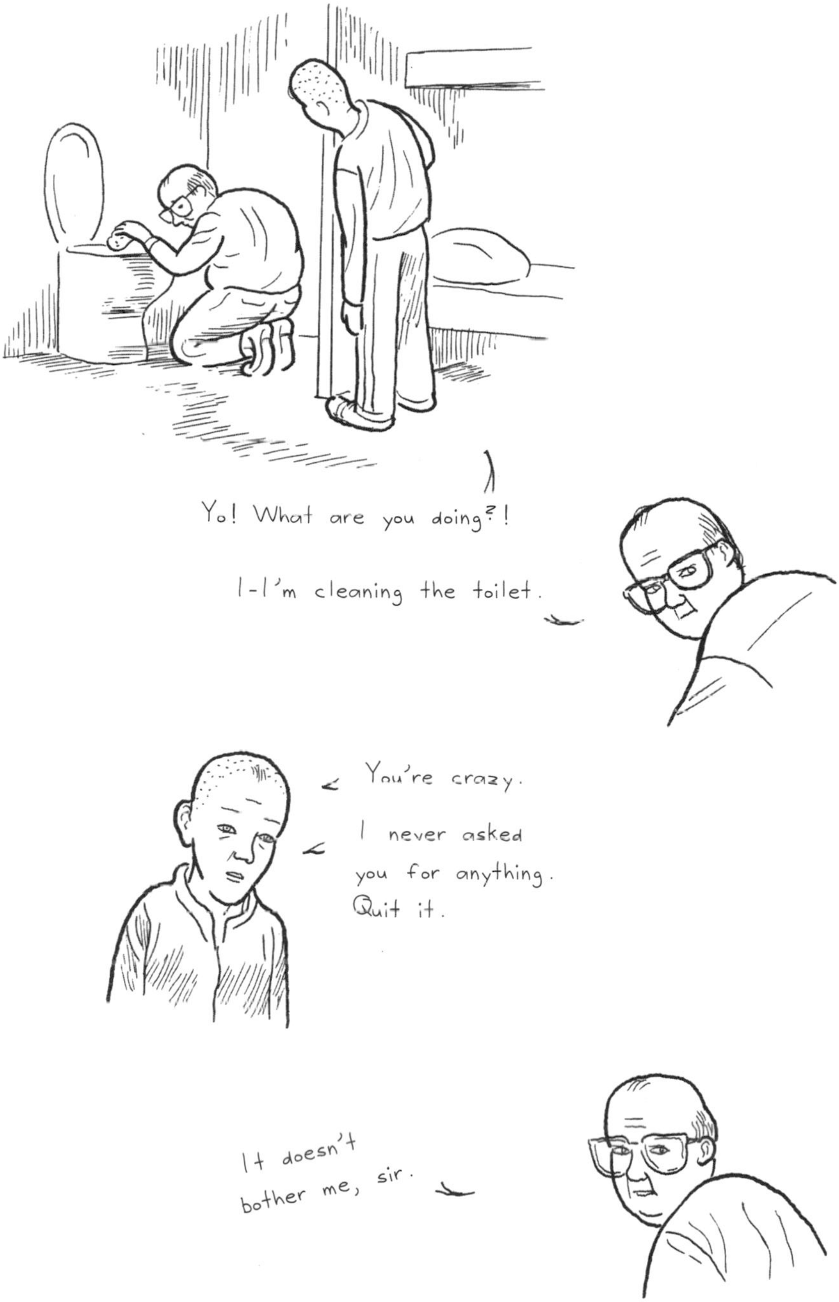
Yo! What are you doing?!
I-I'm cleaning the toilet.
You're crazy.
I never asked you for anything. Quit it.
It doesn't bother me, sir.

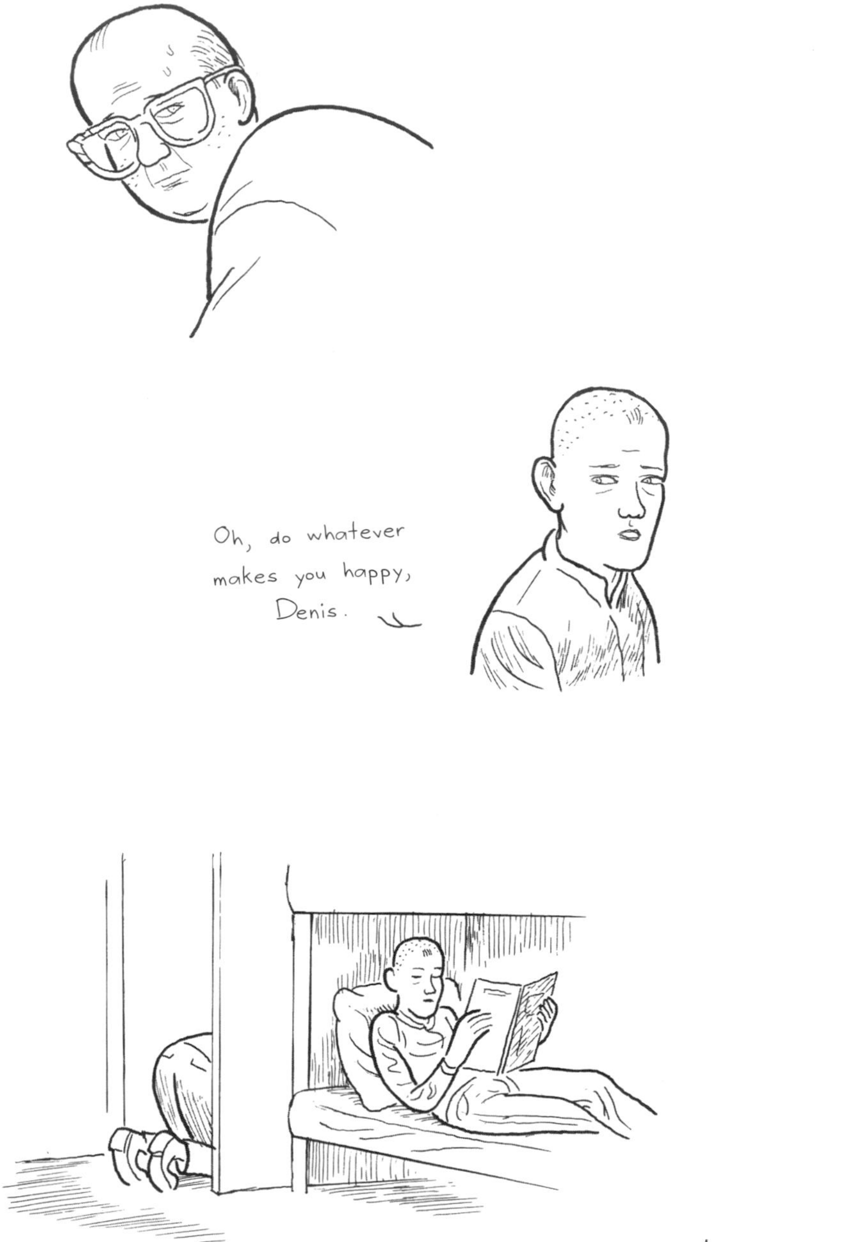
Oh, do whatever makes you happy, Denis.
They must've put you through the wringer, wherever you're from.

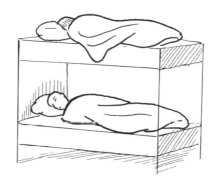

The sound of his breathing...

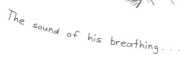

1...2...3...4...

Fuck! I can't start

counting his breaths.

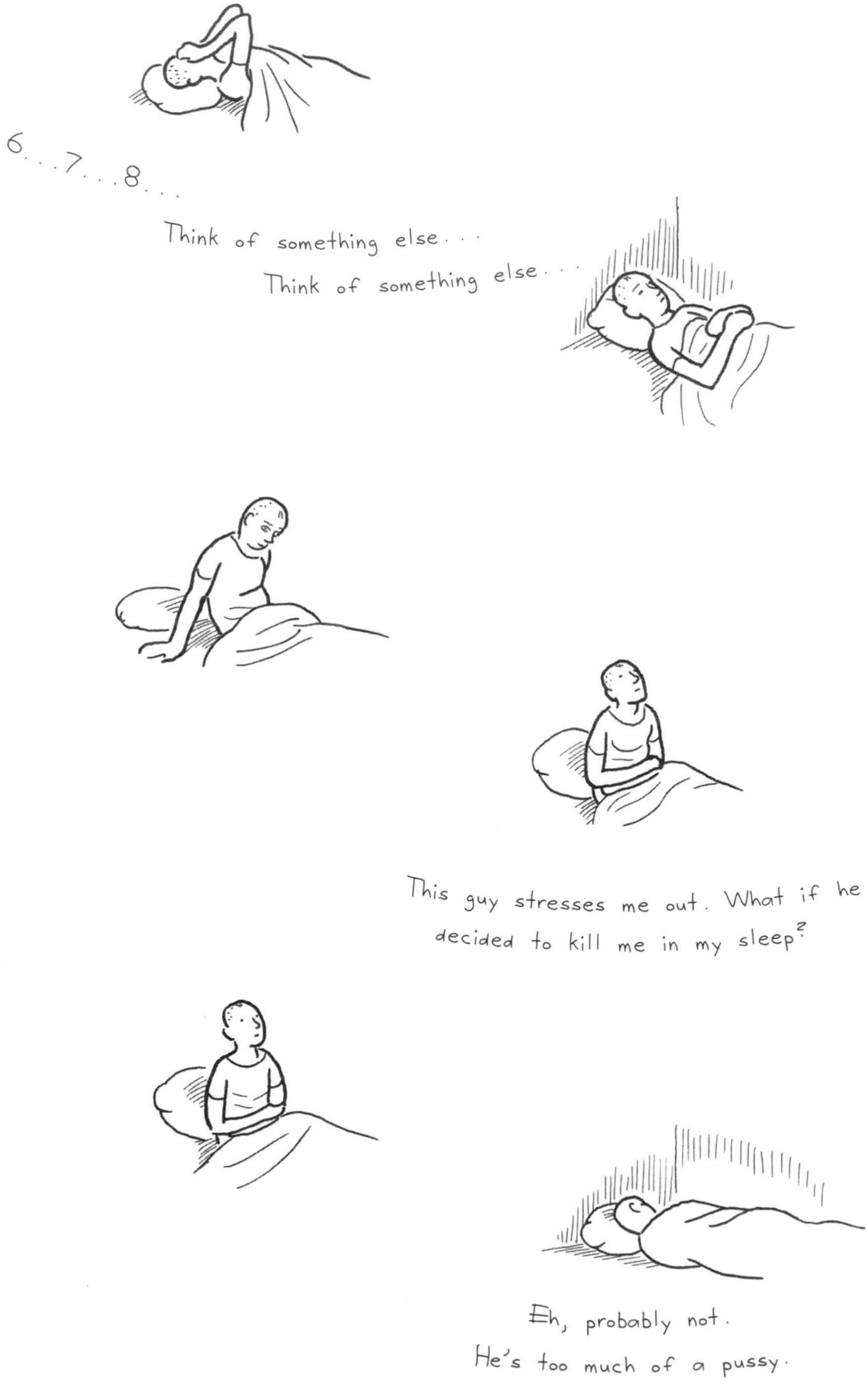

6...7...8...
Think of something else...
Think of something else...
This guy stresses me out. What if he decided to kill me in my sleep?
Eh, probably not.
He's too much of a pussy.

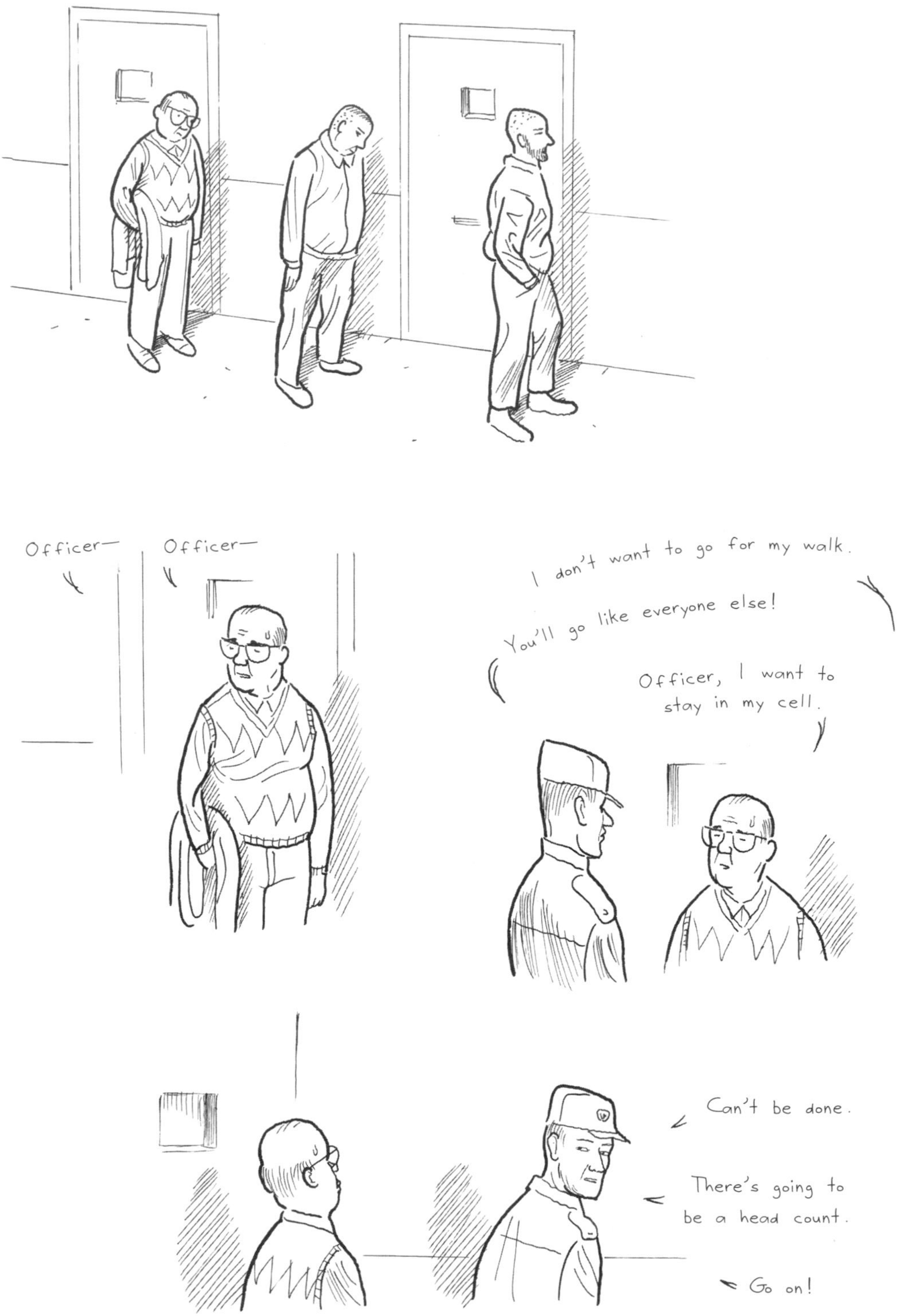

Officer—
Officer—
I don't want to go for my walk.
You'll go like everyone else!
Officer, I want to stay in my cell.
Can't be done.
There's going to be a head count.
Go on!

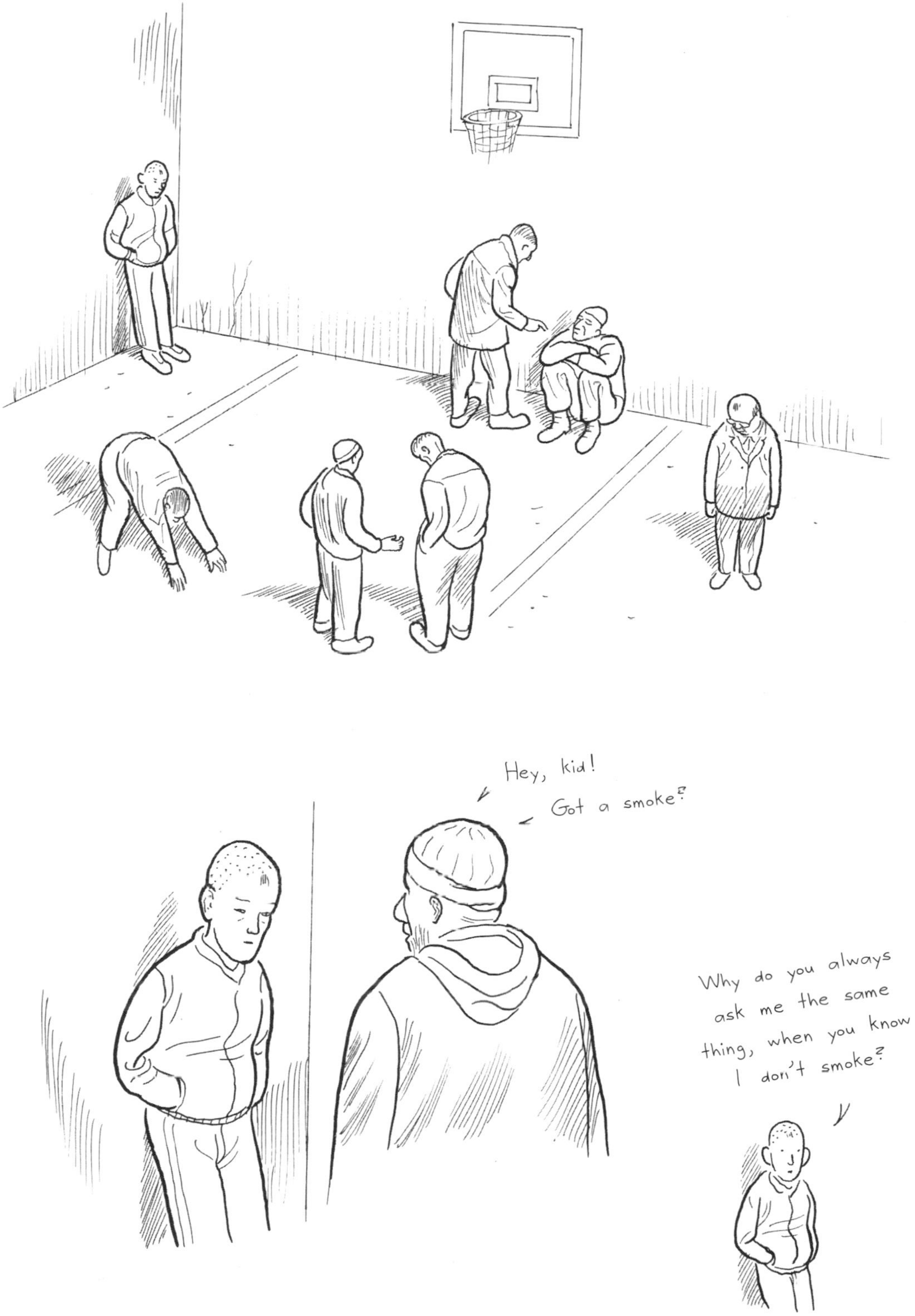
Hey, kid!
Got a smoke?
Why do you always ask me the same thing, when you know I don't smoke?

Huh. True, that. You're right.

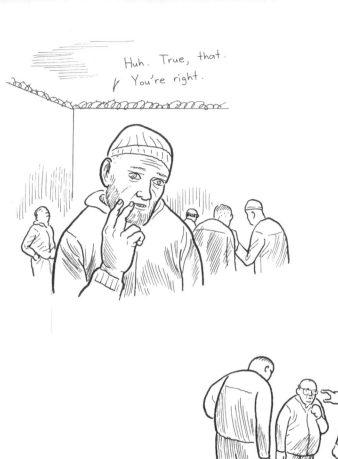

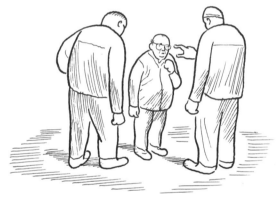

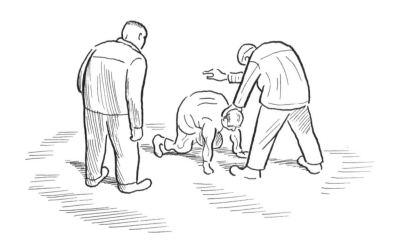

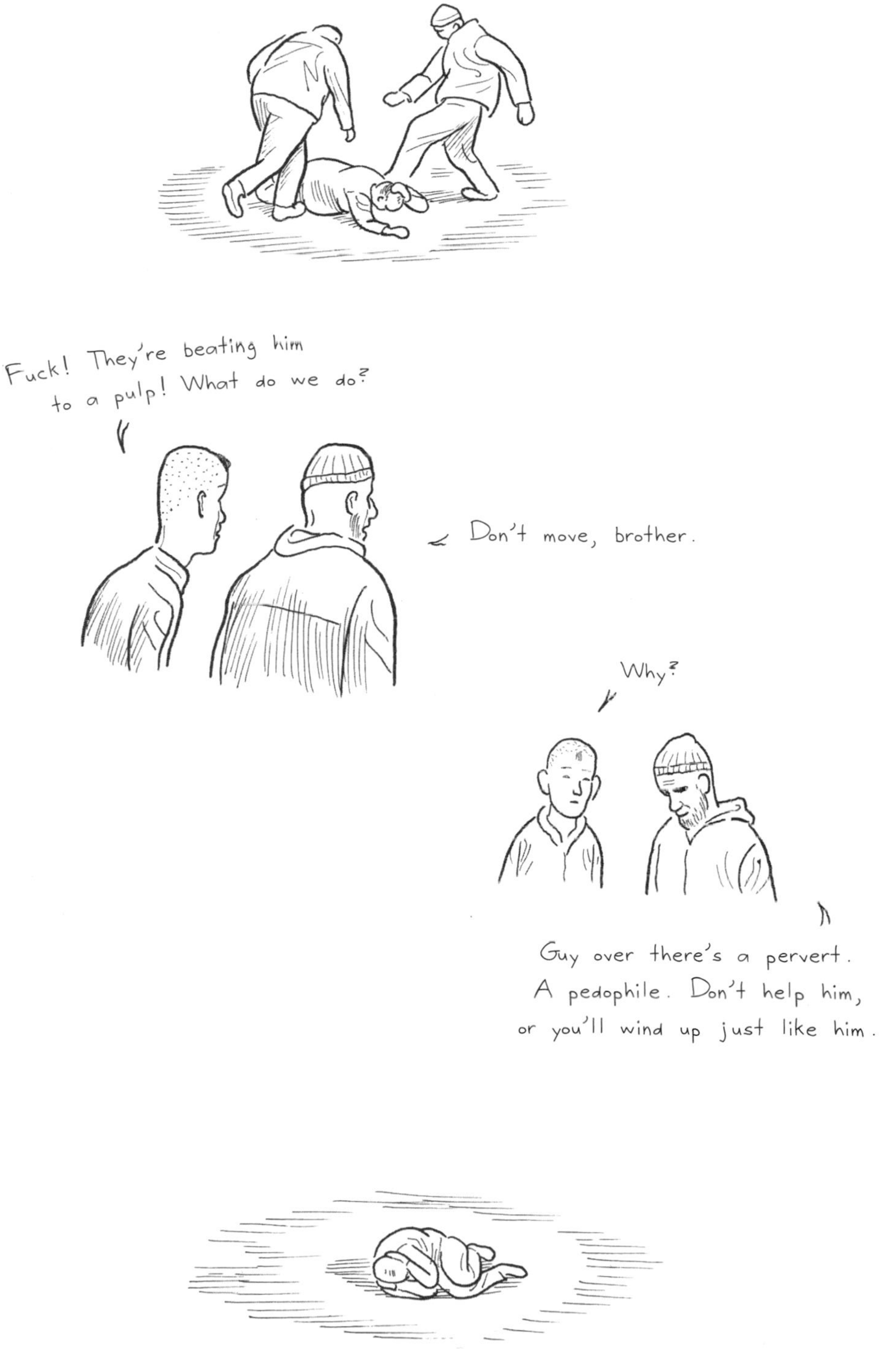
Fuck! They're beating him to a pulp! What do we do?
Don't move, brother.
Why?
Guy over there's a pervert. A pedophile. Don't help him, or you'll wind up just like him.

You know that guy?

...we're cellmates.

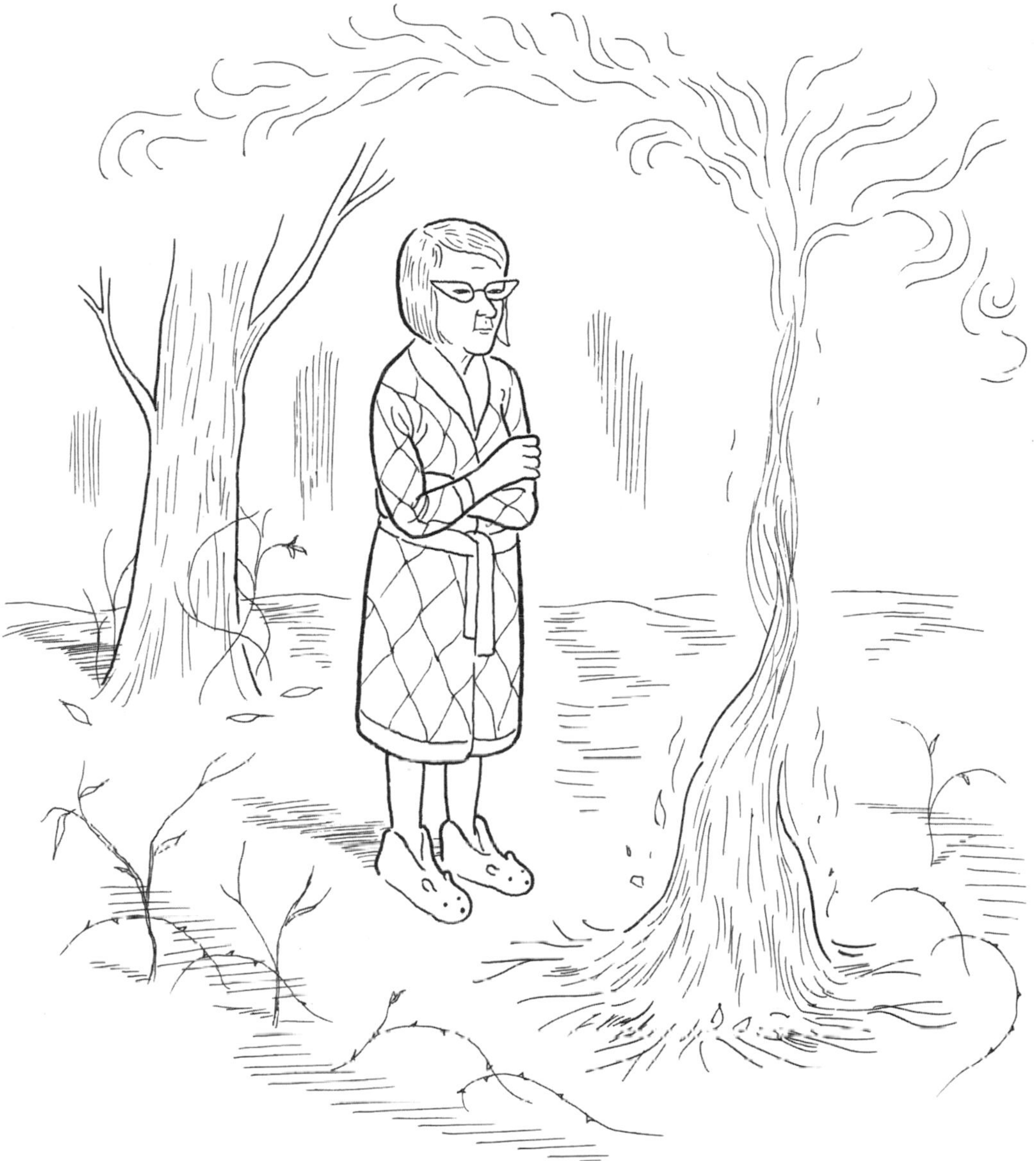

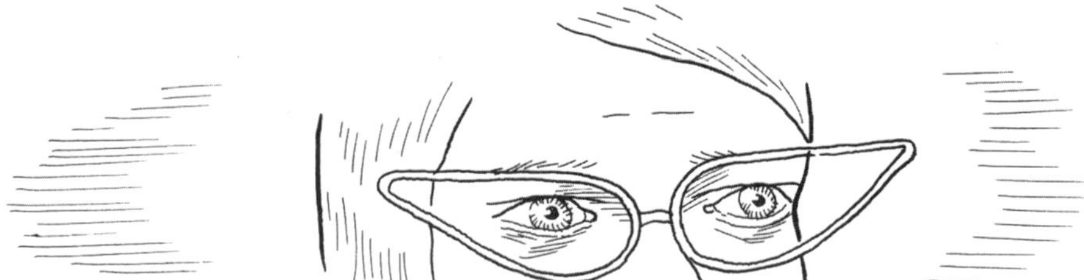

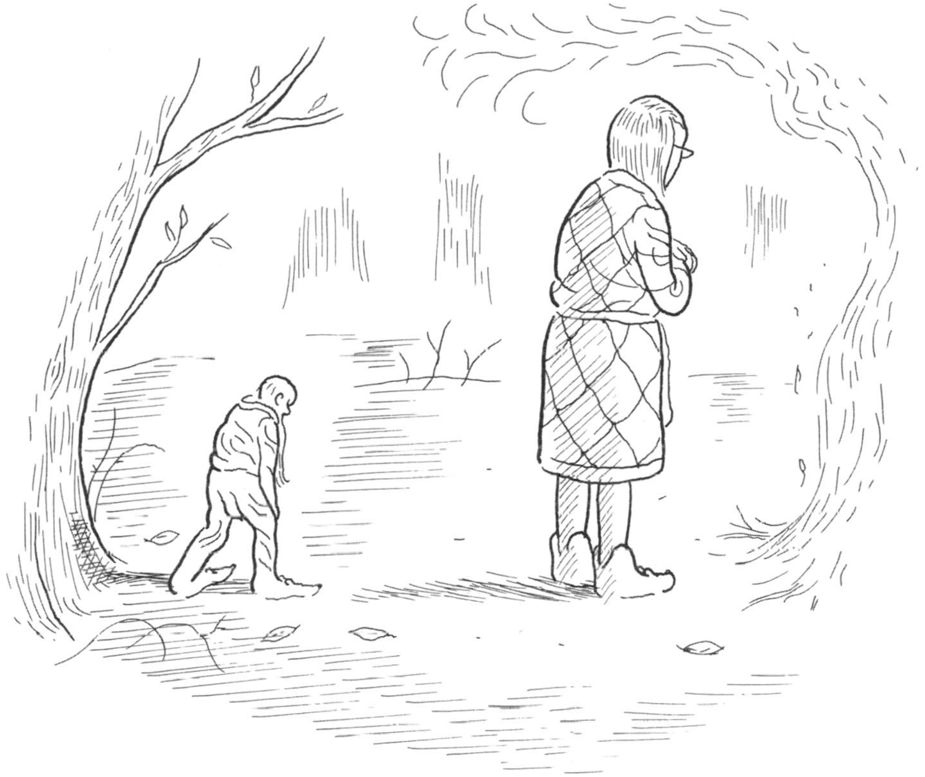

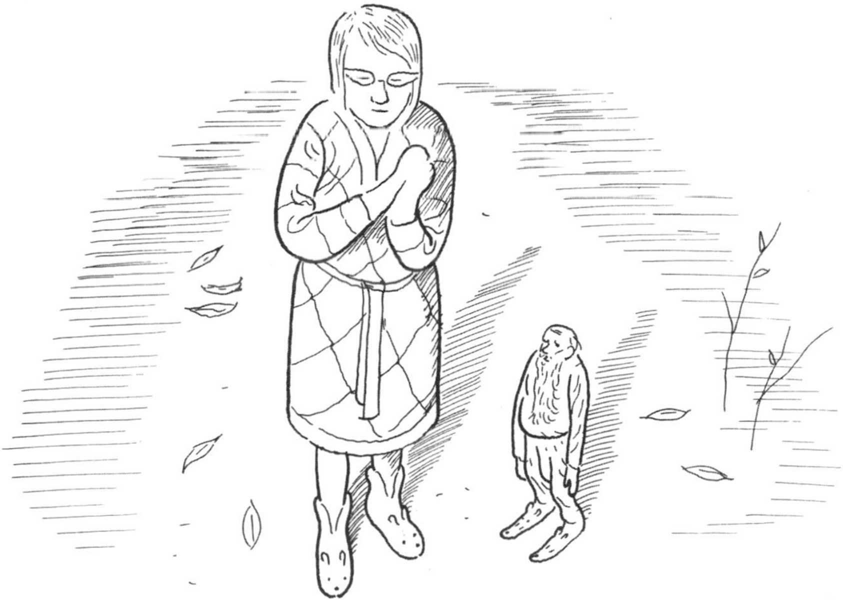

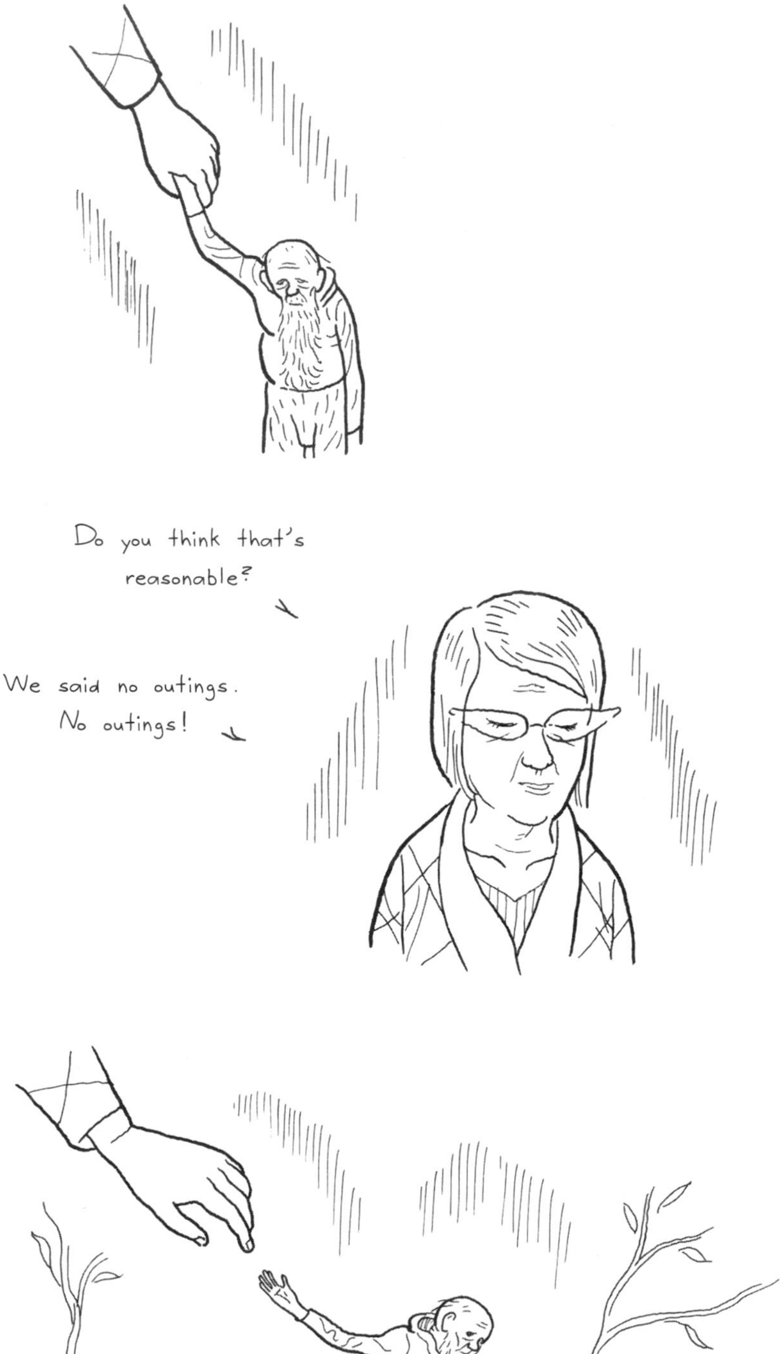
Do you think that's reasonable?
We said no outings. No outings!

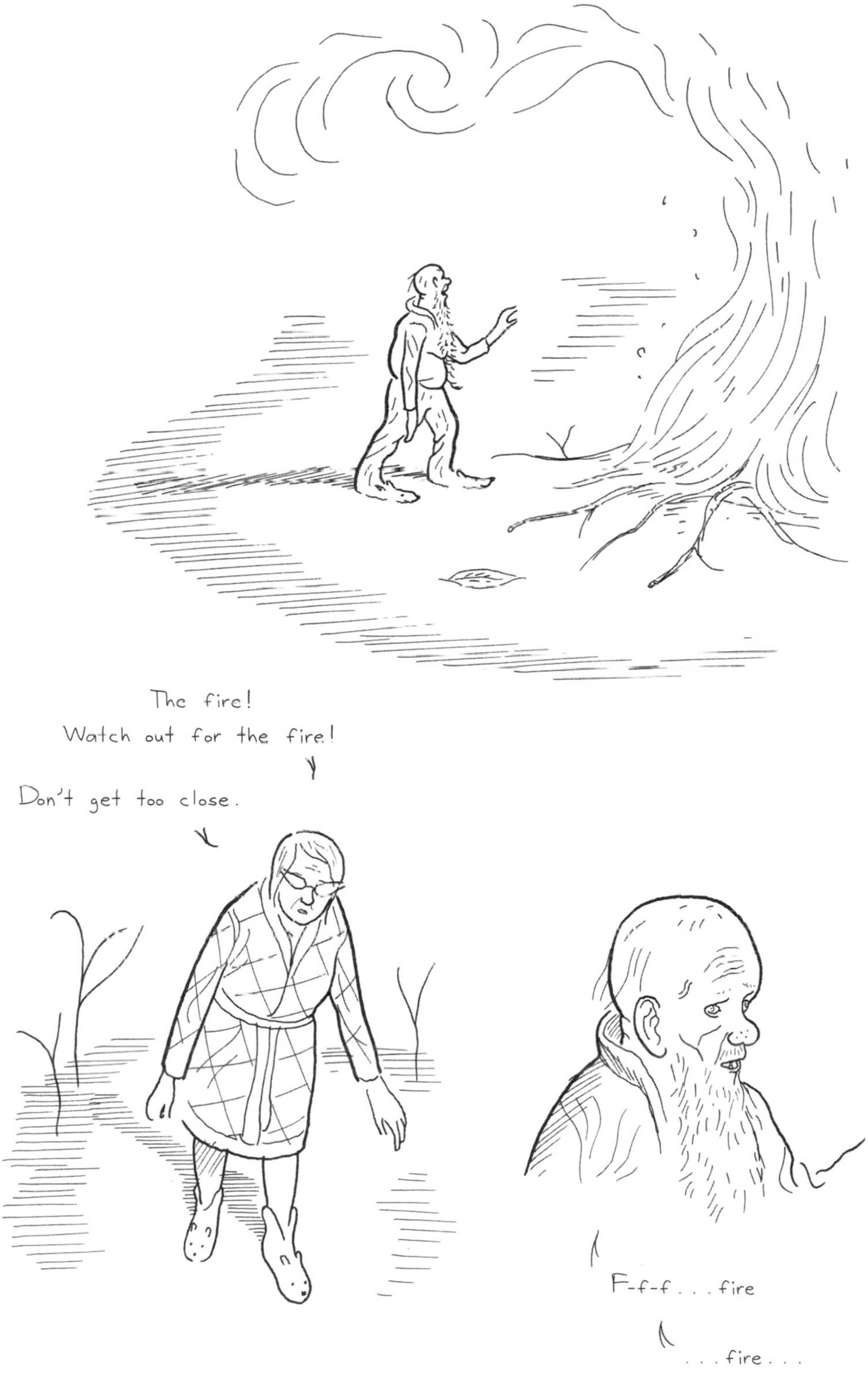
The fire!
Watch out for the fire!
Don't get too close.
F-f-f . . . fire
. . . fire . . .

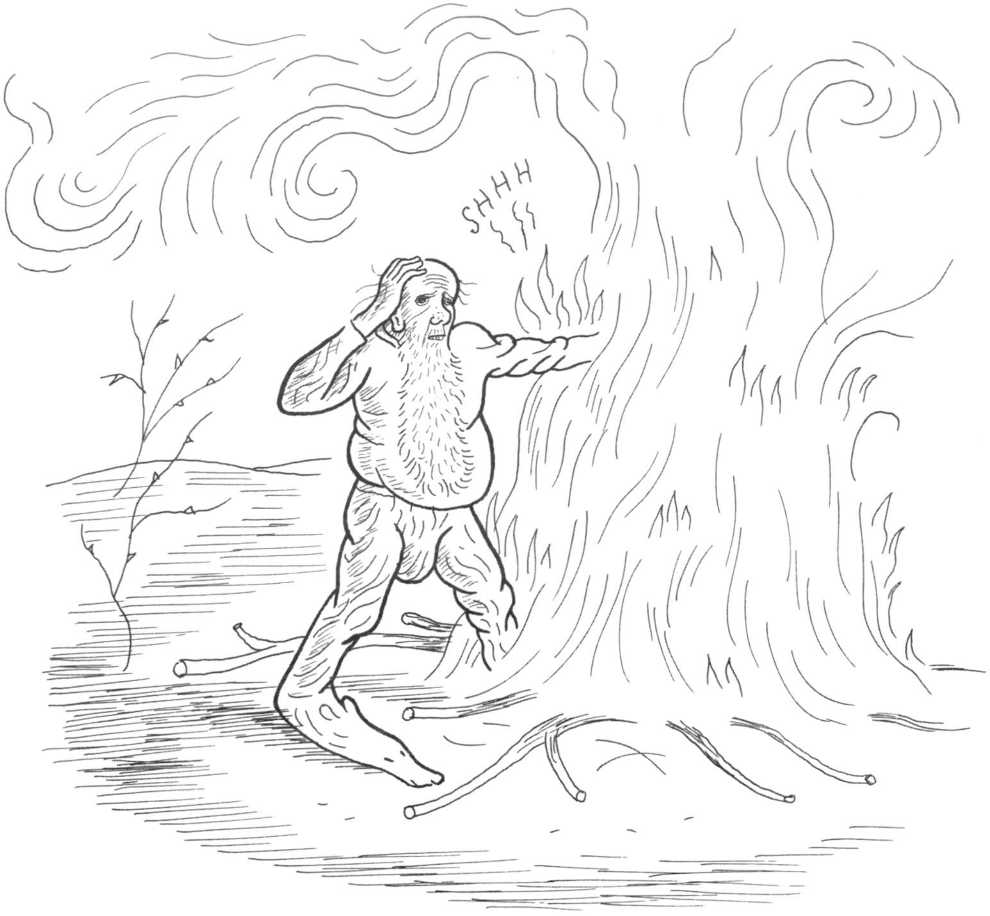
SHHH

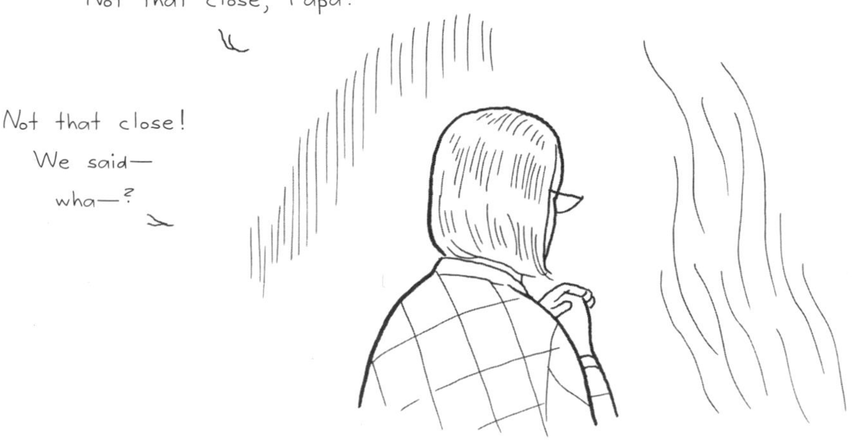
Not that close, Papa.
Not that close! We said— wha—?

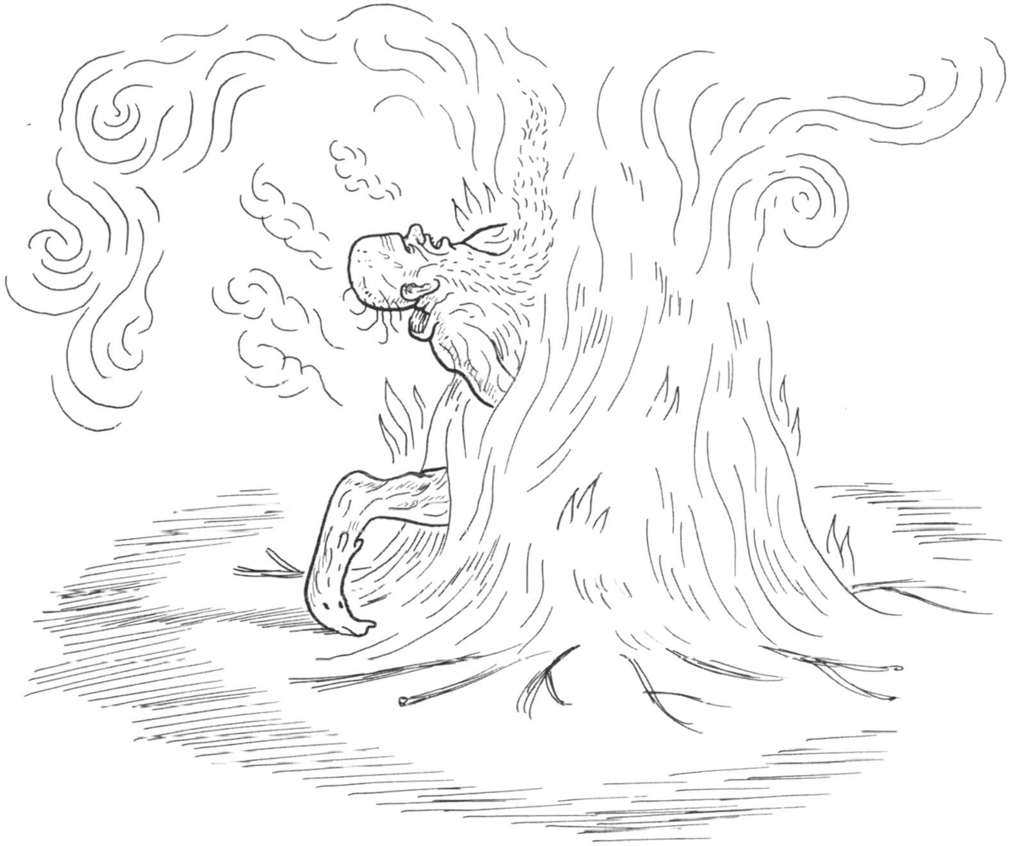

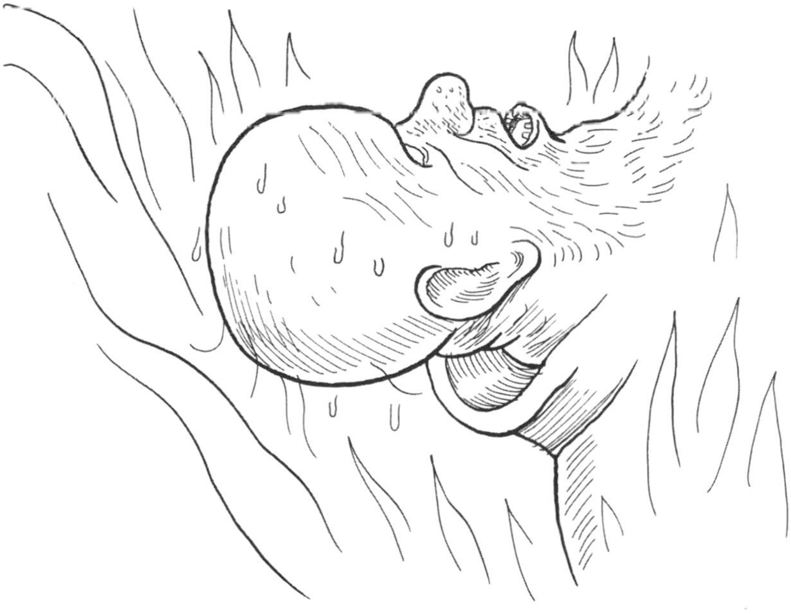

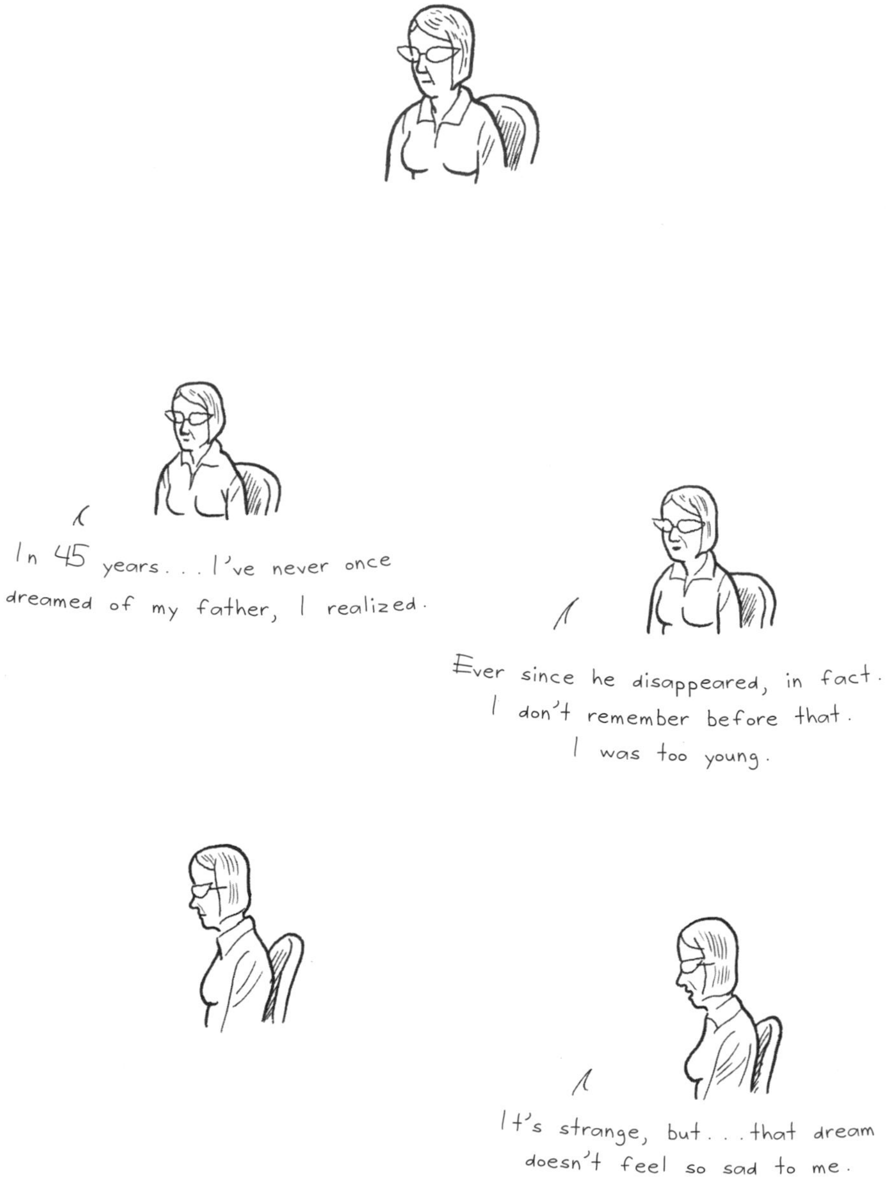
In 45 years. . . I've never once dreamed of my father, I realized.
Ever since he disappeared, in fact. I don't remember before that. I was too young.
It's strange, but. . . that dream doesn't feel so sad to me.

Hm . . .

Yes?

It's—

Hmm . . .

It's like—

It's like something finally happened.

In my life, I mean.

I know it's silly . . .

The fact that you now remember
most of your dreams is a sign that
something is starting to happen again.
That's not insignificant.
As things go.

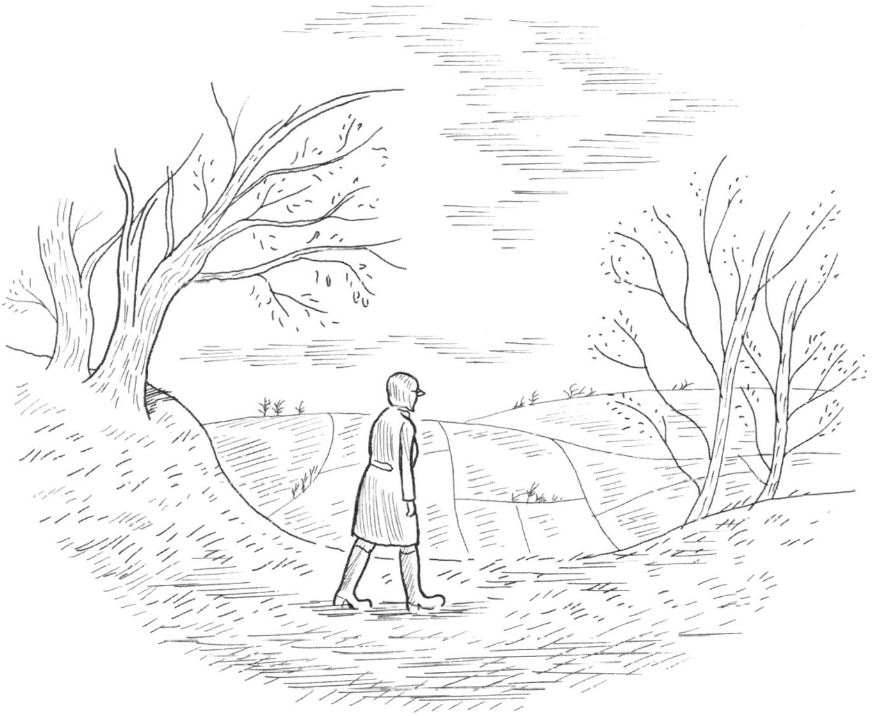

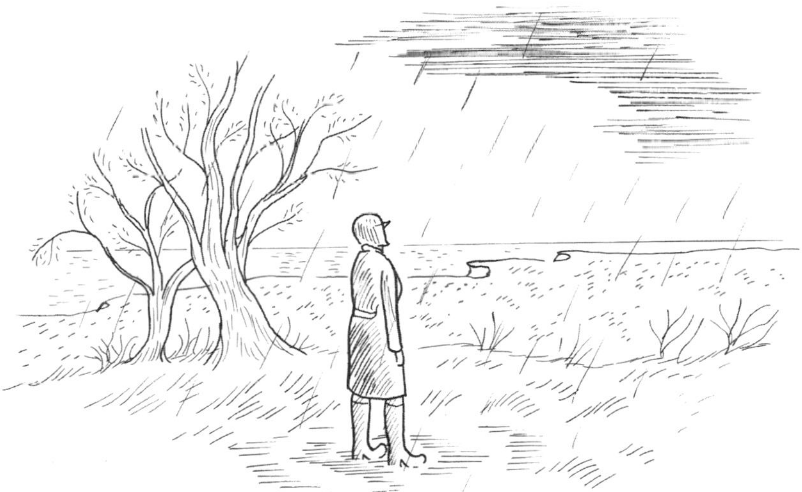

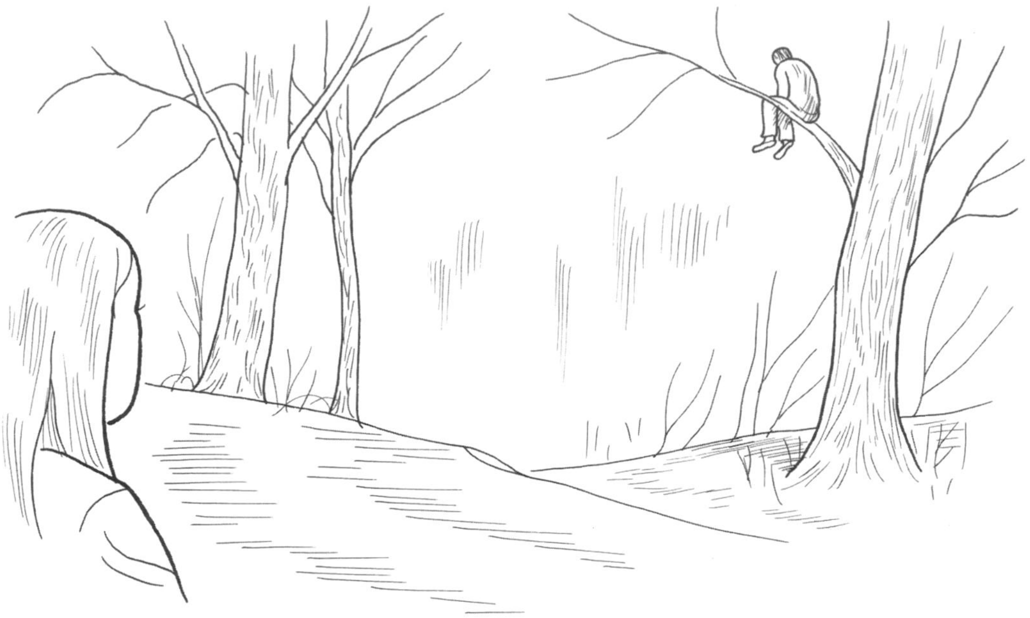
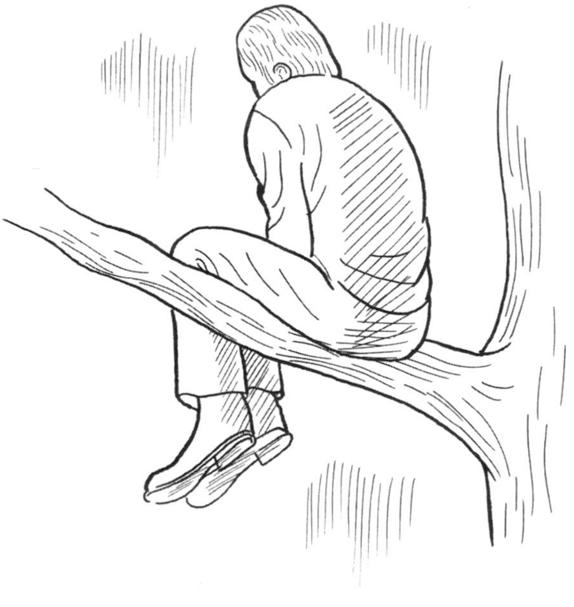
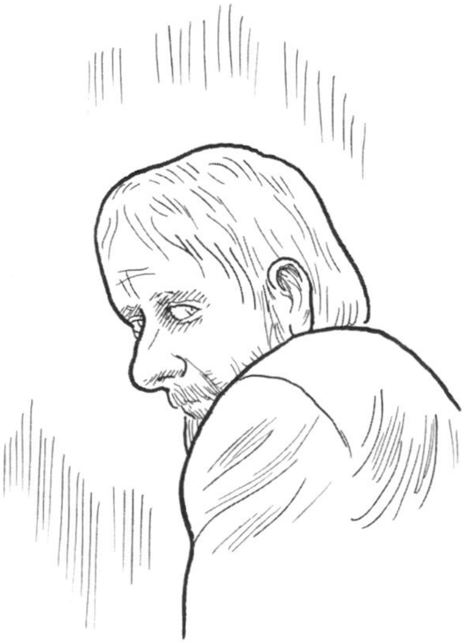

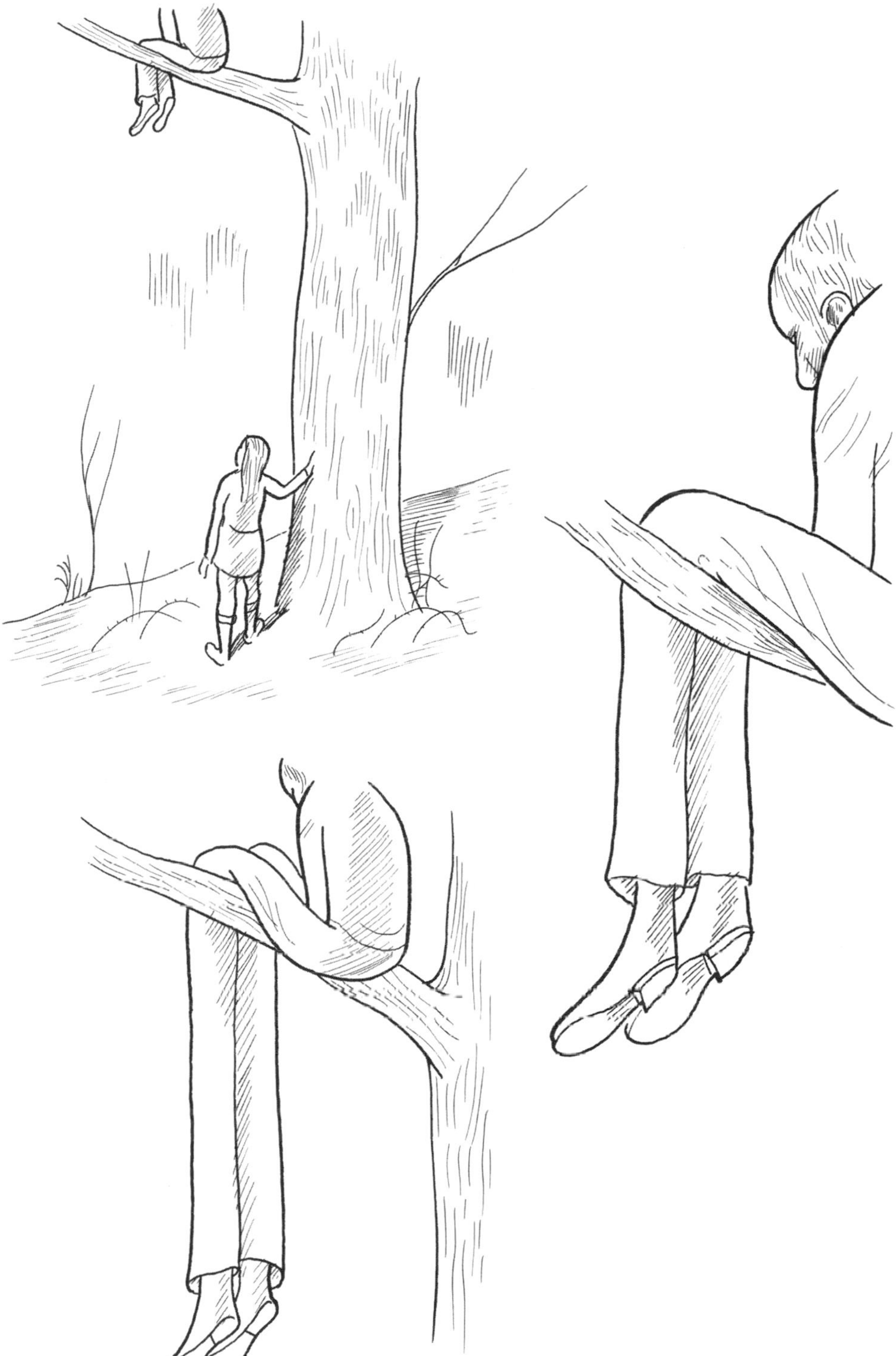

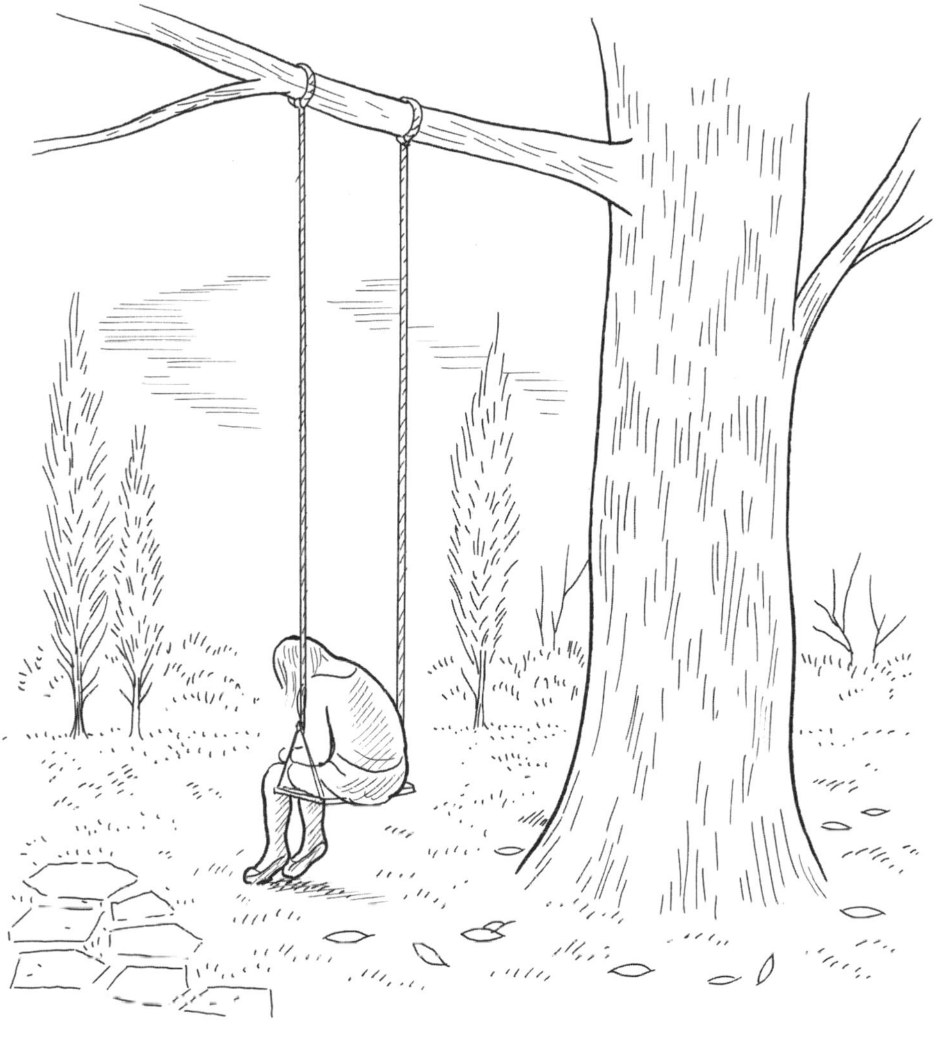

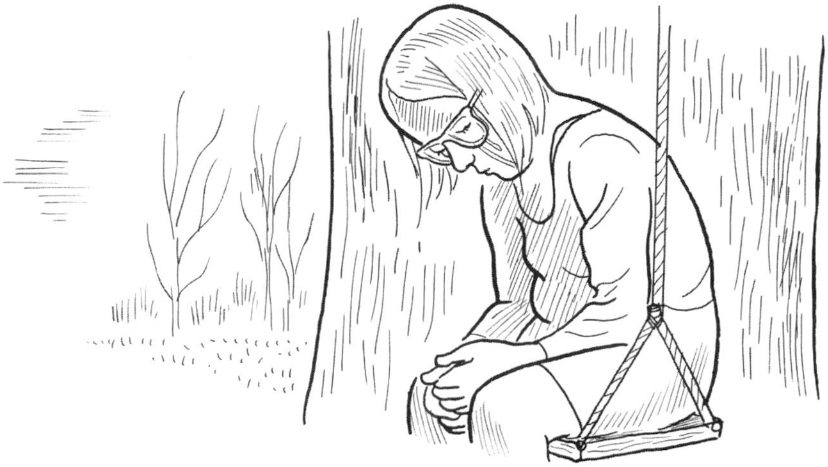

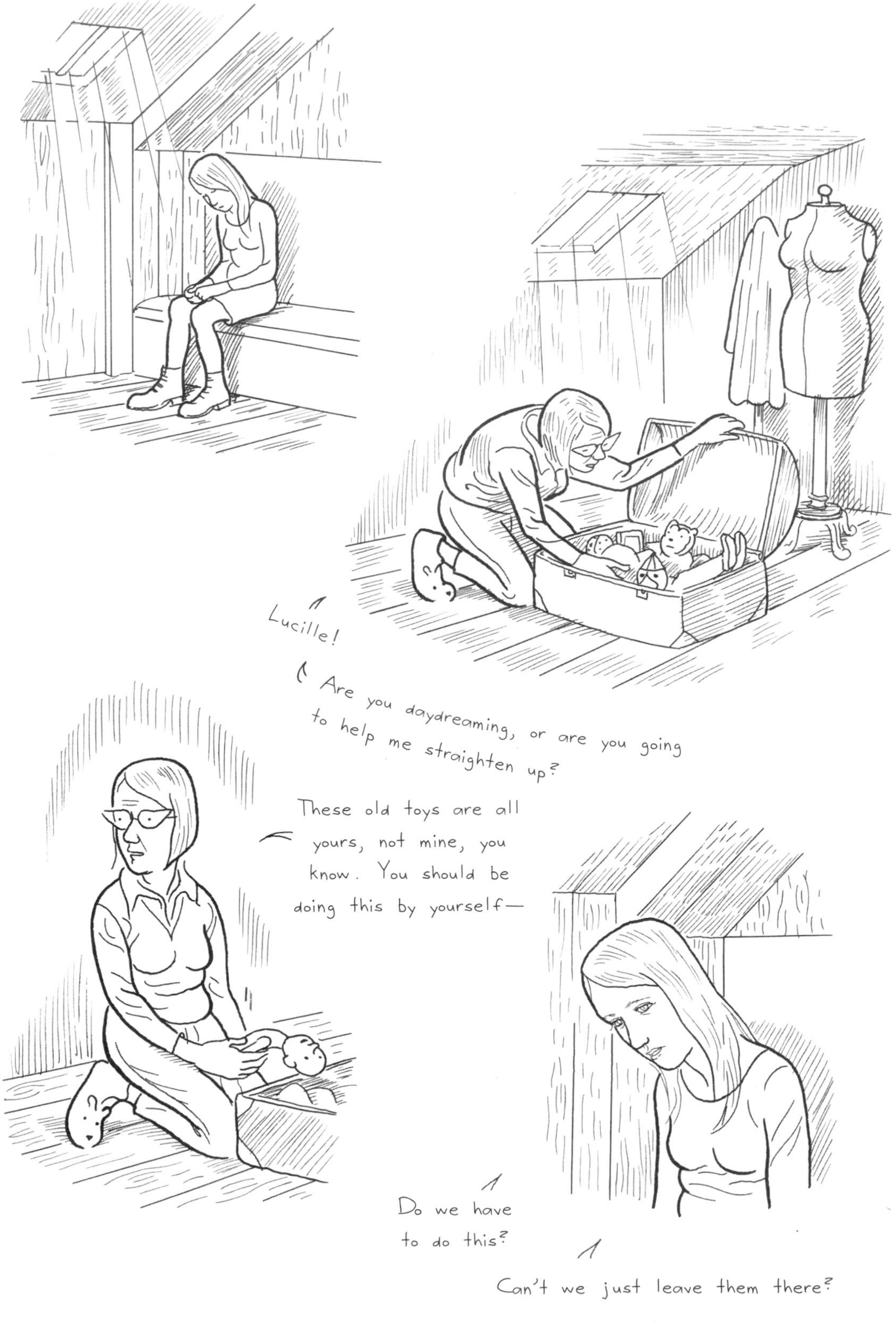
Lucille!
Are you daydreaming, or are you going to help me straighten up?
These old toys are all yours, not mine, you know. You should be doing this by yourself—
Do we have to do this?
Can't we just leave them there?

No! I've already told
you I need the space.

I've lived for other people long enough.
I've finally reached an age when I
want to do some things for me.

And my toys are stopping you?

That's enough, Lucille!

We've already gone over this. Hmph!
Besides, there are plenty of disadvantaged
children who'd love to have these toys.

What if I want to
keep them?

For—I don't know,
my...own children?

When you have your own
house, you can keep everything
you want!

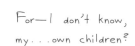

Well, I sure can't keep it all in the 150 square
foot room I'm renting right now. This is stupid.

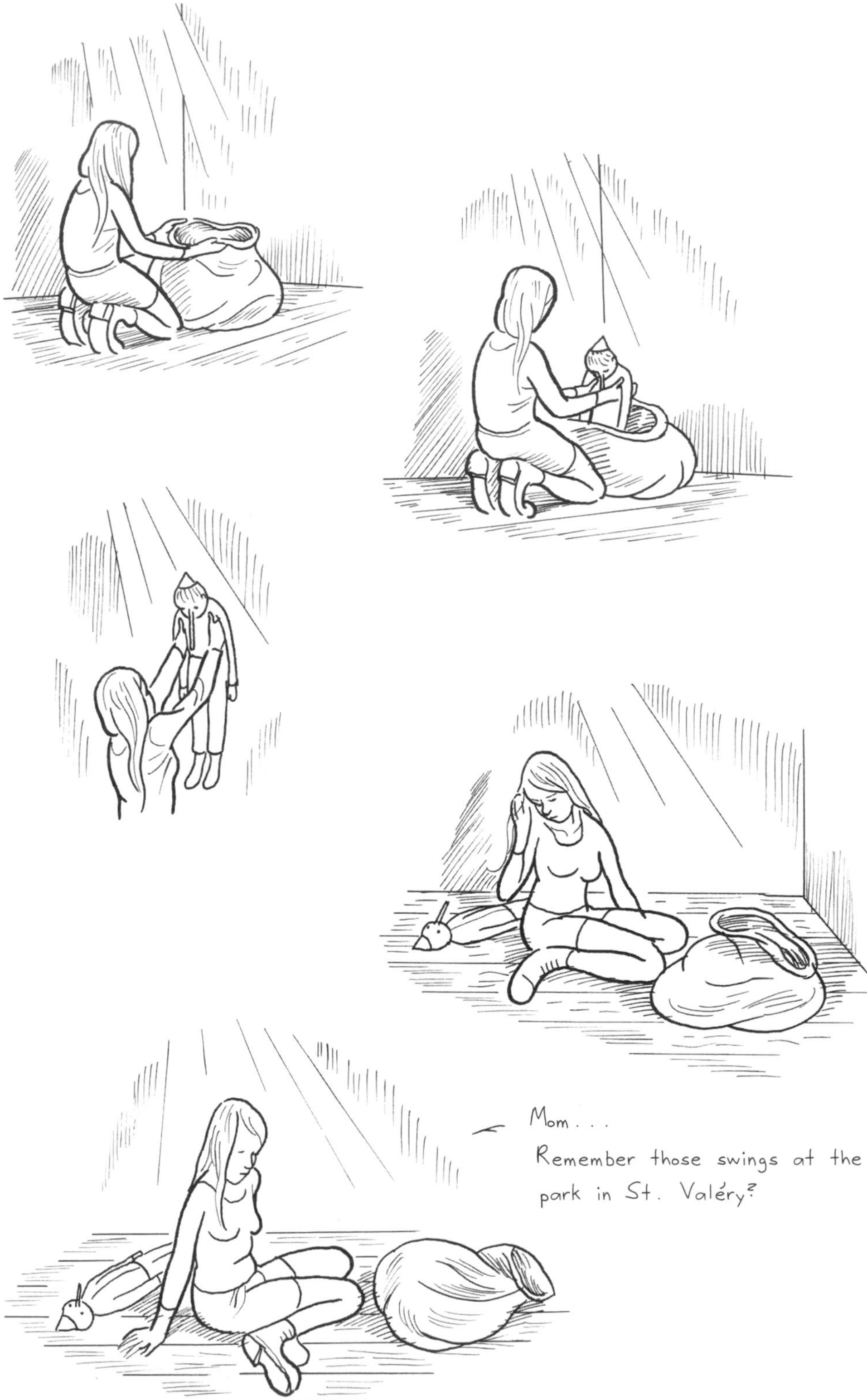
Mom . . .
Remember those swings at the park in St. Valéry?

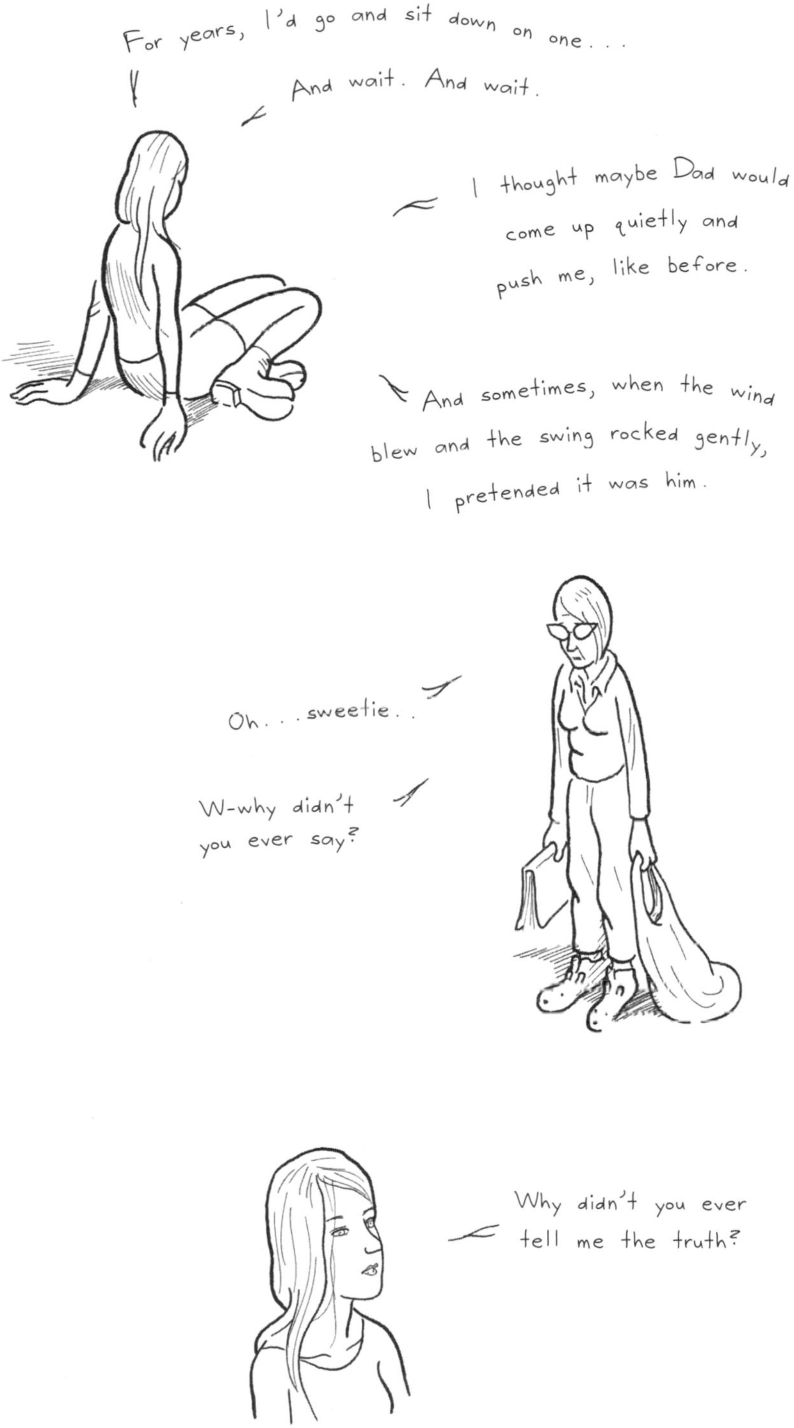
For years, I'd go and sit down on one...
And wait. And wait.
I thought maybe Dad would come up quietly and push me, like before.
And sometimes, when the wind blew and the swing rocked gently, I pretended it was him.
Oh...sweetie..
W-why didn't you ever say?
Why didn't you ever tell me the truth?

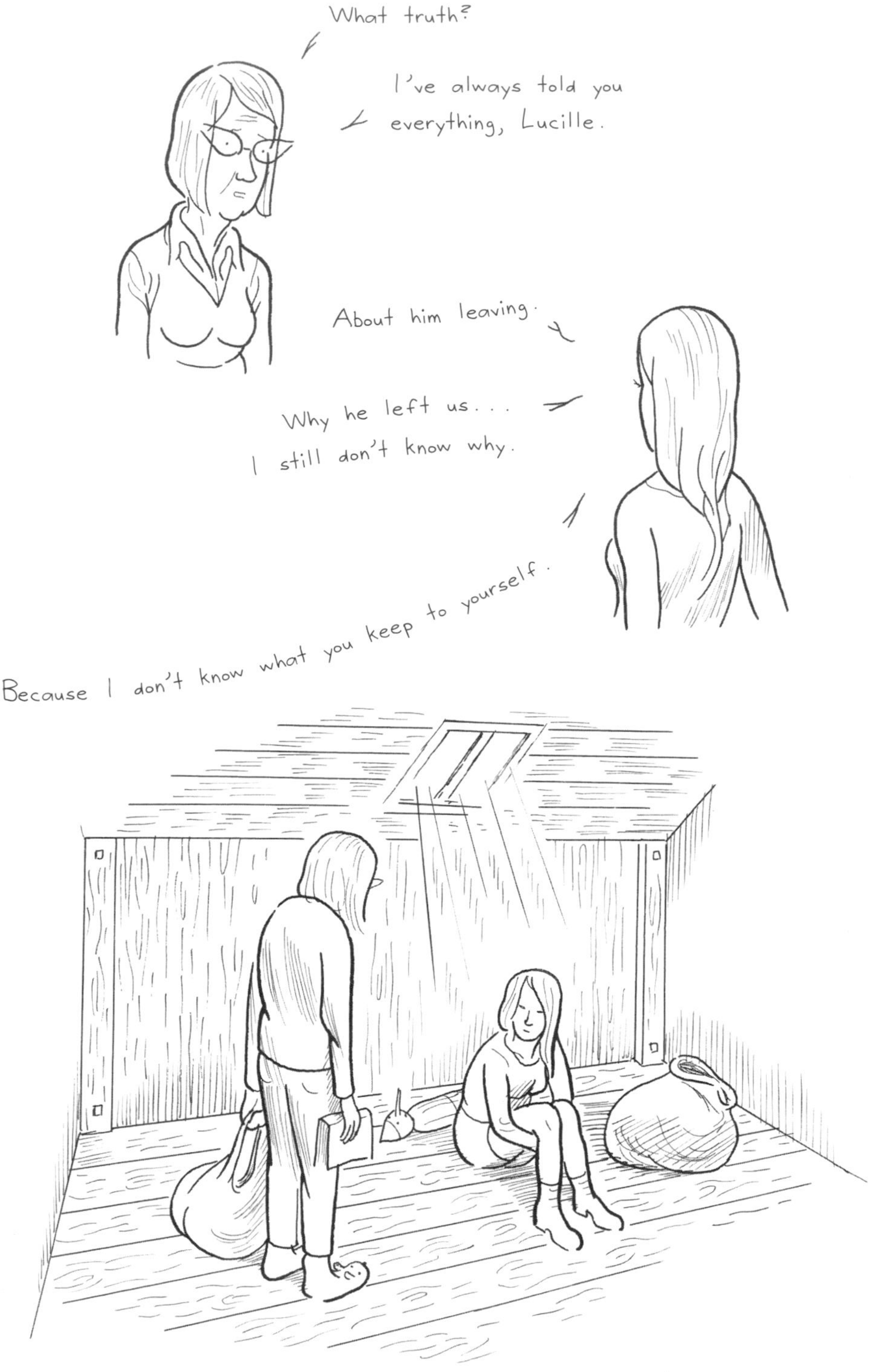
What truth?
I've always told you everything, Lucille.
About him leaving.
Why he left us...
I still don't know why.
Because I don't know what you keep to yourself.

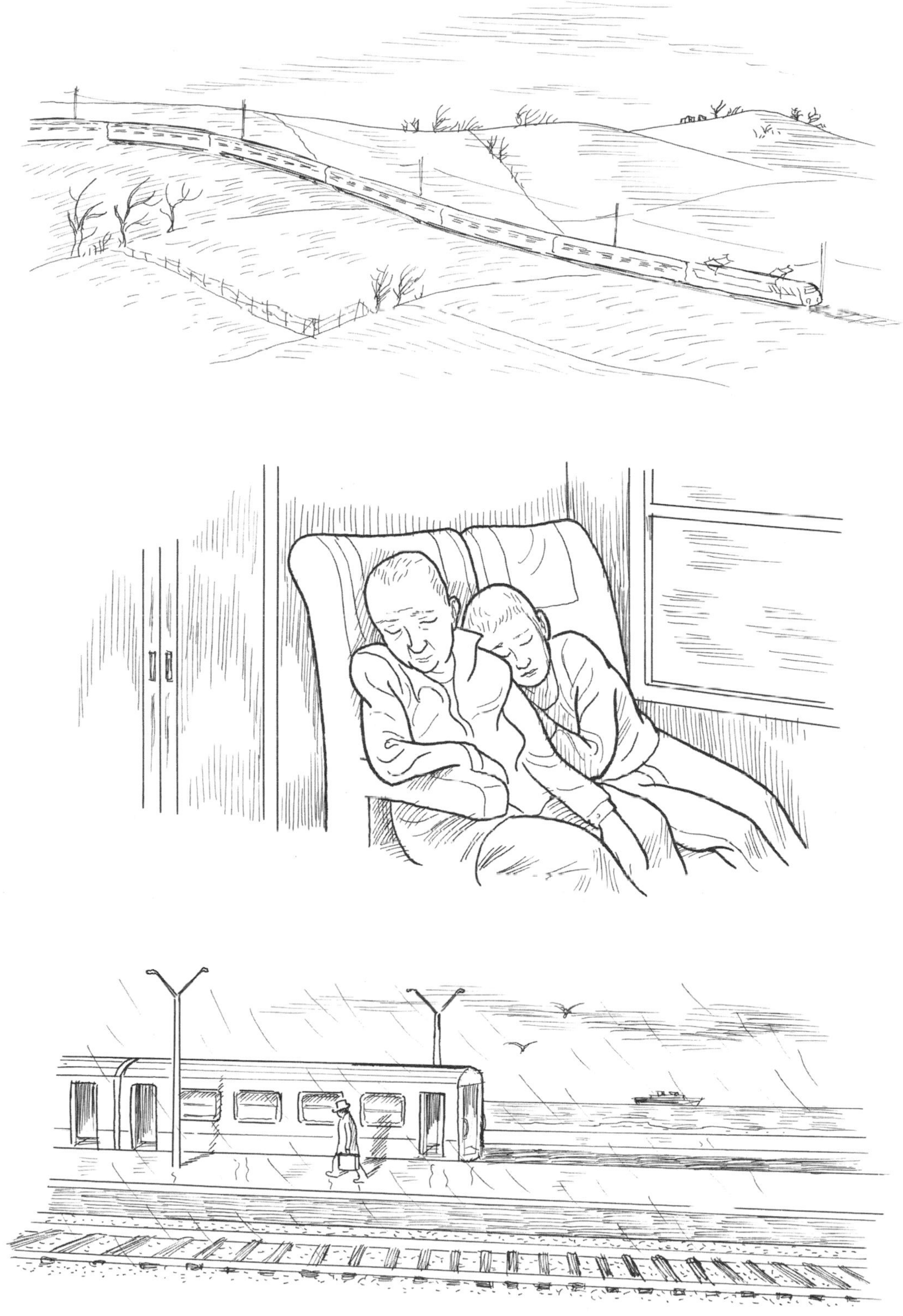

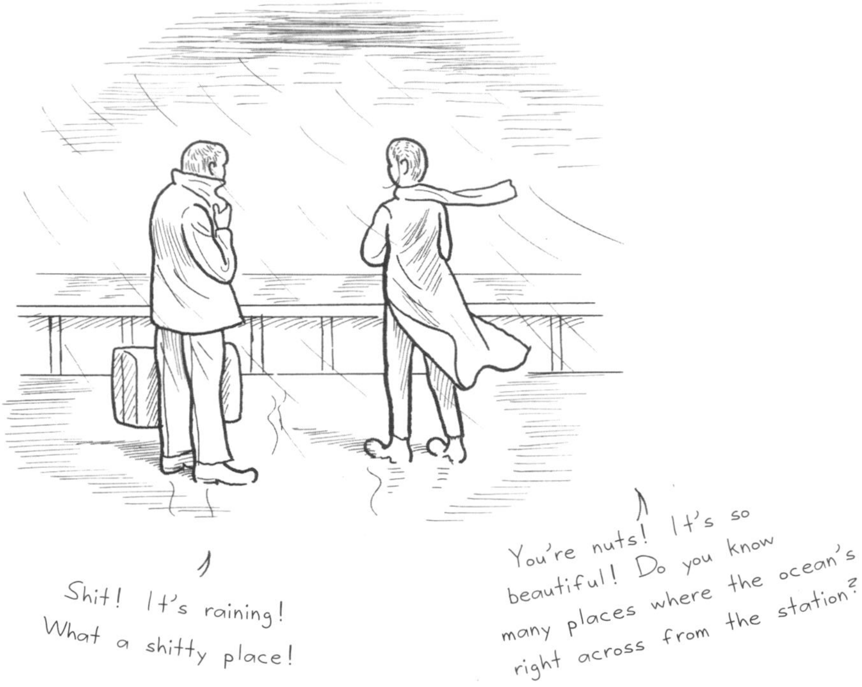
Shit! It's raining! What a shitty place!
You're nuts! It's so beautiful! Do you know many places where the ocean's right across from the station?

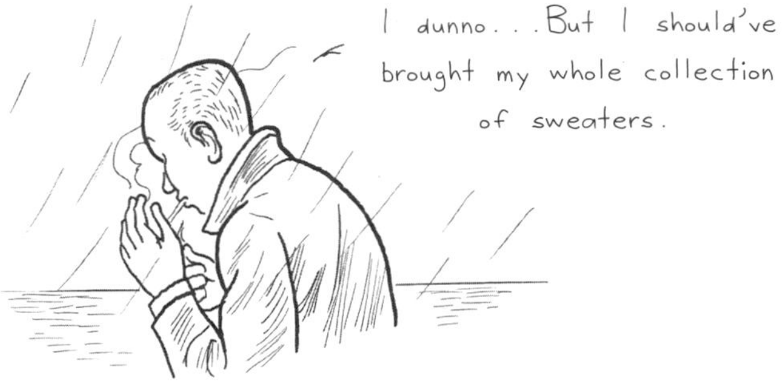
I dunno. . . But I should've brought my whole collection of sweaters.

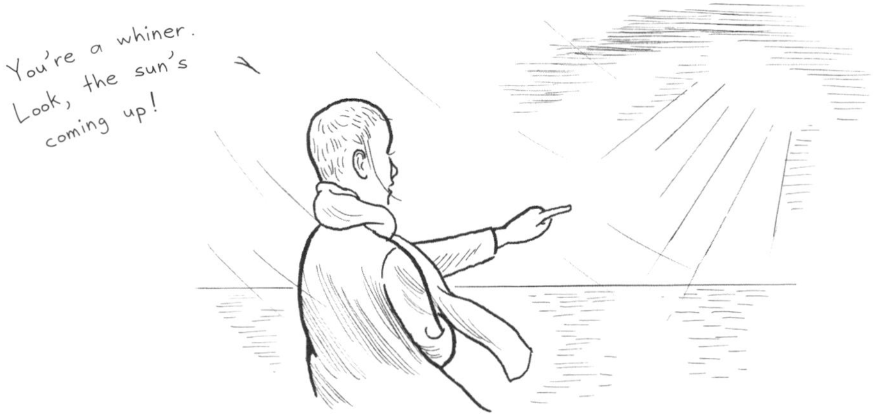
You're a whiner. Look, the sun's coming up!

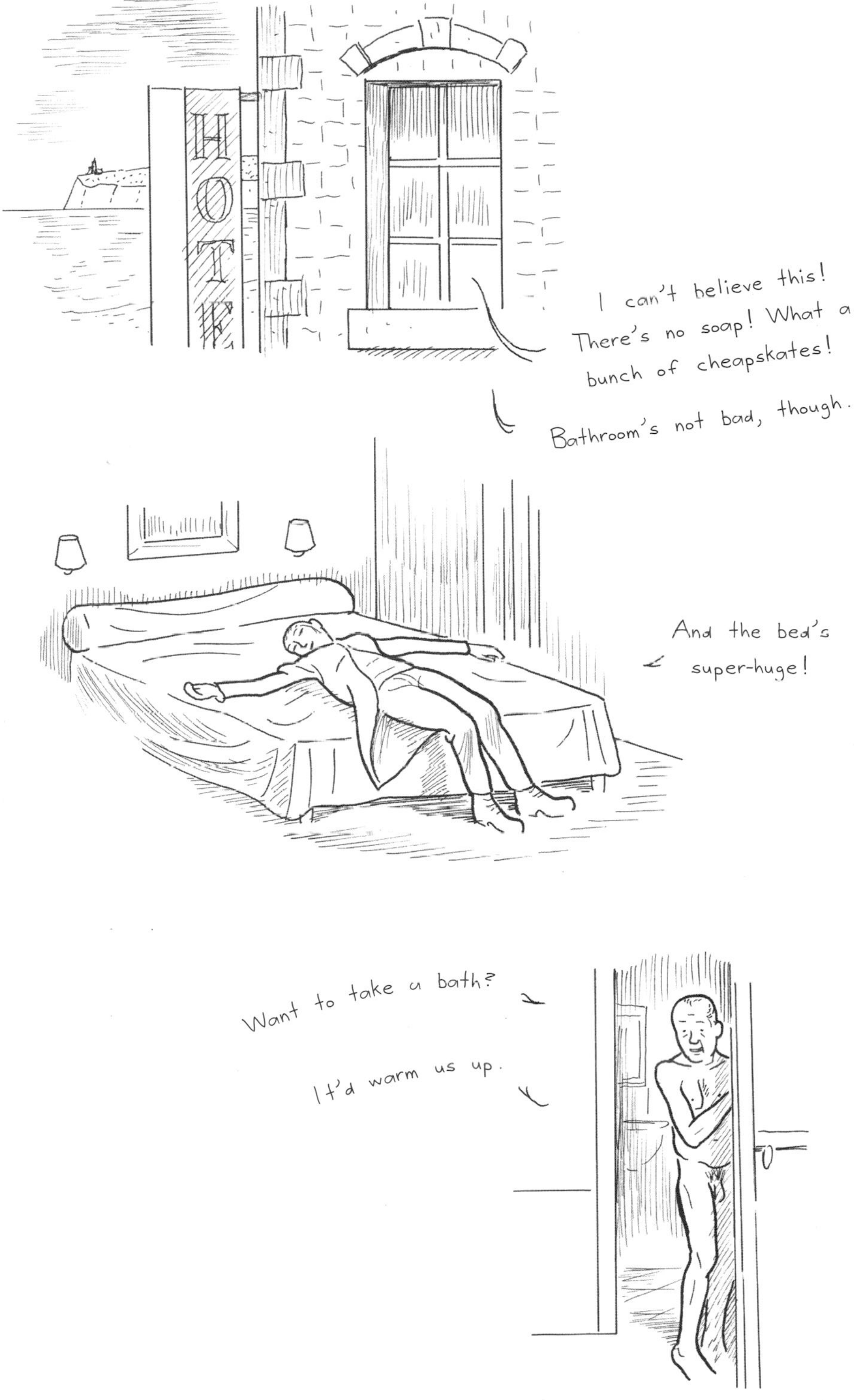
HOT
I can't believe this! There's no soap! What a bunch of cheapskates!
Bathroom's not bad, though.
And the bed's super-huge!
Want to take a bath?
It'd warm us up.

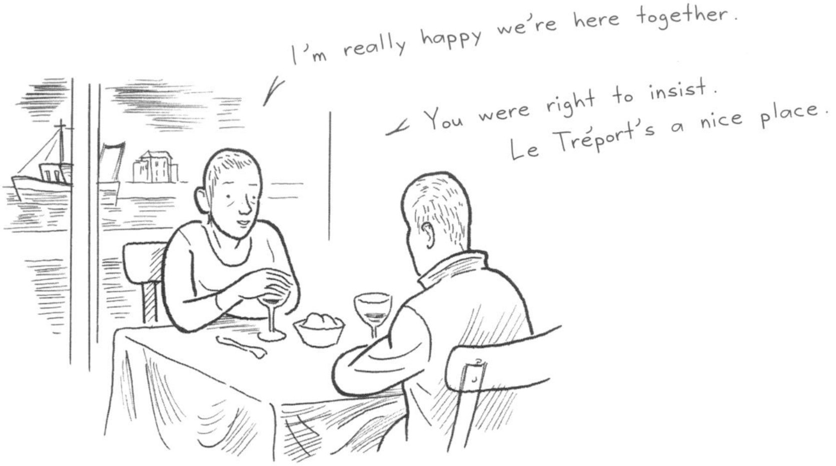
I'm really happy we're here together.
You were right to insist.
Le Tréport's a nice place.

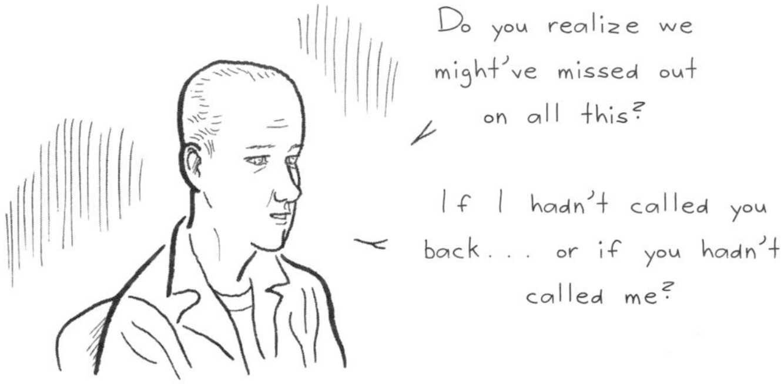
Do you realize we might've missed out on all this?
If I hadn't called you back... or if you hadn't called me?

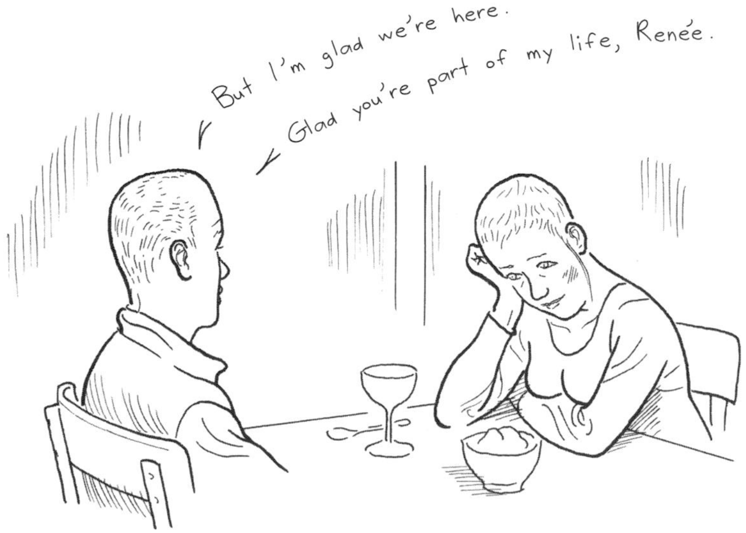
But I'm glad we're here.
Glad you're part of my life, Renée.

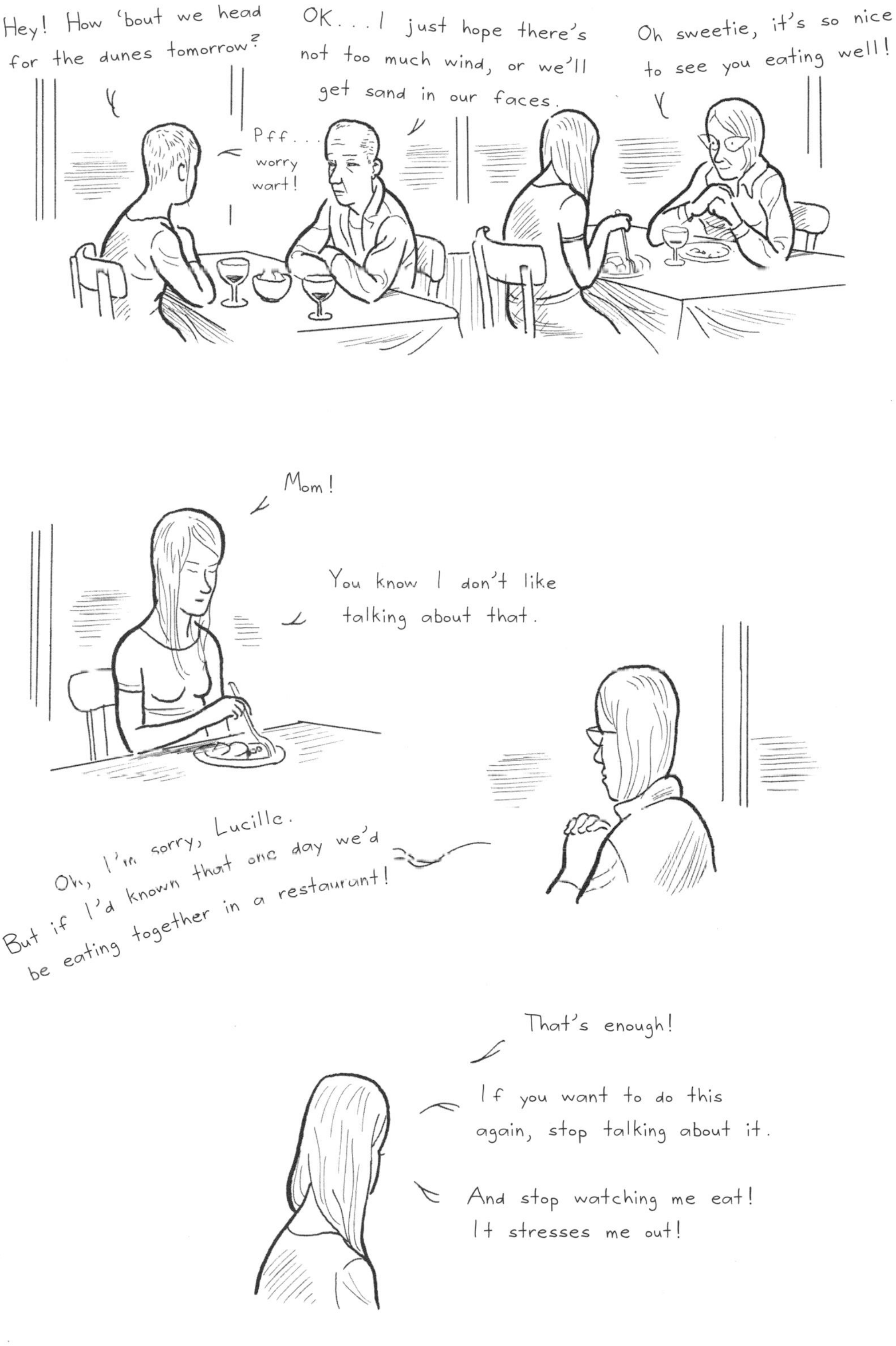
Hey! How 'bout we head for the dunes tomorrow?
Pff... worry wart!
OK... I just hope there's not too much wind, or we'll get sand in our faces.
Oh sweetie, it's so nice to see you eating well!
Mom!
You know I don't like talking about that.
Oh, I'm sorry, Lucille. But if I'd known that one day we'd be eating together in a restaurant!
That's enough!
If you want to do this again, stop talking about it.
And stop watching me eat! It stresses me out!

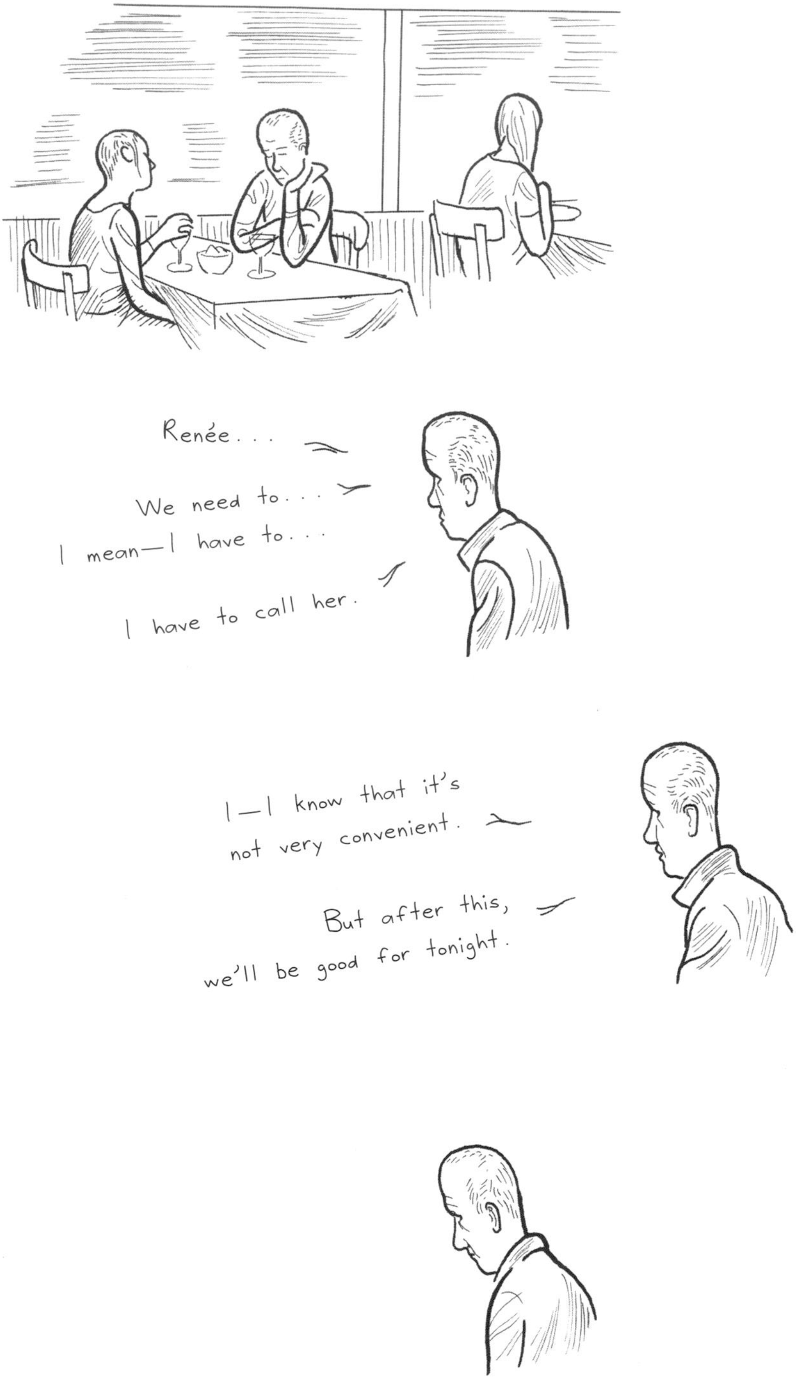
Renée...
We need to...
I mean—I have to...
I have to call her.
I—I know that it's not very convenient.
But after this, we'll be good for tonight.

Well . . .
Well, I'm going.

I'm calling her now.

You—you don't have
anything to say?

What do you want me to say, Pierre?

...I'll be back.

I won't be long.

SCRiii

Yes, darling.
We'll be on any minute now.
It's going to be a shitty
concert.

If you could see this bumfuck town...

What a nice
little restaurant!

Right, sweetie?

Jesus!
Mom, you can be
a real pain.

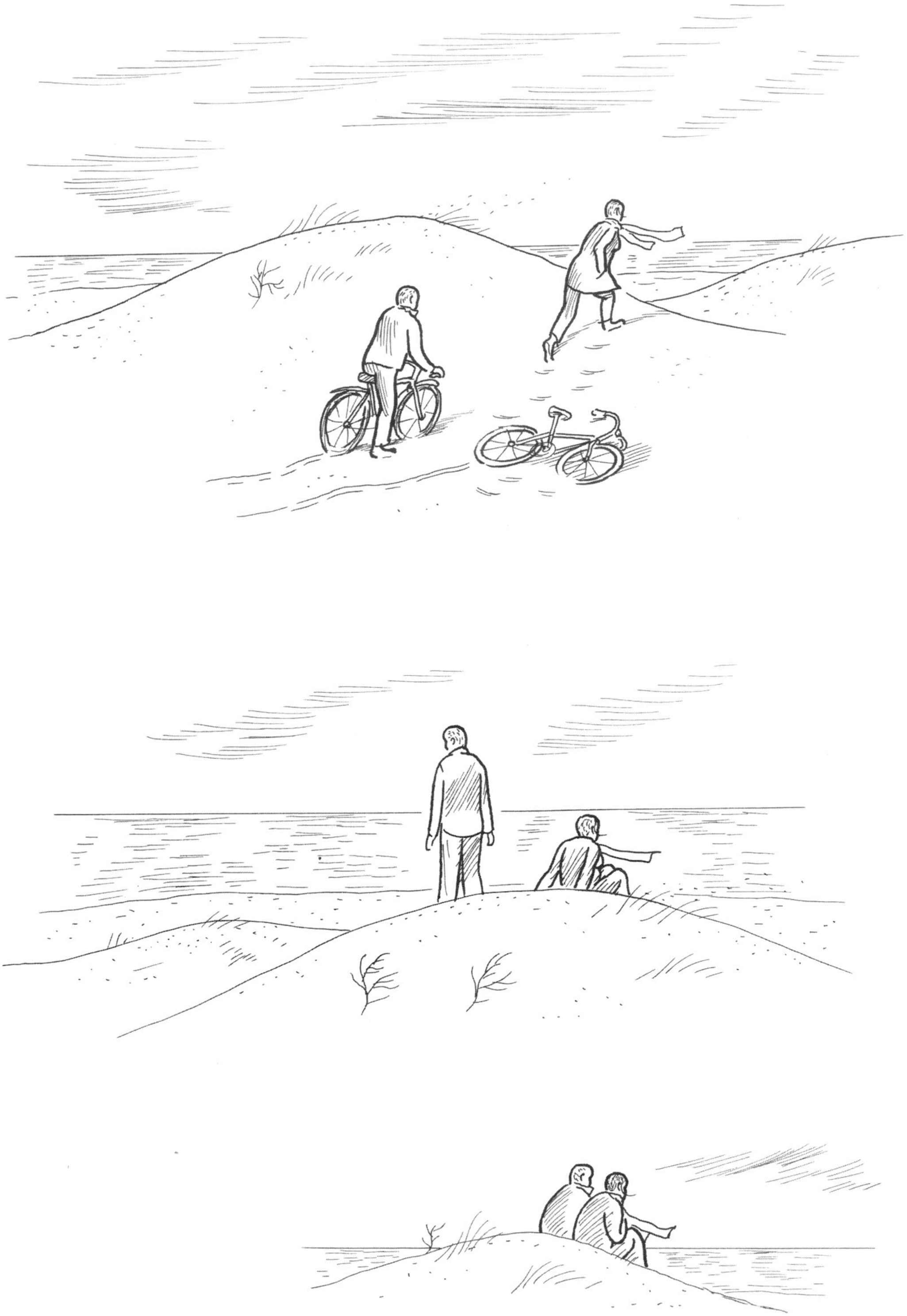

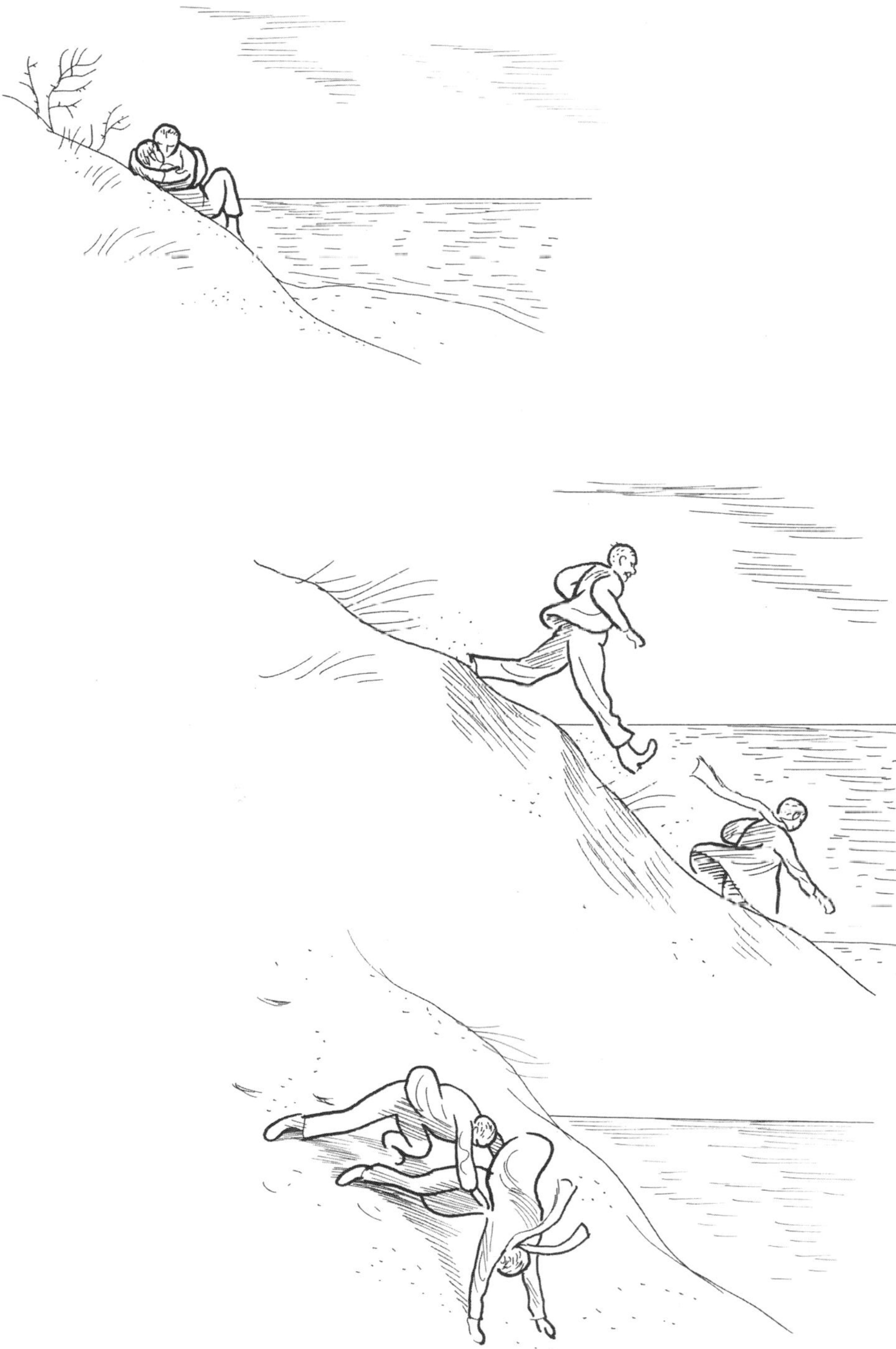

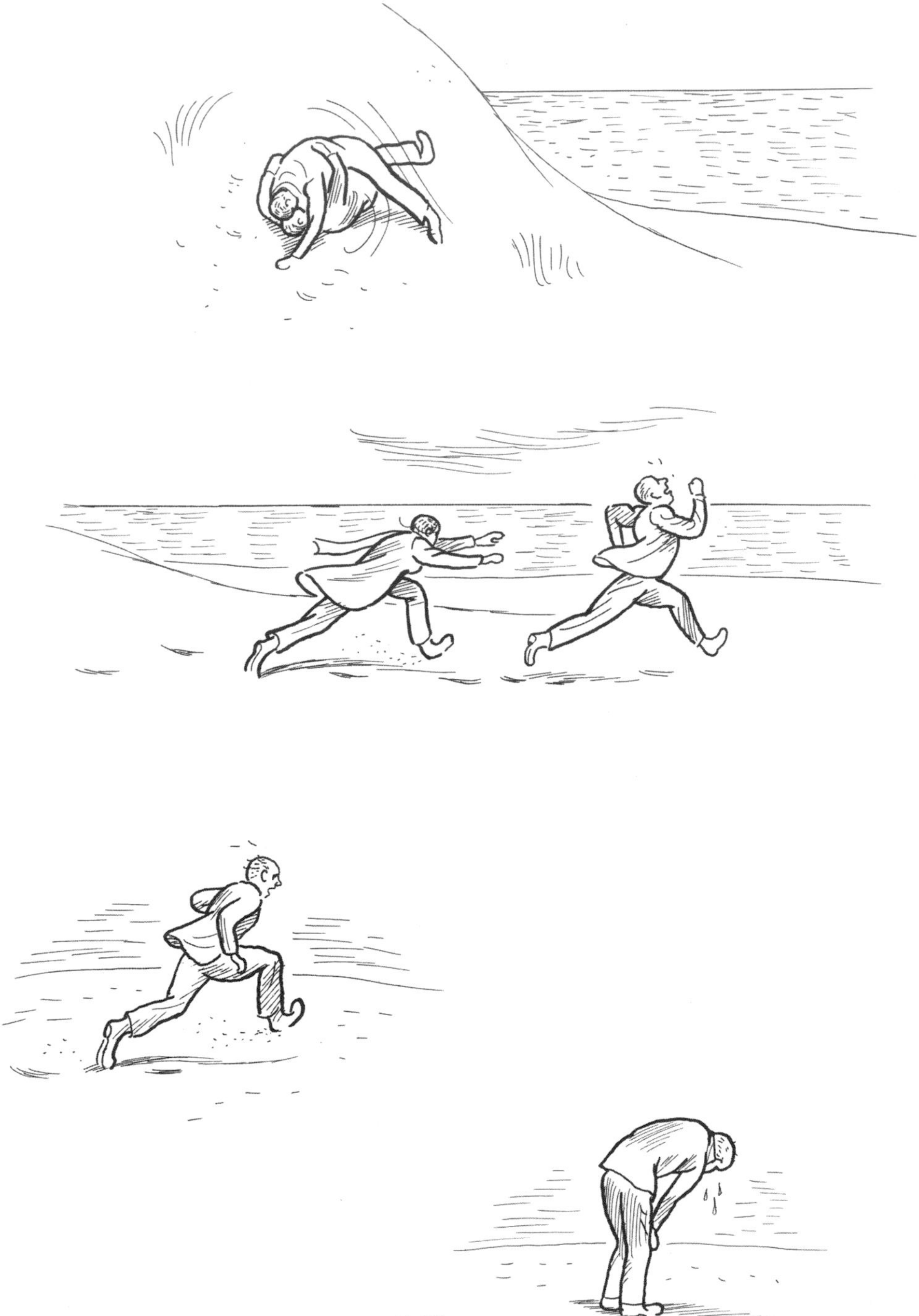

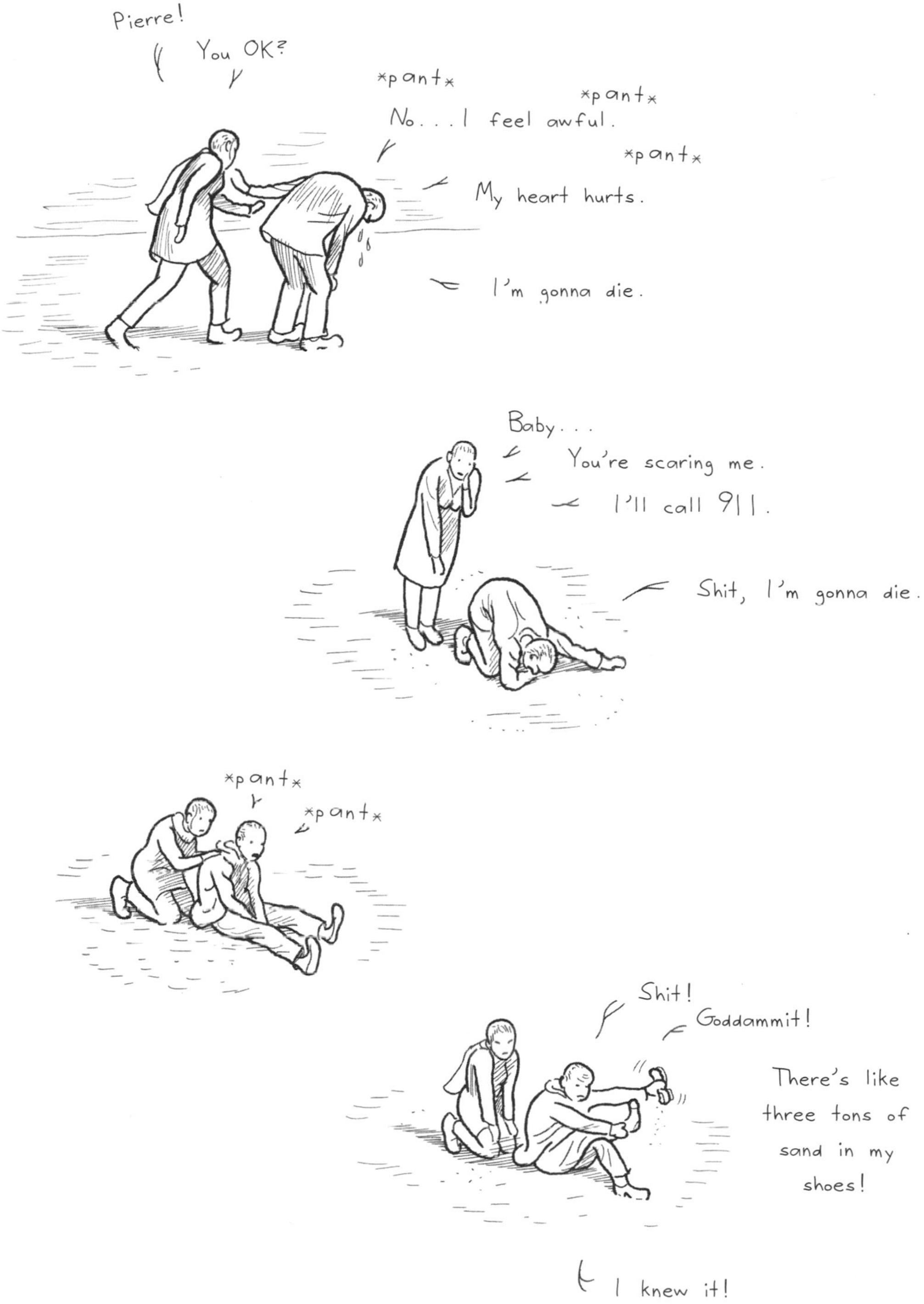
Pierre!
You OK?
pant
No... I feel awful.
pant
pant
My heart hurts.
I'm gonna die.
Baby...
You're scaring me.
I'll call 911.
Shit, I'm gonna die.
pant
pant
Shit!
Goddammit!
There's like three tons of sand in my shoes!
I knew it!

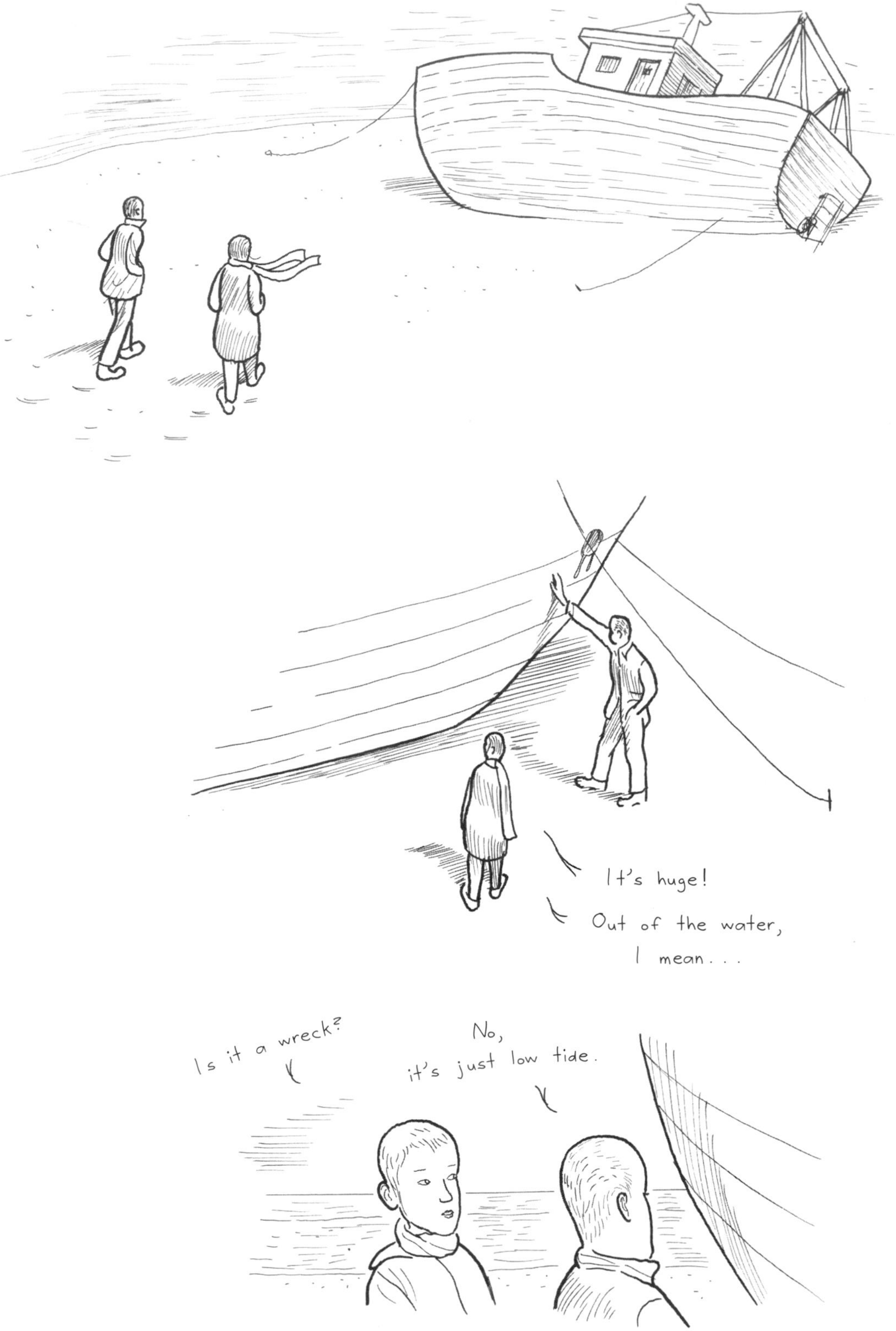
It's huge!
Out of the water, I mean...
Is it a wreck?
No, it's just low tide.

bzz

Head back to the bikes?
I'm getting cold.

Who was it?

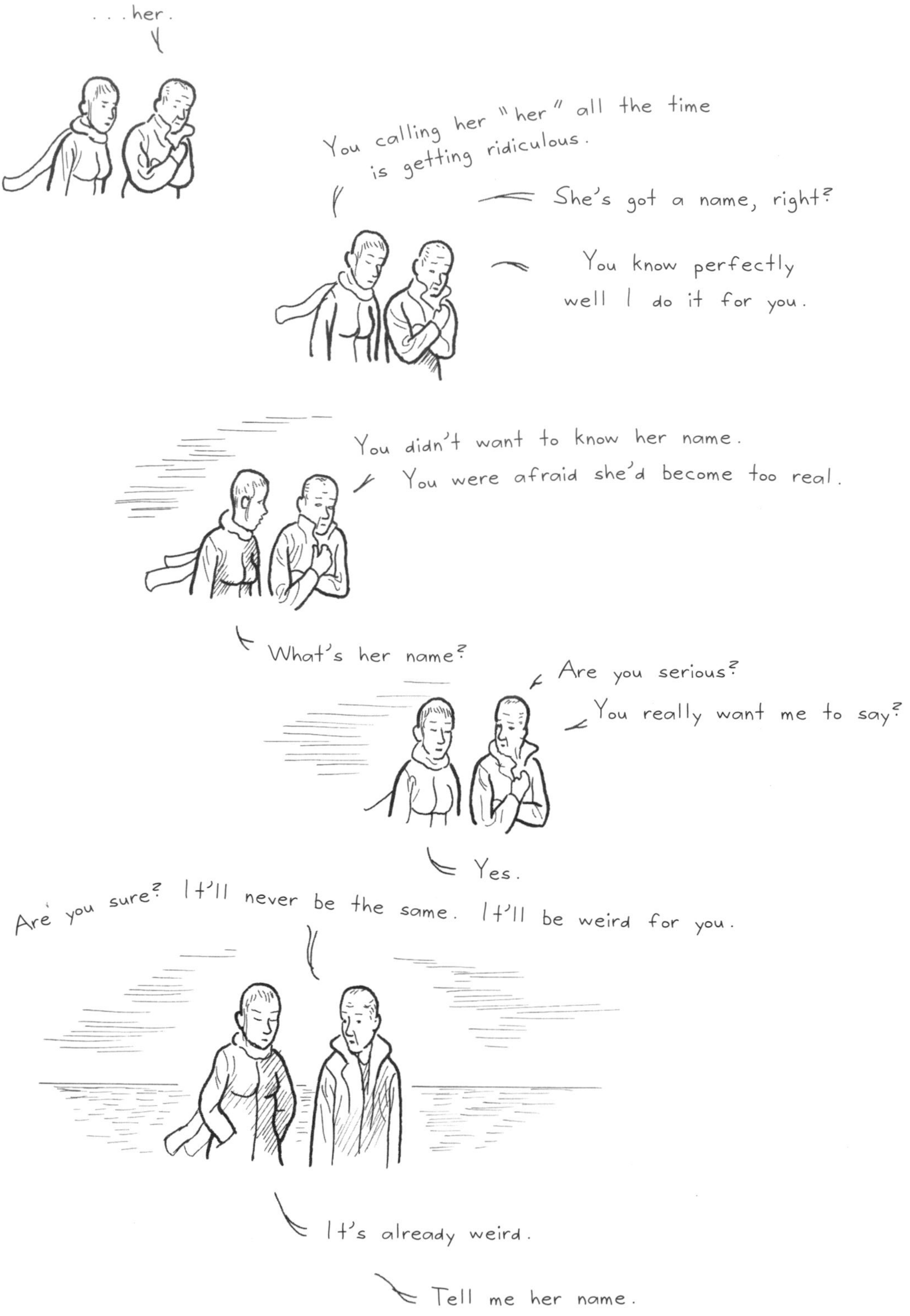
. . . her .
You calling her "her" all the time is getting ridiculous .
She's got a name, right?
You know perfectly well I do it for you .
You didn't want to know her name .
You were afraid she'd become too real .
What's her name?
Are you serious?
You really want me to say?
Yes .
Are you sure? It'll never be the same . It'll be weird for you .
It's already weird .
Tell me her name .

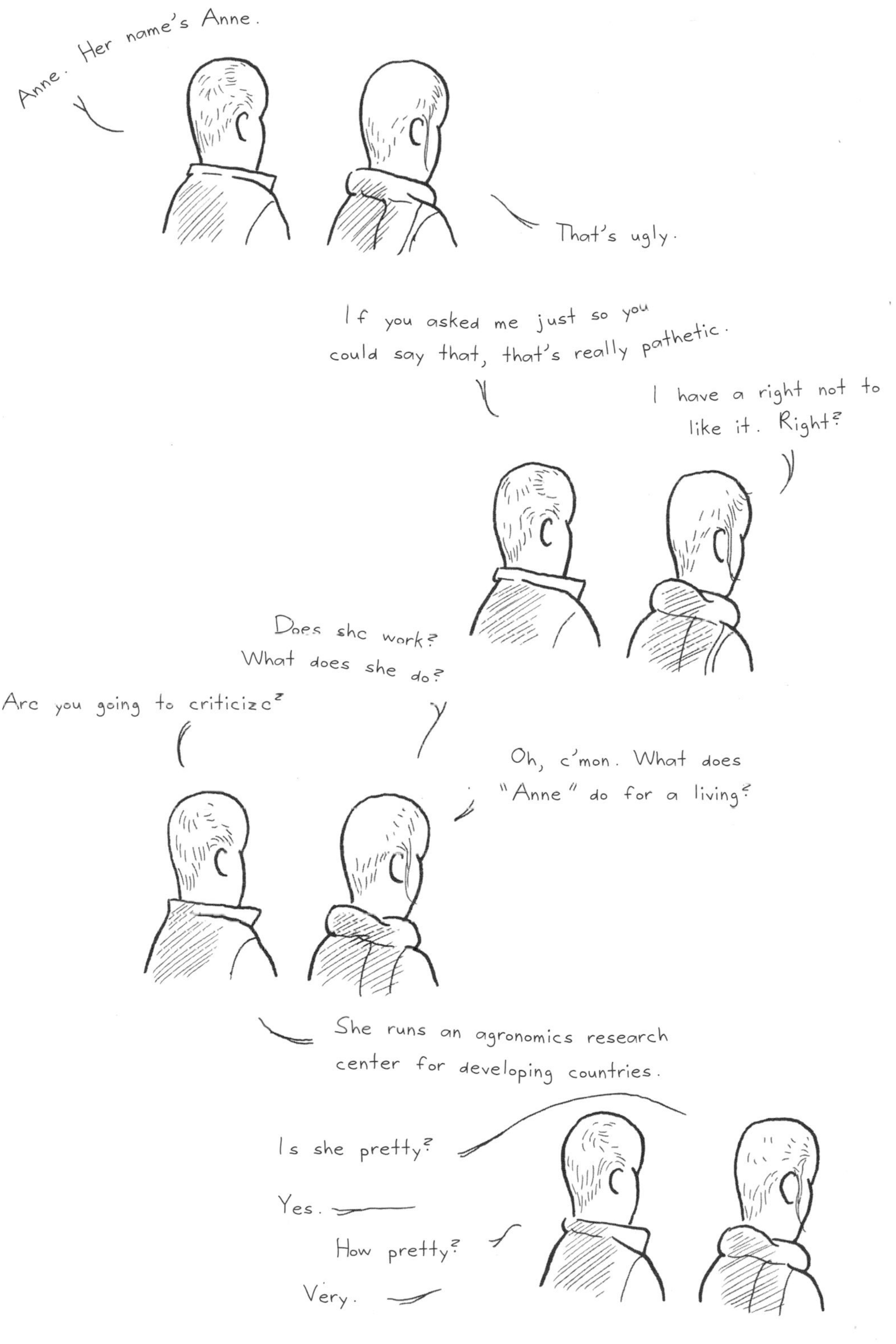
Anne. Her name's Anne.
That's ugly.
If you asked me just so you could say that, that's really pathetic.
I have a right not to like it. Right?
Does she work? What does she do?
Are you going to criticize?
Oh, c'mon. What does "Anne" do for a living?
She runs an agronomics research center for developing countries.
Is she pretty?
Yes.
How pretty?
Very.

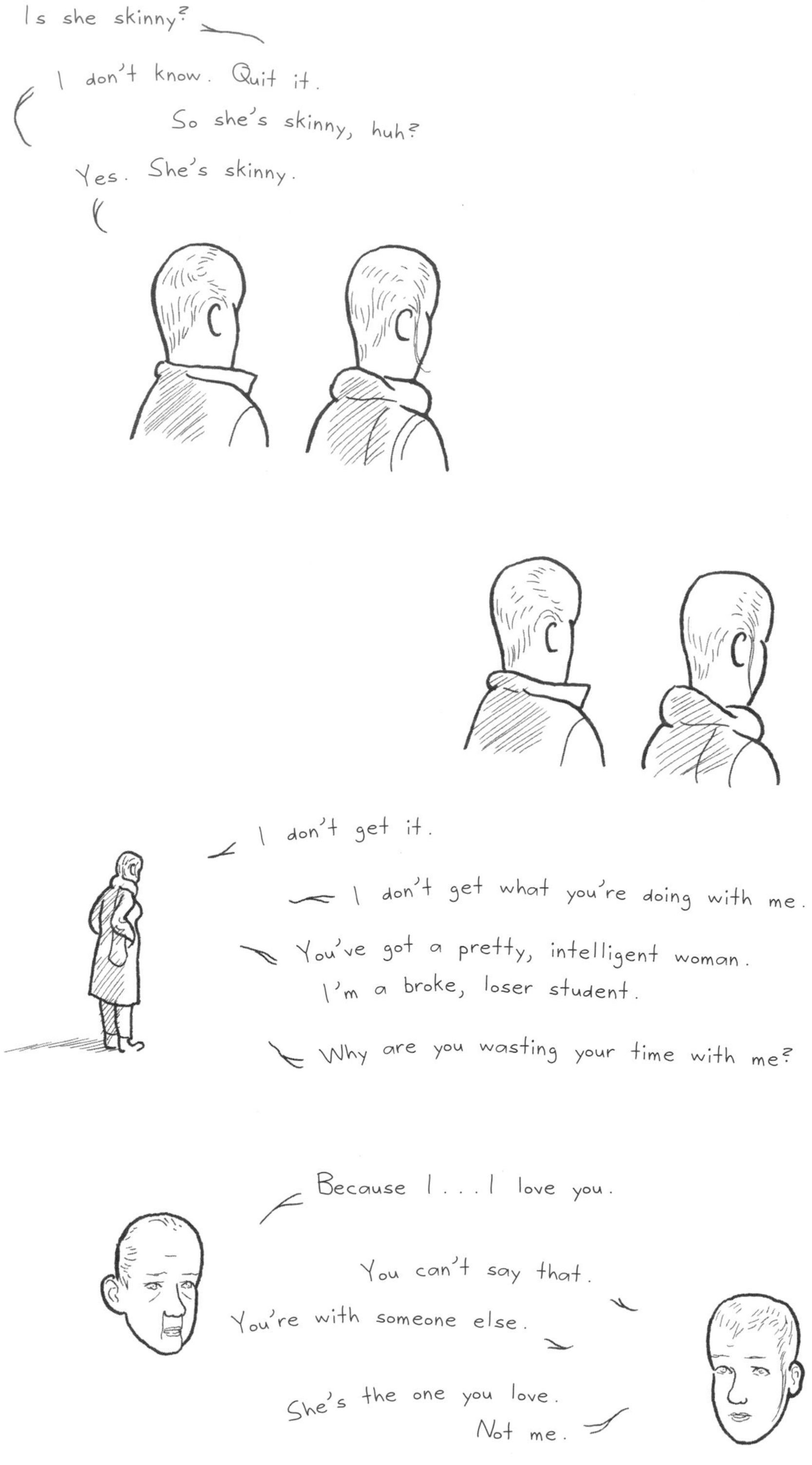
Is she skinny?
I don't know. Quit it.
So she's skinny, huh?
Yes. She's skinny.
I don't get it.
I don't get what you're doing with me.
You've got a pretty, intelligent woman.
I'm a broke, loser student.
Why are you wasting your time with me?
Because I . . . I love you.
You can't say that.
You're with someone else.
She's the one you love.
Not me.

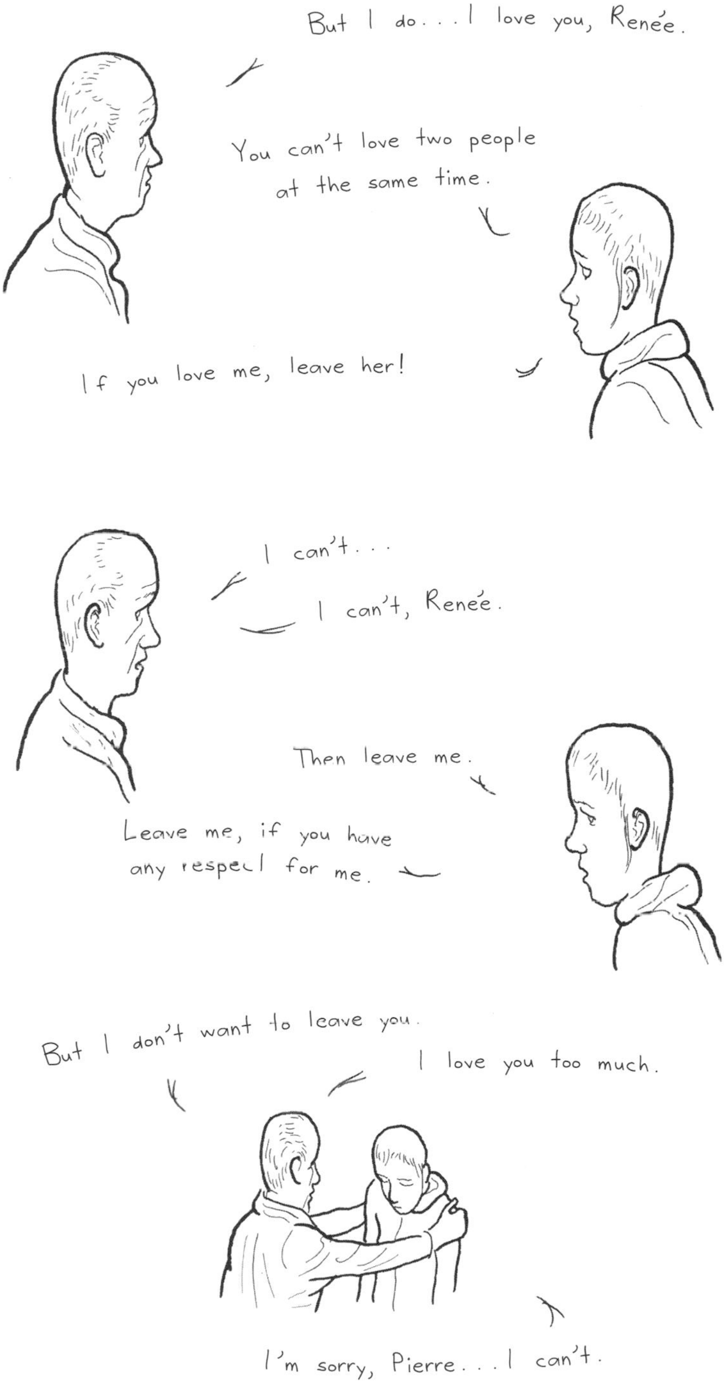
But I do...I love you, Renée.
You can't love two people at the same time.
If you love me, leave her!
I can't...
I can't, Renée.
Then leave me.
Leave me, if you have any respect for me.
But I don't want to leave you.
I love you too much.
I'm sorry, Pierre...I can't.

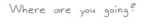

Where are you going?

If you really wanted me, you wouldn't make me live like this.

Don't fucking touch me!

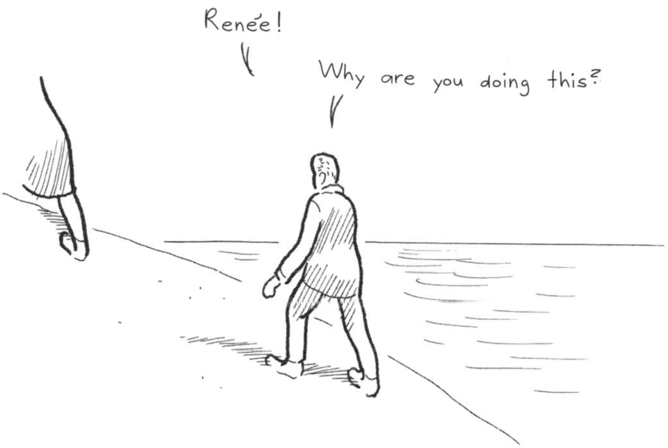

Renée!
Why are you doing this?

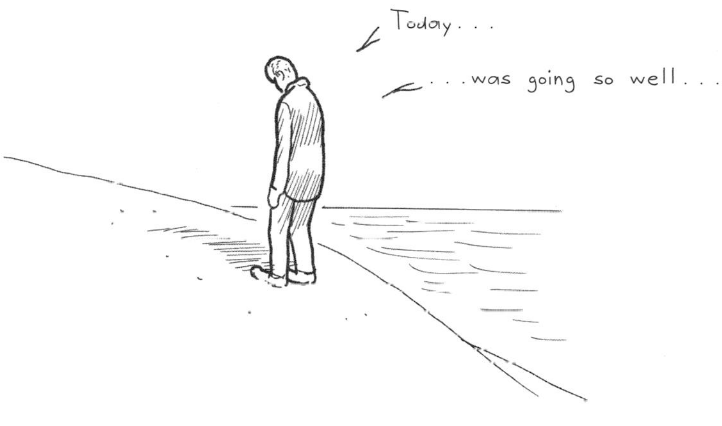

Today...
...was going so well...

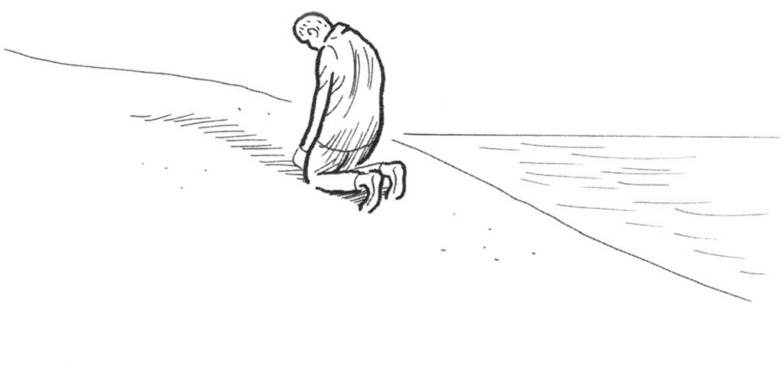

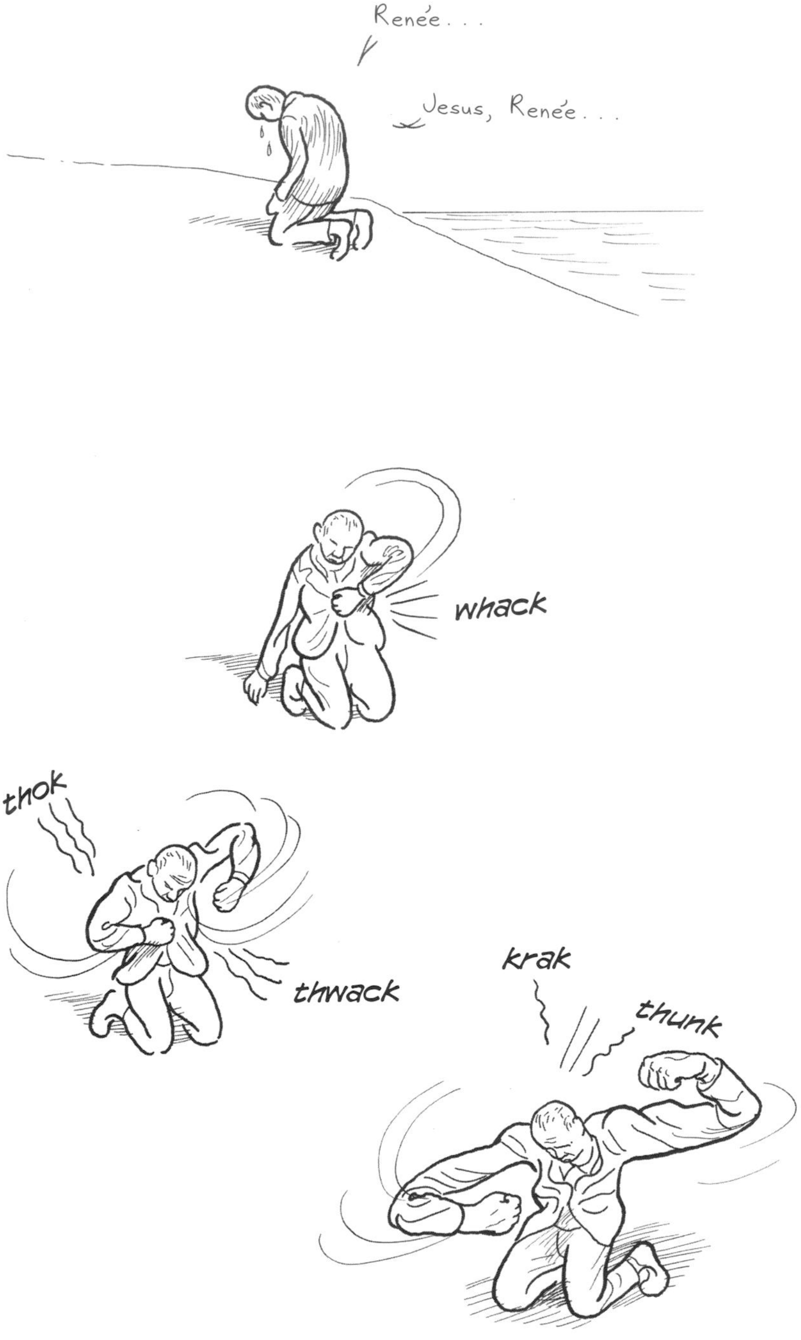
Renée...
Jesus, Renée...
whack
thok
thwack
krak
thunk

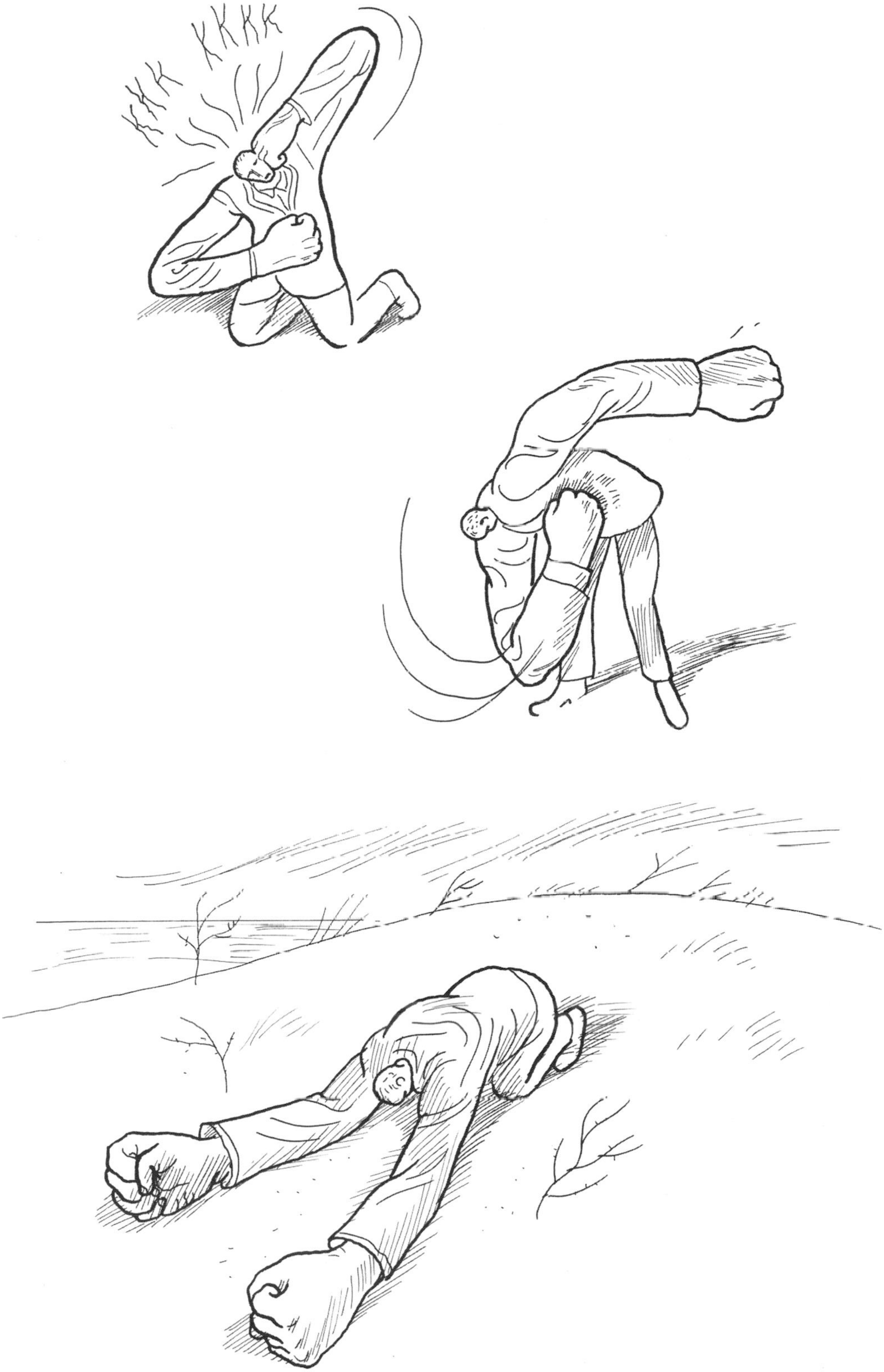

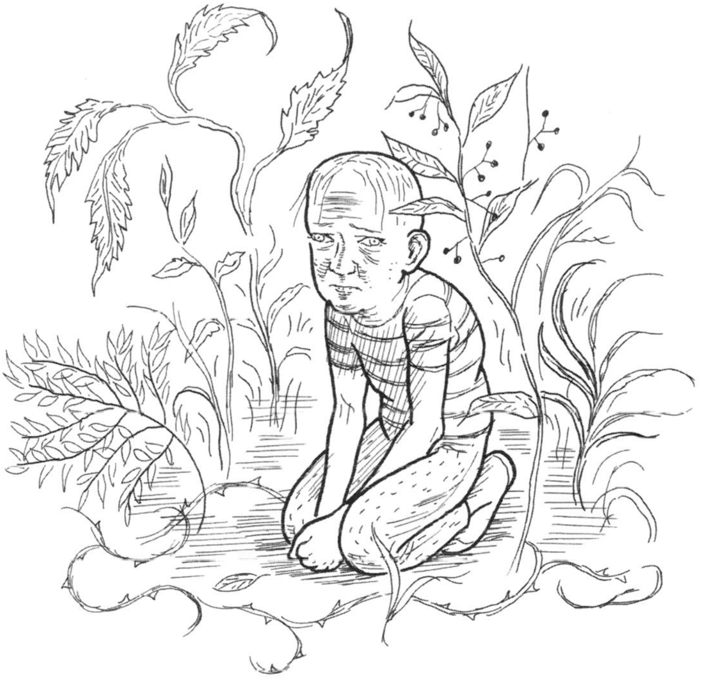

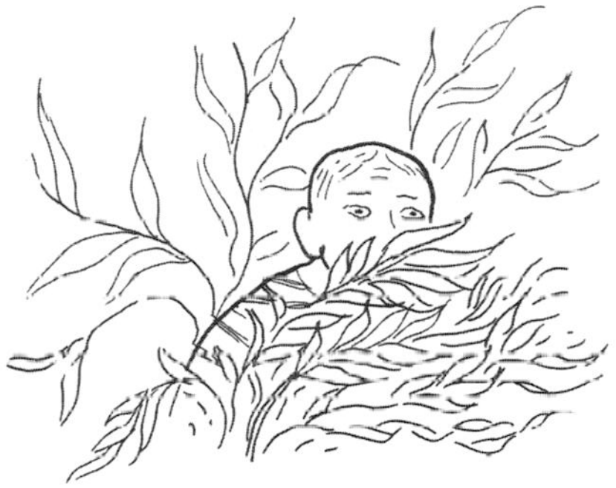

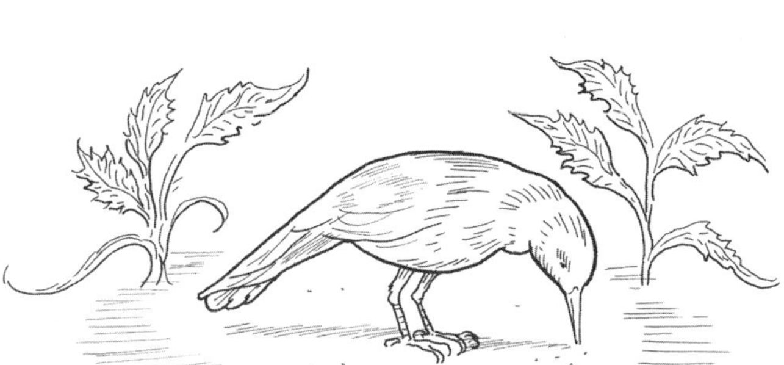

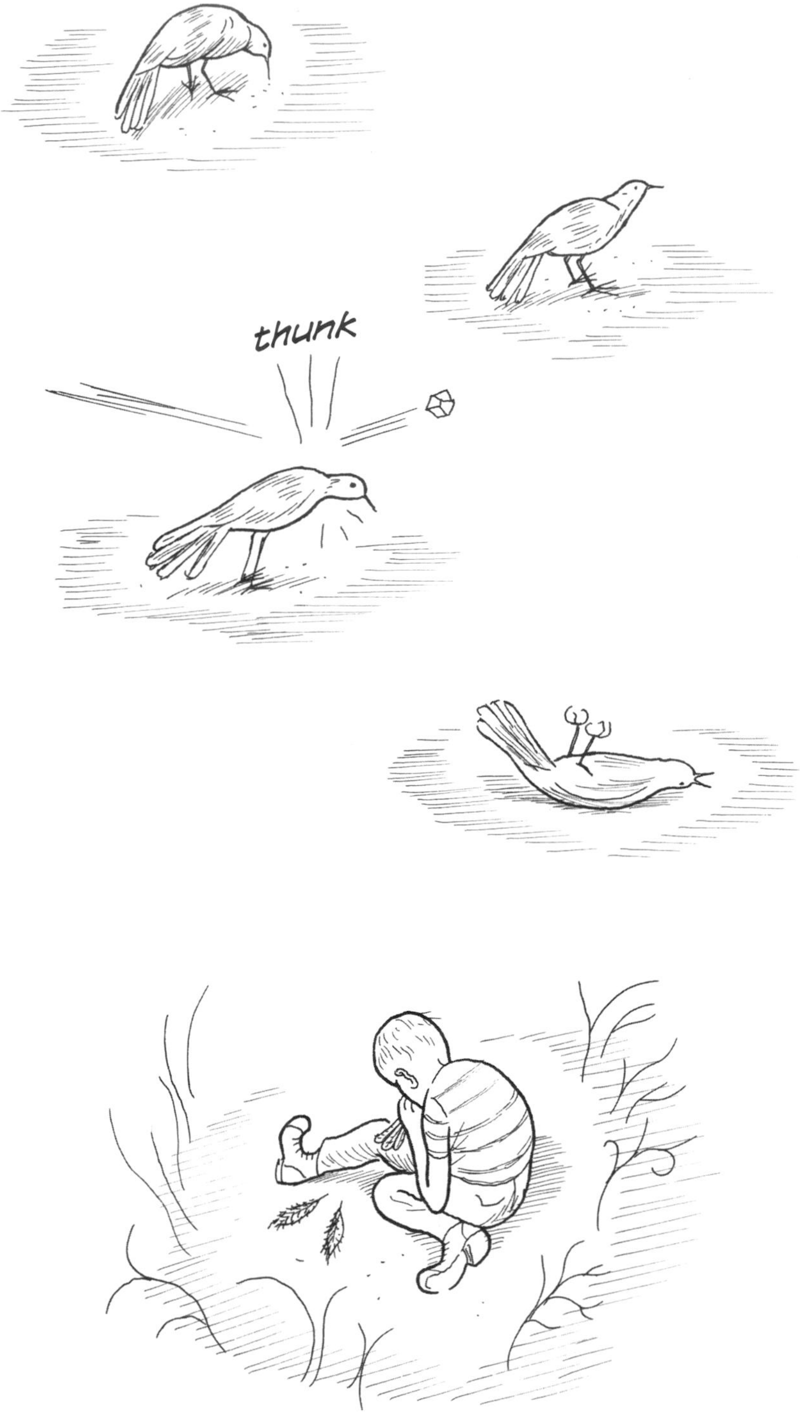
thunk

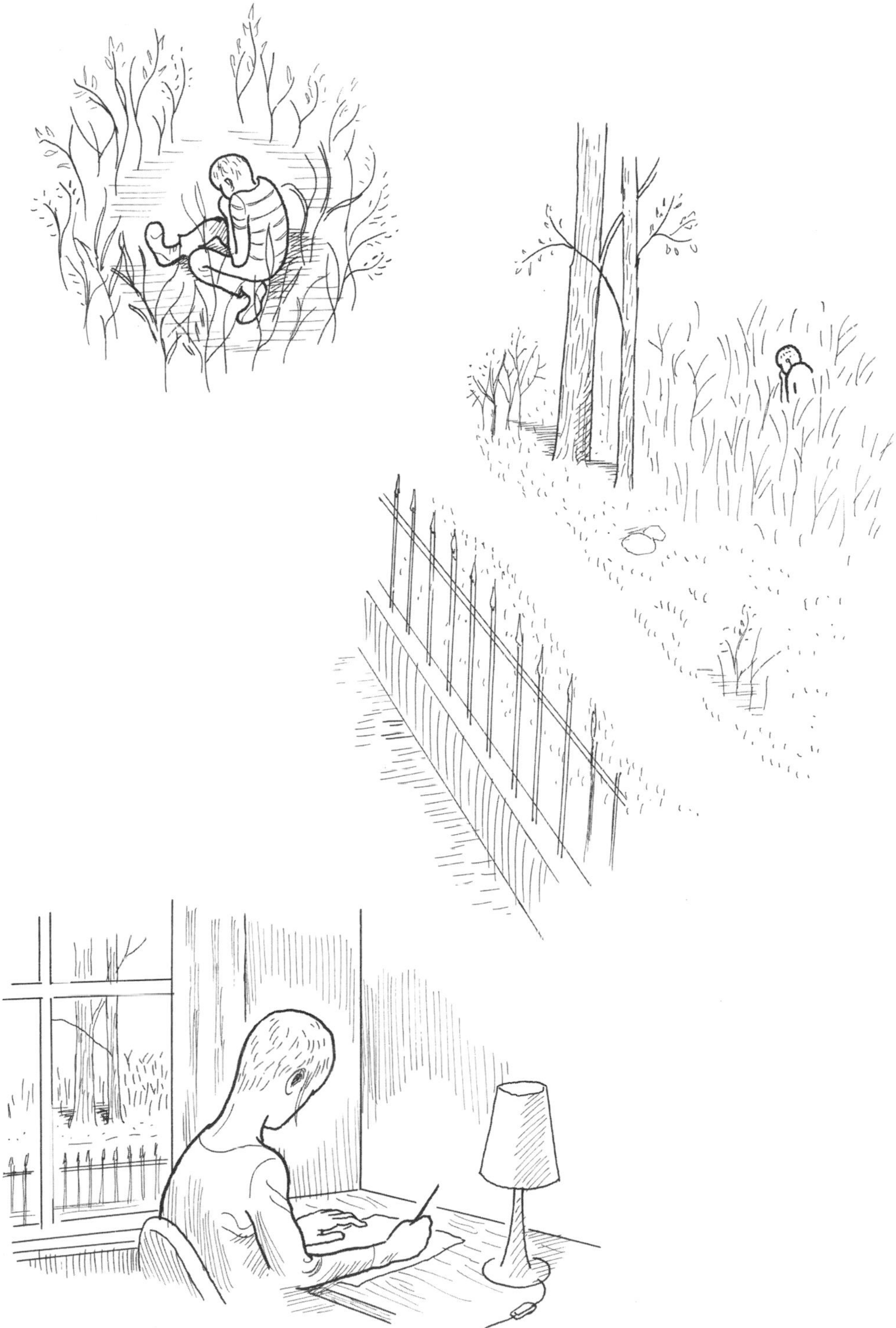

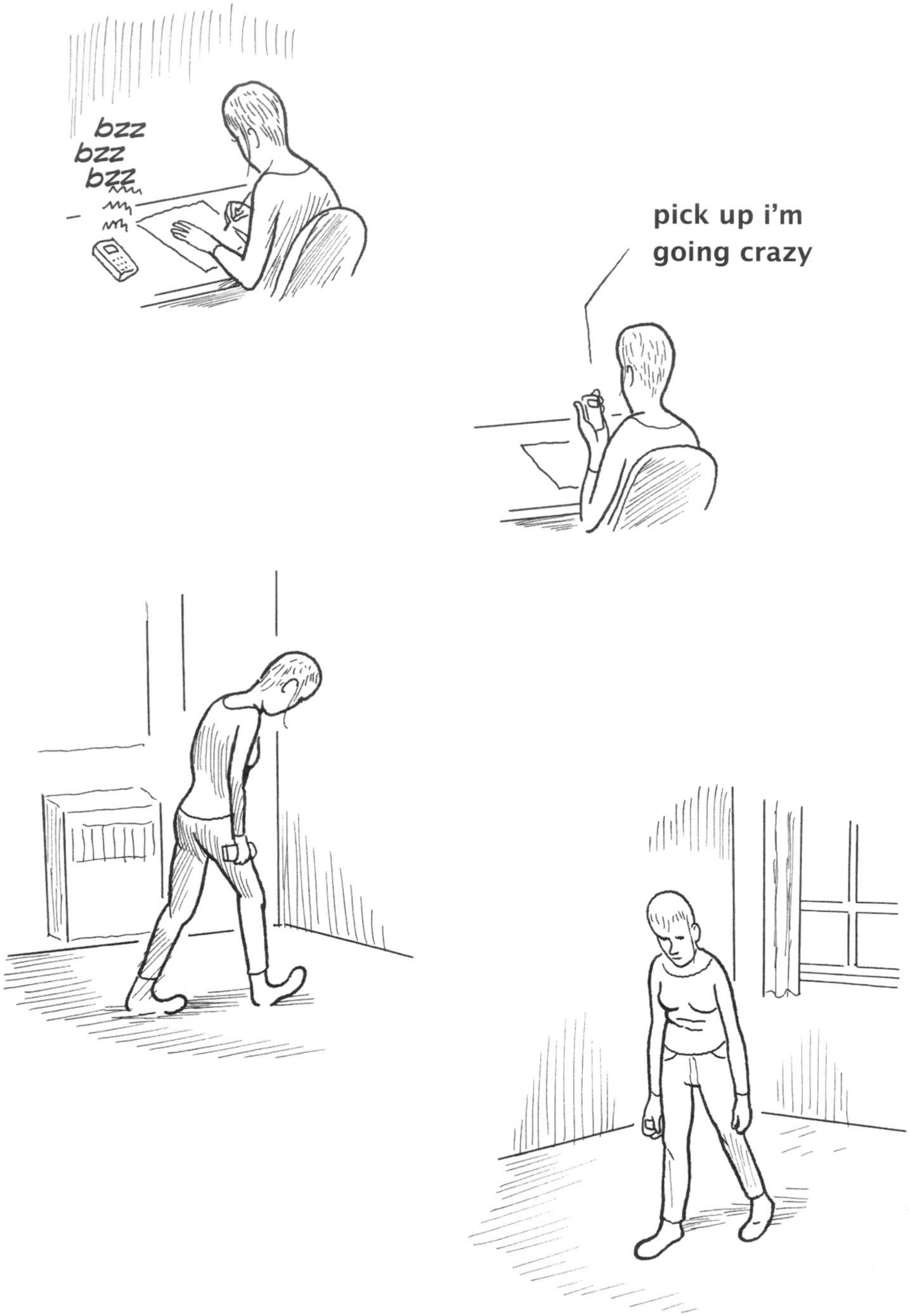
bzz
bzz
bzz
pick up i'm going crazy

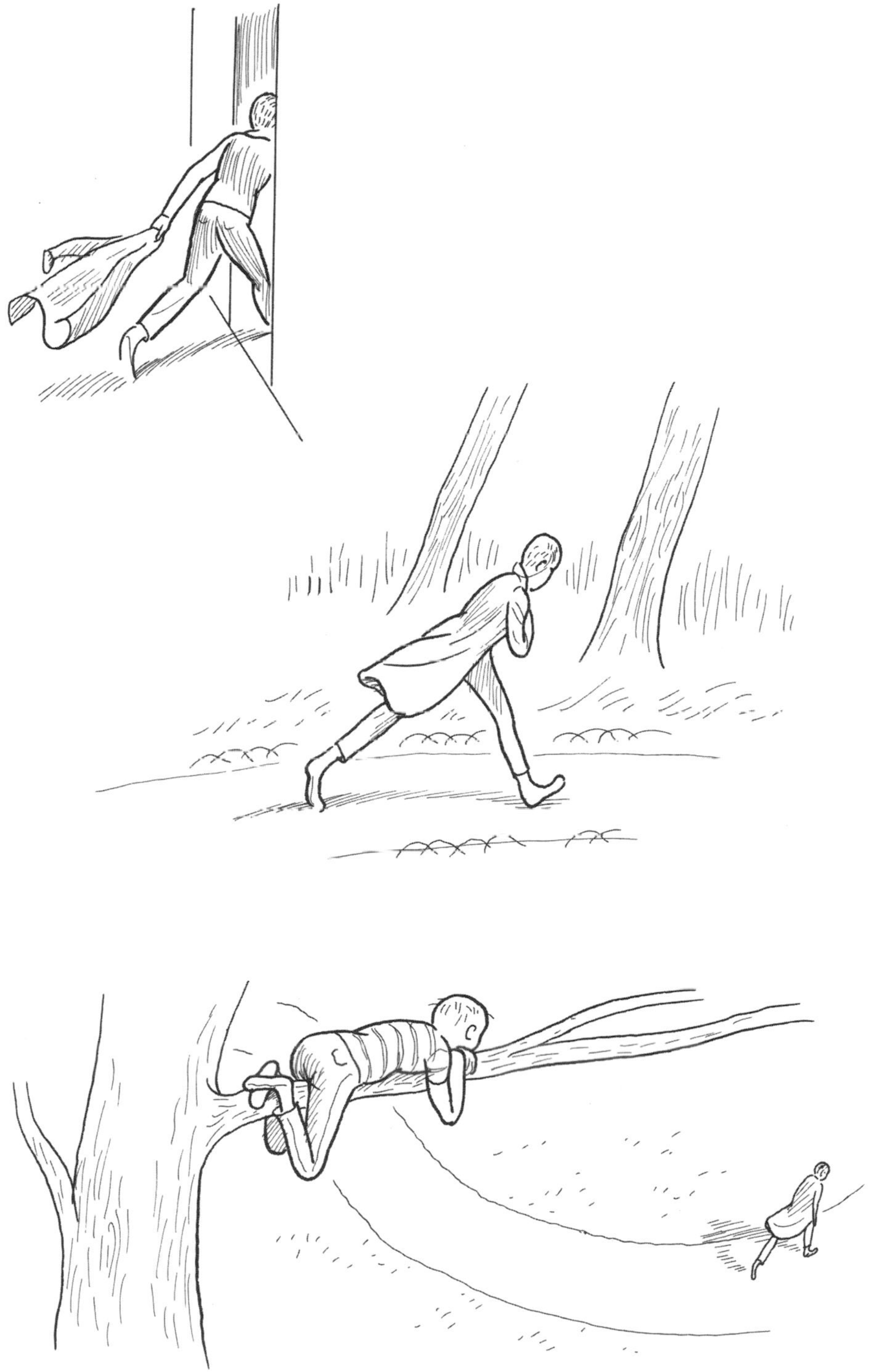

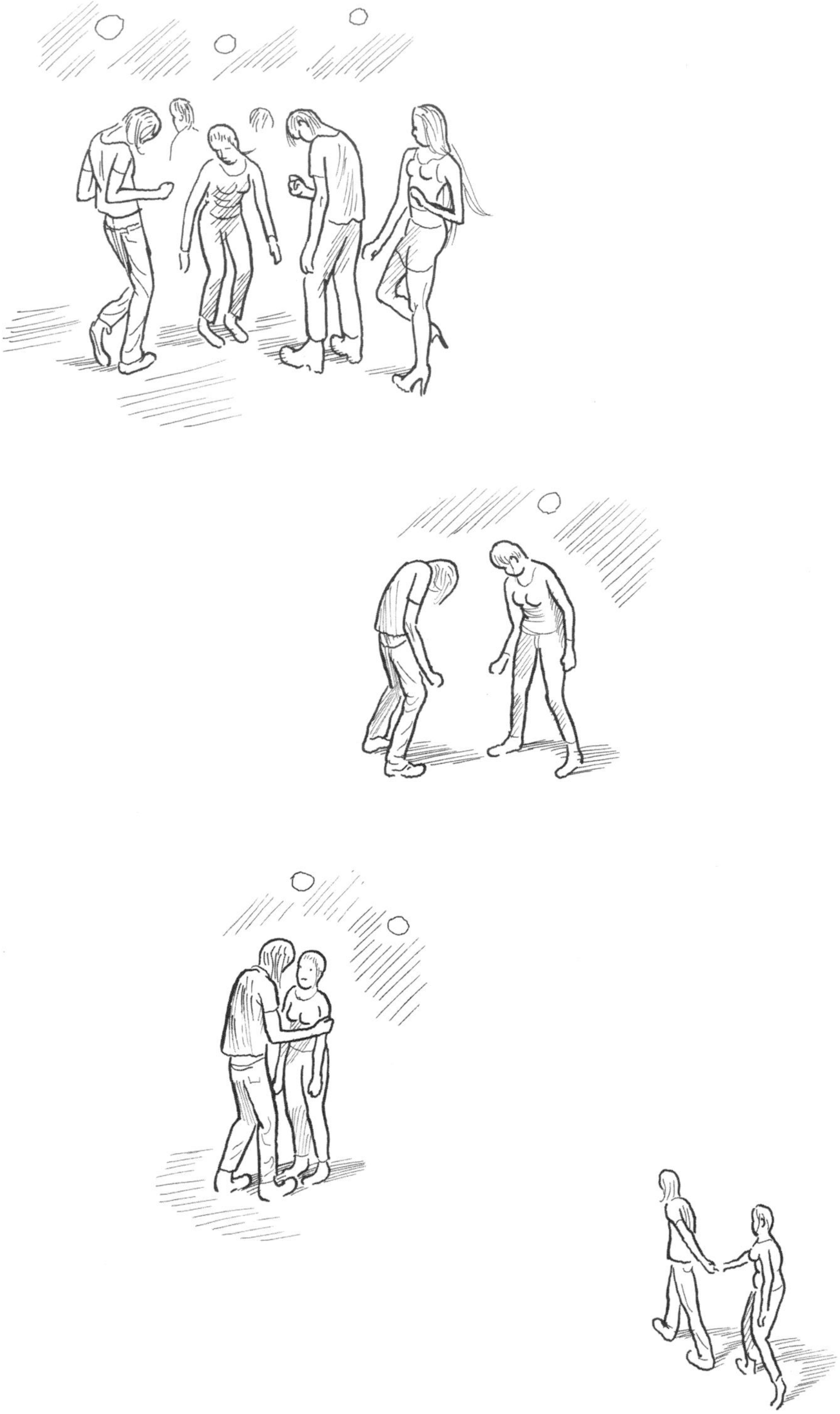

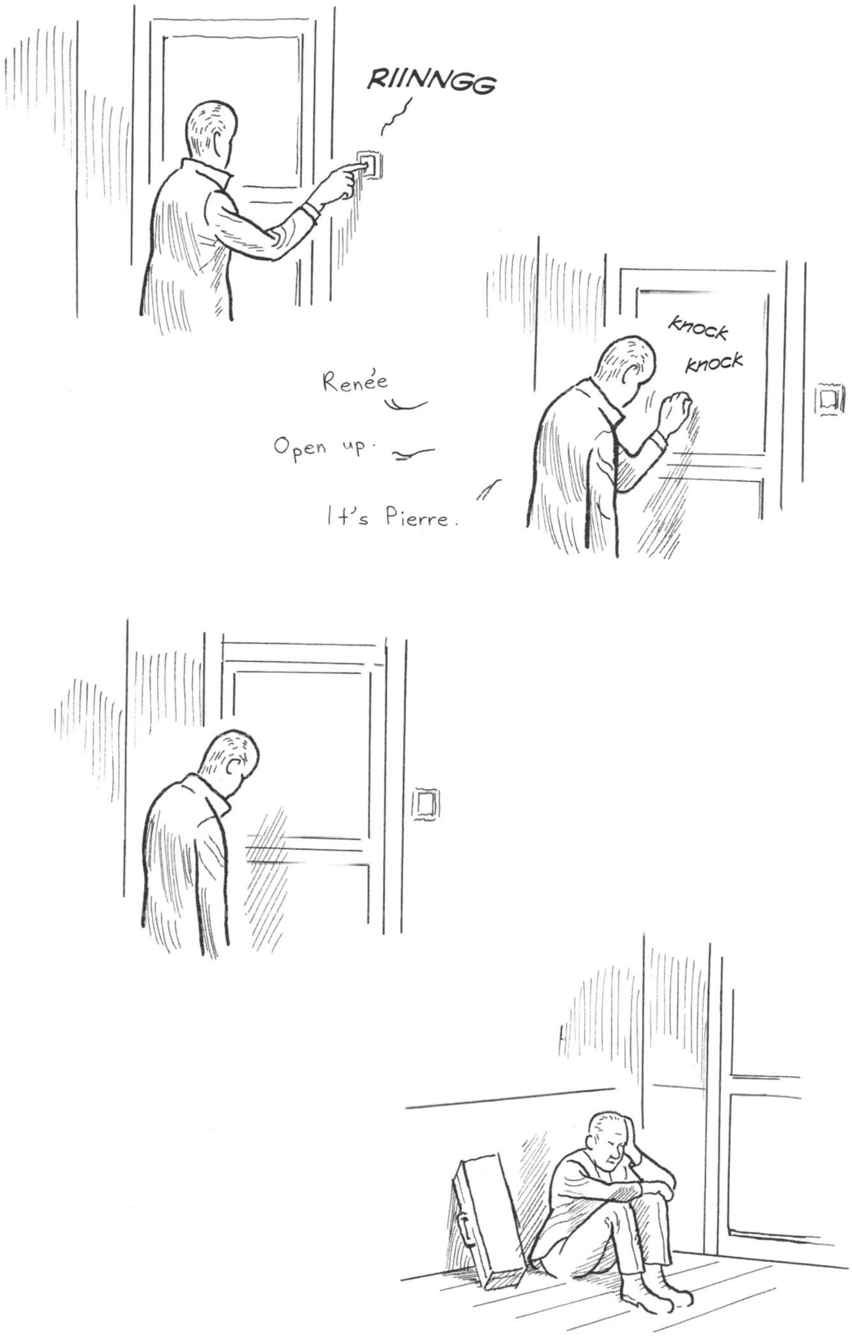
RIINNGG
knock
knock
Renée
Open up.
It's Pierre.

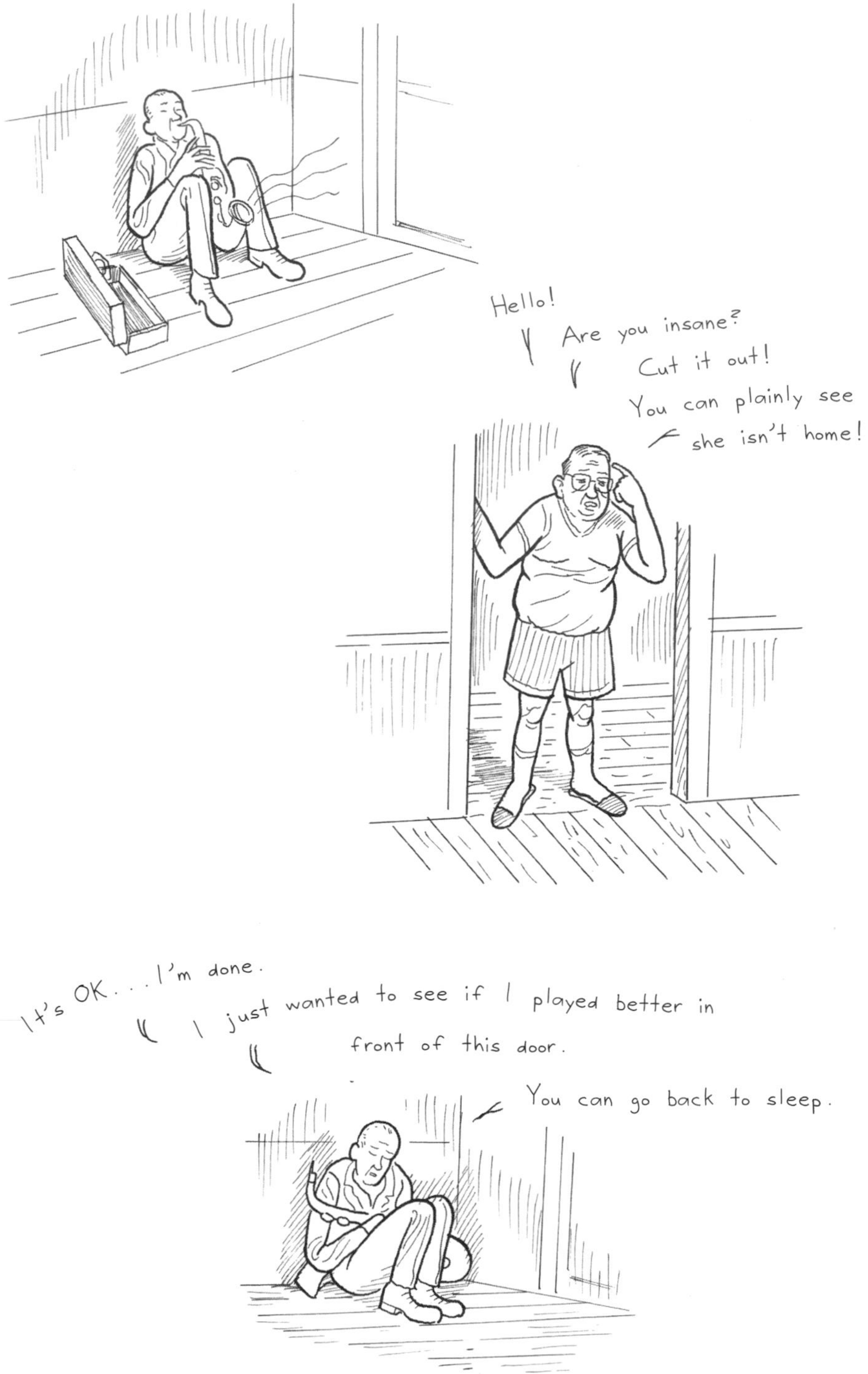
Hello!
Are you insane?
Cut it out!
You can plainly see she isn't home!
It's OK . . . I'm done.
I just wanted to see if I played better in front of this door.
You can go back to sleep.

Well. . . . you gonna let me
come up, or what?

Wait!

C'mon. . . .it'll be cool.
I want you so bad.

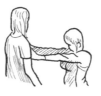

No! Stop, I—I don't know. . .

Sorry.

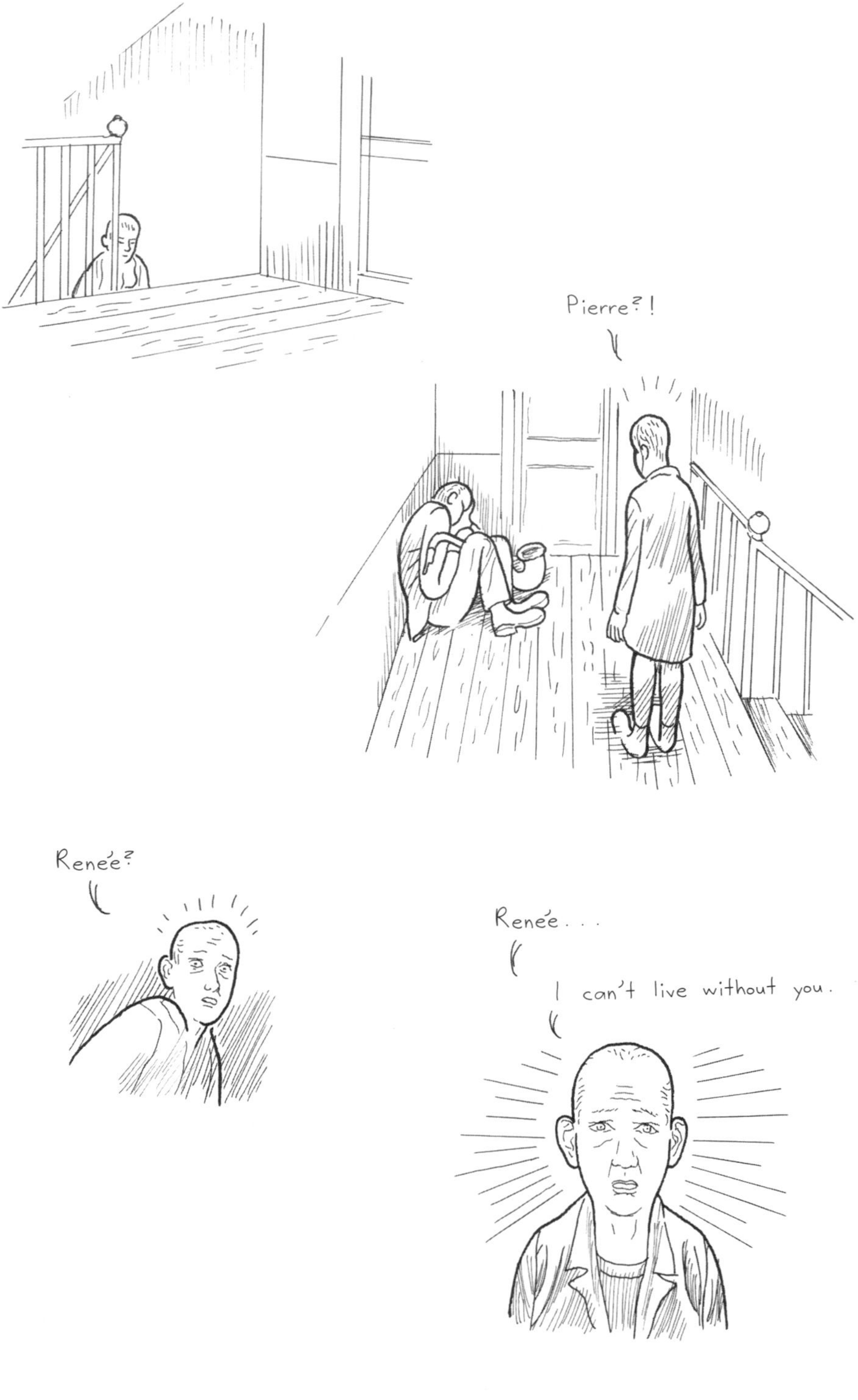
Pierre?!
Renée?
Renée...
I can't live without you.

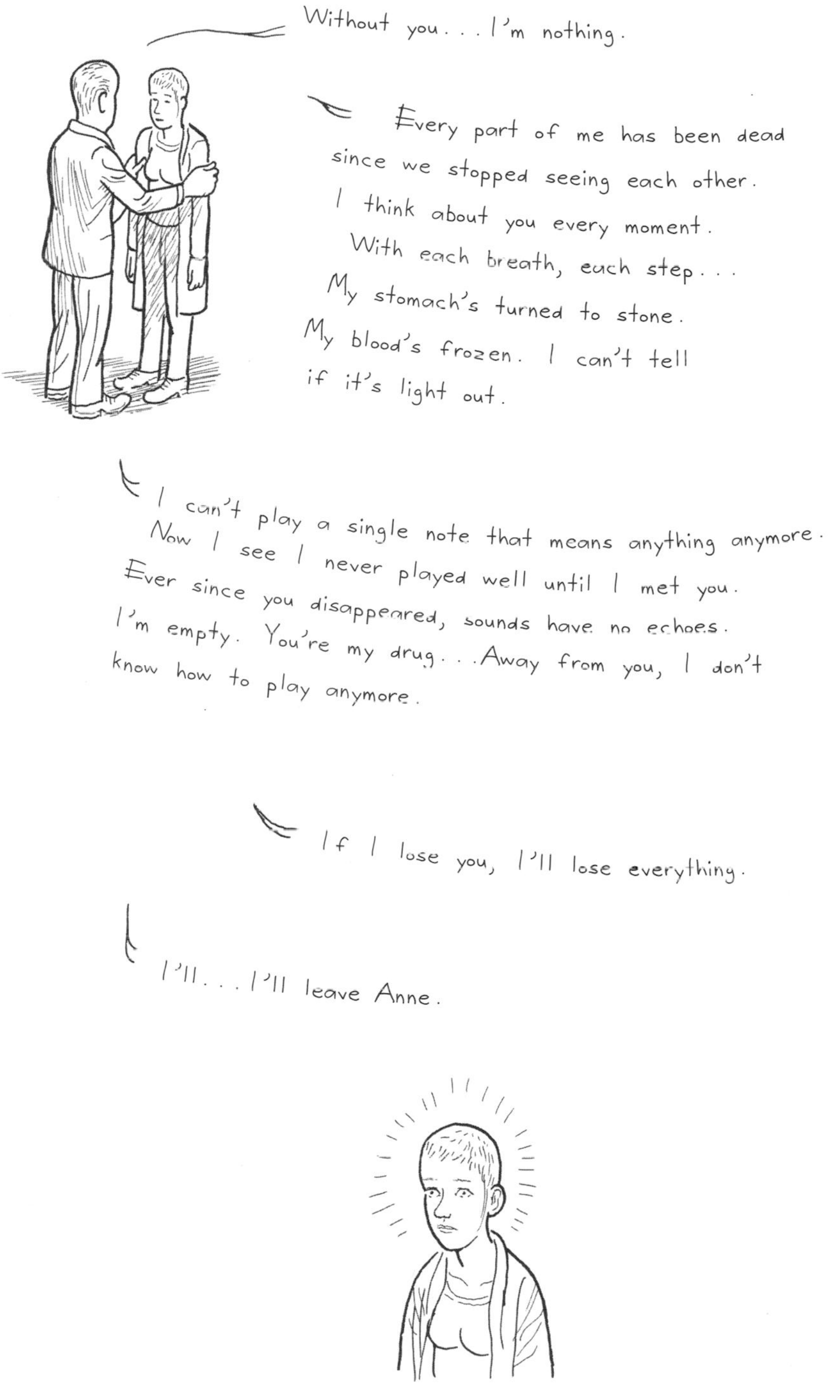
Without you... I'm nothing.
Every part of me has been dead since we stopped seeing each other. I think about you every moment. With each breath, each step... My stomach's turned to stone. My blood's frozen. I can't tell if it's light out.
I can't play a single note that means anything anymore. Now I see I never played well until I met you. Ever since you disappeared, sounds have no echoes. I'm empty. You're my drug... Away from you, I don't know how to play anymore.
If I lose you, I'll lose everything.
I'll... I'll leave Anne.

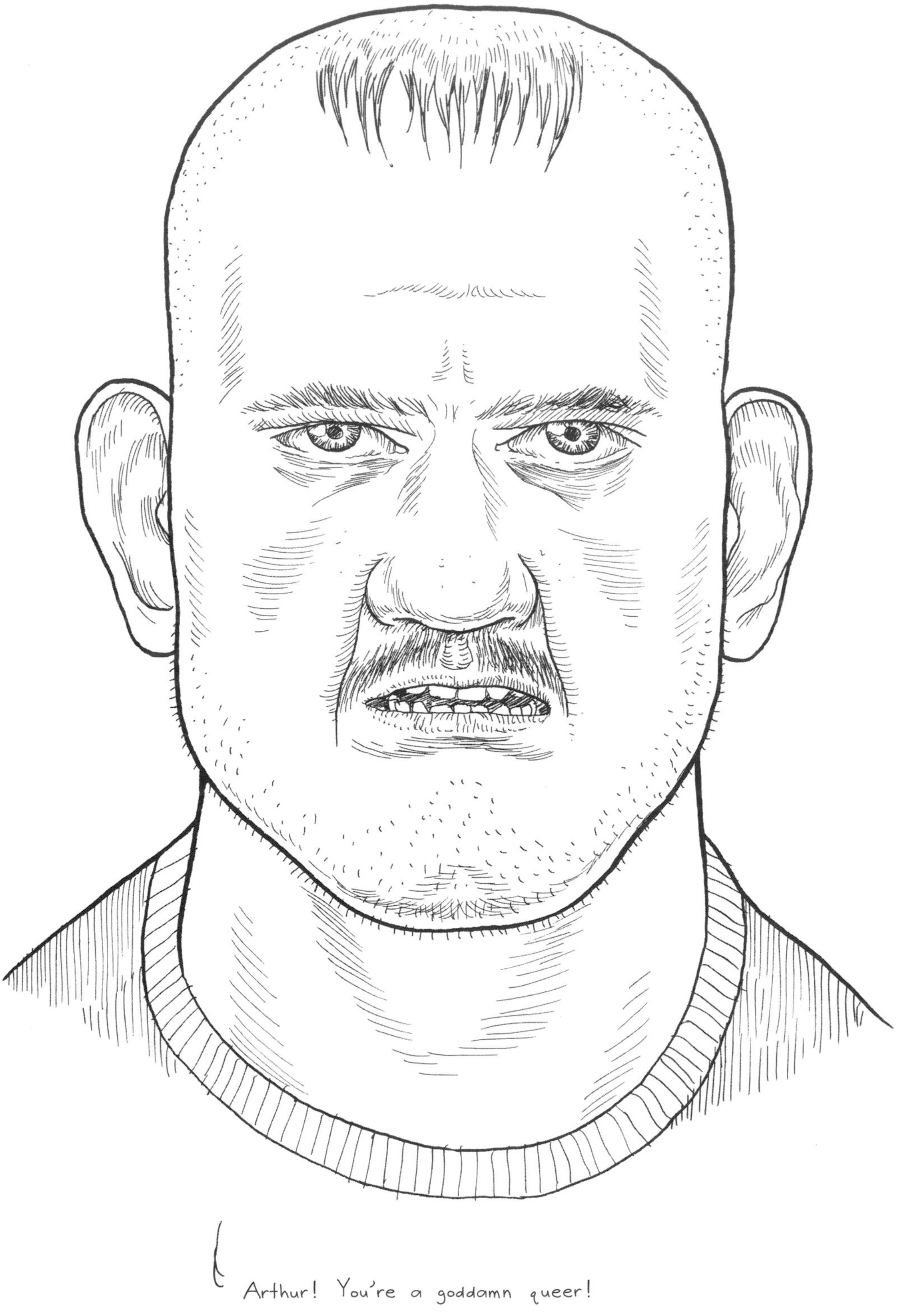
Arthur! You're a goddamn queer!

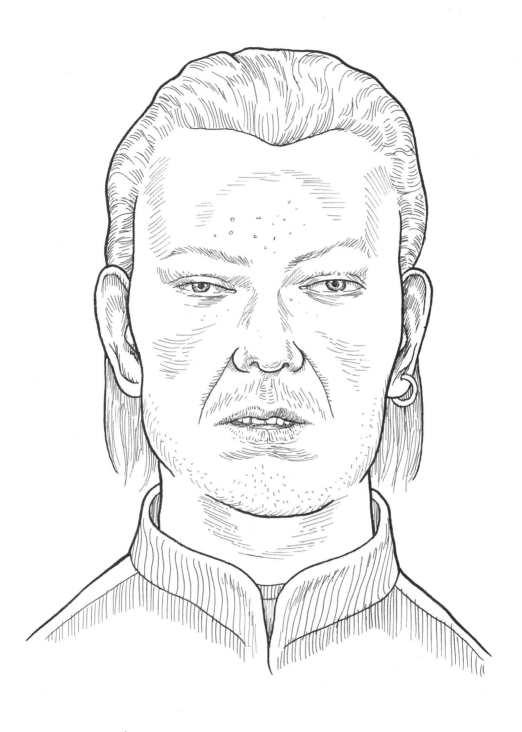

Who likes a little ass-hosing.

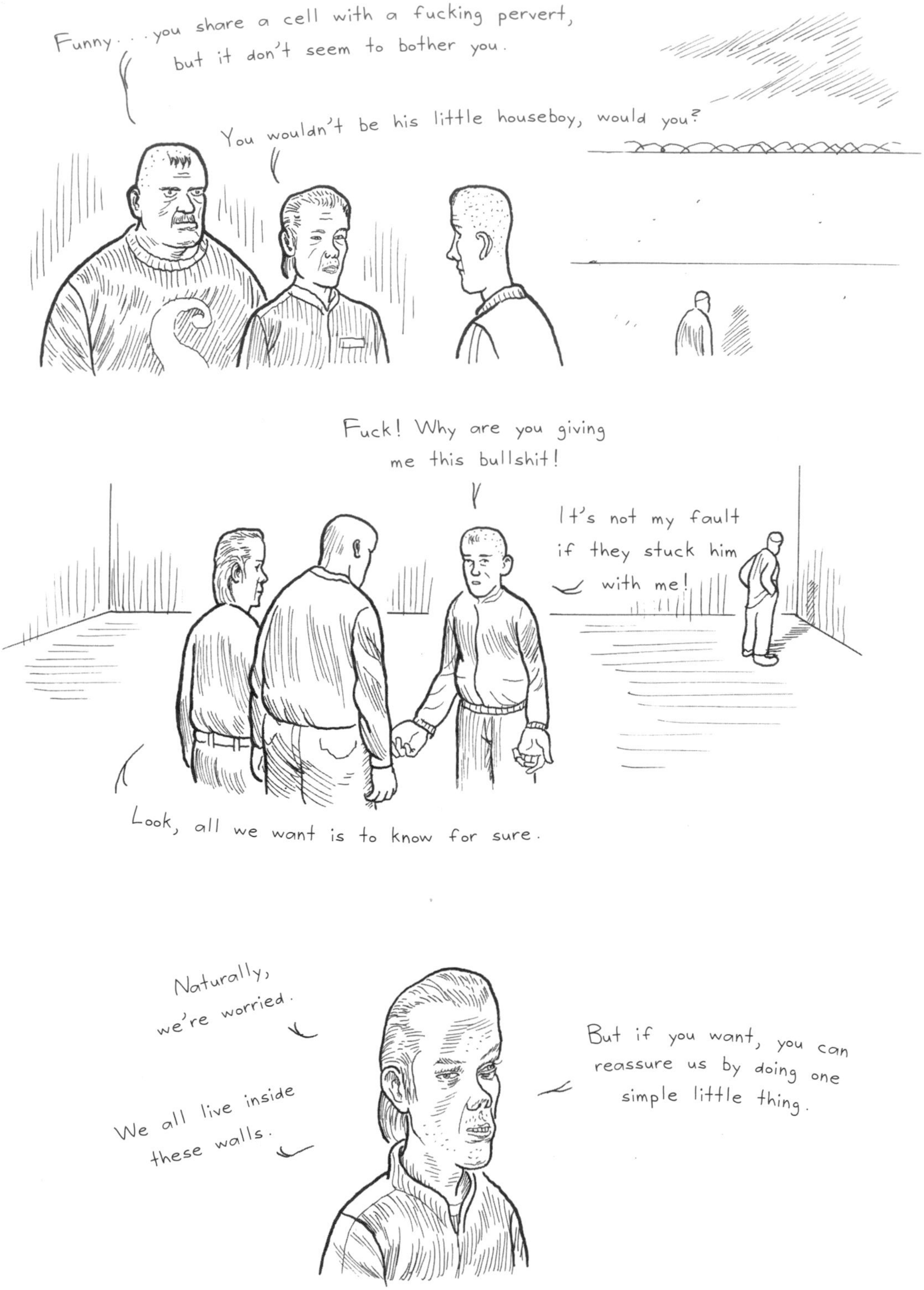
Funny . . . you share a cell with a fucking pervert, but it don't seem to bother you.
You wouldn't be his little houseboy, would you?
Fuck! Why are you giving me this bullshit!
It's not my fault if they stuck him with me!
Look, all we want is to know for sure.
Naturally, we're worried.
We all live inside these walls.
But if you want, you can reassure us by doing one simple little thing.

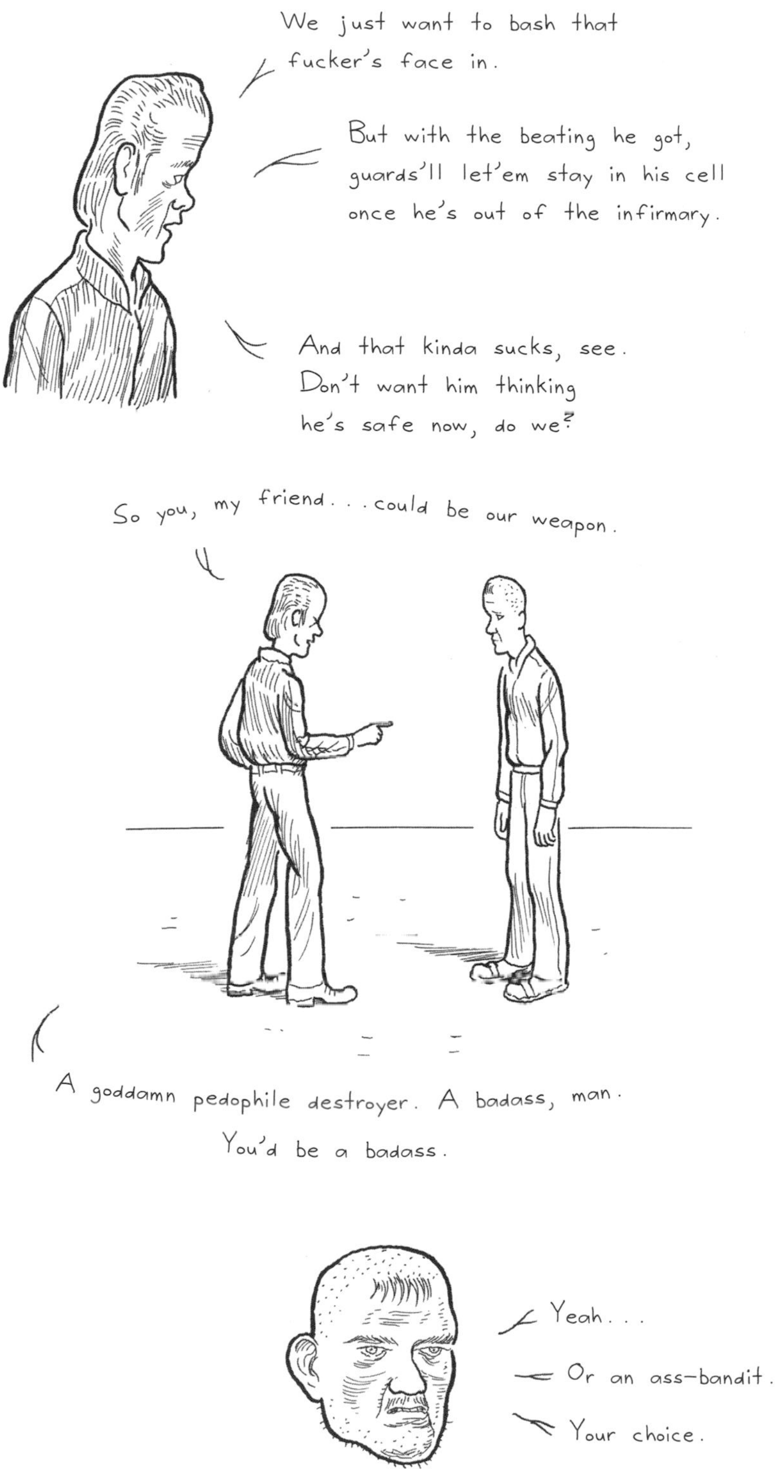

We just want to bash that fucker's face in.
But with the beating he got, guards'll let'em stay in his cell once he's out of the infirmary.
And that kinda sucks, see. Don't want him thinking he's safe now, do we?
So you, my friend...could be our weapon.
A goddamn pedophile destroyer. A badass, man. You'd be a badass.
Yeah...
Or an ass-bandit.
Your choice.

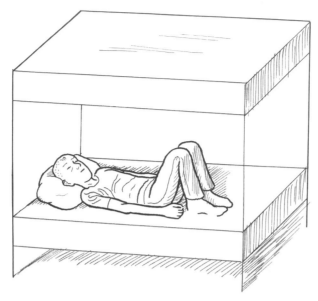

I'm in a box—my bed—in another box—my cell—which is in an even bigger box—the prison. Hmm...no...I'm in a box—my head—which is in another box—my bed—which is locked in my cell which is, in turn, in the box of this prison...

Before, there was this knocking that made me check over and over if the doors were tightly shut.

Now, I want them open...

I whacked off too much today. My dick hurts.

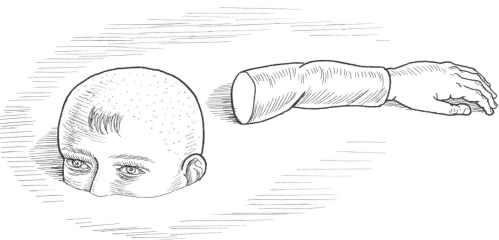

But it calms me down. Even if every time I ejaculate I feel like I'm sinking a little bit deeper into myself.

Sometimes when I come I can't help thinking of my father. Why does my brain do that? It disgusts me . . .

I can't see him clearly. I have an idea of my father in my head.
This used to happen before he died, too. But now, I think about
his death often too.

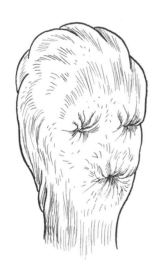

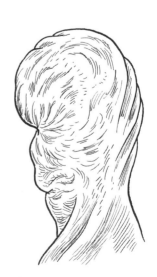

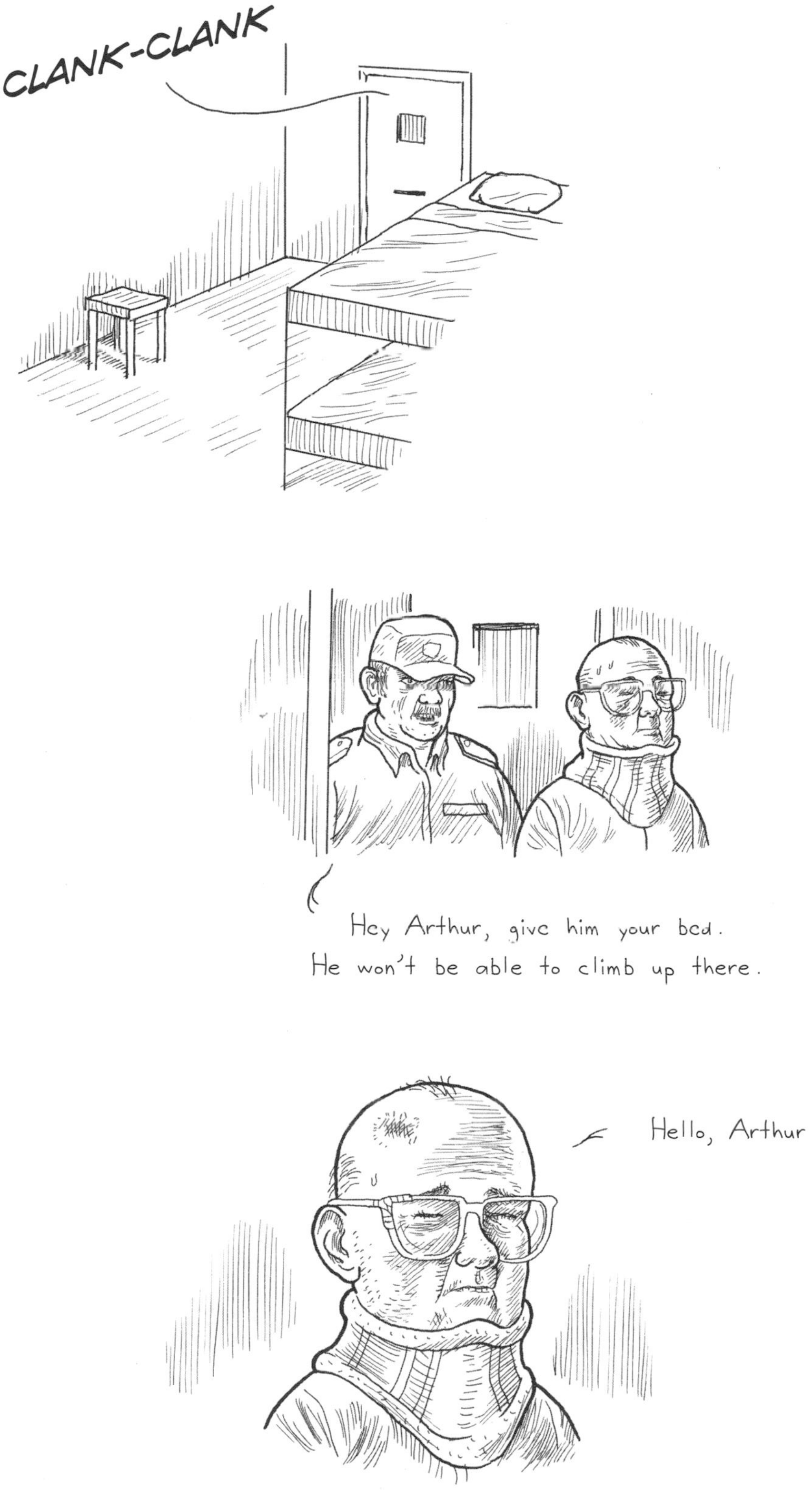
CLANK-CLANK
Hey Arthur, give him your bed.
He won't be able to climb up there.
Hello, Arthur

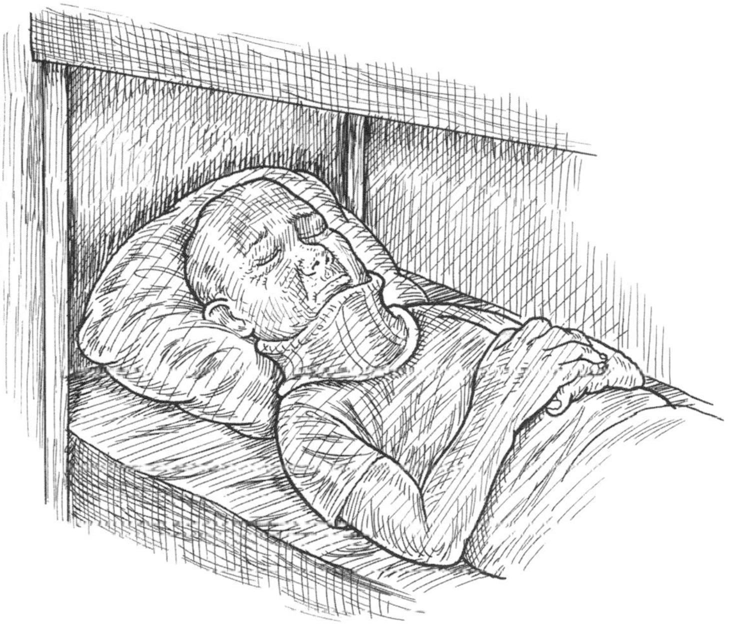

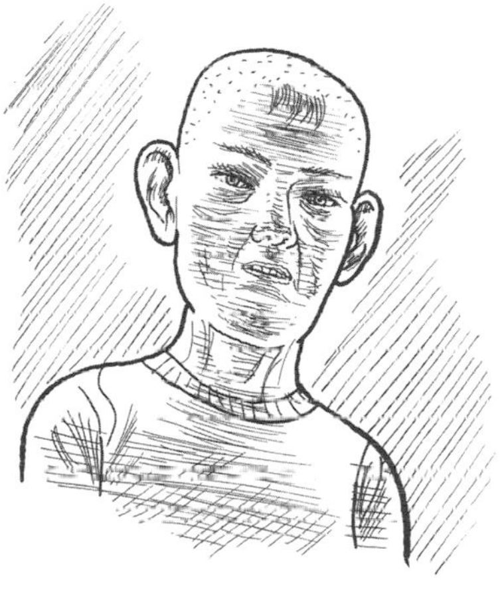

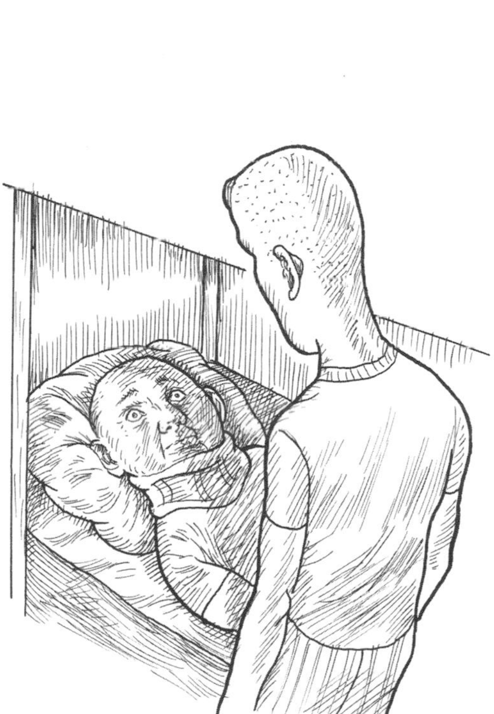

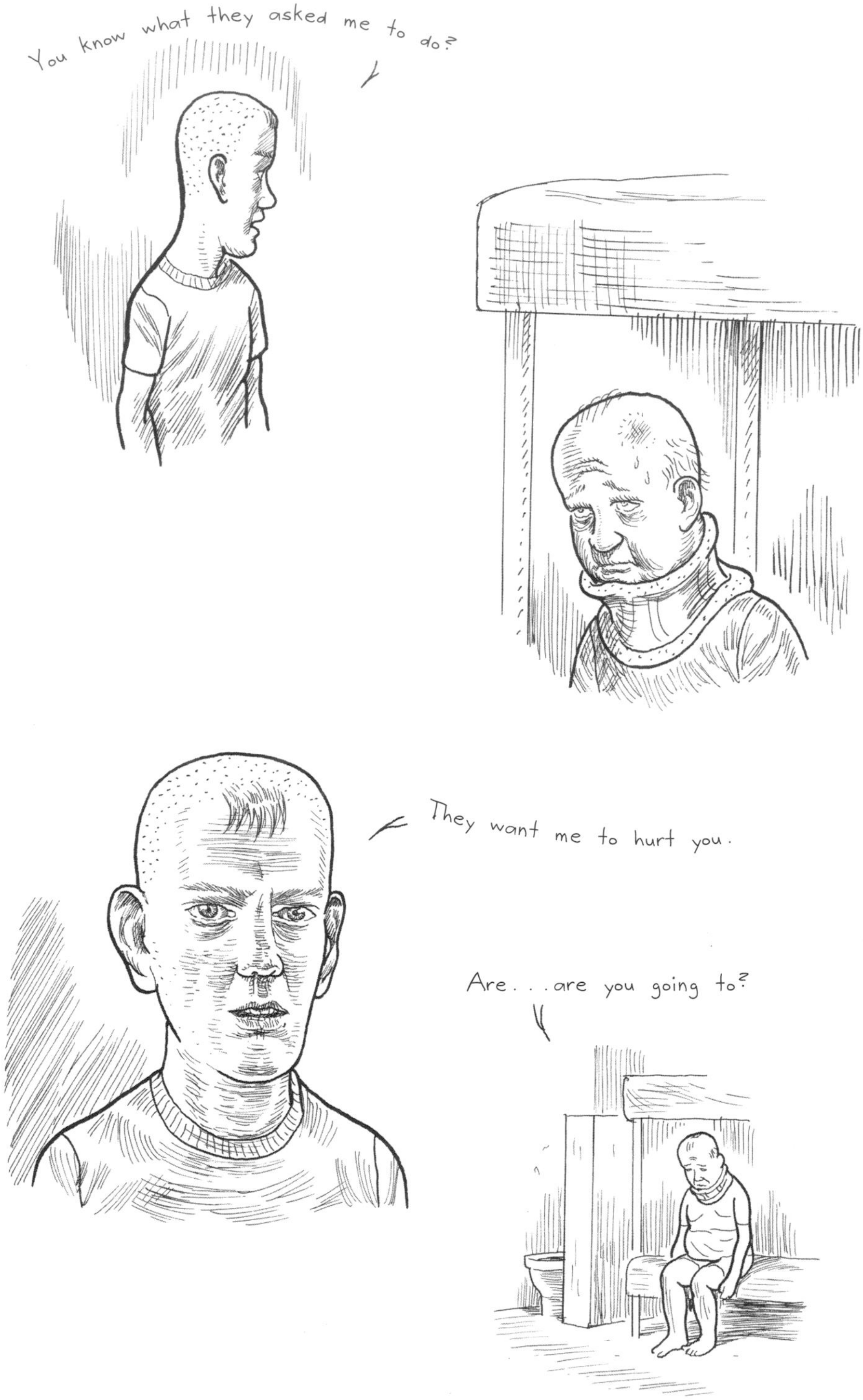
You know what they asked me to do?
They want me to hurt you.
Are. . .are you going to?

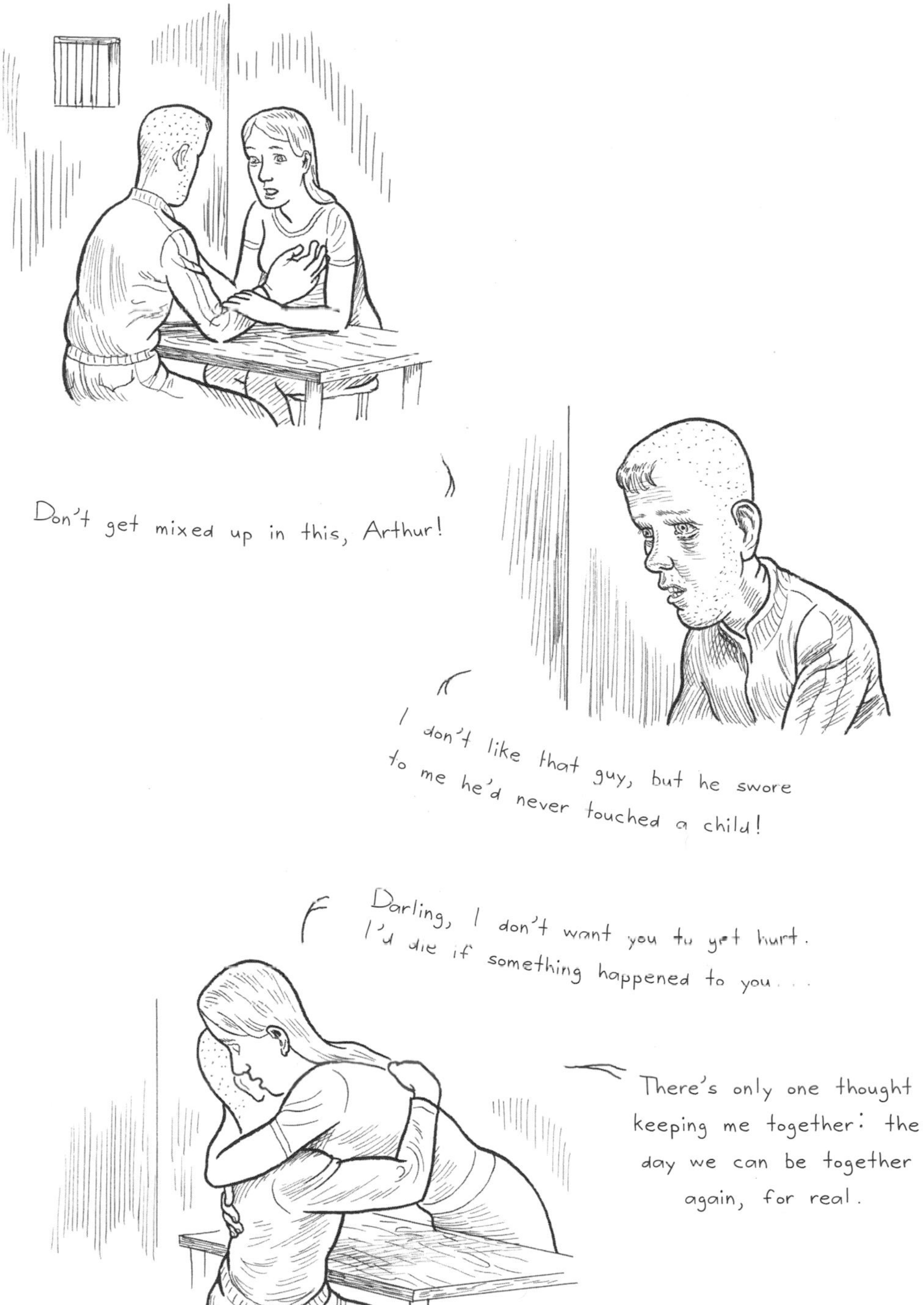
Don't get mixed up in this, Arthur!
I don't like that guy, but he swore to me he'd never touched a child!
Darling, I don't want you to get hurt. I'd die if something happened to you...
There's only one thought keeping me together: the day we can be together again, for real.

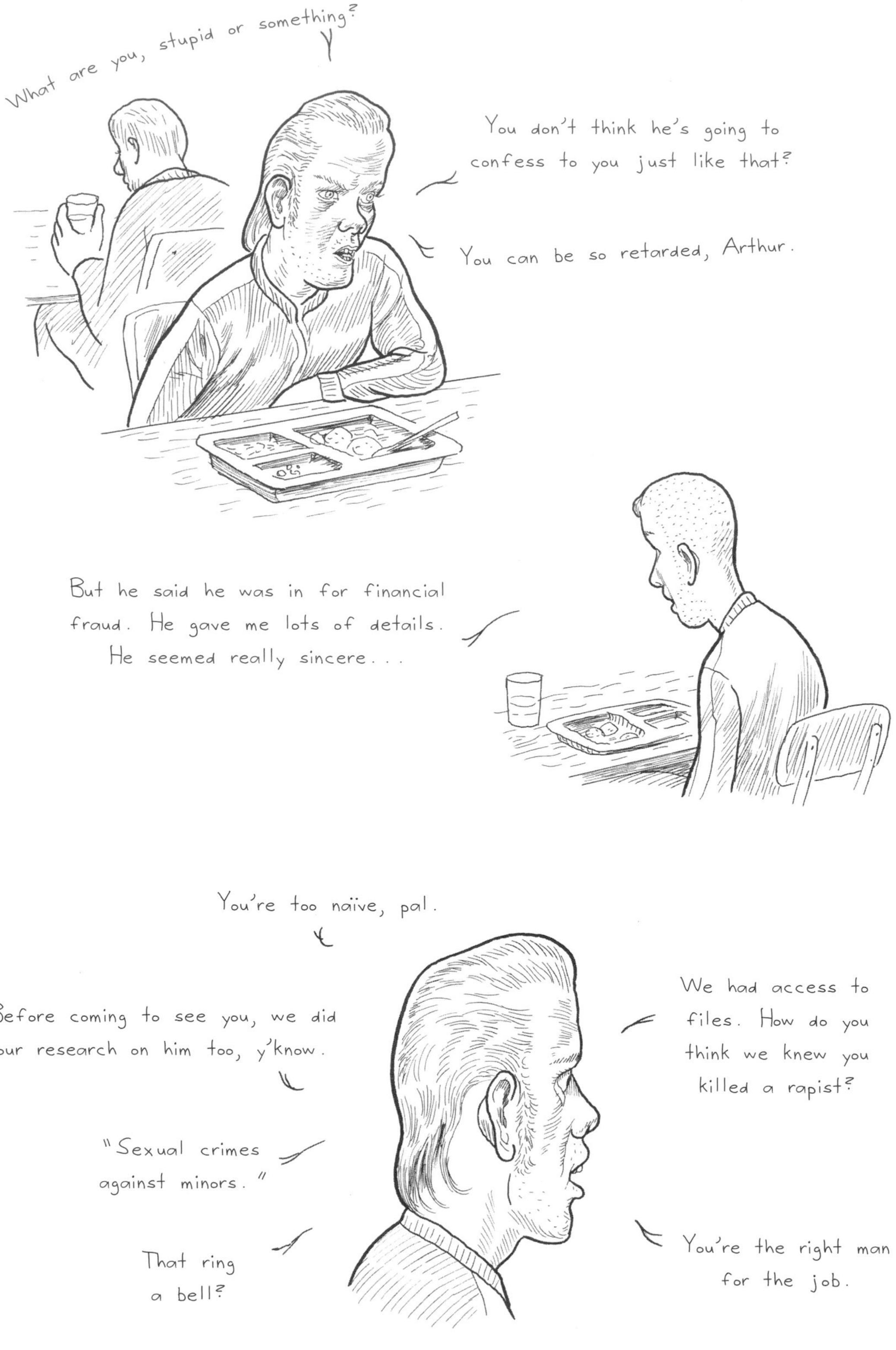
What are you, stupid or something?
You don't think he's going to confess to you just like that?
You can be so retarded, Arthur.
But he said he was in for financial fraud. He gave me lots of details. He seemed really sincere...
You're too naïve, pal.
Before coming to see you, we did our research on him too, y'know.
"Sexual crimes against minors."
That ring a bell?
We had access to files. How do you think we knew you killed a rapist?
You're the right man for the job.

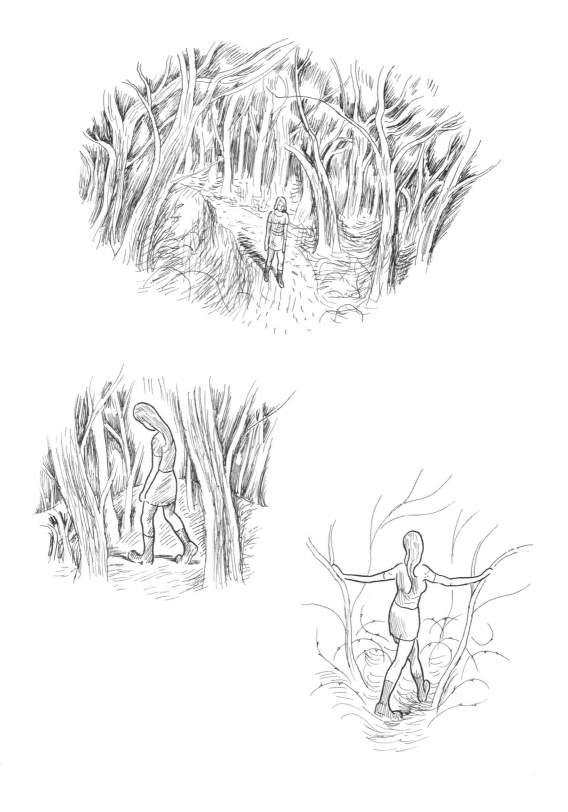

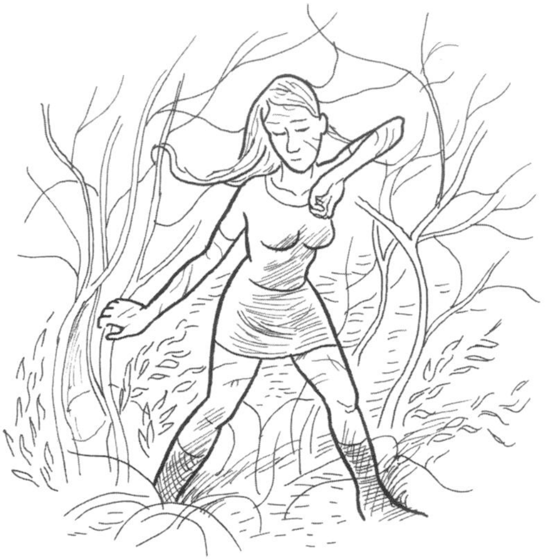

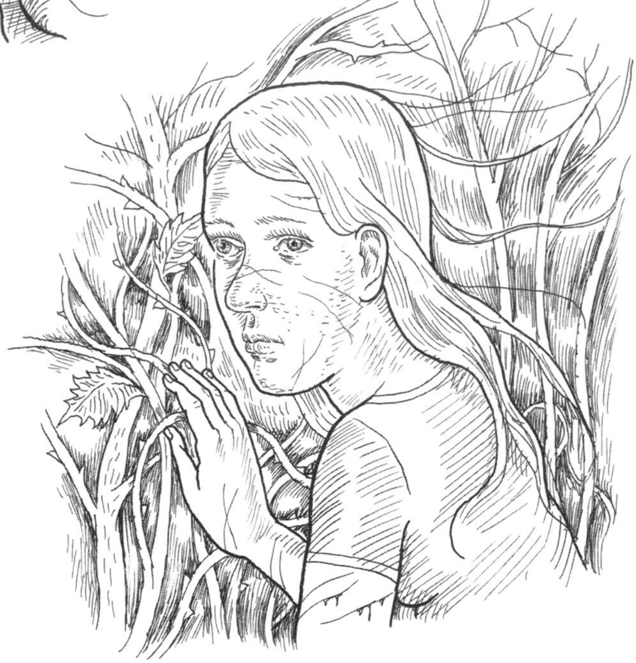

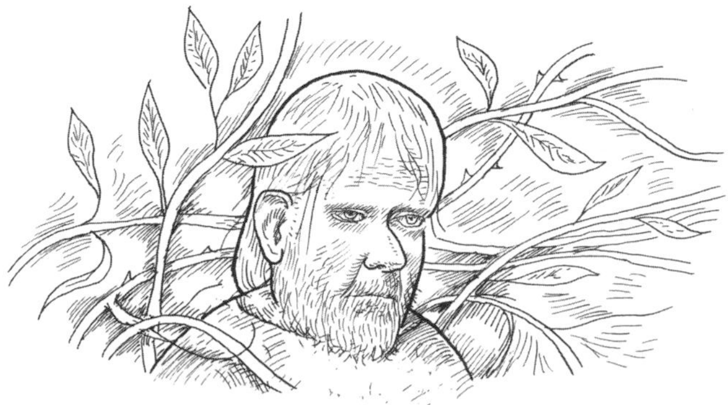

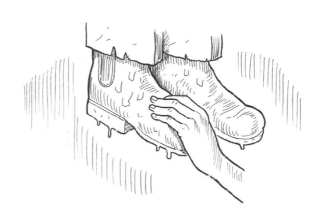

Daddy... do you love me?

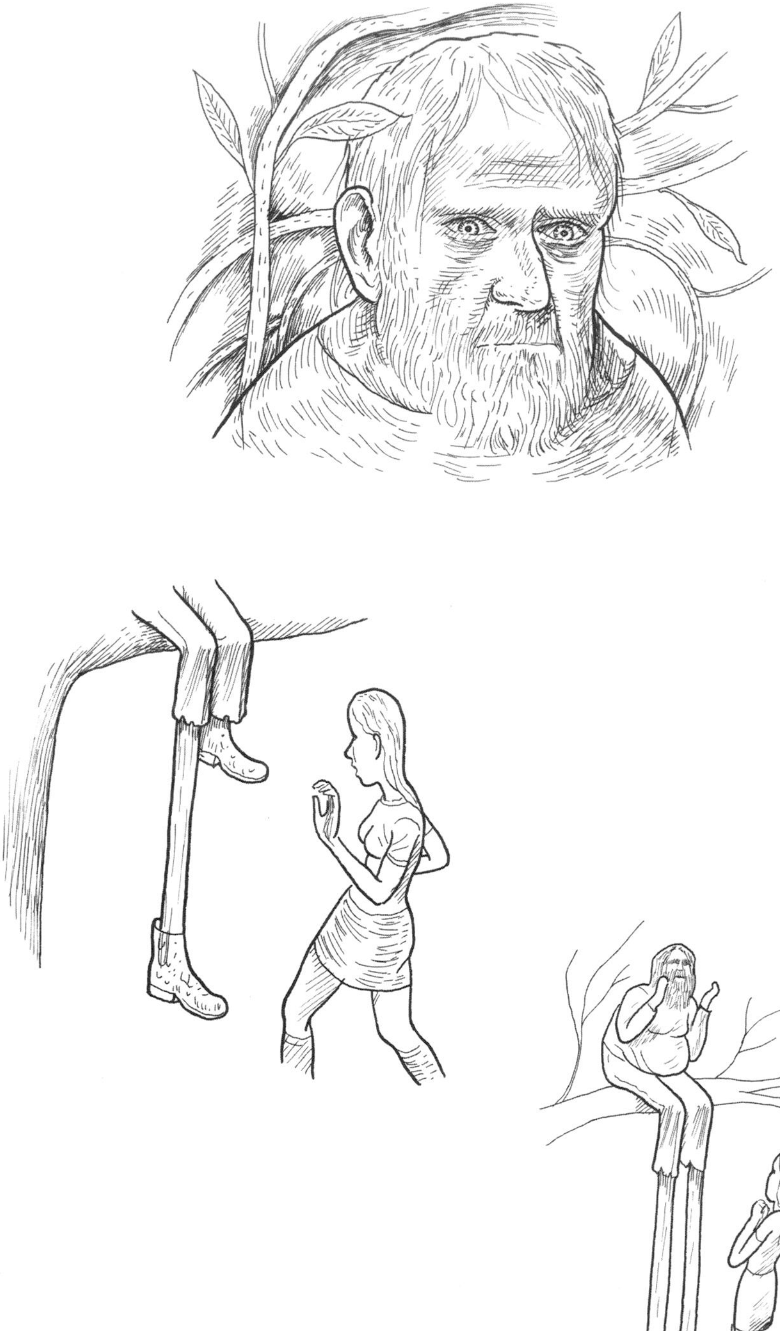

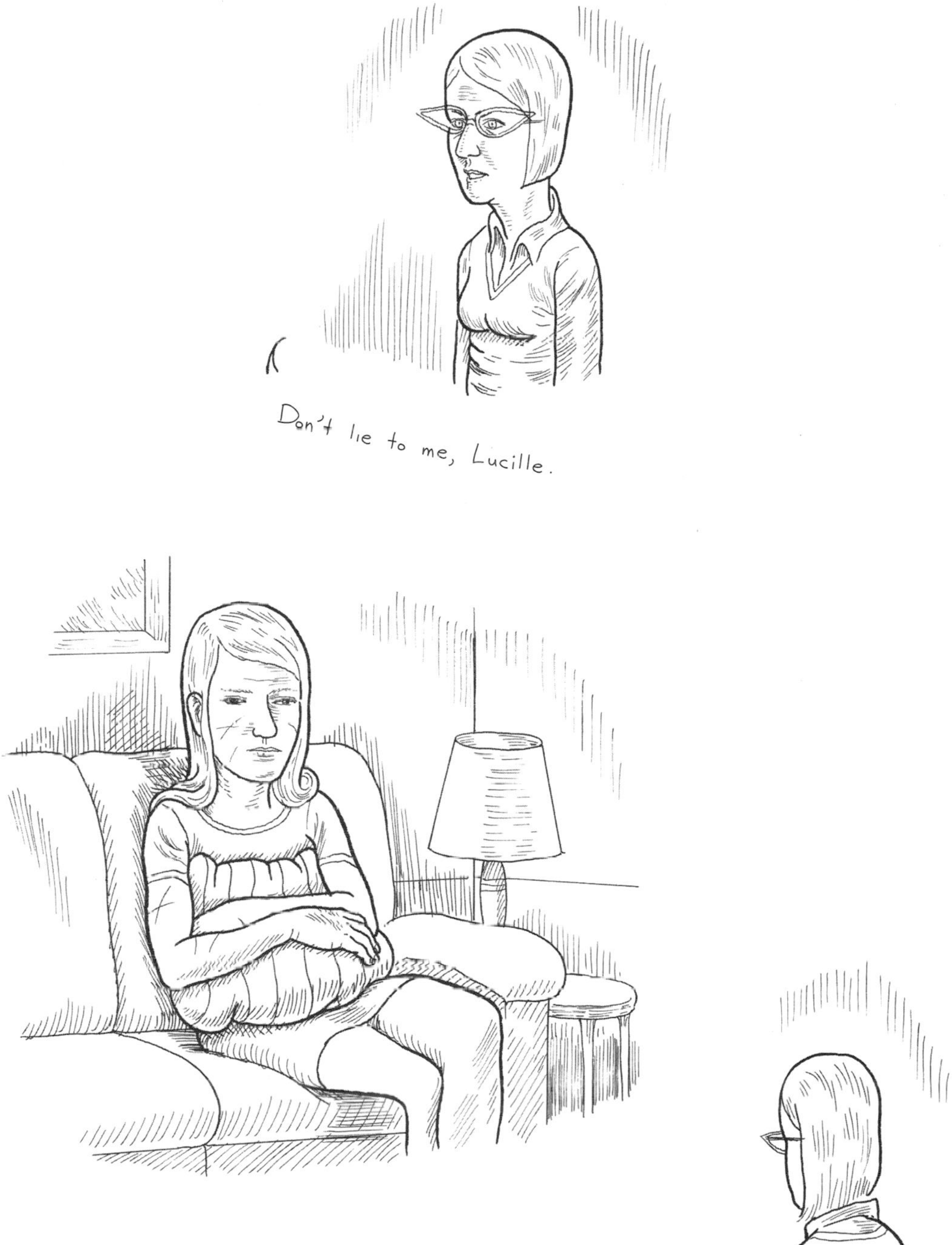
Don't lie to me, Lucille.
I'm worried, Lucille.

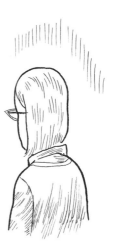

How long are you going to wait?

Look at me. I spent my
life hoping your father
would return.

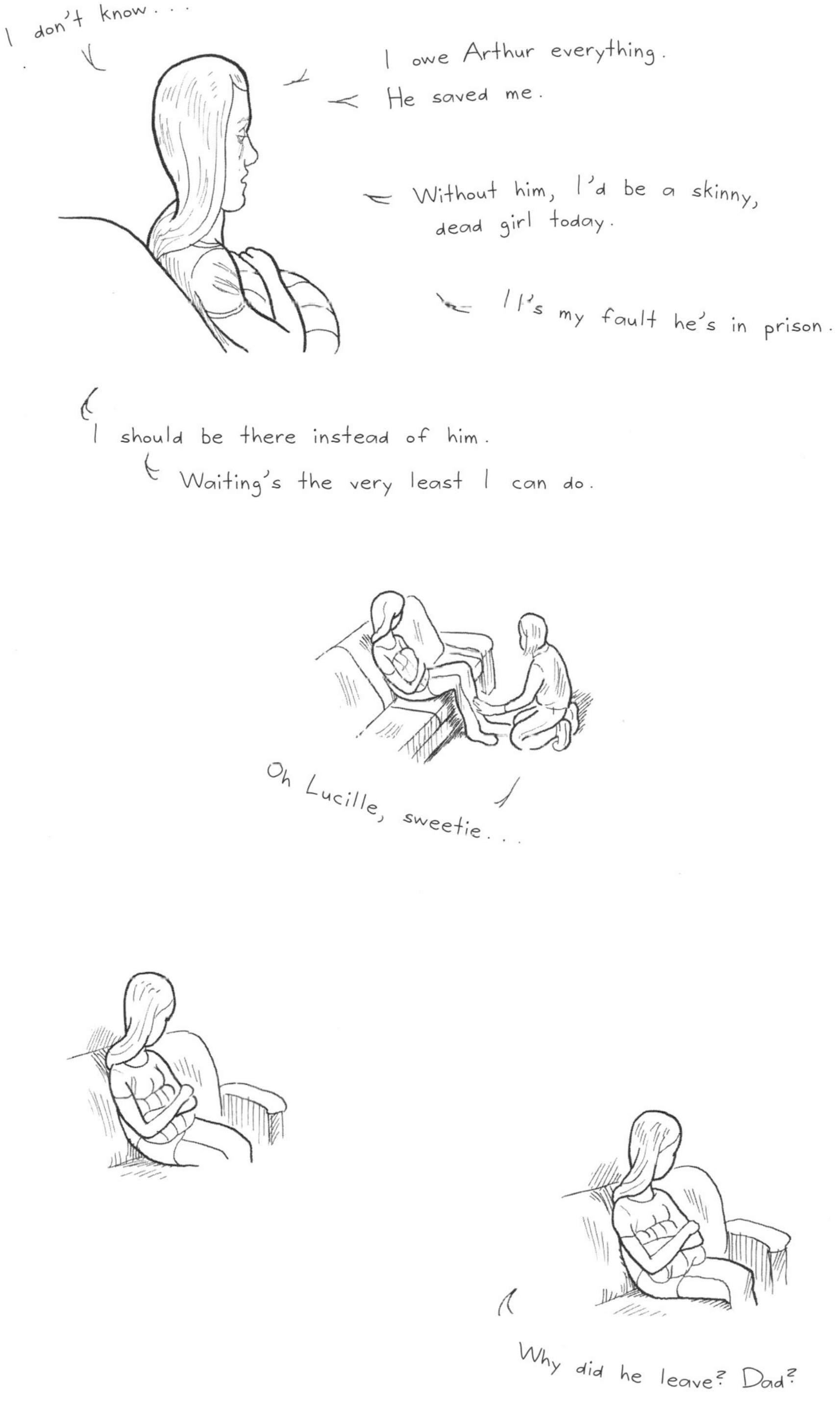
I don't know . . .
I owe Arthur everything.
He saved me.
Without him, I'd be a skinny, dead girl today.
It's my fault he's in prison.
I should be there instead of him.
Waiting's the very least I can do.
Oh Lucille, sweetie . . .
Why did he leave? Dad?

I was angry.

He left because I got angry.

I hated him for dying....my father. He left me.
Do you understand? Deep down, that's it.
I was full of resentment that he'd deprived
me of his love.

I didn't know it. So I hated your father instead.
I even picked him so he'd leave me.
He was the kind of man who runs away.

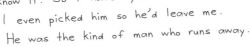

I let it all out at him until
he couldn't take it anymore.

One day, he disappeared.

I still love him. I miss him every day.

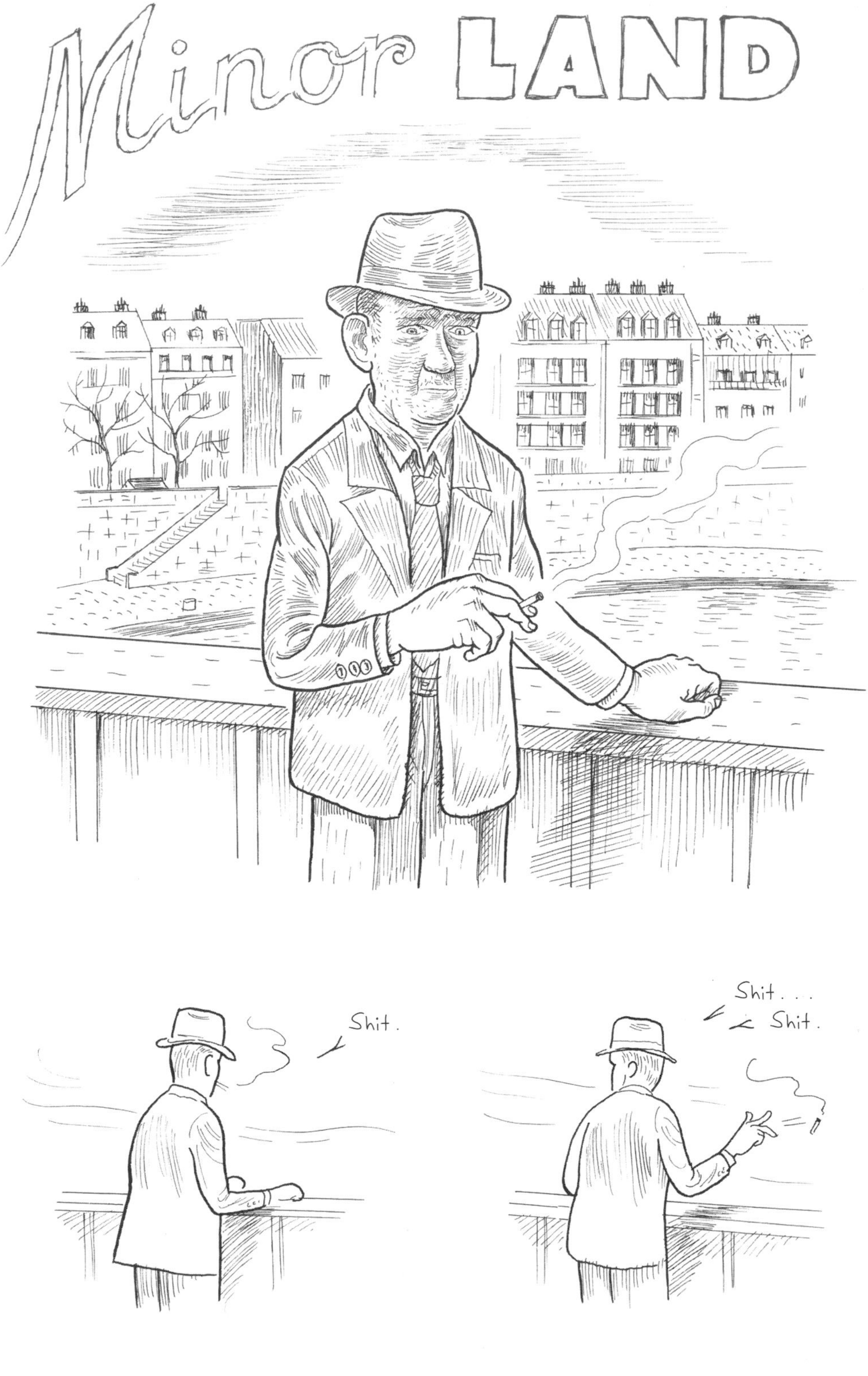
Minor LAND
Shit.
Shit. . .
Shit.

Pierre!?

I left Anne...

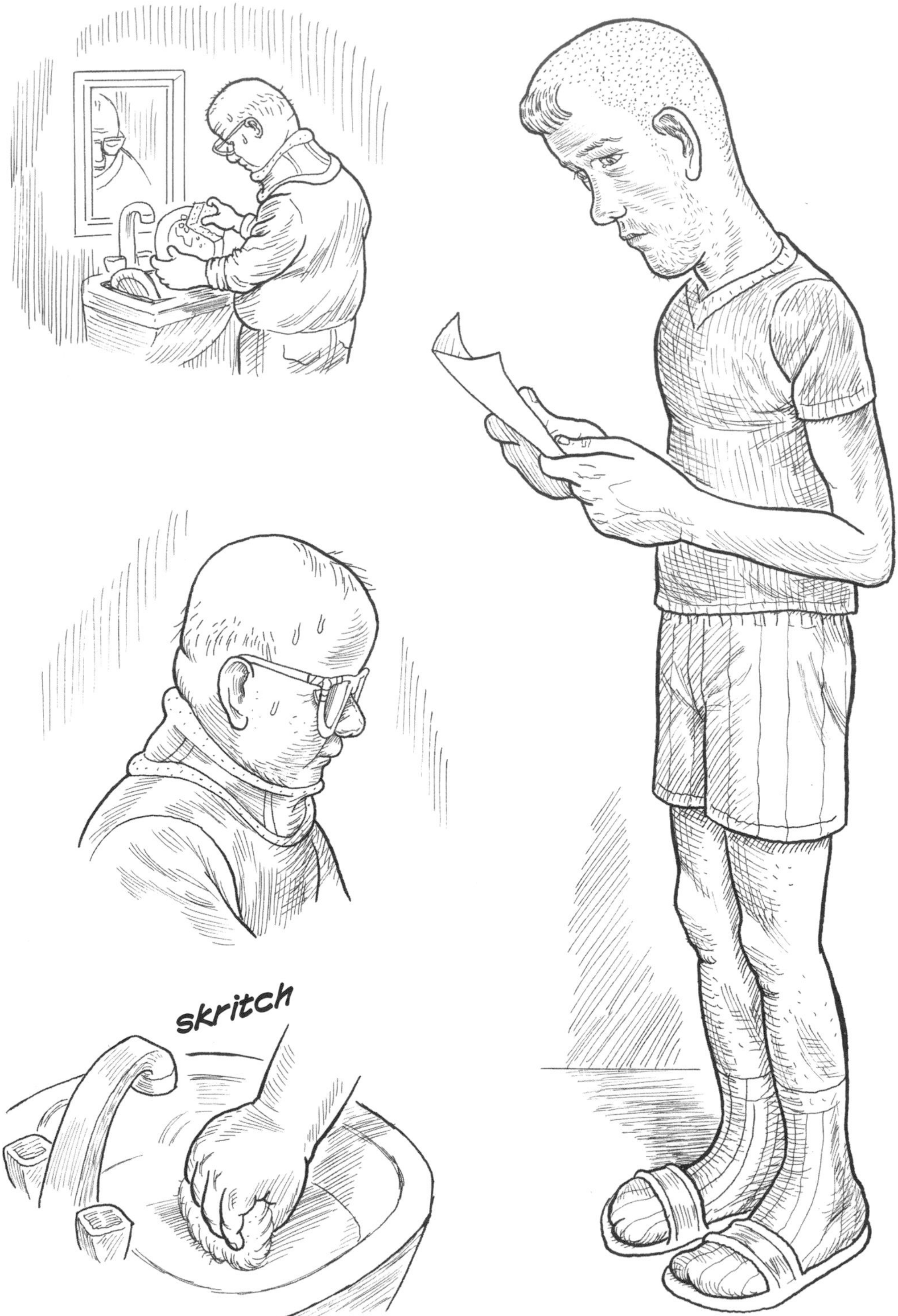
skritch

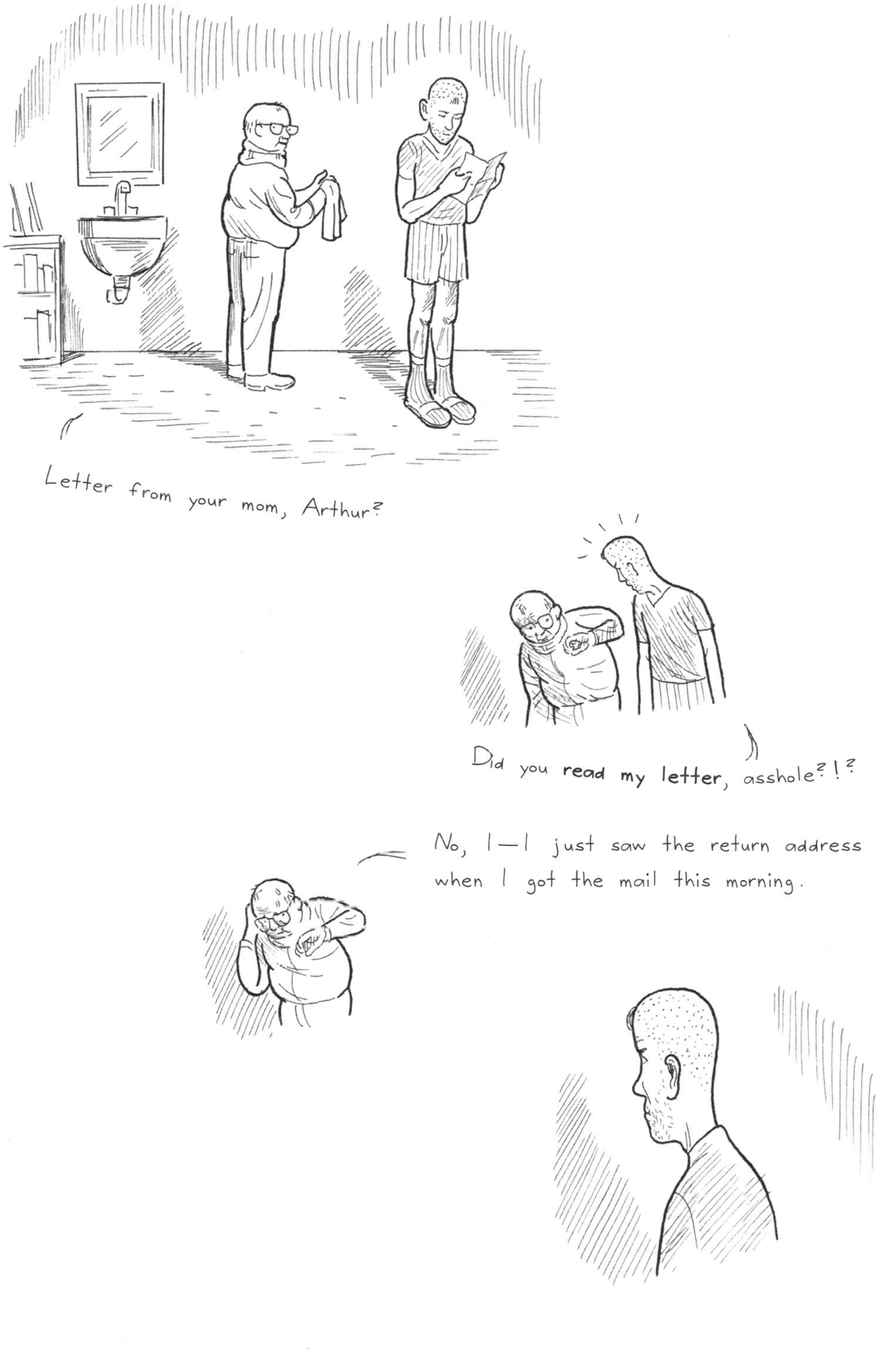
Letter from your mom, Arthur?
Did you **read my letter**, asshole?!?
No, I—I just saw the return address when I got the mail this morning.

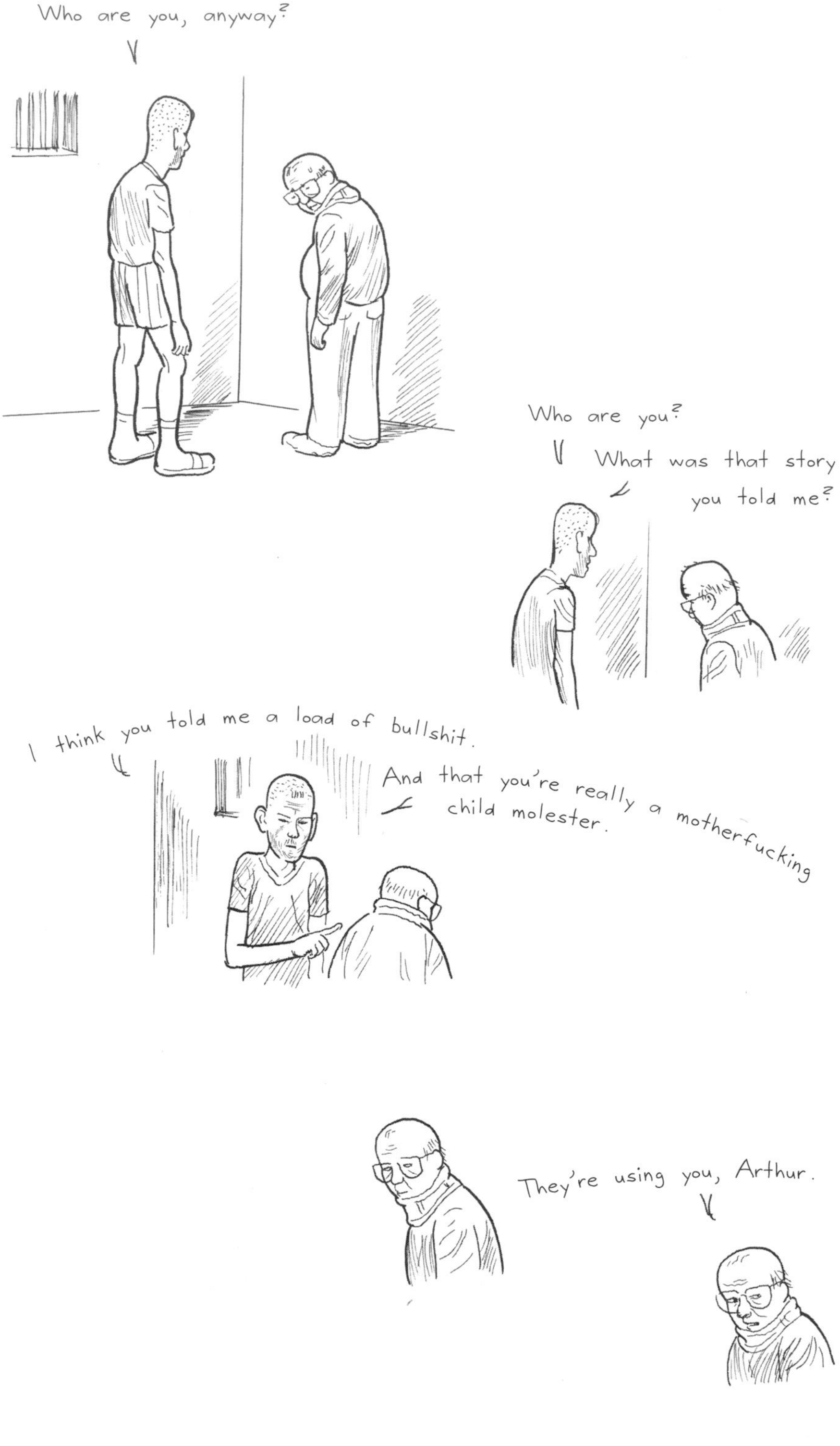
Who are you, anyway?
Who are you?
What was that story you told me?
I think you told me a load of bullshit.
And that you're really a motherfucking child molester.
They're using you, Arthur.

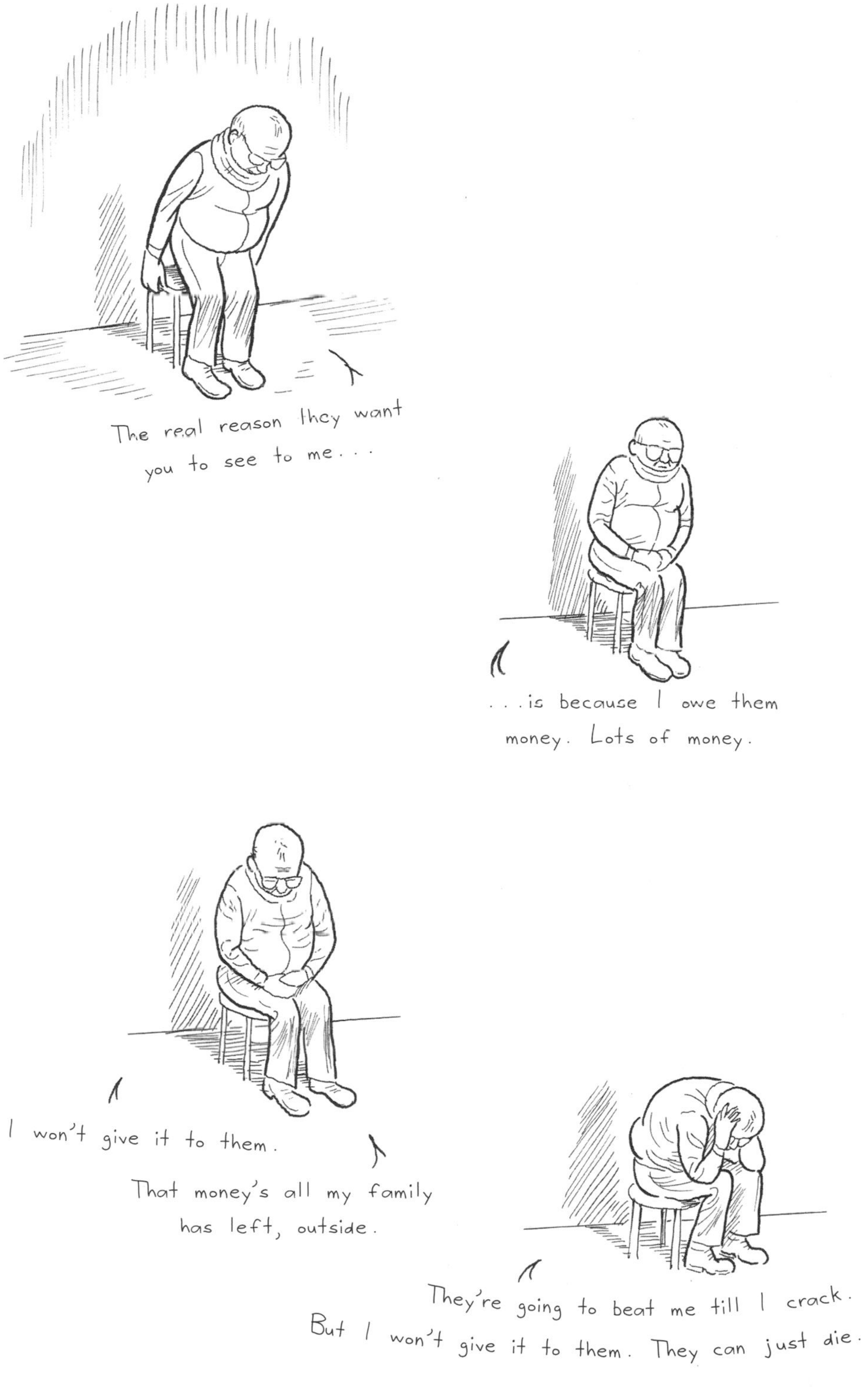
The real reason they want you to see to me...
...is because I owe them money. Lots of money.
I won't give it to them.
That money's all my family has left, outside.
They're going to beat me till I crack.
But I won't give it to them. They can just die.

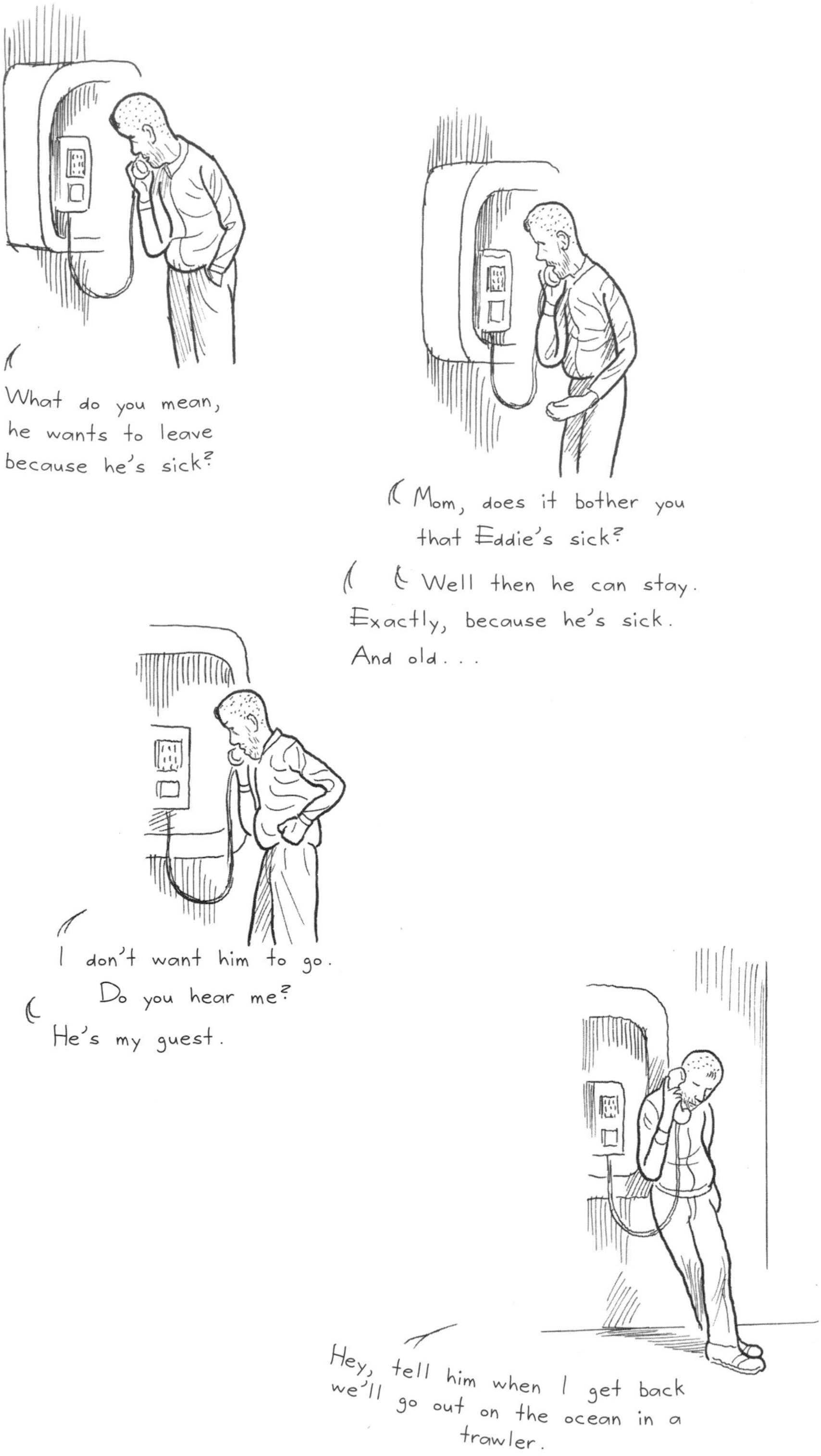
What do you mean, he wants to leave because he's sick?
Mom, does it bother you that Eddie's sick?
Well then he can stay.
Exactly, because he's sick. And old...
I don't want him to go. Do you hear me?
He's my guest.
Hey, tell him when I get back we'll go out on the ocean in a trawler.

Brother!

Hakim.
Can I ask you something?
Maybe...

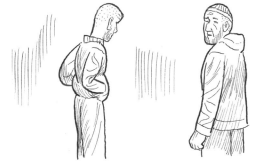

Do you think it's true my cellmate owes the guys here money?

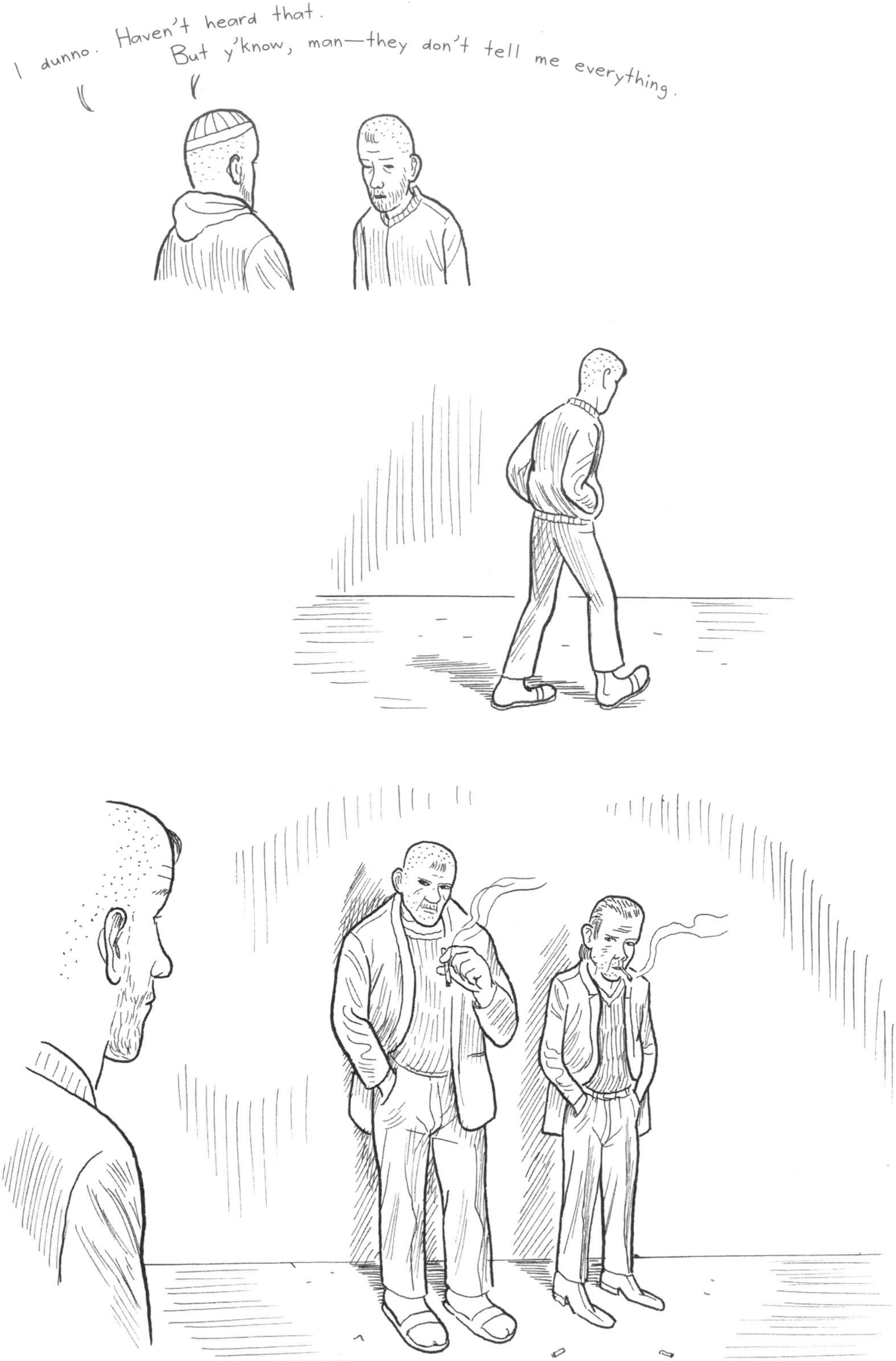
I dunno. Haven't heard that.
But y'know, man—they don't tell me everything.

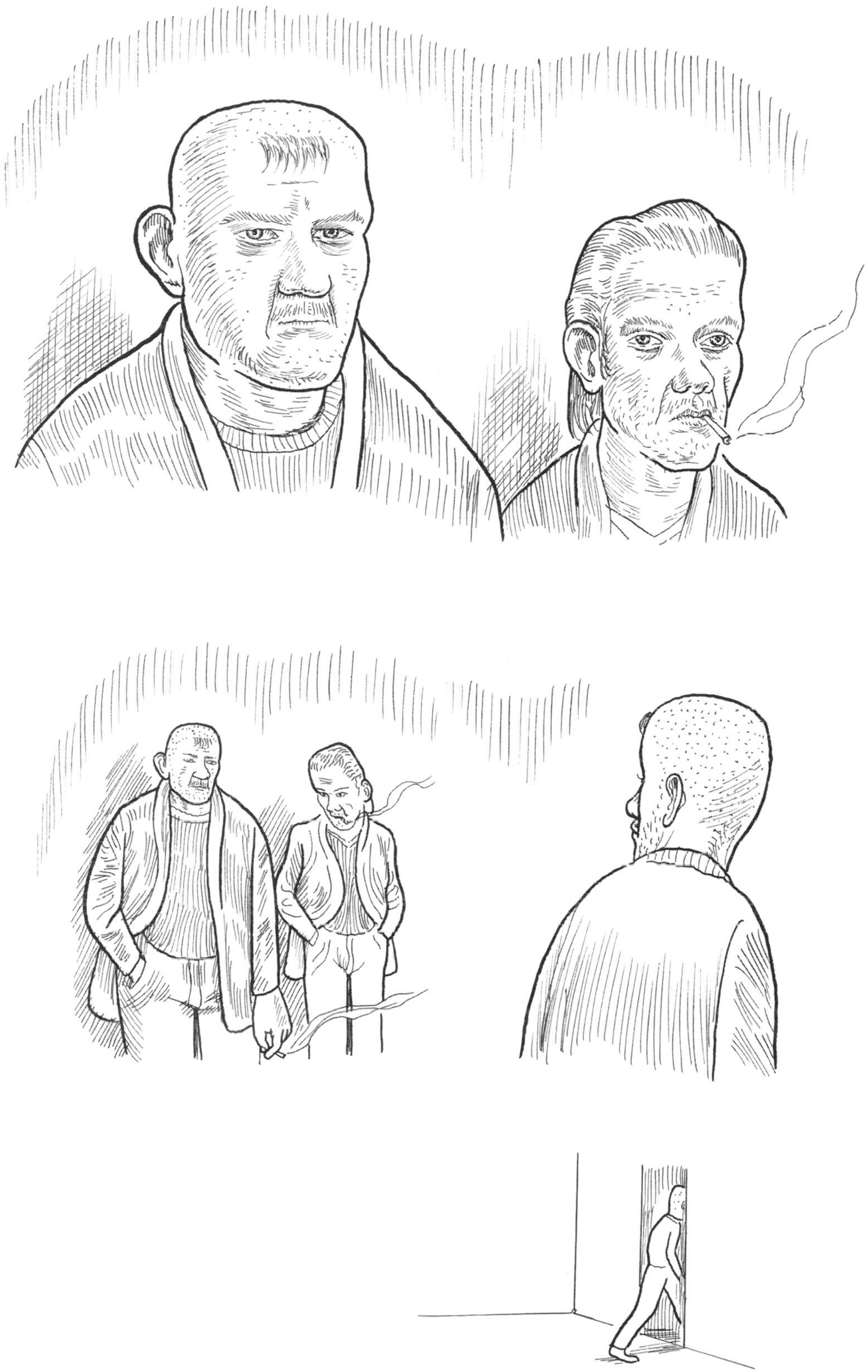

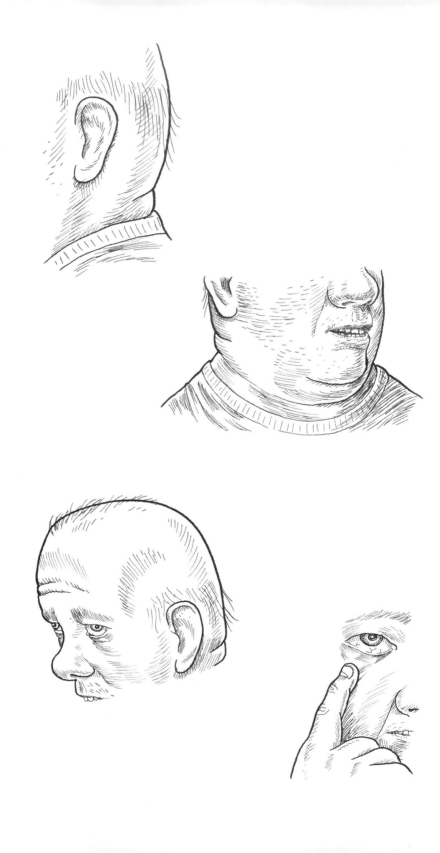

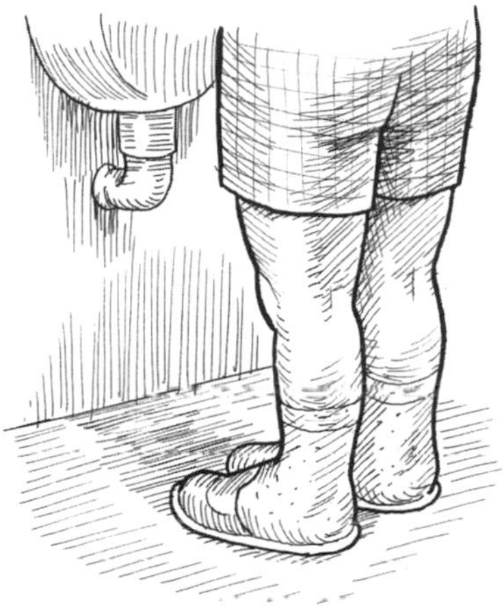

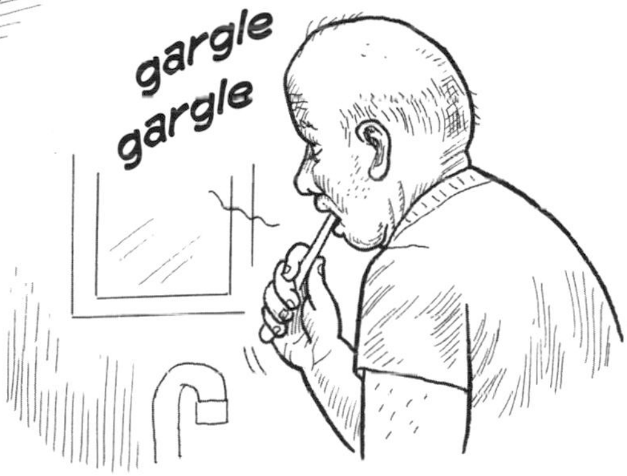
gargle
gargle

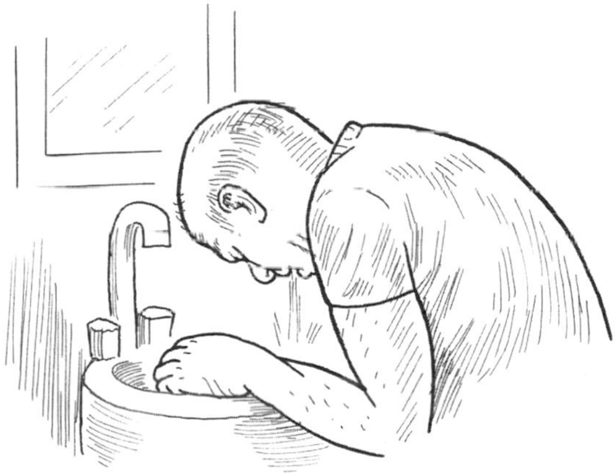

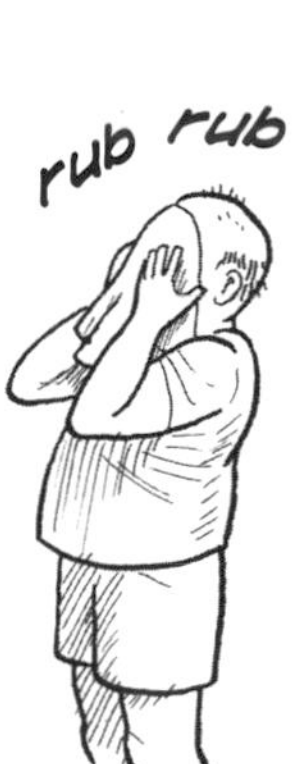
rub rub

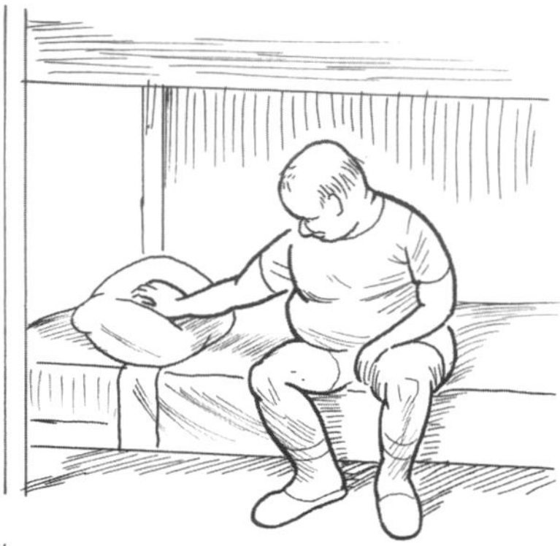

First the pillow. Can't forget to pat the pillow.

Then the socks, tucked between bed and wall.

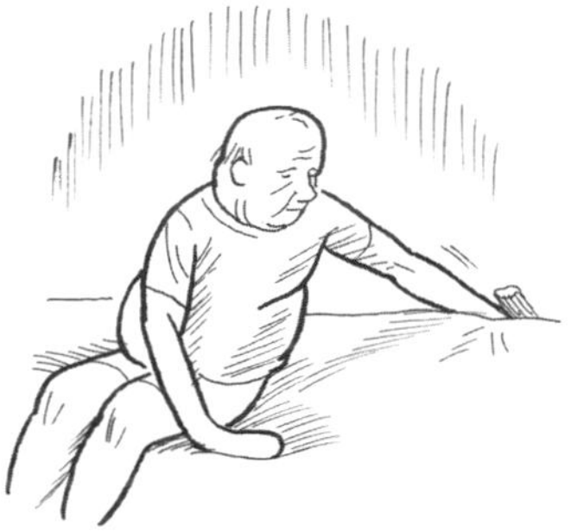

That's right, fatty. Better hide your polyester socks so I don't steal them.

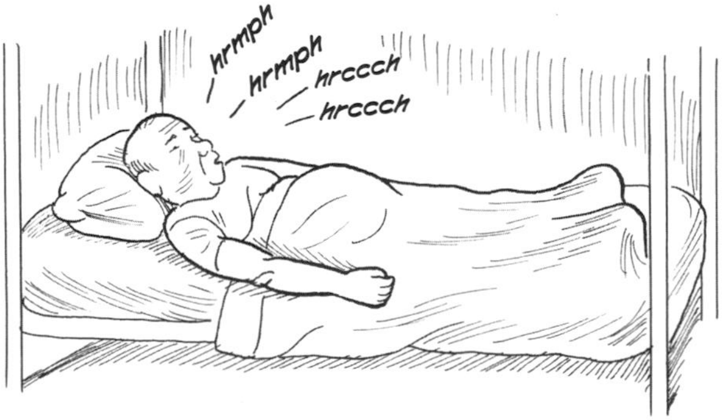
hrmph
hrmph
hrccch
hrccch

Coughing... throat clearing.. ten whole minutes of disgusting noises, punctuated each night by a solemn "Good night, Arthur." And followed by deep breaths I can't keep from counting. I hate this guy.

Who is Denis?

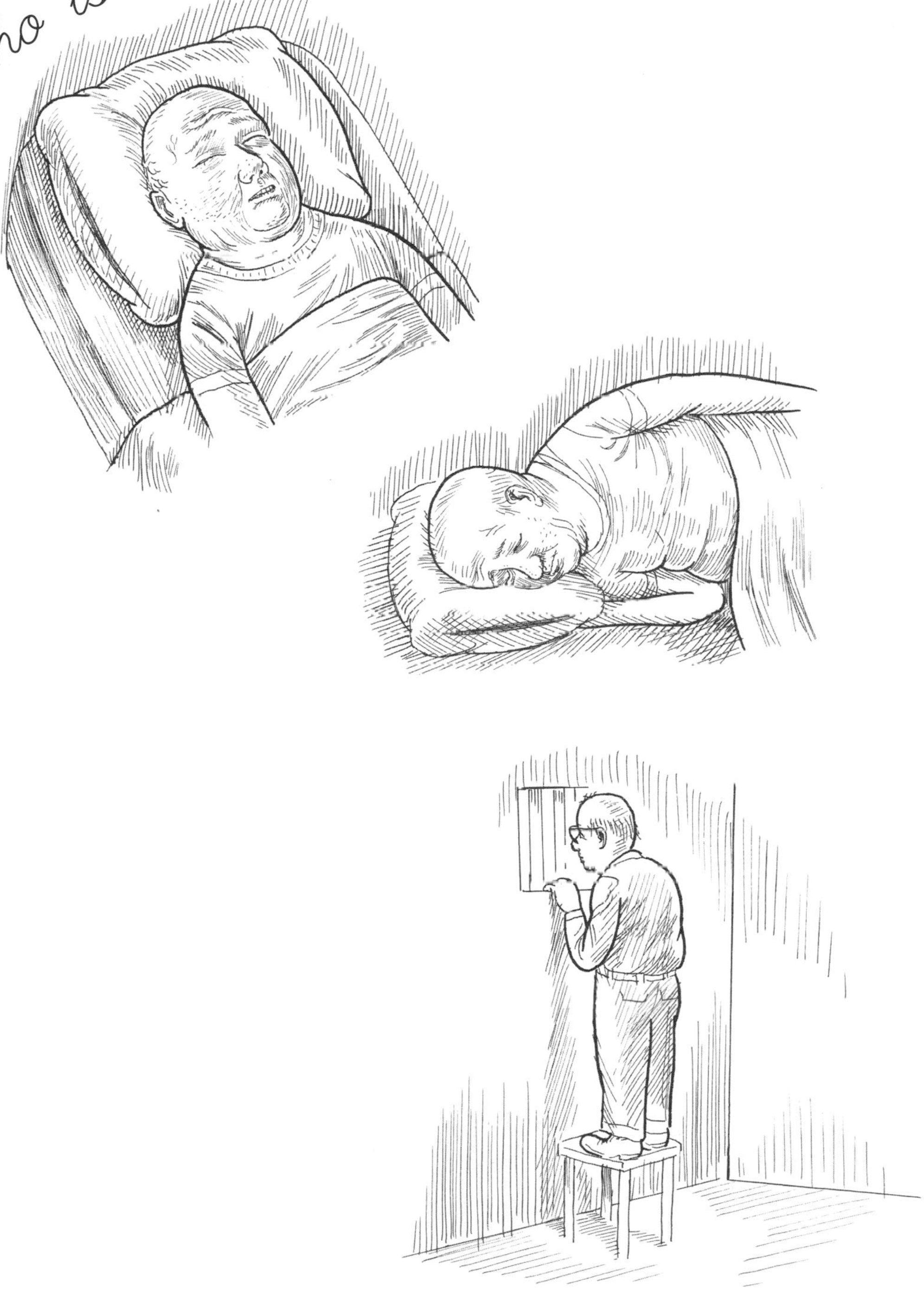

Denis makes lists

Patrick. . .Benjamin. . .Emily. . .Sylviane. . .Jerome. . .Lucy. . .
. . .lists of first names.

Denis tidies

Several hours a day.
Several times a day.

mmm. . . .mm mmmm. . .

Denis talks to himself

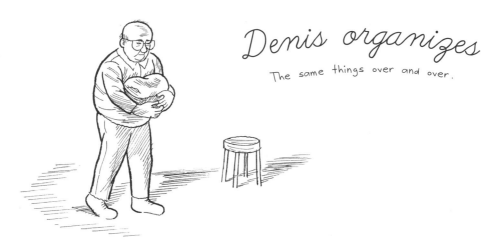

Denis organizes

The same things over and over.

Denis rummages

Through my stuff.

Goddammit!

Why are you fucking touching my stuff, asshole?

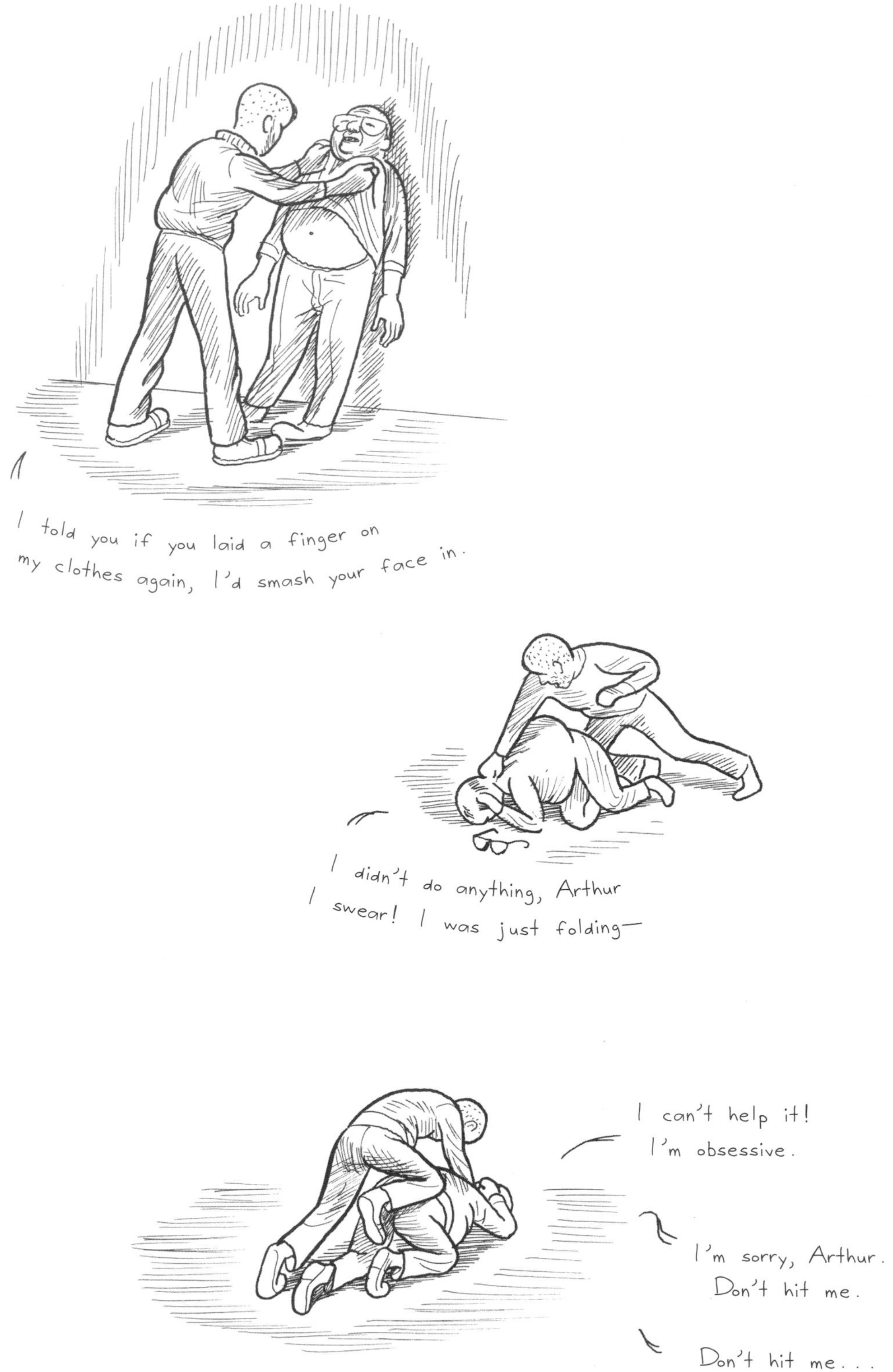
I told you if you laid a finger on my clothes again, I'd smash your face in.
I didn't do anything, Arthur I swear! I was just folding—
I can't help it! I'm obsessive.
I'm sorry, Arthur. Don't hit me.
Don't hit me . . .

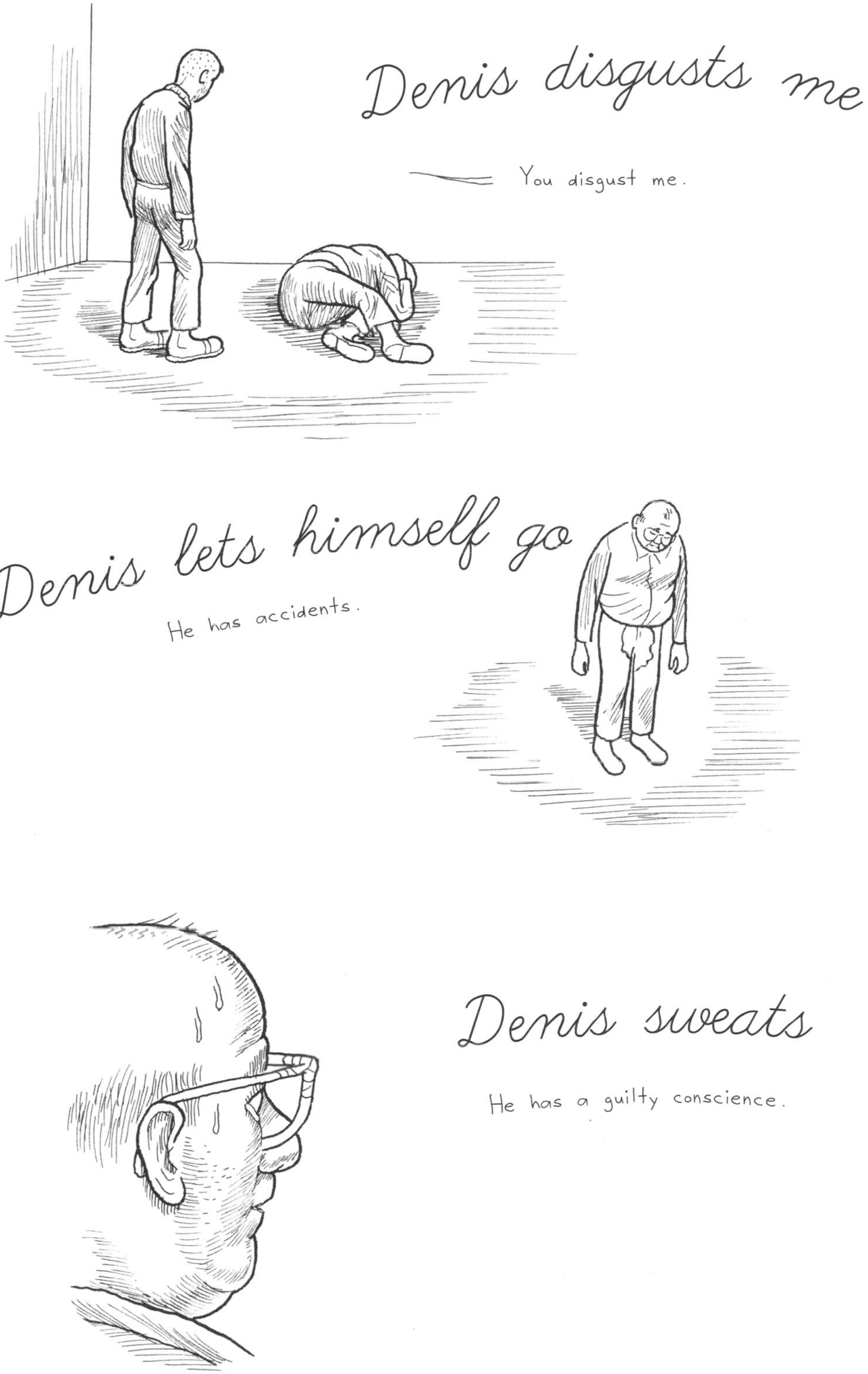
Denis disgusts me
You disgust me.
Denis lets himself go
He has accidents.
Denis sweats
He has a guilty conscience.

Denis drags his feet

At least he doesn't move much.

Denis is depressed

Sometimes he even cries.

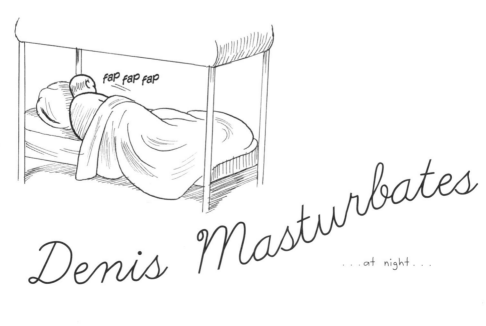

fap fap fap

Denis Masturbates

. . . at night . . .

Goddammit, fatass!

Do you think I can't tell what you're doing?

Don't fucking whack off while I'm here.
It makes me want to hurl.

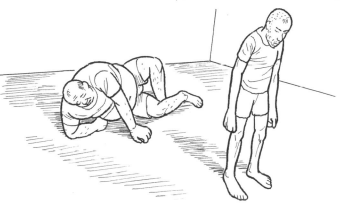

You can't stop me.

I've got a right to, like everyone else.

What?

What did you
say, fuckwad?

You have no rights here!

What are you jacking off to?

Huh? What do you think about, asshole?

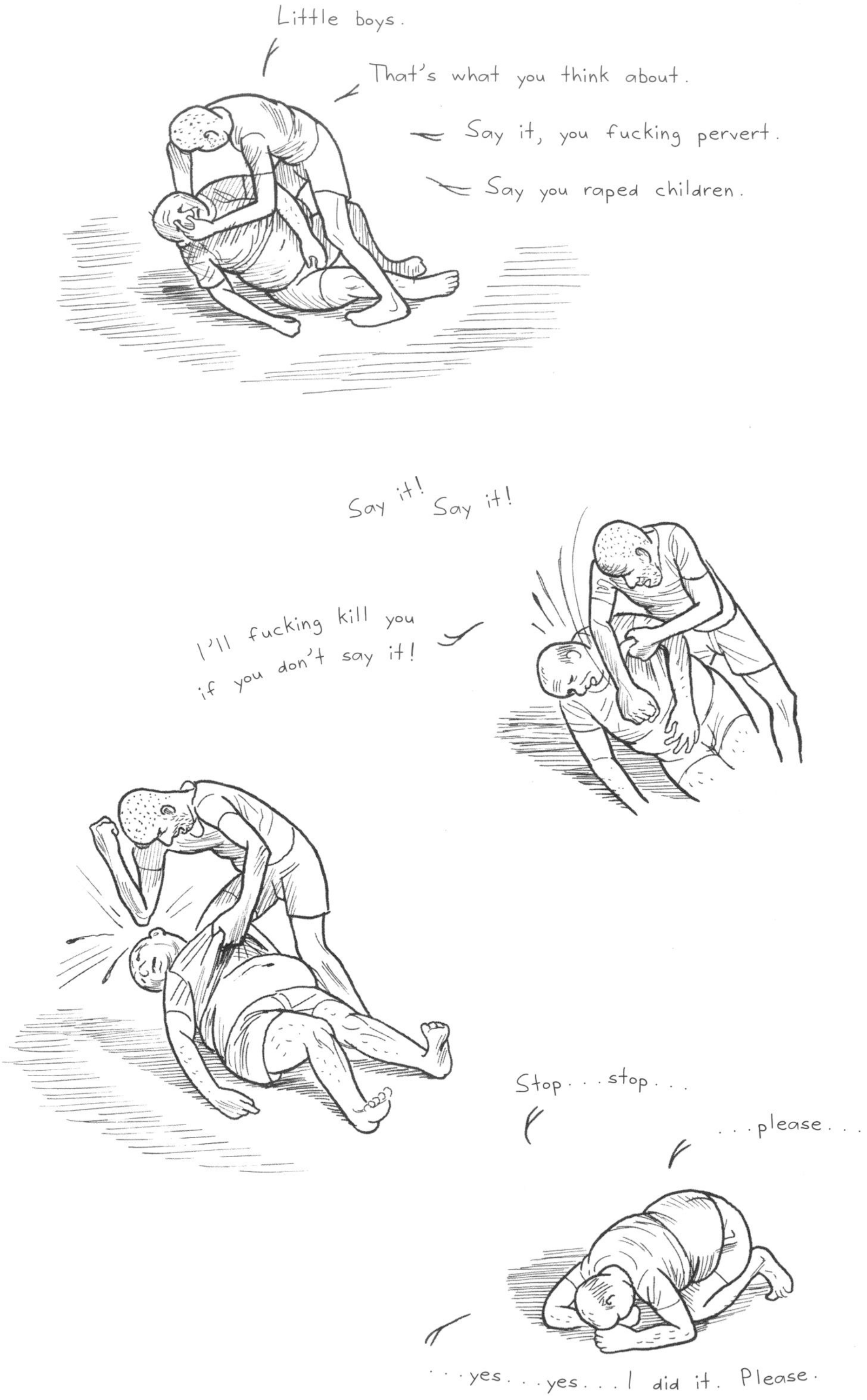
Little boys.
That's what you think about.
Say it, you fucking pervert.
Say you raped children.
Say it! Say it!
I'll fucking kill you if you don't say it!
Stop... stop...
...please...
...yes... yes... I did it. Please.

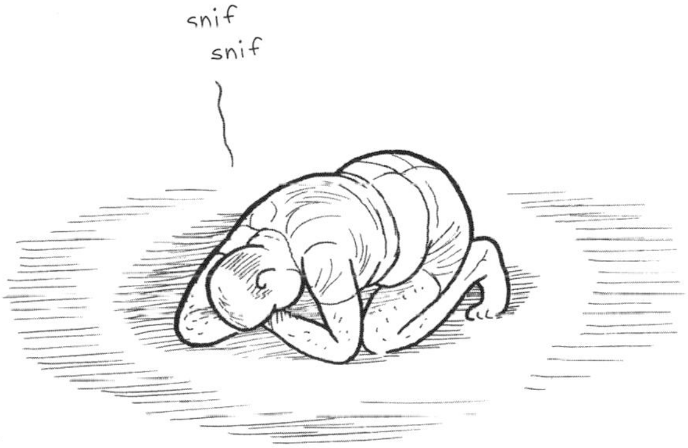
snif
snif

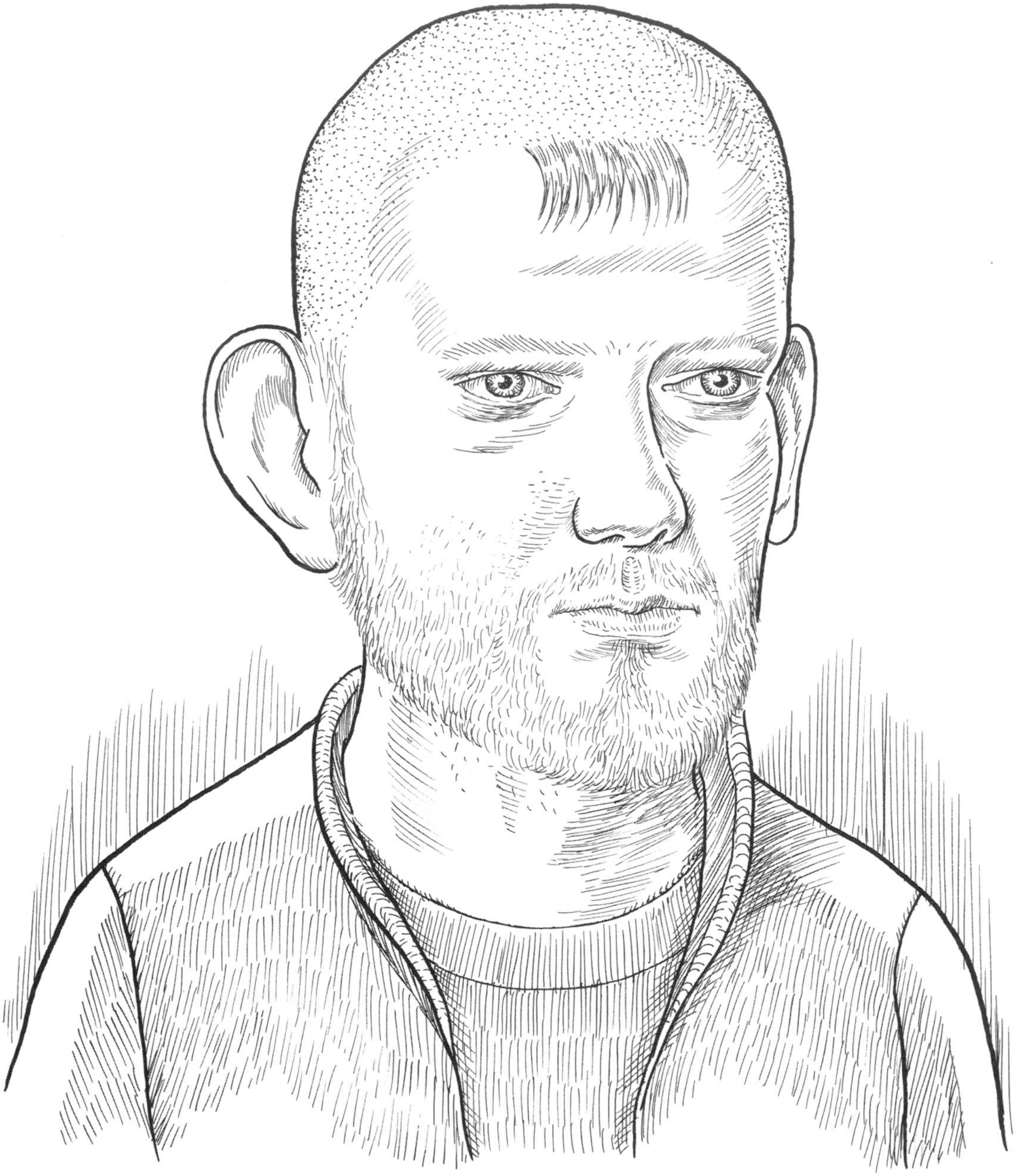

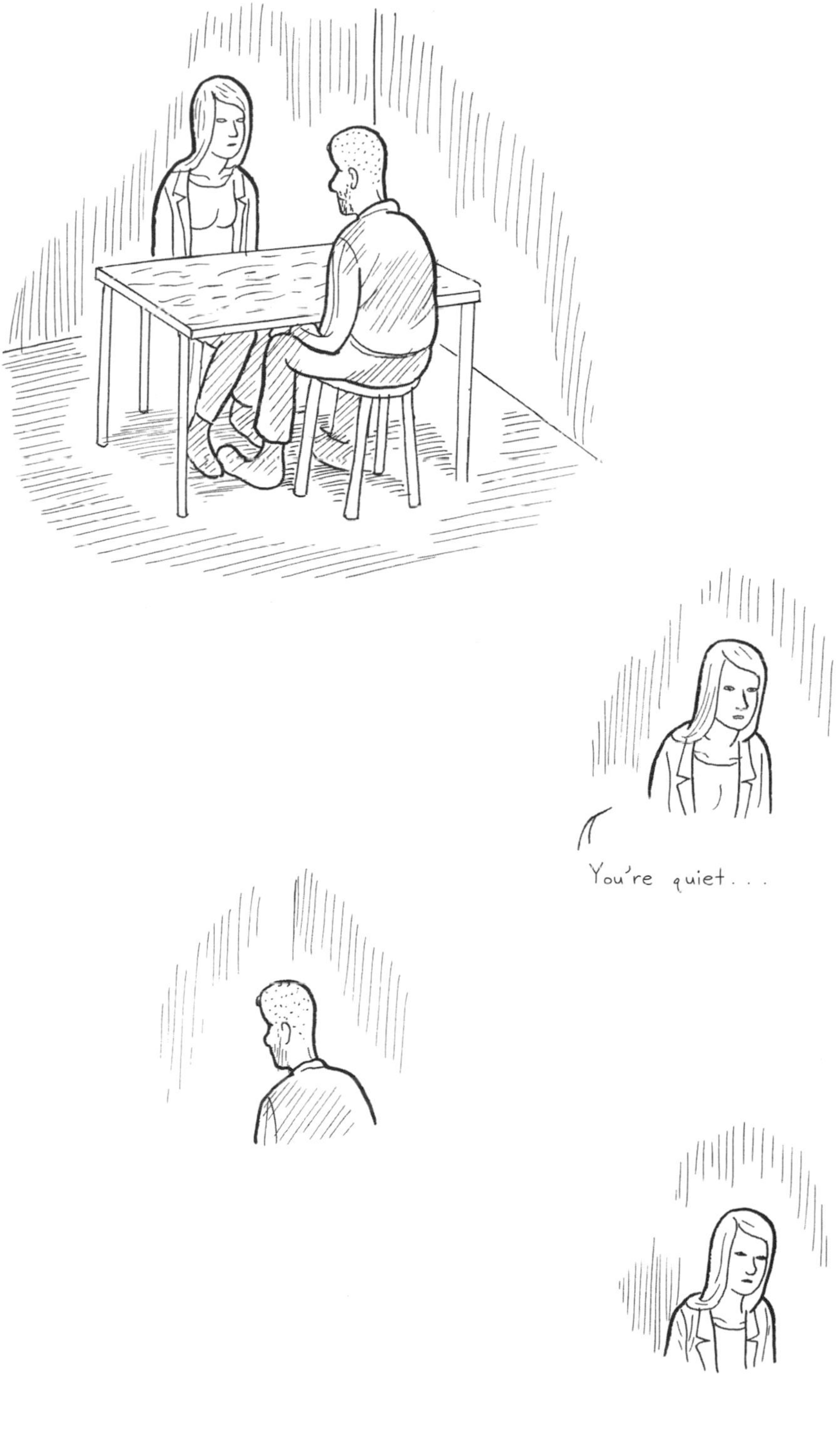
You're quiet...

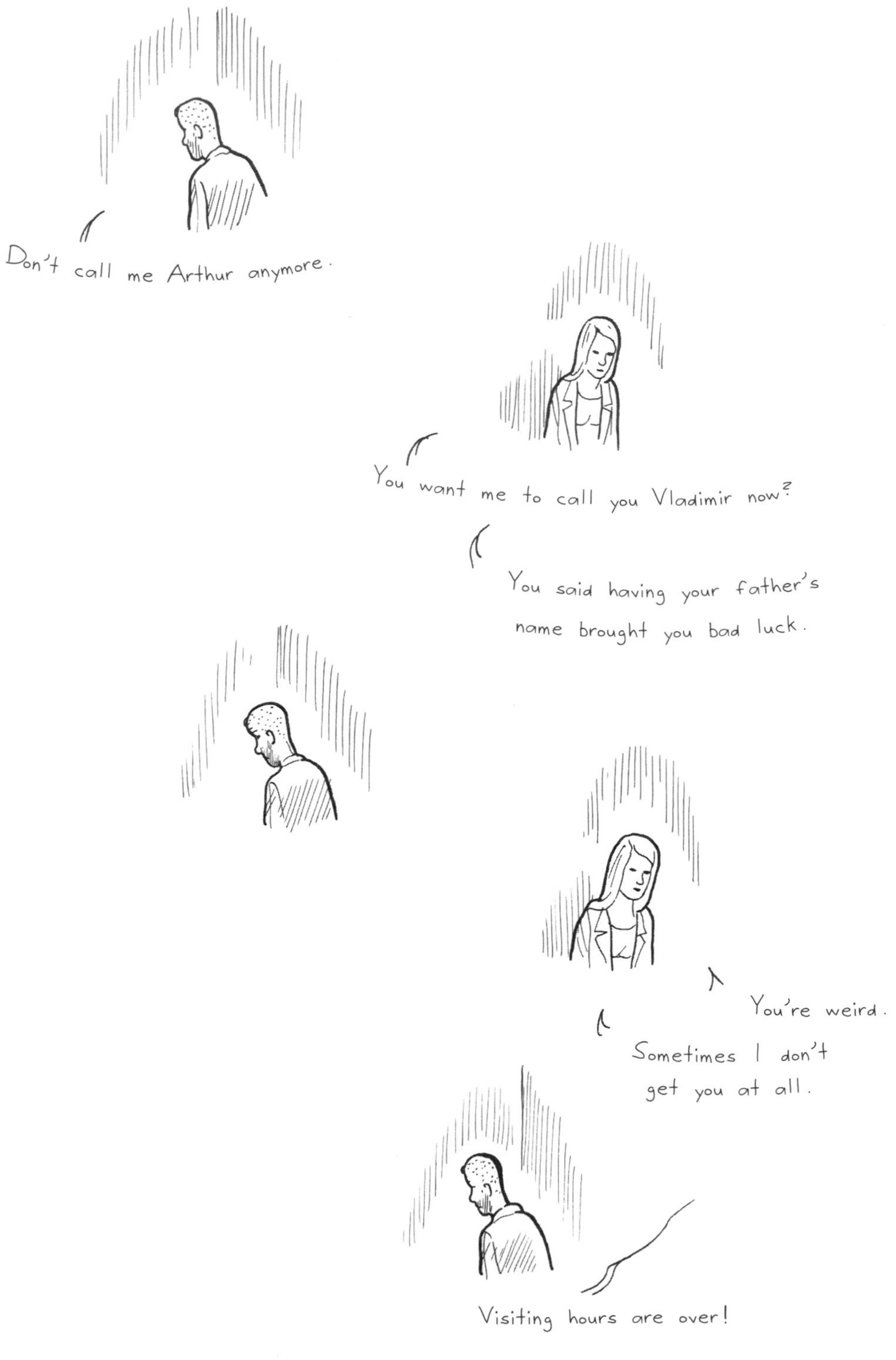
Don't call me Arthur anymore.
You want me to call you Vladimir now?
You said having your father's name brought you bad luck.
You're weird.
Sometimes I don't get you at all.
Visiting hours are over!

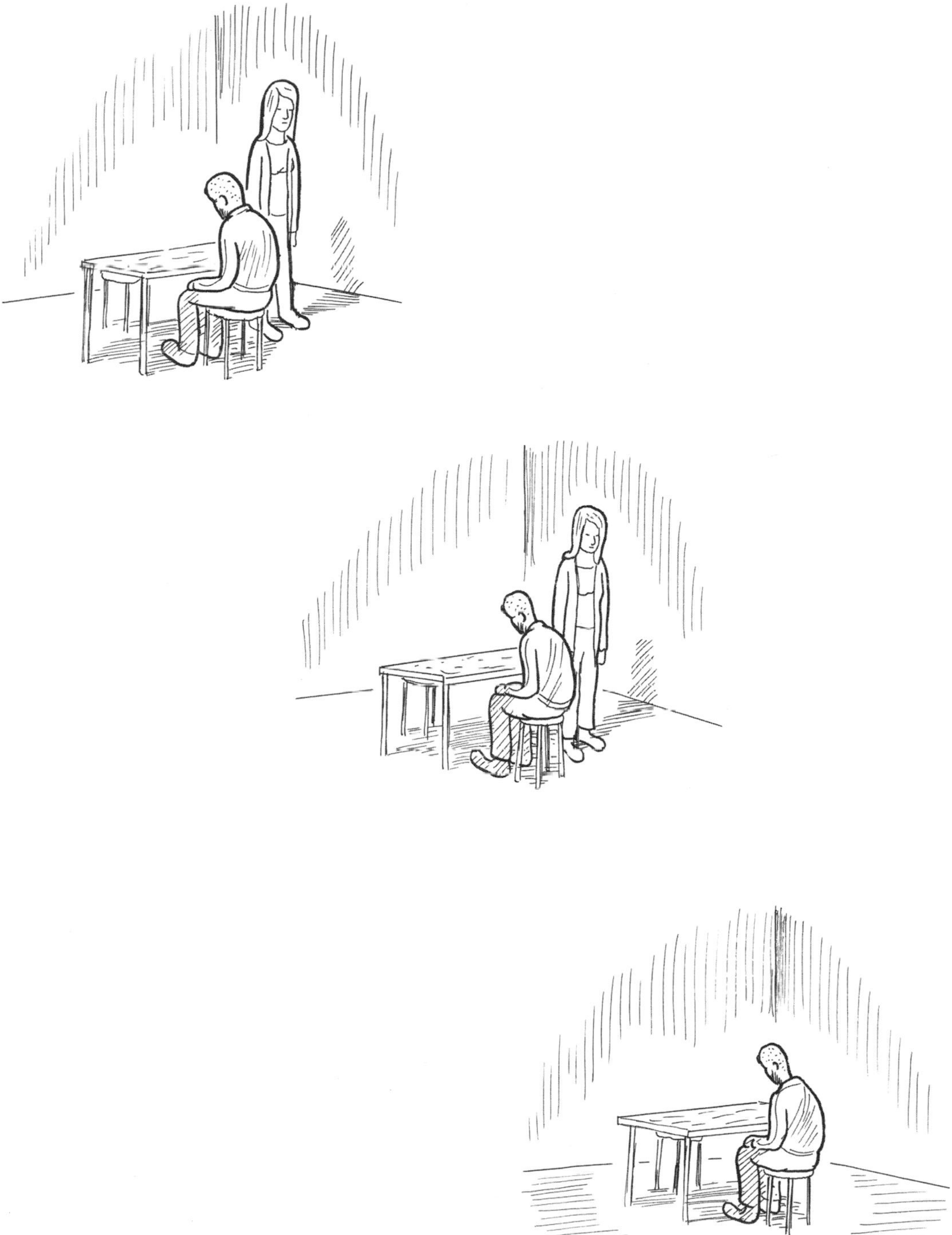

Pierre. . .

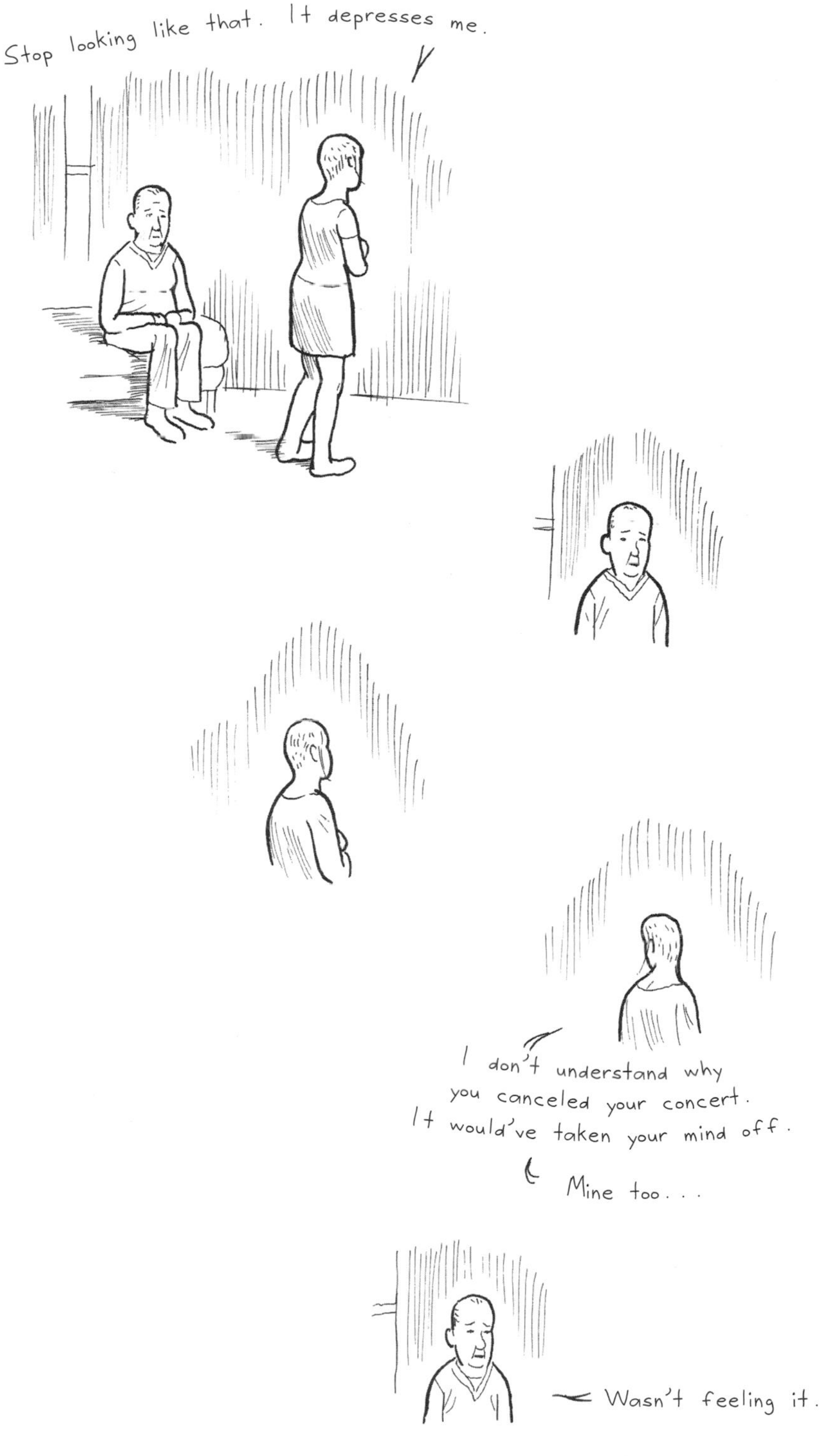
Stop looking like that. It depresses me.
I don't understand why you canceled your concert. It would've taken your mind off.
Mine too...
Wasn't feeling it.

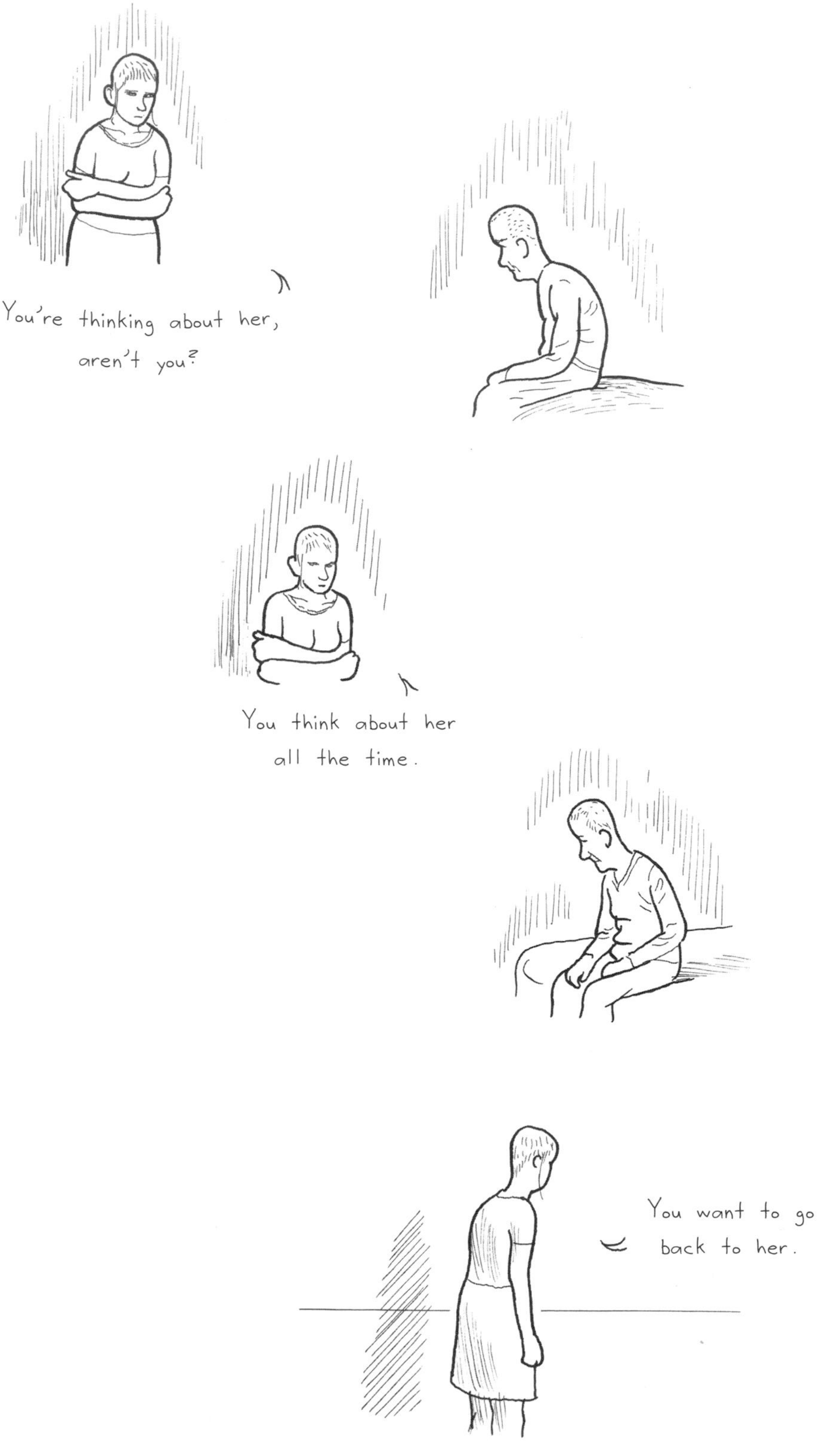
You're thinking about her, aren't you?
You think about her all the time.
You want to go back to her.

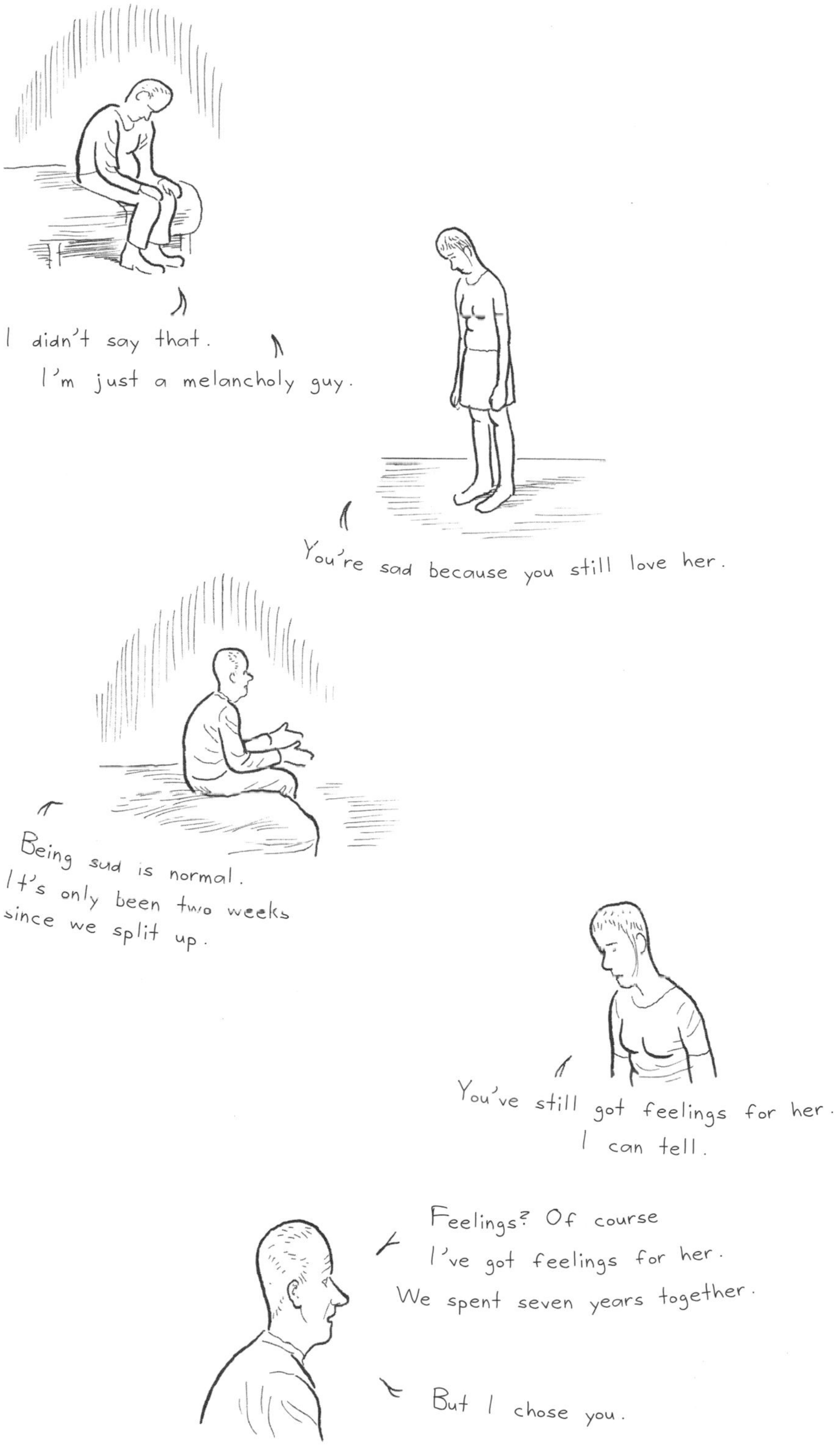

I didn't say that.
I'm just a melancholy guy.
You're sad because you still love her.
Being sad is normal.
It's only been two weeks since we split up.
You've still got feelings for her. I can tell.
Feelings? Of course I've got feelings for her. We spent seven years together.
But I chose you.

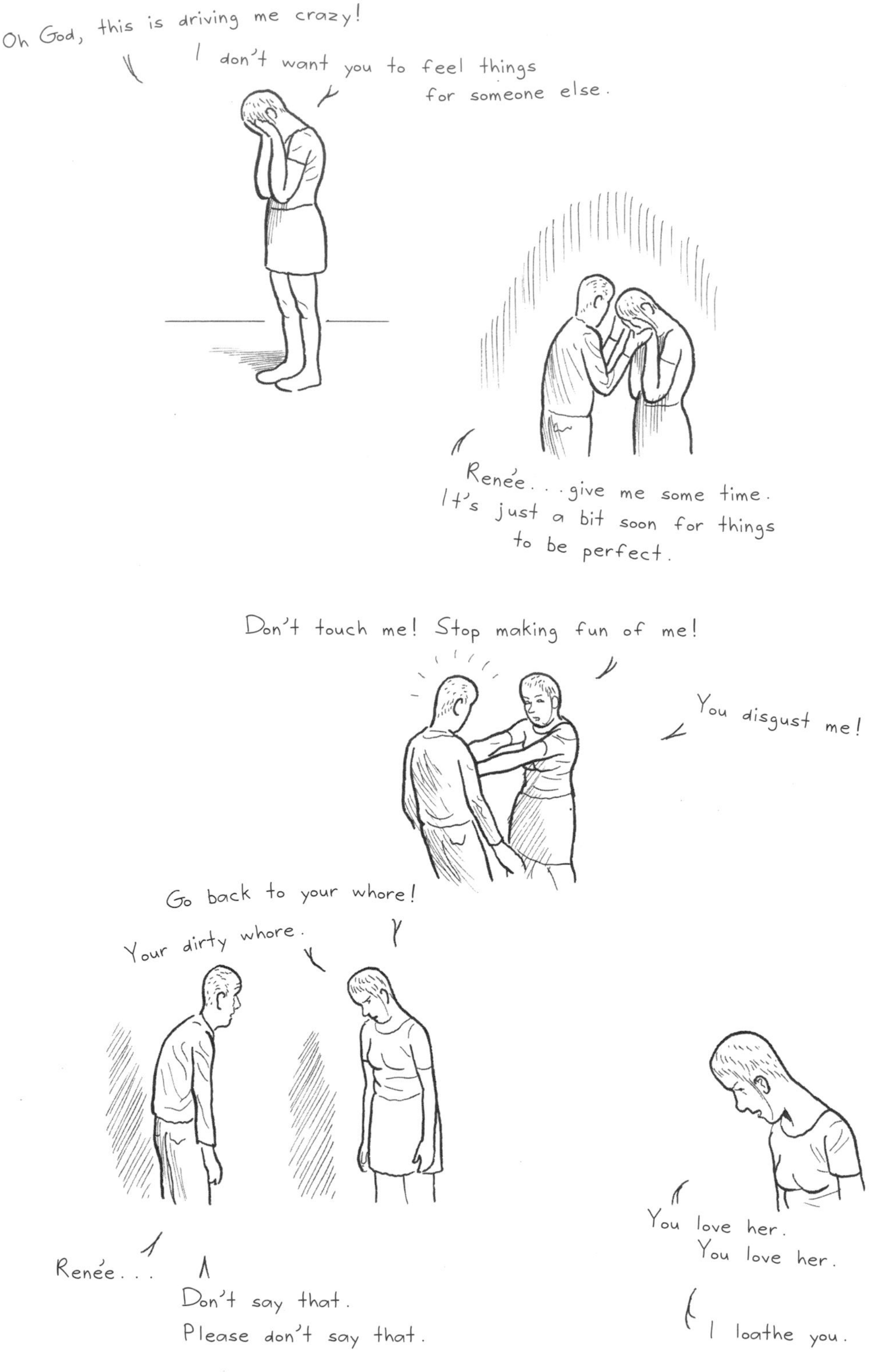
Oh God, this is driving me crazy!
I don't want you to feel things for someone else.
Renée...give me some time. It's just a bit soon for things to be perfect.
Don't touch me! Stop making fun of me!
You disgust me!
Go back to your whore!
Your dirty whore.
Renée...
Don't say that. Please don't say that.
You love her. You love her.
I loathe you.

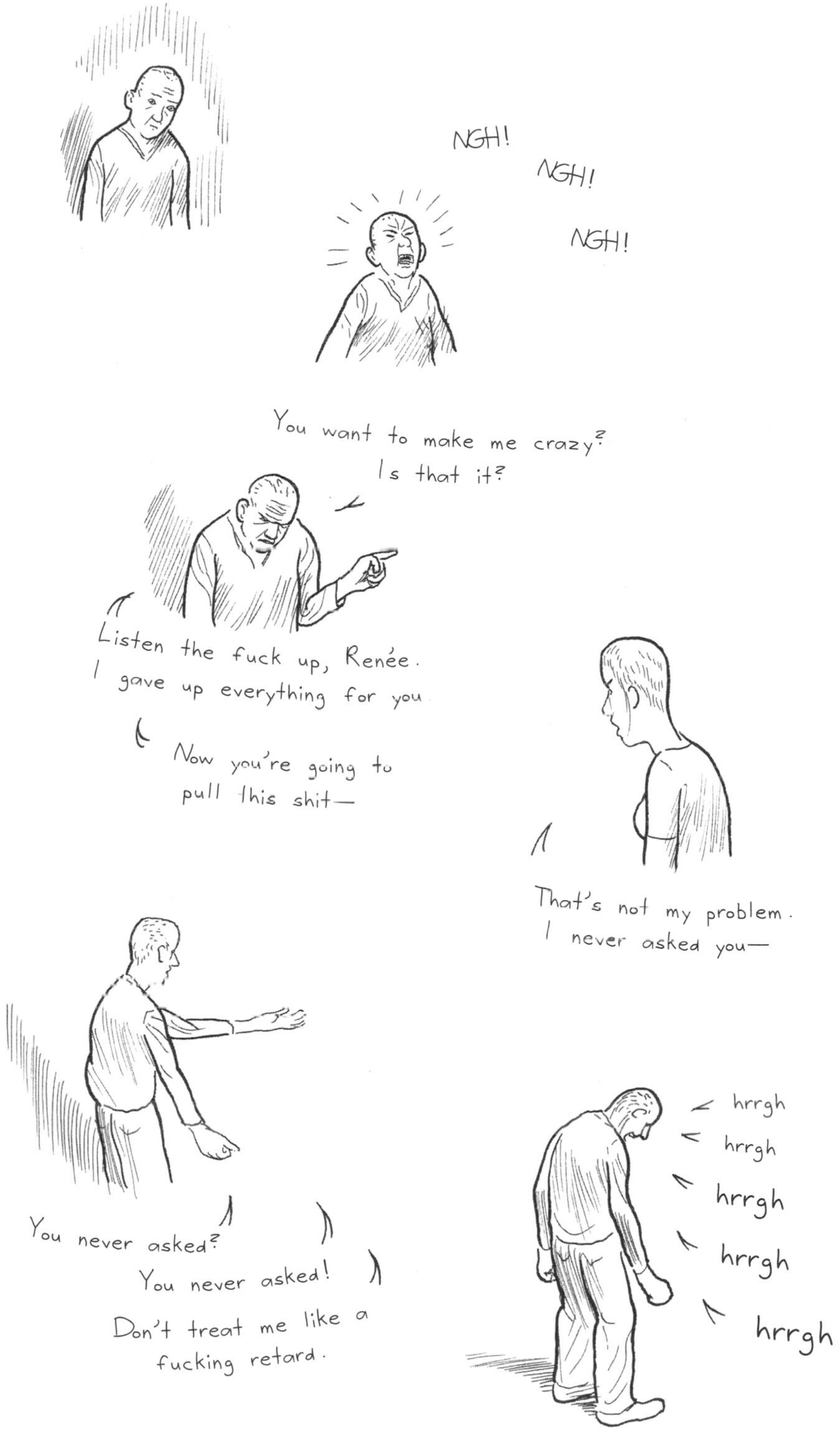
NGH!
NGH!
NGH!
You want to make me crazy? Is that it?
Listen the fuck up, Renée. I gave up everything for you.
Now you're going to pull this shit—
That's not my problem. I never asked you—
You never asked?
You never asked!
Don't treat me like a fucking retard.
hrrgh
hrrgh
hrrgh
hrrgh
hrrgh

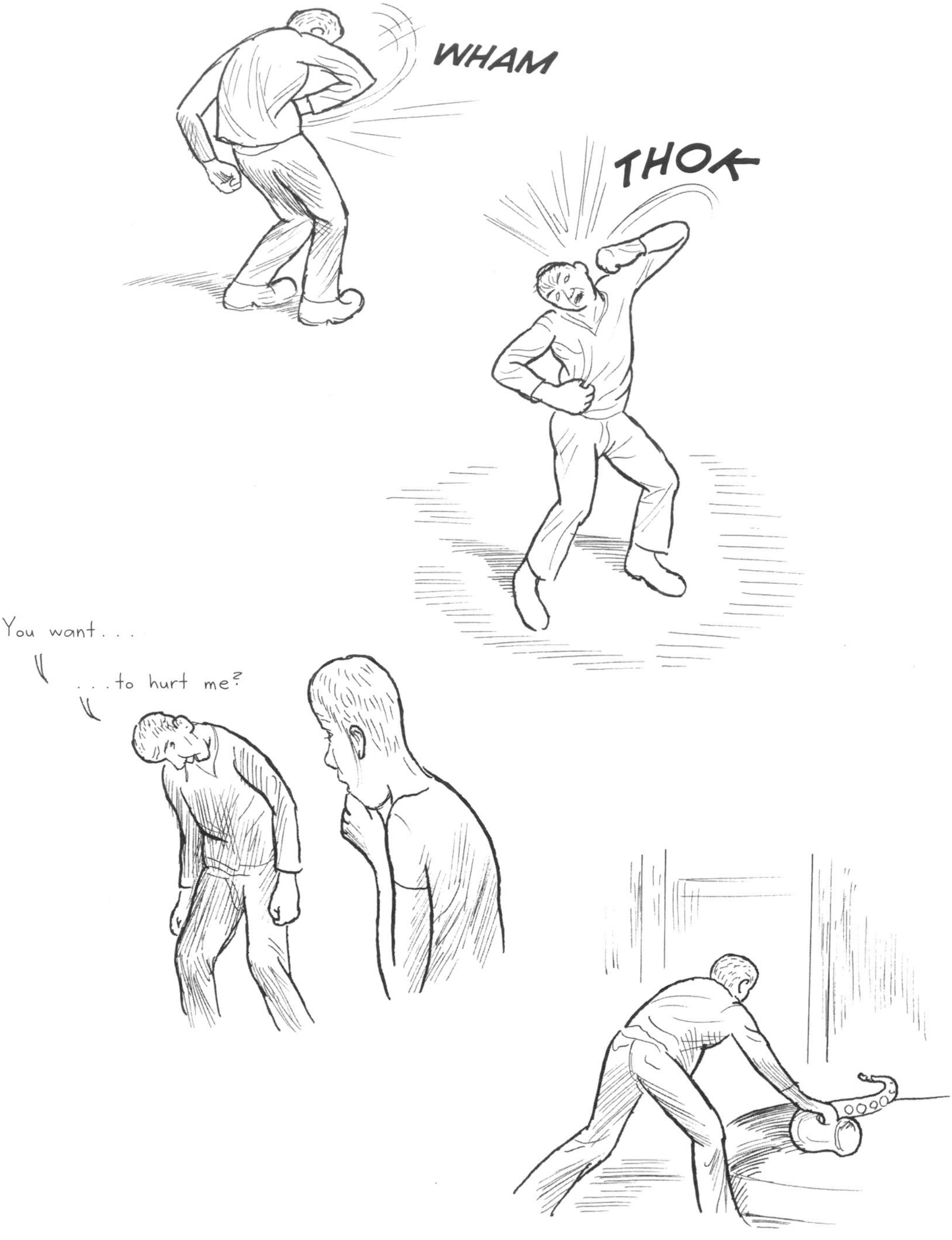
WHAM
THOK
You want...
...to hurt me?

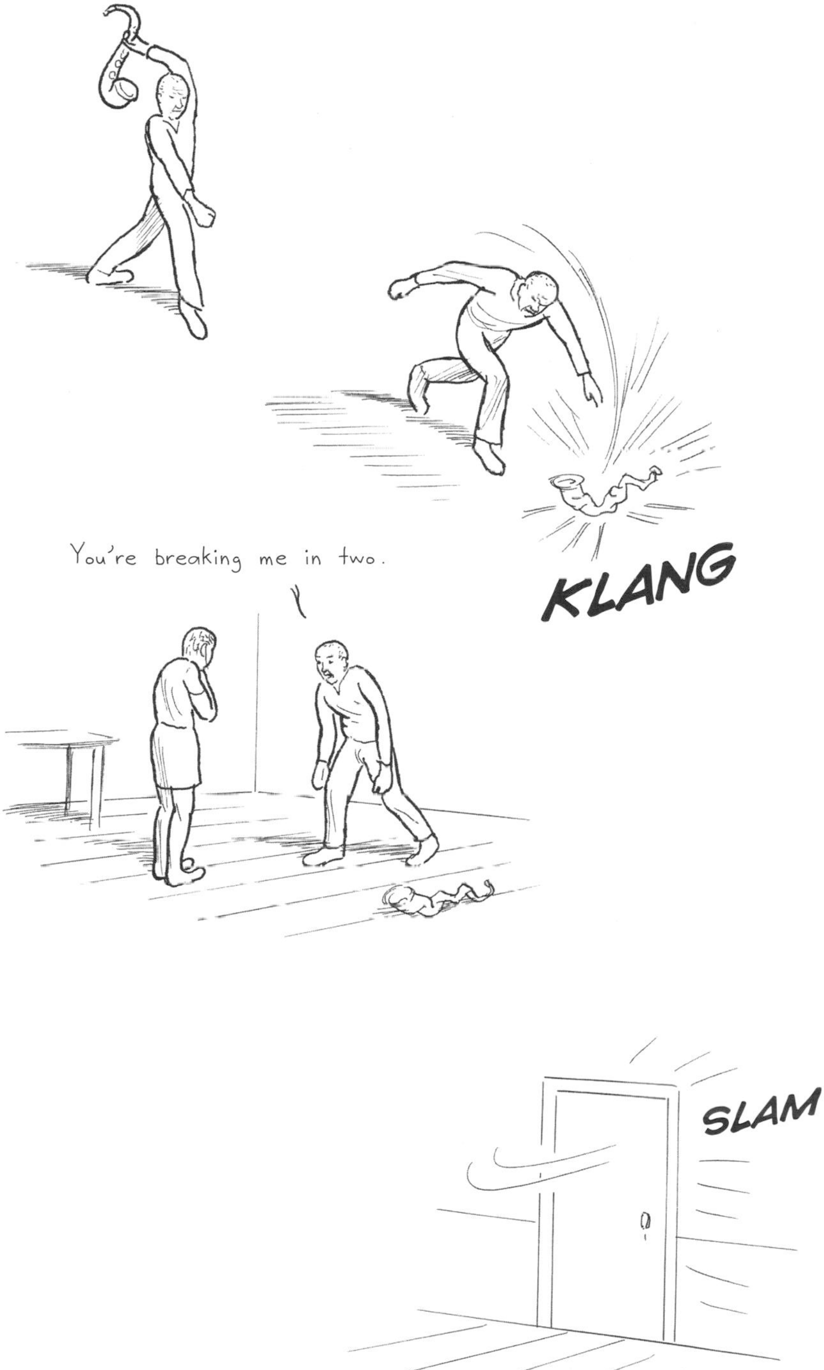
KLANG
You're breaking me in two.
SLAM

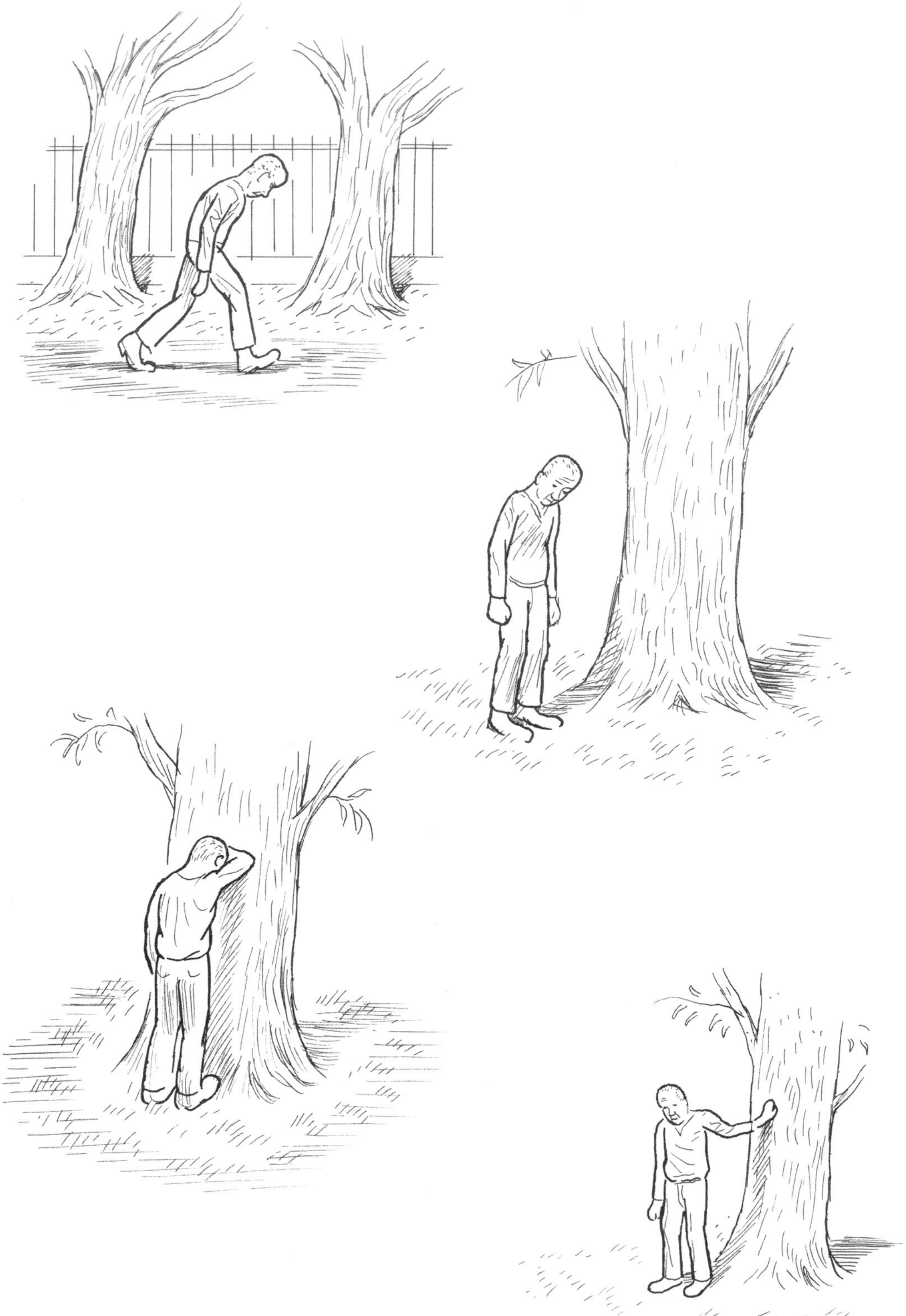

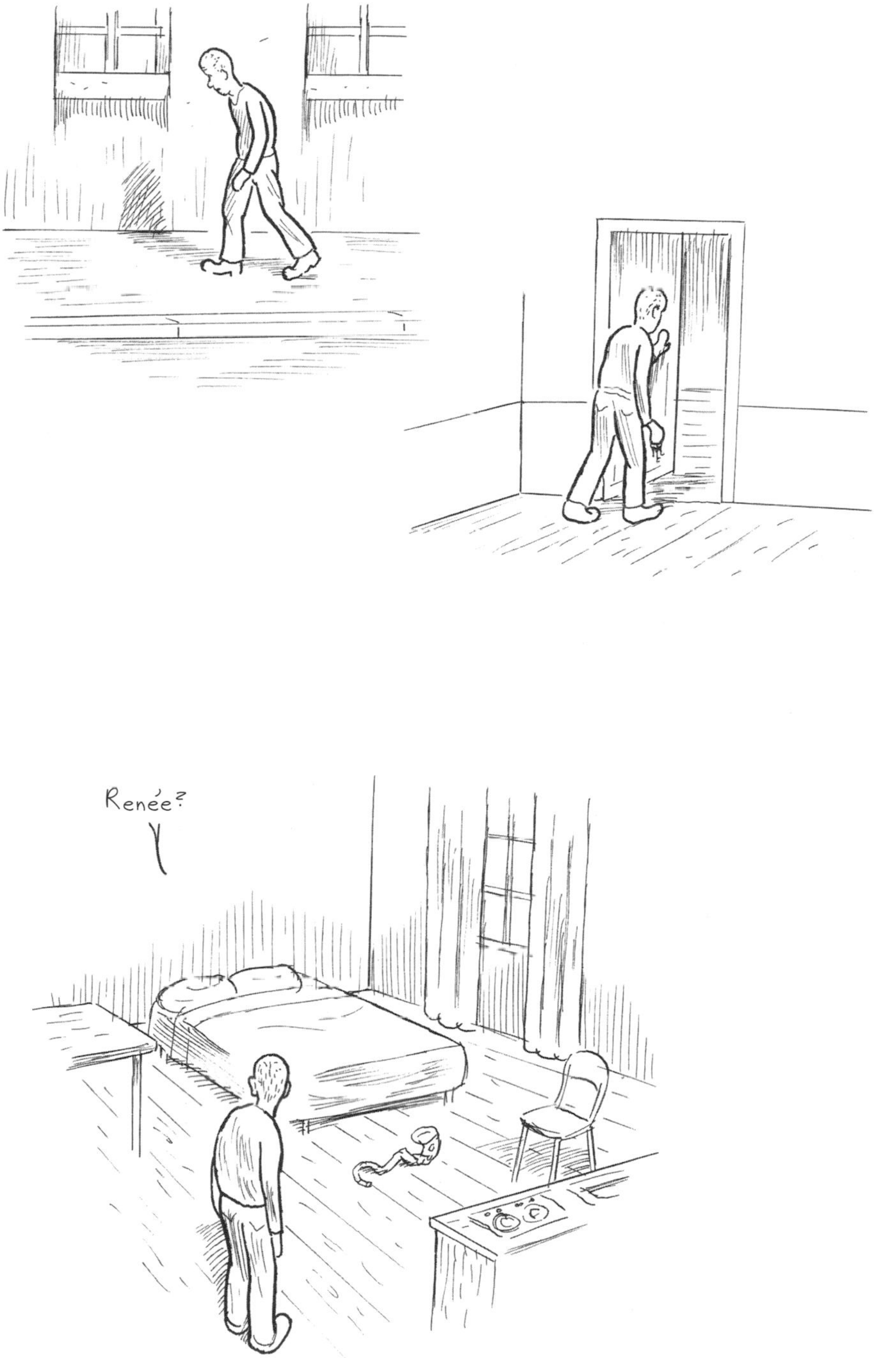
Renée?

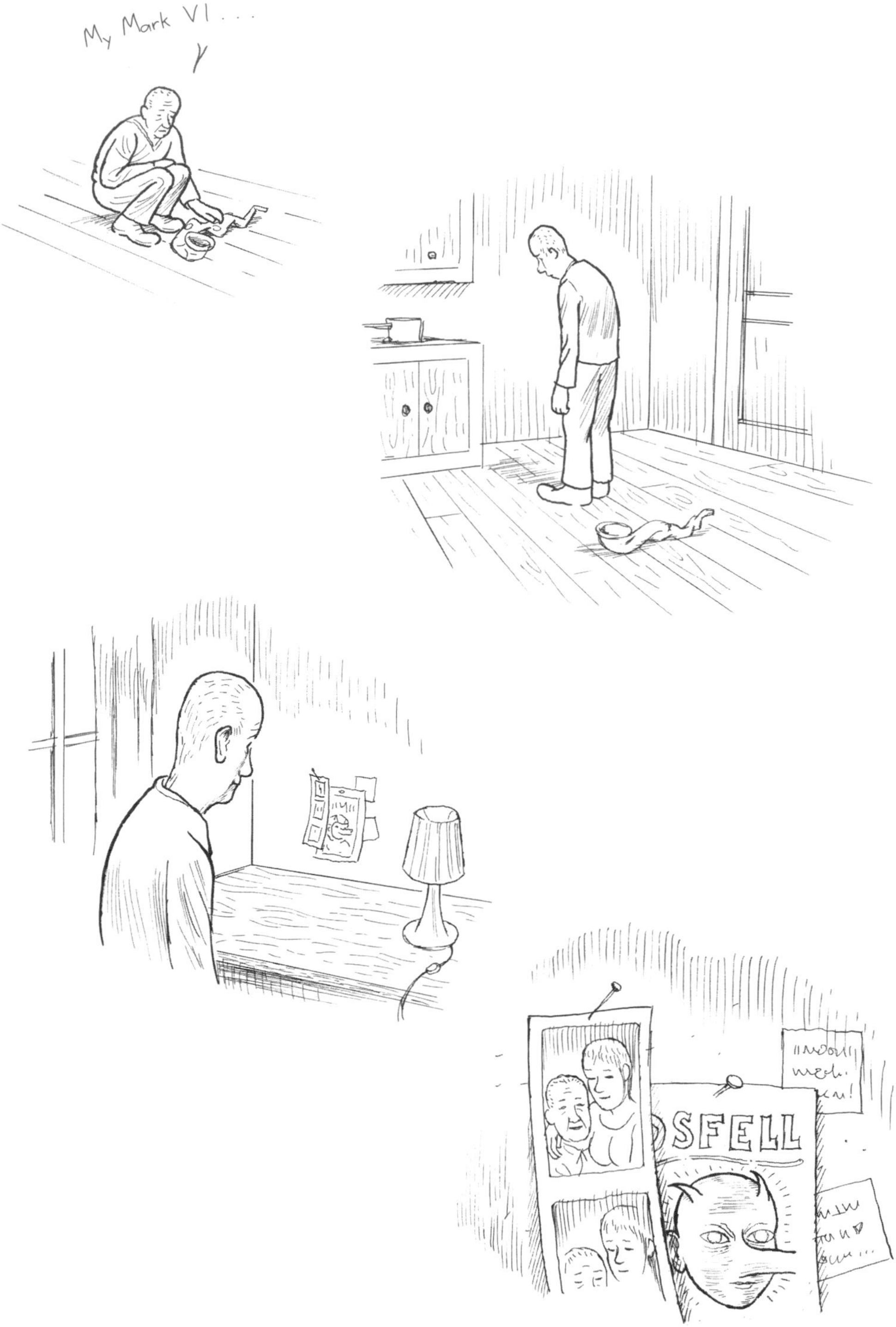
My Mark VI . . .
SFELL

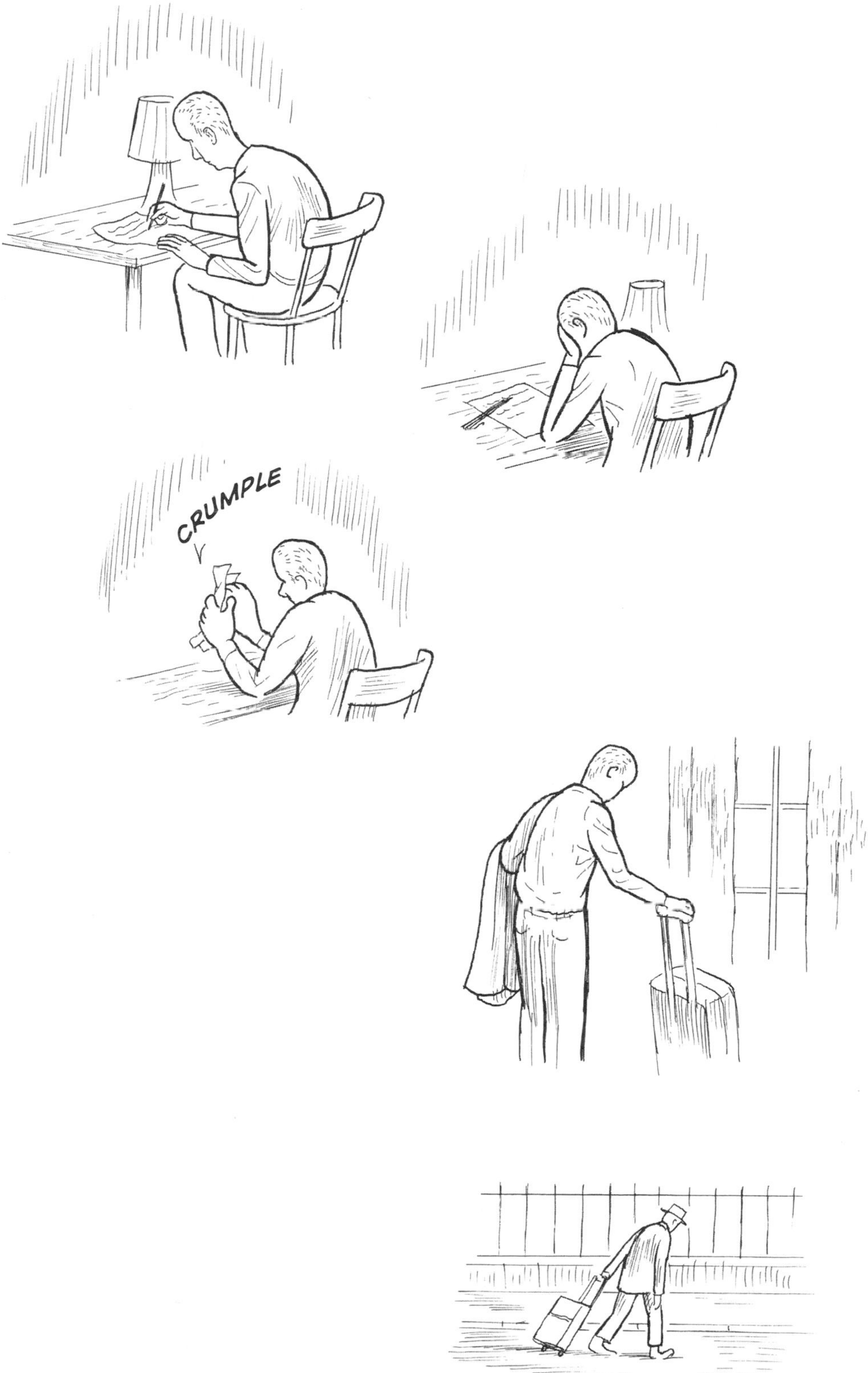
CRUMPLE

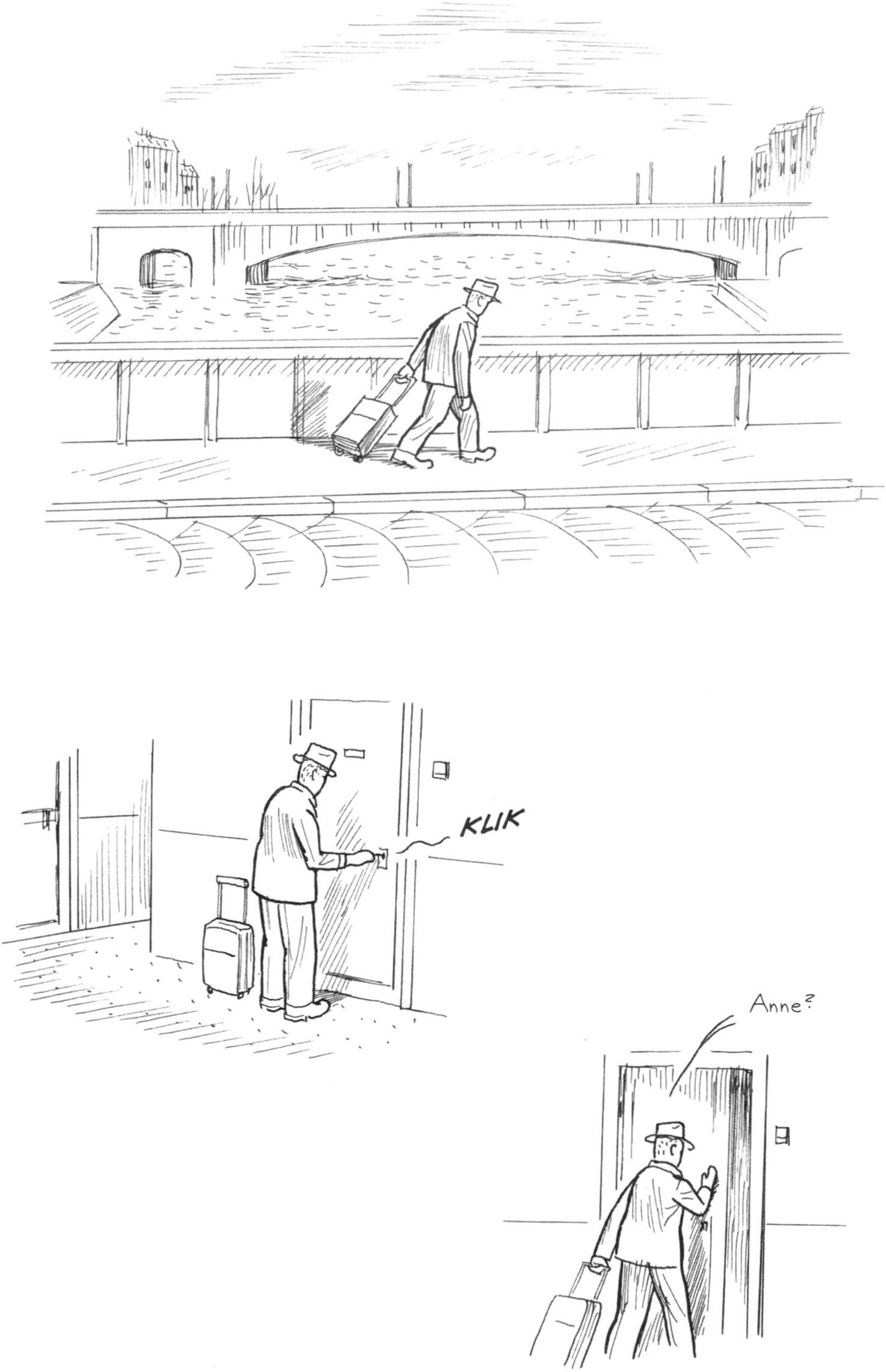
KLIK
Anne?

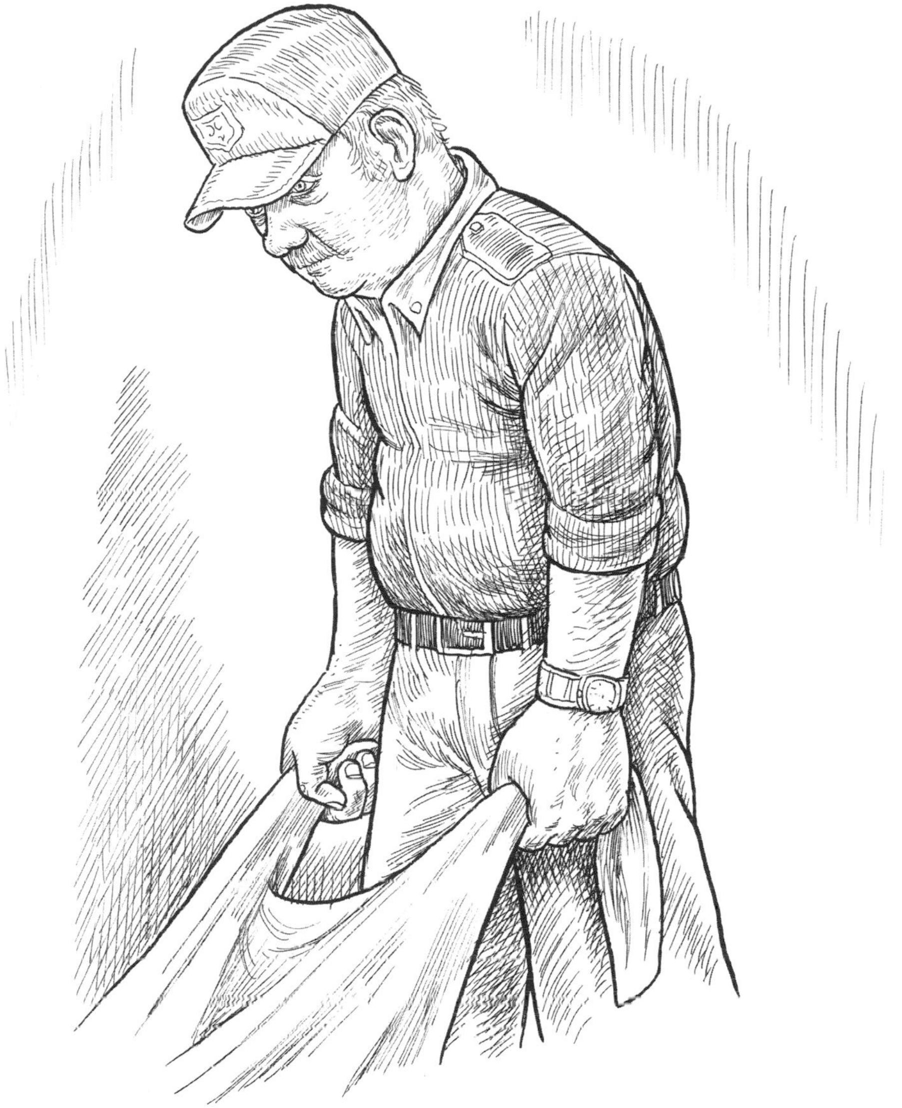

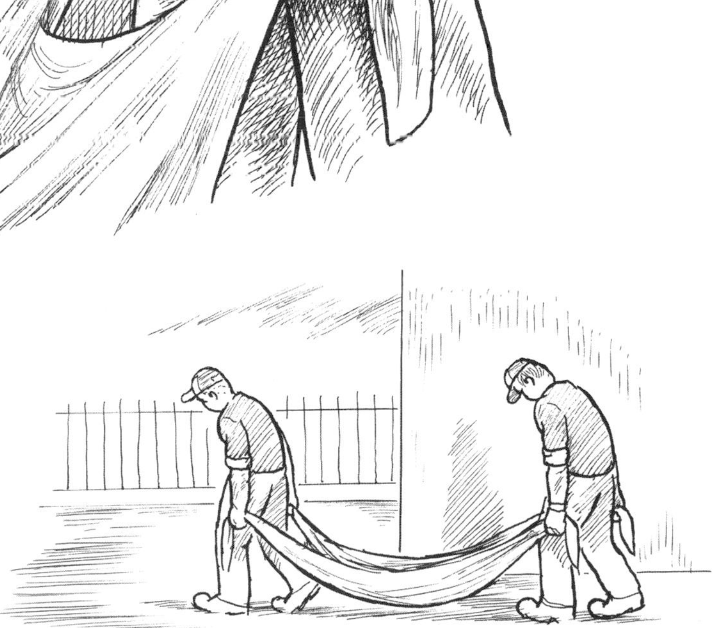

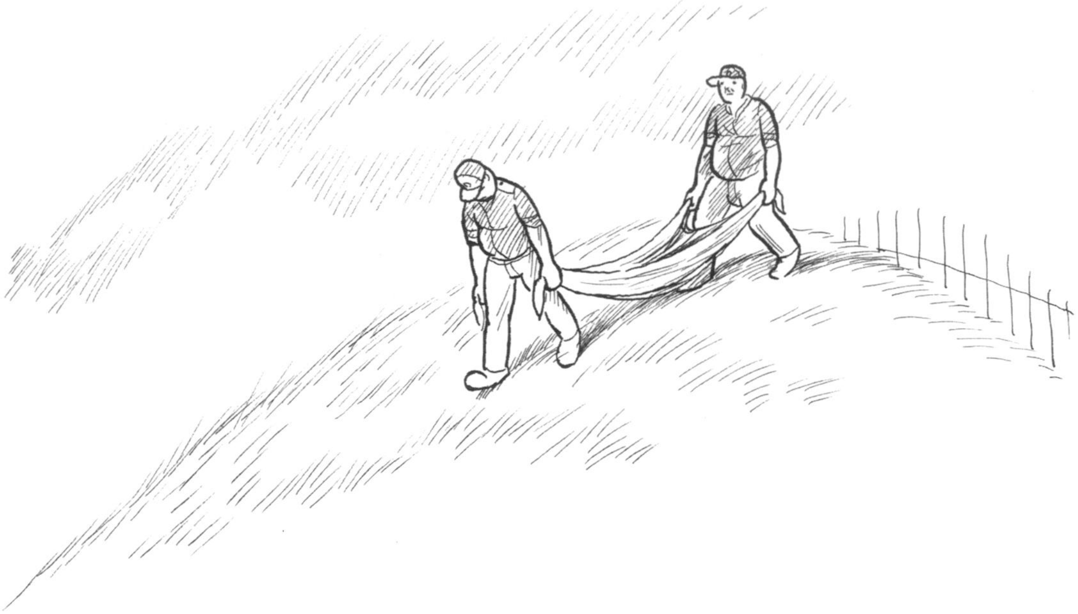

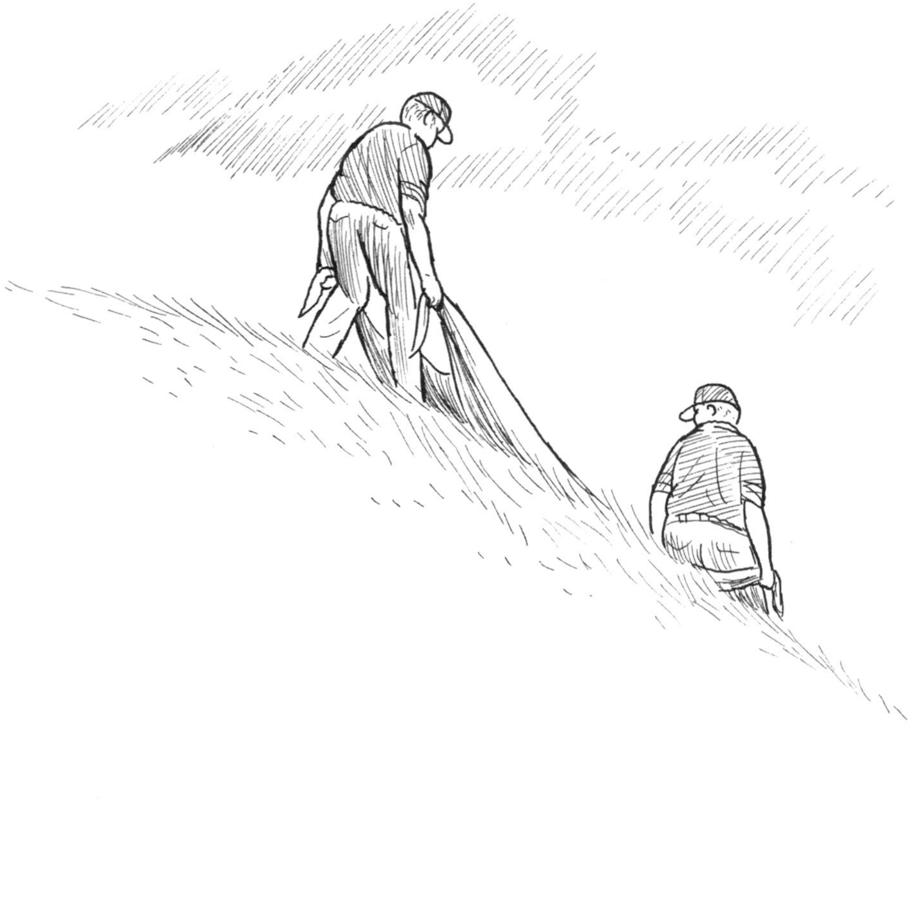

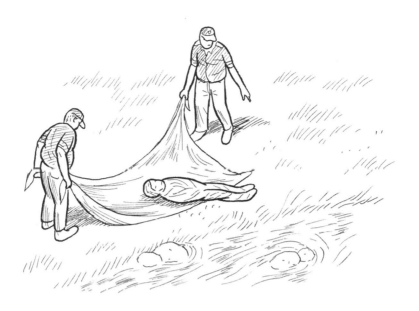

sploosh

SPLAK

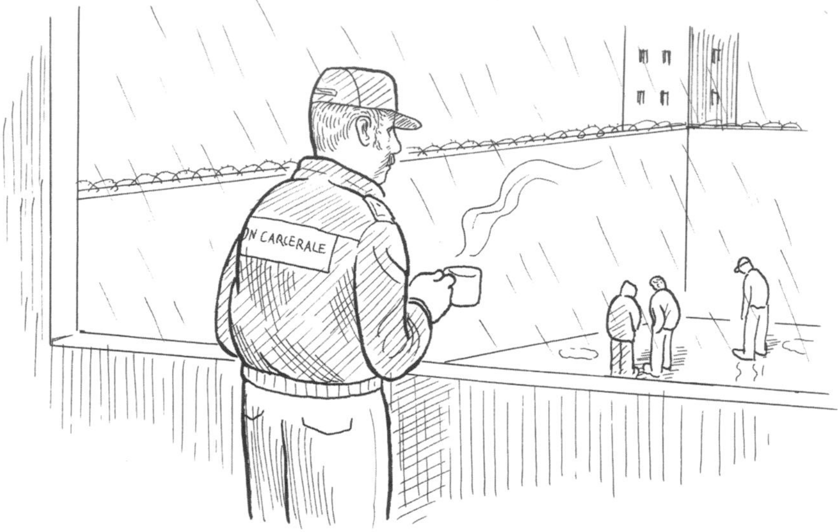
ON CARCERALE

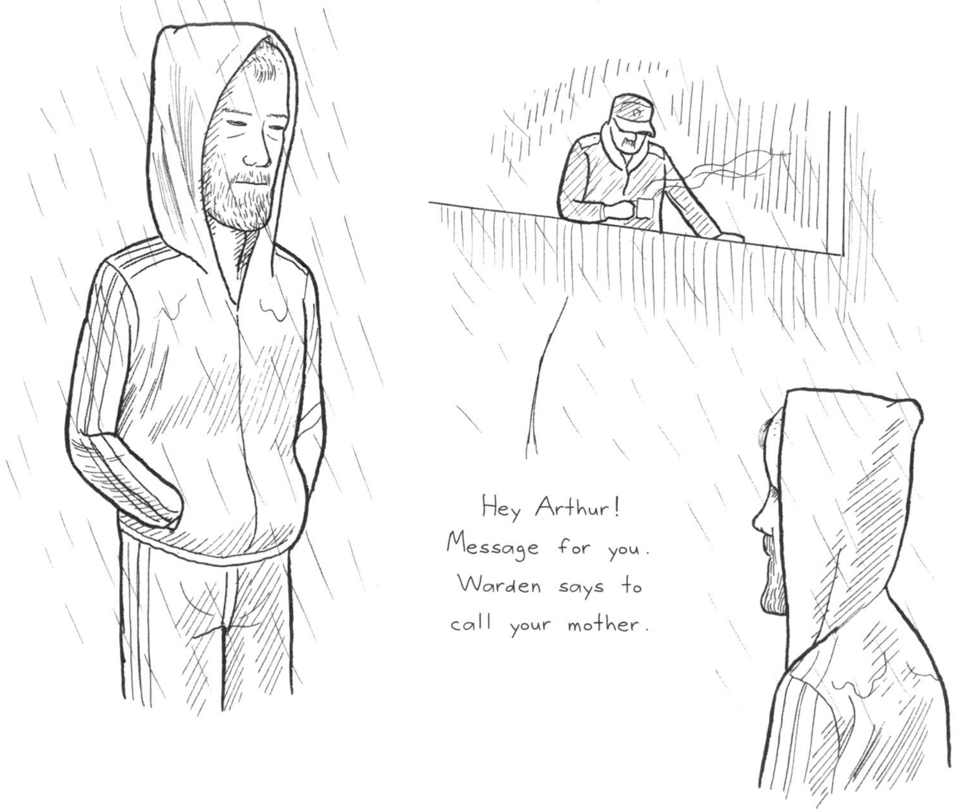
Hey Arthur! Message for you. Warden says to call your mother.

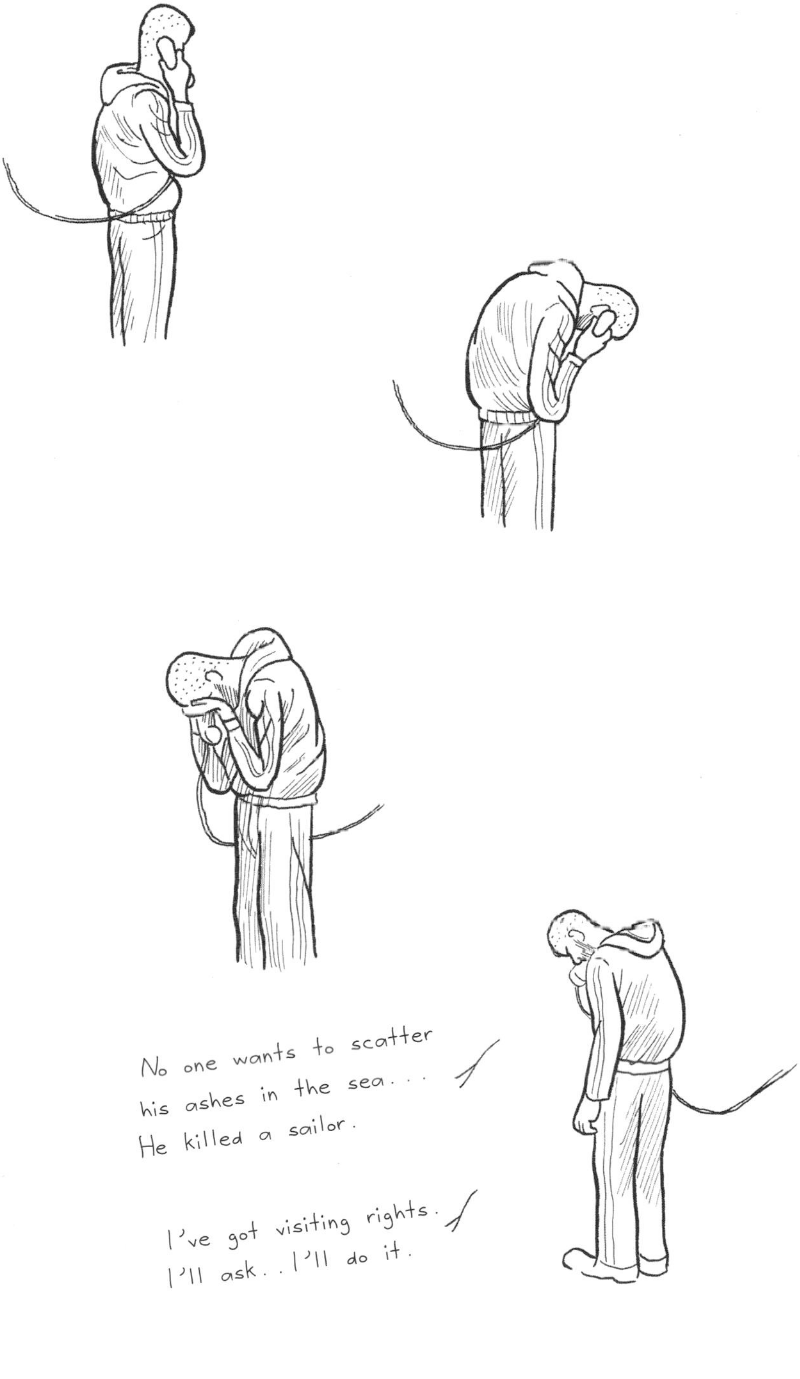
No one wants to scatter
his ashes in the sea...
He killed a sailor.
I've got visiting rights.
I'll ask.. I'll do it.

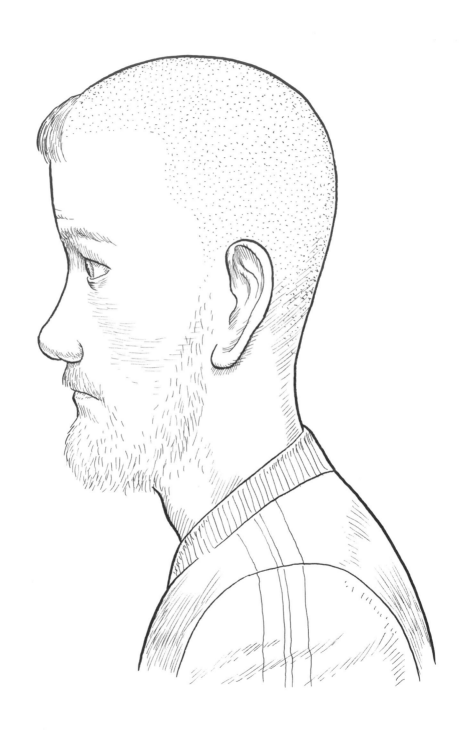

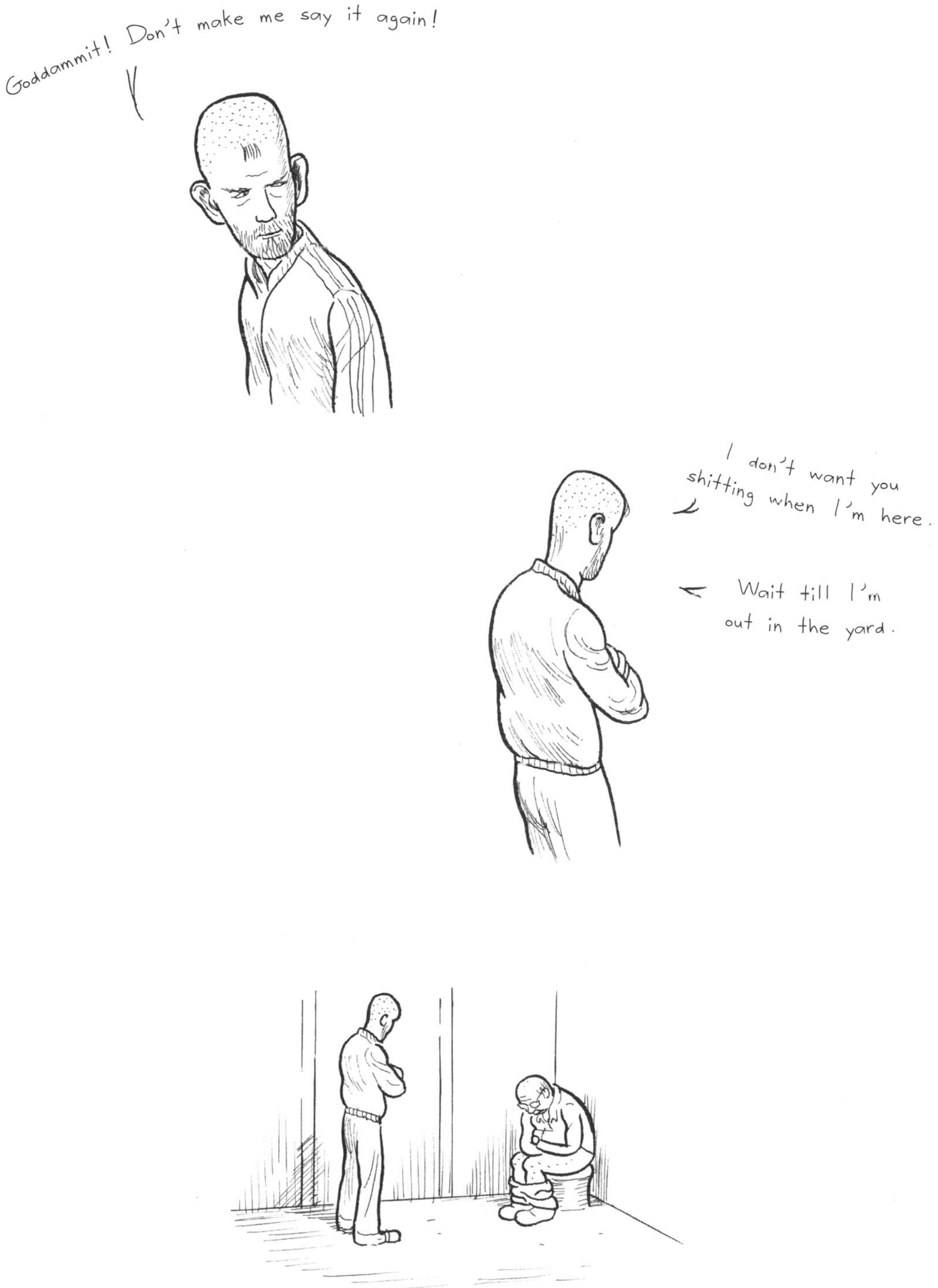
Goddammit! Don't make me say it again!
I don't want you shitting when I'm here.
Wait till I'm out in the yard.

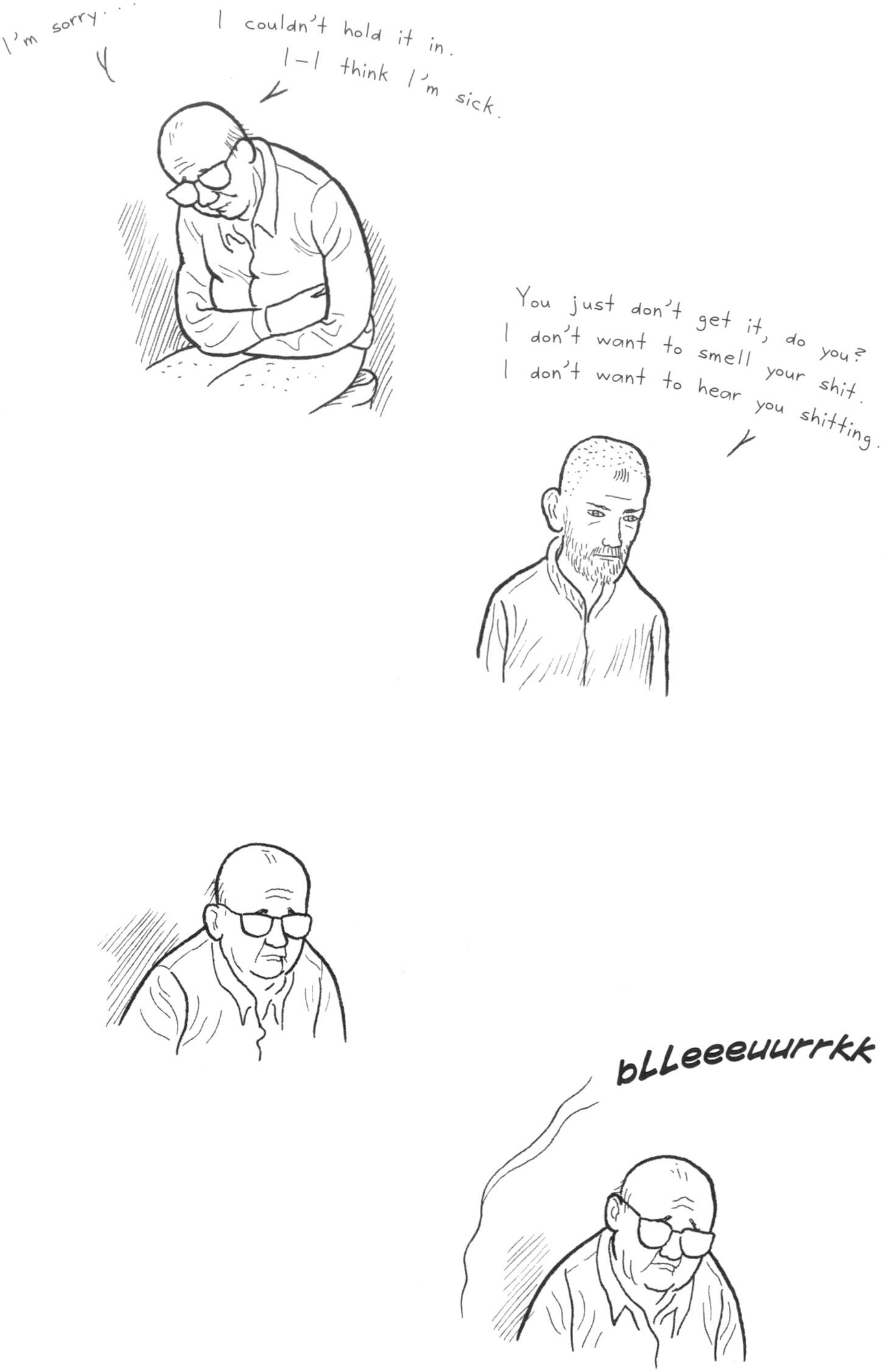
I'm sorry...
I couldn't hold it in.
I-I think I'm sick.
You just don't get it, do you?
I don't want to smell your shit.
I don't want to hear you shitting.
bLLeeeuurrkk

Motherfucking pig!
Get out, you make me want to hurl.

Get up.

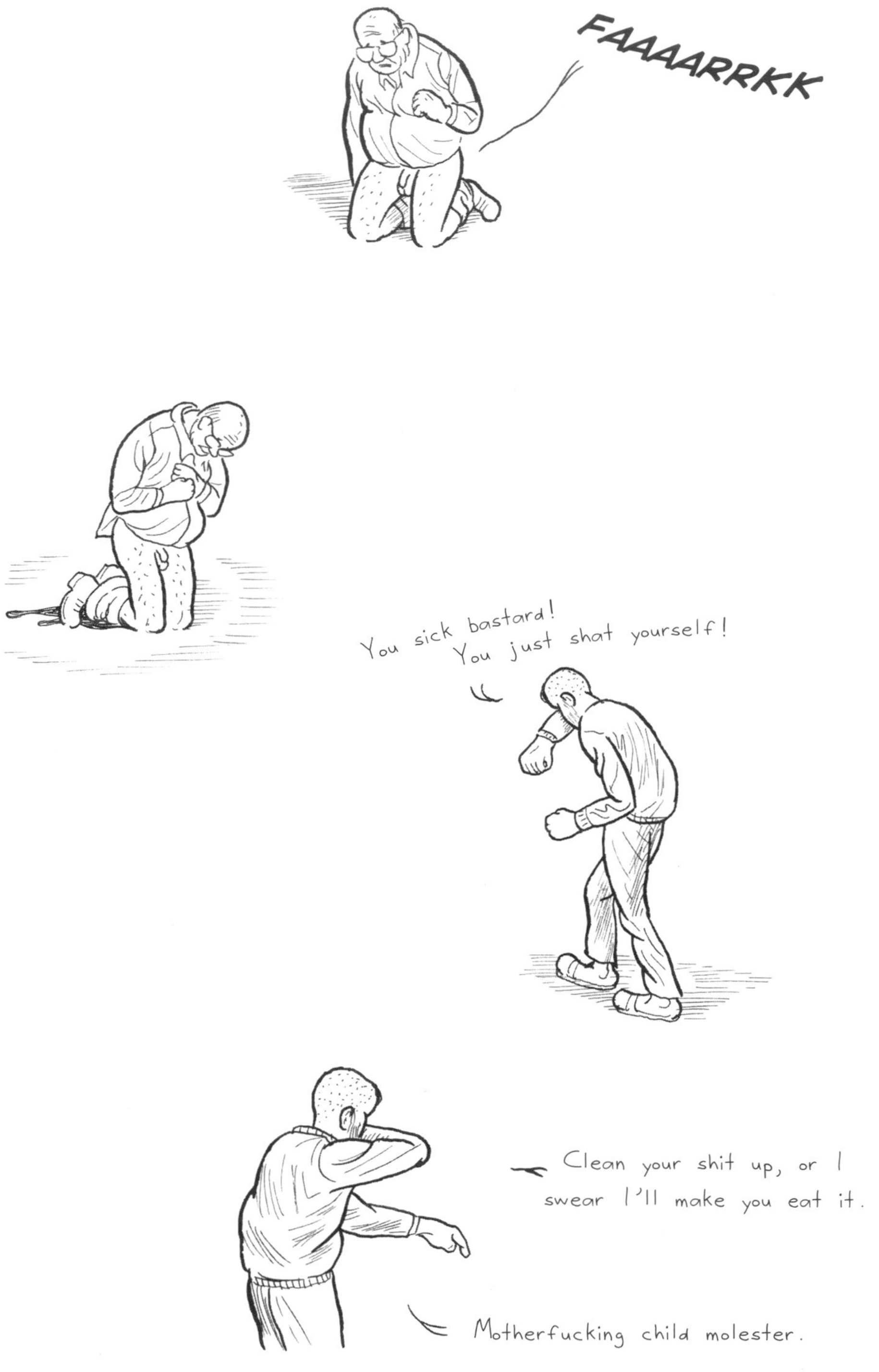
FAAAARRKK
You sick bastard! You just shat yourself!
Clean your shit up, or I swear I'll make you eat it.
Motherfucking child molester.

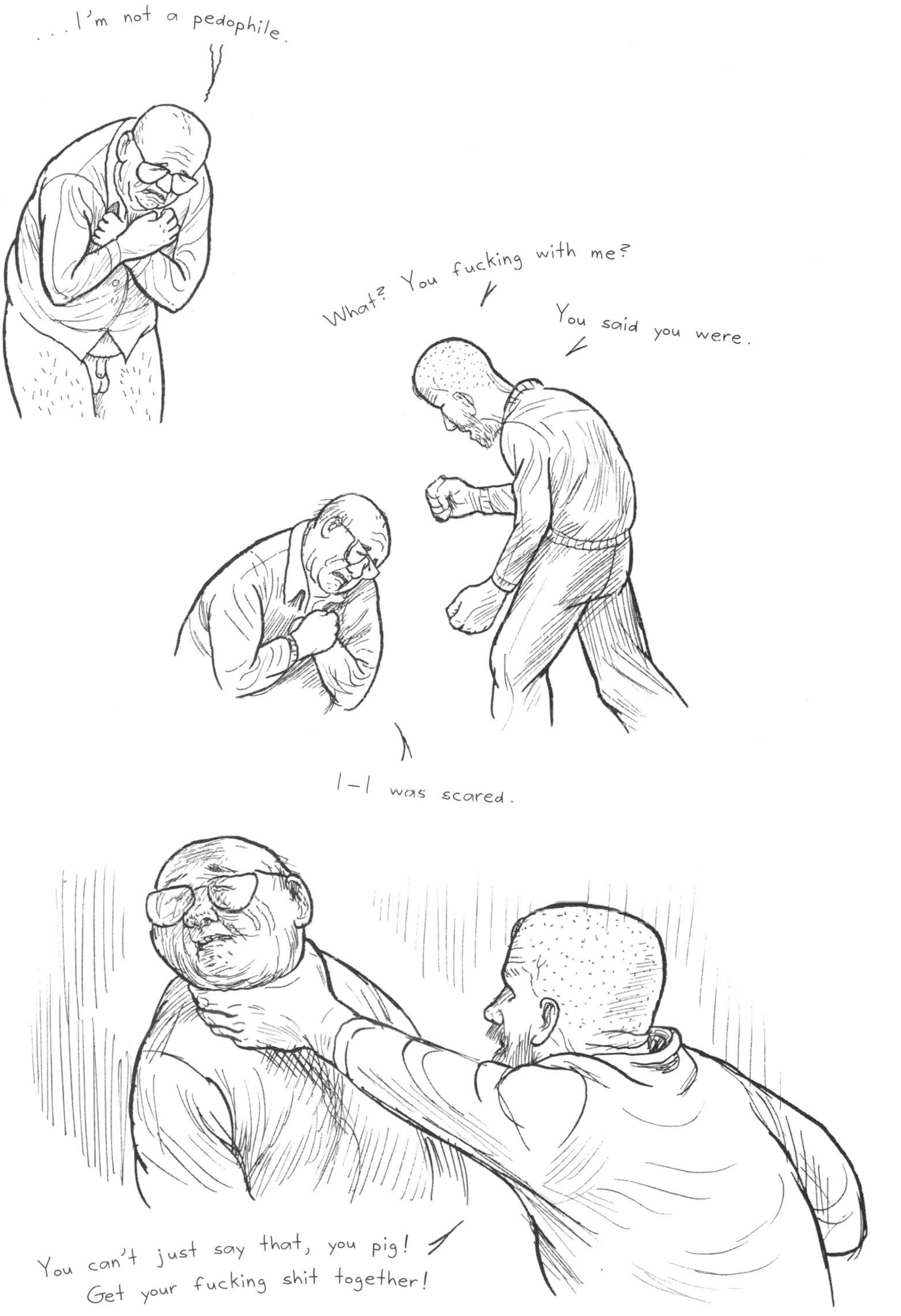
...I'm not a pedophile.
What? You fucking with me?
You said you were.
I-I was scared.
You can't just say that, you pig!
Get your fucking shit together!

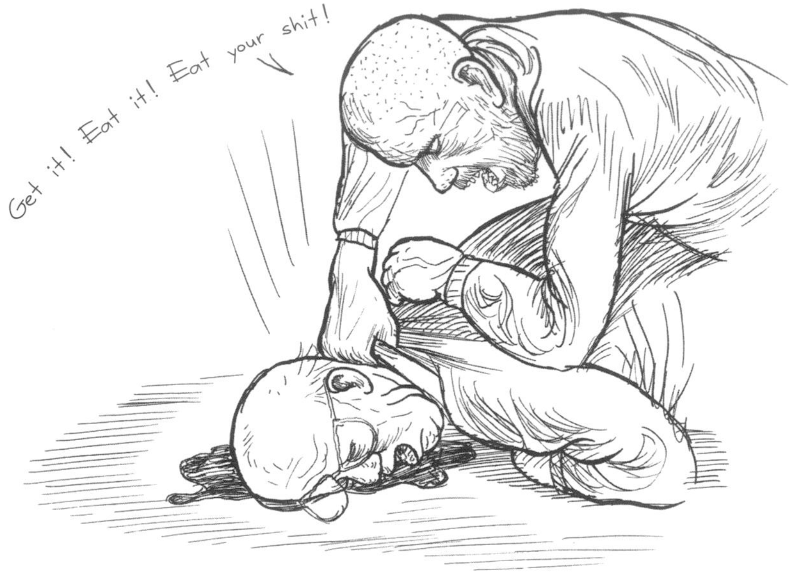
Get it! Eat it! Eat your shit!

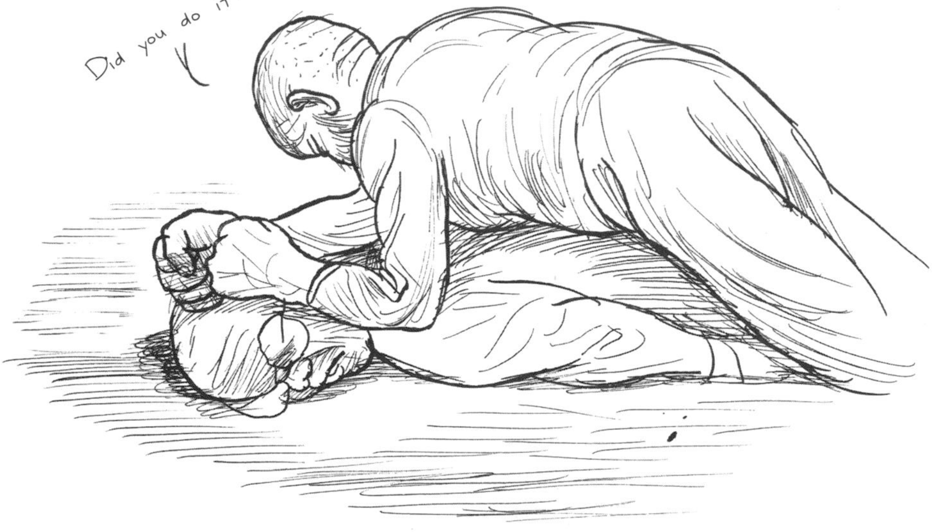
Did you do it?

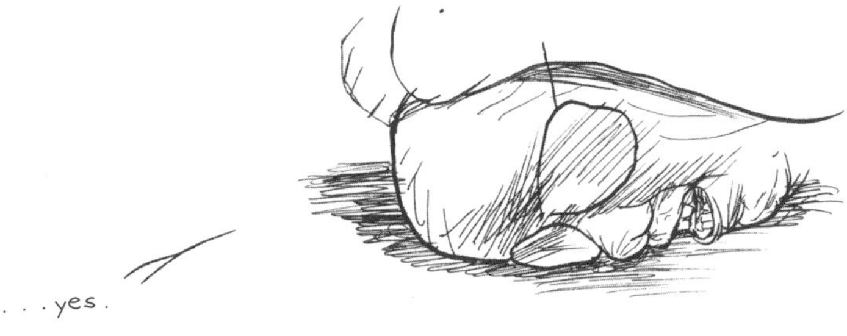
. . . yes.

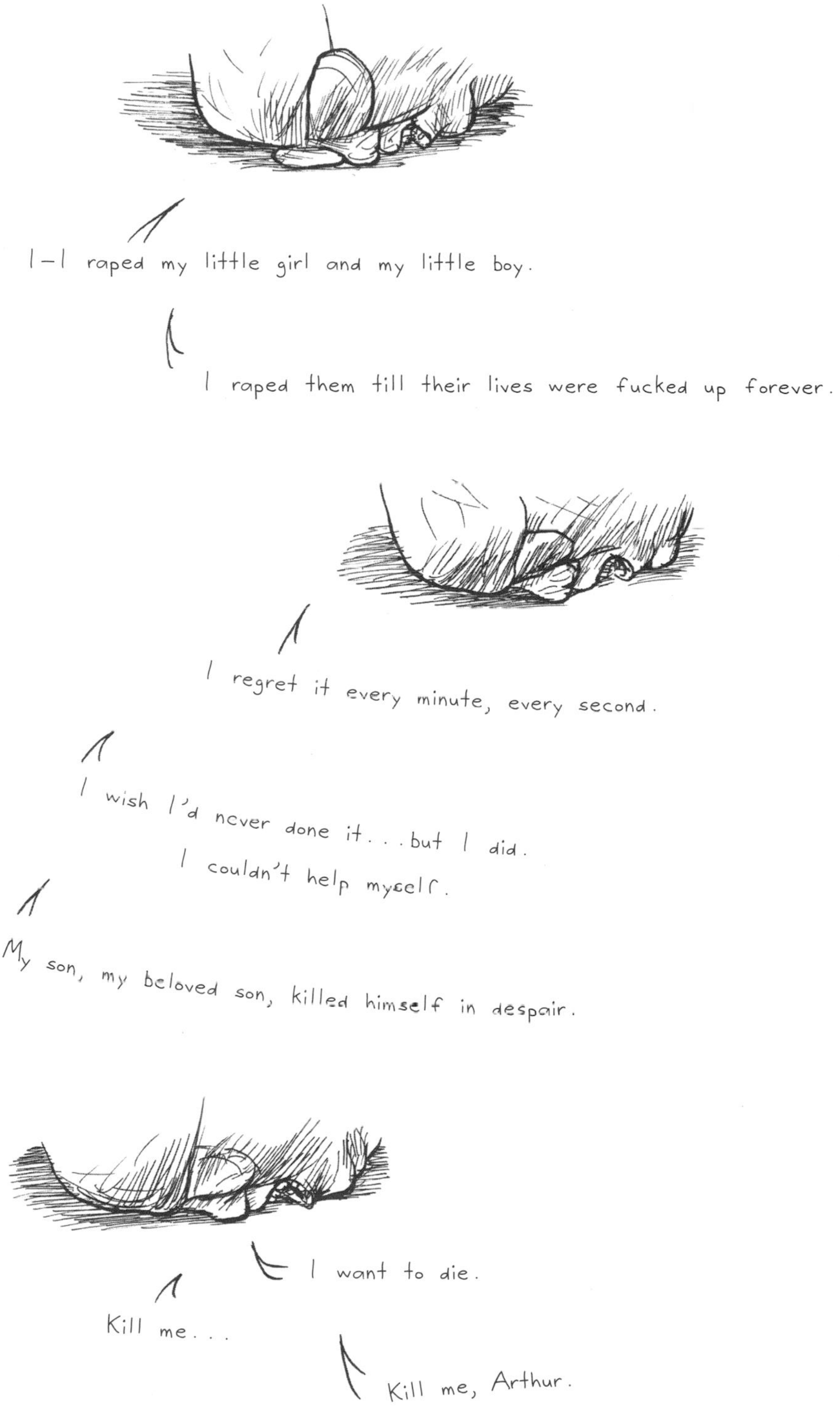

I—I raped my little girl and my little boy.

I raped them till their lives were fucked up forever.

I regret it every minute, every second.

I wish I'd never done it...but I did.
I couldn't help myself.

My son, my beloved son, killed himself in despair.

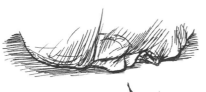

I want to die.

Kill me...

Kill me, Arthur.

Do it!

Shut the fuck up!

Do it, Arthur.

You can't even imagine everything I did to them.

They were begging me—

Fuck! Shut the fucking fuck up, Denis!

I destroyed them. Their bodies and minds...

They were begging me.

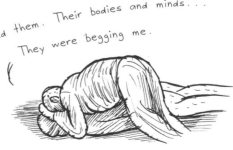

And yet... I know I'd do it all again if I could.

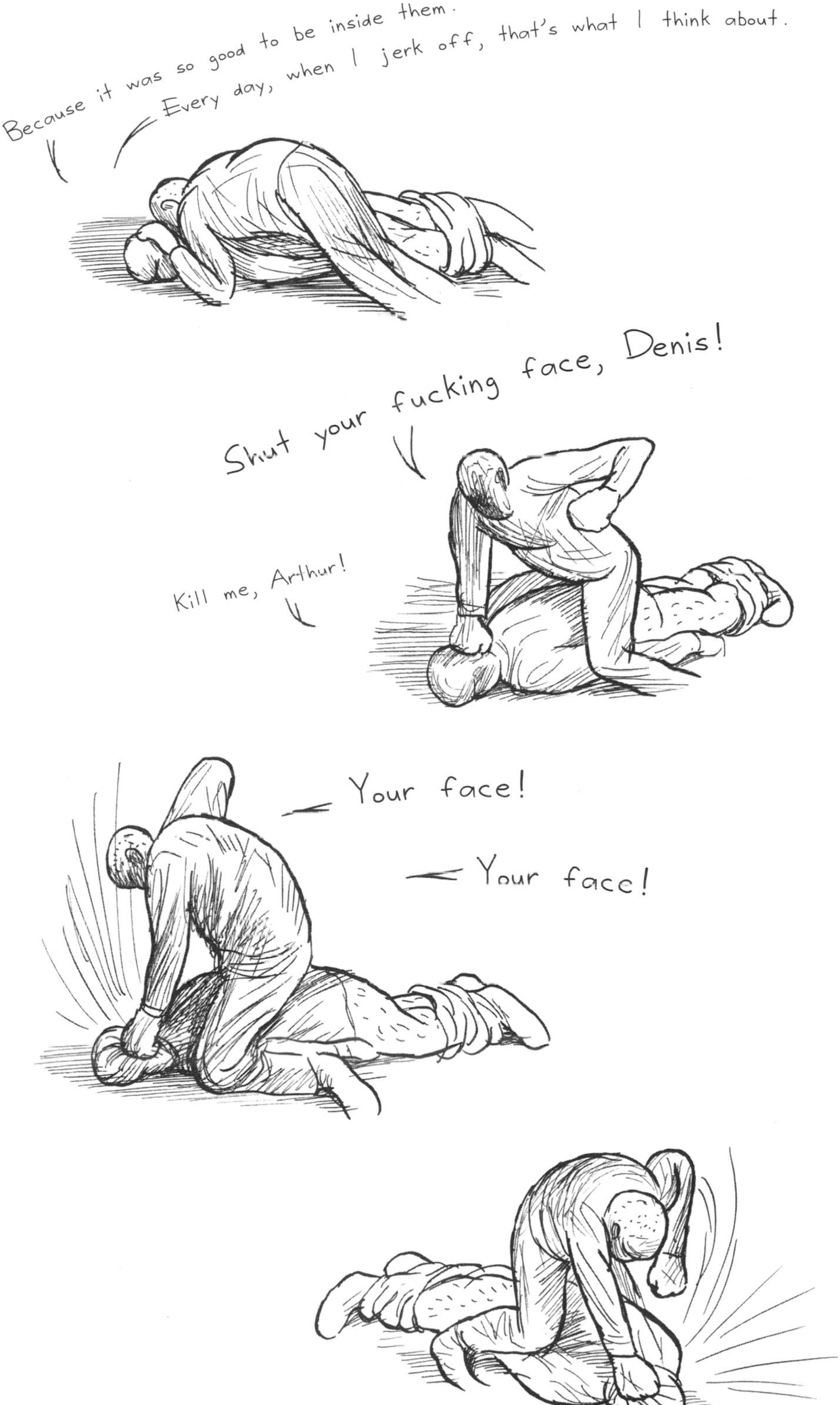
Because it was so good to be inside them.
Every day, when I jerk off, that's what I think about.
Shut your fucking face, Denis!
Kill me, Arthur!
Your face!
Your face!

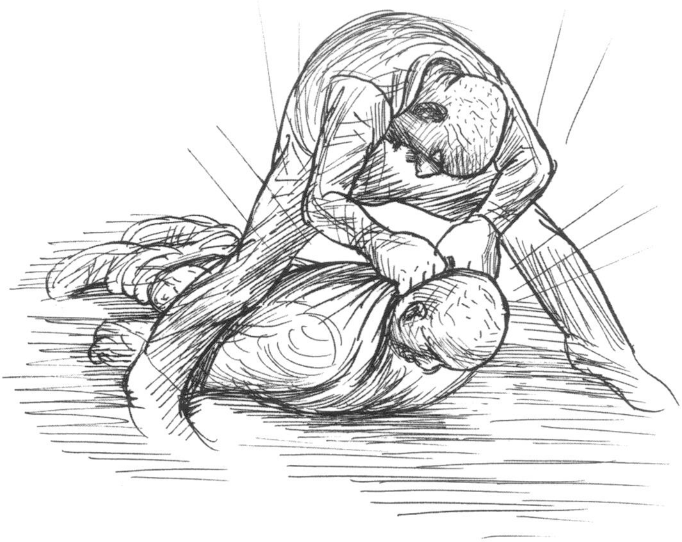

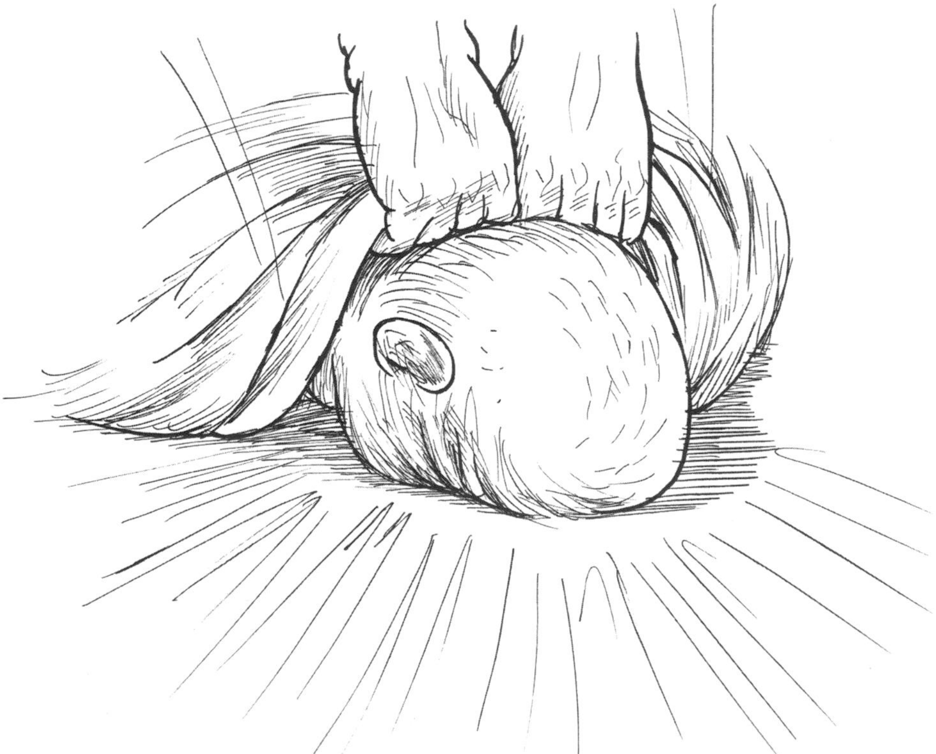

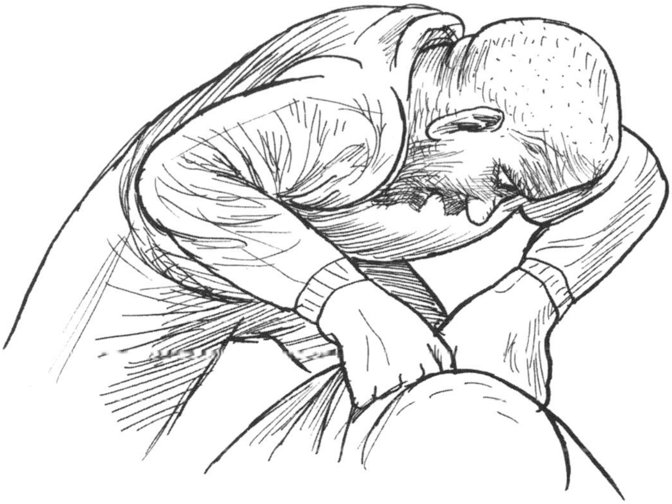

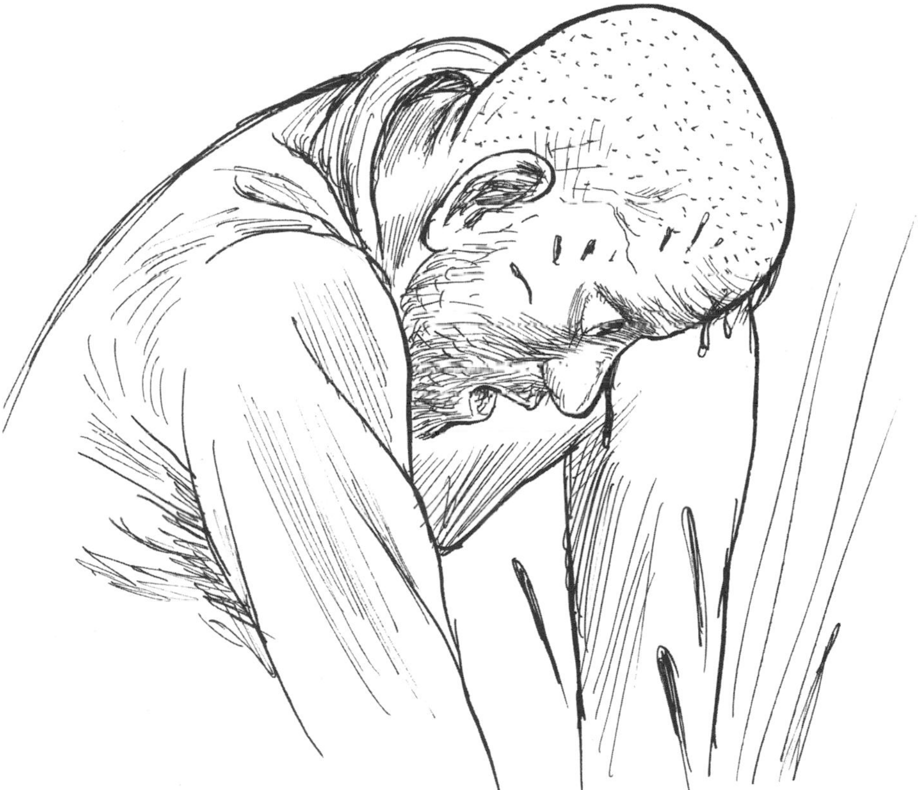

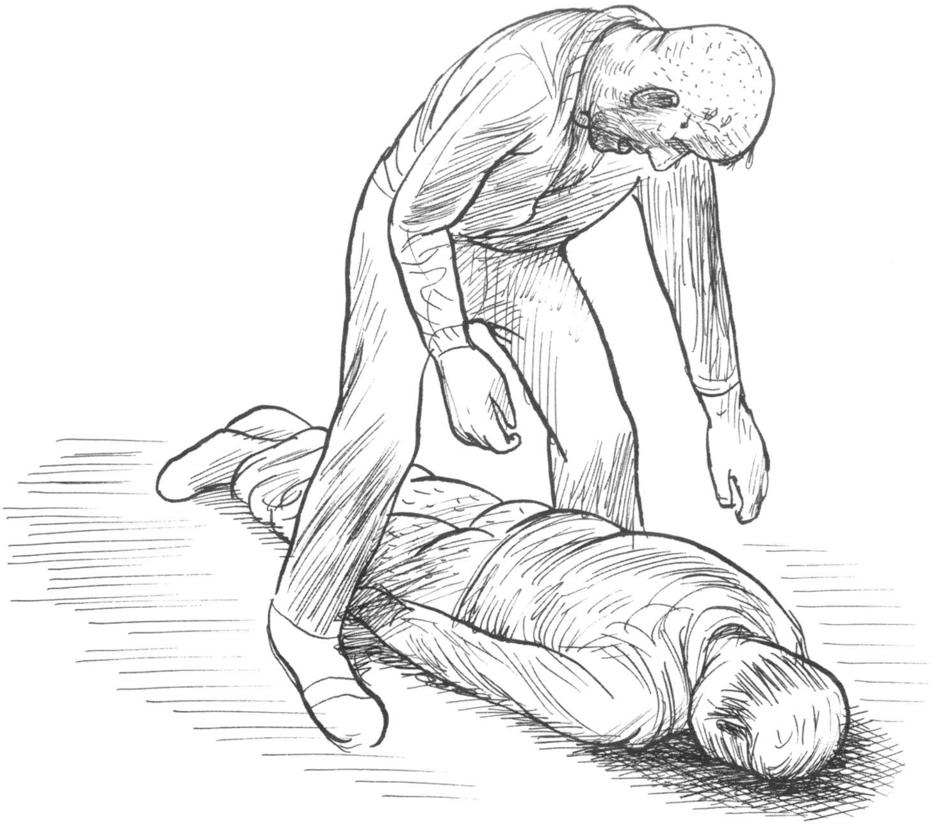

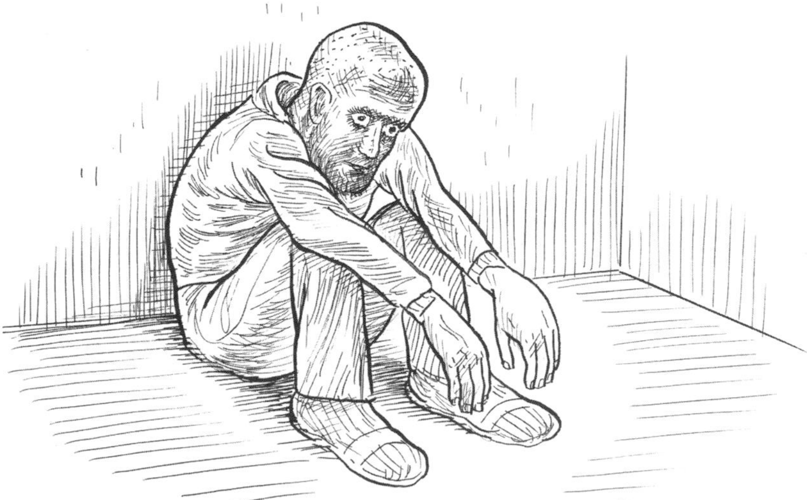

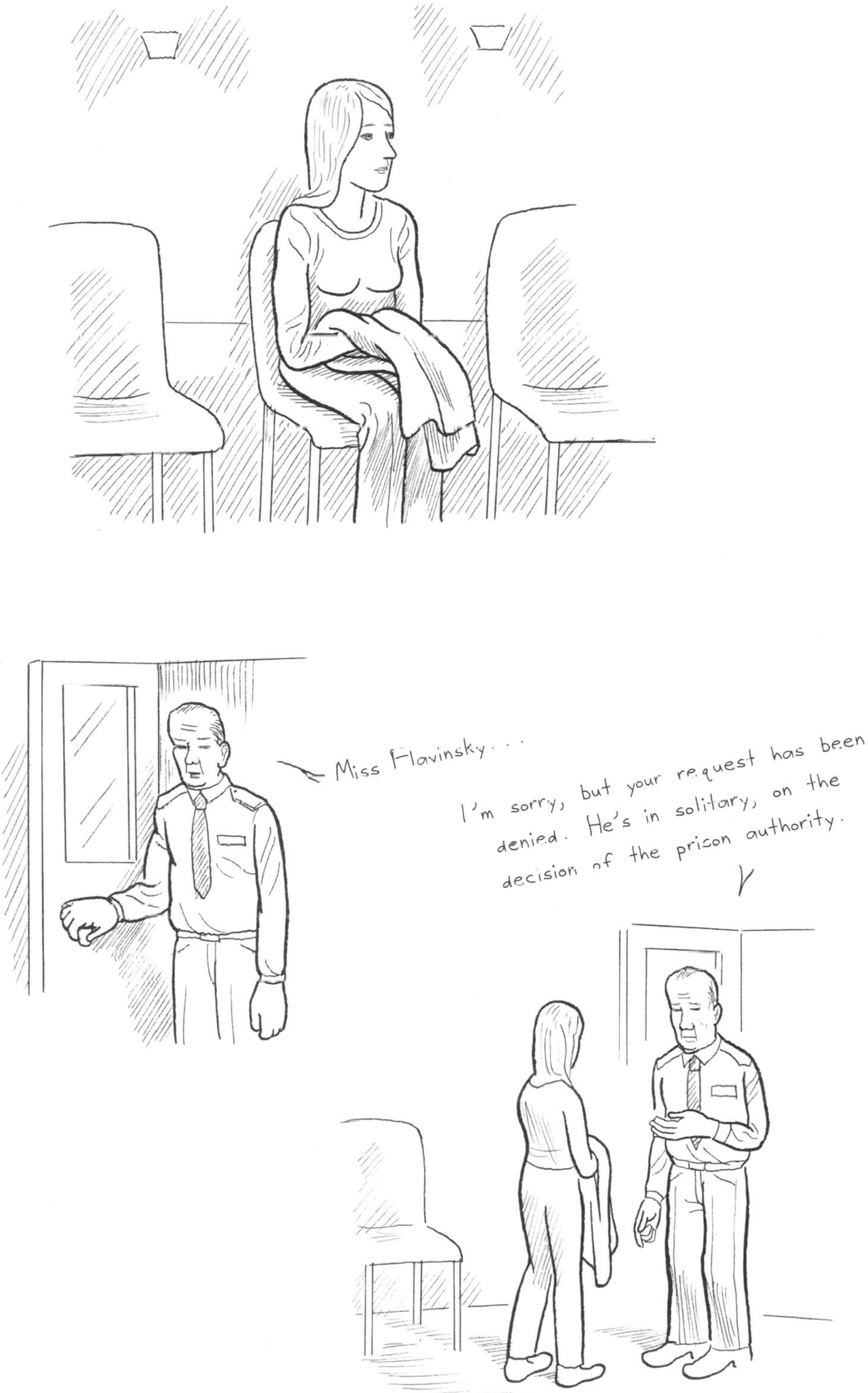
Miss Flavinsky...
I'm sorry, but your request has been denied. He's in solitary, on the decision of the prison authority.

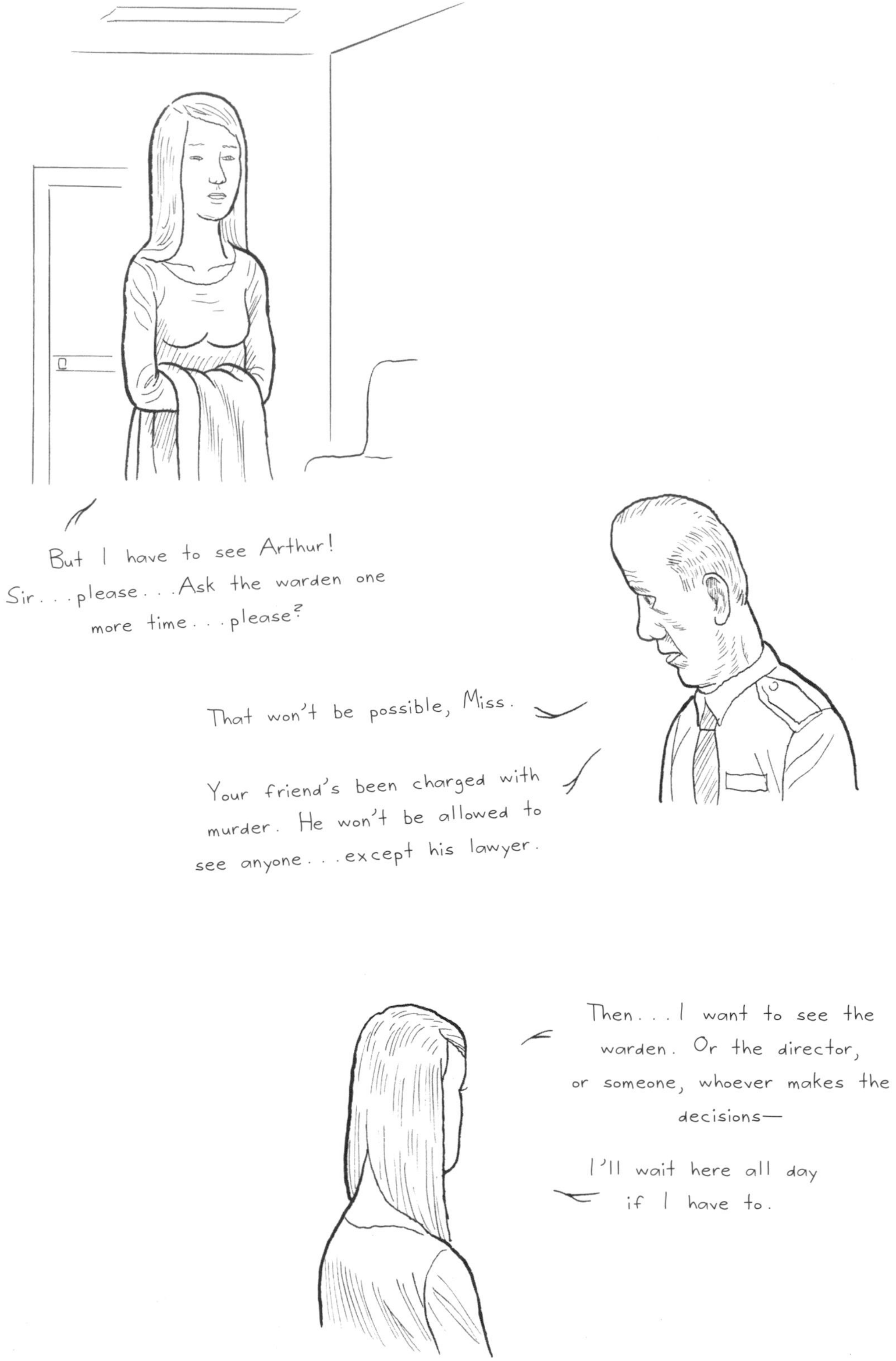
But I have to see Arthur! Sir. . . please. . . Ask the warden one more time. . . please?
That won't be possible, Miss.
Your friend's been charged with murder. He won't be allowed to see anyone. . . except his lawyer.
Then. . . I want to see the warden. Or the director, or someone, whoever makes the decisions—
I'll wait here all day if I have to.

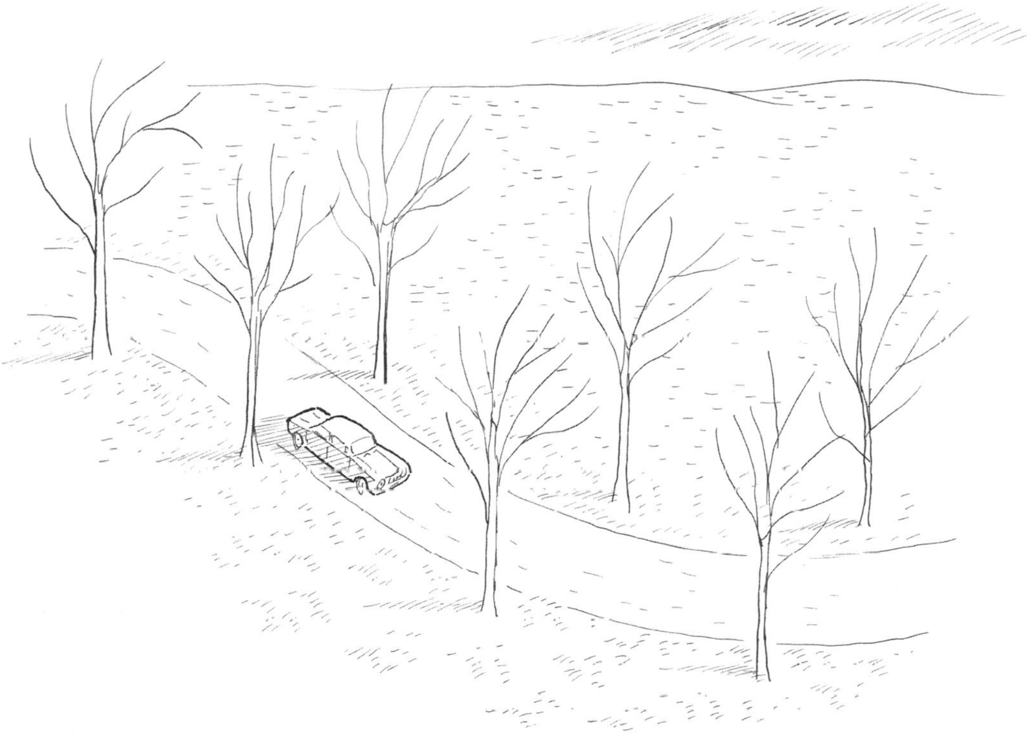

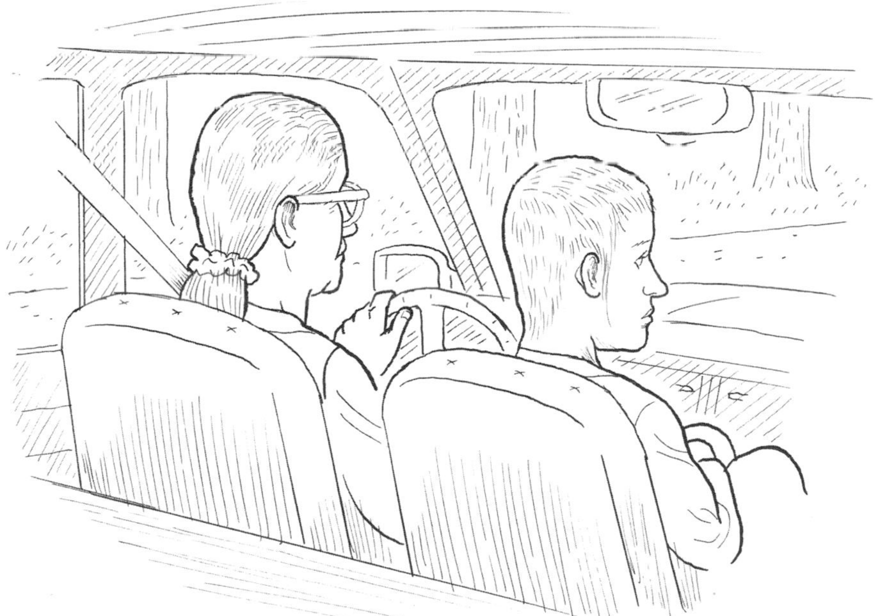

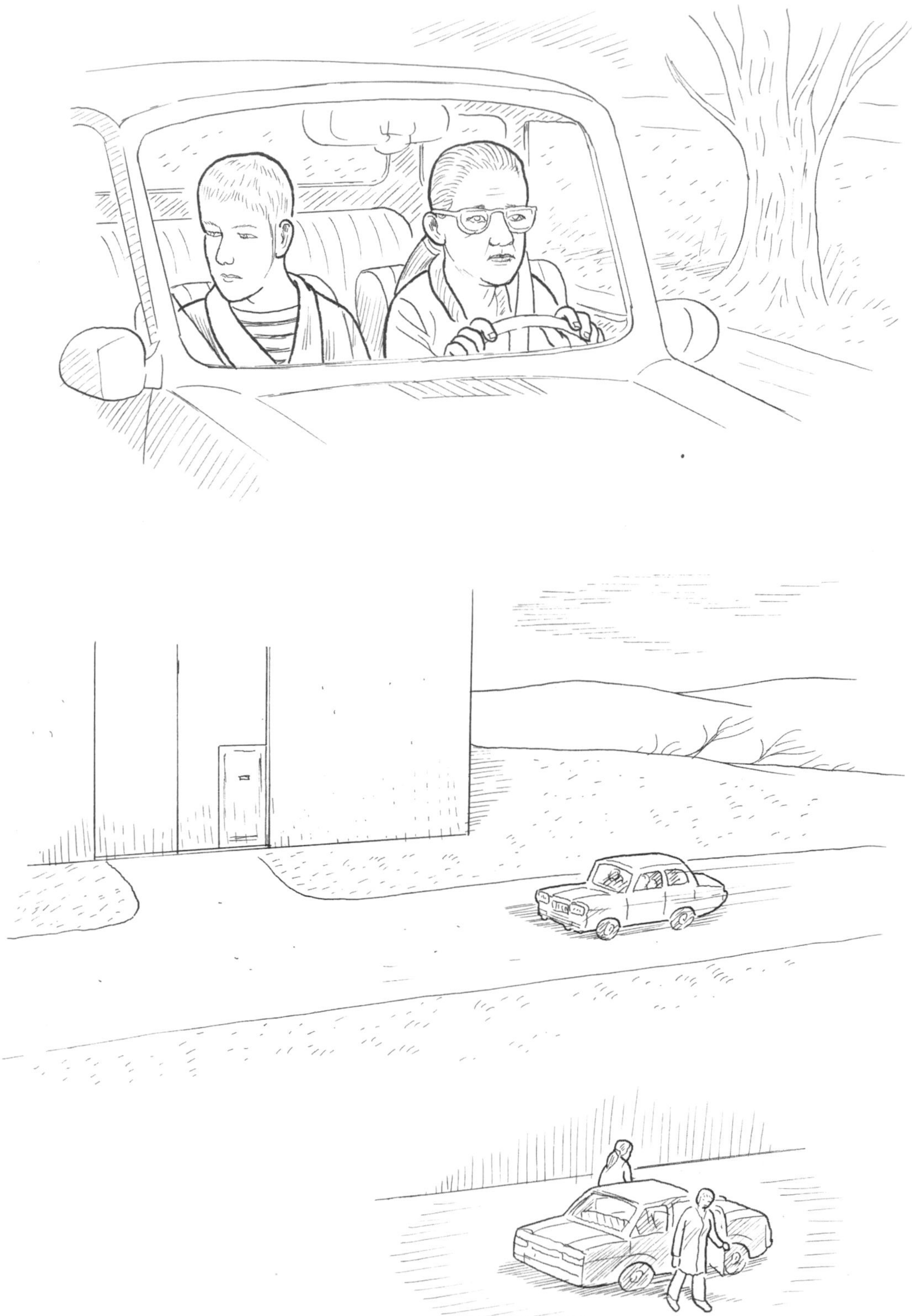

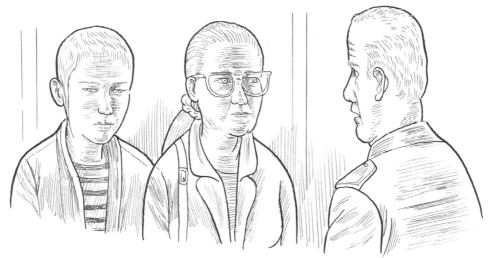

Are you the wife and daughter of
Denis Bruissiez?

Yes. We've—we've come to identify. . .the body.

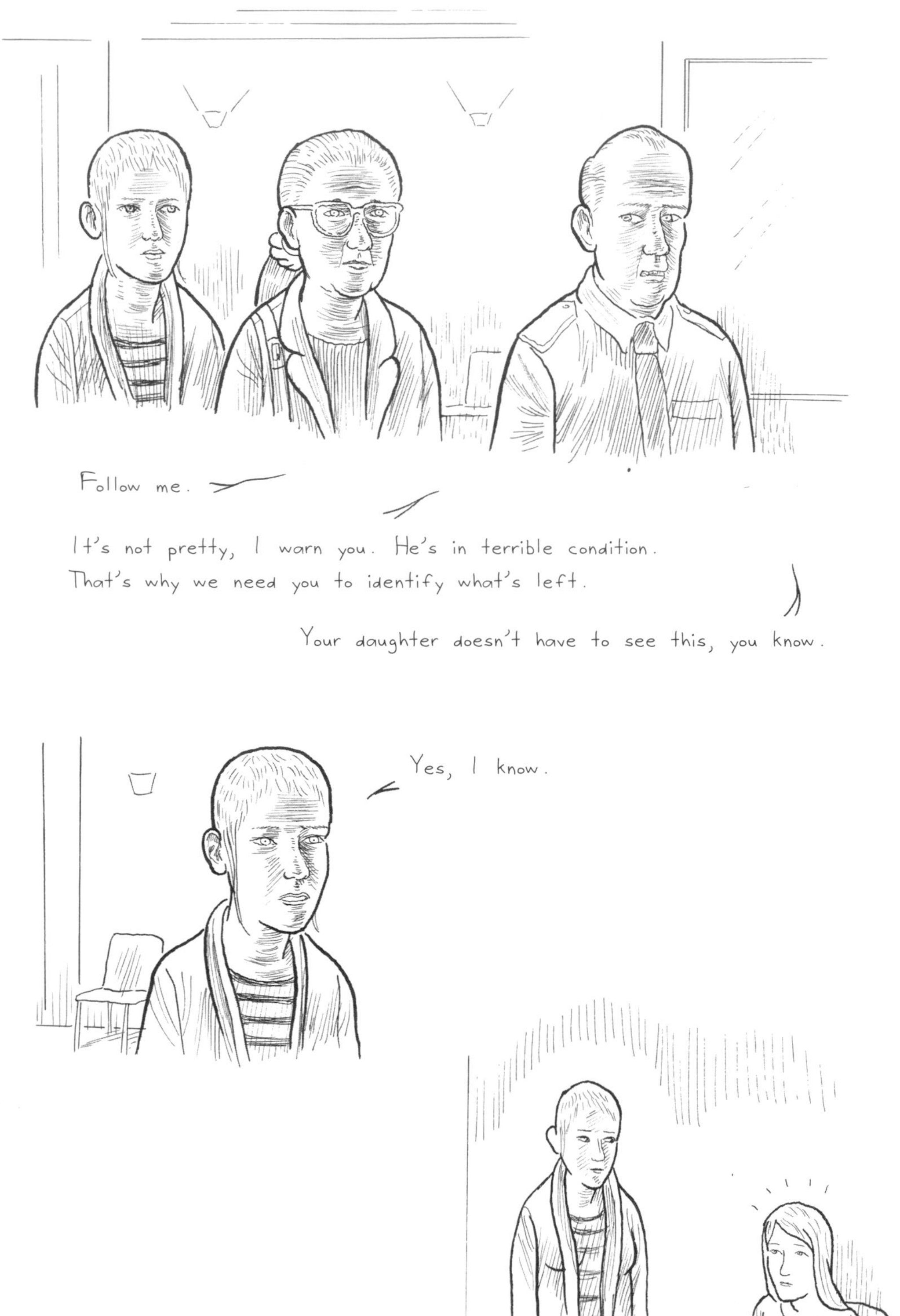
Follow me.
It's not pretty, I warn you. He's in terrible condition. That's why we need you to identify what's left.
Your daughter doesn't have to see this, you know.
Yes, I know.

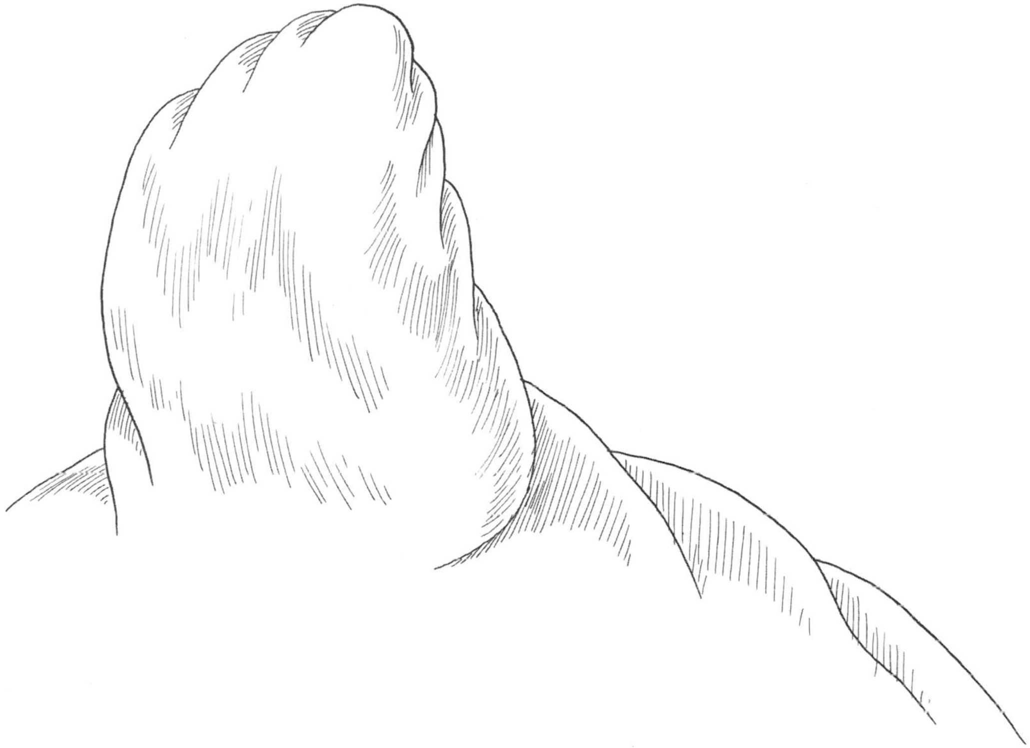

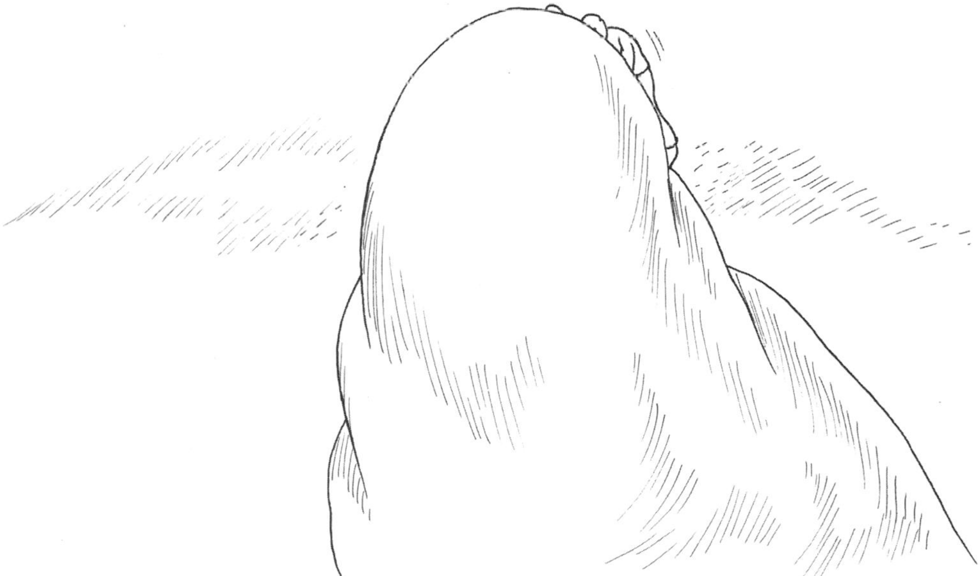

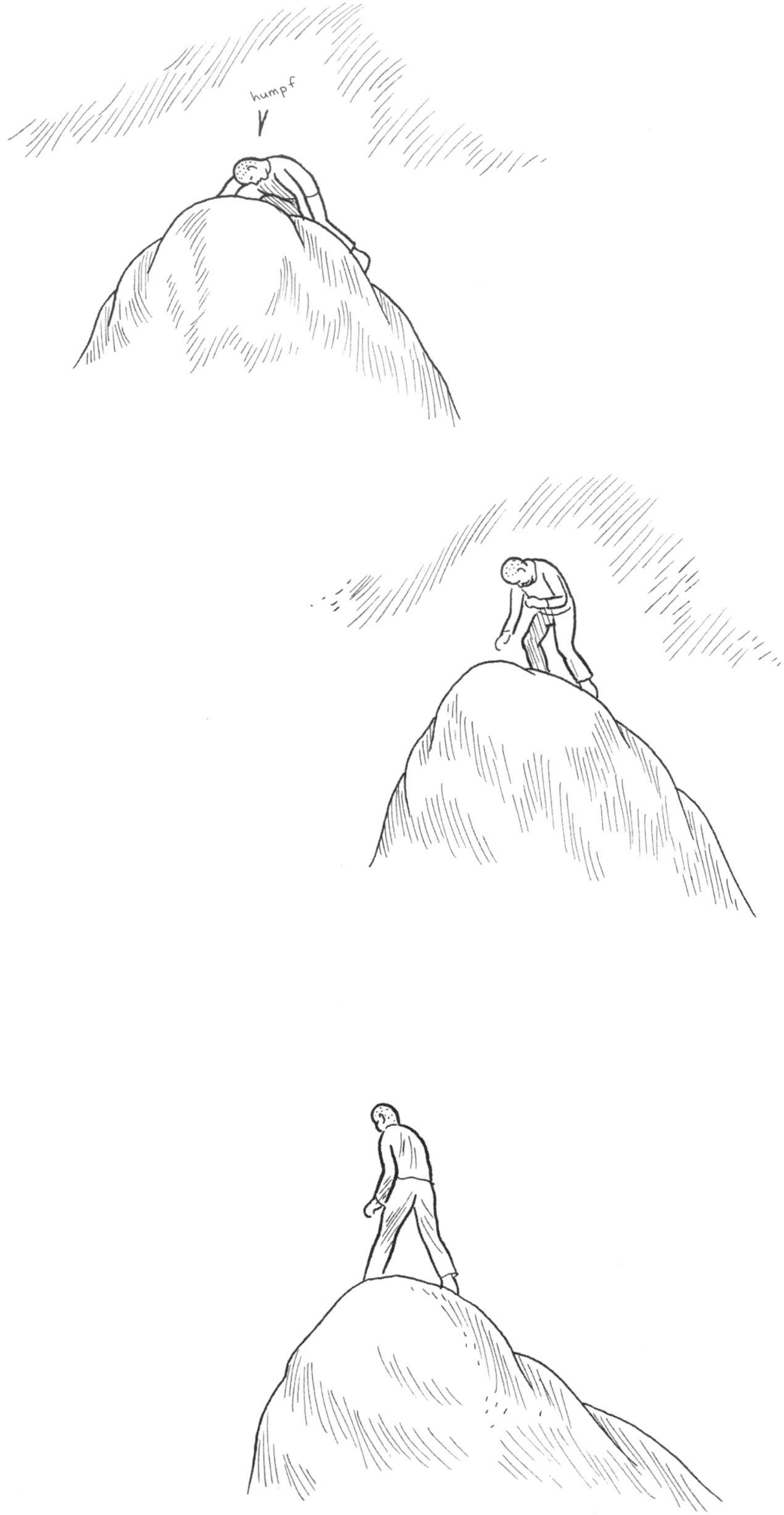
humpf

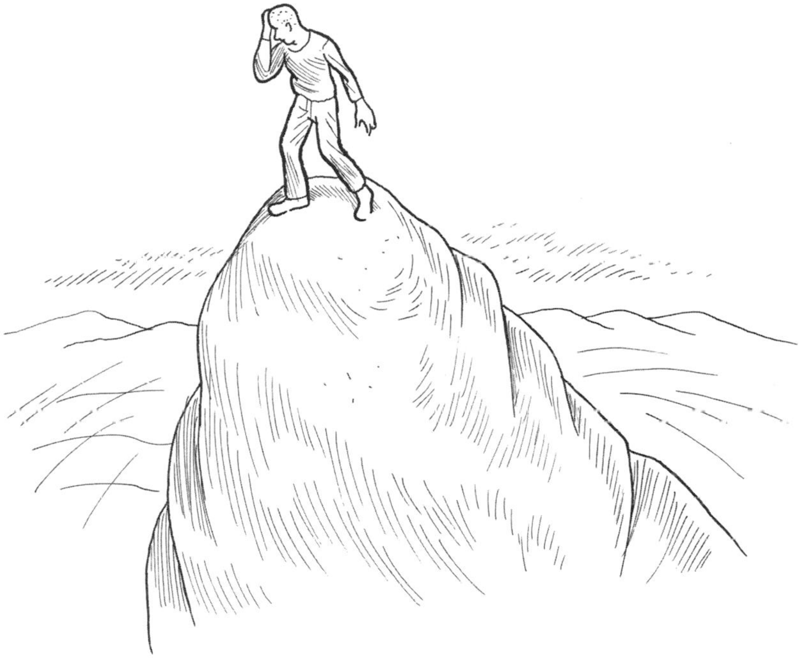
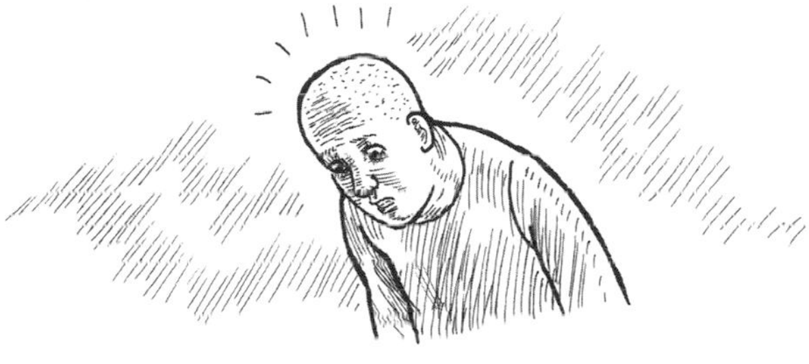
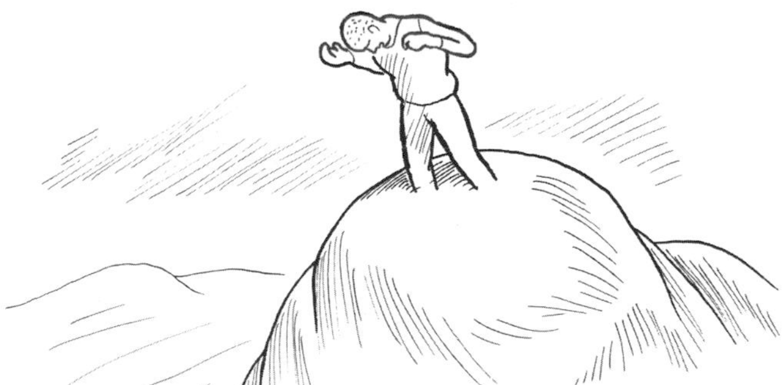

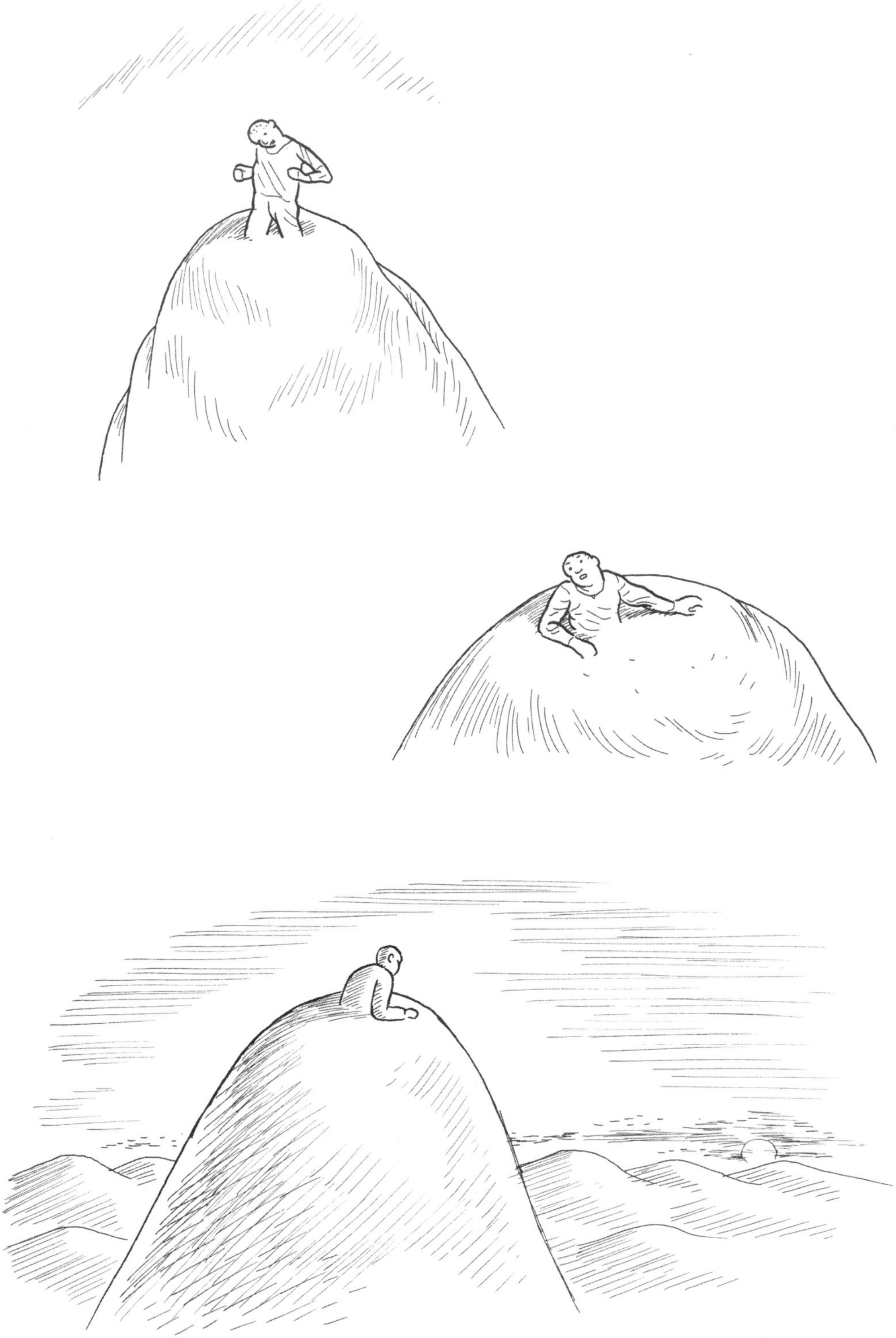

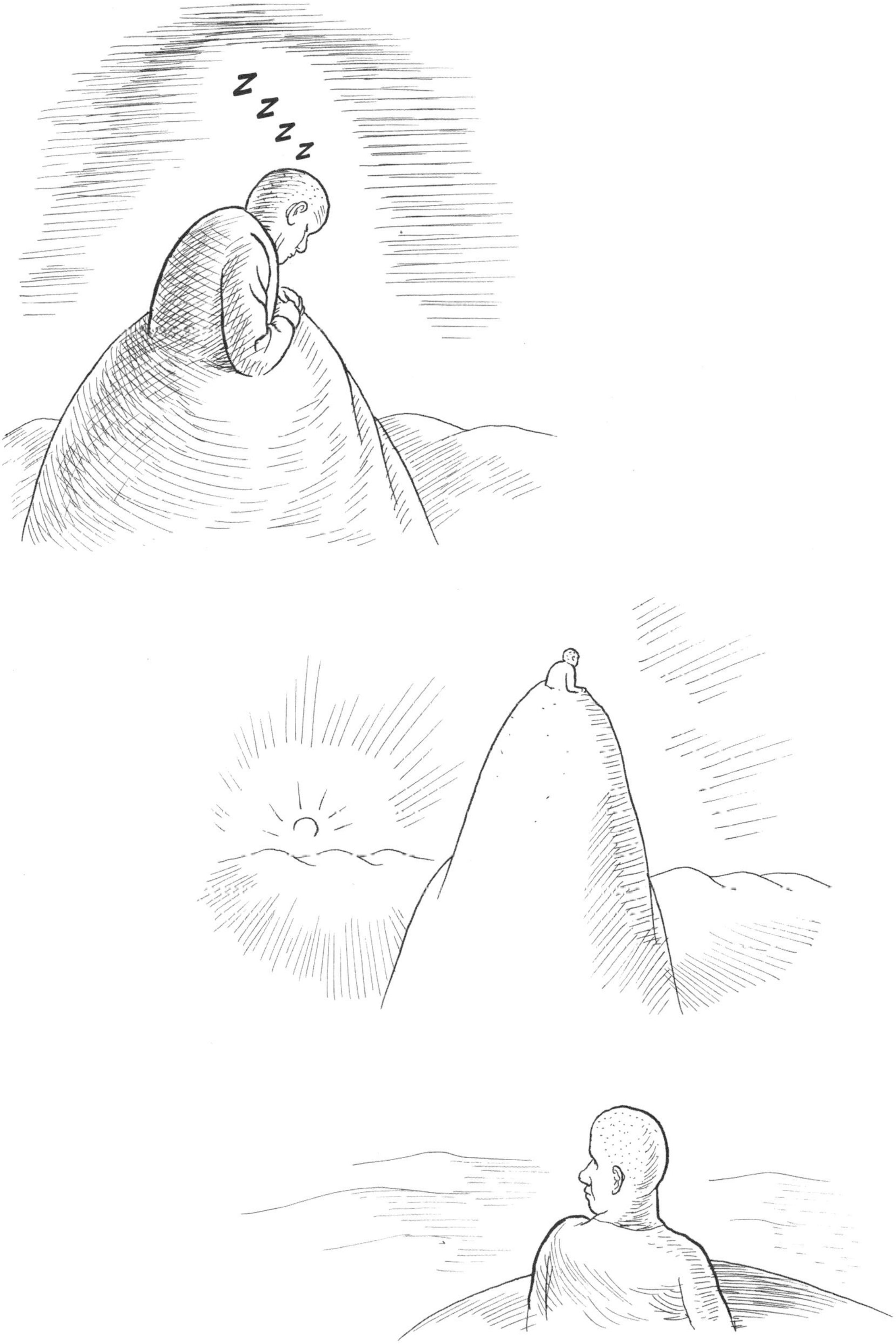
ZZZZ

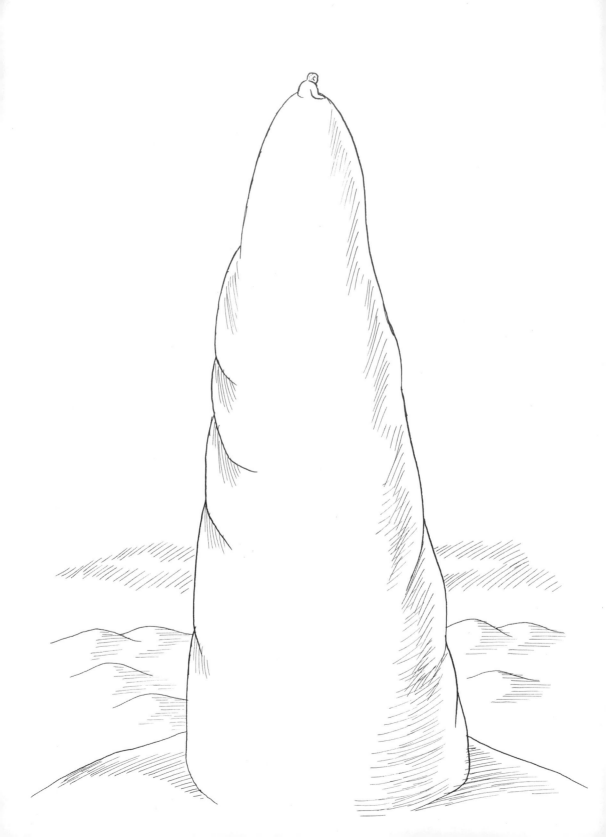

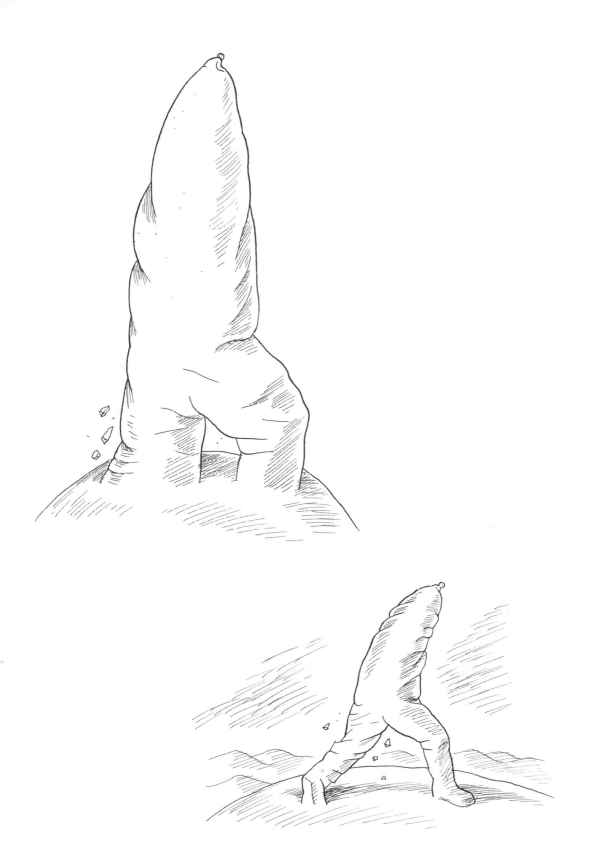

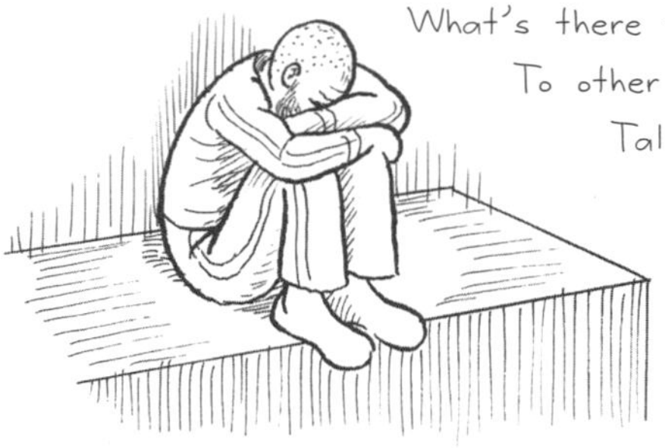

What's there to say?
To other people. . . Just to talk.
Talk about insignificant thoughts.
What's eating me up. . .

Night dreams that hobble my days.
Will they even listen to dreams?
Who cares?

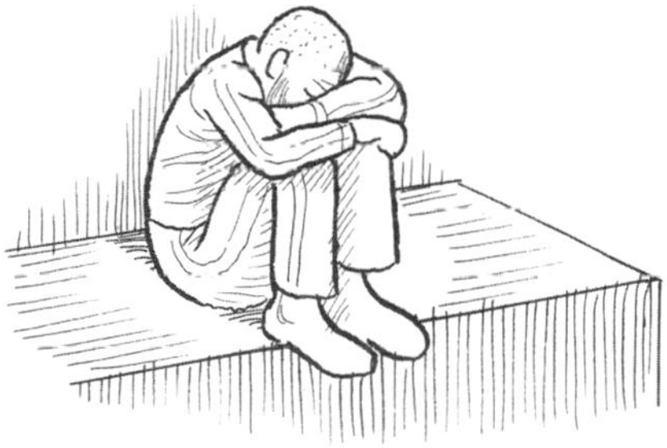

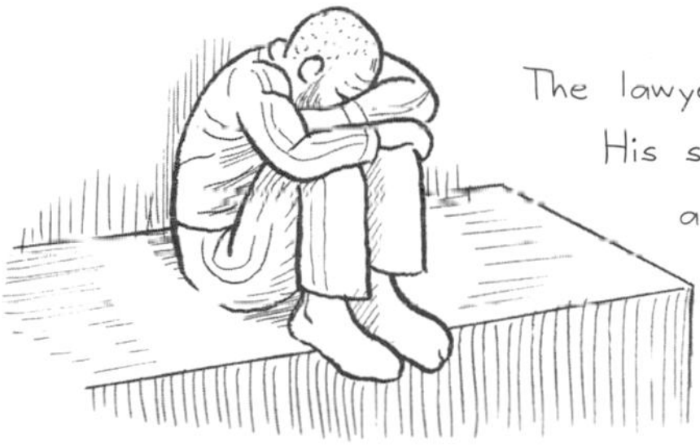

The lawyer wants to talk about my father.
His suicide. . . But I'm the one who's
already dead. . .

. . . smothered by anger.

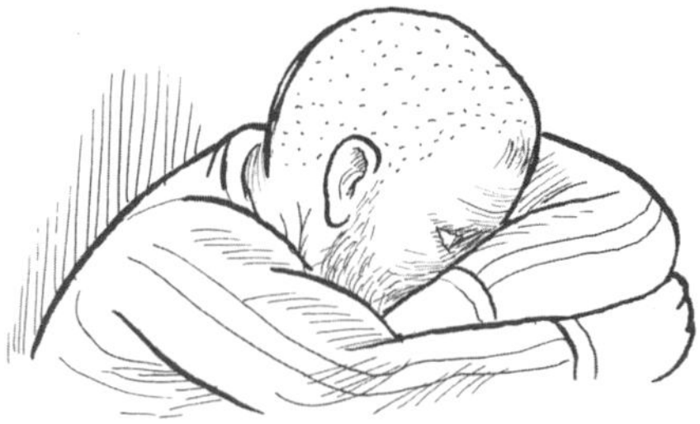

KLANG

Arthur, get your shoes on!

The hour of your final judgment
is at hand! Ha ha!

You put your best pajamas
on to impress the judge?

Ha ha ha!

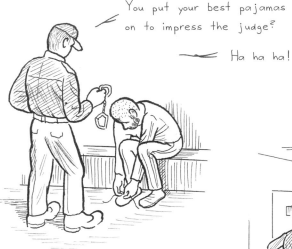

C'mon, hurry it up.
They'll start without you.

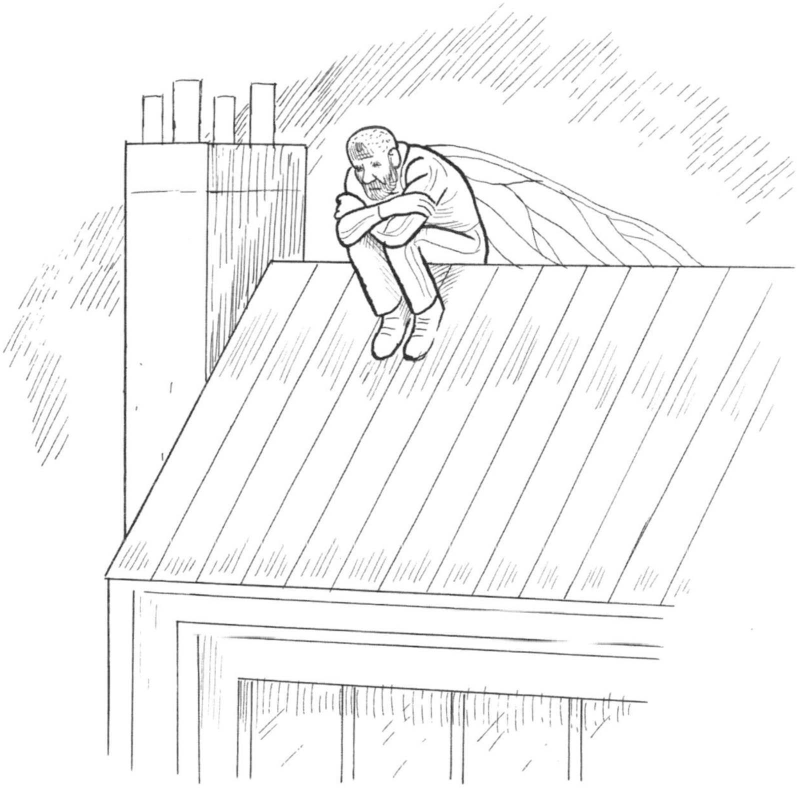

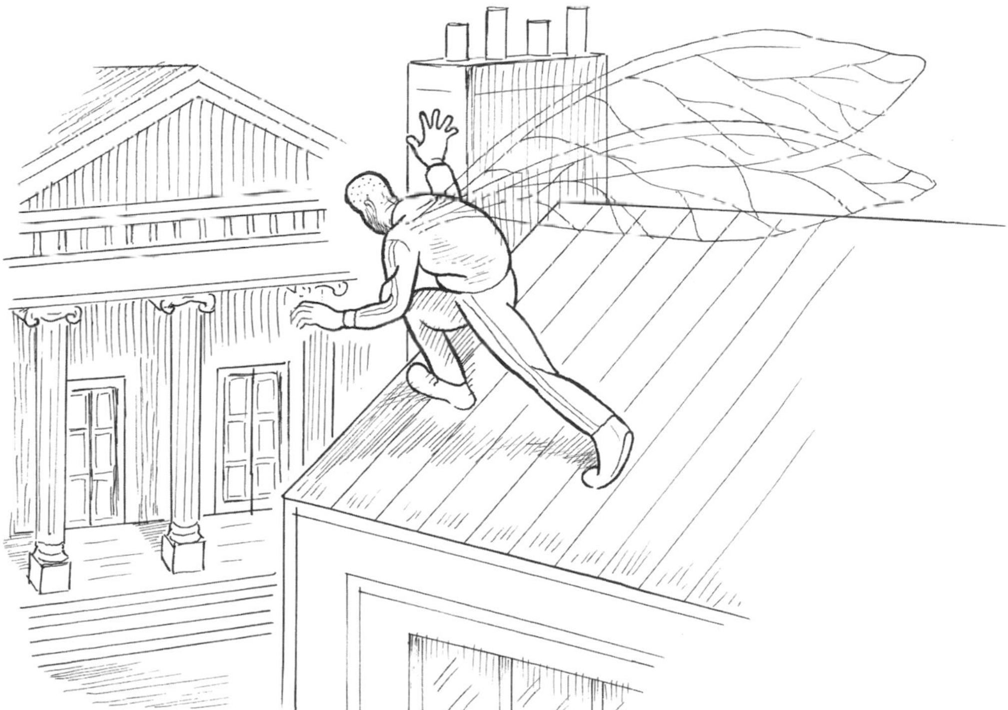

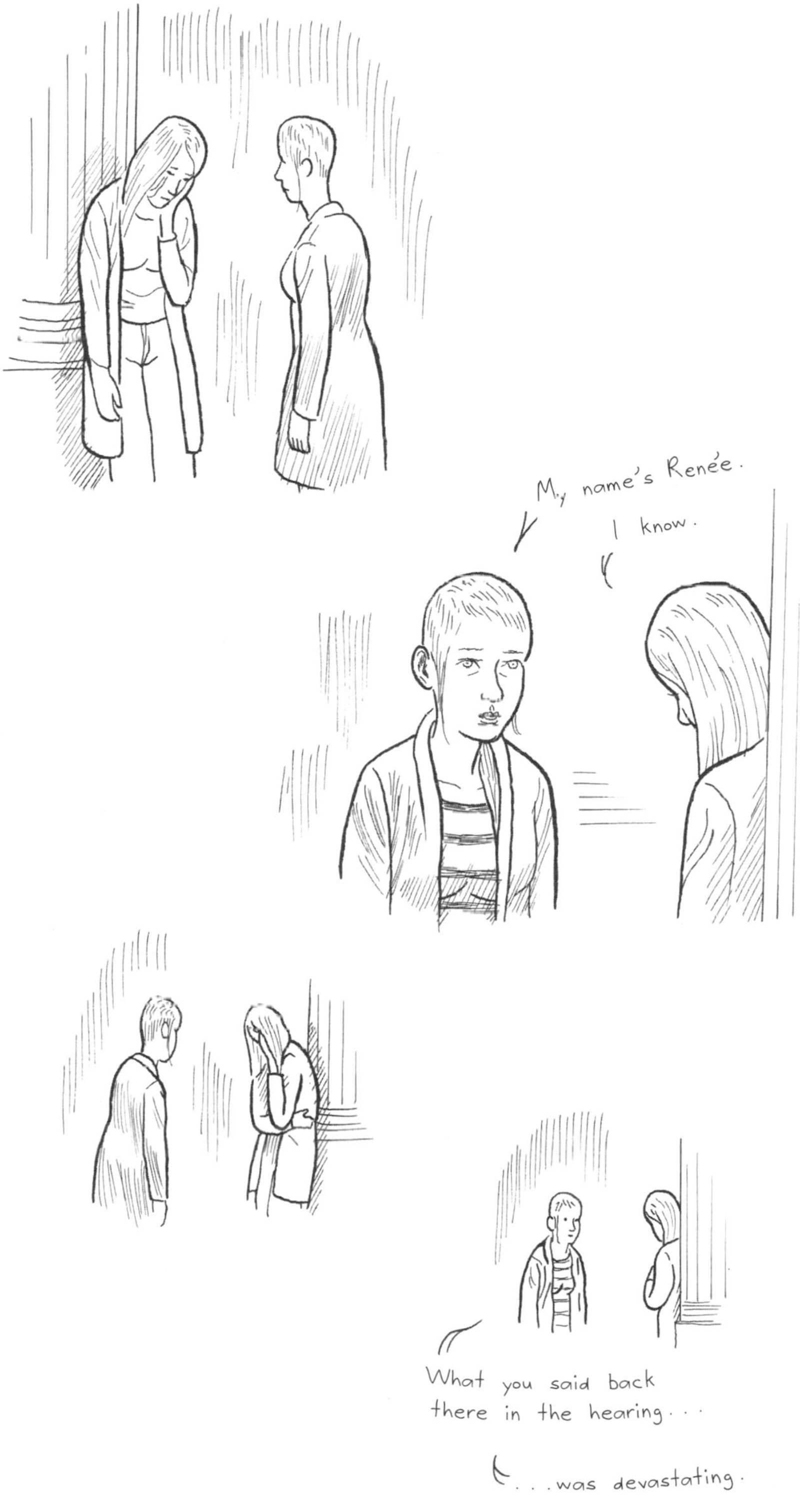
My name's Renée.
I know.
What you said back there in the hearing...
...was devastating.

It didn't do any good.

Don't be afraid to cry.

I can't seem to.

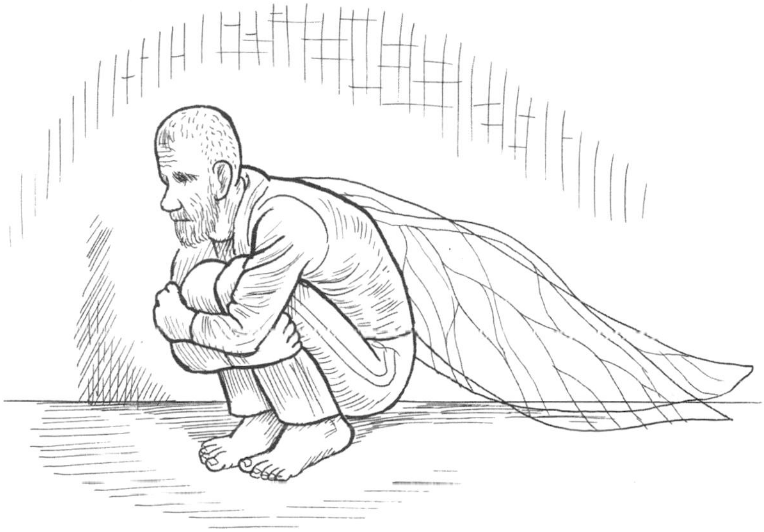

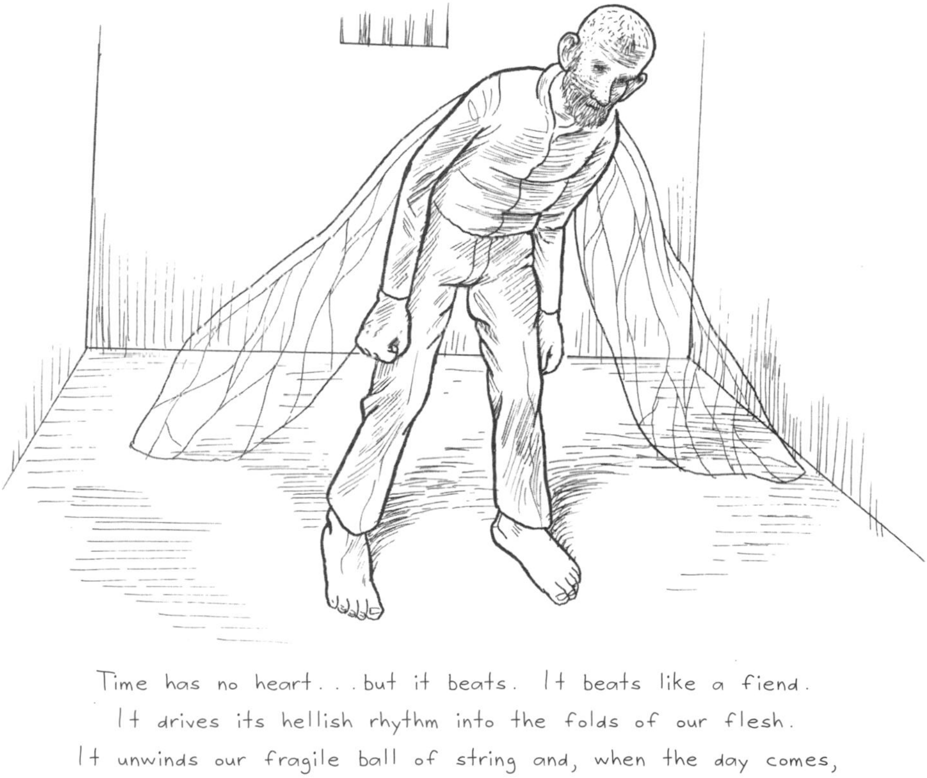

Time has no heart... but it beats. It beats like a fiend.
It drives its hellish rhythm into the folds of our flesh.
It unwinds our fragile ball of string and, when the day comes,
holds out to us one dangling end...

Twenty-five years. A whole career. A full-time job...
And all I did was tug on the string, hour after hour.

Counting every time the toilet flushed, the doors squeaked
on their hinges, the uneven breathing from the damp and
the stone...

Counting words in silent prayers...words that fled
their sentences...Counting. I had a thousand rituals.
An entire rosary. It should've been enough. "It"...
"It" should have held my anger back.

"It" turned out to be nothing at all. An apprentice attempt. A college try.

There are some unhinged people you just shouldn't stick together.
Nothing good comes of it.

Poor Denis...Poor me...
I won't see the day again. It won't see me either.

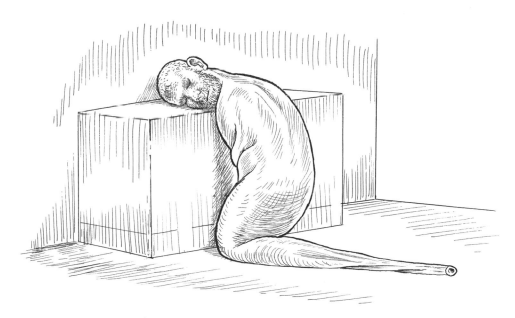

Lucille...my Lucille...Forgive me.

You were my beloved. Beloved above all.

We'll never go see the ocean swell from the trawlers of Tréport.

My arms around the full sink,
I embrace death, mouth open.

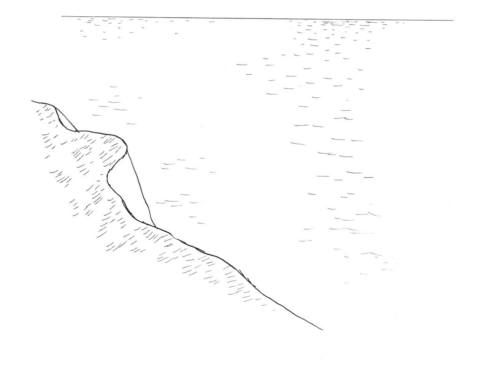

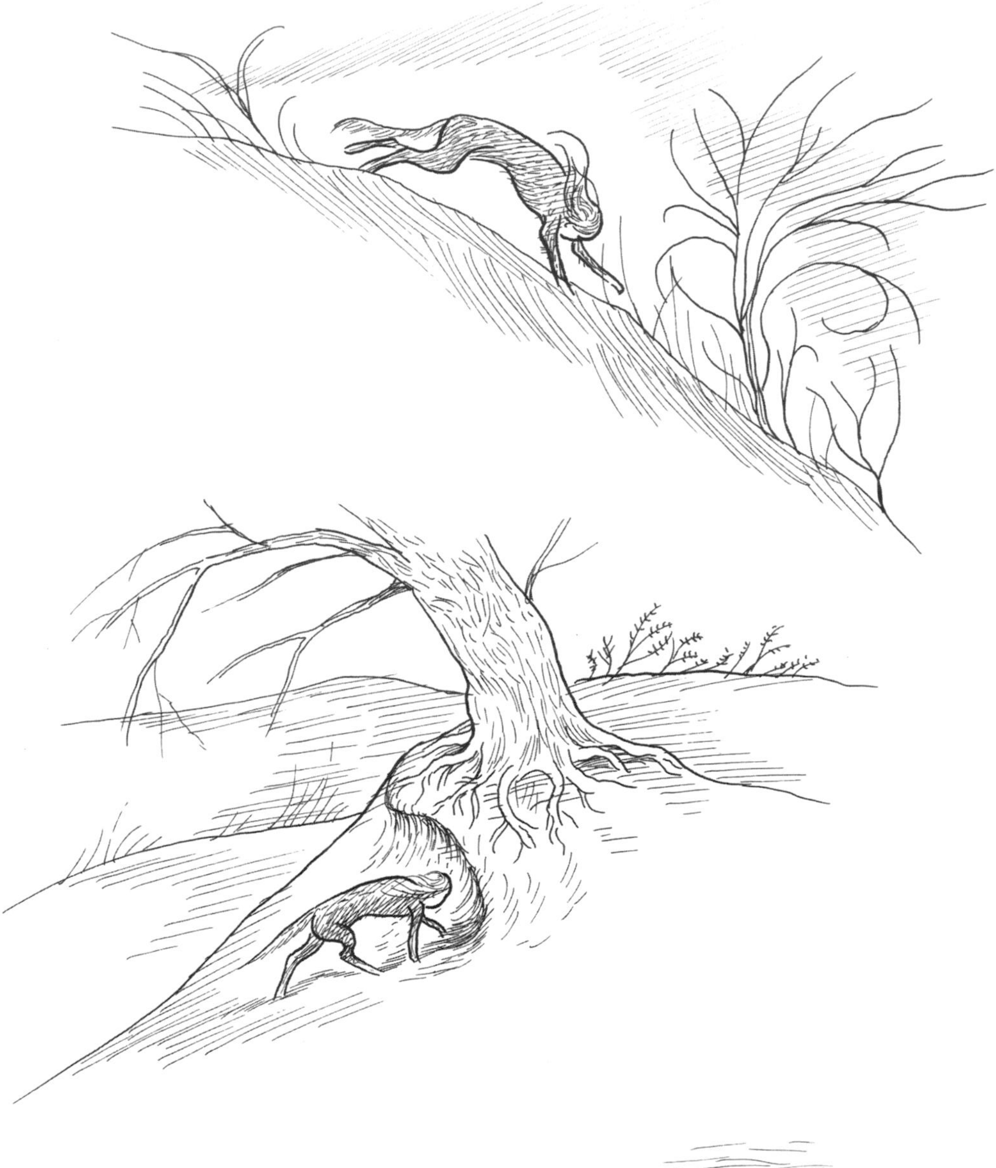

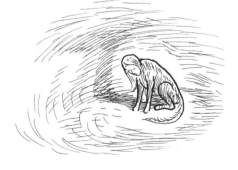

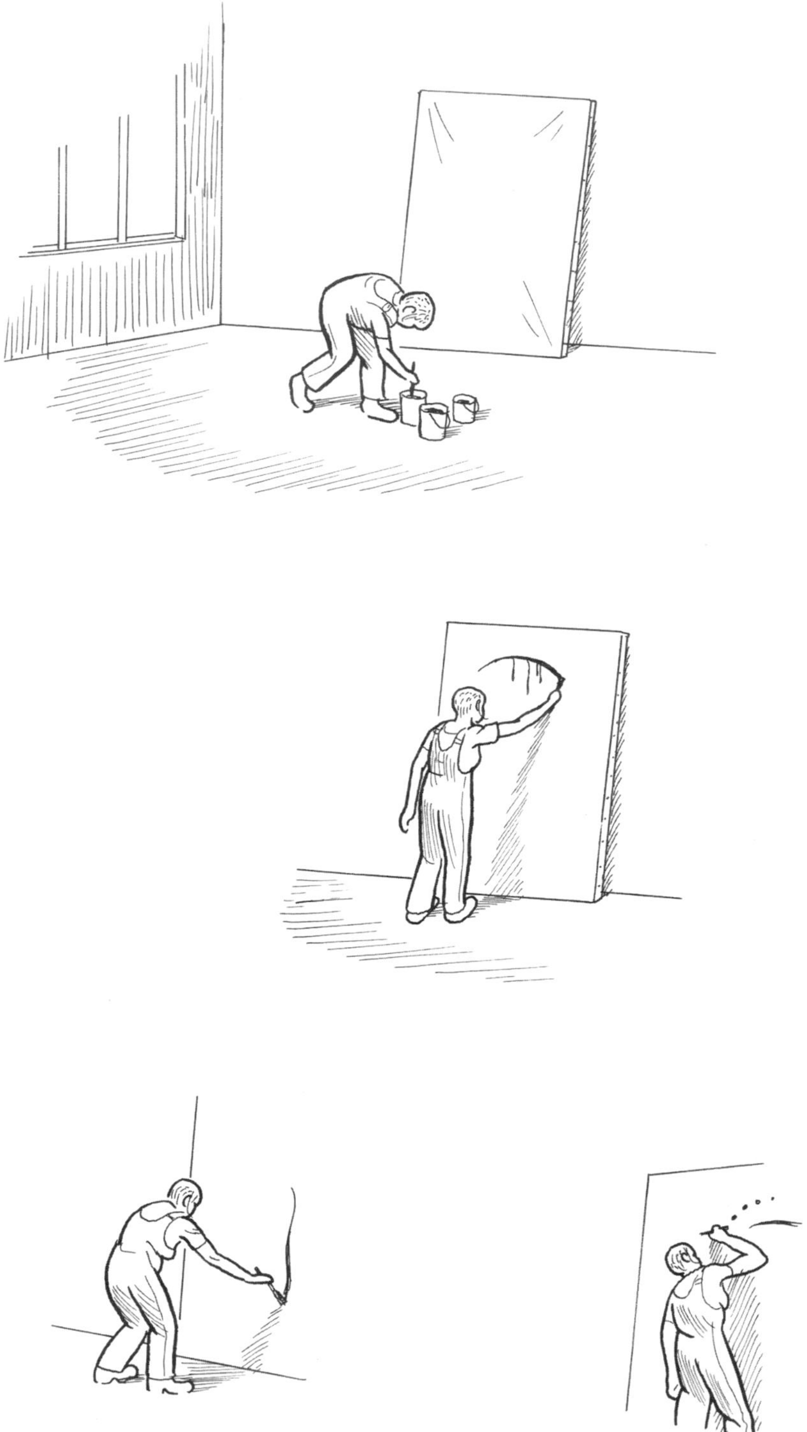

No, no, no!

What the hell is this shit, Reneé?

You think I'm lending you my studio and my paints so you can put out this hackwork?

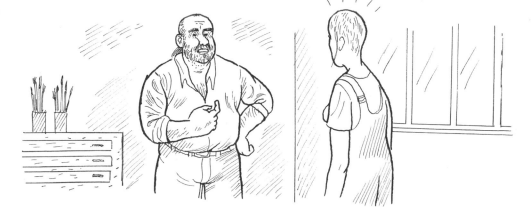

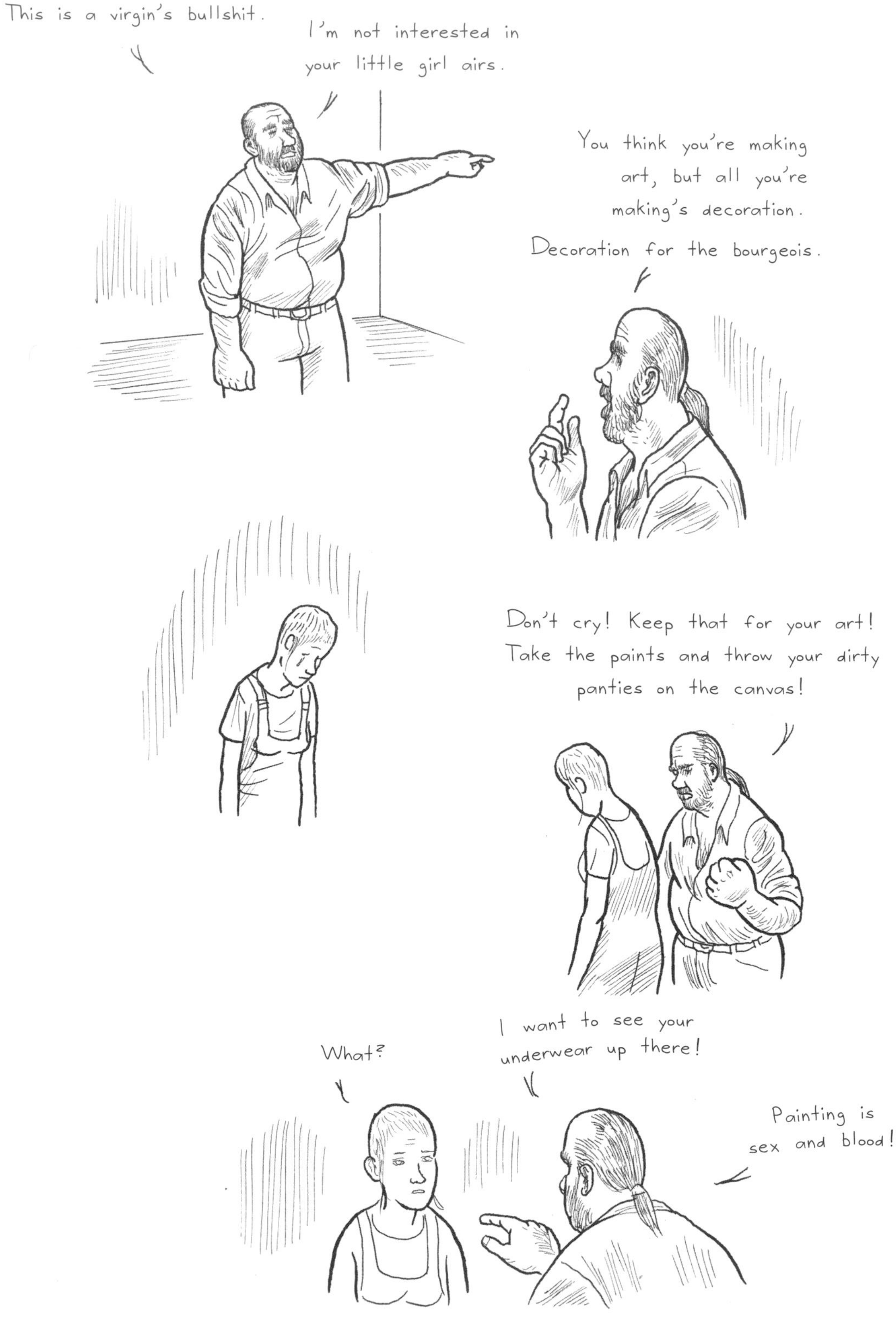
This is a virgin's bullshit.
I'm not interested in your little girl airs.
You think you're making art, but all you're making's decoration.
Decoration for the bourgeois.
Don't cry! Keep that for your art! Take the paints and throw your dirty panties on the canvas!
What?
I want to see your underwear up there!
Painting is sex and blood!

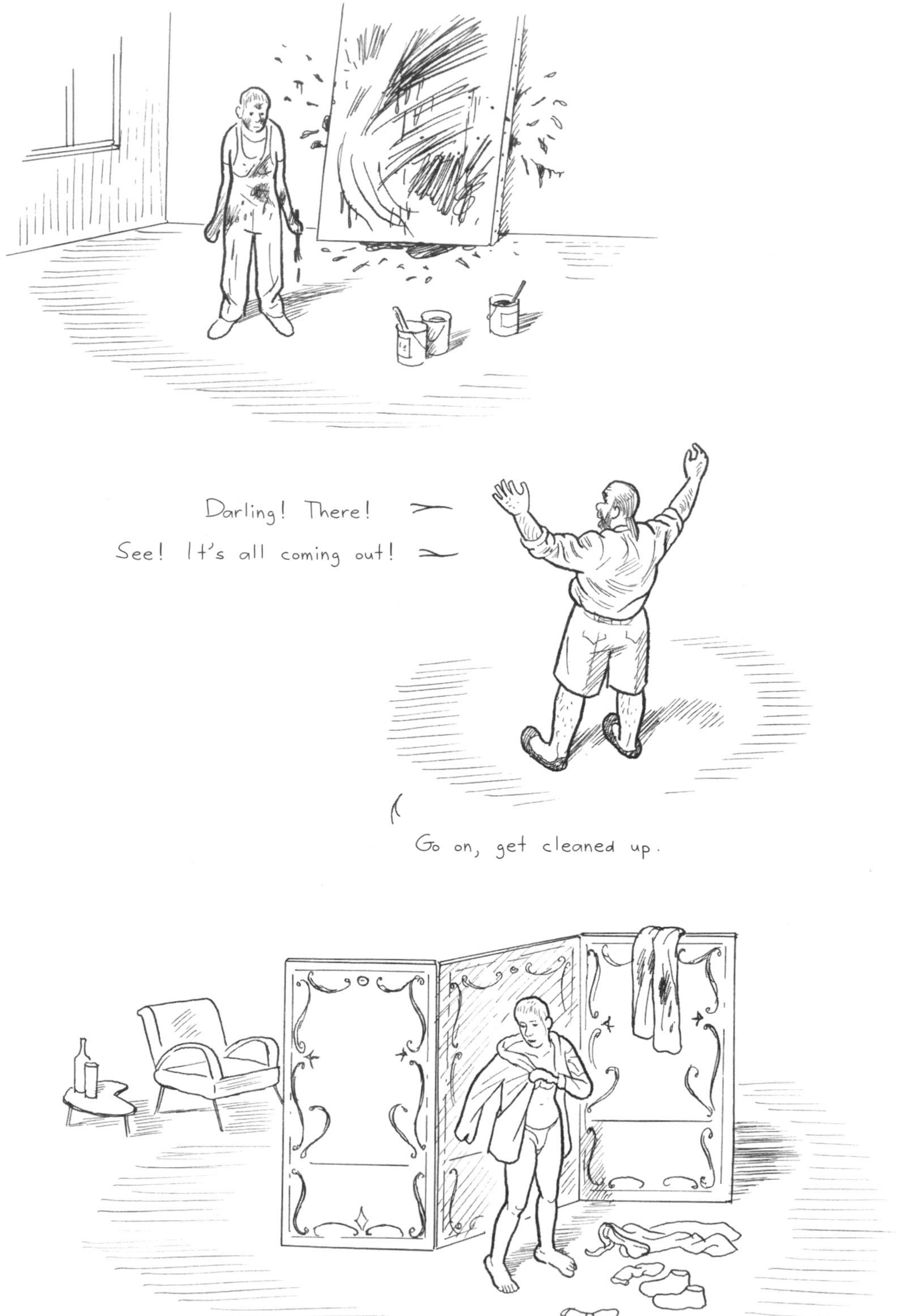

Darling! There!
See! It's all coming out!
Go on, get cleaned up.

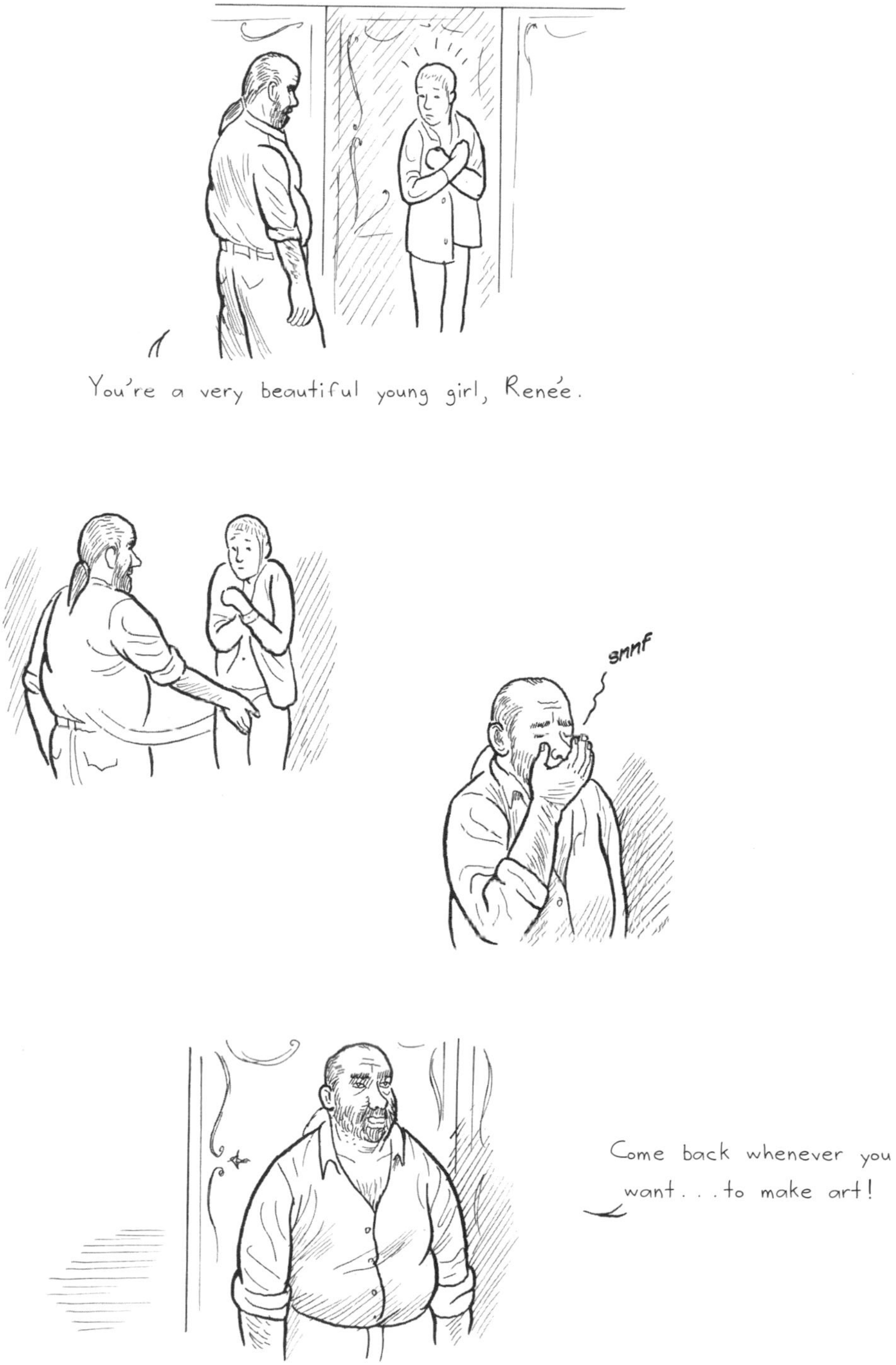
You're a very beautiful young girl, Renée.
smnf
Come back whenever you want. . . to make art!

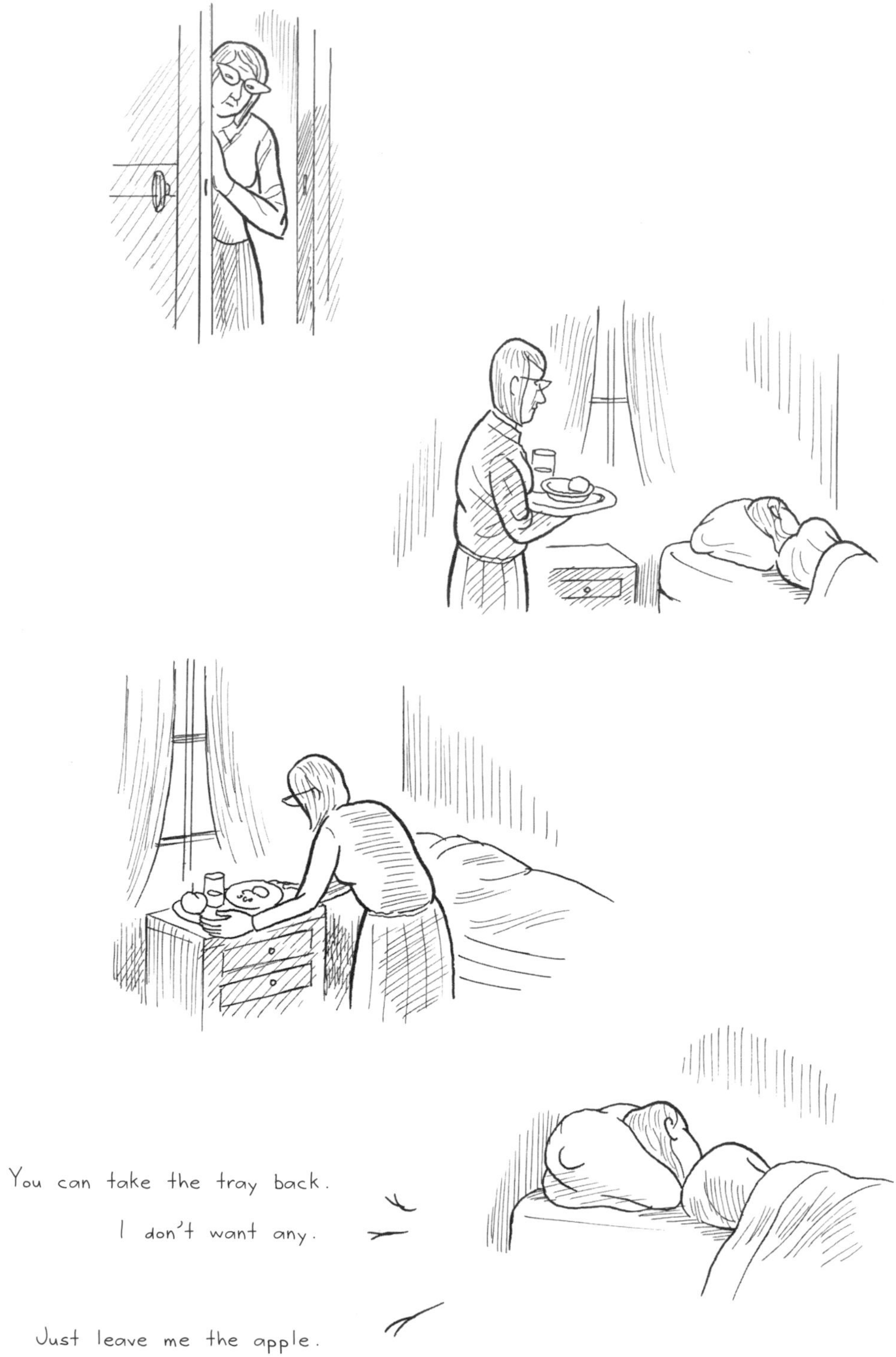
You can take the tray back.
I don't want any.
Just leave me the apple.

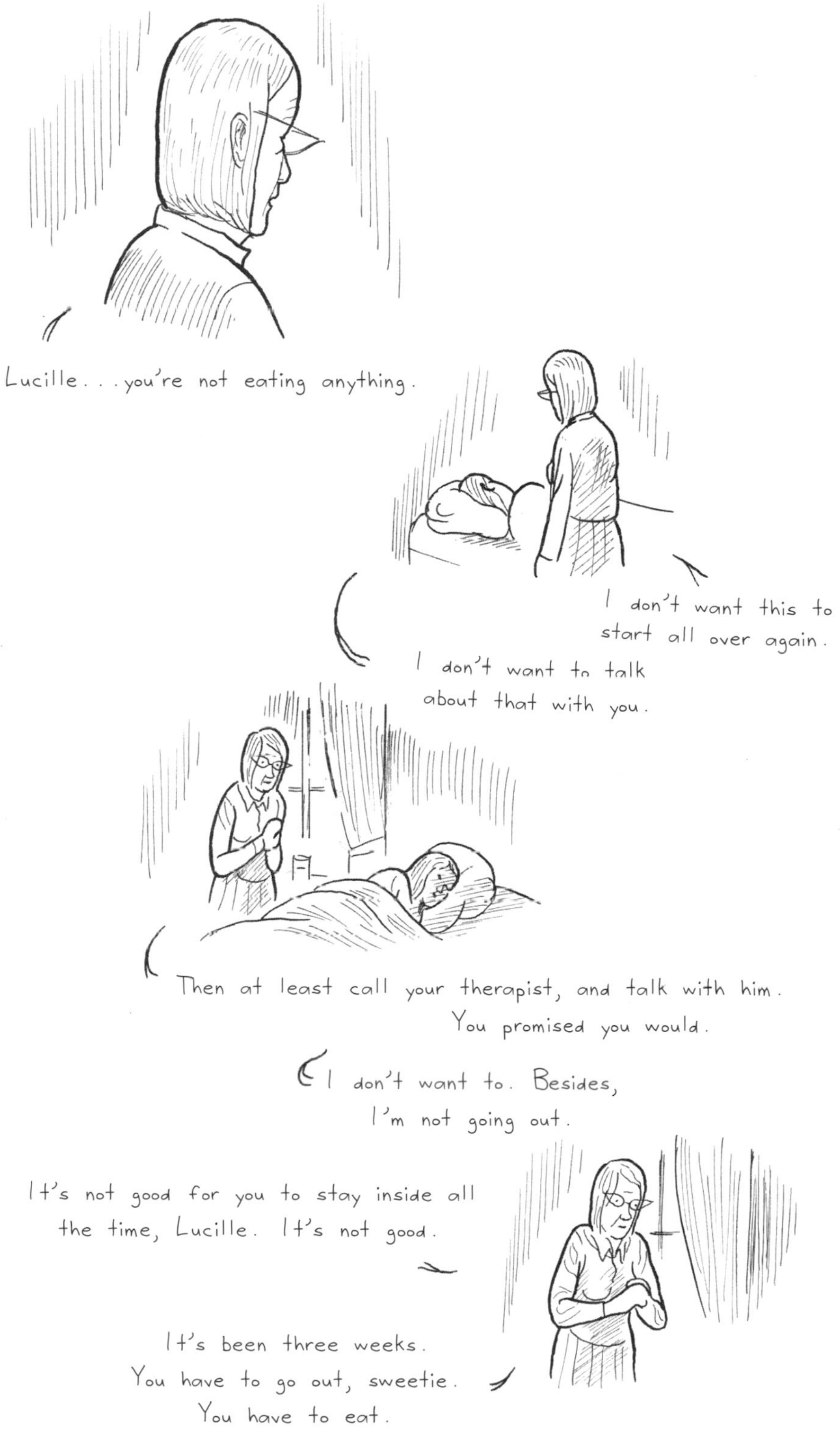

Lucille . . . you're not eating anything.
I don't want this to start all over again.
I don't want to talk about that with you.
Then at least call your therapist, and talk with him. You promised you would.
I don't want to. Besides, I'm not going out.
It's not good for you to stay inside all the time, Lucille. It's not good.
It's been three weeks. You have to go out, sweetie. You have to eat.

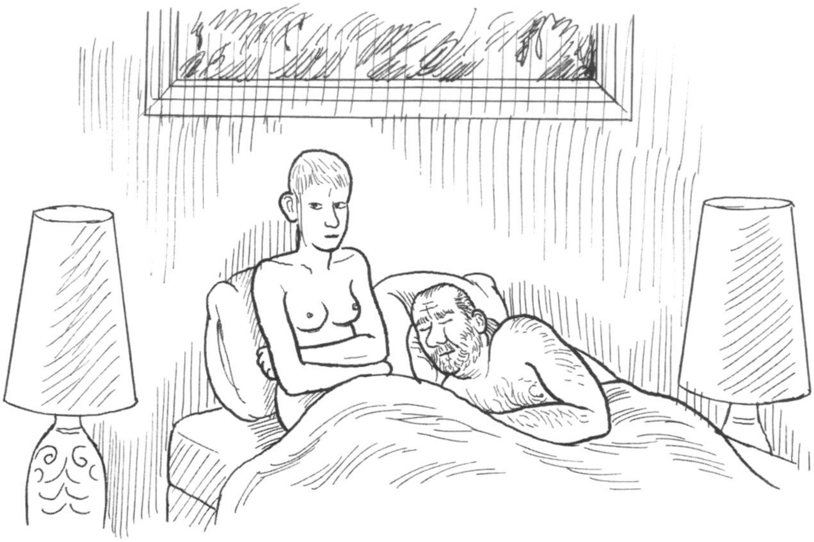
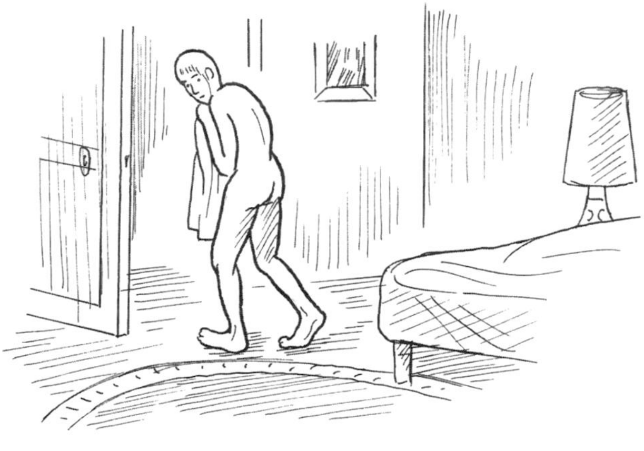
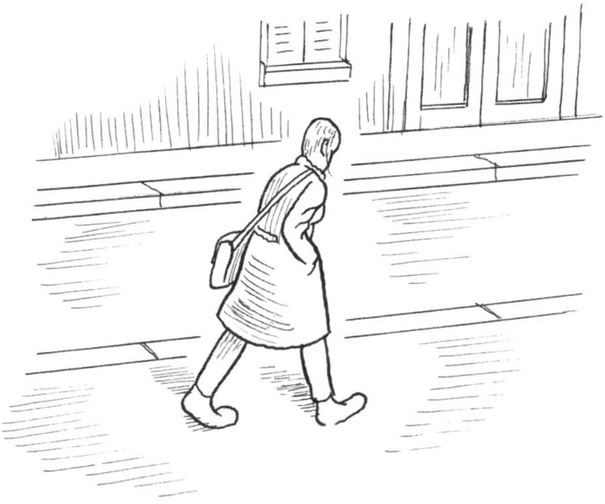

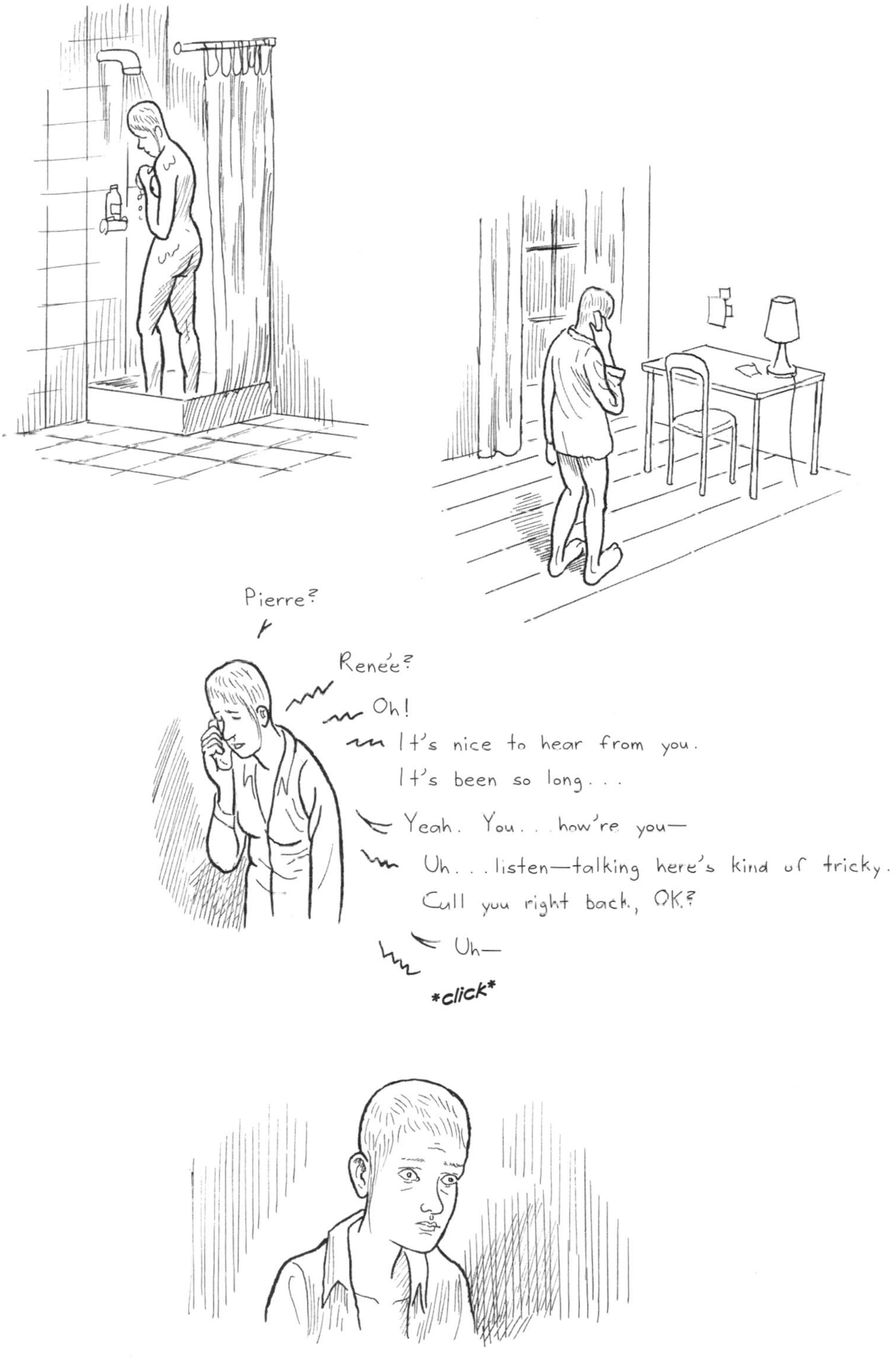
Pierre?
Renée?
Oh!
It's nice to hear from you.
It's been so long...
Yeah. You... how're you—
Uh... listen—talking here's kind of tricky.
Call you right back, OK?
Uh—
click

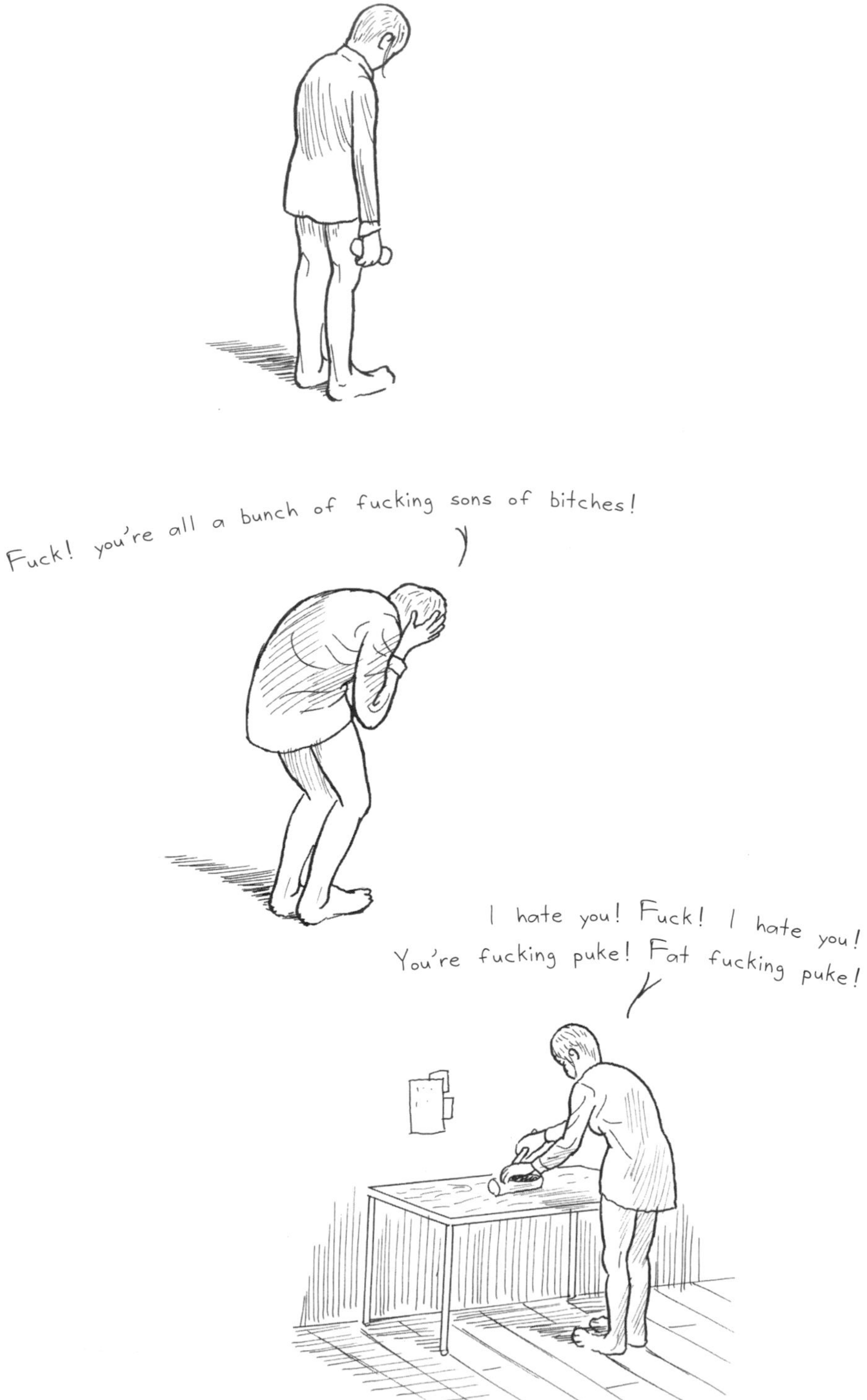
Fuck! you're all a bunch of fucking sons of bitches!
I hate you! Fuck! I hate you! You're fucking puke! Fat fucking puke!

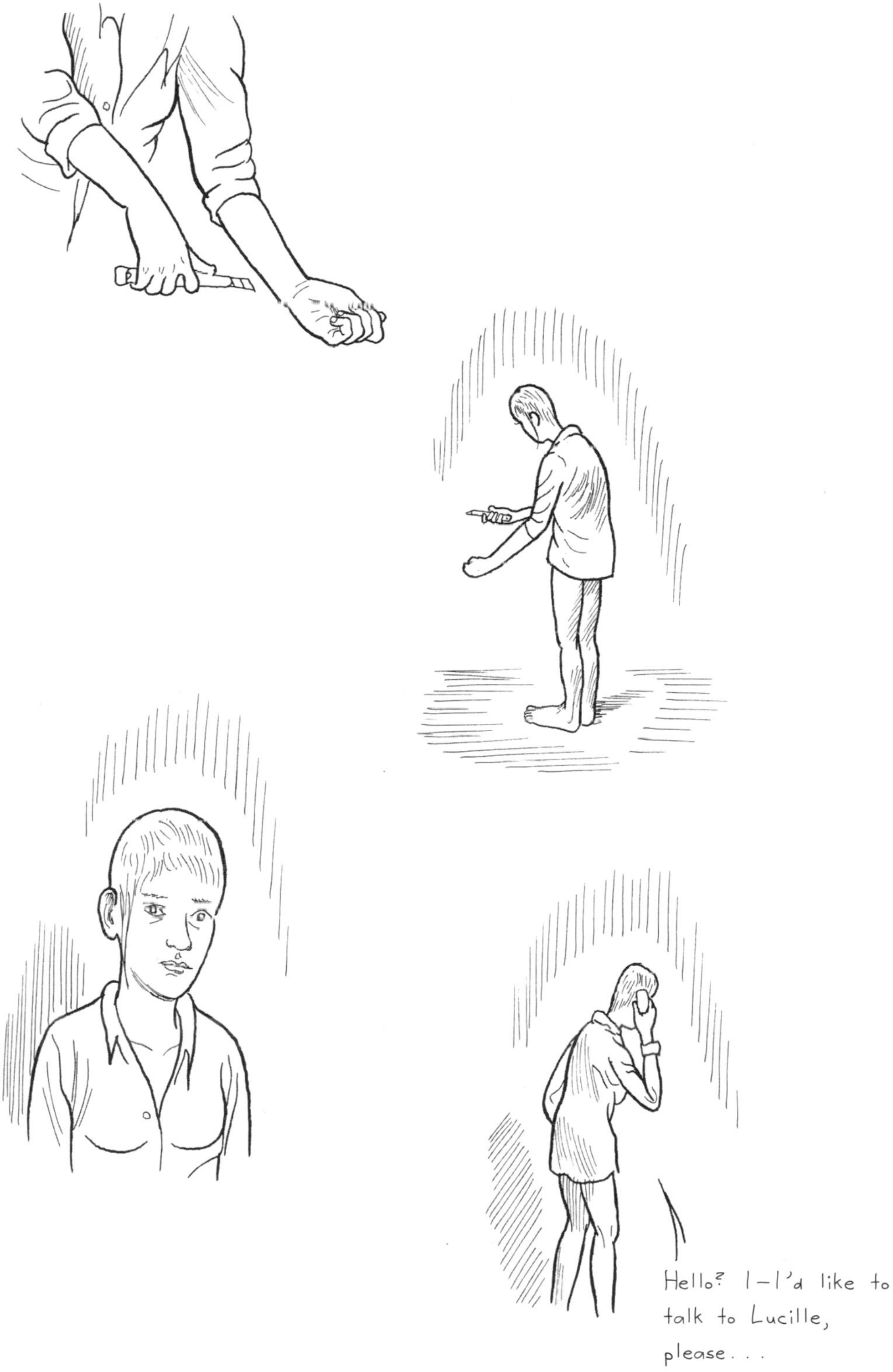
Hello? I—I'd like to talk to Lucille, please...

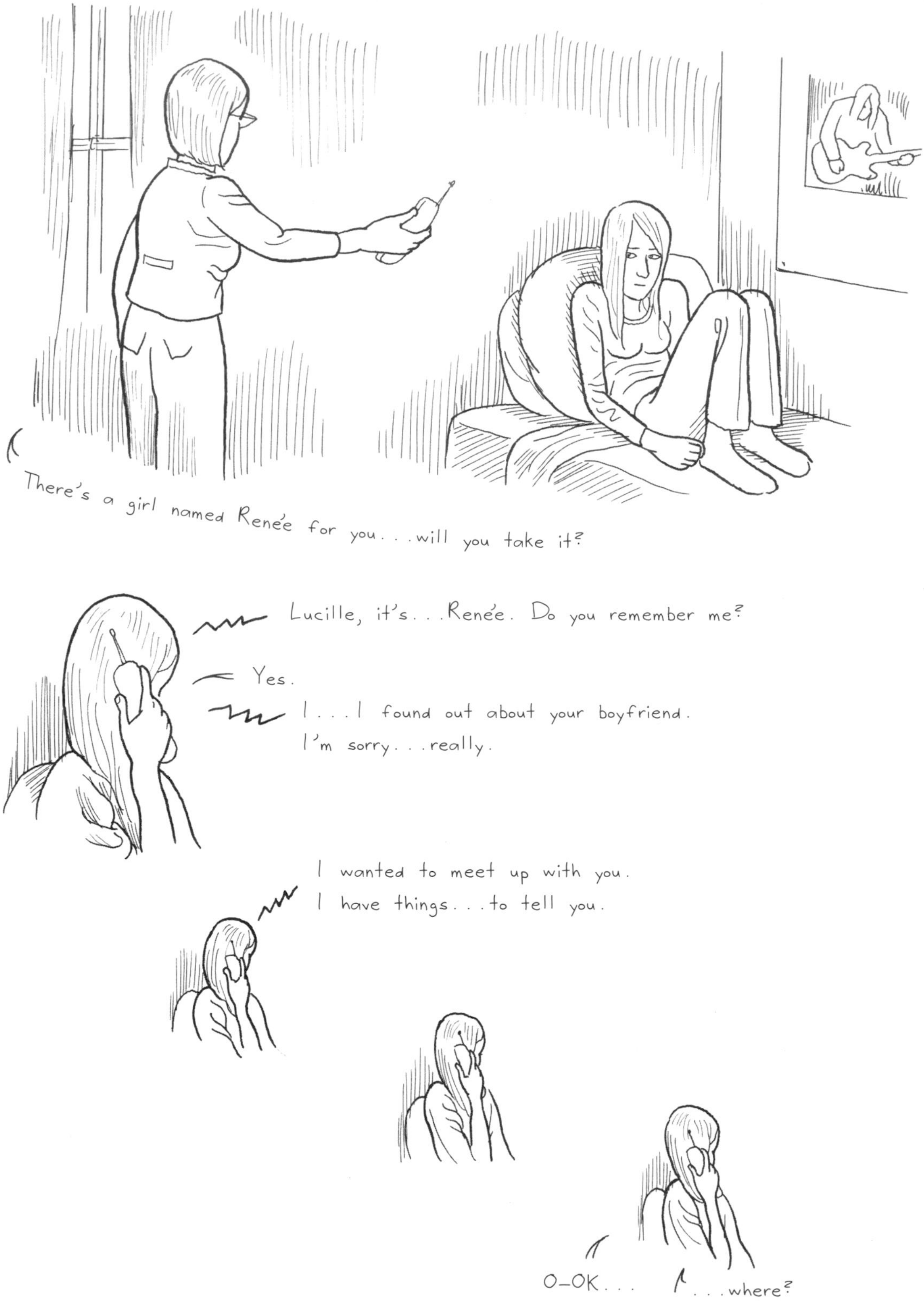
There's a girl named Renée for you...will you take it?
Lucille, it's...Renée. Do you remember me?
Yes.
I...I found out about your boyfriend.
I'm sorry...really.
I wanted to meet up with you.
I have things...to tell you.
O-OK...
...where?

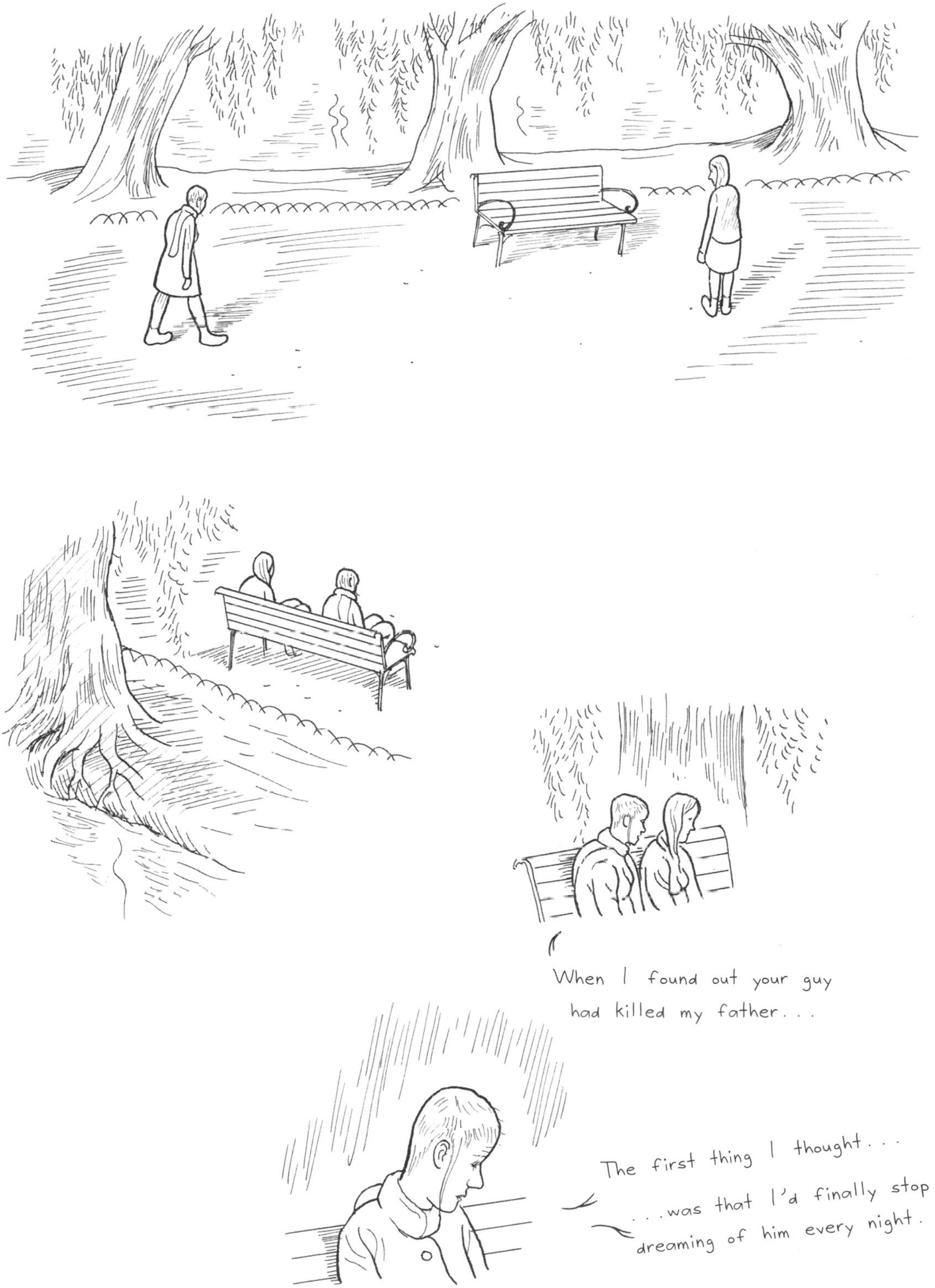
When I found out your guy had killed my father...
The first thing I thought...
...was that I'd finally stop dreaming of him every night.

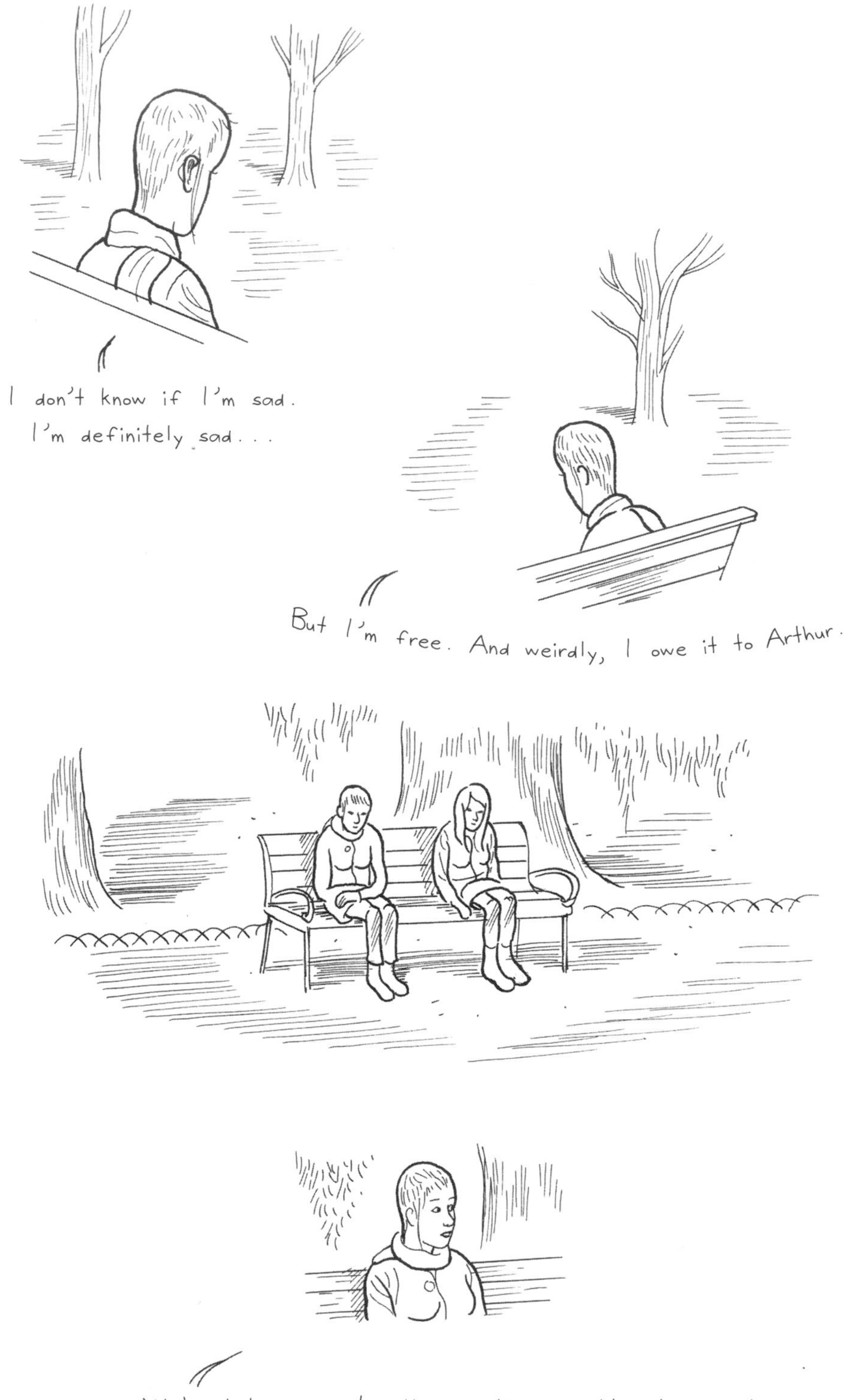
I don't know if I'm sad.
I'm definitely sad...
But I'm free. And weirdly, I owe it to Arthur.
We're linked now, Lucille, whether you like it nor not.

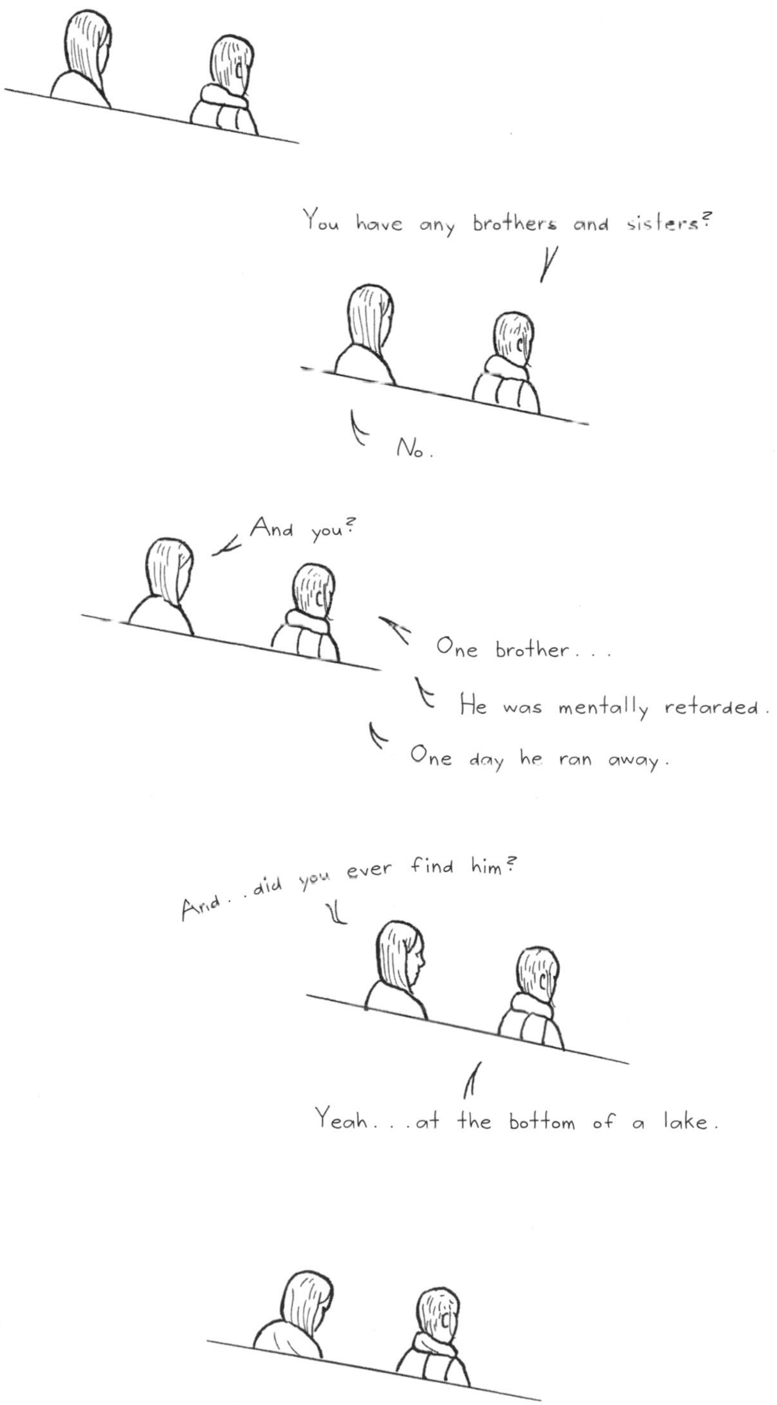
You have any brothers and sisters?
No.
And you?
One brother...
He was mentally retarded.
One day he ran away.
And.. did you ever find him?
Yeah... at the bottom of a lake.

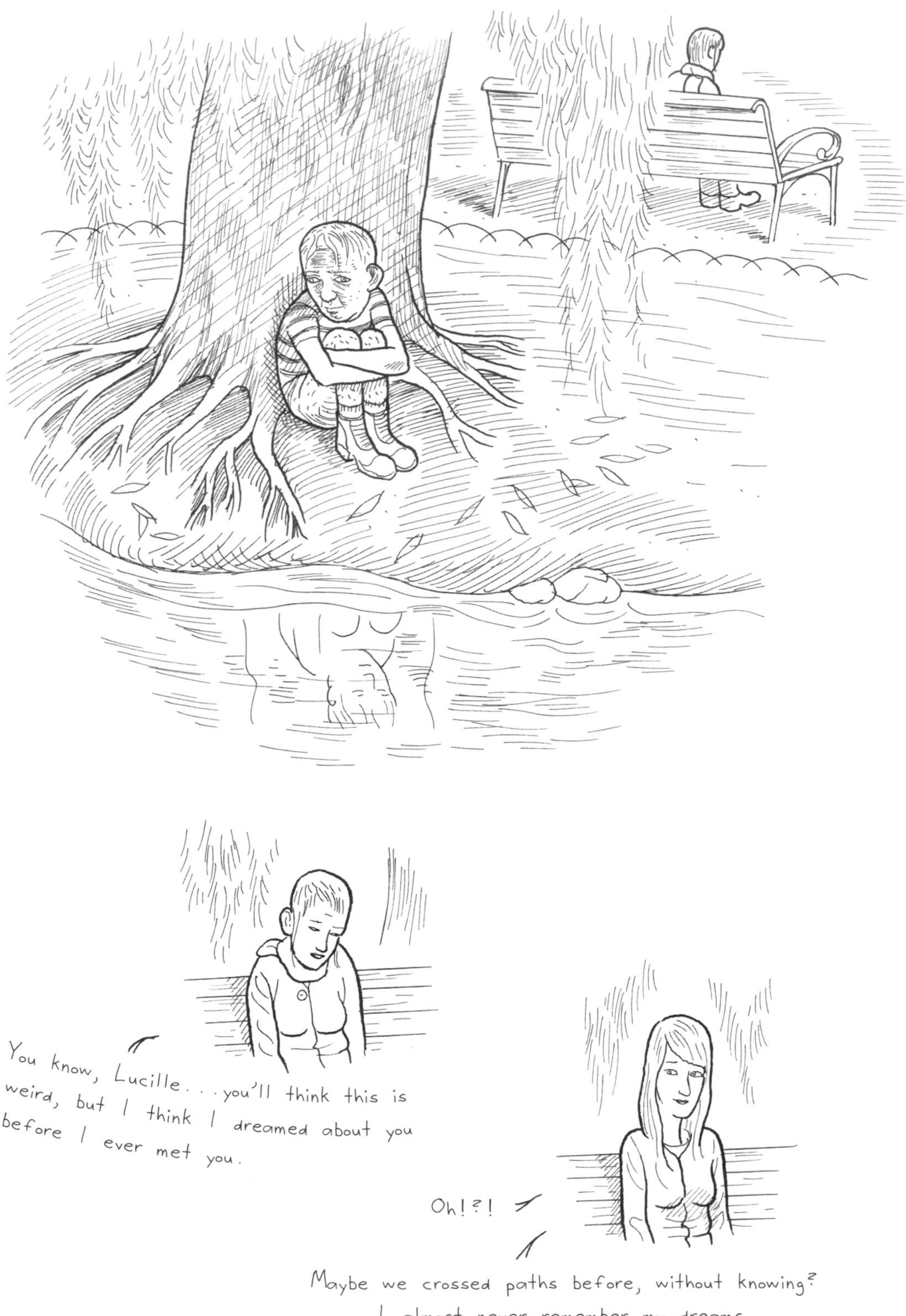
You know, Lucille... you'll think this is weird, but I think I dreamed about you before I ever met you.
Oh!?!
Maybe we crossed paths before, without knowing? I almost never remember my dreams.

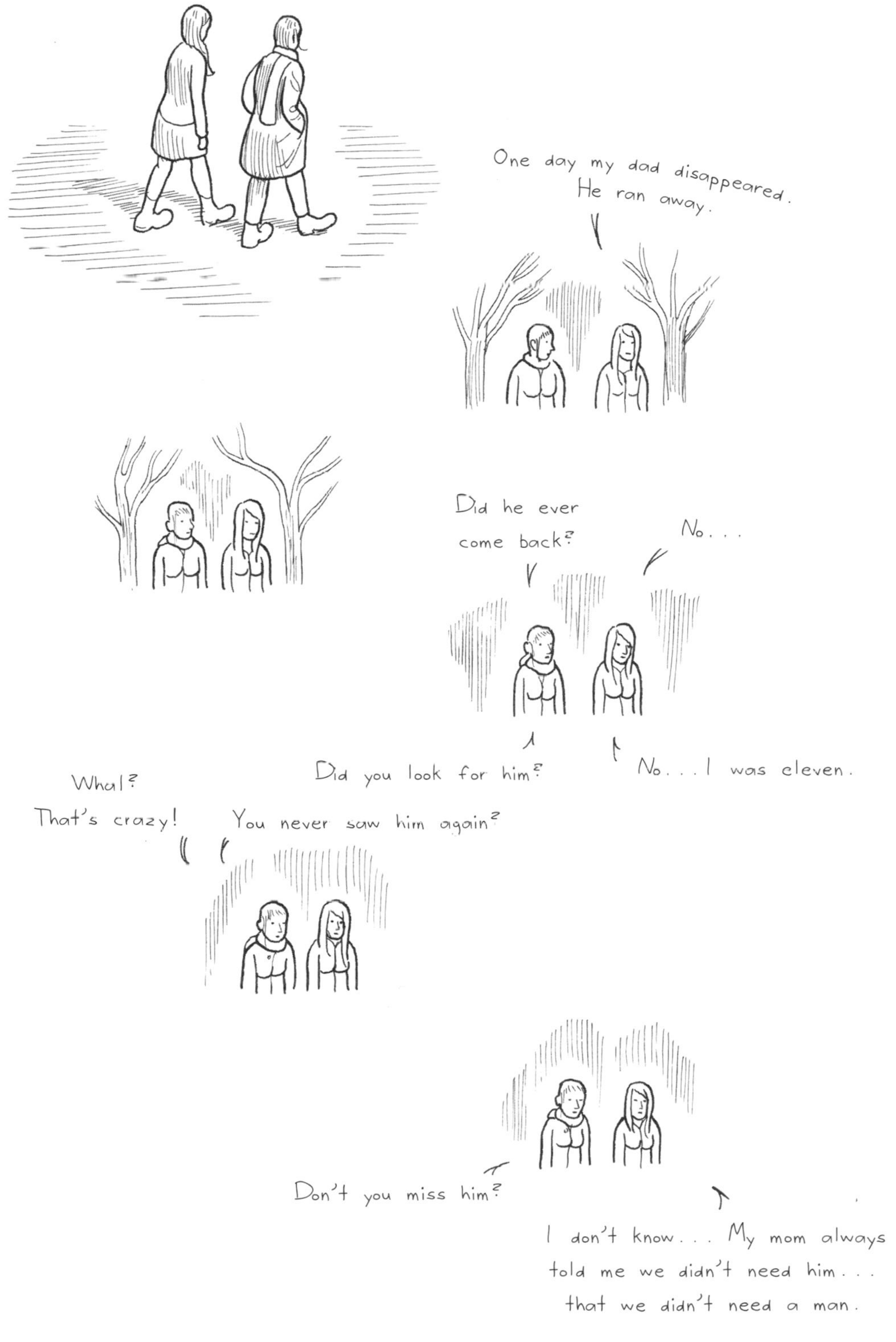
One day my dad disappeared. He ran away.
Did he ever come back?
No...
Did you look for him?
No... I was eleven.
What? That's crazy!
You never saw him again?
Don't you miss him?
I don't know... My mom always told me we didn't need him... that we didn't need a man.

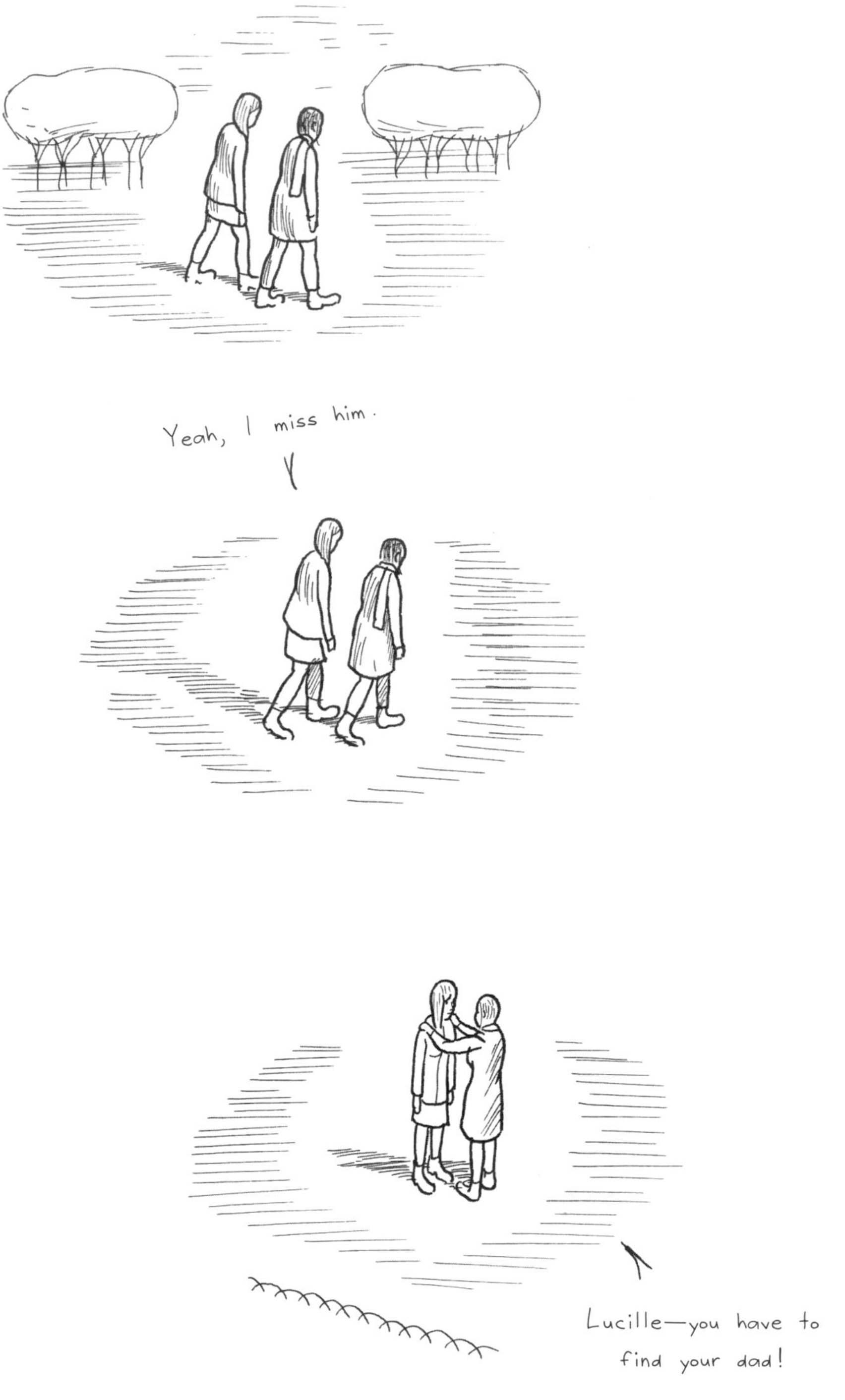
Yeah, I miss him.
Lucille—you have to find your dad!

My mom went into hysterics when I asked if she knew where my dad lived.
She wound up confessing he'd sent her letters.
At least one a year!
She'd hidden them from me! She said she burned them.
I'm sure she's lying.
Anyway, now I know he lives on a little island.
Probably not even 200 people live there.

Lucille . . .

Let's go!

I'll go with you! If you want.

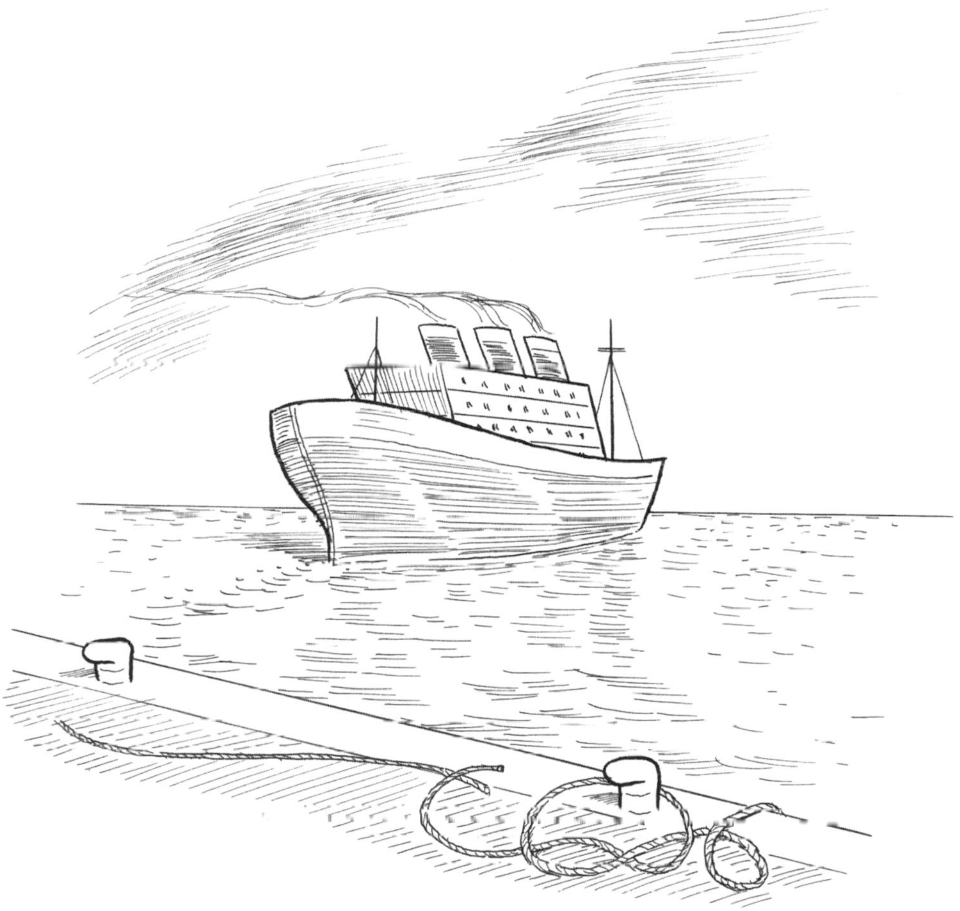

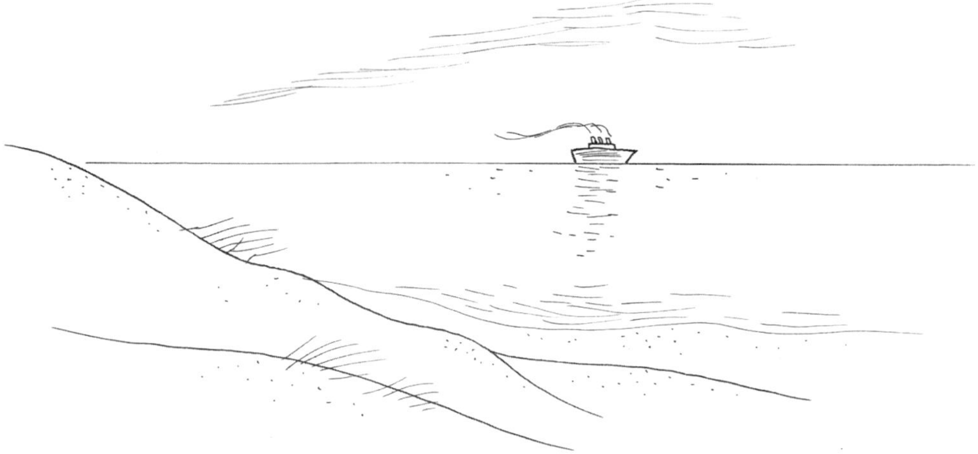

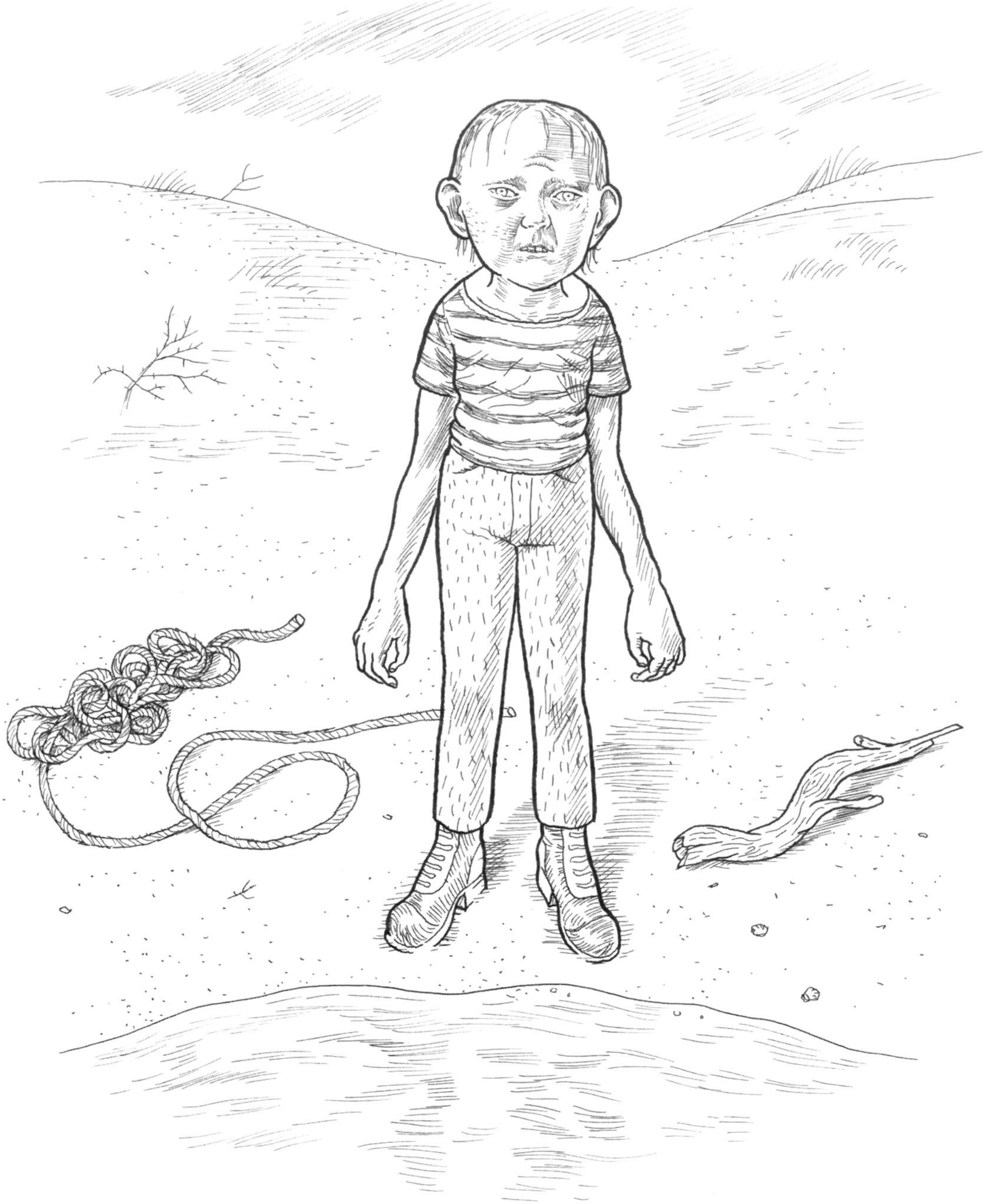

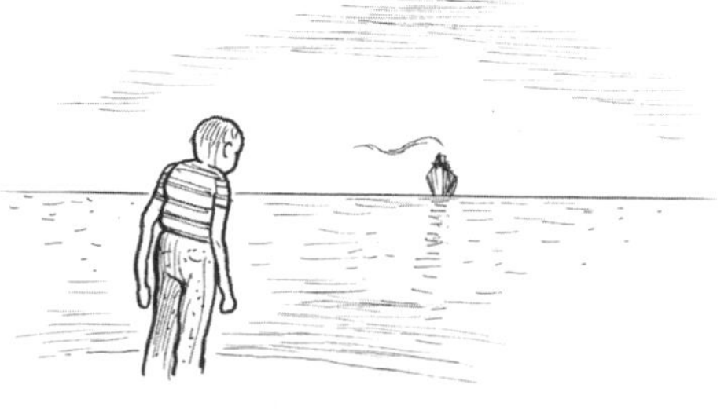

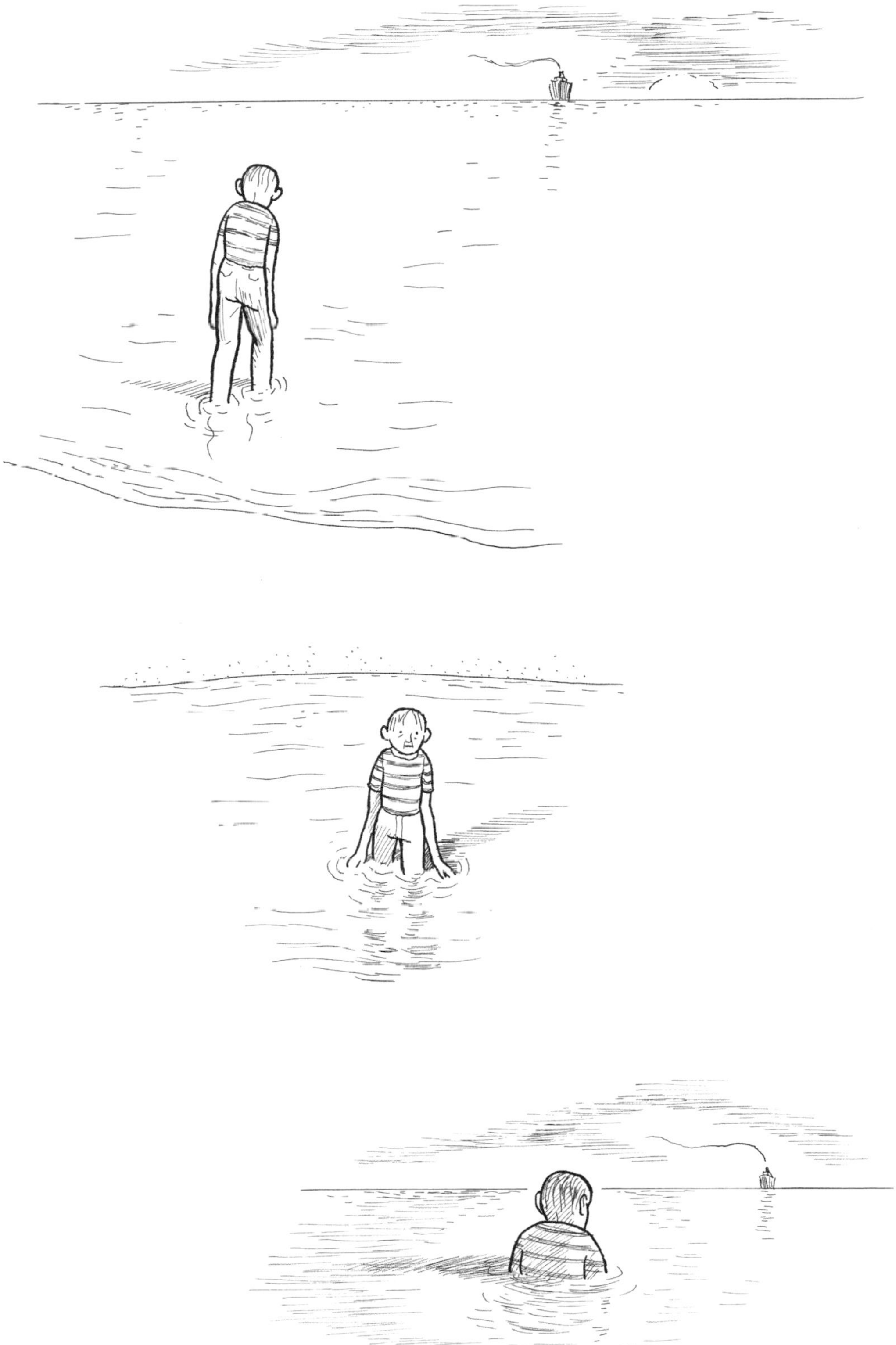

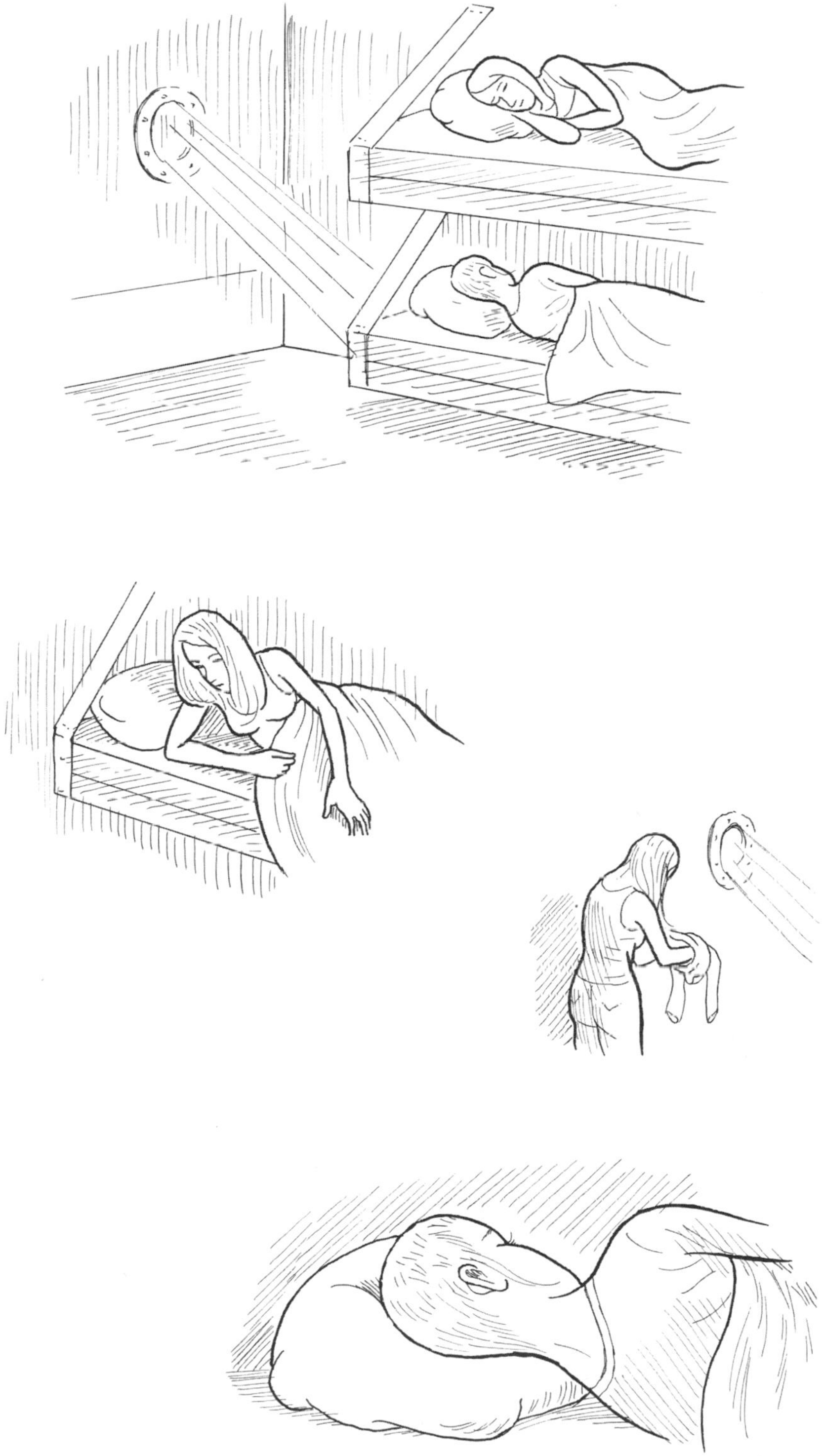

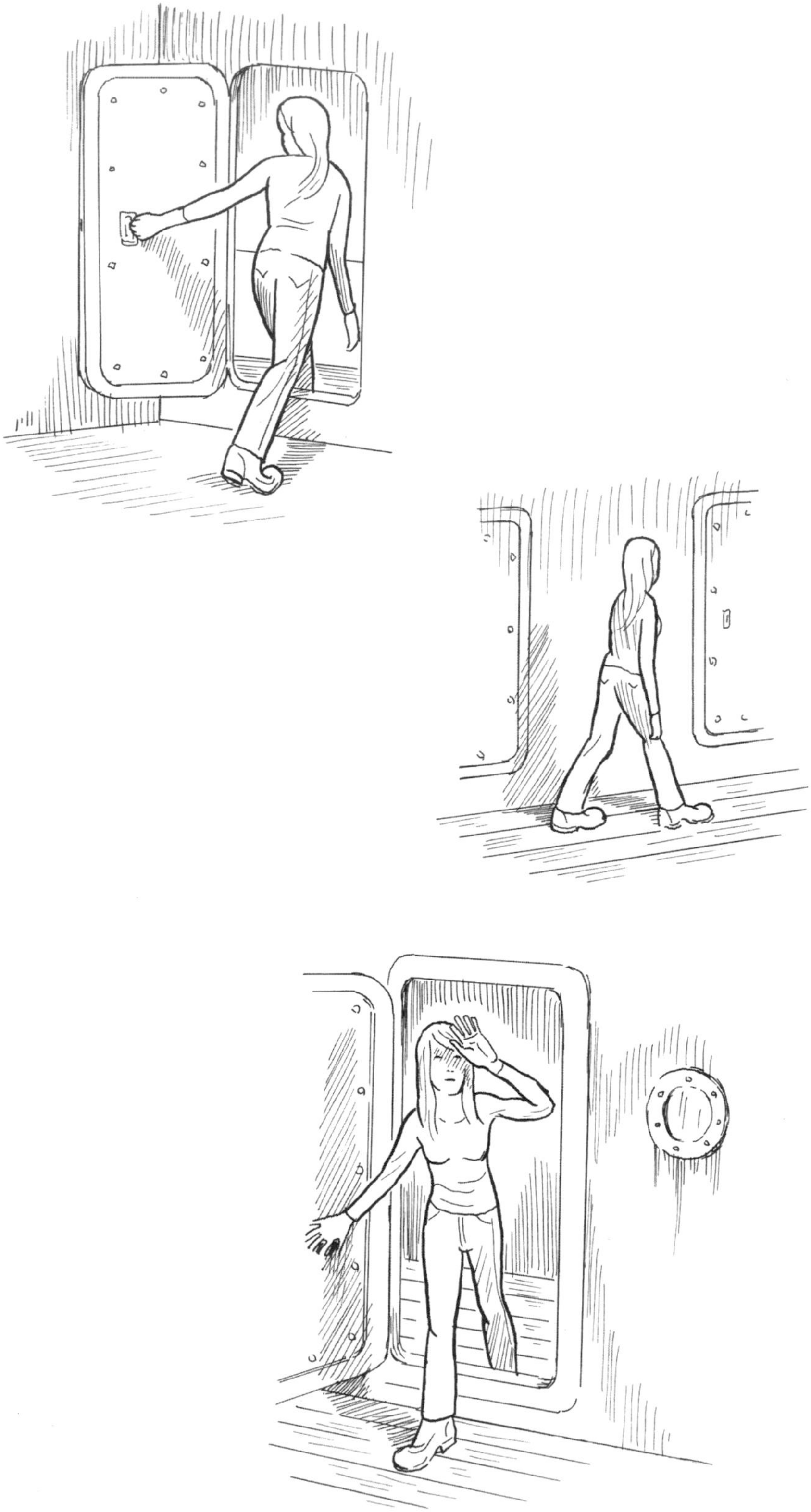

There it is...the ocean swell...spangled with shifting ramparts, shortened shadows, gauzy salt rains. Just like you said it would be...my love.

Your voice....your voice plows a furrow through the waves to me.... I hear you, Arthur. The walls of castles made of water tumble into the ocean. And I—here I am, where echoes of their great falling bear me your murmur. I hear you...

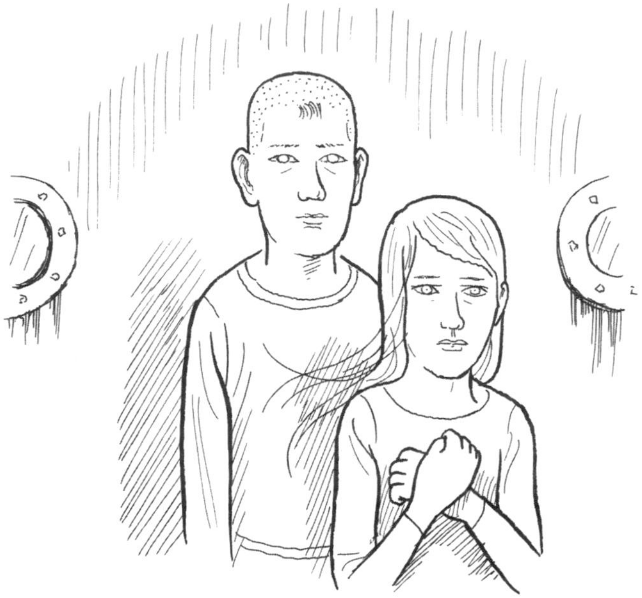

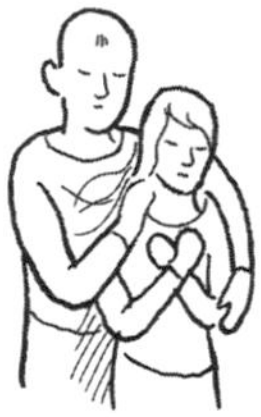

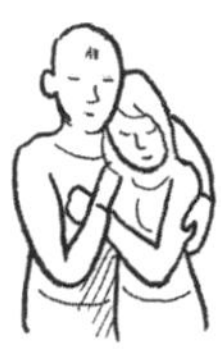

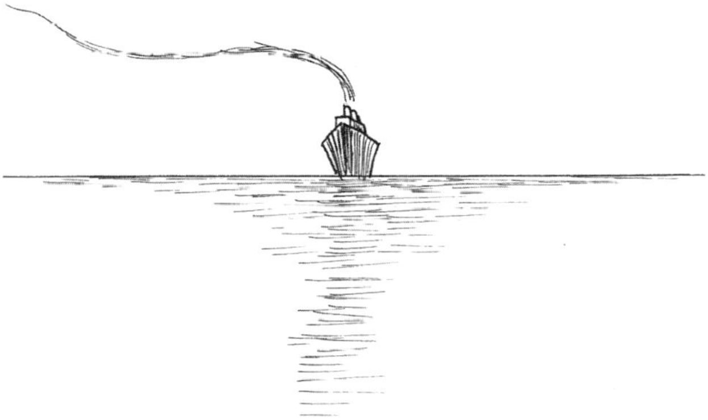

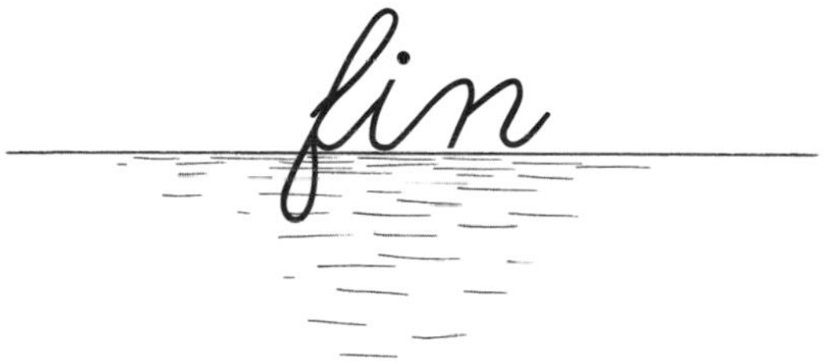
fin

Wednesday, October 20th, 2010 Ludovic Debeurme

Renée by Ludovic Debeurme © 2011 Futuropolis (Paris, France)

First English-language edition published by
Top Shelf Productions
PO Box 1282
Marietta, GA 30061-1282
USA

Editor-in-Chief: Chris Staros

Top Shelf Productions is an imprint of IDW Publishing,
a division of Idea and Design Works, LLC. Offices: 2765 Truxtun Road,
San Diego, CA 92106. Top Shelf Productions®, the Top Shelf logo,
Idea and Design Works®, and the IDW logo are registered trademarks
of Idea and Design Works, LLC. All Rights Reserved. With the exception
of small excerpts of artwork used for review purposes, none of the
contents of this publication may be reprinted without the permission of
IDW Publishing. IDW Publishing does not read or accept unsolicited
submissions of ideas, stories, or artwork.

Visit our online catalog at www.topshelfcomix.com.

Printed in Korea.

18   17   16   15   5   4   3   2   1

Also available from Ludovic Debeurme and Top Shelf
is the prequel to this book, *Lucille*.

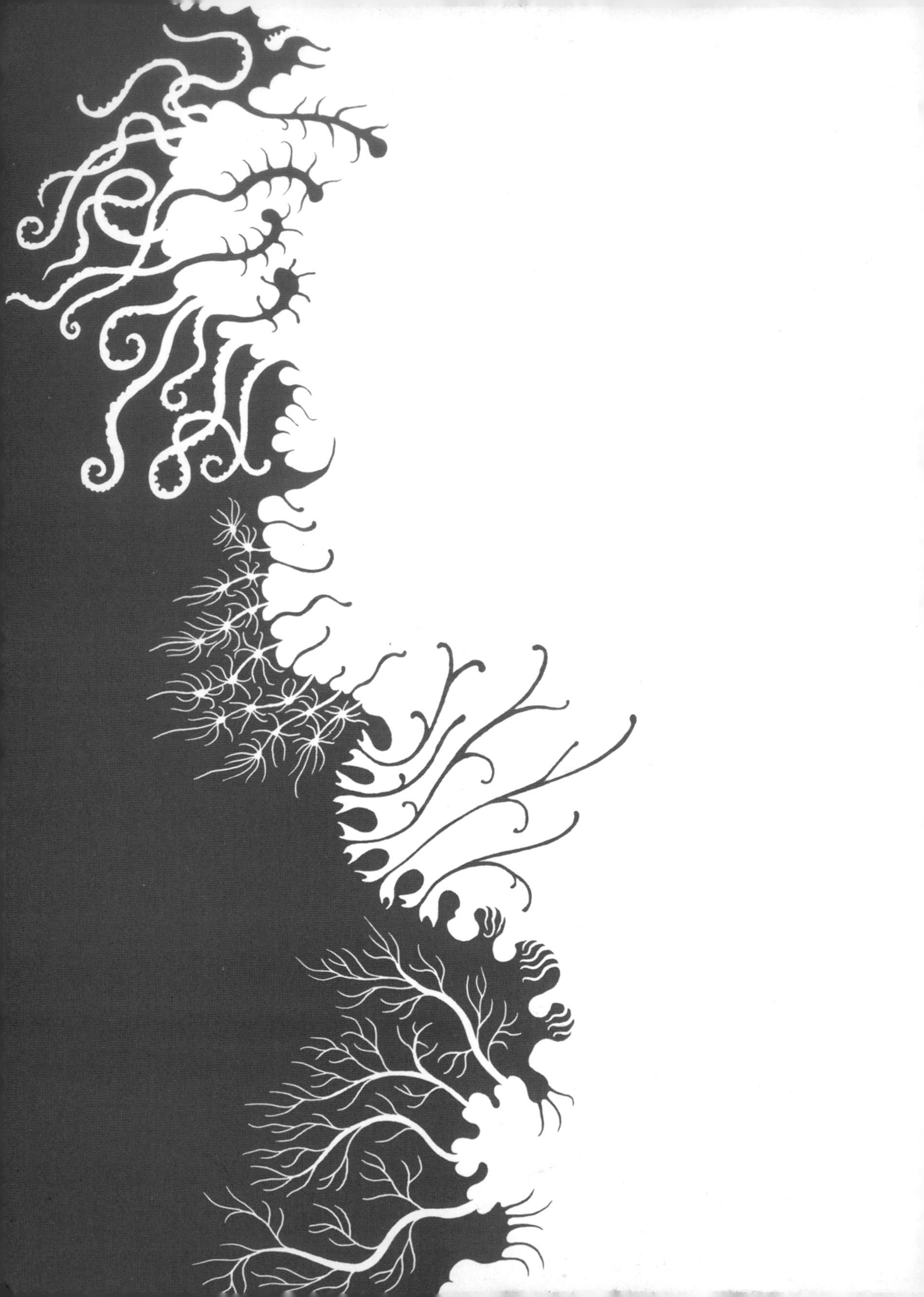